The Mathematical Aspects of Barrier Options

The Mathematical Aspects of Barrier Options

Mehmet Fuat Beyazıt
Istanbul Bilgi University, Turkey

World Scientific

NEW JERSEY • LONDON • SINGAPORE • BEIJING • SHANGHAI • HONG KONG • TAIPEI • CHENNAI • TOKYO

Published by

World Scientific Publishing Co. Pte. Ltd.
5 Toh Tuck Link, Singapore 596224
USA office: 27 Warren Street, Suite 401-402, Hackensack, NJ 07601
UK office: 57 Shelton Street, Covent Garden, London WC2H 9HE

Library of Congress Control Number: 2025015490

British Library Cataloguing-in-Publication Data
A catalogue record for this book is available from the British Library.

THE MATHEMATICAL ASPECTS OF BARRIER OPTIONS

ISBN 978-981-98-1262-2 (hardcover)
ISBN 978-981-98-1263-9 (ebook for institutions)
ISBN 978-981-98-1264-6 (ebook for individuals)

For any available supplementary material, please visit
https://www.worldscientific.com/worldscibooks/10.1142/14297#t=suppl

Desk Editors: Nambirajan Karuppiah/Pui Yee Lum

Typeset by Stallion Press
Email: enquiries@stallionpress.com

Printed in Singapore

To my family

Preface

First of all, I should draw the reader's attention to this point: Most of the information, calculations, and formulas in this book can indeed be found in other resources, but not with this much detail. Most derivations, especially partial barriers, are given here with much more detail and clarity.

In financial mathematics lectures, we often refer to formulae. However, we have difficulty explaining to students how the formulae of these sophisticated models, which the masters and academics working in this field produce with extraordinary creativity, are derived. A more transparent and detailed explanation of these models' methods and techniques is meaningful and useful for academicians and students in this field. The detailed derivation of the formulae will also help practitioners working in the financial world to understand these sophisticated products better and, in turn, to provide better solutions to their client's needs. For this reason, the book was designed to make many topics more understandable to the reader.

Secondly, it is assumed that the reader has basic theoretical knowledge and tools often used in financial mathematics and stochastic calculus. However, adding an introductory section and an Appendix on the basic concepts and theories that form the basis of mathematical finance was deemed appropriate. Considering that the book's readership will be undergraduate students of the Financial Mathematics program and master's and doctoral students, we repeat this information here, which may be found more comprehensively in other resources.

Thirdly, this book, which consists of seven chapters, can be seen as a detailed review and explanation of various articles referred to in the text when necessary. Therefore, the reader may witness that the notation used to show the same process is sometimes shown in a different notation. Although I have tried to ensure uniformity, for example, the barrier value may be shown as "a" in one section, "b" in another section, and "m" in another section. I hope this issue is not large enough to overshadow the book's real purpose.

As mentioned above, the first chapter conveys mathematical finance's fundamental tools and concepts. The book's second part is devoted to the reflection principle and the probability density functions that form the basis of barrier options. The reflection principle is given in essential detail first for discrete processes and then for continuous processes. The third chapter examines the barrier options and derives formulae using the univariate normal density function. Rubinstein and Reiner (1991) were the primary sources in this section. The uses of barriers and hedging barrier options are explained in the fourth chapter. The fifth chapter is the most specific part and deals with partial barrier options. Many formulae for partial barriers are derived in detail. In this chapter, Carr (1995) and Heynen and Kat (1994) were the primary resources used in the detailed derivations. Chapter 6 discusses double barrier options. Finally, Chapter 7 examines some exotic types of barrier options, including step barriers, partial step barriers, and step double barriers. Guillaume (2003, 2004, 2010, 2012, 2021, and 2023) was the primary source for these barrier options. The introductory section of the Appendix presents a review of the probability concept. In Appendix B, the reader may find some simple Matlab codes for various Double Barrier option formulae requiring iterations. Since the codes are only for double barrier call options, the reader is encouraged to develop codes for put options and A and B-type partial barriers for both calls and puts. Appendix C gives the derivation of put-call symmetry in Carr and Chou (1996, 1998). I hope that the approach, especially the applied methods in deriving partial barriers, will help broaden the horizons of students and academics working on this subject and guide them. On this occasion, I would like to thank Professor John C. Hull, Professor Don M. Chance, Professor Sam Howison, and Professor Y. Kuen Kwok for allowing me to use the sections from their valuable publications. I must also express my heartfelt gratitude to Professor Tristan Guillaume for his contribution, guidance, and advice. Finally, I would like to extend a special thanks to my editors Lum Pui Yee and Nambirajan Karuppaiah. Without their support and cooperation, this work would not have been possible.

All errors in the book are my own. I can only be grateful to readers who send any errors they find to fuat.beyazit@bilgi.edu.tr.

Wish you have fun by reading and applying...

About the Author

Mehmet Fuat Beyazit holds BSc, MSc, and PhD degrees from Istanbul Technical University, Istanbul, Turkey. He has served as a Financial Controller and Manager for various companies, including multinationals. Currently, he is a Lecturer at Istanbul Bilgi University, Istanbul, Turkey, where he teaches several courses on Financial Mathematics. His main areas of interest include Financial Derivative Pricing, Computational Methods in Finance, and Risk Management.

Contents

List of Figures

List of Tables

Chapter 1

Mathematical Background

1.1. Introduction

In this section, before moving on to pricing barrier options, we will examine the basic building blocks, basic concepts, and theories related to financial mathematics. Options are called "redundant assets." This is because they can be produced unnaturally by creating a suitable portfolio. However, this portfolio should not allow arbitrage in the market; otherwise, the price will not be right and will not last long. Therefore, we will start this section with arbitrage theory in discrete markets. Secondly, we will examine some concepts related to stochastic processes and continue with Brownian motion and Martingale topics. Finally, we will see the Girsanov theorem and equivalent martingale measures and be ready to examine the concepts related to barrier pricing.

1.2. Market Model

(a) We can choose the market model with two periods as $t = 0, 1$. It is possible to trade and consume in both periods.

(b) We can define the sample space containing each possible state ω (state of the world) as

$$\Omega = \{\omega_1 \dots \omega_K\}$$

with $K < \infty$. The values of these states will become certain at $t = 1$.

(c) Let's define a probability measure on Ω such that $\mathbb{P}(\omega) > 0$ for all $\omega \in \Omega$.

(d) Let's define a bank/deposit account as $B = \{B_t : t = 0,\ 1\}$ where $B_0 = 1$ and B_1 is a random variable. However, this value is strictly positive for every $\omega \in \Omega$, in fact, $B_1 \geq 1$. Therefore, we can define the interest rate as $r = B_1 - 1$. We generally accept this process as deterministic rather than random.

(e) Let's define $S = \{S_t : t = 0,\ 1\}$ with $N < \infty$ risky financial assets (stocks) as

$$S_t = \{S_1(t), \ldots, S_N(t)\}$$

Let $S_n(t)$ show the price of the n'th stock at time t.

(f) Let's define a trading strategy as $\theta = \{\theta_0, \theta_1 \ldots \theta_N\}$. θ_0 shows the amount of money in the deposit account, and other parameters $\theta_1 \ldots \theta_N$ shows the number of each risky asset in the portfolio. This parameter can generally be positive or negative. However, when there is a short sale restriction, we take $\theta_n \geq 0$.

If we want to express financial asset prices for Ω in the period $t = 1$, we can express them in the matrix structure with the $K \times N$ matrix as follows:

$$S(1,\Omega) = \begin{matrix} S_1(1,\omega_1) & S_2(1,\omega_1) \ldots. & S_N(1,\omega_1) \\ S_1(1,\omega_2) & S_2\,(1,\omega_2) \ldots & S_N\,(1,\omega_2) \\ S_1(1,\omega_K) & S_2\,(1,\omega_K) \ldots. & S_N(1,\omega_K) \end{matrix}$$

The matrix $S(1,\ \Omega)$ consists of positive scalar numbers. If we want to add the bank account, the extended matrix is

$$S(1,\Omega) = \begin{bmatrix} B_1 & S_1(1,\omega_1) & S_2(1,\omega_1) & \ldots & S_N(1,\omega_1) \\ B_1 & S_1(1,\omega_2) & S_2(1,\omega_2) & \ldots & S_N(1,\omega_2) \\ B_1 & S_1(1,\omega_K) & S_2(1,\omega_K) & \ldots & S_N(1,\omega_K) \end{bmatrix}$$

or

$$\begin{bmatrix} 1+r & S_1(1,\omega_1) & S_2(1,\omega_1)\ldots & S_N(1,\omega_1) \\ 1+r & S_1(1,\omega_2) & S_2(1,\omega_2)\ldots & S_N(1,\omega_2) \\ 1+r & S_1(1,\omega_K) & S_2(1,\omega_K)\ldots & S_N(1,\omega_K) \end{bmatrix}$$

where

$$S(1,\Omega) \in \mathbb{R}^{K\times(N+1)}$$

1.2.1. *Portfolio value process*

We can define the value process $V = \{V_t : t = 0, 1\}$ as the total value of the portfolio for each period

$$V_t = \theta_0 B_t + \sum_{n=1}^{N} \theta_n S_n(t) \quad t = 0,\ 1 \tag{1.1}$$

The value process depends on the choice of θ Trading Strategy, but V_1 is a random variable.

1.2.2. *Gain process*

The gain process represents the change in portfolio value between $t = 0$ and $t = 1$.

Since $\theta_n(S_n(t) - S_n(t-1))$ shows the profit or loss caused by each financial asset, and since the deposit account also provides profit (interest) as

$$\theta_0(B(1) - B(0)) = \theta_0(B(0)r) = \theta_0 r$$

we can write this process as

$$G = \theta_0 r + \sum_{n=1}^{N} \theta_n(S_n(t) - (S_n(t-1)) \quad t = 1$$

or

$$G = \theta_0 r + \sum_{n=1}^{N} \theta_n \Delta S_n(t)$$

$$\text{where} \quad \Delta S_n(t) = S_n(1) - S_n(0) \tag{1.2}$$

A simple algebra shows that

$$V_0 = \theta_0 B_0 + \sum_{n=1}^{N} \theta_n S_n(0) = \theta_0 + \sum_{n=1}^{N} \theta_n S_n(0)$$

$$V_1 = \theta_0 B_1 + \sum_{n=1}^{N} \theta_n S_n(1) = \theta_0(1+r) + \sum_{n=1}^{N} \theta_n S_n(1)$$

$$G = V_1 - V_0 = \theta_0 r + \sum_{n=1}^{N} \theta_n \Delta S_n(t) \tag{1.3}$$

1.2.3. *Discounted price process*

Let's define the discounted price processes of risky financial assets as $S^* = \{S_t^* : t = 0,\ 1\}$ and $S_t^* = \{S_1^*(t), \dots, S_N^*(t)\}$. Let $S_n^*(t)$ represent the discounted price of the n'th stock at time t. Let's perform the discounting process with the deposit account we use as the unit of measurement. In other words, let's define

$$S_n^*(t) = S_n(t)/B_t$$

or

$$S_n^*(t) = \frac{S_n(t)}{B(t)} \quad n = 1 \dots N \quad t = 0, 1 \tag{1.4}$$

1.2.4. *Discounted value process*

Similar to 1.1.3. We can show the discounted value process by $V^* = \{V_t^* : t = 0, 1\}$. That is

$$V_t^* = \frac{\theta_0(1+r)}{(1+r)} + \sum_{n=1}^{N} \theta_n S_n(1)/(1+r)$$

$$V_t^* = \theta_0 + \sum_{n=1}^{N} \theta_n S_n^*(t) \quad t = 0, 1 \tag{1.5}$$

We can also write the discounted gain process as

$$G^* = V_1^* - V_0^*$$

and this yields

$$V_1^* = \theta_0 + \sum_{n=1}^{N} \theta_n S_n^*(1)$$

$$V_0^* = \theta_0 + \sum_{n=1}^{N} \theta_n S_n^*(0)$$

$$G^* = \sum_{n=1}^{N} \theta_n (S_n^*(1) - S_n^*(0)) = \sum_{n=1}^{N} \theta_n \Delta S_n^* \tag{1.6}$$

In general, we can state the process as $V_t^* = \frac{V_t}{B_t}$ $t = 0, 1$. The discounted financial asset prices in expanded matrix form can be written as

$$S^*(1,\Omega) = \begin{matrix} 1 & S_1^*(1,\omega_1) & S_2^*(1,\omega_1)\ldots & S_N^*(1,\omega_1) \\ 1 & S_1^*(1,\omega_2) & S_2^*(1,\omega_2)\ldots & S_N^*(1,\omega_2) \\ 1 & S_1^*(1,\omega_K) & S_2^*(1,\omega_K)\ldots & S_N^*(1,\omega_K) \end{matrix}$$

where

$$S(1,\Omega) \in \mathbb{R}^{K\times(N+1)}$$

Example 1.1 (Pliska, 1997, p. 3).

$$S_0 = 5 \quad r = \frac{1}{9} \quad K = 2 \quad S_1(\omega_1) = \frac{20}{3} \quad S_1(\omega_2) = \frac{40}{9}$$

Then, we can calculate

$$1 + r = \frac{10}{9} \; S_1^*(\omega_1) = 6 \; veS_1^*(\omega_2) = 4$$

For any arbitrary strategy θ, we have

$$V_0 = \theta_0 + 5\theta_1 = V_0^*$$

The value and gain processes for each state of the world are

ω_1

$$V_1 = 10/9\theta_0 + 20/3\theta_1$$
$$V_1^* = \theta_0 + 6\theta_1$$
$$G = V_1 - V_0 = 1/9\theta_0 + 5/3\theta_1$$
$$G^* = \theta_1$$

ω_2

$$V_1 = 10/9\theta_0 + 40/9\theta_1$$
$$V_1^* = \theta_0 + 4\theta_1$$
$$G = V_1 - V_0 = 1/9\theta_0 - 5/9\theta_1$$
$$G^* = -\theta_1$$

1.3. Arbitrage and Trading Strategies

1.3.1. *Dominant trading strategies*

In the presence of any two trading strategies $\widehat{\theta}$ and $\widetilde{\theta}$, if $\hat{V}_0 = \tilde{V}_0$ and $\hat{V}_1(\omega) > \tilde{V}_1(\omega)$ for all $\omega \in \Omega$ then the $\widehat{\theta}$ strategy is considered dominant. Both trades start with the same investment, but at the end of the period, the dominant strategy earns more returns in all states.

$$V_0 = 0, \; V_1(\omega) > 0, \quad \forall \omega \in \Omega$$

is a dominant strategy. Defining $\theta = \widehat{\theta} - \widetilde{\theta}$ we have

$$V_0 = \widehat{V}_0 - \tilde{V}_0 = 0$$

Since we have $\widehat{V}_1(\omega) > \tilde{V}_1(\omega)$ we can write $V_1 = \widehat{V}_1(\omega) - \tilde{V}_1(\omega) > 0$.

Proposition 1.1. *If and only if there is a trading strategy that satisfies the condition*

$$V_0 = 0, \; V_1(\omega) > 0, \quad \forall \omega \in \Omega$$

then there is a dominant trading strategy. In this case, it is also possible to convert the negative investment (wealth) at the beginning of the period into a non-negative value at the end.

Let's assume that θ is a strategy that satisfies Proposition 1.1. We know that $\{\theta_1, \theta_2, \ldots, \theta_N\}$ is a strategy and that $G^* > 0$ for each $\omega \in \Omega$.

Now, let us define a new strategy $\widetilde{\theta}$, $\delta = \min_\omega G^*(\omega)$ and $\theta_n = \widetilde{\theta}_n \quad n = 1, N$ where

$$\widetilde{\theta}_0 = -\sum_{n=1}^{N} \theta_n S_n^*(0) - \delta$$

Instead of having $\widetilde{\theta}_0 = -\sum_{n=1}^{N} \theta_n S_n^*(0)$ or $\widetilde{\theta}_0 + \sum_{n=1}^{N} \theta_n S_n^*(0) = 0$ and $\widetilde{V}_0^* = 0$ now we have

$$\widetilde{V}_0^* = \widetilde{\theta}_0 + \sum_{n=1}^{N} \theta_n S_n^*(0) = \sum_{n=1}^{N} \theta_n S_n^*(0) - \sum_{n=1}^{N} \theta_n S_n^*(0) - \delta = -\delta < 0$$

But, by definition $G^*(\omega) \geq \delta$ *for all* $\omega \in \Omega$*, therefore,*

$$\widetilde{V}_1^* = \widetilde{V}_0^* + G^*(\omega) \geq 0$$
$$\widetilde{V}_1^* = -\delta + G^*(\omega) \geq 0$$

has been converted into a non-negative value for all $\omega \in \Omega$*. Therefore, a situation equivalent to Proposition* 1.1 *is obtained.*

Proposition 1.2. *A dominant trading strategy exists if and only if there is a trading strategy that satisfies the condition* $V_0 < 0$ *and* $V_1(\omega) \geq 0$ *for all* $\omega \in \Omega$*.*

1.3.2. *Linear pricing measure*

The dominant trading strategy does not have a consistent logic in terms of the market. In other words, this is not a sustainable strategy. If there is a linear pricing measure as a non-negative vector

$$\pi = \{\pi(\omega_1), \pi(\omega_2) \dots \ \pi(\omega_K)\}$$

providing that

$$V_0^* = \sum_{\omega=1}^{K} \pi(\omega) V_1^*(\omega) = \sum_{\omega=1}^{K} \pi(\omega) V_1(\omega)/B_1(\omega) \tag{1.7}$$

then the pricing of the contingent claims will be logically consistent. For an arbitrary trading strategy θ we can write

$$\theta_0 + \sum_{n=1}^{N} \theta_n S_n^*(0) = \sum_{\omega=1}^{K} \pi(\omega) \left[\theta_0 + \sum_{n=1}^{N} \theta_n S_n^*(1)(\omega)\right]$$

If,

$$\theta_1 = \theta_2 = \dots \theta_N = 0$$

we must have

$$\sum_{\omega=1}^{K} \pi(\omega) = 1 \tag{1.8}$$

to protect the equality of both sides of the equation. Therefore, we can interpret π as a probability measure on Ω.

For any arbitrary strategy $i \in \{1 \dots N\}$ and assuming $\theta_n = 0$ all $i \neq n$, the equation also implies

$$S_n^*(0) = \sum_{\omega=1}^{K} \pi(\omega) S_n^*(1)(\omega) \quad n = 1 \dots N \tag{1.9}$$

Proposition 1.3. *The vector π is considered a linear pricing measure if and only if it is a probability measure on Ω that satisfies* (1.9).

This means that the present value of each financial asset is equal to its expected discounted value under the probability measure π. We can say the same thing for portfolio value. Thus, the close relationship between the linear pricing measure and dominant trading strategies emerges.

Proposition 1.4. *A linear pricing measure exists if and only if there are no dominant trading strategies.*

This principle can be explained (Pliska, 1997, pp. 6 − 8) *with linear programming duality theory.*

We have

$$\boldsymbol{\pi} \in \mathbb{R}^{\boldsymbol{K}}, \quad \{\boldsymbol{w_1}, \boldsymbol{w_2}, \dots, \boldsymbol{w_K}\}, \text{ as a column vector}$$

$Z = \begin{pmatrix} S_1^*(0) \\ S_2^*(0) \\ S_N^*(0) \\ 1 \end{pmatrix}$, $Z \in R^{N+1}$ *is also a column vector of initial prices, including the bank account and*

$$\mathbb{Z} = \begin{matrix} S_1^*(1, w_1) & S_1^*(1, w_2) & S_1^*(1, w_K) \\ S_N^*(1, w_1) & S_N^*(1, w_2) & S_N^*(1, w_K) \\ 1 & 1 & 1 \end{matrix}$$

is the transposed expanded payoff matrix.

The existence of a linear pricing measure indicates the existence of a solution to the following linear programming problem.

$$\max\ (0, 0, \dots, 0)\pi$$

$$\mathbb{Z}\pi = Z$$

$$\pi \geq 0 \quad \mathbb{Z}\pi \to Z \quad (N+1) \times K * (K \times 1) \to (N+1) \times 1 \tag{1.10}$$

According to the duality theorem, the dual of (1.10)

$$\min \theta Z$$

$$\theta \mathbb{Z} \geq 0 \tag{1.11}$$

must have a solution of $\theta = \{\theta_1 \ldots \theta_{N+1}\}$*, and the two optimal objective values must coincide and be equal to zero. We interpret the solution of* θ *as a trading strategy with the last component corresponding to* θ_0*.*

The minimization of (1.11) *means* $V_0^* = \theta Z = 0$*, but according to constraint* $V_1^* = \theta \mathbb{Z} \geq 0$ *for all* $\omega \in \Omega$*. Since the minimizing strategy,* θ *has an objective value equal to zero; there cannot be any trading strategy with* $V_0^* < 0$ *and* $V_1^*(\omega) \geq 0$ *for all* $\omega \in \Omega$*. Hence, the existence of linear pricing measure implies there cannot be any dominant strategies.*

Therefore, if no dominant strategy exists, the solution to (1.11) *is* $\theta = 0$*. According to the duality theorem, there is a linear pricing measure* π *that satisfies the conditions in* (1.10)*.*

$$\max\ (0, 0, \ldots, 0)\pi$$

$$\mathbb{Z}\pi = Z$$

$$\pi \geq 0$$

In other words, the solution $\theta = 0$ *requires the existence of* π*.*

1.3.2.1. *Farkas lemma*

If and only if there exists a vector $\pi(w) \geq 0$ and $\pi(\omega) \in \mathbb{R}^K$ (linear pricing measure) such that $S^*(0) = \pi(w)S^*(1,\ \Omega)$ then there is no vector $\theta \in \mathbb{R}^{N+1}$ such that $S^*(1,\ \Omega)\theta > 0$ *ve* $S^*(0)\theta = 0$.

Note that when we multiply the $S^*(0)$ vector by the θ vector and the $\pi(w)S^*(1,\ \Omega)$ equation by the θ vector again, let's assume that the left side is "0". In this case, $\pi(w)S^*(1,\ \Omega)\theta$ on the right side should be equal to zero. Since π (w) is positive, we need $S^*(1,\ \Omega)$ $\theta = 0$ to be satisfied. However, we want the $S^*(1,\ \Omega)\theta > 0$ property. Therefore, for this, the $\pi(\omega)$ vector would not have existed. However, if this vector exists, the opposite, i.e., the θ vector, should not exist.

Market models that incorporate any dominant trading strategy are not reasonable and sustainable from an economic point of view. However, markets with non-dominant trading strategies are more acceptable and sensible as they include a pricing measure.

1.3.3. *Law of one price*

If there do not exist two different trading strategies, such as $\widehat{\theta}$ *ve* $\widetilde{\theta}$ satisfying the conditions $\widehat{V}_0 > \widetilde{V}_0$ and $\widehat{V}_1(\omega) = \widetilde{V}_1(\omega)$ for all $\omega \in \Omega$, we say the law of one price holds for securities market model. However, if the two strategies provide the same payoff by the time $t = 1$ but have different initial values, the law of one price does not hold.

For $\widehat{\theta}$ *ve* $\widetilde{\theta}$ assuming $\widehat{V}_1^*(\omega) = \widetilde{V}_1^*(\omega)$ $\widehat{V}_0^* > \widetilde{V}_0^*$ imply that $\widehat{G}^*(\omega) < \widetilde{G}^*(\omega)$ for all $\omega \in \Omega$. Defining a new trading strategy

$$\theta_n = \widetilde{\theta}_n - \widehat{\theta}_n$$

$n = 1 \ldots N$ it is evident that we have $G^*(w) > 0$ for all $\omega \in \Omega$. Taking

$$H_0 = -\sum_{n=1}^{N} H_n S_n^*(0)$$

we have $V_0^* = 0$ and $V_1^* = V_0^* + G^*(w) > 0$ for all $\omega \in \Omega$. That is, the law of one price fails to hold.

Proposition 1.5. *If no dominant trading strategies exist, then the law of one price holds. The converse is not necessarily true* (Pliska, 1997, p. 8). *We may have one price for security, but there may be dominant trading strategies.*

Consider a market with

$$K = 2, \quad N = 1, \quad r = 1, \quad S_0 = 10, \quad S_1(w_1) = S_1(w_2) = 12$$

Thus, in all cases, $V_1 = \alpha$ is constant and provides the same payment.

$$2\theta_0 + 12\theta_1 = \alpha$$

There can be infinite trading strategies, all of which have different V_0 values. The law of one price did not hold. Now, assume $S_1(w_2) = 8$.

$\theta_0 = 10$, $\theta_1 = -1$ trading strategy will yield $V_0 = 0$, however, we have

$$B_1 + S_1(\omega_1) = V_1(\omega_1) = 20 - 12 = 8$$
$$B_1 + S_1(\omega_2) = V_1(\omega_2) = 20 - 8 = 12$$

at time $t = 1$. So, in this case, we have one price, but the dominant strategy exists.

1.3.4. *The law of one price and asset span*

The set of payments provided by portfolios created with different transaction strategies $\theta = \{\theta_0 \dots \theta_N\}$ is called the Asset Span (concepts such as value and financial asset space can also be considered). In other words, the set of payments of all portfolios is given this name. The value span can also be regarded as the payment matrix's column space.

Example:

$$S_1^*(1) = \begin{pmatrix} 1 \\ 2 \\ 3 \end{pmatrix} \; S_2^*(1) = \begin{pmatrix} 3 \\ 1 \\ 2 \end{pmatrix} \; S^*(0) = (1\ 2)$$

The asset span consists of all vectors as a combination of

$$\theta_1 \begin{pmatrix} 1 \\ 2 \\ 3 \end{pmatrix} + \theta_2 \begin{pmatrix} 3 \\ 1 \\ 2 \end{pmatrix}$$

Also, we can write the payoff matrix as

$$\mathbb{Z}' = S^*(1) = \begin{pmatrix} 1 & 3 \\ 2 & 1 \\ 3 & 2 \end{pmatrix}$$

and the asset span as

$$\mathbb{S} = \begin{pmatrix} 1 & 3 \\ 2 & 1 \\ 3 & 2 \end{pmatrix} \begin{pmatrix} \theta_1 \\ \theta_2 \end{pmatrix}$$

where θ_1 and θ_2 are scalars.

Naturally, more than one financial asset can be added to this portfolio. If these financial assets remain within the value region, their payoffs can be produced as linear combinations of $S_1^*(1)$ and $S_2^*(1)$. Such assets are called redundant financial assets. Since there are only 3 different states, the size of the value region cannot be larger than 3. Therefore, the maximum number of non-redundant financial assets can be 3. Let's add a third financial asset to the model with the following payoff vector:

$$S_3^*(1) = \begin{pmatrix} 1 \\ 3 \\ 4 \end{pmatrix}$$

Now, the space of financial assets is the entire space $\mathbb{R}^3$ spanned by $S_1^*(1), S_2^*(1), S_3^*(1)$. Any added financial asset will be "redundant" since the discounted payoff vector will remain inside this space. Such markets where the discounted payoff vectors remain inside the financial asset space are called "complete market models." This is possible only if the dimension of the asset span is equal to the number of possible states. Let X be the discounted payoff of some contingent claim; then, the payoff can be replicated by some linear combination of the financial assets in the model.

$$X = S^*(1)\theta \quad S^*(0) \in \mathbb{R}^{+(N+1)} \quad \theta \in \mathbb{R}^{N+1}$$

Then, we can define

$$F(X) = S^*(0)\theta$$

as a pricing functional of the payoff X.

1.3.5. *State prices*

A contingent claim is a value whose payment depends on a particular outcome. These outcomes are called states (states of nature), and financial assets are called state-contingent claims. A contingent value whose payment is "1" if a particular outcome occurs and "0" otherwise (non-occurrence) is also called an Arrow–Debreu financial asset or a primary financial asset (Arrow–Debreu security, pure security).

The state prices for two stocks and one risk-free asset are as follows

State/Asset	X_1	X_2	X_f
w_1	110	105	102
w_2	100	101	102
w_3	90	98	102

Now, let's consider that a contingent claim will pay "1" if the first state occurs and "0" in all other cases, a second contingent claim will pay "1" in the second state and "0" in all other cases, and a third contingent claim will pay "1" in the third state and "0" in all other cases.

In this case, the first stock can be thought of as a portfolio consisting of three contingent claims:

110 units of contingent claim 1 (cc1), 100 units of cc2 and 90 units of cc3. Thus, for example, if the 2nd state occurs, the share value will be 100; if the 3rd state occurs, the share value will be 90, etc.

Likewise, we can write the second stock as a combination of 105 units of cc1, 101 units of cc2, and 98 units of cc3.

We will call the prices of contingent claims state prices. Therefore, stock/financial asset prices can be calculated in terms of state prices if the state prices are known since stocks are written as a portfolio of state-contingent assets or claims.

In order to calculate, there must be as many underlying financial assets or state prices as complex securities. We call this the spanning property. $i = 1, \ldots, n$ represents the number of states, and $j = 1 \ldots n$ represents the number of complex securities. Let X_{ij} represent the payoff of the j'th financial asset in state i, and let α_{ij} be the number of shares that must be held from the j'th financial asset in state i, then we can write

$$\alpha_{11}X_{11} + \alpha_{12}X_{12} + \cdots + \alpha_{1n}X_{1n} = 1$$

$$\alpha_{11}X_{21} + \alpha_{12}X_{22} + \cdots + \alpha_{1n}X_{2n} = 0$$

$$\cdots\cdots\cdots\cdots\cdots\cdots\cdots\cdots\cdots\cdots\cdots\cdots$$

$$\alpha_{11}X_{n1} + \alpha_{12}X_{n2} + \cdots + \alpha_{1n}X_{nn} = 0$$

$$\alpha_{21}X_{11} + \alpha_{22}X_{12} + \cdots + \alpha_{2n}X_{1n} = 0$$

$$\alpha_{21}X_{21} + \alpha_{22}X_{22} + \cdots + \alpha_{2n}X_{2n} = 1$$

$$\alpha_{21}X_{n1} + \alpha_{22}X_{n2} + \cdots + \alpha_{2n}X_{nn} = 0$$

$$[\alpha_{n1}X_{11} + \alpha_{n2}X_{12} + \cdots + \alpha_{nn}X_{1n} = 0$$

$$\alpha_{n1}X_{21} + \alpha_{n2}X_{22} + \cdots + \alpha_{nn}X_{2n} = 0$$

$$\alpha_{n1}X_{n1} + \alpha_{n2}X_{n2} + ... + \alpha_{nn}X_{nn} = 1 \tag{1.12}$$

The entire system can be written as a system of simultaneous equations.

$$X = \begin{bmatrix} X_{11} & X_{12} & X_{1n} \\ X_{21} & X_{22} & X_{2n} \\ X_{n1} & X_{n2} & X_{nn} \end{bmatrix}$$

$$A = \begin{bmatrix} \alpha_{11} & \alpha_{12} & \alpha_{1n} \\ \alpha_{21} & \alpha_{22} & \alpha_{2n} \\ \alpha_{n1} & \alpha_{n2} & \alpha_{nn} \end{bmatrix}$$

$$I = \begin{bmatrix} 1 & 0 & 0 \\ 0 & 1 & 0 \\ 0 & 0 & 1 \end{bmatrix}$$

$$XA' = I$$

The coefficients α_{ij} can be calculated easily as

$$A = (X^{-1}I)'$$

If we know the stock prices, then the state prices can be calculated as

$$\varphi = AS(0)$$

$$\varphi = (X')^{-1}S(0) \tag{1.13}$$

Example:

$X =$

	Security 1	Security 2	Security 3	Security 4
State 1	100	75	20	85
State 2	100	100	65	72
State 3	100	125	90	135
State 4	100	150	118	110

You can show that the state prices are
0.06
0.18
0.26
0.42
and the risk-free rate is

$$r_f = \frac{1}{0.06 + 0.18 + 0.26 + 0.42} - 1 = \frac{1}{0.92} - 1 = 0.086957$$

1.3.6. *Arbitrage*

Suppose we do not have any dominant strategy. In that case, we cannot have a trading strategy generating a strictly positive amount of wealth at time $t = 1$, with zero investment. However, suppose investors can profit from a transaction without being exposed to any risk of losing money. In that case, such an investment opportunity is called an arbitrage opportunity, and the portfolio is an arbitrage portfolio. Formally, we can define an arbitrage opportunity for an arbitrary trading strategy θ as

$$\begin{aligned} &\text{(a)} \quad V_0 = 0 \\ &\text{(b)} \quad V_1 \geq 0 \\ &\text{(c)} \quad EV_1 > 0 \end{aligned} \tag{1.14}$$

In another words, it must be $V_1(w_k) \geq 0$ for all $k = 1, \ldots, K$, but the terminal wealth must be

$$V_1(w_k) > 0 \quad \text{for at least one } w_k.$$

Since $V_t^* = \frac{V_t}{B_t}$ and $B_t > 0$, a similar idea is also valid for discounted prices and portfolio values.

$$\begin{aligned} &(\text{a}^*) \quad V_0^* = 0 \\ &(\text{b}^*) \quad V_1^* \geq 0 \\ &(\text{c}^*) \quad EV_1^* > 0 \end{aligned} \tag{1.15}$$

Another equivalent condition is the following proposition.

Proposition 1.6. *θ is an arbitrage strategy if and only if we have*

$$\begin{aligned} &(\text{a}) \quad G^* \geq 0 \\ &(\text{b}) \quad EG^* > 0 \\ &(\text{c}) \quad V_0^* = 0 \end{aligned} \tag{1.16}$$

Proposition 1.7. *An arbitrage opportunity exists if a dominant trading strategy exists. However, arbitrage does not imply a dominant trading strategy, i.e., the converse is not always true.*

Example (Pliska, 1997, p. 9).

$K = 2 \quad N = 1 \quad r = 0 \quad S_0 = 10 \quad S_1(w_1) = 12 \quad S_1(w_2) = 10$

$S_1(0)$	$S_1(\omega_1)$	$S_1(\omega_2)$
10	12	10

$\theta = (-10,\ 1)$ is an arbitrage strategy, because $V_0 = 0$ and $V_1 = (2,\ 0)$.

$$\begin{aligned} \theta_0 B_0 + \theta_1 S_0 &= -10 * 1 + 1 * 10 = V_0 = 0 \\ V_1(\omega_1) &= -10 + 1 * 12 = 2 \\ V_1(\omega_2) &= -10 + 1 * 10 = 0 \end{aligned}$$

$V_1 = (2,\ 0)$ creates an arbitrage opportunity. However, if the linear pricing measure is taken as $\pi(0,\ 1)$, we have

$$EV_1 = \pi_1 V_1(\omega_1) + \pi_2 V_1(\omega_2) = 0 * 2 + 1 * 0 = 0$$

Since the expected value of final wealth equals 0, there is no dominant strategy even if we have an arbitrage opportunity.

In general, single-period financial asset market models can be grouped into four groups (Pliska, 1997, pp. 9–10)

(1) Strategies where there is no arbitrage opportunity.
(2) There are arbitrage opportunities but no dominant trading strategy.
(3) Situations where there are dominant strategies but the law of one price holds.
(4) Situations where the law of one price does not hold.

Of course, only Category 1 will make economic sense. The absence of arbitrage will be possible with the existence of a risk-neutral probability measure, which means a linear pricing measure, together with discounted price processes.

1.3.7. *Risk-neutral probability measure*

Although finding a dominant strategy in the presence of a linear pricing measure is impossible, arbitrage is still possible in the system. To eliminate arbitrage in the system, there must be a strictly positive "risk neutral" probability measure for each $\omega \in \Omega$.

A probability measure Q defined on Ω is called a risk-neutral probability measure if

$$\begin{aligned} &\text{(a)} \quad Q(\omega) > 0 \ ve \\ &\text{(b)} \quad E^Q(\Delta S_n^*) = 0 \quad n = 1, \ldots, N \end{aligned} \tag{1.17}$$

By this definition, it can be easily shown that $E^Q\left(S_n^*(1)\right) = S_n^*(0)$. Thus, it is seen that the risk-neutral probability measure is a linear pricing measure that assigns a strictly positive probability density for each $\omega \in \Omega$.

Example: $K = 2$, $N = 1$, $1 + r = 1.1$, $S(0) = 5$, $S_1(\omega_1) = 7.7$, $S_1(\omega_2) = 4.4$.

There must be a strictly positive probability measure for 1.17 to be satisfied

$$5 = 7q_1 + 4q_2$$

$$1 = q_1 + q_2$$

$$q_1 = \frac{1}{3} \quad q_2 = \frac{2}{3}$$

Since $q_1,\ q_2 > 0$, the model has no arbitrage.

Let

$K = 2,\ N = 1,\ 1 + r = 1.1,$

$$S(0) = 5,\ S_1(\omega_1) = 7.7,\ S_1(\omega_2) = 4.4,\ S_1(\omega_3) = 3.3$$

$$5 = 7q_1 + 4q_2 + 3q_3$$

$$1 = q_1 + q_2 + q_3$$

The situation is slightly different because we have three states but two instruments. The solution is

$$q_2 = 2 - 4q_1$$

$$q_3 = -1 + 3q_1$$

and in terms of q_1. Since all the probabilities have to be strictly positive, we must have

$$q_1 < 1/2$$

$$q_1 > 1/3$$

So, there is no arbitrage for $1/3 < q_1 < 1/2$.

However, the system may have more than one risky financial asset. Now, let's consider the case of $N = 2$ and $K = 3$, where the prices are as follows:

$$S_1(0) = 5,\ S_1(\omega_1) = \frac{20}{3},\ S_1(\omega_2) = \frac{20}{3},\ S_1(\omega_3) = \frac{40}{9}$$

$$S_2(0) = 10,\ S_1(\omega_1) = \frac{40}{3},\ S_1(\omega_2) = \frac{80}{9},\ S_1(\omega_3) = \frac{80}{9}$$

The discounted prices are

$$S_1^*(\omega_1) = 6, \quad S_1^*(\omega_2) = 6, \; S_1^*\,(\omega_3) = 4$$
$$S_2^*(\omega_1) = 12, \quad S_2^*(\omega_2) = 8, \; S_2^*\,(\omega_3) = 8$$

and we have

$$q_1 = q_3 = \frac{1}{2}, \qquad q_2 = 0$$

Then, there is an arbitrage opportunity. It is possible to find a strictly positive probability measure for individual risky assets satisfying: $E^Q[S_1(1)] = 5$ and $E^Q[S_2(1)] = 10$. However, the existence of more than one financial asset will increase their interaction, and it will be challenging to find a strictly positive risk-neutral probability measure together. Therefore, arbitrage opportunities will emerge in the model as the number of assets increases.

1.3.8. *Arbitrage and separating hyperplane theorem*

Theorem 1.1. *A linear pricing measure exists if and only if no dominant strategies exist.*

Theorem 1.2 (Fundamental Theorem of Asset Pricing). *There are no arbitrage opportunities if and only if the risk-neutral probability measure Q exists.*

Let

$$\mathcal{W} = \left\{X \in \mathbb{R}^K : X = G^*\right\}$$

We know that G^* is the payoff value for some trading strategies θ, and $\mathcal{W}$ is a set of random variables. Let X be a vector of these payoff situations. Therefore, the $X \in \mathcal{W}$ values represent the discounted values of the payoffs obtained at $t = 1$ for a strategy with an initial investment of $V_0 = 0$. $\mathcal{W}$ is the linear subspace of $\mathbb{R}^K$ and for $X, \tilde{X} \in \mathcal{W}$, and two scalars u and v, we can write

$$uX + v\tilde{X} \in \mathcal{W}$$

Let's define another set as

$$\mathbb{A} = \left\{X \in \mathbb{R}^K : X \geq 0\right\}$$

That is a non-negative orthant (K-dimensional space) of $\mathbb{R}^K$. In this case, since the initial investment will be zero, arbitrage opportunities will exist if and only if a subspace of $\mathcal{W}$ intersects with A, that is, if $\mathcal{W} \cap \mathbb{A} \neq \emptyset$. It can be seen that there is an arbitrage opportunity if and only if the subspace of $\mathcal{W}$ intersects with the non-negative orthant of $\mathbb{R}^K$.

Now, let's define the orthogonal subspace corresponding to a subspace of $\mathcal{W}$ as $\mathcal{W}^\perp = \{Y \in R^K : X.Y = 0, \ \forall X \in \mathcal{W}\}$. The $X.Y$ product is the inner product defined as $X(w_1) * Y(w_1) + \cdots + X(w_K) * Y(w_K)$.

If $\mathcal{W} \cap \mathbb{A} \neq \emptyset$, then every point (on the Cartesian axes) around the perpendicular $\mathcal{W}^\perp$ (which intersects $\mathcal{W}$ at 90 degrees) will be strictly positive. $\mathcal{W} \cap \mathbb{A} = 0$ implies the existence of $\mathcal{W}^\perp$, which is perpendicular to $\mathcal{W}$ with every point not at the origin is strictly positive. In particular, there will be a point on this perpendicular for which all components are equal to 1. We can define the geometry of this specific point as

$$\mathbb{Q}^+ = \left\{q \in R^K : q_1 + \cdots + q_K = 1, \quad q > 0\right\}$$

($P^+ = \{X \in R^K : X_1 + \cdots + X_K = 1, \ X_K > 0\}$ in Pliska, 1997, p. 13). This geometry suggests that $\mathcal{W} \cap \mathbb{A} = 0$ if and only if $\mathcal{W}^\perp \cap \mathbb{Q}^+ \neq 0$.

For all $\Delta S_n^* \in \mathcal{W}$, any element of the set $\mathbb{Q}^+ \cap \mathcal{W}^\perp$ is a risk-neutral probability measure. Conversely, if Q is any risk-neutral probability measure, then for any $G^* \in \mathcal{W}$ corresponding to the trading strategy θ, we can write

$$E^Q G^* = E^Q \left[\sum_{n=1}^{N} \theta_n \Delta S_n^*\right] = \sum_{n=1}^{N} \theta_n E^Q \left[\Delta S_n^*\right] = 0$$

and $Q \in \mathbb{Q}^+ \cap \mathcal{W}^\top$. Let M be the set of all risk-neutral probability measures; $M = \mathbb{Q}^+ \cap \mathcal{W}^\top$.

Arbitrage opportunities will exist if the convex sets $\mathbb{A}$ and $\mathcal{W}$ have a non-zero intersection. That is, at the beginning of the period, investment is zero, and the set of returns is positive in all cases. However, if this intersection is zero, arbitrage is not present, and a hyperplane will separate these two disjoint convex sets. Let

$$\mathbb{A}^+ = \{X \in \mathbb{A} : EX = 1\}$$

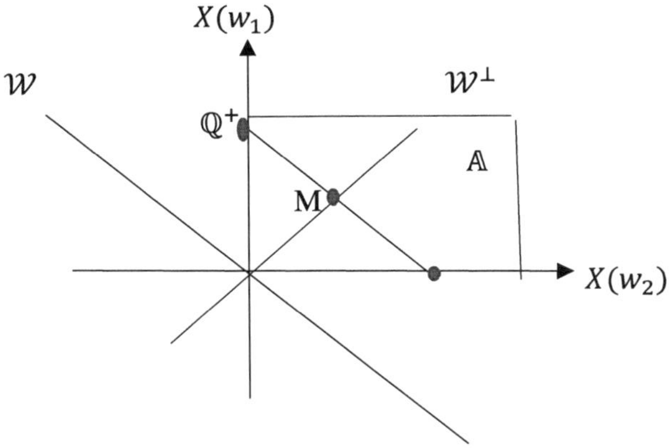

Figure 1.1. Geometric interpretation of risk-neutral probabilities.
Source: Figure is excerpted from Pliska, 1997, p. 14.

be a closed, bounded, and convex subset of R^K. No-arbitrage implies $\mathbb{A}^+$ and $\mathcal{W}$ are disjoint sets as they are shown in Figure 1.1. By the separating plane theorem, there exists $Y \in \mathcal{W}^\top$ such that $X.Y > 0$ for all $X \in \mathbb{A}^+$. Accordingly, it is possible to have vector $X \in \mathbb{A}$ having all components $k = 1 \ldots K$ zero except with the positive k'th element. Then, every component of Y must be strictly positive. By setting

$$Q\left(w_k\right) = \frac{Y\left(w_k\right)}{Y\left(w_1\right) + \cdots + Y\left(w_K\right)} \tag{1.18}$$

we obtain a probability measure Q with $Q \in \mathcal{W}^\top$. Conversely, if Q is a risk-neutral probability measure, the trading strategy θ cannot satisfy $E^Q G^* > 0$ and $G^* \geq 0$, so there cannot be an arbitrage strategy.

Example: Let our price set be

$$S_1(0) = 5,\ S_1\left(\omega_1\right) = \frac{20}{3},\quad S_1(\omega_2) = \frac{20}{3},\ S_1(\omega_3) = \frac{40}{9}$$

$$S_2(0) = 10,\ S_1(\omega_1) = \frac{40}{3},\quad S_1(\omega_2) = \frac{80}{9},\ S_1\left(\omega_3\right) = \frac{80}{9}$$

and the discounted prices be

$$S_1^*(\omega_1) = 6,\ S_1^*(\omega_2) = 6,\quad S_1^*\left(\omega_3\right) = 4$$

$$S_2^*(\omega_1) = 12,\ S_2^*(\omega_2) = 8,\quad S_2^*\left(\omega_3\right) = 8$$

We can write gain vectors as ($K = 3$)

n	$\Delta S_n^*(\omega_1)$	$\Delta S_n^*(\omega_2)$	$\Delta S_n^*(\omega_3)$
1	1	1	−1
2	2	−2	−2

It follows that

$$\mathcal{W} = \left\{X \in \mathbb{R}^3 : X = \theta_1 + 2\theta_2, \quad \theta_1 - 2\theta_2, \ -\theta_1 - 2\theta_2\right\}$$

for some $\theta_1, \theta_2 \ \in \mathbb{R}$. Then, we can find such a $\theta = (2 - 1)$ that we have

$$\mathcal{W} = \left\{X \in \mathbb{R}^3 : X_1 + X_3 = 0\right\}$$

and $X_2 > 0$. Notice that $V_0 = 0$. It can be shown that $\lambda \in R$

$$\mathcal{W}^{\perp} = \left\{Y \in \mathbb{R}^3 : Y = (\lambda, 0, \lambda) \ \lambda \in R\right\}$$

satisfies the condition

$$X \cdot Y = 0$$

but cannot satisfy the condition of $\mathcal{W}^{\perp} \cap \mathbb{Q}^{+} \neq 0$.

Now, we observe that

$$\mathcal{W} \cap \mathbb{A} = \left\{X \in \mathbb{R}^3 : X_1 = X_3 = 0, \ X_2 > 0\right\}$$

The portfolio's time $t = 1$ value is $(0, X_2, 0)$, and the solution to θ is

$$\theta_1 + 2\theta_2 = 0$$

$$\theta_1 - 2\theta_2 = X_2$$

$$\theta_1 = \frac{X_2}{2}\theta_2 = -\frac{X_2}{4}$$

Setting

$$\theta_0 = -\theta_1 S_1(0) - \theta_2 S_2(0)$$

$$\theta_0 = -\frac{5X_2}{2} + \frac{10X_2}{4} = 0 = V_0$$

we have an arbitrage opportunity for every $X_2 \ > 0$ for the trading strategy $\theta = \left(0, \frac{X_2}{2}, -\frac{X_2}{4}\right)$.

Subsection 1.3.8.1 more rigorously explains the relation between the arbitrage opportunity and the separating hyperplane theorem.

1.3.8.1. *Separating hyperplane theorem*

Let f be a vector in $\mathbb{R}^n$. A hyperplane $H = [f, \alpha]$, is a projection of vectors X onto f such that $X \in \mathbb{R}^n$ has magnitude α. For example, let

$\mathcal{W} = \begin{pmatrix} X_1 \\ X_2 \\ X_3 \end{pmatrix}$ then, $X_1 + 3X_2 + 2X_3 = 2$ is a hyperplane in $\mathbb{R}^3$ where

$$f = \begin{pmatrix} 1 \\ 3 \\ 2 \end{pmatrix}, \quad \alpha = 2$$

Any set C in $\mathbb{R}^n$ is called a convex set if any pair of vectors X and Y in C can be written as

$$(\gamma X + (1 - \gamma) Y) \in C, \quad 0 \leq \gamma \leq 1$$

In other words, if this linear combination also lies in, C we call the set convex. For example

$$C = \left\{ \begin{pmatrix} X_1 \\ X_2 \\ X_3 \end{pmatrix} : X_1 \geq 0, X_2 \geq 0, X_3 \geq 0 \right\} \tag{1.19}$$

is a convex set in $\mathbb{R}^3$.

If for any two sets A and B and for every $X \in A$ and $Y \in B$, there exists a value of α such that $f \cdot X \geq \alpha$ and $f \cdot Y < \alpha$, then the hyperplane $H = [f, \alpha]$ separates the sets A and B. For example, the hyperplane

$$\left[\begin{pmatrix} 1 \\ 1 \\ 1 \end{pmatrix}, 0 \right]$$

separates two disjoint convex sets

$$A = \left\{ \begin{pmatrix} X_1 \\ X_2 \\ X_3 \end{pmatrix} : X_1 \geq 0,\ X_2 \geq 0,\ X_3 \geq 0 \right\}$$

$$B = \left\{ \begin{pmatrix} Y_1 \\ Y_2 \\ Y_3 \end{pmatrix} : \; Y_1 < 0, \; Y_2 < 0, \; Y_3 < 0 \right\}$$

in $\mathbb{R}^3$.

We will establish its relation with the arbitrage portfolio as follows. $f \cdot Y < \alpha$ represents the set formed by the initial investment if α is assumed to be zero. Therefore, $f \cdot X \geq \alpha$ shows the arbitrage profit obtained at the end of the investment/period. If a hyperplane such as $\left[\begin{pmatrix} 1 \\ 1 \\ 1 \end{pmatrix}, 0 \right]$ can provide this separation, arbitrage will exist since a positive return is received in any case for a negative investment. The only condition for this not to exist is that the f vector is zero or the two sets have only a common vector, "0".

To prove the theorem, let us first assume that the risk-neutral probability measure exists and is expressed as $\pi = [q_1, q_2 \cdots q_K]$

$$S^*(1,\Omega) = \begin{matrix} 1 \; S_1^*(1,\omega_1) \; S_2^*(1,\omega_1) \ldots \; S_N^*(1,\omega_1) \\ 1 \; S_1^*(1,\omega_2) \; S_2^*(1,\omega_2) \ldots \; S_N^*(1,\omega_2) \\ 1 \; S_1^*(1,\omega_K) \; S_2^*(1,\omega_K) \ldots \; S_N^*(1,\omega_K) \end{matrix}$$

is the expanded payoff matrix, and we can write

$$\begin{aligned} S^*(0) &= \pi S^*(1,\Omega) = [q_1, q_2 \ldots q_K] \\ &= \begin{pmatrix} 1 \; S_1^*(1,\omega_1) \; S_2^*(1,\omega_1) \ldots \; S_N^*(1,\omega_1) \\ 1 \; S_1^*(1,\omega_2) \; S_2^*(1,\omega_2) \ldots \; S_N^*(1,\omega_2) \\ 1 \; S_1^*(1,\omega_K) \; S_2^*(1,\omega_K) \ldots \; S_N^*(1,\omega_K) \end{pmatrix} \end{aligned}$$

Assuming there is a trading strategy

$$\theta = \{\theta_0, \; \theta_1 \ldots \theta_N\} \quad \theta \in \mathbb{R}^{N+1}$$

such that

$$S^*(1, \; \Omega)\, \theta^T \geq 0$$

for all $w \in \Omega$ and strictly positive for some cases.

We consider the case

$$S^*(0)\theta^T = \pi S^*(1,\Omega)\,\theta^T$$

It is evident that $S^*(0)\theta^T > 0$ is satisfied since the vector π is strictly positive and $S^*(1,\ \Omega)\,\theta^T \geq 0$ for all $w \in \Omega$. Hence, there are no arbitrage opportunities.

Now, we define another subset, $U \in \mathbb{R}^{K+1}$ with $\theta \in \mathbb{R}^{N+1}$.

$$U = \begin{pmatrix} -S^*(0)\theta^T \\ S^*(1,w_1)\,\theta^T \\ S^*(1,w_2)\,\theta^T \\ S^*(1,w_K)\,\theta^T \end{pmatrix}$$

These vectors in U are the rows of the expanded payoff matrix. $S^*(1,w_K)$ is the k'th row of $S^*(1,\ \Omega)$. For example, the second row can be obtained as

$$S_0^*(1,w_1)\ S_1^*(1,w_1)\ldots\ S_N^*(1,w_1)\ \begin{matrix}\theta_0\\ \theta_1\\ \theta_N\end{matrix}$$

The first row is the initial investment and has the opposite sign. The case where all vectors are zero is also in the subset $U \in \mathbb{R}^{K+1}$. We also note that U is convex. (The linear sum of two operation strategies will remain in subset U.)

Let us define another convex subset in $\mathbb{R}_+^{K+1}$

$$\mathbb{R}_+^{K+1} = \{(X_0X_1\ldots X_K)^T \in R^{K+1},\ X_i \geq 0\},\quad i = 0\ldots K$$

The lack of arbitrage possibilities will mean that the subsets $\mathbb{R}_+^{K+1}$ and U have only the zero vector in common: $\mathbb{R}_+^{K+1} \cap U = \{0\}$. That is, each set can have only the zero vector in common. Therefore, these two sets will be separated by a hyperplane $[f,\alpha]$.

First, consider the converse; let us assume that there is a non-zero vector $X \in U \cap R_+^{K+1}$. Since there is a trading strategy θ that accompanies each vector in U, we can show that θ, together with $X \in U \cap R_+^{K+1}$, always provides an arbitrage opportunity.

Consider the

$$-S^*(0)\theta^T = 0 \quad \text{and} \quad -S^*(0)\theta^T > 0 \text{ cases.}$$

If $-S^*(0)\theta^T = 0$, then since $X \neq 0$ and $X \in \mathbb{R}_+^{K+1}$ the entries (all vectors in U) in $S^*(1, w_k)\theta^T$, $k = 1, \ldots, K$ are all positive with at least one strict inequality. With an initial investment of zero, this represents an arbitrage opportunity.

For the second case $-S^*(0)\theta^T > 0$ can be written as $S^*(0)\theta^T < 0$. Once again, all the entries in $S^*(1, w_k)\theta^T$, $k = 1, \ldots, K$ are all non-negative. So, this exhibits a dominant strategy and, in turn, an arbitrage strategy.

To avoid arbitrage, we must have $U \cap R_+^{K+1} = \{0\}$. Then U and R_+^{K+1} are disjoint convex subsets in $\mathbb{R}^{K+1}$. By the Separating Hyperplane Theorem, there exists a hyperplane that separates non-empty convex sets U and R_+^{K+1}.

If $f \in R^{K+1}$ is an orthogonal vector (normal) of this hyperplane, then we must have

$$f \cdot X > f \cdot Y$$

where $X \in R_+^{K+1} \backslash \{0\}$ and $Y \in U$.

Since U is a linear subspace, the negative multiples of $Y \in U$ must also belong to U as $-f \cdot Y$.

For example, let

$$f = [1\ 1\ 1],\ X = [2\ 3\ 1] \text{ and } Y[-3 - 6\ 1]$$

$$1 \times 2 + 1 \times 3 + 1 \times 1 > 1 \times (-3) + 1 \times (-6) + 1 \times 1$$

$$7 > -8$$

that is, it must be

$$f \cdot X > f \cdot Y$$

However, the condition

$$f \cdot X > -f \cdot Y$$

cannot be satisfied. This inequality is satisfied if and only if $f \cdot Y = 0$ for all $Y \in U$. In this case, we have

$$f \cdot X > 0 \tag{1.20}$$

for all $X \in R_+^{K+1} \backslash \{0\}$.

This requires that all elements in f be strictly positive since it is possible to make $f \cdot X = 0$ by choosing the i'th element in f as non-positive and choosing all elements in X other than the i'th one as zero, which contradicts the result that $f \cdot X > 0$ for every $X \in R_{+}^{K+1} \backslash \{0\}$.

From $f \cdot Y = 0$, for all $\theta \in R^{N+1}$ we can write

$$-f_0 S^*(0)\theta^T + \sum_{k=1}^{K} f_k S^*(1, w_k)\, \theta^T = 0$$

where f_k $k = 0, \ldots, K$ are the components of vector f. By $q(w_k) = q_k = \frac{f_k}{f_0}$ for $k = 0 \ldots K$, we can deduce the result that

$$S^*(0) = \sum_{k=1}^{K} q_k S^*(1, w_k)$$

q_k are the strictly positive risk-neutral probabilities for $f_k > 0$ for all $k = 0, \ldots, K$ where

$$\sum_{k=1}^{K} q_k = 1 \quad f_0 = \sum_{k=1}^{K} f_k$$

Example: Let

$$\begin{matrix} 1 \\ S_1(0) \\ S_2(0) \end{matrix} = [q_1 \quad q_2 \quad q_3] \begin{matrix} 1 & S_1^*(1, w_1) & S_2^*(1, w_1) \\ 1 & S_1^*(1, w_2) & S_2^*(1, w_2) \\ 1 & S_1^*(1, w_3) & S_2^*(1, w_3) \end{matrix}$$

$$\begin{matrix} 1 \\ 3 \\ 3 \end{matrix} = [q_1 \quad q_2 \quad q_3] \begin{matrix} 1 & 4 & 3 \\ 1 & 3 & 2 \\ 1 & 2 & 4 \end{matrix}$$

For any arbitrary trading strategy $\theta = \{\theta_1, \theta_2\}$, we can calculate the gain process as

$$\begin{matrix} 4 & 3 \\ 3 & -3 \\ 2 & 3 \end{matrix} = \begin{matrix} 1 \\ 0 \\ -1 \end{matrix}$$

and

$$\begin{matrix} 3 \\ 2 \\ 4 \end{matrix} - \begin{matrix} 3 \\ 3 \\ 3 \end{matrix} = \begin{matrix} 0 \\ -1 \\ 1 \end{matrix}$$

$$\mathcal{W} = \begin{Bmatrix} 1 & 0 \\ 0 & -1 \\ -1 & 1 \end{Bmatrix} \begin{matrix} \theta_1 \\ \theta_2 \end{matrix}$$

Since we must have

$$E^Q G^* = E^Q \left[\sum_{n=1}^{N} \theta_n \Delta S_n^* \right] = \sum_{k=1}^{K} Q(w_k) \sum_{n=1}^{N} \theta_n \left[\Delta S_n^* \right] = 0$$

to avoid arbitrage, the risk-neutral probability measure vector $Q(w_k)$ will lie within the orthogonal $\mathcal{W}^\top$ of the payoff set. $\mathcal{W}^\top$ is the line orthogonal to the vectors

$$\mathcal{W} = \begin{Bmatrix} 1 & 0 \\ 0 & -1 \\ -1 & 1 \end{Bmatrix}$$

This line can be arbitrarily chosen as $\lambda(1\ 1\ 1)^\top$ with λ being scalar. That gives

$$\lambda(1\ 1\ 1) \begin{Bmatrix} 1 & 0 \\ 0 & -1 \\ -1 & 1 \end{Bmatrix} = 0 \quad (f \cdot X = 0)$$

Remembering that $Q \in \mathcal{W}^\top$ with every component of Q must be strictly positive and

$$Q(w_k) = \frac{Y(w_k)}{Y(w_1) + \cdots + Y(w_K)}$$

we can calculate our risk-neutral probabilities as

$$\begin{pmatrix} \frac{1}{3} & \frac{1}{3} & \frac{1}{3} \end{pmatrix} \in \mathbb{Q}^+ \cap \mathcal{W}^\perp$$

where the sum of components is equal to one and all strictly positive.

Summary: Up to this point, we have seen the concept of arbitrage and the technical conditions for the existence of arbitrage. We have seen that if there are two different disjoint sets satisfying the property

$$f \cdot X > f \cdot Y$$

they can be separated by a separating hyperplane $[f, \alpha]$, but it must be $f \cdot Y = 0$ due to the property of convex linear subspace.

Therefore, we have seen that for arbitrage not to occur, the only common point of these two convex sets is the zero vector where $X \in R_+^{K+1} \backslash \{0\}$, $Y \in U$ and $U \cap R_+^{K+1} = \{0\}$.

1.3.9. *Valuation of contingent claims*

A contingent value is a random value $X(w)$ that makes a specific payment to the investor at $t = 1$ according to a particular $\omega_k \in \Omega$ state. Therefore, a price determination is required that the buyer and seller can accept. Although it may be thought that this price may depend on the risk preferences and utility functions of the buyer and seller, arbitrage pricing theory shows that the prices of contingent claims at $t = 0$ have a fair and correct price that is independent of the buyer and seller risk preferences.

Suppose there is a portfolio value V_1 that can replicate the value of a contingent claim X at $t = 1$, and there is a trading strategy θ that can replicate this portfolio. In that case, the contingent value X is called attainable or marketable. For each $\omega_k \in \Omega$, $V_1 = X$ must be satisfied by the trading strategy θ. The portfolio produced by the trading strategy θ is called a replicable portfolio.

If the price of X at $t = 0$ is p_0 and $p_0 > V_0$ or $p_0 < V_0$, there will be a situation of making a profit without taking any risk, namely an arbitrage opportunity. (How?)

In this case, the correct price should be $p_0 = V_0$. However, if there is another $\widehat{\theta}$ strategy that provides the property $\widehat{V}_1 = X$ and $\widehat{V}_0 \neq V_0$, arbitrage profits can still be generated through this strategy. The problem is that the law of one price does not work. The uniqueness of V_0 depends on the law of one price working.

As is known, if arbitrage opportunities do not exist, the dominant strategy does not exist. If there is no dominant strategy, the law of one price is valid. Therefore, the existence of a risk-neutral probability measure will show that the law of one price is valid.

Proposition 1.8. *If Q is a risk-neutral measure, then for each trading strategy θ we can write*

$$V_0 = V_0^* = E^Q V_0^* = E^Q[V_1^* - G^*] = E^Q[V_1^*] - E^Q\left[\sum_{n=1}^{N} H_n \Delta S_n^*\right]$$

$$E^Q[V_1^*] - E^Q\left[\sum_{n=1}^{N} H_n \Delta S_n^*\right] = E^Q[V_1^*] - 0 = E^Q[V_1/B_1]$$

$E^Q[V_1^*]$ is constant with respect to the risk-neutral measure Q and does not depend on the choice of Q. Therefore, there is only one, trading strategy that yields the price V_0, and there is no other $\widehat{\theta}$ such that $\widehat{V}_1 = X$ and $\widehat{V}_0 \neq V_0$.

Proposition 1.9. *If the law of one price is valid, the price of an attainable conditional value X at $t = 0$ is calculated as*

$$V_0 = H_0 B_0 + \sum_{n=1}^{N} H_n S_n(0)$$

Proposition 1.10 (Risk Neutral Valuation Principle). *If the market model does not contain arbitrage opportunities, time $t = 0$ price of an attainable contingent claim X is calculated as*

$$E^Q[X/B_1]$$

where Q is a risk-neutral measure.

Example:

$$q_1 = q_2 = 1/2 \ r = 0.1$$

$$B_1 = 1.1 = \frac{10}{9}, \quad X(\omega_1) = 7.7, \ X(\omega_2) = 2.2$$

$$S_0 = 5, \quad K = 2, \quad S_1(\omega_1) = 6.6, \ S_1(\omega_2) = 4.4$$

$$S_1^*(\omega_1) = 6, \quad S_1^*(\omega_2) = 4$$

we can calculate $E^Q\left[\frac{X}{B_1}\right]$

$$E^Q\left[\frac{X}{B_1}\right] = \frac{1}{2} * \frac{7.7}{1.1} + \frac{1}{2} * \frac{2.2}{1.1} = 4.5$$

providing X is attainable. Therefore, we need to show that there is a trading strategy that can achieve this.

$$\begin{aligned}
&V_1^* = V_0^* + G^* = 4.5 + \theta_1 \Delta S_1^* \\
&7 = 4.5 + \theta_1.(6-5) \\
&2 = 4.5 + \theta_1.(4-5) \\
&\theta_1 = 2.5
\end{aligned}$$

To determine θ_0

$$\begin{aligned}
&V_0 = \theta_0 * 1 + \theta_1 S_1(0) = \\
&4.5 = \theta_0 + 2.5 * 5 \\
&\theta_0 = -8
\end{aligned}$$

That is, by borrowing -8 in addition to the initial cost of 4.5, we can buy $\frac{12.5}{5} = 2.5$ shares of risky asset.

$$\begin{aligned}
&X(w_1) = 2.5 * 6.6 - 8.8 = 7.7 \\
&X(w_2) = 2.5 * 4.4 - 8.8 = 2.2
\end{aligned}$$

It is obvious that with the trading strategy $\theta = (\theta_0, \theta_1)$ and with the risk-neutral probabilities $q = (q_1, q_2)$ time $t = 1$ payoffs of the contingent claim X are exactly replicated by one risk-free and one risky asset.

Example: Consider an arbitrary contingent claim $X = (X_1, X_2, X_3)$. This value is attainable/marketable if and only if

$$V_0 = \theta_0 B_1 + \theta_1 S_1$$

for the pair θ_0, θ_1. Each state's portfolio with strategy θ must replicate the contingent claim's payoffs.

$$\omega_1 : \ 1.1\theta_0 + 6.6\theta_1 = X_1$$
$$\omega_2 : \ 1.1\theta_0 + 4.4\theta_1 = X_2$$
$$\omega_3 : \ 1.1\theta_0 + 2.2/3\theta_1 = X_3$$
$$\theta_1 = X_1 - 1.5X_2$$
$$\theta_1 = X_1 - 3X_3$$

The contingent claim is attainable if we obtain the same θ_1 value in both cases. Therefore, it is not always possible to price the contingent claims in situations with many risk-neutral probabilities.

1.3.10. *Complete and incomplete markets*

It may not be possible to apply the risk-neutral valuation principles in calculating the $t = 0$ price of the contingent claim just because there is a risk-neutral probability measure because we may face a problem regarding the marketability of the contingent claim. In other words, it may not be evident and definite what the $t = 0$ price is. In other words, we may not be sure that $E^Q[X/B_1]$ is the correct price. Therefore, it is necessary to test whether the contingent claim is marketable. One way is to obtain the solution of the above equation system for a specific trading strategy. If the solution of the equation system exists, the contingent claim is marketable.

The market model is called complete (complete market) if every contingent claim X can be produced by some trading strategy. Otherwise, the model is incomplete.

Proposition 1.11. *Assume that there are no arbitrage possibilities. In this case, the model is complete if and only if the number of states in Ω equals the number of elements in the vector $\{B_1, S_1(1) \ldots S_N(1)\}$. Let's write the expanded payoff matrix as $A \in \mathbb{R}^{K\times(N+1)}$*

$$A = \begin{matrix} B_1(\omega_1) & S_1(1)(\omega_1) \ldots & S_N(1)(\omega_1) \\ B_1(\omega_2) & S_1(1)(\omega_2) \ldots & S_N(1)(\omega_2) \\ B_1(\omega_K) & S_1(1)(\omega_K) \ldots & S_N(1)(\omega_K) \end{matrix}$$

Let

$$\theta = [\theta_0, \theta_1, \ldots, \theta_N]'$$
$$X = [X_1, X_2, \ldots, X_K]'$$

Then, If the $A\theta = X$ solution exists, the model will be complete. With linear algebra terms, if the rank of matrix A is K, that is, if the matrix has K independent columns, it is possible to say that the model is complete.

Example (Pliska, 1997, p. 22): With two financial assets and three states ($N = 2,\ K = 3$), let

$$A = \begin{bmatrix} 10/9 & 20/3 \\ 10/9 & 40/9 \\ 10/9 & 10/3 \end{bmatrix} \qquad S(0) = 5$$

where $1 + r = 10/9$. Since the rank is not 3, the model is not complete.

The risk-neutral probabilities must satisfy the equations

$$1 = q_1 + q_2 + q_3$$
$$5 = 6q_1 + 4q_2 + 3q_3$$

Then, we can find a λ that $\frac{1}{2} < \lambda < 2/3\ q_1 = \lambda$

$$Q = (\lambda, 2 - 3\lambda, -1 + 2\lambda)$$
$$E^Q\left[X/B_1\right] = \frac{9}{10} * \left[\lambda X_1 + (2 - 3\lambda)\, X_2 + (-1 + 2\lambda) X_3\right]$$

However, for X to be marketable, this value must be the same for all λs since it must coincide with the transaction strategy that produces V_0. This value is the same if and only if $X_1 - 3X_2 + 2X_3 = 0$. In other words, in this model, if and only if the $E^Q[X/B_1]$ value gives the same result for every risk-neutral probability, then the contingent claim X is marketable. Conversely, if X is attainable, then $E^Q[X/B_1]$ is a constant value according to the risk-neutral probability measure because V_0 is the initial value of the portfolio and $V_0 = E^Q\left[X/B_1\right]$.

If X is not attainable, there will be no solution of θ in the $A\theta = X$ system. Therefore, according to Farkas Lemma, there must be a vector $\pi = (\pi_1, \pi_2, \ldots, \pi_K))$ that satisfies the conditions $\pi A = 0$ and $\pi X > 0$.

Let $\mathbb{M}$ be the set of risk-neutral probabilities. $\hat{Q} \in \mathbb{M}$ and λ is an arbitrarily small scalar $\lambda > 0$. For all $k = 1 \ldots K$, we can write

$$Q(\omega_k) = \hat{Q}(\omega_k) + \lambda \pi_k B_1(\omega_k) > 0$$

The discounted price process is

$$E^Q S_n^*(1) = \sum Q(\omega_k) S_n(1, \omega_k)/B_1(\omega_k)$$

$$E^Q S_n^*(1) = \sum \hat{Q}(\omega_k) S_n(1, \omega_k)/B_1(\omega_k)$$
$$+ \lambda \sum \pi_k S_n(1, \omega_k) B_1(\omega_k)/B_1(\omega_k)$$

and since

$$\sum \pi_k S_n(1, \omega_k) = 0$$

$$E^Q S_n^*(1) = \sum \hat{Q}(\omega_k) S_n(1, \omega_k)/B_1(\omega_k)$$

$$E^Q S_n^*(1) = \sum \hat{Q}(\omega_k) S_n^*(1, \omega_k) = S_n^*(0)$$

So, we have $Q \in \mathbb{M}$ and $\hat{Q} \in \mathbb{M}$. Now, we have to show that the expected value of X/B_1 is different under the different probability measures Q and $\hat{Q}$. Since $\delta = \pi X > 0$

$$E^Q[X/B_1] = \sum Q(\omega_k) X(\omega_k)/B_1(\omega_k)$$

$$E^Q[X/B_1] = \sum \hat{Q}(\omega_k) X(\omega_k)/B_1(\omega_k) + \lambda \sum \pi_k X(\omega_k)$$

$$E^Q[X/B_1] = E^{\hat{Q}}[X/B_1] + \lambda \delta$$

$$E^Q[X/B_1] \neq E^{\hat{Q}}[X/B_1]$$

X is not attainable.

Proposition 1.12. *The contingent claim X is attainable if and only if $E^Q[X/B_1]$ has the same value for all $Q \in \mathbb{M}$.*

Proposition 1.13. *The model is complete if $\mathbb{M}$ contains only one risk-neutral probability measure.*

Up to this point, we have examined some concepts related to arbitrage theory and the risk-neutral probability measure using discrete models. In the following sections, we will discuss continuous markets and models, particularly the concepts and tools used in continuous models, focusing on pricing issues.

1.4. Continuous Processes and Pricing Principles

In option markets, pricing is mainly done with continuous time models. At least in the modern sense, the Black–Scholes–Merton (BSM) formula, which we can call the first option formula, was formulated considering the continuous time model (Black and Scholes, 1973; Merton, 1973). In the following years, discrete models such as the Binomial model (Cox *et al.*, 1976) and trinomial models (Boyle, 1988; Boyle and Gibbs, 1989; Kamrad and Ritchken, 1991) were developed. In the limiting case, i.e., for the infinitesimal time ($dt \to 0$), it can be shown that discrete models converge to continuous models (Cox and Rubinstein, 1985). In this subsection, Martingales and Brownian motion, which are the basic building blocks of continuous models, will be examined. The following subsections will provide the scope, basics, and framework for option pricing.

1.4.1. *Martingales*

The martingales have a broad scope of applications in general probability theory. They are used for calculating absorption probabilitics, analyzing the path structure of continuous-time processes, deriving inequalities for stochastic processes, analyzing sequential and control models, and for a variety of other purposes (Karlin and Taylor, 1975, p. 238). The name martingale derives from a French acronym for the gambling strategy of doubling one's bets until a win is secured. However, our general definition is different than this misleading and restrictive meaning.

Definition 1.1. A stochastic process $\{X_n; n = 0,\ 1\ldots\}$ is a martingale if for $n = 0,\ 1\ldots$

$$\begin{aligned} &\text{(i) } E\left[|X_n|\right] < \infty \\ &\text{(ii) } E\{X_{n+1}|X_0, X_1, \ldots, X_n\} = X_n \end{aligned} \tag{1.21}$$

In a gambling context, the martingale property implies that in a fair game, the player's fortune in the next play is equal to her current fortune and is not affected by the previous history of plays/fortunes. We may use the same property for stock prices in a financial setting. The best estimate for $t+1$ time price of a stock is equal to the previous price.

$$E\{S_{t+1}|S_0, S_1, \ldots, S_t\} = S_t$$

However, by an iterative process and reasoning, we can also write

$$E\{S_t|S_0\} = S_0$$

Another similar definition is as follows:

Definition 1.2. Let $\{X_n; n = 0,\ 1\ldots.\}$ and $\{Y_n;\ n = 0,\ 1\ldots\}$ be stochastic processes. Then it is said that $\{X_n\}$ is a martingale with respect to $\{Y_n\}$ if for $n = 0,\ 1\ldots$

$$\begin{aligned} &\text{(i)}\ \ E[|X_n|] < \infty \\ &\text{(ii)}\ E\left\{X_{n+1}|Y_0, Y_1, \ldots, Y_n\right\} = X_n \end{aligned} \tag{1.22}$$

In this version, $Y_0, Y_1, \ldots, Y_n$ can be regarded as the information or history up to the stage (time) $n(t)$.

Example: The Variance of a Sum as a Martingale (Karlin and Taylor, 1975, p. 241).

Let $Y_0 = 0$ and $Y_1, \ldots, Y_k$ be independent and identically distributed random variables with $E[Y_k] = 0$ and $E\left[Y_k^2\right] = \sigma^2$ $k = 1,\ 2\ldots.$ Let $X_0 = 0$

$$X_n = \left(\sum_{k=1}^{n} Y_k\right)^2 - n\sigma^2$$

We can prove the first condition that

$$E\left[|X_n|\right] \leq 2n\sigma^2 < \infty$$

Then,

$$
\begin{aligned}
&E\{X_{n+1}|Y_0, Y_1, \ldots, Y_n\} \\
&= E\left\{\left(Y_{n+1} + \sum_{k=1}^{n} Y_k\right)^2 - (n+1)\sigma^2 | Y_0, Y_1, \ldots, Y_n\right\} \\
&= E\left\{Y_{n+1}^2 + 2Y_{n+1}\sum_{k=1}^{n} Y_k + \left(\sum_{k=1}^{n} Y_k\right)^2 - (n+1)\sigma^2 | Y_0, Y_1, \ldots, Y_n\right\} \\
&= X_n + E\left\{Y_{n+1}^2 + 2Y_{n+1}\sum_{k=1}^{n} Y_k - \sigma^2 | Y_0, Y_1, \ldots, Y_n\right\} \\
&= X_n + E\{Y_{n+1}^2|Y_0, Y_1, \ldots, Y_n\} + 2E\{Y_{n+1}|Y_0, Y_1, \ldots, Y_n\}\sum_{k=1}^{n} Y_k - \sigma^2 \\
&= X_n + \sigma^2 + 0 - \sigma^2 = X_n
\end{aligned}
$$

So, $\{X_n\}$ is a martingale with respect to $\{Y_n\}$.

1.4.1.1. *Supermartingales and submartingales*

Definition 1.3. Let $\{X_n; n = 0,\ 1\ldots\}$ and $\{Y_n; n = 0,\ 1\ldots\}$ be stochastic processes. Then $\{X_n\}$ is called a supermartingale with respect to $\{Y_n\}$ if for all n

$$
\begin{aligned}
&\text{(i)} \quad E[|X_n^-|] > -\infty \text{ where } x^- = \min(x, 0) \\
&\text{(ii)} \quad E\{X_{n+1}|Y_0, Y_1, \ldots, Y_n\} \leq X_n \\
&\text{(iii)} \quad X_n \text{ is a function of } (Y_0, Y_1, \ldots, Y_n)
\end{aligned}
\tag{1.23}
$$

We call $\{X_n\}$ a submartingales with respect to $\{Y_n\}$ if for all n

$$
\begin{aligned}
&\text{(i)} \quad E[|X_n^+ t|] < \infty \text{ where } x^+ = \max(x, 0) \\
&\text{(ii)} \quad E\{X_{n+1}|Y_0, Y_1, \ldots, Y_n\} \geq X_n \\
&\text{(iii)} \quad X_n \text{ is a function of } (Y_0, Y_1, \ldots, Y_n)
\end{aligned}
\tag{1.24}
$$

It is observed that an inequality replaces the martingale equality.

1.4.1.2. *Local martingales and semimartingales*

There are still a few more definitions and classifications of martingales. They are the integral and inextricable part of option pricing theory. The following are their further definitions, and the reader is referred to other comprehensive resources for the theoretical details. [(For example, Protter, 1992; Jacod and Shiryaev, 2000; Harrison and Kreps, 1979; Harrison and Pliska, 1981, 1983) are the fundamental resources on the subject.]

Definition 1.4. Let $\mathcal{M}$ be the class of uniformly integrable martingales. This class includes all martingales X such that the family of random variables $(X_t)_{t\in\mathbb{R}_+}$ is uniformly integrable.

Definition 1.5. $\mathcal{M}^2$ is the class of all square-integrable martingales, that is, of all martingales X such that $sup_{t\in\mathbb{R}_+} E(X_t^2) < \infty$. Then we have $\mathcal{M}^2 \subset \mathcal{M}$.

Definition 1.6. A local martingale is a process that belongs to the localized class $\mathcal{M}_{\text{loc}}$ constructed from the class of uniformly integrable martingales $\mathcal{M}$.

The last definition is on semimartingales.

Definition 1.7.

(a) A semimartingale is a process X of the form

$$X = X_0 + M + A$$

where X_0 is finite-valued and $\mathcal{F}_0$-measurable, $M \in \mathcal{M}$, and $A \in \wp$. $\wp$ is the set of all real-valued adapted processes (cadlag) with finite variation.

(b) A special semimartingale is a semimartingale X, which admits a decomposition

$$X = X_0 + M + A \tag{1.25}$$

with process A being predictable.

1.4.2. *Brownian motion*

The concept of the Brownian movement goes back to 1828 when observations were made by botanist Robert Brown of the irregular movement of pollen suspended in water. Then, the dispersal or the diffusion process of the pollen/particles in water found a wide range of application areas, such as thermal noise in electrical circuits, queuing and inventory systems, and other physical, biological, economic, and management systems with random perturbations. Then, it was constructed more formally by Wiener in 1923 and Levy in 1948 and simplified by Ciesielski in 1961. The stock price is one of these application areas, and it was first used in 1900 by Bachelier in his thesis *La theorie de la speculation*. Today, it is the basic building block of mathematical finance and continuous models in finance and financial markets. We will first give a simple construction of Brownian motion (Shreve, 2004, Chapter 3) and then present the Levy construction of it due to (Etheridge, 2002, pp. 56–59; Harrison, 1985, pp. 2–5).

1.4.2.1. *Symmetric random walk (SRW)*

Let X be the result of an infinite coin tossing where

$$X = \begin{cases} 1 & \text{if } w_j = H \\ -1 & \text{if } w_j = T \end{cases}$$

Let us define $M_0 = 0$

$$M_k = \sum_{j=1}^{k} X_j \quad k = 1,\ 2\dots$$

The process M_k is called a symmetric random walk. At each step(toss) the process steps up or down one unit with equal probability. This type of random walk has independent increments. For

$$0 = k_0 < k_1 < \dots k_m$$
$$M_{k_1},\ ((M_{k_2} - M_{k_1})\dots M_{k_m} - M_{k_{m-1}})$$

are all independent. Note that $M_{k_1} = (M_{k_1} - M_{k_0})$. Then, we can write the increment of the random walk as

$$M_{k_{i+1}} - M_{k_i} = \sum_{j=k_i+1}^{k_{i+1}} X_j$$

For instance, for $i = 2$

$$M_{k_3} - M_{k_2} = \sum_{j=k_2+1}^{k_3} X_j = X_{k_2+1} + \cdots + X_{k_3}$$

This is the change in position of the random walk between the times k_i and k_{i+1}. The expected value of the increments is zero, and the variance is equal to $k_{i+1} - k_i$.

Since

$$E\left(M_{k_3} - M_{k_2}\right) = \sum_{j=k_2+1}^{k_3} E(X_j) = E\left(X_{k_2+1}\right) + \cdots + E\left(X_{k_3}\right) = 0 \tag{1.26}$$

$$E(X_j) = \frac{1}{2} * 1 - \frac{1}{2} * 1 = 0$$

the expected value is zero. The variance is

$$Var\left[M_{k_{i+1}} - M_{k_i}\right] = E\left(\sum_{j=k_i+1}^{k_{i+1}} (X_j) - \sum_{j=k_i+1}^{k_{i+1}} E(X_j)\right)^2$$

$$= \sum_{j=k_i+1}^{k_{i+1}} Var(X_j) = \sum_{j=k_i+1}^{k_{i+1}} E(X_j^2)$$

But since

$$= \frac{1}{2} 1^2 + (-1)^2 \frac{1}{2} = 1$$

and we have

$$\sum_{j=k_i+1}^{k_{i+1}} 1$$

That is, we have $k_{i+1} - k_i$ times 1 in the summation. Therefore, the variance is equal to

$$Var\left[M_{k_{i+1}} - M_{k_i}\right] = k_{i+1} - k_i \tag{1.27}$$

Since the rate of accumulation of the variance is equal to this difference, it can be written as

$$l - k$$

for any time interval $k < l$. We can also write the quadratic variation of the SRW up to time k as

$$[M, M]_k = \sum_{j=1}^{k} (M_j - M_{j-1})^2 = k \tag{1.28}$$

Because all the one-step increments of the random walk along the time k will be equal to X_j (1 or $-$ 1), which will mean

$$\sum_{j=1}^{k} (M_j - M_{j-1})^2 = \sum_{j=1}^{k} 1 = k$$

1.4.2.2. *Martingale property*

For non-negative integers $k < l$ we must show that

$$E[M_l | \mathcal{F}_k] = M_k$$

based on the Definition 1.2. We can write the equation as

$$E[M_l - M_k + M_k | \Im_k] = E[(M_l - M_k) | \Im_k] + E[M_k | \Im_k]$$

But $E[M_k | \Im_k]$ is equal to M_k, and the first part equals zero due to (1.27). Therefore,

$$E[(M_l - M_k) | \Im_k] + E[M_k | \Im_k] = M_k \tag{1.29}$$

1.4.2.3. *Scaled SRW*

The way to approximate Brownian motion is to scale down the SRW step size and speed up the time steps. We define the scaled SRW for a positive integer as

$$W^{(n)}(t) = \frac{1}{\sqrt{n}} M_{nt} \tag{1.30}$$

where nt is an integer. Like RW, the increments of scaled RW are independent of each other. For instance,

$$(W^{(n)}(t_1) - W^{(n)}(t_0)), (W^{(n)}(t_2) - W^{(n)}(t_1)), \ldots, (W^{(n)}(t_m) - W^{(n)}(t_{m-1}))$$

are all independent.

For example, $(W^{(100)}(0.3) - W^{100}(0))$ will depend on the first 30 coin tosses (price movements), $(W^{(100)}(0.7) - W^{100}(0.3))$ will depend on subsequent 40 coin tosses, etc.

For $0 \leq s \leq t$ and with integers ns, nt we can write

$$E\left[W^{(n)}(t) - W^{(n)}(s)\right] = 0$$

$$Var(W^{(n)}(t) - W^{(n)}(s)) = t - s$$

Because the variable $(W^{(n)}(t) - W^{(n)}(s))$ consists of independent random variables with an expected value of "0" and a variance $\frac{1}{n}$.

Since

$$E\left[W^{(n)}(t) - W^{(n)}(s)\right] = \frac{1}{\sqrt{n}} E(M_{nt} - M_{ns})$$

and

$$M_{k_{i+1}} - M_{k_i} = \sum_{j=k_i+1}^{k_{i+1}} X_j$$

we obtain

$$M_{nt} - M_{ns} = \sum_{j=ns+1}^{nt} X_j \Rightarrow E(M_{nt} - M_{ns}) = \sum_{j=ns+1}^{nt} E(X_j)$$

$$E[W^{(n)}(t) - W^{(n)}(s)] = \frac{1}{\sqrt{n}} E(M_{nt} - M_{ns}) = \frac{1}{\sqrt{n}} \sum_{j=ns+1}^{nt} E(X_j) = 0$$

Also, we can calculate the variance as

$$Var(W^{(n)}(t) - W^{(n)}(s)) = Var\left(\frac{1}{\sqrt{n}}(M_{nt} - M_{ns})\right)$$

$$= \frac{1}{n} Var\left(\sum_{j=ns+1}^{nt} (X_j)\right) = \frac{1}{n} 1 \cdot (nt - ns) = t - s$$

In other words, if we scale X_j by $\frac{1}{\sqrt{n}}$, instead of writing

$$X_j = 1 \text{ or } X_j = -1, \text{ we write } X_j = 1\frac{1}{\sqrt{100}} = \frac{1}{10} \text{ or}$$

$$X_j = -1\frac{1}{\sqrt{100}} = -\frac{1}{10}$$

For each X_j the expected value and the variance will be

$$E(X_j) = \frac{1}{2}\frac{1}{10} - \frac{1}{2}\frac{1}{10} = 0 \quad Var(X_j) = \frac{1}{2}\frac{1}{100} + \frac{1}{2}\frac{1}{100} = \frac{1}{100}$$

Then, for example, for $t = 0.7$, $s = 0.3$ we obtain the variance as $Var(W^{(100)}(0.7) - W^{100}(0.3)) = 40 * \frac{1}{100} = 0.4$ or $t - s = 0.4$. Because this variable contains 40 random variables with variance $\frac{1}{100}$.

The quadratic variation of scaled random walk can be written as

$$\left[W^{(n)}, W^{(n)}\right](t) = \sum_{j=1}^{nt} \left(W\left(\frac{j}{n}\right) - W\left(\frac{j-1}{n}\right)\right)^2$$

For example, for $t = 1.15, s = 0, n = 100$ the quadratic variation after the 115.th step or at time 1.15 is

$$[W^{(100)}, W^{(100)}](1.15) = \sum_{j=1}^{115} \left(W^{(100)}\left(\frac{j}{100}\right) - W^{(100)}\left(\frac{j-1}{100}\right)\right)^2$$

$$[W^{(100)}, W^{(100)}](1.15) = \sum_{j=ns+1}^{nt} \left(\frac{1}{\sqrt{n}}(M_j - M_{j-1})\right)^2$$

$$= \sum_{j=ns+1}^{nt} \frac{1}{100}(M_j - M_{j-1})^2 = \sum_{j=ns+1}^{nt} \frac{1}{100}(X_j)^2$$

$$\sum_{j=ns+1}^{nt} \left(\frac{1}{10}X_j\right)^2 = \frac{1}{100} \sum_{j=ns+1}^{nt} X_j{}^2$$

$$= \frac{1}{100} 1 \cdot (nt - ns) = \frac{115}{100} = 1.15 = (t - s)$$

In general, the quadratic variation is

$$\left[W^{(n)}, W^{(n)}\right](t) = \sum_{j=1}^{nt}\left(W\left(\frac{j}{n}\right) - W\left(\frac{j-1}{n}\right)\right)^2$$

$$= \sum_{j=1}^{nt}\left(\frac{1}{\sqrt{n}}X_j\right)^2 = \frac{nt \cdot 1}{n} = t \tag{1.31}$$

This is also equal to $Var(W^{(n)}(t))$.

1.4.2.4. *From scaled random walk to Brownian motion*

We obtain Brownian motion as the limit of the scaled random walks. In other words, we formalize the Brownian motion for $n \to \infty$ or for infinitesimal time intervals.

Definition 1.8. Let $(\Omega,\ \mathcal{F},\ \mathbb{P})$ be a probability space. For each $w \in \Omega$, suppose there is a continuous real-valued stochastic process $(W(t))_{t \geq 0}$. $W(t)t \geq 0$ is a $\mathbb{P}$–Brownian motion, if for $0 = t_0 < t_1 \cdots < t_m$

(a) the increments

$$W(t_1),\ (W(t_2) - W(t_1)) \ldots (W(t_m) - W(t_{m-1}))$$

are independent

(b) for each $t \geq s$, the random variable $W(t) - W(s)$ has the normal distribution with mean zero and variance $t - s$, and

(c) $W(0) = 0$ almost surely (technically, $P(W(0, w) = 0) = 1$).

1.4.2.5. *Distribution of Brownian motion*

Since $W(t_1) = W(t_1) - W(t_0), W(t_2) - W(t_1), \ldots, W(t_m) - W(t_{m-1})$ are independently and normally distributed, they are jointly normally distributed.

Their joint normal distributions are determined by their means and covariances. We know that the mean of each variable is zero.

For any two different periods, $0 \leq s \leq t$, the covariance of $W(s)$ and $W(t)$ is

$$\begin{aligned}
&E[(W(s) - E(W(s)))(W(t) - E(W(t))] \\
&\quad = E\left[W(s)W(t)\right] = E[W(s)(W(t) - W(s)) + W^2(s)] \\
&\quad = E[W^2(s)] = Var(W(s)) = s
\end{aligned}$$

Because the first term

$$E\left[W(s)(W(t) - W\left(s\right))\right]$$

is equal to zero due to the independence property of Brownian motion increments. Therefore, the covariance matrix of the Brownian motion vector is

$$\begin{bmatrix}
E(W^2(t_1)) & E\left[W(t_1)W(t_2)\right]\ldots & E\left[W(t_1)W(t_m)\right] \\
E\left[W(t_1)W(t_2)\right] & E\left(W^2\left(t_2\right)\right)\ldots & E\left[W\left(t_2\right)W\left(t_m\right)\right] \\
E\left[W\left(t_m\right)W(t_1)\right] & E\left[W\left(t_m\right)W(t_2)\right]\ldots & E(W^2\left(t_m\right))
\end{bmatrix}$$

$$= \begin{bmatrix}
t_1 & t_1 & t_1 \\
t_1 & t_2 & t_2 \\
t_1 & t_2 & t_m
\end{bmatrix}$$

Practically, we will take the covariance between the two time periods as the earlier period, such as

$$\begin{aligned}
E\left[W(s)W(t)\right] &= s \quad s < t \\
E\left[dW(s)dW(t)\right] &= ds \quad s < t
\end{aligned}$$

or

$$Cov\left(W(t), W\left(s\right)\right) = s \wedge t \tag{1.32}$$

1.4.2.6. *First and second variations of Brownian motion*

The first variation of Brownian motion is infinite. We can write the first variation for a differentiable function f and for a time partition

$\pi = (0 = t_0, t_1, \ldots, t_n = T)$

$FV_T(f) = [f(t_1) - f(t_0)] - [f(t_2) - f(t_1)] + [f(T) - f(t_2)]$

$FV_T(f) = \int_{t_0}^{t_1} f'(t)dt + \int_{t_1}^{t_2} (-f'(t))dt + \int_{t_2}^{T} f'(t)dt = \int_{t_0}^{T} |f'(t)|\, dt$

Choosing $\|\pi\| = \max_{0<j\leq n-1}(t_{j+1} - t_j)$ and using the mean value theorem, we can write

$$FV_T(f) = \lim_{\|\pi\|\to 0} \sum_{j=0}^{n-1} \left| f'(t_j^*)(t_{j+1} - t_j) \right|$$

$$FV_T(f) = \lim_{\|\pi\|\to 0} \sum_{j=0}^{n-1} \left| f'(t_j^*)(t_{j+1} - t_j) \right| = \int_{t_0}^{T} |f'(t)|\, dt$$

where

$$f'(t_j^*) = \frac{f(t_{j+1}) - f(t_j)}{t_{j+1} - t_j}$$

However, we cannot write the same calculation for Brownian motion because the increments of Brownian motion are sharp (pointy) and indifferentiable. Then, $\frac{d}{dt}W(t)$ is not defined. However, the quadratic variation of Brownian motion is defined.

Theorem 1.3 (Shreve, 2004, pp. 102–103). *Let W be a Brownian motion. Then $[W, W](T) = T$ for all $T \geq 0$ almost surely.*

Let $\pi = \{0 = t_0, t_1, \ldots, t_n = T\}$ be the partition of $[0, T]$. Let's define the quadratic variation as

$$Q_\pi = \sum_{j=0}^{n-1} (W(t_{j+1}) - W(t_j))^2$$

It must be shown that as $\|\pi\| \to 0$, $Q_\pi \to T$. We know that

$$E(Q_\pi) = E\left[\sum_{j=0}^{n-1} (W(t_{j+1}) - W(t_j))^2\right] = Var(W(t_{j+1}) - W(t_j))$$

Since

$$Var(W(t_{j+1}) - W(t_j)) = t_{j+1} - t_j$$

we have

$$E(Q_\pi) = \sum_{j=0}^{n-1} E(W(t_{j+1}) - W(t_j))^2 = \sum_{j=0}^{n-1} t_{j+1} - t_j = t_n = T$$

In addition to this, it can be shown that

$$\begin{aligned}
&Var(Q_\pi) = Var[(W(t_{j+1}) - W(t_j))^2] \\
&= E[(W(t_{j+1}) - W(t_j))^2 - E((W(t_{j+1}) - W(t_j))^2]^2 \\
&= E[(W(t_{j+1}) - W(t_j))^2 - (t_{j+1} - t_j)]^2 \\
&= E[(W(t_{j+1}) - W(t_j))^4 - 2(t_{j+1} - t_j)E(W(t_{j+1}) \\
&\quad - W(t_j))^2 + (t_{j+1} - t_j)^2]
\end{aligned}$$

Since

$$\frac{E(W(t_{j+1}) - W(t_j))^4}{\sigma^4} = \frac{E(W(t_{j+1}) - W(t_j))^4}{(t_{j+1} - t_j)^2} = 3$$

$$Var(Q_\pi) = \sum_{j=0}^{n-1} 2(t_{j+1} - t_j)^2 \leq \sum_{j=0}^{n-1} 2\,\|\pi\|\,(t_{j+1} - t_j) = \|\pi\|\,2T \to 0$$

For $dW(t).dt$ *and* $dt.dt$ *we write*

$$\lim_{\|\pi\|\to 0} \sum_{j=0}^{n-1} (W(t_{j+1}) - W(t_j))(t_{j+1} - t_j) = 0$$

$$\lim_{\|\pi\|\to 0} \sum_{j=0}^{n-1} (t_{j+1} - t_j)^2 = 0$$

For $\pi = \{0 = t_0, t_1, \ldots, \; t_n = T\}$ *and for maximum interval* $\|\pi\| = \max_{0<k\leq n-1}(t_{k+1} - t_k)$

$$|(W(t_{j+1}) - W(t_j))(t_{j+1} - t_j)| \leq \max_{0\leq k\leq n-1} |(W(t_{k+1}) - W(t_k))| \times (t_{j+1} - t_j)$$

Taking summation

$$\left|\sum_{j=0}^{n-1}(W(t_{j+1}) - W(t_j))(t_{j+1} - t_j)\right| \leq \max_{0\leq k\leq n-1} |(W(t_{k+1}) - W(t_k))|.T$$

Since W *is continuous,* $\max_{0\leq k\leq n-1} |(W(t_{k+1}) - W(t_k))|$ *has limit zero as* $\|\pi\| = \max_{0<k\leq n-1}(t_{k+1} - t_k) \to 0$.

Therefore, we have $dW(t).dt = 0$.

Also, from

$$\lim_{\|\pi\|\to 0} \sum_{j=0}^{n-1} (t_{j+1} - t_j)^2 \leq \max_{0<k\leq n-1} (t_{k+1} - t_k) \sum_{j=0}^{n-1} (t_{j+1} - t_j) = \|\pi\| * T$$

$$dt.dt = 0$$

as $\|\pi\| = \max_{0<k\leq n-1}(t_{k+1} - t_k) \to 0$. ⊡

There are some practical results when these principles are applied in financial applications.

$$\begin{array}{ll} \text{(i)} & \text{We write } dW = \varepsilon\sqrt{dt} \text{ where } \varepsilon \sim \mathcal{N}(0,1) \;\; E(\varepsilon^2) = 1 \\ \text{(ii)} & dW^2 = dW \,.\, dW = dt \\ \text{(iii)} & dW_1 \,.\, dW_2 = 0 \quad \text{if} \quad W_1 \text{ and } W_2 \text{ are independent} \\ \text{(iv)} & dW_1 \,.\, dt = 0 \quad dt.dt = 0 \\ \text{(v)} & dW_1 \,.\, dW_2 = \rho dt \end{array} \tag{1.33}$$

where ρ is the correlation coefficient between W_1 and W_2 if correlated.

We can construct correlated Brownian motion as follows. Assume Z_1 and Z_2 are uncorrelated and independent Brownian motions. We can write

$$dW_1(t) = dZ_1(t)$$
$$dW_2 = \rho dZ_1(t) + \sqrt{1-\rho^2}dZ_2(t)$$

It can be shown that the variance of dW_1 and dW_2 is dt and

$$Cov\left(dW_1(t), dW_2(t)\right) = \rho dt$$

since

$$E(dZ_1(t)dZ_2(t)) = 0$$

The properties of Brownian motion, the basic building block of continuous time models, have been shown until now. We will now proceed with stochastic integrals, the essential parts of financial models, and derivative pricing principles.

1.5. Stochastic Integration and Ito's Integral

For a positive number of T, consider an integral such as

$$\int_0^T \Delta(t).dW(t) \tag{1.34}$$

$W(t)$ is the Brownian motion with $\mathcal{F}_t$ $t \geq 0$, and the integrand $\Delta(t)$ is $\mathcal{F}_t$ adapted, which means the value of it is known at time t. In other words, the information in $\mathcal{F}_t$ is sufficient to evaluate $\Delta(t)$ at that time. $\Delta(t)$ can be interpreted as the number/position of assets held, and $W(t)$ can be construed as the price of risky assets. $\Delta(t)$ depends on the price path of the asset up to time t. However, the integral variable $dW(t)$ is random, and the increments after time t are independent of $\mathcal{F}_t$. We know the $W(t)$ but not sure about the $W(t+1)$. If $f(t)$ is a differentiable function, we can write

$$\int_0^T \Delta(t).df(t) = \int_0^T \Delta(t).f'(t)dt$$

However, since Brownian motion paths cannot be differentiated, we have to develop different types of tools for integration with respect to Brownian paths, which are called Ito integrals (see Oksendal, 2003, pp. 21–42).

1.5.1. The construction and the properties of integral

Consider the partition $\pi = \{0 = t_0, t_1, \ldots, t_n = T\}$ again as the trading dates $t_0, t_1, \ldots, t_n$ and $\Delta(t_0), \Delta(t_1), \ldots, \Delta(t_{n-1})$ as the positions held by the investor up to the next trading date. The gain from trading can be presented as a summation

$$\begin{aligned} I(t) &= \Delta(t_0)\left[W(t) - W(t_0)\right] = \Delta(t_0)W(t)\ 0 \le t \le t_1 \\ I(t) &= \Delta(t_0)W(t_1) + \Delta(t_1)[W(t) - W(t_1)] \quad t_1 \le t \le t_2 \\ I(t) &= \Delta(t_0)W(t_1) + \Delta(t_1)[W(t_2) - W(t_1)] + \Delta(t_2)[W(t) - W(t_3)] \\ &= \Delta(t_0)W(t) \quad t_2 \le t \le t_3 \end{aligned}$$

and so on (Shreve, 2004, pp. 126–128). In general, it can be written as

$$I(t) = \sum_{j=0}^{k-1} \Delta(t_j)\left[W\left(t_{j+1}\right) - W\left(t_j\right)\right] + \Delta(t_k)\left[W(t) - W\left(t_k\right)\right]$$

for $t_k \le t \le t_{k+1}$.

We obtain the Ito integral from this summation as a limiting case for infinitesimal time intervals

$$I(t) = \int_0^t \Delta\left(u\right) dW(u) \tag{1.35}$$

This notation is valid for upper integration limit T and every t between 0 and T.

Theorem 1.3. *The Ito integral is a martingale.*

We will refer to the proof in Shreve, 2004, pp. 128–129. Let $0 \le s \le t \le T$ and we have the partition π with partition points t_l and t_k such that $s \in [t_l, t_{l+1})$ and $t \in [t_k, t_{k+1})$.

We must show that

$$E\left(I(t) \mid \mathcal{F}_s\right) = I(s)$$

Then, we can expand the integral as

$$\begin{aligned} I(t) = &\sum_{j=0}^{l-1} \Delta(t_j)\left[W\left(t_{j+1}\right) - W\left(t_j\right)\right] + \Delta(t_l)\left[W\left(t_{l+1}\right) - W\left(t_l\right)\right] \\ &+ \sum_{j=0}^{k-1} \Delta(t_j)\left[W\left(t_{j+1}\right) - W\left(t_j\right)\right] + \Delta(t_k)\left[W(t) - W\left(t_k\right)\right] \end{aligned}$$

Since $t_l \leq s$, all the terms in the first sum are $\mathcal{F}_s$-measurable. By conditioning on $\mathcal{F}_s$, we can write the first sum as

$$E\left(\Delta(t_l)\left[W\left(t_{l+1}\right)-W\left(t_l\right)\right] \mid \mathcal{F}_s\right)=\Delta(t_l)\left[W\left(t_{l+1}\right)|\mathcal{F}_s - W\left(t_l\right)\right]$$
$$\Delta(t_l)\left[W\left(t_{l+1}\right)|\mathcal{F}_s\right]=\Delta(t_l) W(s)$$

$$I(s)=\sum_{j=0}^{l-1} \Delta(t_j)\left[W\left(t_{j+1}\right)-W\left(t_j\right)\right]+\Delta(t_l)\left[W(s)-W\left(t_l\right)\right]$$

and this is equal to $I(s)$. The second sum can be made zero by iterated conditioning and taking out what is known principle (see Appendix A) where $t_j \geq t_{l+1} > s$.

So, conditioning on each term in the sum with respect to $\mathcal{F}_{t_j}$

$$\begin{aligned} &E(\Delta(t_j)[W(t_{j+1})-W(t_j)]|\mathcal{F}_s) \\ &\quad = E(E(\Delta(t_j)[W(t_{j+1})-W(t_j)]|\mathcal{F}_{t_j})|\mathcal{F}_s) \end{aligned}$$
$$E\left(\sum_{j=l+1}^{k-1} \Delta(t_j)[W(t_j)-W(t_j)]\,|\mathcal{F}_s\right)=0$$

Conditioning on the last term in the sum with respect to $\mathcal{F}_{t_k}$ will also yield

$$E(E(\Delta(t_k)[W(t_{k+1})-W(t_k)]|\mathcal{F}_{t_k})|\mathcal{F}_s)=0$$

So we are done. Because $I(t)$ is a martingale and $I(0)=0$, Ito integral will always be zero

$$E(I(t))=E\int_0^t \Delta(u)dW(u)=0 \tag{1.36}$$

Theorem 1.4. *The Ito integral satisfies (Ito isometry)*

$$EI^2(t)=\int_0^t \Delta^2(u)du \tag{1.37}$$

$$I(t) = \sum_{j=0}^{k-1} \Delta(t_j)[W(t_{j+1}) - W(t_j)] + \Delta(t_k)[W(t) - W(t_k)]$$

$$I^2(t) = \sum_{j=0}^{k-1} \Delta^2(t_j)[W(t_{j+1}) - W(t_j)]^2 + \Delta^2(t_k)[W(t) - W(t_k)]^2$$

$$+ 2 \sum_{0 \le i < j}^{k-1} \Delta(t_i)\Delta(t_j)(W(t_{i+1}) - W(t_i))(W(t_{j+1}) - W(t_j))$$

$$+ 2 \sum_{j=0}^{k-1} \Delta(t_j)\Delta(t_k)(W(t_{j+1}) - W(t_j)(W(t) - W(t_k))$$

Because of the property of Brownian motion $E(W(t_{j+1}) - W(t_j)|\mathcal{F}_{t_j}) = 0$. *Therefore, we have*

$$EI^2(t) = \sum_{j=0}^{k-1} E\Delta^2(t_j)[W(t_{j+1}) - W(t_j)]^2 + E\Delta^2(t_k)[W(t) - W(t_k)]^2 =$$

$$EI^2(t) = \sum_{j=0}^{k-1} E\Delta^2(t_j)(t_{j+1} - t_j) + E\Delta^2(t_k)(t - t_k)$$

However, $\Delta(t_j)$ *is constant on the interval* $[t_j, t_{j+1})$ *and the expectation can be written*

$$\Delta^2(t_j)(t_{j+1} - t_j) = \int_{t_j}^{t_{j+1}} \Delta^2(u)\, du$$

$$\Delta^2(t_k)(t - t_k) = \int_{t_k}^{t} \Delta^2(u)\, du$$

$$EI^2(t) = \sum_{j=0}^{k-1} E \int_{t_j}^{t_{j+1}} \Delta^2(u)\, du + E \int_{t_k}^{t} \Delta^2(u)\, du$$

Finally, we obtain

$$EI^2(t) = E \int_0^t \Delta^2(u)\, du$$

Theorem 1.5. *The quadratic variation accumulated up to time t by the Ito integral is*

$$[I, I](t) = \int_0^t \Delta^2(u)\, du$$

(For proof, see Shreve, 2004, pp. 131–132*).*

We can write the integral in differential form as

$$dI(t) = \Delta(t) dW(t)$$

Then, the equation tells us the change in the Ito integral I is $\Delta(t)$ times the change in the Brownian motion W when the time moves a little bit forward from time t. This is the differential form of Ito's integral. When we use the integral form, we write as

$$I(t) = I(0) + \int_0^t \Delta(u)\, dW(u) \tag{1.38}$$

by adding the constant of integration. Since the integration constant is always $I(0) = 0$, they have the same meaning.

The Ito integral is special, and the integration results are different from the ordinary integration of differentiable functions. The reason is Brownian motion as an integral variable and the integrand.

Example (Shreve, 2004, pp. 134–137): We want to compute the integral $\int_0^T W(t)dW(t)$. Since the integrand is Brownian motion, we may choose $\Delta(t) = W(t)$, and for a large integer n we divide the integrand with simple processes as follows

$$\Delta_n(t) = \begin{cases} W(0) = 0 \quad 0 \leq t < \frac{T}{n} \\ W\left(\frac{T}{n}\right) \quad \frac{T}{n} \leq t < \frac{2T}{n} \dots \\ W\left(\frac{(n-1)T}{n}\right) \frac{(n-1)T}{n} \leq t < T \end{cases}$$

Then, we can write

$$\int_0^T W(t)dW(t) = \lim_{n\to\infty} \int_0^T \Delta_n(t)dW(t)$$

Now, it is possible to write the integral as a summation

$$\lim_{n\to\infty}\sum_{j=0}^{n-1} W\left(\frac{jT}{n}\right)\left[W\left(\frac{(j+1)T}{n}\right)-W\left(\frac{jT}{n}\right)\right]$$

Let $W\left(\frac{jT}{n}\right)=W_j$

$$\lim_{n\to\infty}\sum_{j=0}^{n-1} W\left(\frac{jT}{n}\right)\left[W\left(\frac{(j+1)T}{n}\right)-W\left(\frac{jT}{n}\right)\right]$$

$$=\lim_{n\to\infty}\sum_{j=0}^{n-1} W_jW_{j+1}-W_j^2$$

Now, consider

$$\frac{1}{2}\sum_{j=0}^{n-1}(W_{j+1}-W_j)^2=\frac{1}{2}\sum_{j=0}^{n-1}W_{j+1}^2-\sum_{j=0}^{n-1}W_jW_{j+1}+\frac{1}{2}\sum_{j=0}^{n-1}W_j^2$$

Then, since

$$\frac{1}{2}\sum_{j=0}^{n-1}W_{j+1}^2+\frac{1}{2}\sum_{j=0}^{n-1}W_j^2=\frac{1}{2}\,W_n^2+\sum_{j=0}^{n-1}W_j^2$$

we take all of them as

$$\frac{1}{2}\,W_n^2+\sum_{j=0}^{n-1}W_j^2\;-\sum_{j=0}^{n-1}W_jW_{j+1}=\frac{1}{2}\,W_n^2+\sum_{j=0}^{n-1}W_j(W_j-W_{\,j+1})$$

$$\frac{1}{2}\sum_{j=0}^{n-1}(W_{j+1}-W_j)^2=\frac{1}{2}\,W_n^2+\sum_{j=0}^{n-1}W_j(W_j-W_{\,j+1})$$

$$\frac{1}{2}\,W_n^2-\frac{1}{2}\sum_{j=0}^{n-1}(W_{j+1}-W_j)^2=\sum_{j=0}^{n-1}W_j(W_{\,j+1}-W_j)$$

Since

$$W\left(\frac{(j+1)T}{n}\right) = W\left(\frac{(n-1+1)T}{n}\right) = W(T)$$

$$\sum_{j=0}^{n-1} W_j(W_{j+1} - W_j) \quad \text{or}$$

$$\lim_{n\to\infty} \sum_{j=0}^{n-1} W\left(\frac{jT}{n}\right)\left[W\left(\frac{(j+1)T}{n}\right) - W\left(\frac{jT}{n}\right)\right]$$

is equal to

$$\frac{1}{2}\, W^2(T) - \frac{1}{2}\sum_{j=0}^{n-1}\left(W\left(\frac{(j+1)T}{n}\right) - W\left(\frac{jT}{n}\right)\right)^2$$

But the last term is when $n \to \infty$.

$$-\frac{1}{2}[W,W](T) = -\frac{1}{2}T$$

Finally, we obtain the result as

$$\int_0^T W(t)dW(t) = \frac{1}{2}\, W^2(T) - \frac{1}{2}T$$

If $W(t) = f(t)$ is a differentiable function with $f(0) = 0$

$$\int_0^T f(t)df(t) = \int_0^T f(t)f'(t)dt = \frac{1}{2}f^2(T)$$

(How?) The reason for the extra term $-\frac{1}{2}T$ in the integral is the non-zero quadratic variation of Brownian motion and also the construction of Ito integral, evaluating the integrand $W\left(\frac{jT}{n}\right)$ at the left-hand point of subinterval $\left[W\left(\frac{(j+1)T}{n}\right) - W\left(\frac{jT}{n}\right)\right]$.

Still, we can show that the expected value of the Ito integral is equal to zero. By writing

$$E\left[I(t)\right] = E\int_0^T W(t)dW(t) = \frac{1}{2}\ E[W^2(T)] - \frac{1}{2}T$$

we obtain

$$\frac{1}{2}\ E[W^2(T)] - \frac{1}{2}T = 0$$

If there were not the term $-\frac{1}{2}T$, then we would not have the martingale property in the integral.

1.6. Ito Processes

1.6.1. *Ito–Doeblin formula for stochastic processes*

Theorem 1.6 (Shreve, 2004, pp. 138–143). *Let $f(t,x)$ be a function for which the partial derivatives $f_t(t,x), f_x(t,x), f_{xx}(t,x)$ are defined and continuous and let $W(t)$ be a Brownian motion. Then, for every $T \geq 0$,*

$$\begin{aligned} f(T, W(T)) &= f(0, W(0) + \int_0^T f_t\left(t, W\left(t\right)\right) dt \\ &\quad + \int_0^T f_x\left(t, W(t)\right) dW(t) + \frac{1}{2}\int_0^T f_{xx}\left(t, W(t)\right) dt \end{aligned} \tag{1.39}$$

By applying Taylor expansion for $f\left(x\right) = \frac{1}{2}x^2$ we can write

$$f\left(x_{j+1}\right) - f\left(x_j\right) = f'\left(x_j\right)\left(x_{j+1} - x_j\right) + \frac{1}{2}f''\left(x_j\right)\left(x_{j+1} - x_j\right)^2$$

f''' and higher order derivatives are zero, and the expansion is exact. But we can apply the idea considering $x_j = W(t_j)$. In this case, we

can write

$$f(W(T)) - f(W(0)) = \sum_{j=0}^{n-1} (f(W(t_{j+1})) - f(W(t_j))$$

Applying Taylor expansion, we have

$$\sum_{j=0}^{n-1} (f(W(t_{j+1})) - f(W(t_j)) = \sum_{j=0}^{n-1} f'(W(t_j)) [W(t_{j+1}) - W(t_j)] + \frac{1}{2}\sum_{j=0}^{n-1} f''(W(t_j)) [W(t_{j+1}) - W(t_j)]^2$$

But replacing the first and second derivatives in the formula, the right-hand side is equal to

$$= \sum_{j=0}^{n-1} W(t_j)[W(t_{j+1}) - W(t_j)] + \frac{1}{2}\sum_{j=0}^{n-1} [W(t_{j+1}) - W(t_j)]^2$$

As $\|\pi\| \to 0$, *taking the limits*

$$\begin{aligned} &f(W(T)) - f(W(0)) \\ &= \lim_{\|\pi\|\to 0} \sum_{j=0}^{n-1} W(t_j)[W(t_{j+1}) - W(t_j)] \\ &\quad + \lim_{\|\pi\|\to 0} \frac{1}{2}\sum_{j=0}^{n-1} [W(t_{j+1}) - W(t_j)]^2 = \int_0^T W(t)dW(t) + \frac{1}{2}T \end{aligned}$$

which means

$$f(W(T)) - f(W(0)) = \int_0^T f'(W(t))dW(t) + \frac{1}{2}\int_0^T f''(W(t))dt$$

This is called the Ito-Doeblin formula in integral form for the function $f(x) = \frac{1}{2}x^2$. *Instead of this particular function, if we have a general function such as* $f(t,x)$ *replacing* $x_j = W(t_j)$ *and* $x_{j+1} = W(t_{j+1})$ *again, we can write*

$$f(W(T)) - f(W(0)) = \sum_{j=0}^{n-1} (f(t_{j+1}, W(t_{j+1})) - f(t_j, W(t_j))$$

$$\sum_{j=0}^{n-1} f_t(t_j, W(t_j))(t_{j+1} - t_j) + \sum_{j=0}^{n-1} f_x(t_j, W(t_j))(W(t_{j+1}) - W(t_j))$$

$$+ \frac{1}{2}\sum_{j=0}^{n-1} f_{xx}(t_j, W(t_j))(W(t_{j+1}) - W(t_j))^2$$

$$+ \sum_{j=0}^{n-1} f_{tx}(t_j, W(t_j))(t_{j+1} - t_j)(W(t_{j+1}) - W(t_j))$$

$$+ \frac{1}{2}\sum_{j=0}^{n-1} f_{tt}(t_j, W(t_j))(t_{j+1} - t_j)^2$$

$$+ \textit{higher order terms}$$

As $\|\pi\| \to 0$, *taking the limits we obtain*

$$\begin{aligned} & f(W(T)) - f(W(0)) \\ & = \int_0^T f_t(t_j, W(t_j))dt + \int_0^T f_x(t_j, W(t_j))dW(t) \\ & + \frac{1}{2}\int_0^T f_{xx}(t_j, W(t_j))dt \end{aligned}$$ ⊡

and other terms and higher-order terms do not contribute to the sum. The general type of Ito-Doeblin formula can be written in differential form as

$$df = f_t(t, W(t))\,dt + f_x(t, W(t))\,dW(t) + \frac{1}{2}f_{xx}(t, W(t))\,dt \quad (1.40)$$

1.6.2. *Ito processes*

Ito processes are also known as drift-diffusion processes.

Definition 1.9. Let $W(t)$ $t \geq 0$ be a Brownian motion, and let $\mathcal{F}(t)$ be an associated filtration. An Ito process is a stochastic process of the form

$$X(t) = X(0) + \int_0^t a\,(X(s), s)\,ds + \int_0^t b\,(X(s), s)\,dW(t) \qquad (1.41)$$

where $a(X(s), s)$ and $b(X(s), s)$ are adapted stochastic processes. The second integral is the Ito integral, and $a(X(s), s)$ is called the drift, and $b\,(X\,(s)\,, s)$ is called the volatility of the process.

The Ito process can be written in differential form as

$$dX(t) = a\,(X(t), t)\,dt + b\,(X(t), t)\,dW(t)$$

The differential form is generally used in financial theory. Still, it should be remembered that it is only meaningful if the process's integral form is consistent with the Ito stochastic integral.

Lemma 1.1. *The quadratic variation of the Ito process is*

$$[X, X](t) = \int_0^t b(X(s), s)^2 ds$$

Definition 1.10. Let $X(t)$ $t \geq 0$ be an Ito process, let $\theta(t)$ $t \geq 0$ be an adapted process, and let $\mathcal{F}(t)$ be an associated filtration. We define the integral with respect to the Ito process as

$$\int_0^t \theta(s)dX(s) = \int_0^t \theta(s)a(X(s), s)ds + \int_0^t \theta(s)b(X(s), s)dW(t)$$

Now, instead of Brownian motion, we can write the Ito process:

$$f(T, X(T)) - f(0, X(0)) = \sum_{j=0}^{n-1} (f(t_{j+1}, X(t_{j+1})) - f(t_j, X(t_j))$$

$$= \sum_{j=0}^{n-1} f_t(t_j, X(t_j))(t_{j+1} - t_j) + \sum_{j=0}^{n-1} f_x(t_j, X(t_j))(X(t_{j+1}) - X(t_j))$$

$$+\frac{1}{2}\sum_{j=0}^{n-1} f_{xx}(t_j, X(t_j))(X(t_{j+1}) - X(t_j))^2$$

$$+\sum_{j=0}^{n-1} f_{tx}(t_j, X(t_j))(t_{j+1} - t_j)(X(t_{j+1}) - X(t_j))$$

$$+\frac{1}{2}\sum_{j=0}^{n-1} f_{tt}(t_j, X(t_j))(t_{j+1} - t_j)^2$$

$$+\, higher\ order\ terms$$

Similarly, as $\|\pi\| \to 0$, taking the limits we obtain

$$\sum_{j=0}^{n-1} f_t(t_j, X(t_j))(t_{j+1} - t_j) = \int_0^T f_t\,(t, X(t))\,dt$$

$$\sum_{j=0}^{n-1} f_x(t_j, X(t_j))(X(t_{j+1}) - X(t_j)) = \int_0^T f_x\,(t, X(t))\,dX(t)$$

But this is equal to

$$\int_0^T f_x(t, X(t))dX(t) = \int_0^T f_x(t, X(t))a(X(t), t)dt + \int_0^T f_x(t, X(t))b(X(t), t)dW(t)$$

Finally, the last term is

$$\frac{1}{2}\sum_{j=0}^{n-1} f_{xx}(t_j, X(t_j))(X(t_{j+1}) - X(t_j))^2 = \frac{1}{2}\int_0^T f_{xx}\,(t, X(t))\,b\,(X(t), t)^2 dt$$

Then, we are led to the following theorem.

Theorem 1.7. *Ito-Doeblin formula for an Ito process.*

Let $X(t)$ $t \geq 0$ be an Ito process and let $f(t,x)$ be a function for which the partial derivatives $f_t, f_x(t,x)$, $f_{xx}(t,x)$ are defined and continuous. For every $T \geq$,

$$f(T,X(T)) - f(0,X(0)) = \int_0^T f_t(t,X(t))dt + \int_0^T f_x(t,X(t))\,dX(t) + \frac{1}{2}\int_0^T f_{xx}(t,X(t))\,dX(t)^2$$

and replacing dX, we obtain

$$\begin{aligned} f(T,X(T)) = f(0,X(0)) &+ \int_0^T f_t(t,X(t))\,dt \\ &+ \int_0^T f_x(t,X(t))a(X(t),t)\,dt \\ &+ \frac{1}{2}\int_0^T f_{xx}(t,X(t))\,b(X(t),t)^2 dt \\ &+ \int_0^T f_x(t,X(t))\,b(X(t),t)dW(t) \end{aligned}$$

The differential form is

$$df(t,X(t)) = f_t(t,X(t))dt + f_x(t,X(t))dX(t) + \frac{1}{2}f_{xx}(t,X(t))\,dX(t)^2$$

and

$$\begin{aligned} df(t,X(t)) = f_t(t,X(t))\,dt &+ f_x(t,X(t))a(X(t),t)dt \\ &+ f_x(t,X(t))b(X(t),t)dW(t) \\ &+ \frac{1}{2}f_{xx}(t,X(t))b(X(t),t)^2 dt \end{aligned} \tag{1.42}$$

These results are also known as Ito's Lemma or Ito's formula.

1.6.3. Multidimensional Ito's lemma

Assume a function $f(X(t), Y(t), t)$ and let $X(t), Y(t)$ are the Ito processes given by

$$dX(t) = \mu_X dt + \sigma_X dW(t)$$
$$dY(t) = \mu_Y dt + \sigma_Y dW(t)$$

and $W(t)\ t \geq$ is a Brownian motion. By Ito's Lemma, applying Taylor expansion to $f(X(t), Y(t), t)$, we have

$$df\,(X(t), Y(t), t)$$
$$= \frac{\partial f}{\partial t}dt + \frac{\partial f}{\partial X}dX + \frac{1}{2}\frac{\partial^2 f}{\partial X^2}dX.dX + \frac{\partial f}{\partial Y}dY + \frac{\partial^2 f}{\partial X \partial Y}dXdY$$
$$+ \frac{1}{2}\frac{\partial^2 f}{\partial Y^2}dY.dY$$

Replacing dX, dY, and $dXdY$, we obtain

$$df(X(t), Y(t), t)$$
$$= \frac{\partial f}{\partial t}dt + \frac{\partial f}{\partial X}\left[\mu_X dt + \sigma_X dW(t)\right] + \frac{1}{2}\frac{\partial^2 f}{\partial X^2}\sigma_X^2 dt$$
$$+ \frac{\partial f}{\partial Y}[\mu_Y dt + \sigma_Y dW(t)] + \frac{\partial^2 f}{\partial X \partial Y}\sigma_X \sigma_Y dt + \frac{1}{2}\frac{\partial^2 f}{\partial Y^2}\sigma_Y^2 dt$$

Now, we assume we have uncorrelated Brownian motions $W_1(t)$, $W_2(t)$, $t \geq$, and $X(t), Y(t)$ are Ito processes given by in integral form as

$$X(t) = X(0) + \int_0^t \mu_1 dt + \int_0^t \sigma_{11} dW_1(t) + \int_0^t \sigma_{12} dW_2(t)$$

$$Y(t) = Y(0) + \int_0^t \mu_2 dt + \int_0^t \sigma_{21} dW_1(t) + \int_0^t \sigma_{22} dW_2(t)$$

and in differential form as

$$dX(t) = \mu_1 dt + \sigma_{11} dW_1(t) + \sigma_{12} dW_2(t)$$
$$dY(t) = \mu_2 dt + \sigma_{21} dW_1(t) + \sigma_{22} dW_2(t)$$

where $\mu_1, \mu_2, \sigma_{ij}$ are constants and $\sigma_{ij} > 0$.

σ_{ij} shows the sensitivity of i'th process to the j'th risk factor (Brownian motion). Applying Ito's Lemma to $f(t, x, y)$, we obtain

$$\begin{aligned} df(t,x,y) = {} & \frac{\partial f(t,x,y)}{\partial t} dt \\ & + \frac{\partial f(t,x,y)}{\partial X} \left[\mu_1 dt + \sigma_{11} dW_1(t) + \sigma_{12} dW_2(t)\right] \\ & + \frac{1}{2}\frac{\partial^2 f}{\partial X^2}\left[\sigma_{11}^2 + \sigma_{12}^2\right] dt \\ & + \frac{\partial f}{\partial Y}\left[\mu_2 dt + \sigma_{21} dW_1(t) + \sigma_{22} dW_2(t)\right] \\ & + \frac{\partial^2 f}{\partial X \partial Y}\left[\sigma_{11}\sigma_{21} + \sigma_{12}\sigma_{22}\right] dt + \frac{1}{2}\frac{\partial^2 f}{\partial Y^2}\left[\sigma_{21}^2 + \sigma_{22}^2\right] dt \end{aligned}$$

Then, we can write the Ito-Doeblin formula in integral form as

$$\begin{aligned} f(X(t), Y(t), t) = {} & f(X(0), Y(0), 0) \\ & + \int_0^t \left[f_t + f_x \mu_1 + \frac{1}{2} f_{xx}\left[\sigma_{11}^2 + \sigma_{12}^2\right] + f_y \mu_2 \right. \\ & \left. + \frac{1}{2} f_{yy}\left[\sigma_{21}^2 + \sigma_{22}^2\right] + f_{xy}\left[\sigma_{11}\sigma_{21} + \sigma_{12}\sigma_{22}\right] \right] du \\ & + \int_0^t [\sigma_{11} f_x + \sigma_{21} f_y] dW_1(u) \\ & + \int_0^t [\sigma_{12} f_x + \sigma_{22} f_y] dW_2(u) \end{aligned} \tag{1.43}$$

Corollary 1.1. *Let $X(t)$and $Y(t)$ are Ito processes. Then*

$$d\left(X(t)Y(t)\right) = dX(t)Y(t) + X(t)dY(t) + dX(t).dY(t) \quad (1.44)$$

The proof is simple. Applying Ito's Lemma' for $f = xy$ yields the formula.

1.7. Stochastic Differential Equations

A stochastic differential equation (SDE), in general, is written as

$$dX(t) = a\left(X(t), t\right) dt + b\left(X(t), t\right) dW(t)$$

The solution to this SDE is

$$dX(t) = X(0) + \int_0^t a\left(X\left(u\right), u\right) du + \int_0^t b\left(X\left(u\right), u\right) dW(u)$$

Since the models are based on the SDEs for most cases in mathematical finance, we need the solutions of these equations. These solutions are simple for a few instances but can be quite difficult for others. For example, the solution for

$$dX(t) = adt + bdW(t)$$

for constant a and b, the solution is

$$X(t) = X(0) + \int_0^t adu + \int_0^t bdW\left(u\right) = X(0) + at + bW(t)$$

since $W(0) = 0$.

1.7.1. *SDE for geometric Brownian motion*

Geometric Brownian motion (GBM) is the most commonly used process in continuous-time financial modeling. The stock prices are assumed to follow such a process, and the celebrated BSM option pricing formula is based on GBM. The process is shown by the SDE as

$$dS(t) = rS(t)dt + \sigma S(t)dW(t)$$

If we work with the log prices instead of prices, we can apply Ito's Lemma as follows;

$$y = \ln S(t) \rightarrow dy = d(\ln S(t))$$
$$dy = \frac{\partial y}{\partial S}dS + \frac{1}{2}\frac{\partial^2 y}{\partial S^2}dS^2 + \cdots$$

Note that there is no dt term, and all higher-order terms are zero.
Then,

$$d(\ln S(t)) = \frac{1}{S}\left[rS(t)dt + \sigma S(t)dW(t)\right] - \frac{1}{2}\frac{1}{S^2}\sigma^2 S^2 dt$$
$$d(\ln S(t)) = \left[r - \frac{1}{2}\sigma^2\right]dt + \sigma dW\,(t)$$
$$\ln S(T) - \ln S(0) = \int_0^T \left(r - \frac{1}{2}\sigma^2\right)du + \int_0^T \sigma dW(u)$$
$$\ln\,(S(T)/S(0)) = \left(r - \frac{1}{2}\sigma^2\right)T + \sigma W(T) \qquad (1.45)$$

and finally, we can write the solution of SDE as

$$S(T) = S(0)e^{\int_0^T \left(r-\frac{1}{2}\sigma^2\right)du + \int_0^T \sigma dW(u)}$$
$$S(T) = S(0)e^{\left(r-\frac{1}{2}\sigma^2\right)T + \sigma W(T)} \qquad (1.46)$$

This can be regarded as the time T solution of the stock-price process, which is the base for option pricing. Other than this, various SDEs are used in interest rate models, stochastic volatility models, and so on. A few of them are as follows.

Vasicek Interest Rate Model:

$$dr(t) = [a - br(t)]\,dt + \sigma dW(t)$$

This is called the Ornstein–Uhlenbeck process and contains mean reversion property.

Hull and White Short Rate Model:

$$dr(t) = [a(t) - br(t)]\, dt + \sigma dW(t)$$

It is very similar to the Vasicek model, but the coefficient θ is time-dependent. It is also known as the extended Vasicek model.

Cox–Ingersoll–Ross Short Rate Model:

$$dr(t) = [a(t) - b(t)r(t)]\, dt + \sqrt{r(t)}\sigma dW(t)$$

This is the model preventing interest rates from being negative. All the coefficients except the volatility are time-dependent.

The last example is Heston's stochastic volatility model

$$\begin{aligned} dS(t) &= rS(t)dt + \sigma S(t)dW_1(t) \\ dV(t) &= k\,[\theta - V(t)]\, dt + \sigma V(t)dW_2(t) \end{aligned}$$

where $S(t)$ is the time t asset price, r is the risk-free rate, $\sqrt{V(t)}$ is the asset price volatility, σ volatility of volatility, k is the speed of mean-reversion, θ is the long-term variance, and Ws are correlated Brownian motions.

1.7.2. *Markov property*

A process $X(u)$, $t \geq u$ is Markovian if the process value conditional on information at time u only depends on the value of the process at time u. This means the previous values taken by the process before the observation date do not affect the current value. So, the process is said to have memoryless properties. Technically, we can write the following expectations for a Markovian process;

$$E_u\,[X(t)] = E_{u,X(u)}\,[X(t)] \quad t \geq u \tag{1.47}$$

This means the only relevant information at time θ is only (θ), and the process does not remember the other values in the trajectory.

1.7.3. *The Feynman–Kac theorem*

With three scalar functions $\mu(t,x), \sigma(t,x),\ \varphi(x)$, we try to find a solution C to a boundary value problem on $[0,T]\,x\mathbb{R}$

$$\frac{\partial C(t,x)}{\partial t} + \mu(t,x)\frac{\partial C(t,x)}{\partial x} + \frac{1}{2}\sigma^2(t,x)\frac{\partial^2 C\,(t,x)}{\partial x^2} = 0$$

$$C\,(T, X(T)) = \varphi(X(T))$$

Now, let us define an SDE as

$$dX\,(s) = \mu(s, X\,(s)\,ds + \sigma\,(s, X\,(s))\,dW(s)$$

Let us fix a point in time t and a point in space x.

$$X(T) = x$$

Applying the Ito's Lemma to $C\,(t,x)$ yields us

$$\begin{aligned} C(T,X(T)) = C(t,X(t)) & \\ &+ \int_t^T \left(\frac{\partial C(s,X(s))}{\partial s} + \mu(s,X(s))\frac{\partial C(s,X(s))}{\partial x}\right. \\ &\left. + \frac{1}{2}\sigma^2(s,X(s))\frac{\partial^2 C(s,X(s))}{\partial x^2}\right) ds \\ &+ \int_t^T \sigma(s,X(s))\frac{\partial C(s,X(s))}{\partial x} dW(s) \end{aligned}$$

The first integral is equal to zero by construction. Taking expectations, the second integral also vanishes since this becomes an Ito integral. Therefore, we obtain

$$E[C\,(T, X(T))] = C\,(t, X(t))$$

So, the solution to the boundary value problem is

$$C\,(t, X(t)) = E\,[C\,(T, X(T))] = E_{t,x}\,[\varphi(X(T))]$$

This result is known as the Feynman–Kac stochastic representation formula.

Proposition 1.14 (Feynman–Kac). *Assume that C is a solution to the boundary value problem*

$$\begin{aligned} &\frac{\partial C(t,x)}{\partial t} + \mu(t,x)\frac{\partial C(t,x)}{\partial x} + \frac{1}{2}\sigma^2(t,x)\frac{\partial^2 C(t,x)}{\partial x^2} = 0 \\ &C(T,x) = \varphi(x) \end{aligned} \tag{1.48}$$

Also, assume that the process

$$\sigma(s, X(s))\frac{\partial C(s,X(s))}{\partial x}$$

is square integrable. Then, C has the representation

$$C(t, X(t)) = E_{t,x}[\varphi(X(T))] \tag{1.49}$$

where X satisfies the following stochastic representation, which is an SDE:

$$\begin{aligned} &dX(s) = \mu(s, X(s)ds + \sigma(s, X(s))dW(s) \\ &X(T) = x \end{aligned}$$

The following proposition presents a closely related boundary value problem we use in option pricing.

Proposition 1.15 (Feynman–Kac). *Assume that C is a solution to the boundary value problem*

$$\begin{aligned} &\frac{\partial C(t,x)}{\partial t} + \mu(t,x)\frac{\partial C(t,x)}{\partial x} + \frac{1}{2}\sigma^2(t,x)\frac{\partial^2 C(t,x)}{\partial x^2} - rC(t,x) = 0 \\ &C(T,x) = \varphi(x) \end{aligned} \tag{1.50}$$

Assume further that the process

$$\sigma(s, X(s))\frac{\partial C(s,X(s))}{\partial x}$$

is square integrable. Then C has the representation

$$C(t, X(t)) = e^{-r(T-t)}E_{t,x}[\varphi(X(T))]$$

where X satisfies the following stochastic representation:

$$dX(s) = \mu(s, X(s)ds + \sigma(s, X(s))dW(s)$$
$$X(T) = x$$

This partial differential equation (PDE) given by (1.50) *is called a parabolic one, the base for the celebrated BSM formula. The option class, whether it is call or put, changes according to the expression of boundary or terminal conditions (see the details in* Björk, 2004, pp. 68–75*).*

1.8. Measure Change and Girsanov Theorem

In finance, most pricing issues are handled in a risk-neutral probability world rather than the world of actual probabilities. This requires assigning risk-neutral probabilities to outcomes and, in turn, changing the probability measure. Let $\mathbb{P}$ and $\widetilde{\mathbb{P}}$ be the real and risk-neutral probability measures, respectively. By using a positive number $Z(w)$, we can write

$$Z(w)d\mathbb{P} = d\widetilde{\mathbb{P}}$$

This means that when we need to revise the probability upward (downward), we apply $Z > 1(Z < 1)$. However, the outcomes with zero probability in the real world must also have zero probability in the risk-neutral world to call them equivalent probability measures.

What follows are the theorems (without proofs; for proofs, see Shreve 2004, pp. 33–39) and the definitions of measure change. The following sub-section explains the role of the Girsanov theorem in measure change.

1.8.1. *Measure change*

Theorem 1.8. *Let* $(\Omega,\ \mathcal{F},\ \mathbb{P})$ *be a probability space, and let* Z *be an almost surely nonnegative random variable with* $E[Z] = 1$*. For* $A \in \mathcal{F}$ *define*

$$\widetilde{\mathbb{P}}(A) = \int_A Z(w)dP(w)$$

then $\widetilde{\mathbb{P}}$ *is a probability measure. Furthermore, if* X *is a nonnegative random variable, then*

$$\tilde{E}[X] = E[XZ]$$

where $\tilde{E}\left[X\right] = \int_{\Omega} X(w)d\widetilde{\mathbb{P}}(w)$.

If Z is almost surely strictly positive, we also have

$$\tilde{E}\left[\frac{Y}{Z}\right] = E[Y]$$

Note that if $P(w) = 0$, then $\widetilde{\mathbb{P}}(w) = 0$.

Since $\tilde{E}\left[X\right] = \int_{\Omega} X(w)d\widetilde{\mathbb{P}}(w)$ and $\int_{\Omega} Z(w)X(w)dP(w)$ we can write

$$d\widetilde{\mathbb{P}}(w) = Z(w)dP(w) \rightarrow Z\left(w\right) = \frac{d\widetilde{\mathbb{P}}(w)}{dP(w)} \tag{1.51}$$

Definition 1.11. Let Ω be a nonempty set, and $\mathcal{F}$ be a $\sigma-$ algebra (see Appendix A) of subsets of Ω. Two probability measures $\mathbb{P}$ and $\widetilde{\mathbb{P}}$ on $(\Omega,\ \mathcal{F})$ are equivalent if they have zero probability for the same sets in $\mathcal{F}$.

Definition 1.12. Let $(\Omega,\ \mathcal{F},\ \mathbb{P})$ be a probability space and let $\widetilde{\mathbb{P}}$ be the equivalent probability measure on $(\Omega,\ \mathcal{F})$ and let Z be an almost surely positive random variable with $E[Z] = 1$ that relates $\mathbb{P}$ and $\widetilde{\mathbb{P}}$ then, Z is called the Radon–Nikodym derivative of $\widetilde{\mathbb{P}}$ with respect to $\mathbb{P}$. We can write

$$Z(w) = \frac{d\widetilde{\mathbb{P}}(w)}{dP(w)}$$

Example: Let X be a standard normal variable with $\sim N(0,1)$. Let $Y = X + \theta$ with $\sim N(\theta, 1)$. Then, we want to change the distribution of Y as $\sim N(0,1)$ without changing the Y itself. For example, without changing the asset prices, we change the asset price distribution.

We can do this by defining a positive random variable as

$$Z(w) = \exp\left\{-\theta X - \frac{1}{2}\theta^2\right\}$$

satisfying the positivity and $E[Z] = 1$.

Now, under $\widetilde{\mathbb{P}}$

$$\tilde{P}(Y \leq b) = \int_{\{w;Y(w)\leq b\}} Z(w)dP(w) = \int_{\{\Omega\}} 1_{Y(w)\leq b} Z(w)dP(w)$$

$$= \int_{\{\Omega\}} 1_{X(w)\leq b-\theta} Z(w)dP(w)$$

$$\tilde{P}(Y \leq b) = \int_{-\infty}^{b-\theta} e^{-\theta X - \frac{1}{2}\theta^2} dP(w) = \int_{-\infty}^{b-\theta} e^{-\theta x - \frac{1}{2}\theta^2} e^{-\frac{1}{2}x^2} dx$$

Replacing $y = x + \theta$

$$\tilde{P}(Y \leq b) = \int_{-\infty}^{b} e^{-\frac{1}{2}y^2} dy$$

What we have done is, by multiplying the random variable with $Z(w)$, we have changed the mean of Y from θ to zero.

1.8.2. *Girsanov theorem*

Let's design a measurement change for the entire process. For this, we consider the process related to the Radon–Nikodym derivative in the probability space $(\Omega,\ \mathcal{F},\ \mathbb{P})$, as a process

$$Z(t) = E\left[(Z \mid \mathcal{F}(t))\right] \tag{1.52}$$

with $E[Z] = 1$ under the filtering $\mathcal{F}(t), 0 \leq\ t \leq T$. Due to iterative conditioning, the Radon–Nikodym derivative is a martingale. When we take the conditional expectation of both sides of the equation with respect to the information set $\mathcal{F}(s)$, by the tower property and by definition, we can write

$$E\left[(Z(t)|\mathcal{F}(s))\right] = E\left[(E\left[(Z|\mathcal{F}(t))\right]|\mathcal{F}(s))\right] = E\left[(Z|\mathcal{F}(s))\right] = Z(s)$$

We will write 2 Lemmas (Shreve, 2004, pp. 211–212) and then proceed to Girsanov's theorem.

Lemma 1.2. *Let $0 \leq t \leq T$ and Y be a $\mathcal{F}(t)$ — measurable random variable. In this case, we can write*

$$\tilde{E}Y = E[YZ(t)]$$

The proof is simple. By using the unbiasedness of conditional expectations and taking out what is known and by definition, we can write;

$$\tilde{E}Y = E[YZ]$$

$E[YZ] = E[E(YZ|\mathcal{F}(t))] = E[YE(Z|\mathcal{F}(t))]$ *and since* $E(Z|\mathcal{F}(t)) = Z(t)$ *we have*

$$\tilde{E}Y = E[YZ(t)]$$

Lemma 1.3. *Let Y be a $\mathcal{F}(t)-$measurable random variable with $0 \leq s \leq t \leq T$. Then, we can write*

$$\tilde{E}\left[(Y \mid \mathcal{F}(s))\right] = \frac{1}{Z(s)}E\left[(YZ(t) \mid \mathcal{F}(s))\right] \tag{1.53}$$

Note that the equation $\frac{1}{Z(s)}E\left[(YZ(t)|\mathcal{F}(s))\right]$ is $\mathcal{F}(s)$ — measurable. Therefore, using the partial averaging property, for all $A \in \mathcal{F}(s)$ (see Appendix A for partial averaging), we can write

$$\int_A \frac{1}{Z(s)}E\left[(YZ(t) \mid \mathcal{F}(s))\right] d\tilde{P} = \int_A Y d\tilde{P}$$

Since the conditional expectation of Y is according to the probability measure $\widetilde{P}$, we perform the integration according to this measure.

The left side can be expressed as

$$\tilde{E}\left[1_A \frac{1}{Z(s)} E\left[(YZ(t)|\mathcal{F}(s))\right]\right]$$

Since $\tilde{E}[X] = E[ZX]$ multiplying this expression by $Z(s)$ yields

$$E\left[1_A E\left[(YZ(t)|\mathcal{F}(s))\right]\right]$$

Then, applying the same properties of martingales and the Lemma 1.1, we obtain

$$\begin{aligned} E[1_A E[(YZ(t)|\mathcal{F}(s))]] &= E[E[1_A(YZ(t)|\mathcal{F}(s))]] \\ &= E[1_A YZ(t)] = \tilde{E}[1_A Y] = \int_A Y d\tilde{P} \end{aligned}$$

Theorem 1.9 (Girsanov Theorem). *Let $W(t)$ be a Brownian motion in the probability space $(\Omega,\ \mathcal{F},\ \mathbb{P})$, with $0 \le t \le T$ and $\mathcal{F}(t)$ be the filtration associated with this. Let $\theta(s)$ be an adapted process (adapted to filtration $\mathcal{F}(t)$ with $0 \le t \le T$). Define*

$$Z(t) = \exp\left\{-\int_0^t \theta(u)\, dW(u) - \frac{1}{2}\int_0^t \theta^2(u) du\right\}$$

$$\widetilde{W}(t) = W(t) + \int_0^t \theta(u)\, du \tag{1.54}$$

and assume

$$\int_0^T \theta^2(u) Z^2(u) du < \infty$$

Let us define $Z = Z(T)$. Then $E[Z] = 1$ and under the probability measure $\widetilde{\mathbb{P}}$

$$\widetilde{\mathbb{P}}(A) = \int_A Z(w) dP(w)$$

the process $\tilde{W}(t)$ is a Brownian motion with $0 \le t \le T$.

The proof requires that we must show

(i) $\tilde{W}(0) = 0$
(ii) $d\tilde{W}(t)d\tilde{W}(t) = dt$
(iii) $Z(t)$ *is a martingale*
(iv) $Z(t)\tilde{W}(t)$ *has the martingale property under* $\mathbb{P}$
(v) $\tilde{W}(t)$ *has the martingale property under* $\widetilde{\mathbb{P}}$

First, it is clear that for $t = 0$

$$\tilde{W}(0) = W(0) + \int_0^0 \theta(u)du = 0$$

Secondly

$$d\tilde{W}(t)d\tilde{W}(t) = (dW(t) + \theta(u)du)^2 = dt$$

Furthermore since

$$Z(t) = \exp\left\{-\int_0^t \theta\,(u)\,dW\,(u) - \frac{1}{2}\int_0^t \theta^2(u)du\right\}$$

we have $Z(t) = e^X$ where $X = -\int_0^t \theta(u)dW(u) - \frac{1}{2}\int_0^t \theta^2(u)du$. By applying Ito's Lemma

$$dZ(t) = df\,(X(t)) = f'\,(X(t))\,dX(t) + \frac{1}{2}f'\,(X(t))\,dX^2(t).$$

$$dZ(t) = df\,(X(t)) = e^{X(t)}dX(t) + \frac{1}{2}e^{X(t)}dX^2(t)$$

$$= e^{X(t)}\left(-\theta(t)dW(t) - \frac{1}{2}\theta^2\,(t)\,dt\right) + \frac{1}{2}e^{X(t)}\theta^2(t)dt$$

Since the last terms cancel out we obtain

$$dZ(t) = -\theta(t)dW(t)e^{X(t)} = -\theta(t)dW(t)Z(t)$$

and

$$Z(t) = Z(0) - \int_0^t \theta(u)\, dW(u)$$

That is, this is an Ito integral and Ito integrals are martingales;

$$\begin{aligned}
&E\left[dZ(t)\right] = 0 \\
&Z(t) = E\left\{Z(T)|\mathcal{F}(t)\right\} = E\left\{Z|\mathcal{F}(t)\right\}, \quad 0 \leq t < T
\end{aligned}$$

Now, let us show that $Z(t)\tilde{W}(t)$ is a martingale under measure $\mathbb{P}$. Applying Ito's product rule, we get

$$\begin{aligned}
d(\tilde{W}(t)Z(t)) &= d\tilde{W}(t)Z(t) + \tilde{W}(t)dZ(t) + d\tilde{W}(t)dZ(t) \\
&= Z(t)dW(t) + \theta(t)Z(t)dt - \tilde{W}(t)\theta(t)Z(t)dW(t) + (dW(t) \\
&\quad + \theta(t)dt)(-\theta(t)Z(t)dW(t) = (1 - \tilde{W}(t)\theta(t))Z(t)dW(t)
\end{aligned}$$

Since there is no deterministic dt term in the last term, $\tilde{W}(t)Z(t)$ is a martingale under the measure $\mathbb{P}$. Taking expectations, we obtain

$$E\left[d\left(\tilde{W}(t)Z(t)\right)\right] = E\left[\left(1 - \tilde{W}(t)\theta(t)\right)Z(t)dW(t)\right] = 0$$

Finally, we need to show that $\tilde{W}(t)$ is a martingale under the measure $\widetilde{\mathbb{P}}$. From Lemma 1.3 and the property that $\tilde{W}(t)Z(t)$ is a martingale under measure $\mathbb{P}$, we can write

$$\begin{aligned}
\tilde{E}(\tilde{W}(t)|\mathcal{F}(s)) &= \frac{1}{Z(s)}E(\tilde{W}(t)Z(t)|\mathcal{F}(s)) \\
&= \frac{1}{Z(s)}Z(s)\tilde{W}(s) = \tilde{W}(s)
\end{aligned}$$

So, the proof is done.

1.9. Risk-Neutral Measure and the Pricing

1.9.1. *Risk-neutral measure*

Let $W(t)$ be a Brownian motion in the probability space $(\Omega, \mathcal{F}, \mathbb{P})$, with $0 \leq t \leq T$ and $\mathcal{F}(t)$ be the filtration associated with this. Then, the stock price process is modeled through the following SDE

$$dS(t) = \mu(t)S(t)dt + \sigma(t)S(t)\,dW(t)$$

The mean rate of return $\mu(t)$ and volatility $\sigma(t)$ are adapted processes to filtration $\mathcal{F}(t)$. $\sigma(t) > 0$ for every $t \in [0, T]$ almost surely. The solution to SDE is

$$S(t) = S(0)e^{\int_0^t (\mu - \frac{1}{2}\sigma^2)du + \int_0^t \sigma dW(u)}$$

Suppose we have an $\mathcal{F}(t)-$adapted interest rate process $r(t)$. Then, we can define a discount process as

$$D(t) = \exp\left\{-\int_0^t r(s)ds\right\} \tag{1.55}$$

and

$$dD(t) = -r(t)D(t)dt$$

Defining $I(t) = \int_0^t r(s)ds$ *ve* $dI(t) = r(t)dt$ and

$$D(t) = f\left(I(t)\right) = e^{-I(t)}$$

and applying Ito's Lemma, we obtain

$$\begin{aligned} dD(t) = df\left(I(t)\right) &= f'\left(I(t)\right)dI(t) + \frac{1}{2}f''\left(I(t)\right)dI(t)dI(t) \\ &= r(t)dt \cdot (-e^{-I(t)}) = -r(t)D(t)dt \end{aligned}$$

Note that although $D(t)$ is random, its quadratic change is zero. This is because it is a "smooth" function.

The discounted price process is

$$D(t)S(t) = D(t)S(0)\exp\left\{\int_0^t \sigma(s)\,dW(s) + \int_0^t (\mu(s) - \frac{1}{2}\sigma^2(s))ds\right\}$$

$$D(t)S(t) = S(0)\exp\left\{\int_0^t \sigma(s)dW(s) + \int_0^t (\mu(s) - r(s) - \frac{1}{2}\sigma^2(s))ds\right\} \tag{1.56}$$

Defining

$$X = \int_0^t \sigma(s)dW(s) + \int_0^t (\mu(s) - r(s) - \frac{1}{2}\sigma^2(s))ds$$

and

$$D(t)S(t) = f\left(X(t)\right) = e^{X(t)}$$

and applying Ito's lemma to $D(t)S(t)$ we obtain

$$\begin{aligned} d\left(D(t)S(t)\right) &= f'\left(X\right)dX + \frac{1}{2}f''\left(X\right)dX^2 \\ &= D(t)S(t)\sigma(t)dW(t) + D(t)S(t)\left(\mu(t) - r(t) - \frac{1}{2}\sigma^2\left(t\right)\right)dt \\ &\quad + D(t)S(t)\frac{1}{2}\sigma^2(t)dt \\ &= D(t)S(t)\sigma(t)dW(t) + D(t)S(t)\left(\mu(t) - r(t)\right)dt \end{aligned}$$

Defining

$$\lambda = \frac{\mu(t) - r(t)}{\sigma(t)} \tag{1.57}$$

as the market price of risk, which is the Sharpe ratio, we can restate the process as

$$d(D(t)S(t)) = D(t)S(t)\sigma(t)[dW(t) + \lambda dt]$$

But $dW(t) + \lambda dt$ is equal to $d\widetilde{W}(t)$ under $\widetilde{\mathbb{P}}$. Therefore, we call $\widetilde{\mathbb{P}}$ as the equivalent risk-neutral probability measure under which the discounted price process behaves like a martingale and the risk factor is removed.

$$d\left(D(t)S(t)\right) = D(t)S(t)\sigma(t)d\tilde{W}(t)$$

By integration, we obtain

$$D(t)S(t) = D(0)S(0) + \int_0^t D\left(u\right)S\left(u\right)\sigma\left(u\right)d\tilde{W}\left(u\right)$$

which is an Ito integral and a martingale. One step further is the solution to the SDE before. With the new perspective, we can change from

$$dS(t) = \mu(t)S(t)dt + \sigma(t)S\left(t\right)dW\left(t\right)$$

to

$$dS(t) = \mu(t)S(t)dt + \sigma(t)S(t)[d\tilde{W}(t) - \lambda dt]$$
$$dS(t) = r(t)S(t)dt + \sigma(t)S(t)d\tilde{W}(t)$$

and the solution is

$$S(t) = S(0)e^{\int_0^t \left(r-\frac{1}{2}\sigma^2\right)du+\int_0^t \sigma dW(u)} \tag{1.58}$$

under the risk-neutral measure $\widetilde{\mathbb{P}}$.

1.9.2. *The pricing issues and the asset pricing theorems revisited*

Until now, we have used the discount process or risk-free bank account as a numeraire for risk-neutral processes.

$$D(t) = \exp\left\{-\int_0^t r(s)ds\right\}, \quad B(t) = \exp\left\{\int_0^t r(s)ds\right\}$$

$$B(t) = \frac{1}{D(t)}$$

Once again, applying Ito's product rule, we can write

$$d\left(\frac{S}{B}\right) = \frac{1}{B}dS + Sd\left(\frac{1}{B}\right) + dSd\left(\frac{1}{B}\right)$$

$$d\left(\frac{1}{B}\right) = -\frac{1}{B^2}dB + \frac{1}{B^3}dB^2 = -\frac{1}{B}rdt$$

$$dSd\left(\frac{1}{B}\right) \to 0 \quad \frac{1}{B^3}dB^2 \to 0$$

$$d\left(\frac{S}{B}\right) = \frac{S}{B}\left(\mu - r\right)dt + \frac{S}{B}\sigma dW$$

Since

$$d\tilde{W} = dW + \lambda dt \quad \lambda = \frac{\mu - r}{\sigma}$$

where λ is the risk premium, the discounted stock price, or the stock price expressed in terms of the risk-free asset price is found to be a martingale.

$$d\left(\frac{S}{B}\right) = \frac{S}{B}\left(\mu - r\right)dt + \frac{S}{B}\sigma\left[d\tilde{W} - \frac{\mu - r}{\sigma}dt\right] = \frac{S}{B}\sigma d\tilde{W}$$

Then, we may transform the SDE of the stock price as

$$dS(t) = \mu(t)S(t)dt + \sigma(t)S(t)[d\tilde{W}(t) - \lambda dt]$$
$$dS(t) = r(t)S(t)dt + \sigma(t)S(t)d\tilde{W}(t)$$

The probability measure $\widetilde{\mathbb{P}}(B)$ is risk-neutral with the numeraire. However, the unit of measurement may not always be a risk-free asset, and we may have to change it according to our needs.

Theorem 1.10 (Fundamental Theorem of Financial Asset Pricing II). *Under the risk-neutral measure, all components of the risk price vector vanish, for λ_α $\alpha = 1, \ldots, M$ and the drift term of the financial asset price equation is expressed by the risk-free interest* *rate. In this case, the price process of any attainable instrument is represented by*

$$\frac{S(t)}{B(t)} = E^{Q(B)}\left[\frac{S(T)}{B(T)}\right]$$

$$S(t) = B(t)E^{Q(B)}\left[\frac{S(T)}{B(T)}\right] = E^{Q(B)}\left[\frac{S(T)}{B(T)}\right]$$

$$= E^{Q(B)}\left[\exp\left\{-\int_0^t r(s)ds\right\} S(T)\right]$$

for any exit time.

Now, assume $\alpha = 1, \ldots, M$ risk factors, $i = 1 \ldots N$ risky assets and portfolio V with portfolio weights $\vartheta^i \quad i = 0 \ldots N$. Suppressing the time dimension, we can write the portfolio value as

$$V = \vartheta^0 B + \sum_{i=1}^{N} \vartheta^i S^i \tag{1.59}$$

The change in the portfolio is

$$dV = \vartheta^0 dB + \sum_{i=1}^{N} \vartheta^i dS^i = \vartheta^0 r B dt + \sum_{i=1}^{N} \vartheta^i dS^i$$

The condition for the self-financing portfolio is

$$d\vartheta^0 B + \sum_{i=1}^{N} d\vartheta^i (S^i + dS^i) = 0 \tag{1.60}$$

In other words, changes in the asset holdings are made without transferring funds from inside to outside and from outside to inside the portfolio.

Now, with the no-arbitrage condition and a self-financing strategy, we can write

$$\sum_{i=1}^{N} d\vartheta^i (S^i + dS^i) = 0$$

for $\vartheta^i \quad i = 0 \ldots N$. Then, the value and the change in the value of the portfolio with this strategy is

$$\pi = \sum_{i=1}^{N} \vartheta^i S^i$$

$$d\pi = \sum_{i=1}^{N} \vartheta^i dS^i$$

$$r\pi dt = \sum_{i=1}^{N} \vartheta^i \left[\mu^i S^i dt + \sum_{\alpha=1}^{M} S^i \sigma_\alpha^i dW_\alpha \right]$$

This strategy will be completely risk-free if the stochastic component is zero, and we must have

$$\sum_{i=1}^{N} \vartheta^i S^i \sigma_\alpha^i = 0$$

for all $\alpha = 1, \ldots, M$. (1.61)

That is, $\mathbb{R}^N$ dimensional vector components $\vartheta^i S^i$ are orthogonal to the subspaces $(\alpha = 1, \ldots, M)$ of the vectors in it, that is, to their σ_α^i components.

Now, we have only

$$r\pi dt = \sum_{i=1}^{N} \vartheta^i \mu^i S^i dt$$

and since

$$\pi = \sum_{i=1}^{N} \vartheta^i S^i$$

we obtain

$$\sum_{i=1}^{N} \vartheta^i S^i \left(\mu^i - r\right) = 0 \tag{1.62}$$

Here again, we see that the $\vartheta^i S^i$ vector components are orthogonal to the $(\mu^i - r)$ vector components. Our knowledge of linear algebra tells us that the $\vartheta^i S^i$ components are orthogonal to both vector components if and only if the components $(\mu^i - r)$ and can be written as a linear combination of σ^i_α. That is,

$$\mu^i = r + \sum_{\alpha=1}^{M} \lambda_\alpha \sigma^i_\alpha \tag{1.63}$$

λ_α is called risk price and are independent of the financial asset price.

Example: Assume we have two risky assets, S and A (we are ignoring the time indices). We have

$$\begin{aligned} dS &= \mu^S S dt + \sigma^S S dW \\ dA &= \mu^A A dt + \sigma^A A dW \\ d(S/A) &= \frac{1}{A} dS + d\left(\frac{1}{A}\right) S + dSd\left(\frac{1}{A}\right) = \\ \frac{d\left(\frac{S}{A}\right)}{\frac{S}{A}} &= (\mu^S - \mu^A)dt + \sigma^A(\sigma^A - \sigma^S)dt + (\sigma^S - \sigma^A)dW \end{aligned}$$

But since

$$\mu^i = r + \sum_{\alpha=1}^{M} \lambda_\alpha \sigma^i_\alpha$$

we can write

$$\frac{d\left(\frac{S}{A}\right)}{\frac{S}{A}} = \lambda\left(\sigma^S - \sigma^A\right) dt - \sigma^A(\sigma^S - \sigma^A) + (\sigma^S - \sigma^A)dW$$

To make $\frac{d\left(\frac{S}{A}\right)}{\frac{S}{A}}$ a martingale, we need to have $\lambda = \sigma^A$; that is, the market price of risk (risk premium) must be equal to the volatility of the numeraire asset. Then

$$E\left(\frac{d\left(\frac{S}{A}\right)}{\frac{S}{A}}\right) = E\left[(\sigma^S - \sigma^A)dW\right] = 0$$

Therefore, when we are in a risk-neutral word with the stock price as numeraire, our SDE is

$$dS = \mu S dt + \sigma S d\tilde{W} \ \lambda = \sigma \ \mu = r + \sigma^2$$

which yields

$$dS = (r + \sigma^2) S dt + \sigma S d\tilde{W}$$

and applying Ito's lemma for ln $S(t)$, we obtain the solution as

$$S(t) = S(0) e^{\int_0^t \left(r + \frac{1}{2}\sigma^2\right) du + \int_0^t \sigma dW(u)}$$

or

$$S(t) = S(0) e^{\left(r + \frac{1}{2}\sigma^2\right) t + \sigma W(t)}$$

For more than one risk factor

$$\mu^S = r + \sum_{\alpha=1}^{M} \lambda_\alpha \sigma_\alpha^S \quad \mu^A = r + \sum_{\alpha=1}^{M} \lambda_\alpha \sigma_\alpha^A$$

$$E\left(\frac{d\left(\frac{S}{A}\right)}{\frac{S}{A}}\right) = \left[\sum_{\alpha=1}^{M} \lambda_\alpha \sigma_\alpha^S - \sum_{\alpha=1}^{M} \lambda_\alpha \sigma_\alpha^A + \sum_{\alpha=1}^{M} \sigma_\alpha^A \left(\sigma_\alpha^A - \sigma_\alpha^S\right)\right] dt$$

$$E\left(\frac{d\left(\frac{S}{A}\right)}{\frac{S}{A}}\right) = \left[\sum_{\alpha=1}^{M} \left(\lambda_\alpha - \sigma_\alpha^A\right)\left(\sigma_\alpha^S - \sigma_\alpha^A\right)\right] dt$$

The feature that allows the process $\frac{S}{A}$ to be martingale is that $\lambda_\alpha = \sigma_\alpha^A$. In other words, the price of risk for each factor should be equal to the volatility of the financial asset, which is the unit of measurement, against each factor. Since this is accepted as zero for the risk-free unit of measurement, we can write $\mu = r$, as mentioned above, in a risk-neutral world with a risk-free asset as the numeraire (see Delbaen and Schachermayer, 1994 and 1998 for the fundamental asset pricing theorems).

1.10. Option Pricing

An option is a right to buy or sell a risky asset at a specific price at a certain maturity or period. We categorize such contingent claims into two main categories: call options and put options. In this subsection, we will provide a solution to the celebrated BSM formula and present some justifications for the existence and wide range of use of options.

1.10.1. *Why options?*

An option can be replicated with stock and cash positions. Then, when it is possible to replicate the option with stock and cash positions, the question of why one should buy an option may arise. Indeed, options are referred to as "redundant securities" in the financial literature. An excellent explanation of the reasons for using options is given in Cox and Rubinstein (1985, pp. 44–59).

Let's summarize these explanations below:

Even if it were possible to synthetically produce an option that would make precisely the same return pattern as a portfolio of stocks and bonds, this cannot always be done for various reasons. For example, changes in volatility and the firm's dividend policy may cause changes in option prices, but no change may occur in the portfolio of stocks and bonds. Similarly, if there is a significant jump in stock prices and the stock value crashes, the loss that a call option will suffer will be limited to the option premium only. Therefore, options offer a much wider variety and pattern of returns.

Options offer more favorable borrowing and lending rates. Since option prices are generally designed for large investors, the rates used here will be at rates that are not accessible to small investors.

Options offer more suitable opportunities to overcome collateral restrictions. For example, a put option purchase or a call option sale (put purchase and call write) can be produced alternatively with a short selling and lending portfolio. However, in this case, short-selling restrictions will make it challenging to obtain the same option payoff. The same situation applies even when purchasing a call option. Because even when buying shares by borrowing, collateral obligations will come into play as possible restrictions.

Tax advantages are another factor, and options help to defer profits. For example, an option spread strategy can defer taxes until one year later by making a loss on a short-term option and a profit on a long-term option.

Institutional investors, especially if not small investors, face lower transaction costs. Suppose the portfolio is frequently switched between stocks and bonds. In that case, options are the desired investment vehicle, and if it is to be less frequent, the portfolio itself is the preferred investment vehicle.

Options can also be effective in enabling us to make a profit using private information. By choosing overvalued or undervalued options, and if we have special knowledge about stocks, we can achieve an excellent portfolio performance by using both. For example, if we have special knowledge about the volatility parameter, we can easily choose overvalued or undervalued options. We know that a company will make a new investment, but we may not know whether this investment will cause the stock to increase or decrease. However, if we predict that volatility will grow in any case, buying call and put options simultaneously can make a profit on our position.

Option positions are preferred instead of buying stocks in highly uncertain situations because they protect against unexpected volatility increases.

Options can protect against unexpected changes in a firm's dividend policy. They can also provide a separation between price gains and dividend yields. Let's assume we invest in a mutual fund of stocks that pay high dividends and expect dividends. Let's also assume that a firm will make a significant policy change in not making dividend payments. If you had created a portfolio consisting of a call and a short sale as an investor, you would have protected yourself against a decrease in dividends (Why?) and also against other possible risks. (Why?)

Options also help to overcome regulations and restrictions on short selling. For example, in a falling market, we may have to wait for the stock price to increase to short sell, i.e., we may not be able to sell on consecutive days of decline. Borrowing a particular stock from a brokerage firm may also be impossible. In such cases, options are the best way to produce short-selling synthetically.

Undoubtedly, the fact that the market volume of options has reached trillions of dollars shows that many of the abovementioned reasons are valid. However, let's not forget that the emergence of a pricing system that will bring supply and demand together and be used as a market compass impacts this result.

1.10.2. *Black–Scholes–Merton formula*

Fischer Black and Myron Scholes significantly contributed to option pricing with their famous article "The Pricing of Options and Corporate Liabilities," published in 1973. This formula was vital in quickly calculating the option price, providing the hedge ratio and option sensitivities, and reaching the necessary simple and observable parameters by the market players. The same year, Merton's article "Theory of Rational Option Pricing" was published. Merton produced the same formula using the error function and significantly contributed to option pricing theory. For this reason, the formula is often referred to as the BSM formula. We will stick to this approach. This subsection will present brief information on the BSM formula.

There is a specific correlation between the value of a stock and the option price. For example, in a call option, this correlation is positive (the stock and option prices increase together), and in a put option, it is negative (if the stock price decreases, the option price increases). This correlation can be used to create risk-free portfolios. This understanding also lies at the basis of the BSM model.

Now, let us make a portfolio by selling one-unit option and buying Δ units of stock.

$$\pi = -F + \Delta S$$

We expect the portfolio return to equal a risk-free rate in a risk-neutral world. Therefore, we can write;

$$\begin{aligned} d\pi &= -dF + \Delta dS = r\pi dt \\ F &= F(S,t)\ dS = rSdt + \sigma SdW \end{aligned} \tag{1.64}$$

and

$$\begin{aligned} dF = {} & \frac{\partial F(t,S)}{\partial t}dt + rS\frac{\partial F(t,S)}{\partial S}dt + \frac{1}{2}\sigma^2\frac{\partial^2 F(t,S)}{\partial S^2}dt \\ & + \frac{\partial F(t,S)}{\partial S}\ \sigma SdW \end{aligned}$$

Replacing in (1.64), we obtain

$$\begin{aligned} r(-F + \Delta S)dt = {} & -\frac{\partial F(t,S)}{\partial t}dt - rS\frac{\partial F(t,S)}{\partial S}dt - \frac{1}{2}\sigma^2\frac{\partial^2 F(t,S)}{\partial S^2}dt \\ & - \frac{\partial F(t,S)}{\partial S}\ \sigma SdW + \Delta dS \end{aligned}$$

Defining $\Delta = \frac{\partial F(t,S)}{\partial S}$ eliminates the second and the last terms on the right-hand side, and we obtain the PDE of second-order;

$$\frac{\partial F(t,S)}{\partial t} + rS\frac{\partial F(t,S)}{\partial S} + \frac{1}{2}\sigma^2\frac{\partial^2 F(t,S)}{\partial S^2} - rF = 0 \qquad (1.65)$$

The solution to this PDE requires some boundary or terminal conditions. For call options, the terminal condition is

$$\max(S_T - K, 0) = (S_T - K)^+$$

and put options

$$\max(K - S_T, 0) = (K - S_T)^+$$

which are known as the payoff functions of calls and puts, respectively.

There are various ways to derive the BSM formula and solutions to the SDE in (1.65). However, since we know the Feynman–Kac representation,

$$C(t, X(t)) = e^{-r(T-t)}E_{t,x}[\varphi(X(T))]$$

and using the lognormal distribution parameters for the log-asset price, we claim that the solution for the put option is

$$p(t, S) = e^{-r(T-t)}E_t[(K - S(T))^+]$$

Keeping in mind that

$$E[\ln S(T)] = \ln S(0) + \left(r - \frac{1}{2}\sigma^2\right)T$$

$$Var[\ln S(T)] = \sigma^2 T$$

and $x_T = \ln S(T)$ the expectation is

$$p(0, S) = p_0 = \int_{-\infty}^{K} (K - S(T)f(S(T)dS$$

$$p(0,S) = p_0 = \frac{e^{-rT}}{\sigma\sqrt{2\pi T}}\int_{-\infty}^{\ln K}(K-e^x)e^{-\frac{1}{2}\left(\frac{x-\ln S_0-\left(r-\frac{1}{2}\sigma^2\right)T}{\sigma\sqrt{T}}\right)^2}dx$$

$$\varepsilon = \frac{x-\ln S_0-\left(r-\frac{1}{2}\sigma^2\right)T}{\sigma\sqrt{T}} = \frac{-\ln\left(S_0/K\right)-\left(r-\frac{1}{2}\sigma^2\right)T}{\sigma\sqrt{T}}$$

where we have used $x = x_T$.

The first integral is

$$K\frac{e^{-rT}}{\sqrt{2\pi}}\int_{-\infty}^{\frac{-\ln(S_0/K)-\left(r-\frac{1}{2}\sigma^2\right)T}{\sigma\sqrt{T}}} e^{-\frac{1}{2}(\varepsilon)^2}d\varepsilon$$

which is Ke^{-rT} times the standard cumulative normal distribution

$$N\left(\frac{-\ln\left(S_0/K\right)-\left(r-\frac{1}{2}\sigma^2\right)T}{\sigma\sqrt{T}}\right) = N(-d_2)$$

where

$$d_2 = \frac{\ln\left(S_0/K\right)+\left(r-\frac{1}{2}\sigma^2\right)T}{\sigma\sqrt{T}}$$

Then, the first integral is equal to

$$Ke^{-rT}N(-d_2)$$

The second integral is

$$-\frac{e^{-rT}}{\sqrt{2\pi}}\int_{-\infty}^{\frac{-d_2}{\sigma\sqrt{T}}} e^x e^{-\frac{1}{2}(\varepsilon)^2}d\varepsilon = \frac{-S_0}{\sqrt{2\pi}}\int_{-\infty}^{\frac{-d_2}{\sigma\sqrt{T}}} e^{-\frac{1}{2}\sigma^2+\sigma\sqrt{\varepsilon T}}e^{-\frac{1}{2}(\varepsilon)^2}d\varepsilon$$

$$= \frac{-S_0}{\sqrt{2\pi}}\int_{-\infty}^{\frac{-d_2}{\sigma\sqrt{T}}} e^{-\frac{1}{2}\left(\varepsilon-\sigma\sqrt{T}\right)^2}d\varepsilon$$

$$= \frac{-S_0}{\sqrt{2\pi}}\int_{-\infty}^{\frac{-\ln(S_0/K)-\left(r+\frac{1}{2}\sigma^2\right)T}{\sigma\sqrt{T}}} e^{-\frac{1}{2}(y)^2}dy$$

where we have written

$$x_T = \ln S(0) + \left(r - \frac{1}{2}\sigma^2\right)T + \sigma W(T)$$
$$= \ln S(0) + \left(r - \frac{1}{2}\sigma^2\right)T + \sigma\varepsilon\sqrt{T}$$

Then, the second integral is

$$-S_0 N(-d_1)$$

where

$$d_1 = \frac{\ln\left(S_0/K\right) + \left(r + \frac{1}{2}\sigma^2\right)T}{\sigma\sqrt{T}}$$

So, we obtain the put option price as

$$p = e^{-rT} KN(-d_2) - S_0 N(-d_1) \tag{1.66}$$

Similarly, we can find the call option price as

$$c = S_0 N\left(d_1\right) - e^{-rT} KN(d_2) \tag{1.67}$$

by changing the payoff function and the integral limits only.

1.11. Barrier Options

Barrier options are among the oldest exotic options. They were traded in American financial markets before the Chicago Board of Options Exchange (CBOE) was established. If options are to be classified according to their path, we classify barrier options as path-dependent. Path dependency requires that the option payoff is determined depending on the path followed by the financial asset price, so they are defined as path-dependent options.

Barrier options can be classified into two groups: knock-out or knock-in. In the first case, the option expires worthless if the asset price reaches/hits a specific barrier value. Therefore, the option's payoff function is no longer functional. The option will only be activated in the second case if the financial asset price reaches or hits a specific value. However, the option's payoff still depends on whether the option is in or out of the money at the end of the maturity.

This depends on whether the option is traded as a call or put, apart from the barrier feature. Since barriers can be designed as up and down, in this case, we will encounter four different types of barrier features: down-and-out, up-and-out, down-and-in, and up-and-in. In addition, considering that each option has a call or put feature, we will have eight different option types. In addition, the option variety may increase depending on whether the barrier value is below or above the strike value.

There are some variations on barrier options. The barriers with different features are called exotic-type barriers. The first of these is partial barrier options. In these options, the barrier is not activated for a certain period. This period can be from the current time to a particular time before maturity or from a specific time after the current time to the end of maturity. Another theme is related to the monitoring frequency. Monitoring can be done daily, weekly, or monthly rather than continuously. In this case, it is possible to talk about discrete barriers rather than continuous barriers (see Kat and Verdonk, 1994; Heynen and Kat, 1996; Kou, 2003).

Another variation is that the barrier variable and the underlying asset of the payoff function can be different variables. In this case, we are talking about outside barriers.

Double-barrier options exist for cases where the barrier variable is designed as an upper and lower barrier. Different versions include situations such as which barrier to reach first or both barriers to be hit.

Apart from these, there are exotic barrier options with different features, such as Asian barrier options, window or limited-time barrier options, step barriers, etc. Their common feature is that their payments depend on reaching one or more barrier values during the option's maturity period.

Finally, there may be cases where the option holder is given a Rebate to compensate for his/her loss, usually in cases where the barrier is knocked out. The rebate may be embedded in the option as an additional cost to the barrier premium.

Barrier options are cheaper instruments than vanilla options because they impose additional restrictions on the option payoff. These restrictions eliminate some price levels that financial asset prices can reach, reducing the expected value of these contributions at these levels to zero.

The closer the financial asset price is to the barrier value, the lower the price will be for knock-out options, and vice versa, the higher the price will be for knock-in options. Also, a knock-out option is less sensitive to volatility than a vanilla option bearing the same features. The reason is simple: higher volatility increases the probability of being in the money but also increases the probability of being knocked out and becoming worthless.

Which barrier options should investors prefer in which situations? We can answer this question by assuming that the markets are rising or falling.

For example, if the markets are rising, investors can buy up-and-in calls or down-and-out calls. Because when the markets rise, both payoff functions will be in the money. The price will be lower than vanilla options because if the price does not rise enough or when there is a fall, the barrier payoff will be zero. However, vanilla options will still possibly provide positive payoffs. It is known that down-and-out call options are generally traded on stocks with high volatility in financial markets. When the markets are falling, investors will buy up-and-out or down-and-in puts. Investors will benefit from falling markets at lower costs than vanilla options. The barrier options will be worthless if the markets move in the opposite direction or do not fall enough. However, the payoff of vanilla options may remain positive at maturity.

Some barrier options, called reverse barriers, are not attractive to investors. These are knock-out barriers, which are in the money, and knock-in barriers, which are out of the money. In these options, the barrier value is considered to be on the wrong side of the spot price. As the financial asset price moves toward in (out of) the money, the option will be knocked out (in). However, for option writers, these are attractive products regarding risk management. For example, an up-and-out call write will mean that all losses are eliminated when the price rises sufficiently. Although this is an alternative transaction to a call spread in a sense, it is not the same as a call spread. Here, the loss incurred is wholly eliminated, but the loss is capped in the call spread (see Heynen and Kat, 1997, p. 127).

We need to make three different choices regarding barrier options. First, the payoff function for the barrier option, whether the option will be a call or a put, must be determined. After this, whether the option should be knock-in or knock-out must be determined, and finally, the barrier level must be determined. It is observed that knock-out options are more popular than knock-in options in the markets, and barrier values are generally selected to differ by 5–10% from the spot price. However, barrier selection is vital for special situations. For example, for out-of-the-money calls and out-of-the-money puts, there is no point in the barrier value between the spot and exercise prices because the option will always be knocked out before being in the money. The opposite is true for in-the-money options. The option will be knocked in before it is in the money, thus becoming an ordinary vanilla option.

The literature on barrier options dates back to 1969 with Snyder, "Alternative Forms of Options." Merton (1973) gives the formulation of a down-and-out call. Hudson (1991) then explains how to use barrier options, specifically up-and-out calls and puts. Benson and Daniel (1991) give a general explanation of barrier options. Beaglehole (1992) is a comprehensive study of down-and-out and up-and-in barriers. The formulae for all vanilla barrier options are given in Rubinstein and Reiner (1991). There is a pervasive literature on exotic-type barriers. We will refer to these sources frequently in the relevant sections when appropriate.

1.12. Conclusion

In this introductory chapter, we examined theorems and concepts related to the basic principles and tools of financial mathematics. We moved from discrete markets to markets based on continuous time and reviewed the concept of arbitrage in these markets. We studied the technical meaning of arbitrage and the relationship between the separating hyperplane theorem and arbitrage theory. We saw how the risk-neutral probability measure is used in pricing contingent claims. We examined the meaning of the stochastic integral and the Ito-Doeblin formula. We explained the risk-neutral probability measure, the Girsanov theorem, and how the probability measure was changed. We explained how risk-neutral pricing is used in pricing contingent claims based on the put option example and solved the BSM equation. Finally, we examined what barrier options are, what types exist, and how they are used. In the following chapters, Chapter 3 will derive the formulae for all vanilla options based on Rubinstein and Reiner (1991) and Rich (1994), while Chapter 4 will give examples of how barrier options can be used and hedged.

Chapter 2

Extremes of Brownian Motion and Reflection Principle

2.1. Introduction

Regarding the valuation of barrier options, we are often concerned with whether the underlying variable (we will take as the stock price for most cases), which is random by construction, has reached a certain level. This critical level is called the barrier (barrier), which activates or deactivates the option. Therefore, barrier option pricing has to be done by analyzing the stochastic process of the stock price in connection with the probability of reaching the barrier. We will leave the barrier classification aside for now (in-out) and examine the probability of the share price reaching the barrier.

Assume $X(t)$ as a random variable with a stochastic process, and we investigate the probability that this value is greater than or equal to b at a given time interval $0 \leq t \leq T$. We show this probability as

$$P(\max X(t) \geq b)$$

Although the term "supremum", the least upper limit (bound), is used instead of the max term, we will adapt to the term maximum since our aim is related to size. (We use minimum instead of infimum, which is the greatest lower limit (bound).)

Sometimes, we may want to calculate the following probability to use in barrier option pricing:

$$P(\max X(t) < b \; X(T) \geq k) \quad k < b \quad 0 \leq t \leq T$$

This representation expresses the probability that the share price will be higher than the strike price at time T but always smaller than the barrier value b during the entire time interval, with $k < b$, i.e., the strike price is less than the barrier value.

We will calculate these and similar probabilities using the reflection principle or the method of images.

2.2. Reflection Principle for a Discrete Time Stochastic Process

This section is based on Professor Don M. Chance's teaching notes (*The Reflection Principle in Finance*, Teaching Note 00-07, 2010). Examining discrete processes before moving on to continuous processes will be very useful in understanding the reflection principle.

Let $X(t)$ be a stochastic process taking the values

$$X(t) = \mp 1$$

and $t = 1, 2, 3, 4 = T$.

Let's define $Y(t)$ as

$$Y(t) = \sum_{1}^{4} X(t)$$

Then, at time T, $Y(t)$ will have taken values between -4 and $+4$. Table 2.1, lists all the random walk paths of $X(t)$ and $Y(t)$. Depending on these paths, we can simply calculate some probabilities of $Y(t)$ for $t \leq 4$ by counting. For example;

$$P(\max Y(t) \geq 3) = 2/16 \quad P(\max Y(t) \geq 2) = 6/16$$
$$P(\max Y(t) \geq 1) = 10/16$$

The number of paths is $2^4 = 16$.

Table 2.1. Random walk.

Outcome	$t = 1$	$t = 2$	$t = 3$	$t = 4$	max	min
1	1	2	3	4	4	1
2	1	0	1	2	2	0
3	1	2	1	2	2	1
4	1	2	3	2	3	1
5	−1	0	1	2	2	−1
6	1	2	1	0	2	0
7	1	0	−1	0	1	−1
8	1	0	1	0	1	0
9	−1	−2	−1	0	0	−2
10	−1	0	−1	0	0	−1
11	−1	0	1	0	1	−1
12	−1	0	−1	−2	0	−2
13	−1	−2	−1	−2	−1	−2
14	−1	−2	−3	−2	−1	−3
15	1	0	−1	−2	1	−2
16	−1	−2	−3	−4	−1	−4

Alternatively, we can calculate the same probabilities with the following formula:

$$P(\max Y(t) \geq b) = 2 * P(Y(T) \geq b) - P(Y(T) = b)$$

For $b = 1, 2, 3$ and $T = 4$ we have the same probabilities:

$$\begin{aligned}
P(\max Y(t) \geq 3) &= 2 * P(Y(4) \geq 3) - P(Y(4) = 3) \\
&= 2 * 1/16 - 0 = 2/16 \\
P(\max Y(t) \geq 2) &= 2 * P(Y(4) \geq 2) - P(Y(4) = 2) \\
&= 2 * 5/16 - 4/16 = 6/16 \\
P(\max Y(t) \geq 1) &= 2 * P(Y(4) \geq 1) - P(Y(4) = 1) \\
&= 2 * 5/16 - 0 = 10/16
\end{aligned}$$

(Calculate for $T = 3$ and $b = 2$).

Think about why the formula is correct.

For the probability $P(\max Y(t) \geq 2)$, there are six states where Y takes at least the value 2 at and before time $t = 4$. The reflection principle claims that this probability can be calculated by multiplying the probability of $P(\max Y(4) \geq 2)$ with 2 and subtracting the probabilities of $Y(4) = 2$.

Let's look at the paths that $Y(t)$ takes the value 2 before time $t = 4$. We can see that the paths 1, 3, 4, 6 satisfy this condition. So, if Y takes the value 2 by the time $t = 2$, it will follow paths symmetrically until arriving time $t = 4$. For example:

(1) Path for $t = 2, 3, 4$ $Y(t)$ will take the values $Y(t) = 2, 3, 4$

(2) Path for $t = 2, 3, 4$ $Y(t)$ will take the values $Y(t) = 2, 1, 0$

Both paths are mirror images of each other and follow an opposite and symmetrical path.

Similarly,

(3) Path $t = 2, 3, 4$ $Y(t) = 2, 1, 2$

(4) Path $t = 2, 3, 4$ $Y(t) = 2, 3, 2$

constitute a mirror image of each other. In addition to these four paths, $Y(t)$ takes the value of 2 on the 2 and 5 paths by the time $t = 4$.

We are concerned with the paths in which $Y(t)$ takes the value 2 at and before $t = 4$.

Now, we can see five states where $Y(4) \geq 2$. Therefore, the probability is 5/16.

However, since there are situations $Y(t) = 2$ before $t = 4$ and $Y(T) < 2$ at time T, the probability of $P(\max Y(T) \geq 2)$ is higher and using the features of these paths we can calculate this probability.

The paths for $P(Y(T) \geq 2)$ follow two different ways or contain two different groups:

(1) $Y(t)$ takes the value of 2 for the first time at the time $t = 4$.
(2) $Y(t)$ takes the value of 2 before time $t = 4$ and $Y(T) \geq 2$ by the time $T = 4$.

However, there is another path that $Y(t)$ takes the value of 2 before time $t = 4$ and becomes $Y(T) \leq 2$.

By the reflection principle, we know this path constitutes the mirror image of the 2 way mentioned above. Therefore, there is no problem multiplying the number of paths with $Y(T) \geq 2$ by 2. That will give us the number of all the paths that $Y(t)$ hits the value 2.

However, when we multiply this probability by 2, the situations where $Y(t) = 2$ before time $t = 4$ and becomes $Y(T) = 2$ are counted twice. To avoid double counting, we have to subtract the situations where $Y(T)$ is precisely equal to 2, from $2 * P(Y(T) \geq 2$.

Stating simpler, paths 1 and 6 in our table form images of each other, and both meet the situation we desire: $Y(2) = 2$, but $Y(T) =\ 0$, $Y(\mathrm{T}) = 4$. Therefore, multiplying the first path by two and adding the 4 cases with $Y(T) = 2$ will give the same result because these four states are already mirror images of each other no need to be multiplied by 2.

So, the rule

$$P(\max Y(t) \geq b) = 2 * P(Y(T) \geq b) - P(Y(T) = b)$$

is correct.

Then the probability P, (which is the maximum value of $Y(t)$ is less than a specific (barrier) value can be stated as

$$P(\max Y(t) < b) = 1 - P(\max Y(t) \geq b)$$

and

$$P(\max Y(t) < b) = 1 - 2 * P(Y(T) \geq b) + P(Y(T) = b)$$

A similar calculation method can be used for the minimum values of the underlying variable. In this case, we may want to find cases where the minimum value of the random variable $Y(t)$ is less than or equal to a certain value of b. The mirror image of the same formula can be written as follows using the same way of thinking;

$$P(\min Y(t) \leq b) = 2 * P(Y(T) \leq b) - P(Y(T) = b)$$

For example, for $b = -1$, we can count ten paths that $P(\min Y(t) \leq -1)$.

For the paths 12–16, $\min Y(T) \leq -1$, there is no case for $\min Y(T) = -1$.

Therefore, the probability is

$$2 * P(Y(T) \leq -1) - P(Y(T) = -1) = 2 * 5 - 0 = 10/16$$

(Calculate for $b = -2$).

Similarly, we can show the probability that the minimum value is above a certain b value as

$$P(\min Y(t) > b) = 1 - P(\min Y(t) \leq b)$$

As it should be noted, since we work with discrete (discrete) values, we include the probability of the random variable being equal to a specific value in the calculations. However, when we work with continuous values, we evaluate these probabilities as "0". Therefore, in the case of barrier values, we tend to express the probabilities as $P(\max Y(t) > b)$ or $P(\min Y(t) < b)$ instead of $\geq$ or $\leq$ because the option is knocked in or out when the underlying variable hits this value.

In this case, we can state the problem alternatively as

$$P(\max Y(t) > b) = P(\max Y(t) \geq b + \Delta)$$

for $\max Y(t) > b$.

Similarly, for minimum values, we can replace $b - \Delta$ and

$$P(\min Y(t) < b) = P(\min Y(t) \leq b - \Delta)$$

In summary, we have the equations:

(1) $P(\max Y(t) \geq b) = 2 * P(Y(T) \geq b) - P(Y(T) = b)$
(2) $P(\max Y(t) > b) = P(\max Y(t) \geq b + \Delta)$
(3) $P(\max Y(t) < b) = 1 - P(\max Y(t) \geq b)$
(4) $P(\max Y(t) \leq b) = 1 - P(\max Y(t) > b)$
(5) $P(\min Y(t) \leq b) = 2 * P(Y(T) \leq b) - P(Y(T) = b)$
(6) $P(\min Y(t) < b) = P(\min Y(t) \leq b - \Delta)$
(7) $P(\min Y(t) > b) = 1 - P(\min Y(t) \leq b)$
(8) $P(\min Y(t) \geq b) = 1 - P(\min Y(t) < b)$

For pricing the barrier options, we need joint outcomes or probabilities in most cases. For example, we may need the probability of $Y(4) \geq w, \min Y(t) \leq a$ at the same time. That is, by the time $T = 4$, we may need the random variable to take the value equal or greater than w but at the same time hit the barrier or take the value less than a between $0 \leq t \leq T$. For $w = 0$ and $a = -1$, let's check the probability of

$$P(Y(4) \geq 0, \min Y(t) \leq -1)$$

This condition is satisfied on the 5, 7, 9, 10, and 11 paths.

Path	$t = 1$	$t = 2$	$t = 3$	$t = 4$	max	min
5	−1	0	1	2	2	−1
7	1	0	−1	0	1	−1
9	−1	−2	−1	0	0	−2
10	−1	0	−1	0	0	−1
11	−1	0	1	0	1	−1

This probability is 5/16. By using the reflection principle, we can calculate the same probability as follows.

Let $Y(t)$ hit the critical barrier value −1 by moving down in that direction. Then, we may expect that it takes the value "0" in the next step. But its probability is the same with the path that $Y(t)$ travels from −1 to −2. That is, we need the probability of $Y(4) \leq -2$, and this probability is 5/16 (number of paths 12–16 is 5).

We find the critical value as $2a - w = -2\text{–}0 = -2$. As we did before, we multiply the paths that have taken value ≤ -1 by two and subtract the values that have taken values "0" and greater than "0" to avoid double counting. That means, we have been calculating the probability of $P(Y(T) \leq 2a - w)$.

Therefore, we can write

$$P(Y(T) \geq w, \min Y(t) \leq a) = P(Y(T) \leq 2a - w)$$

Similarly, assuming $w = 0$ and the upper barrier $M = 1$, let's find the probability of $P(Y(T) \leq 0, \max Y(t) \geq 1)$. This can be calculated through paths 6, 7, 8, 11, and 15. The probability is also 5/16 here.

Path	$t = 1$	$t = 2$	$t = 3$	$t = 4$	max	min
6	1	2	1	0	2	0
7	1	0	−1	0	1	−1
8	1	0	1	0	1	0
11	−1	0	1	0	1	−1
15	1	0	−1	−2	1	−2

Considering the reflection principle, when $Y(t)$ hits the barrier value 1, it may be expected to move forward to zero and less, but it may travel from 1 to 2 with the same probability. Therefore, the probability that we need is $Y(4) \geq 2$. The critical value is

$$2M - w = 2 * 1 - 0 = 2$$

the condition $Y(4) \geq 2$ is satisfied with 5/16 probability for the first 5 paths. Then, the probability that we need is

$$P(Y(T) \leq w, \max Y(t) \geq M) = P(Y(T) \geq 2M - w)$$

One of the crucial problems is related to the design of the process. For example, the following process

$$P\left(Y(T) \geq -1\right), \quad P(\max Y(t) \geq -3)$$

is flawed because $Y(T) \geq -1$ already requires it to be max $Y(t) \geq -3$.

In this case, the structure has to be corrected and reconstructed. We can write the basic probabilities that we are going to use in pricing the barrier and partial barrier options as

$$P\left(Y(T) \leq w, \max Y(t) \geq a\right) = P(Y(T) \geq 2a - w$$
$$P\left(Y(T) \geq w, \min Y(t) \leq a\right) = P(Y(T) \leq 2a - w$$

2.3. Reflection Principle for Continuous Time Stochastic Processes

We use the Brownian motion as the stochastic process instead of the Binomial steps for the continuous-time case. We will first use the Brownian process without the deterministic term (drift) and only with the local volatility term σ. We will then extend the structure to include the deterministic term. Let's define the Brownian process with W, with $W(0) = 0$ at the time interval $[0, T]$. If $X(T)$ is another process with $X(T) = \sigma W(T)$ its variance is

$$Var(X(T)) = \sigma^2 T$$

To calculate joint probabilities, we can no longer simply calculate the number of paths as we did in the discrete case because there are infinite paths. Let's try to calculate these probabilities by going through an example.

Let's define a fixed positive time t and a barrier level a. We aim to determine the number of Brownian motion paths $W(t)$ that reach the barrier level at or before time t. In continuous terms, we would like to calculate the probability of hitting the barrier until time t.

Figure 2.1. Reflection principle.

This is called the first passage time to barrier level a, and we will denote it by τ_a.

A Brownian motion may move in two ways concerning the barrier. It reaches the barrier before time t but at time t remains below the barrier value, say, w, or it exceeds the barrier value a at time t. The probability of having the exact barrier value a is zero, for we assume the random variable has a continuous distribution.

Figure 2.1 shows the paths' number and nature after the Brownian motion hits the barrier at time $t^* = \tau_a$. This illustrates a kind of symmetry in the structure of Brownian paths. This is called reflection property. The assumption is that if the Brownian motion, after hitting the barrier, goes down to the value w, with the same probability, it may go up to value $a + a - w = 2a - w$, which reflects the assumed w value.

The value of $2a - w$ is the mirror image of w, and using the mirror analogy, it is reflected by the barrier.

We may then state that the joint probability of the Brownian motion reaching the barrier and ending up below w at time t is the same as the probability that it exceeds the value $2a - w$ at time t due to the reflection principle. Formally,

$$P\{\tau_a \leq T,\ W(T) \leq w\} = P\{W(T) \geq 2a - w\} \tag{2.1}$$

Assume $W_t > w > a$ $t \in [0, T]$. We want to calculate the probability

$$P(W(T) > w, \min \quad W(t) > a)$$

This is the probability of the situations where the minimum value of the Brownian process never hits the barrier value a. At the same time, it takes a value greater than w at the end of the maturity T.

Because

$$\begin{aligned} &P(W(T) > w, \min W(t) > a) + P(W(T) > w, \min W(t) \leq a) \\ &\quad = P(W(T) > w) \end{aligned}$$

we can write

$$\begin{aligned} &P(W(T) > w,\ \min W(t) > a) \\ &= P(W(T) > w) - P(W(T) > w, \min W(t) \leq a) \end{aligned} \tag{2.2}$$

The first term on the right-hand side is the cumulative probability of the standard normal distribution. As for the second term, this is the probability that $W(t)$ will fall and hit a, but bounce back at maturity and take a value greater than w. However, due to the reflection principle, this probability is equal to the probability that $W(t)$ falls to a and takes a distance $w - a$ towards the downward direction. Therefore, the total distance traveled down will be $a - (w - a) = 2a - w$.

Then, the probability we are looking for is

$$P(W(T) > w, \min W(t) \leq a) = P(W(T) \leq 2a - w)$$

This is the standard normal probability for the Brownian motion with standard deviation $\sigma\sqrt{T}$ and can be presented

$$P(W(T) \leq 2a - w) = P(\varepsilon\sigma\sqrt{T} \leq 2a - w) = N\left(\frac{2a - w}{\sigma\sqrt{T}}\right)$$

The equation (2.2)

$$P(W(T) > w, \quad \min W(t) > a)$$
$$= P\left(W(T) > w\right) - P(W(T) > w, \quad \min W(t) \leq a)$$

Now, can be stated as

$$P(W(T) > w, \quad \min W(t) > a) = 1 - N\left(\frac{w}{\sigma\sqrt{T}}\right) - N\left(\frac{2a - w}{\sigma\sqrt{T}}\right)$$

$$P(W(T) > w, \quad \min W(t) > a) = \left(\frac{-w}{\sigma\sqrt{T}}\right) - N\left(\frac{2a - w}{\sigma\sqrt{T}}\right)$$

If the process $X(t)$ has a drift term μ and is presented by

$$X(t) = \mu t + \sigma W(t)$$

then, we were going to formulate the equation by adding the term μt and write the equation (1.2) as

$$P(X(T) > w, \min X(t) > a) = N\left(\frac{-w + \mu T}{\sigma\sqrt{T}}\right) - e^{\frac{2\mu a}{\sigma^2}} N\left(\frac{2a - w + \mu T}{\sigma\sqrt{T}}\right) \quad (2.3)$$

We will examine the term $e^{\frac{2\mu a}{\sigma^2}}$ later.

2.4. Distribution of First Passage Time

Now, let's find the distributional properties of the first passage time τ_a.

Theorem 2.1 (Shreve, 2004, pp. 112–115). *For all $a \neq 0$ and, $t \geq 0$, the random variable τ_a has a cumulative distribution function and density function*

$$P\{\tau_a \leq t\} = \frac{2}{\sqrt{2\pi}} \int_{\frac{|a|}{\sqrt{t}}}^{\infty} e^{-\frac{y^2}{2}} dy \quad (2.4)$$

and

$$f_{\tau_a}(t) = \frac{d}{dt} P\{\tau_a \leq t\} = \frac{|a|}{t\sqrt{2\pi t}} e^{-\frac{a^2}{2t}} \tag{2.5}$$

respectively.

Proof. For $a > 0$. We assume that if $w = a$, w hits the a from above. Then, using equation (2.1), we can write

$$P\{\tau_a \leq t,\ W(t) \leq a\} = P\{W(t) \geq 2a - w\}$$
$$P\{\tau_a \leq t,\ W(t) \leq a\} = P\{W(t) \geq a\}$$

But we have the same probability for

$$P\{\tau_a \leq t,\ W(t) \geq a\} = P\{W(t) \geq a\}$$

implying that it hits the barrier from below.

Since

$$P\{\tau_a \leq t\} = P\{\tau_a \leq t,\ W(t) \leq a\} + P\{\tau_a \leq t, W(t) \geq a\}$$

this is equal to

$$P\{\tau_a \leq t\} = 2P\{W(t) \geq a\}$$

Therefore,

$$P\{\tau_a \leq t\} = 2P\{W(t) \geq a\} = \frac{2}{\sqrt{2\pi t}} \int_a^\infty e^{-\frac{x^2}{2t}} dx$$

for the Brownian motion with zero drift and variance t.

Transforming,

$$y = \frac{x}{\sqrt{t}}$$

with $dy\sqrt{t} = dx$ and $y \to \frac{a}{\sqrt{t}}$ while $x \to a$ we obtain

$$P\{\tau_a \leq t\} = \frac{2}{\sqrt{2\pi}} \int_{\frac{|a|}{\sqrt{t}}}^\infty e^{-\frac{y^2}{2}} dy$$

If a is negative, we can write the integral lower limit as $\frac{|a|}{\sqrt{t}}$ in absolute terms because τ_a and $\tau_{|a|}$ have the same distribution.

To derive the density, we need to differentiate the distribution function with respect to t.

$$\frac{d}{dt}P\{\tau_a \le t\} = \frac{d}{dy}\left(\frac{2}{\sqrt{2\pi}}\int_{\frac{|a|}{\sqrt{t}}}^{\infty} e^{-\frac{y^2}{2}}dy\right)\frac{dy}{dt}$$

Since $y = |a|t^{-1/2}$

$$f_{\tau_a}(t) = -\frac{2}{\sqrt{2\pi}}e^{-\frac{y^2}{2}}.\left(-\frac{1}{2}\,|a|\,t^{-3/2}\right)$$

and we simply obtain

$$f_{\tau_a}(t) = \frac{|a|}{t\sqrt{2\pi t}}e^{-\frac{a^2}{2t}} \qquad \boxdot$$

2.4.1. *Brownian motion with variance*

Assume

$$W(t) = \sigma\widehat{W}(t)$$

Now, the distributional parameters for Brownian motion are zero and $\sigma^2 t$. Therefore, we can write

$$P\{\tau_a \le t\} = 2P\{\widehat{W}(t) \ge a/\sigma\}$$

$$P\{\tau_a \le t\} = 2P\left\{\widehat{W}(t) \ge \frac{a}{\sigma}\right\} = \frac{2}{\sigma\sqrt{2\pi t}}\int_a^{\infty} e^{-\frac{x^2}{2\sigma^2}t}dx$$

Similarly, making the transformation

$$y = \frac{x}{\sigma\sqrt{t}}$$

with $\sigma dy\sqrt{t} = dx$ and $y \to \frac{a}{\sigma\sqrt{t}}$ while $x \to a$ we obtain

$$P\{\tau_a \le t\} = \frac{2}{\sqrt{2\pi}}\int_{\frac{|a|}{\sigma\sqrt{t}}}^{\infty} e^{-\frac{y^2}{2}}dy \qquad (2.4')$$

If a is negative, we can write the integral lower limit as $\frac{|a|}{\sigma\sqrt{t}}$ in absolute terms because τ_a and $\tau_{|a|}$ have the same distribution. To derive the density, we need to differentiate the distribution function with respect to t.

$$\frac{d}{dt}P\{\tau_a \leq t\} = \frac{d}{dy}\left(\frac{2}{\sqrt{2\pi}}\int_{\frac{|a|}{\sigma\sqrt{t}}}^{\infty} e^{-\frac{y^2}{2}}dy\right)\frac{dy}{dt}$$

Since $y = \frac{|a|}{\sigma}t^{-1/2}$

$$f_{\tau_a}(t) = -\frac{2}{\sqrt{2\pi}}e^{-\frac{y^2}{2}}.\left(-\frac{1}{2}\frac{|a|}{\sigma}t^{-3/2}\right)$$

and we simply obtain

$$f_{\tau_a}(t) = \frac{|a|}{t\sigma\sqrt{2\pi t}}e^{-\frac{a^2}{2\sigma^2 t}} \tag{2.5'}$$

2.4.2. *Distribution of Brownian motion with variance and its maximum*

Let's define the maximum for Brownian motion as

$$M(t) = \max_{0\leq s\leq t}\sigma W(s) \tag{2.6}$$

Then, the probability of being greater than a barrier value or exceeding a barrier value at any time but remaining below a certain value at time t can be expressed as

$$\begin{aligned} P(W(t) < w,\ M(t) > a) &= P(W(t) > 2a - w) \\ &= 1 - P(W(t) < 2a - w) \end{aligned}$$

regarding equation (2.1). This is the cumulative probability of

$$1 - N\left(\frac{2a - w}{\sigma\sqrt{t}}\right) = N\left(\frac{w - 2a}{\sigma\sqrt{t}}\right)$$

But it is also clear that

$$P(W(t) < w,\ M(t) > a) + P(W(t) < w,\ M(t) < a) = P(W(t) < w)$$

we can write

$$P(W(t) < w, M(t) < a) = N\left(\frac{w}{\sigma\sqrt{t}}\right) - N\left(\frac{w - 2a}{\sigma\sqrt{t}}\right) \tag{2.7}$$

This is the probability that the maximum of Brownian motion can never reach/exceed the barrier, and it is less than a certain value w at time t. This corresponds to the number of all Brownian paths minus the paths the barrier is reached or exceeded.

For $a = 0$, it can be easily seen that the function is "0". The maximum cannot be below zero. Also, for $a > 0$ and $w > a$, we can write $M(t) < w$ instead of $M(t) < a$. Therefore, we can write

$$P(W(t) < w, \quad M(t) < w) = N\left(\frac{w}{\sigma\sqrt{t}}\right) - N\left(\frac{-w}{\sigma\sqrt{t}}\right)$$

2.4.3. *Joint distribution of Brownian motion and its maximum*

For a positive barrier value a, $M(t) \geq a$ is possible if and only if $\tau_a \leq t$.

Remembering the reflection principle,

$$P\{M(t) \geq a, \ W(t) \leq w\} = P\{W(t) \geq 2a - w\}, \ w \leq a, \ a > 0$$

we are to search for the joint probability of Brownian motion and its maximum. We want the barrier hit by the Brownian motion, but we also want it to be less than a certain value at time t. Therefore, we can determine the joint distribution of $M(t)$ and $W(t)$ with reference to the theorem in Shreve (2004) as follows.

Theorem 2.2 (Shreve, 2004, pp. 114–115). *For $t \geq 0$, the joint density function of $(M(t), W(t))$ is*

$$f_{M(t),W(t)}(a, w) = \frac{2(2a - w)}{t\sigma^3\sqrt{2\pi t}} \exp\left\{-\frac{(2a - w)^2}{2\sigma^{2t}}\right\}, \quad w \leq a, \ a > 0 \tag{2.8}$$

Proof. The integration limits for x and y are $a \leq x \leq \infty$ and $-\infty \leq y \leq w$, respectively, for $a > 0$. Then, the cumulative distribution function is

$$P\{M(t) \geq a, \ W(t) \leq w\} = \int_a^\infty \int_{-\infty}^w f_{(M(t),W(t))}(x, y) dy dx$$

Since we know that this is equal to the cumulative probability

$$P\{W(t) \geq 2a - w\} = \frac{1}{\sigma\sqrt{2\pi t}} \int_{2a-w}^{\infty} \exp\left\{-\frac{z^2}{2\sigma^2 t}\right\} dz$$

we can write

$$\int_{a}^{\infty}\int_{-\infty}^{w} f_{(M(t),W(t))}(x,y)dydx = \frac{1}{\sigma\sqrt{2\pi t}} \int_{2a-w}^{\infty} \exp\left\{-\frac{z^2}{2\sigma^2 t}\right\} dz$$

Differentiation with respect to $x(a)$ and then $y(w)$ yields

$$-\int_{-\infty}^{w} f_{(M(t),W(t))}(a,y)dy = -\frac{2}{\sigma\sqrt{2\pi t}}\exp\left\{-\frac{(2a-w)^2}{2\sigma^2 t}\right\}$$

Differentiation with respect to w yields equation (2.8)

$$-f_{(M(t),W(t))}(a,w) = -\frac{2(2a-w)}{\sigma^3 t\sqrt{2\pi t}}\exp\left\{-\frac{(2a-w)^2}{2\sigma^2 t}\right\}$$

$$f_{(M(t),W(t))}(a,w) = \frac{2(2a-w)}{\sigma^3 t\sqrt{2\pi t}}\exp\left\{-\frac{(2a-w)^2}{2\sigma^2 t}\right\}$$

since

$$z = 2a - w$$

The conditional distribution of maximum $M(t)$ when $W(t) = w$ is

$$f_{(M(t)|W(t))(a|w)} = \frac{2(2a-w)}{\sigma^2 t}\exp\left\{-\frac{2a(a-w)}{2\sigma^2 t}\right\} w \leq a, \quad a > 0$$

because

$$f_{(M(t)|W(t))(a|w) = \frac{f_{(M(t),W(t))}(a,w)}{f_{W(t)}(w)}}$$

and

$$\frac{f_{(M(t),W(t))}(a,w)}{f_{W(t)}(w)} = \frac{\frac{2(2a-w)}{\sigma^3 t\sqrt{2\pi t}}\exp\left\{-\frac{(2a-w)^2}{2\sigma^2 t}\right\}}{\frac{\exp\left\{-\frac{w^2}{2\sigma^2 t}\right\}}{\sigma\sqrt{2\pi t}}}$$

$$= \frac{2(2a-w)}{\sigma^2 t}\exp\left\{-\frac{2a(a-w)}{2\sigma^2 t}\right\}$$

$\boxdot$

2.4.4. *Brownian motion and its maximum with drift and variance*

Let's define a probability space $(\Omega, \mathcal{F}, \tilde{P})$ with risk-neutral probability measure $\widetilde{P}$. A Brownian motion $\widetilde{W}(t)$ under $\tilde{P}$ is a martingale for it has no drift term. For $0 \leq t \leq T$, we can define another Brownian motion under the probability measure $\tilde{P}$ as

$$\widehat{W}(t) = \mu t + \widetilde{W}(t) \tag{2.9}$$

with drift coefficient μ. Similar to driftless Brownian motion, let's define the maximum as

$$\widehat{M}(T) = \max_{0\leq t\leq T} \widehat{W}(t)$$

for Brownian motion with drift and $\widehat{W}(0) = 0$. Therefore, we have $\widehat{M}(T) \geq 0$ and $\widehat{W}(T) \leq \widehat{M}(T)$, and the domain for our pair $(\widehat{M}(T), \widehat{W}(T))$ is

$$\{(a,w) : w \leq a, a \geq 0\}$$

Theorem 2.3 (Shreve, 2004, pp. 296–299). *Under $\widetilde{P}$, the joint density function of $(\widehat{M}(T)\widehat{W}(T))$ is*

$$\tilde{f}_{\widehat{M}(T),\widehat{W}(T)}(a,w) = \frac{2(2a-w)}{T\sqrt{2\pi T}} e^{\mu w - \frac{1}{2}\mu^2 T - \frac{1}{2T}(2a-w)^2} w \leq a, a \geq 0 \tag{2.10}$$

and is zero for other values of a and w.

Proof. $\widehat{W}(t)$ is a martingale under $\widehat{P}$ but has drift under $\widetilde{P}$. From stochastic calculus, we know that the relation between the risk-neutral and the objective probability measures is established by the Girsanov theorem and the Radon–Nikodym derivative as

$$\widetilde{P}(1_A) = P(Z1_A)$$

$$\widetilde{P}(A) = \int_A Z(T)dP$$

where $E[Z(T)] = 1$.

Likewise, we will establish a relation between $\widehat{P}$ and $\widetilde{P}$ through the martingale $\widehat{Z}(T)$. Similarly, we can write

$$\widehat{P}(A) = \widehat{E}(1_A) = \int_A \widehat{Z}(T)d\widetilde{P} = \tilde{E}(\widehat{Z}1_A)$$

and

$$\tilde{E}(1_A) = \widehat{E}\left(\frac{1}{\widehat{Z}(T)}1_A\right)$$

Define an exponential martingale

$$\widehat{Z}(t) = e^{-\mu\widetilde{W}(t)-\frac{1}{2}\mu^2 t}$$

But since $\widehat{W}(t) = \mu t + \widetilde{W}(t)$ we can write

$$\widehat{Z}(t) = e^{-\mu\widehat{W}(t)+\frac{1}{2}\mu^2 t}$$

Now, we can transform the Brownian motion with drift under $\widehat{P}$ into a martingale under $\widetilde{P}$ by simply writing

$$\tilde{E}\,(1_A) = \widehat{E}\left(\frac{1}{\widehat{Z}(T)}1_A\right)$$

Since the event A is,

$$A = \{\widehat{M}(T) \leq a, \widehat{W}(T) \leq w\}$$

then,

$$\tilde{E}\left\{\mathbb{I}_{\{\widehat{M}(T)\leq a,\widehat{W}(T)\leq w\}}\right\} = \widehat{E}\left\{\frac{1}{\widehat{Z}(T)}\mathbb{I}_{\{\widehat{M}(T)\leq a,\widehat{W}(T)\leq w\}}\right\} \quad (2.11)$$

Remember that $\widehat{W}(T)$ has zero drift under $\widehat{P}$ but has a drift under $\widetilde{P}$. Now, we can use the density function (2.8) and write:

$$\hat{f}_{\widehat{M}(T),\widehat{W}(T)}(a,w) = \frac{2(2a-w)}{T\sqrt{2\pi T}}\exp\left\{-\frac{(2a-w)^2}{2T}\right\}$$

(no drift).

Applying equation (2.11)

$$\widetilde{P}\left\{\widehat{M}(T)\leq a,\widehat{W}(T)\leq w\right\} = \widehat{E}\left\{\frac{1}{\widehat{Z}(T)}\mathbb{I}_{\{\widehat{M}(T)\leq a,\widehat{W}(T)\leq w\}}\right\}$$

and using Radon–Nikodym derivative

$$\widehat{Z}(t) = e^{-\mu\widetilde{W}(t)-\frac{1}{2}\mu^2 t} = e^{-\mu\widehat{W}(t)+\frac{1}{2}\mu^2 t}$$

we can write

$$\widetilde{P}\left\{\widehat{M}(T)\leq a,\widehat{W}(T)\leq w\right\} = \widehat{E}\left\{e^{\mu\widehat{W}(T)-\frac{1}{2}\mu^2 T}\mathbb{I}_{\{\widehat{M}(T)\leq a,\widehat{W}(T)\leq w\}}\right\}$$

Integration over the region $-\infty\leq y\leq w$ and $-\infty\leq x\leq a$

$$\widetilde{P}\{\widehat{M}(T)\leq a,\widehat{W}(T)\leq w\} = \widehat{E}\left\{e^{\mu\widehat{W}(T)-\frac{1}{2}\mu^2 T}\mathbb{I}_{\{\widehat{M}(T)\leq m,\widehat{W}(T)\leq w\}}\right\}$$

$$\widetilde{P}\{\widehat{M}(T)\leq a,\widehat{W}(T)\leq w\} = \int_{-\infty}^{w}\int_{-\infty}^{a} e^{\mu y-\frac{1}{2}\mu^2 T}\hat{f}_{\widehat{M}(T),\widehat{W}(T)}(x,y)\,dxdy$$

will give us the cumulative joint probability of $\widehat{M}(T), \widehat{W}(T)$ pair. To obtain the density function, we differentiate first with respect to a and then w. Then

$$\frac{\partial^2}{\partial a \partial w}\widetilde{P}\{\widehat{M}(T) \le a, \widehat{W}(T) \le w\} = \tilde{f}_{\widehat{M}(T),\widehat{W}(T)}(a,w)$$

$$= \frac{2(2a-w)}{T\sqrt{2\pi T}}e^{\mu w - \frac{1}{2}\mu^2 T - \frac{1}{2T}(2a-w)^2}$$

$$\tilde{f}_{\widehat{M}(T),\widehat{W}(T)}(a,w) = \frac{2(2a-w)}{\sigma^2 T\sigma\sqrt{2\pi T}}e^{\frac{\mu}{\sigma^2}w - \frac{1}{2}\frac{\mu^2}{\sigma^2}T - \frac{1}{2\sigma^2 T}(2a-w)^2}$$

is the density function for Brownian motion with drift and variance σ and its maximum under $\widetilde{P}$ with $w \le a,\ a > 0\ \sigma > 0$. For other values, the density (2.10) is zero. ⊡

Corollary 2.1 (Shreve, 2004, pp. 297–299). *The Density and the Cumulative Probability of Maximum under* $\widetilde{P}$.

The cumulative probability of $\widehat{M}(T)$ with drift term under $\widetilde{P}$ and $a \ge 0$ is

$$\widetilde{P}\{\widehat{M}(T) \le a\} = N\left(\frac{a-\mu T}{\sqrt{T}}\right) - e^{2\mu a}N\left(\frac{-a-\mu T}{\sqrt{T}}\right) \qquad (2.12)$$

and the risk-neutral density function is

$$\tilde{f}_{\widehat{M}(T)}(a) = \frac{2}{\sqrt{2\pi T}}e^{-\frac{1}{2T}(a-\mu T)^2} - 2\mu e^{2\mu a}N\left(\frac{-a-\mu T}{\sqrt{T}}\right) \qquad (2.13)$$

and zero for $a < 0$.

Proof. First, write

$$\widetilde{P}\{\widehat{M}(T) \le a\} = \widetilde{P}\{\widehat{M}(T) \le a, \widehat{W}(T) \ge 0\}$$
$$+ \widetilde{P}\{\widehat{M}(T) \le a, \widehat{W}(T) \le 0\}$$

But this is the combination of $\widehat{W}(T) \geq 0$ and $\widehat{W}(T) \leq 0$. Therefore, we need to integrate equation (2.11) as follows:

$$\widetilde{P}\{\widehat{M}(T) \leq a\} = \int_0^a \int_w^a \frac{2(2x-w)}{T\sqrt{2\pi T}} e^{\mu w - \frac{1}{2}\mu^2 T - \frac{1}{2T}(2x-w)^2} dxdw$$
$$+ \int_{-\infty}^0 \int_0^a \frac{2(2x-w)}{T\sqrt{2\pi T}} e^{\mu w - \frac{1}{2}\mu^2 T - \frac{1}{2T}(2x-w)^2} dxdw$$

First, double integral takes the values $\widehat{W}(T) \geq 0$ but by construction $\widehat{M}(T) \geq \widehat{W}(T)$. Then, the integral limits for outer and inner integrals are $0 < w < a$ and $w < x < a$. The second double integral takes the values $\widehat{W}(T) \leq 0$, but this time $\widehat{M}(T) \geq 0 \geq \widehat{W}(T)$. Then, the integral limits for outer and inner integrals are $-\infty < w < 0$ and $0 < x < a$.

The integration with respect to x (the inner one) yields

$$-\frac{1}{\sqrt{2\pi T}} e^{\mu w - \frac{1}{2}\mu^2 T - \frac{1}{2T}(2x-w)^2}$$
$$-\int_0^a \frac{1}{\sqrt{2\pi T}} e^{\mu w - \frac{1}{2}\mu^2 T - \frac{1}{2T}(2x-w)^2}\Big|_w^a dw$$
$$= -\int_0^a \frac{1}{\sqrt{2\pi T}} e^{\mu w - \frac{1}{2}\mu^2 T - \frac{1}{2T}(2a-w)^2} dw + \int_0^a \frac{1}{\sqrt{2\pi T}} e^{\mu w - \frac{1}{2}\mu^2 T - \frac{1}{2T}w^2} dw$$

Similarly, for the second integral, we can write

$$-\int_{-\infty}^0 \frac{1}{\sqrt{2\pi T}} e^{\mu w - \frac{1}{2}\mu^2 T - \frac{1}{2T}(2x-w)^2}\Big|_0^a dw$$

and

$$-\int_{-\infty}^0 \frac{1}{\sqrt{2\pi T}} e^{\mu w - \frac{1}{2}\mu^2 T - \frac{1}{2T}(2a-w)^2} dw$$
$$+\int_{-\infty}^0 \frac{1}{\sqrt{2\pi T}} e^{\mu w - \frac{1}{2}\mu^2 T - \frac{1}{2T}w^2} dw$$

Note that the integrals can be combined because the integral limits are $-\infty \leq w \leq a$ for both integrals:

$$-\frac{1}{\sqrt{2\pi T}}\int_{-\infty}^{a} e^{\mu w-\frac{1}{2}\mu^2 T-\frac{1}{2T}(2a-w)^2}dw+\frac{1}{\sqrt{2\pi T}}\int_{-\infty}^{a} e^{\mu w-\frac{1}{2}\mu^2 T-\frac{1}{2T}w^2}dw$$

Completing the squares would give

$$-\frac{1}{2T}(w-2a-\mu T)^2=-\frac{1}{2T}(w-2a)^2-\frac{1}{2}\mu^2 T-2\mu a+\mu w$$

$$-\frac{1}{2T}(w-\mu T)^2=-\frac{1}{2T}w^2-\frac{1}{2}\mu^2 T+\mu w$$

and writing

$$e^{\mu w-\frac{1}{2}\mu^2 T-\frac{1}{2T}(2a-w)^2}=e^{2\mu a}e^{-\frac{1}{2T}(w-2a-\mu T)^2} \quad \text{and}$$

$$e^{\mu w-\frac{1}{2}\mu^2 T-\frac{1}{2T}w^2}=e^{-\frac{1}{2T}(w-\mu T)^2}$$

we obtain

$$-\frac{e^{2\mu a}}{\sqrt{2\pi T}}\int_{-\infty}^{a} e^{-\frac{1}{2T}(w-2a-\mu T)^2}dw+\frac{1}{\sqrt{2\pi T}}\int_{-\infty}^{a} e^{-\frac{1}{2T}(w-\mu T)^2}dw$$

By changing of variables

$$y=\frac{w-2a-\mu T}{\sqrt{T}}$$

$$y=\frac{w-\mu T}{\sqrt{T}}$$

$\sqrt{T}dy = dw$ and replacing w with a the upper integral limits of the normal distribution are obtained as

$$y=\frac{-a-\mu T}{\sqrt{T}}$$

$$y=\frac{a-\mu T}{\sqrt{T}}$$

Therefore, the integral is

$$-\frac{e^{2\mu a}}{\sqrt{2\pi}}\int_{-\infty}^{\frac{-a-\mu T}{\sqrt{T}}} e^{-\frac{1}{2}y^2}dy+\frac{1}{\sqrt{2\pi}}\int_{-\infty}^{\frac{a-\mu T}{\sqrt{T}}} e^{-\frac{1}{2}y^2}dy$$

and

$$\widetilde{P}\{\widehat{M}(T) \le a\} = N\left(\frac{a - \mu T}{\sqrt{T}}\right) - e^{2\mu a} N\left(\frac{-a - \mu T}{\sqrt{T}}\right)$$

This is

$$\widetilde{P}\{\widehat{M}(T) \le a\} = N\left(\frac{a - \mu T}{\sigma\sqrt{T}}\right) - e^{\frac{2\mu a}{\sigma^2}} N\left(\frac{-a - \mu T}{\sigma\sqrt{T}}\right)$$

with variance.

For density function

$$\tilde{f}_{\widehat{M}(T)}(a) = \frac{2}{\sqrt{2\pi T}} e^{-\frac{1}{2T}(a-\mu T)^2} - 2\mu e^{2\mu a} N\left(\frac{-a - \mu T}{\sqrt{T}}\right)$$

we need to differentiate equation (2.12) with respect to a

$$\begin{aligned}\frac{\partial \widetilde{P}\left\{\widehat{M}(T) \le a\right\}}{\partial a} &= \frac{1}{\sqrt{T}} N'\left(\frac{a - \mu T}{\sqrt{T}}\right) - e^{2\mu a} N'\left(\frac{-a - \mu T}{\sqrt{T}}\right) \\ &\quad \times \left(-\frac{1}{\sqrt{T}}\right) - 2\mu e^{2\mu a} N\left(\frac{-a - \mu T}{\sqrt{T}}\right)\end{aligned}$$

This is

$$\frac{1}{\sqrt{2\pi T}} e^{-\frac{1}{2T}(a-\mu T)^2} - 2\mu e^{2\mu a} N\left(\frac{-a - \mu T}{\sqrt{T}}\right) + \frac{e^{2\mu a}}{\sqrt{2\pi T}} e^{-\frac{1}{2T}(-a-\mu T)^2}$$

The exponent in the third term can be opened as

$$\begin{aligned}2\mu a - \frac{(-a - \mu T)^2}{2T} &= \frac{4\mu a T}{2T} - \frac{a^2 + 2\mu a T + \mu^2 T^2}{2T} \\ &= -\frac{a^2 - 2\mu a T + \mu^2 T^2}{2T} = -\frac{(a - \mu T)^2}{2T}\end{aligned}$$

and finally, we obtain

$$\tilde{f}_{\widehat{M}(T)}(a) = \frac{2}{\sqrt{2\pi T}} e^{-\frac{1}{2T}(a-\mu T)^2} - 2\mu e^{2\mu a} N\left(\frac{-a - \mu T}{\sqrt{T}}\right)$$

without variance term.

For the cumulative distribution function, define the Radon–Nikodym derivative:

$$\lambda_T = \exp\left\{\frac{\mu}{\sigma^2}Z_T - \frac{1}{2}\frac{\mu^2}{\sigma^2}T\right\}$$

Since

$$P(Z_T < w, M_T^Z > a) = P(Z_T > 2a - w)$$

$$P(Z_T < w, M_T^Z > a) = E\left[1_A \lambda_t\right]$$

$$= E\left[1_{Z_T < w, M_T^Z > a} \exp\left\{\frac{\mu}{\sigma^2}Z_T - \frac{1}{2}\frac{\mu^2}{\sigma^2}T\right\}\right]$$

$$E\left[1_{Z_T > 2a-w} \exp\left\{\frac{\mu}{\sigma^2}(2a - Z_T) - \frac{\mu^2}{2\sigma^2}T\right\}\right]$$

where we replaced Z_T with its mirror image $2a - Z_T$.

This expectation is

$$e^{\frac{2\mu a}{\sigma^2}} \int_{2a-w}^{\infty} e^{-\frac{1}{2}\frac{z^2}{\sigma^2 T} - \frac{2\mu z T}{2\sigma^2 T} - \frac{\mu^2 T^2}{2\sigma^2 T}} dz =$$

$$e^{\frac{2\mu a}{\sigma^2}} \int_{2a-w}^{\infty} e^{-\frac{1}{2}\frac{(z+\mu T)^2}{\sigma^2 T}} dz = e^{\frac{2\mu a}{\sigma^2}} N\left[\frac{w - 2a - \mu T}{\sigma\sqrt{T}}\right]$$

So, the probability $P(Z_T < w, M_T^Z > a)$ of a Brownian motion with drift μ and variance σ^2 is

$$P(Z_T < w, M_T^Z > a) = e^{\frac{2\mu a}{\sigma^2}} N\left[\frac{w - 2a - \mu T}{\sigma\sqrt{T}}\right] \qquad \boxdot$$

2.4.5. *Brownian motion and its minimum with drift and variance*

Let's define a real-valued process X and write

$$M_t^X = \max_{0 \le s \le t} X_s m_t^X = \min_{0 \le s \le t} X_s$$

If X is defined by

$$X_t = \mu t + \sigma W_t$$

then

$$P(X_t < x) = \Phi\left(\frac{x - \mu t}{\sigma\sqrt{t}}\right)$$

and

$$-X_t = (-\mu)t + \sigma(-W_t)$$

Since the process $(-W_t)$ is also a standard Brownian motion, $-X$ has the same form as X, but it is distributed with mean $-\mu t$. We can also write

$$m_t^X = -M_t^{-X}$$

as the greatest of the negative values (minimum). For the minimum, we can write joint probability as

$$P\{W_T > w, m_T^W < a\}T > 0$$

for $a \leq 0$ and $w \geq a$.

Once again, due to the reflection principle, the probability of being $W_T > w$ is the same as $W_T < 2a - w$

$$a - (w - a) = 2a - w$$

$$P\{W_T > w, m_T^W < a\} = P(W_T < 2a - w)$$

$$= \int_{-\infty}^{a} \int_{w}^{\infty} f^W(T, x, y) dx dy$$

$$\frac{\partial}{\partial x} \int_{-\infty}^{a} \int_{w}^{\infty} f^W(T, x, y) dx dy = - \int_{-\infty}^{a} f^W(T, w, y) dy$$

$$-\frac{\partial}{\partial y} \int_{-\infty}^{a} f^W(T, w, y) dy = -f^W(T, w, a)$$

But this is also

$$P\{W_T < 2a - w\} = \frac{1}{\sqrt{2\pi T}} \int_{-\infty}^{2a-w} e^{-\frac{1}{2T}z^2} dz$$

Let

$$\vartheta = 2a - w$$

$$\frac{\partial}{\partial \vartheta}\left(\frac{1}{\sqrt{2\pi T}}\int_{-\infty}^{\vartheta} e^{-\frac{1}{2}z^2}dz\right)\frac{\partial \vartheta}{\partial a} = \frac{1}{\sqrt{2\pi T}}e^{-\frac{1}{2}\left(\frac{2a-w}{\sqrt{T}}\right)^2} * 2$$

and finally, by differentiating with respect to w

$$\frac{\partial}{\partial w}\left(\frac{1}{\sqrt{2\pi T}}e^{-\frac{1}{2}\left(\frac{2a-w}{\sqrt{T}}\right)^2} *2\right) = 2\frac{(2a-w)}{T}\frac{1}{\sqrt{2\pi T}}e^{-\frac{1}{2}\left(\frac{2a-w}{\sqrt{T}}\right)^2}$$

Since

$$-f^W(T, w, a) = \frac{2(2a-w)}{T}\frac{1}{\sqrt{2\pi T}}e^{-\frac{1}{2}\left(\frac{2a-w}{\sqrt{T}}\right)^2}$$

the equation for the joint density of a Brownian motion and its minimum is

$$f^W(T, w, a) = \frac{2(w-2a)}{T}\frac{1}{\sqrt{2\pi T}}e^{-\frac{1}{2}\left(\frac{2a-w}{\sqrt{T}}\right)^2}$$

The joint density of a Brownian motion with variance σ^2 and its minimum is

$$f^W(T, x, a) = \frac{2(w-2a)}{\sigma^2 T\sigma\sqrt{2\pi T}}e^{-\frac{1}{2}\left(\frac{2a-w}{\sigma\sqrt{T}}\right)^2} \tag{2.14}$$

Adding the drift term involves the multiplication with the Radon–Nikodym derivative to change the probability measure.

Let $z = \sigma W \to z^2 = \sigma^2 T\varepsilon$ where ϵ is a normal variate. Then

$$\lambda_T = \exp\left\{\frac{\mu}{\sigma^2}Z_T - \frac{1}{2}\frac{\mu^2}{\sigma^2}T\right\}$$

$$P\left(Z_T > w, m_T^Z < a\right) = E\left[1_A \lambda_t\right]$$

$$= E\left[1_{Z_T>w, m_T^Z<a}\exp\left\{\frac{\mu}{\sigma^2}Z_T - \frac{1}{2}\frac{\mu^2}{\sigma^2}T\right\}\right]$$

$$E\left[1_{Z_T<2a-w}\exp\left\{\frac{\mu}{\sigma^2}(2a - Z_T) - \frac{\mu^2}{2\sigma^2}T\right\}\right]$$

where we replaced Z_T with its mirror image $2a - Z_T$.

This expectation is

$$e^{\frac{2\mu a}{\sigma^2}} \int_{-\infty}^{2a-w} e^{-\frac{1}{2}\frac{z^2}{\sigma^2 T}-\frac{2\mu z T}{2\sigma^2 T}-\frac{\mu^2 T^2}{2\sigma^2 T}} dz$$

$$= e^{\frac{2\mu a}{\sigma^2}} \int_{-\infty}^{2a-w} e^{-\frac{1}{2}\frac{(z+\mu T)^2}{\sigma^2 T}} dz = e^{\frac{2\mu a}{\sigma^2}} N\left[\frac{2a-w+\mu T}{\sigma\sqrt{T}}\right]$$

So, the probability $P(Z_T > w, m_T^Z < a)$ of a Brownian motion with drift μ and variance σ^2 is

$$P(Z_T > w, m_T^Z < a) = e^{\frac{2\mu a}{\sigma^2}} N\left[\frac{2a-w+\mu T}{\sigma\sqrt{T}}\right] \tag{2.15}$$

Applying the total law of probabilities yields

$$P(Z_T > w, m_T^Z > a) = P(Z_T > w) - P(Z_T > w, m_T^Z < a)$$

$$P(Z_T > w, m_T^Z > a) = N\left[\frac{-w+\mu T}{\sigma\sqrt{T}}\right] - e^{\frac{2\mu a}{\sigma^2}} N\left[\frac{2a-w+\mu T}{\sigma\sqrt{T}}\right]$$

where $a \leq 0$ and $w > a$ $(a \leq \min(w, 0))$.

Z_T is the process with Brownian motion W_T having drift μ and variance $\sigma^2 T$. The process will travel at least down to $a\,(a < 0)$ up to time T, then it will travel up by $w - a$ $(w > a)$, or it will go down further by $w - a$ with equal probability. That means

$$P\left(W_T > w, m_T^W < a\right) = P(W_T < 2a - w)$$

which is

$$N\left[\frac{2a - \mathrm{w}}{\sigma\sqrt{T}}\right]$$

without drift and

$$e^{\frac{2\mu a}{\sigma^2}} N\left[\frac{2a-w+\mu T}{\sigma\sqrt{T}}\right] \quad a < \min(a, 0)$$

with drift under the probability measure $\widetilde{P}$.

2.5. The Summary of Cumulative Probabilities and the Densities

This section presents the cumulative probabilities and densities of the variables we will use in pricing barrier options.

For the maximum $M_t^X = \max_{0\leq t\leq T} X_t$ and X_T

The cumulative probabilities are

$$\begin{aligned}
&\widetilde{P}\{\widehat{M}(T) \leq a, \hat{X}(T) \leq w\} \\
&\quad = \widetilde{P}\left\{\hat{X}(T) \leq w\right\} - \widetilde{P}\left\{\widehat{M}(T) \geq a, \hat{X}(T) \leq w\right\}
\end{aligned}$$

$$\begin{aligned}
&\widetilde{P}\{\widehat{M}(T) \leq a, \hat{X}(T) \leq w\} \\
&\quad = N\left(\frac{w-\mu T}{\sigma\sqrt{T}}\right) - e^{\frac{2\mu a}{\sigma^2}} N\left(\frac{w-2a-\mu T}{\sigma\sqrt{T}}\right)
\end{aligned} \tag{2.16}$$

$$\widetilde{P}\{\widehat{M}(T) \geq a, \hat{X}(T) \leq w\} = e^{\frac{2\mu a}{\sigma^2}} N\left(\frac{w-2a-\mu T}{\sigma\sqrt{T}}\right) \tag{2.17}$$

$$\widetilde{P}\{\widehat{M}(T) \leq a\} = N\left(\frac{a-\mu T}{\sigma\sqrt{T}}\right) - e^{\frac{2\mu a}{\sigma^2}} N\left(\frac{-a-\mu T}{\sigma\sqrt{T}}\right) \tag{2.18}$$

and the densities are

$$\tilde{f}_{\widehat{M}(T),\hat{X}(T)}(a,w) = \frac{2(2a-w)}{\sigma^2 T\sigma\sqrt{2\pi T}} e^{\frac{\mu}{\sigma^2}w - \frac{1}{2}\frac{\mu^2}{\sigma^2}T - \frac{1}{2\sigma^2 T}(2a-w)^2} \tag{2.19}$$

$$\tilde{f}_{\widehat{M}(T)}(a) = \frac{2}{\sigma\sqrt{2\pi T}} e^{-\frac{1}{2T}\left(\frac{a-\mu T}{\sigma\sqrt{T}}\right)^2} - \frac{2\mu}{\sigma^2} e^{\frac{2\mu a}{\sigma^2}} N\left(\frac{-a-\mu T}{\sigma\sqrt{T}}\right) \tag{2.20}$$

For the minimum $m_t^X = \min_{0\leq t\leq T} X_t$ and X_T

$$\begin{aligned}
&P(X_T > w, m_T^X > a) \\
&\quad = P(X_T > w) - P(X_T > w, m_T^Z < a)
\end{aligned} \tag{2.21}$$

$$P(X_T > w, m_T^X > a) = N\left[\frac{-w+\mu T}{\sigma\sqrt{T}}\right] - e^{\frac{2\mu a}{\sigma^2}} N\left[\frac{2a-w+\mu T}{\sigma\sqrt{T}}\right] \tag{2.22}$$

$$P\left(X_T > w, m_T^X < a\right) = e^{\frac{2\mu a}{\sigma^2}} N\left[\frac{2a-w+\mu T}{\sigma\sqrt{T}}\right] \tag{2.23}$$

$$\widetilde{P}\{m_T^X \geq a\} = N\left(\frac{-a+\mu T}{\sigma\sqrt{T}}\right) - e^{\frac{2\mu a}{\sigma^2}} N\left(\frac{a+\mu T}{\sigma\sqrt{T}}\right) \tag{2.24}$$

$$\tilde{f}_{\hat{m}(T),\hat{X}(T)}(a,w) = \frac{2(w-2a)}{\sigma^2 T\sigma\sqrt{2\pi T}} e^{\frac{\mu}{\sigma^2}w - \frac{1}{2}\frac{\mu^2}{\sigma^2}T - \frac{1}{2\sigma^2 T}(2a-w)^2} \tag{2.25}$$

$$\tilde{f}_{\hat{m}(T)}(a) = \frac{2}{\sigma\sqrt{2\pi T}} e^{-\frac{1}{2T}\left(\frac{a-\mu T}{\sigma\sqrt{T}}\right)^2} - \frac{2\mu}{\sigma^2} e^{\frac{2\mu a}{\sigma^2}} N\left(\frac{a+\mu T}{\sigma\sqrt{T}}\right) \tag{2.26}$$

2.6. Density Functions for Restricted Brownian Motions

Let's define a density function $f_{do}(w,a,T)$ of a Brownian motion $W(T)$ with drift μ and barrier $a \leq \min(w,0)$. We call this a down barrier.

$$f_{do}(w,a,T) = P(W(T) \in dw,\ m_0^T > a) \tag{2.27}$$

Taking the derivative of equation (2.22) with respect to w

$$\frac{\partial}{\partial w} P(W_T > w, m_T^X > a)$$
$$= \frac{\partial}{\partial w} N\left[\frac{-w+\mu T}{\sigma\sqrt{T}}\right] - \frac{\partial}{\partial w} e^{\frac{2\mu a}{\sigma^2}} N\left[\frac{2a-w+\mu T}{\sigma\sqrt{T}}\right]$$

and changing the sign because $X_T > w$ we write

$$\begin{aligned} f_{do}(w,a,T) &= P(W(T) \in dw,\ m_0^T > a) \\ &= \frac{1}{\sigma\sqrt{T}} n\left(\frac{w-\mu T}{\sigma\sqrt{T}}\right) - e^{\frac{2\mu a}{\sigma^2}} n\left(\frac{w-2a-\mu T}{\sigma\sqrt{T}}\right) \end{aligned} \tag{2.28}$$

where $a \leq \min(w,0)$

Similarly,

$$f_{up}\,(w,a,T) = P(W(T) \in dw, M_0^T < a)$$

where $a \geq \max(w, 0)$ is the up barrier. Taking the derivative of equation (2.16) with respect to w

$$\frac{\partial}{\partial w}\widetilde{P}\{\widehat{M}(T) \leq a, \hat{X}(T) \leq w\}$$
$$= \frac{\partial}{\partial w}N\left(\frac{w-\mu T}{\sigma\sqrt{T}}\right) - \frac{\partial}{\partial w}e^{\frac{2\mu a}{\sigma^2}}N\left(\frac{w-2a-\mu T}{\sigma\sqrt{T}}\right)$$

we can write

$$\begin{aligned} f_{up}(w,a,T) &= P(W(T) \in dw, M_0^T < a) \\ &= \frac{1}{\sigma\sqrt{T}}n\left(\frac{w-\mu T}{\sigma\sqrt{T}}\right) - e^{\frac{2\mu a}{\sigma^2}}n\left(\frac{w-2a-\mu T}{\sigma\sqrt{T}}\right) \end{aligned} \tag{2.29}$$

where $a \geq \max(w, 0)$.

2.7. First Passage Time Density Functions

Let $f(t, a)$ be a transition density of Brownian motion $W(t)$ when it first hits the down barrier a.

Since $\tau_a > t$ and $m_0^T > a$ are all equivalent, we may write

$$f(t,a)dt = P(\tau_a \in dt)$$

$$P(\tau_a > t) = P(m_0^T > a) = N\left(\frac{-a+\mu t}{\sigma\sqrt{t}}\right) - e^{\frac{2\mu a}{\sigma^2}}N\left(\frac{a+\mu t}{\sigma\sqrt{t}}\right)$$

from (2.24).

Taking the derivative with respect to t; (since $P(\tau_a > t)$ derivative takes $(-)$ sign)

$$-\frac{\partial}{\partial t}\left[N\left(\frac{-a+\mu t}{\sigma\sqrt{t}}\right) - e^{\frac{2\mu a}{\sigma^2}} N\left(\frac{a+\mu t}{\sigma\sqrt{t}}\right)\right]$$

we may write

$$f\left(t,a\right)dt = P\left(\tau_a \in dt\right) = \frac{-a}{\sigma t\sqrt{2\pi t}} e^{-\frac{1}{2}\left(\frac{a-\mu t}{\sigma\sqrt{t}}\right)^2} dt \quad a < 0$$

$$f\left(t,a\right) = \frac{-a}{\sigma t\sqrt{2\pi t}} e^{-\frac{1}{2}\left(\frac{a-\mu t}{\sigma\sqrt{t}}\right)^2} \quad a < 0$$

The derivative is

$$-n\left(\frac{-a+\mu t}{\sigma\sqrt{t}}\right)\left[\frac{\mu\sigma\sqrt{t}}{\sigma^2 t} - \frac{\left(-a+\mu t\right)\sigma}{2\sigma^2 t\sqrt{t}}\right]$$

$$+e^{\frac{2\mu a}{\sigma^2}} n\left(\frac{a+\mu t}{\sigma\sqrt{t}}\right)\left[\frac{\mu\sigma\sqrt{t}}{\sigma^2 t} - \frac{\left(a+\mu t\right)\sigma}{2\sigma^2 t\sqrt{t}}\right]$$

$$= n\left(\frac{a-\mu t}{\sigma\sqrt{t}}\right)\left[-\frac{\mu\sigma\sqrt{t}}{\sigma^2 t} + \frac{\left(-a+\mu t\right)\sigma}{2\sigma^2 t\sqrt{t}} + \frac{\mu\sigma\sqrt{t}}{\sigma^2 t} - \frac{(a+\mu t)\sigma}{2\sigma^2 t\sqrt{t}}\right]$$

$$= n\left(\frac{a-\mu t}{\sigma\sqrt{t}}\right)\left[\frac{-2a\sigma}{2\sigma^2 t\sqrt{t}}\right] = n\left(\frac{a-\mu t}{\sigma\sqrt{t}}\right)\left[\frac{-a}{\sigma t\sqrt{t}}\right]$$

Similarly, we can write the transition density for up barrier

$$P\left(\tau_a > t\right) = P\left(M_0^T < a\right) = N\left(\frac{a-\mu t}{\sigma\sqrt{t}}\right) - e^{\frac{2\mu a}{\sigma^2}} N\left(-\frac{a+\mu t}{\sigma\sqrt{t}}\right)$$

Taking the derivative with respect to t:

$$-\frac{\partial}{\partial t}\left[N\left(\frac{-a+\mu t}{\sigma\sqrt{t}}\right) - e^{\frac{2\mu a}{\sigma^2}} N\left(\frac{a+\mu t}{\sigma\sqrt{t}}\right)\right]$$

$$f\left(t,a\right)dt = P\left(\tau_a \in dt\right) = \frac{a}{\sigma t\sqrt{2\pi t}} e^{-\frac{1}{2}\left(\frac{a-\mu t}{\sigma\sqrt{t}}\right)^2} dt \quad a > 0$$

$$f\left(t,a\right) = \frac{a}{\sigma t\sqrt{2\pi t}} e^{-\frac{1}{2}\left(\frac{a-\mu t}{\sigma\sqrt{t}}\right)^2} \quad a > 0$$

Here, we used the same symbol, "a", for the lower and upper barriers. It can be combined in

$$f\left(t,a\right)=\frac{|a|}{\sigma t\sqrt{2\pi t}}e^{-\frac{1}{2}\left(\frac{a-\mu t}{\sigma\sqrt{t}}\right)^{2}}$$

(For details, see Kwok, 2008, pp. 188–195).

2.8. Example: Up and Out Call

This example has been taken from Shreve (2004, pp. 300–308). After the solution, we will present the solutions given by Rubinstein and Reiner (1991) in the third chapter. The reader may decide on the practicality of the methods, but at least they are all unified in the same code.

Barrier options can be priced within the framework of the Black–Scholes–Merton model using the density functions we have presented above. The stochastic equation of the underlying asset under the risk-neutral measure $\widetilde{P}$ is

$$dS(t)=rS(t)dt+\sigma S(t)d\widetilde{W}(t)$$

for $0\leq t\leq T$, and the solution to the differential equation is

$$S(t)=S\left(0\right)e^{\left(r-\frac{1}{2}\sigma^{2}\right)t+\sigma\widetilde{W}(t)}$$

In addition to the expiry T, strike price K in the option terminology, we will add a barrier value H for barrier options. Since the barrier is up-and-out, the option will be knocked out if the share price hits the barrier. If the stock does not reach this value until the maturity date, the option payment will be $\max(S_T-K,0)$. Therefore, the logical consequence of this setup is to design the relationship between the barrier value and the strike price as $H>K$; otherwise, the share price would have to exceed K for the option to be valuable, but if it exceeds the value of H, the option would also become worthless.

The equation for the Brownian motion with drift term and the maximum term are:

$$\widehat{W}(t) = \alpha t + \widetilde{W}(t) \quad 0 \leq t \leq T$$

$$\widehat{M}(T) = \max_{0 \leq t \leq T} \widehat{W}(t)$$

respectively. Multiplying both sides with σ yields

$$\sigma\widehat{W}(t) = \alpha\sigma t + \sigma\widetilde{W}(t)$$

Let's define

$$\alpha = \frac{1}{\sigma}\left(r - \frac{1}{2}\sigma^2\right)$$

Then we have

$$\sigma\widehat{W}(t) = \left(r - \frac{1}{2}\sigma^2\right)t + \sigma\widetilde{W}(t)$$

(a) and therefore

$$S(t) = S(0)e^{\sigma\widehat{W}(t)}$$

$$maxS(t) = S(0)e^{\sigma\widehat{M}(T)}$$

The option will be knocked out if

$$S(0)e^{\sigma\widehat{M}(T)} \geq H$$

and the option pay off will be equal to

$$(S(T) - K)^+ = \left(S(0)e^{\sigma\widehat{W}(T)} - K\right)^+$$

in case the condition

$$S(0)e^{\sigma\widehat{M}(T)} < H$$

is satisfied. The option value at maturity is

$$V(T) = (S(0)e^{\sigma \widehat{W}(T)} - K)^{+} \mathbb{I}_{\left\{S(0)e^{\sigma \widehat{M}(T)} < H\right\}}$$

$$V(T) = (S(0)e^{\sigma \widehat{W}(T)} - K)\mathbb{I}_{\{S(0)e^{\sigma \widehat{M}(T)} < H,\ S(0)e^{\sigma \widehat{W}(T)} > K\}} \tag{2.30}$$

With transforms

$$k = \frac{1}{\sigma}\ln\frac{K}{S(0)}$$

$$a = \frac{1}{\sigma}\ln\frac{H}{S(0)}$$

we can restate the equation (2.30) as

$$V(T) = (S(0)e^{\sigma \widehat{W}(T)} - K)\ \mathbb{I}_{\{\widehat{W}(T)>k,\ \widehat{M}(T)<a\}}$$

Since the probabilities of $\widehat{W}(T) = k, \widehat{M}(T) = a$ are zero for continuous distributions; there is no issue writing the inequalities as strict ones.

Finally, the price is the discounted expected value of equation (2.30).

$$V(0) = \tilde{E}[e^{-rT}V(T)]$$

Since the integral is valuable when the maximum of the Brownian process is below a certain barrier value, the density function we are going to use is the joint density function

$$\tilde{f}_{\widehat{M}(T),\widehat{W}(T)}(m, w) = \frac{2(2m - w)}{T\sqrt{2\pi T}}\ e^{\alpha w - \frac{1}{2}\alpha^2 T - \frac{1}{2T}(2m-w)^2}$$

of $(\widehat{M}(T), \widehat{W}(T))$ pair where $w \le m,\ m \ge 0$.

If $k \ge 0$ (for a call option), the integration region is:

$$\{(m, w) : k \le w \le m \le a\}$$

That is, the maximum will always be below the barrier, and the log price of the underlying asset will always be above the $ln\,K$ scaled with variance and S_0.

If $k \le 0$, the integration region is:

$$\{(m, w) : k \le w \le m,\ 0 \le m \le a\}$$

that is, the positivity of m will be protected. The region can be shown alternatively as

$$\left\{(m, w) : k \le w \le m,\ w^+ \le m \le a\right\}$$

Since the barrier is an up-and-out type, the initial asset value is designed below the barrier as

$$0 < S(0) \le H$$

Therefore, up-and-out barrier call price can be written

$$V(0) = \int_k^a \int_{w^+}^a e^{-rT}(S(0)e^{\sigma w} - K) \\ \times \frac{2(2m - w)}{T\sqrt{2\pi T}}\, e^{\alpha w - \frac{1}{2}\alpha^2 T - \frac{1}{2T}(2m-w)^2} dm dw$$

The solution of inner integral for m is

$$-e^{-rT}(S(0)e^{\sigma w} - K)\frac{1}{\sqrt{2\pi T}} e^{\alpha w - \frac{1}{2}\alpha^2 T - \frac{1}{2T}(2m-w)^2}$$

(verify the integrand by taking the derivative with respect to m). With integral lower and upper limits (a, w^+), we have

$$\begin{aligned} &-\int_k^a e^{-rT}(S(0)e^{\sigma w} - K)\frac{1}{\sqrt{2\pi T}} e^{\alpha w - \frac{1}{2}\alpha^2 T - \frac{1}{2T}(2m-w)^2}\Big|_{w^+}^a dw \\ &\quad - \frac{1}{\sqrt{2\pi T}} \int_k^a (S(0)e^{\sigma w} - K)e^{-rT + \alpha w - \frac{1}{2}\alpha^2 T - \frac{1}{2T}(2a-w)^2} dw \\ &\quad + \frac{1}{\sqrt{2\pi T}} \int_k^h (S(0)e^{\sigma w} - K)e^{\alpha w - rT - \frac{1}{2}\alpha^2 T - \frac{1}{2T}w^2} dw \\ &= S(0)I_1 - KI_2 - S(0)I_3 + KI_4 \end{aligned}$$

where

$$I_1 = \frac{1}{\sqrt{2\pi T}} \int_k^a e^{\sigma w - rT + \alpha w - \frac{1}{2}\alpha^2 T - \frac{1}{2T}w^2} dw$$

$$I_2 = \frac{1}{\sqrt{2\pi T}} \int_k^a e^{-rT + \alpha w - \frac{1}{2}\alpha^2 T - \frac{1}{2T}w^2} dw$$

$$I_3 = \frac{1}{\sqrt{2\pi T}} \int_k^a e^{\sigma w - rT + \alpha w - \frac{1}{2}\alpha^2 T - \frac{1}{2T}(2a-w)^2} dw$$

$$I_4 = \frac{1}{\sqrt{2\pi T}} \int_k^a e^{-rT + \alpha w - \frac{1}{2}\alpha^2 T - \frac{1}{2T}(2a-w)^2} dw$$

Here,

$$(\sigma w + \alpha w) = w(\alpha + \sigma) \quad \gamma = \alpha + \sigma$$

$$\beta = -rT - \frac{1}{2}\alpha^2 T$$

$$\alpha = \frac{1}{\sigma}\left(r - \frac{1}{2}\sigma^2\right)$$

In Shreve (2004), all integrals are shown in

$$\frac{1}{\sqrt{2\pi T}} \int_k^a e^{\beta + \gamma w - \frac{1}{2T}w^2} dw$$

form, and it can be transformed as

$$\frac{1}{\sqrt{2\pi T}} \int_k^a e^{\beta + \gamma w - \frac{1}{2T}w^2} dw = \frac{1}{\sqrt{2\pi T}} \int_k^a e^{\beta + \frac{1}{2}\gamma^2 T - \frac{1}{2T}(w - \gamma T)^2} dw$$

Taking the constant term outside of the integral

$$\frac{1}{\sqrt{2\pi T}} e^{\beta + \frac{1}{2}\gamma^2 T} \int_k^a e^{-\frac{1}{2T}(w-\gamma T)^2} dw$$

and with new integral limits

$$y = \frac{(w - \gamma T)}{\sqrt{T}} \quad dy\sqrt{T} = dw$$

$$a \to \frac{a - \gamma T}{\sqrt{T}} \quad k \to \frac{k - \gamma T}{\sqrt{T}}$$

the integral

$$\frac{1}{\sqrt{2\pi T}} \int_k^h e^{\beta + \gamma w - \frac{1}{2T}w^2} dw$$

can be stated

$$\frac{1}{\sqrt{2\pi}} e^{\beta + \frac{1}{2}\gamma^2 T} \int_{(k-\gamma T)/\sqrt{T}}^{(a-\gamma T/\sqrt{T})} e^{-\frac{1}{2}y^2} dy$$

$$\frac{1}{\sqrt{2\pi T}} \int_k^a e^{\beta + \gamma w - \frac{1}{2T}w^2} dw$$

$$= e^{\beta + \frac{1}{2}\gamma^2 T} \left[N\left(\frac{a - \gamma T}{\sqrt{T}}\right) - N\left(\frac{k - \gamma T}{\sqrt{T}}\right) \right]$$

Using the relationship

$$N(z) = 1 - N(-z)$$

$$\frac{1}{\sqrt{2\pi T}} \int_k^a e^{\beta + \gamma w - \frac{1}{2T}w^2} dw$$

$$= e^{\beta + \frac{1}{2}\gamma^2 T} \left[N\left(\frac{-k + \gamma T}{\sqrt{T}}\right) - N\left(\frac{-a + \gamma T}{\sqrt{T}}\right) \right]$$

and replacing k and a we find:

$$\frac{1}{\sqrt{2\pi T}} \int_k^a e^{\beta + \gamma w - \frac{1}{2T}w^2} dw$$

$$= e^{\beta + \frac{1}{2}\gamma^2 T} \left[N\left(\frac{1}{\sigma\sqrt{T}} \left[\ln\left(\frac{S(0)}{K}\right) + \gamma\sigma T\right]\right) \right.$$

$$\left. - N\left(\frac{1}{\sigma\sqrt{T}} \left[\ln\left(\frac{S(0)}{H}\right) + \gamma\sigma T\right]\right) \right]$$

Let's define

$$\delta_{\pm}(\tau, s) = \frac{1}{\sigma\sqrt{\tau}}\left[\ln s + \left(r \pm \frac{1}{2}\sigma^2\right)\tau\right]$$

We know that

$$\beta = -rT - \frac{1}{2}\alpha^2 T \quad \text{and} \quad \gamma = \alpha + \sigma \quad \text{in integral}$$

$$I_1 = \frac{1}{\sqrt{2\pi T}} \int_k^a e^{\sigma w - rT + \alpha w - \frac{1}{2}\alpha^2 T - \frac{1}{2T}w^2} dw$$

Then

$$e^{-rT-\frac{1}{2}\alpha^2 T + \frac{1}{2}(\alpha+\sigma)^2 T}\left[N\left(\frac{1}{\sigma\sqrt{T}}\left[\ln\left(\frac{S(0)}{K}\right) + (\alpha+\sigma)\sigma T\right]\right)\right.$$
$$\left. - N\left(\frac{1}{\sigma\sqrt{T}}\left[\ln\left(\frac{S(0)}{H}\right) + (\alpha+\sigma)\sigma T\right]\right)\right]$$

$$\alpha = \frac{1}{\sigma}\left(r - \frac{1}{2}\sigma^2\right)$$

$$-rT - \frac{1}{2}\alpha^2 T + \frac{1}{2}(\alpha+\sigma)^2 T = -rT + \frac{1}{2}\sigma^2 T + (\alpha\sigma)T$$

$$= -rT + \frac{1}{2}\sigma^2 T + (\alpha\sigma)T = -rT + \frac{1}{2}\sigma^2 T + rT - \frac{1}{2}\sigma^2 T = 0$$

So, the initial coefficient is equal to 1, and $\gamma\sigma$ is $\gamma\sigma = r + \frac{1}{2}\sigma^2$. (How?)

Therefore, we can write the first integral as

$$I_1 = N\left(\left(\delta_{+}, \left(T, \frac{S(0)}{K}\right)\right)\right) - N\left(\left(\delta_{+}, \left(T, \frac{S(0)}{H}\right)\right)\right)$$

$$I_1 = \left(N\left(\frac{1}{\sigma\sqrt{T}}\left[\ln\left(\frac{S(0)}{K}\right) + \left(r + \frac{1}{2}\sigma^2\right)T\right]\right)\right)$$
$$- N\left(\frac{1}{\sigma\sqrt{T}}\left[\ln\left(\frac{S(0)}{H}\right) + \left(r + \frac{1}{2}\sigma^2\right)T\right]\right)$$

The second integral is

$$I_2 = \frac{1}{\sqrt{2\pi T}} \int_k^a e^{-rT+\alpha w-\frac{1}{2}\alpha^2 T-\frac{1}{2T}w^2} dw$$

$$\beta = -rT - \frac{1}{2}\alpha^2 T$$

$$\gamma = \alpha$$

Therefore, we can write

$$\frac{1}{\sqrt{2\pi T}} \int_k^a e^{\beta+\gamma w-\frac{1}{2T}w^2} dw$$

$$= e^{\beta+\frac{1}{2}\gamma^2 T} \left[N\left(\frac{1}{\sigma\sqrt{T}} \left[\ln\left(\frac{S(0)}{K} \right) + \gamma\sigma T \right] \right) \right.$$

$$\left. - N\left(\frac{1}{\sigma\sqrt{T}} \left[\ln\left(\frac{S(0)}{H} \right) + \gamma\sigma T \right] \right) \right]$$

$$\beta + \frac{1}{2}\gamma^2 T = -rT - \frac{1}{2}\alpha^2 T + \frac{1}{2}\alpha^2 T = -rT$$

$$\gamma = \alpha$$

$$I_2 = e^{-rT} \left[N\left(\frac{1}{\sigma\sqrt{T}} \left[\ln\left(\frac{S(0)}{K} \right) + \alpha\sigma T \right] \right) \right.$$

$$\left. -N\left(\frac{1}{\sigma\sqrt{T}} \left[\ln\left(\frac{S(0)}{H} \right) + \alpha\sigma T \right] \right) \right]$$

$$I_2 = e^{-rT} \left[N\left(\frac{1}{\sigma\sqrt{T}} \left[\ln\left(\frac{S(0)}{K} \right) + \left(r - \frac{1}{2}\sigma^2 \right) T \right] \right) \right.$$

$$\left. - N\left(\frac{1}{\sigma\sqrt{T}} \left[\ln\left(\frac{S(0)}{H} \right) + \left(r - \frac{1}{2}\sigma^2 \right) T \right] \right) \right]$$

$$I_2 = e^{-rT} \left[N\left(\left(\delta_-, \left(T, \frac{S(0)}{K} \right) \right) \right) - N\left(\left(\delta_-, \left(T, \frac{S(0)}{H} \right) \right) \right) \right]$$

The third integral is

$$I_3 = \frac{1}{\sqrt{2\pi T}} \int_k^a e^{\sigma w - rT + \alpha w - \frac{1}{2}\alpha^2 T - \frac{1}{2T}(2a-w)^2} dw$$

We can write it

$$I_3 = \frac{1}{\sqrt{2\pi T}} \int_k^a e^{\sigma w - rT + \alpha w - \frac{1}{2}\alpha^2 T - \frac{2a^2}{T} - \frac{1}{2T}w^2 + \frac{2aw}{T}} dw$$

$$\beta = -rT - \frac{1}{2}\alpha^2 T - \frac{2a^2}{T}$$

$$\gamma = \alpha + \sigma + \frac{2a}{T}$$

With some algebra

$$\beta + \frac{1}{2}\gamma^2 T = -rT - \frac{1}{2}\alpha^2 T - \frac{2a^2}{T} + \frac{1}{2}\left(\alpha + \sigma + \frac{2a}{T}\right)^2 T$$

$$= -rT - \frac{1}{2}\alpha^2 T - \frac{2a^2}{T} + \frac{1}{2}\alpha^2 T + \frac{1}{2}\sigma^2 T + \frac{2a^2}{T} + \alpha\sigma T$$

$$+ 2\alpha a + 2a\sigma$$

$$= -rT + \frac{1}{2}\sigma^2 T + \alpha\sigma T + 2\alpha a + 2a\sigma$$

$$= -rT + \frac{1}{2}\sigma^2 T + \left(r - \frac{1}{2}\sigma^2\right) T + 2\frac{1}{\sigma}\left(r - \frac{1}{2}\sigma^2\right)\frac{1}{\sigma}\ln\frac{H}{S(0)}$$

$$+ 2\frac{\sigma}{\sigma}\ln\frac{H}{S(0)}$$

$$= 2\frac{1}{\sigma}\left(r - \frac{1}{2}\sigma^2\right)\frac{1}{\sigma}\ln\frac{H}{S(0)} + \frac{2}{\sigma}\ln\frac{H}{S(0)}\sigma = \frac{2r}{\sigma^2}\ln\frac{H}{S(0)} - \ln\frac{H}{S(0)}$$

$$+ 2\ln\frac{H}{S(0)}$$

we simplify the equation as

$$= \left(\frac{2r}{\sigma^2} + 1\right) \ln \frac{H}{S(0)}$$

$$e^{\beta + \frac{1}{2}\gamma^2 T} = e^{(\frac{2r}{\sigma^2}+1)\ln \frac{H}{S(0)}} = \left(\frac{H}{S(0)}\right)^{\frac{2r}{\sigma^2}+1}$$

For

$$\begin{aligned}
\gamma &= \alpha + \sigma + \frac{2a}{T} \\
&= \frac{1}{\sigma}\left(r - \frac{1}{2}\sigma^2\right) + \sigma + \frac{2}{\sigma T}\ln \frac{H}{S(0)} \\
&= \frac{1}{\sigma T}\left[\left(r - \frac{1}{2}\sigma^2\right) T + \sigma^2 T + \ln\left(\frac{H}{S(0)}\right)^2\right]
\end{aligned}$$

we have

$$\begin{aligned}
\gamma\sigma T &= \left[\left(r - \frac{1}{2}\sigma^2\right) T + \sigma^2 T + \ln\left(\frac{H}{S(0)}\right)^2\right] \\
&= \left[\left(r + \frac{1}{2}\sigma^2\right) T + \ln\left(\frac{H}{S(0)}\right)^2\right]
\end{aligned}$$

Putting all together

$$\left(\frac{H}{S(0)}\right)^{\frac{2r}{\sigma^2}+1} \left[N\left(\frac{1}{\sigma\sqrt{T}}\left[\ln\left(\frac{S(0)}{K}\right) + \gamma\sigma T\right]\right) - N\left(\frac{1}{\sigma\sqrt{T}}\left[\ln\left(\frac{S(0)}{H}\right) + \gamma\sigma T\right]\right)\right]$$

$$\left(\frac{H}{S(0)}\right)^{\frac{2r}{\sigma^2}+1} N\left(\frac{1}{\sigma\sqrt{T}}\left[\ln\left(\frac{S(0)}{K}\right) + \left(r + \frac{1}{2}\sigma^2\right) T + \ln\left(\frac{H}{S(0)}\right)^2\right]\right)$$

$$- N\left(\frac{1}{\sigma\sqrt{T}}\left[\ln\left(\frac{S(0)}{H}\right)+\left(r+\frac{1}{2}\sigma^2\right)T+\ln\left(\frac{H}{S(0)}\right)^2\right]\right)$$

$$I_3=\left(\frac{H}{S(0)}\right)^{\frac{2r}{\sigma^2}+1}N\left(\frac{1}{\sigma\sqrt{T}}\left[\ln\left(\frac{H^2}{KS(0)}\right)+\left(r+\frac{1}{2}\sigma^2\right)T\right]\right)$$

$$- N\left(\frac{1}{\sigma\sqrt{T}}\left[\ln\left(\frac{H}{S(0)}\right)+\left(r+\frac{1}{2}\sigma^2\right)T\right]\right)$$

$$I_3=\left(\frac{H}{S(0)}\right)^{\frac{2r}{\sigma^2}+1}\left[N\left(\left(\delta_+,\left(T,\frac{H^2}{KS(0)}\right)\right)\right)-N\left(\left(\delta_+,\left(T,\frac{H}{S(0)}\right)\right)\right)\right]$$

Finally,

$$I_4=\frac{1}{\sqrt{2\pi T}}\int_k^a e^{-rT+\alpha w-\frac{1}{2}\alpha^2T-\frac{1}{2T}(2a-w)^2}\,dw$$

$$I_4=\frac{1}{\sqrt{2\pi T}}\int_k^h e^{-rT+\alpha w-\frac{1}{2}\alpha^2T-\frac{2a^2}{T}+\frac{2aw}{T}-\frac{w^2}{2T}}\,dw$$

$$\beta=-rT-\frac{1}{2}\alpha^2T-\frac{2a^2}{T}$$

$$\gamma=\alpha+\frac{2a}{T}$$

$$\beta+\frac{1}{2}\gamma^2T=-rT-\frac{1}{2}\alpha^2T-\frac{2a^2}{T}+\frac{1}{2}\left(\alpha+\frac{2a}{T}\right)^2T=-rT+2a\alpha$$

$$=-rT+\frac{2}{\sigma}\ln\left(\frac{H}{S(0)}\right)\frac{1}{\sigma}\left(r-\frac{1}{2}\sigma^2\right)=-rT+\left(\frac{2r}{\sigma^2}-1\right)$$

$$\ln\left(\frac{H}{S(0)}\right)=e^{\beta+\frac{1}{2}\gamma^2T}=e^{-rT}e^{\left(\frac{2r}{\sigma^2}-1\right)\ln\left(\frac{H}{S(0)}\right)}$$

$$=e^{-rT}\left(\frac{H}{S(0)}\right)^{\left(\frac{2r}{\sigma^2}-1\right)}$$

$\gamma\sigma T$ is

$$\gamma\sigma T = \alpha\sigma T + \frac{2h}{T}\sigma T$$
$$\alpha\sigma T + 2a\sigma$$

Then, we can write

$$\alpha\sigma T + 2h\sigma = \left(r - \frac{1}{2}\sigma^2\right)T + \ln\left(\frac{H}{S(0)}\right)^2$$

So, putting all in I_4

$$I_4 = e^{-rT}\left(\frac{H}{S(0)}\right)^{\left(\frac{2r}{\sigma^2}-1\right)}\left[N\left(\frac{1}{\sigma\sqrt{T}}\left[\ln\left(\frac{S\,(0)}{K}\right) + \gamma\sigma T\right]\right)\right.$$
$$\left. - N\left(\frac{1}{\sigma\sqrt{T}}\left[\ln\left(\frac{S(0)}{H}\right) + \gamma\sigma T\right]\right)\right]$$

$$I_4 = e^{-rT}\left(\frac{H}{S(0)}\right)^{\left(\frac{2r}{\sigma^2}-1\right)}$$
$$\left[N\left(\frac{1}{\sigma\sqrt{T}}\left[\ln\left(\frac{S(0)}{K}\right) + \left(r - \frac{1}{2}\sigma^2\right)T + \ln\left(\frac{H}{S(0)}\right)^2\right]\right)\right.$$
$$\left. - N\left(\frac{1}{\sigma\sqrt{T}}\left[\ln\left(\frac{S\,(0)}{H}\right) + \left(r - \frac{1}{2}\sigma^2\right)T + \ln\left(\frac{H}{S(0)}\right)^2\right]\right)\right]$$

$$I_4 = e^{-rT}\left(\frac{H}{S(0)}\right)^{\left(\frac{2r}{\sigma^2}-1\right)}$$
$$\left[N\left(\frac{1}{\sigma\sqrt{T}}\left[\ln\left(\frac{H^2}{KS(0)}\right) + \left(r - \frac{1}{2}\sigma^2\right)T\right]\right)\right.$$
$$\left. - N\left(\frac{1}{\sigma\sqrt{T}}\left[\ln\left(\frac{H}{S(0)}\right) + \left(r - \frac{1}{2}\sigma^2\right)T\right]\right)\right]$$

$$I_4 = e^{-rT}\left(\frac{H}{S(0)}\right)^{\left(\frac{2r}{\sigma^2}-1\right)}\left[N\left(\left(\delta_-,\left(T,\frac{H^2}{KS(0)}\right)\right)\right)\right.$$
$$\left.-N\left(\left(\delta_-,\left(T,\frac{H}{S(0)}\right)\right)\right)\right]$$

Finally, the up-and-out barrier call price is given by

$$C_{uo} = S(0)\left[N\left(\left(\delta_+,\left(T,\frac{S(0)}{K}\right)\right)\right)-N\left(\left(\delta_+,\left(T,\frac{S(0)}{H}\right)\right)\right)\right]$$
$$-Ke^{-rT}\left[N\left(\left(\delta_-,\left(T,\frac{S(0)}{K}\right)\right)\right)-N\left(\left(\delta_-,\left(T,\frac{S(0)}{H}\right)\right)\right)\right]$$
$$-S\left(0\left(\frac{H}{S(0)}\right)^{\left(\frac{2r}{\sigma^2}+1\right)}\left[N\left(\left(\delta_+,\left(T,\frac{H^2}{KS(0)}\right)\right)\right)\right.\right.$$
$$\left.-N\left(\left(\delta_+,\left(T,\frac{H}{S(0)}\right)\right)\right)\right]+Ke^{-rT}\left(\frac{H}{S(0)}\right)^{\left(\frac{2r}{\sigma^2}-1\right)}$$
$$\times\left[N\left(\left(\delta_-,\left(T,\frac{H^2}{KS(0)}\right)\right)\right)-N\left(\left(\delta_-,\left(T,\frac{H}{S(0)}\right)\right)\right)\right]$$

The reader may verify that the formula can be restated with Black–Scholes–Merton's formula terms as follows:

$$C_{uo} = e^{-rT}\left(K-H\right)N\left(\left(\delta_-,\left(T,\frac{S(0)}{H}\right)\right)\right)+\left(C_{BS}(S,T;K)\right.$$
$$-C_{BS}(S,T;H)-\left(\frac{H}{S(0)}\right)^{\frac{2r}{\sigma^2}-1}\left[C_{BS}\left(\frac{H^2}{S(0)},T;K\right)\right.$$
$$\left.-C_{BS}\left(\frac{H^2}{S(0)},T;H\right)-e^{-rT}(H-K)N\left(\left(\delta_-,\left(T,\frac{H^2}{HS(0)}\right)\right)\right)\right]$$

We can write a simple Matlab code for an "up and out" barrier call like the following (without rebate).

```
function uo= uocall (S0, K, H, r, T, sig, div)
P2=H^2/S0;
ust=(2*(r-div))/sig^2-1;
mult= (H/S0) ^ ust;
a= (log (S0/H) + (r-div-0.5*sig^2) *T)/ (sig*sqrt (T));
b= (log (P2/H) + (r-div-0.5*sig^2) *T)/ (sig*sqrt (T));
uo= (K-H) *exp(-r*T) *normcdf(a)+blsprice (S0, K, r, T,
 sig, div)-blsprice (S0, H, r, T, sig, div)-mult*...
    (blsprice (P2, K, r, T, sig, div)-blsprice (P2, H, r,
T, sig, div)-(H-K) *exp(-r*T) *normcdf(b))
```

```
typing
uocall (100,102,105,0.08,0.5,0.20,0.03) will produce the
value of
uo =    0.0053
```

2.9. Conclusion

We have examined the basic density and cumulative probability functions in pricing the barrier options in light of the reflection principle. Cox and Miller (1965), Harrison (1985), Shreve (2004), Elliott and Kopp (2004), Kwok (2008), and Privault (2014) are the best resources to consult. They include the basics, theory, and applications as well.

In this introductory chapter, Shreve's (2004) solution for the up-and-out barrier call option is presented; in the next chapter, using only two basic density functions, we will provide all the solutions derived by Rubinstein and Reiner (1991).

Chapter 3

The Derivation of Barrier Option Prices

3.1. Introduction

Barrier options are among the oldest path-dependent exotic options, and their trade volume increased drastically after 1992. Their most important feature is offering risk managers a cheaper hedging method than vanilla options. Since they have knock-in and knock-out features, the cost of some price ranges is saved when pricing the barrier options.

If the market believes that some price ranges are unlikely, it may be advantageous to hedge, for example, with the down-and-out call rather than a vanilla one. There are two types of barrier options or features: knock-in and knock-out. A knock-in barrier option is an option whose holder is entitled to receive the standard option payoff if the barrier level is hit until expiration at any time. Otherwise, the option is not functional (in), and she may be entitled to receive a rebate. On the contrary, a knock-out barrier option is an option whose holder is not entitled to receive the standard option payoff if the barrier level is hit. In this case, the option is out, and she may receive some rebate. If the barrier is never hit until maturity, the holder may receive the option payoff if this is in the money at expiration.

The terminology continues with "down" and "up" terms. It matters whether the barrier is hit from above or below. We also add call and put features on "down and in," "down and out," "up and in," and "up and out" barriers to complete the picture.

We give the formal definition as follows with reference to Rubinstein and Reiner (1991). First, notation:

τ	Elapsed time
t	Maturity of a European option
$S(t)$	Underlying asset price at expiration
$t-\tau$	Time to expiration
K	Exercise/strike price
H	Barrier value
R	Lump-sum rebate or shortly rebate

We will use the following density functions from Section 3.2 and Rubinstein and Reiner (1991). Considering the canonical equation for the log-normal return process

$$\ln S_t = \ln S_0 + \left(r - D - \frac{1}{2}\sigma^2\right) t + \sigma W_t$$

$$\ln \frac{S_t}{S_0} = \left(r - D - \frac{1}{2}\sigma^2\right) t + \sigma W_t$$

we write the density of the natural logarithm of the risk-neutral underlying asset return as

$$f(u) = \frac{1}{\sigma\sqrt{2\pi t}} \exp\left(-\frac{v^2}{2}\right) \tag{3.1}$$

where

$$v = \frac{u - \mu t}{\sigma\sqrt{t}} \quad \mu = \left(r - D - \frac{1}{2}\sigma^2\right) \quad u = \ln \frac{x}{S_0}$$

$x = S_t$ and u is the integral variable in relative terms. We can also choose to write

$$v = \frac{u - \mu}{\sigma\sqrt{t}} \quad \mu = \ln S + \left(r - D - \frac{1}{2}\sigma^2\right) t$$

and u starts from $\ln K$ or $\ln H$, depending on the integral.

The remaining density functions are related to the restricted processes. The density of the log-normal returns when the asset price starts movement from above the barrier H, crosses the barrier and ends up above the barrier at expiration is given by the reflection principle as

$$P\left(S_t > u, \hat{m}\left(t\right) < a\right) = P\left(S_t < 2a - u\right)$$
$$P\left(-S_t > u - 2a\right)$$

By symmetry, we can write it with drift and variance

$$P\left(S_t > \frac{u - 2a - \mu t}{\sigma\sqrt{t}}\right) = \frac{e^{\frac{2\mu a}{\sigma^2}}}{\sigma\sqrt{t}} N\left(\frac{-u + 2a + \mu t}{\sigma\sqrt{t}}\right)$$

$$P\left(S_t > \frac{u - 2a - \mu t}{\sigma\sqrt{t}}\right) = 1 - P\left(S_t < \frac{u - 2a - \mu t}{\sigma\sqrt{t}}\right)$$

$$\frac{e^{\frac{2\mu a}{\sigma^2}}}{\sigma\sqrt{t}} N\left(\frac{-u + 2a + \mu t}{\sigma\sqrt{t}}\right) = \frac{e^{\frac{2\mu a}{\sigma^2}}}{\sigma\sqrt{t}} \left[1 - N\left(\frac{u - 2a - \mu t}{\sigma\sqrt{t}}\right)\right]$$

$$\frac{e^{\frac{2\mu a}{\sigma^2}}}{\sigma\sqrt{t}} \frac{\partial\left[1 - N\left(\frac{u-2a-\mu t}{\sigma\sqrt{t}}\right)\right]}{\partial u} = \frac{e^{\frac{2\mu a}{\sigma^2}}}{\sigma\sqrt{t}} \frac{\partial\left[N\left(\frac{-u+2a+\mu t}{\sigma\sqrt{t}}\right)\right]}{\partial u}$$

$$g\left(u\right) = \tilde{f}\left(S_t > u, \hat{m}\left(t\right) < a\right) = \frac{e^{\frac{2\mu a}{\sigma^2}}}{\sigma\sqrt{t}} n\left(\frac{u - 2a - \mu t}{\sigma\sqrt{t}}\right). \tag{3.2}$$

corresponds to equations (2.14) and (2.16)

$$P\left(Z_T < u,\ M_T^Z > a\right) = e^{\frac{2\mu a}{\sigma^2}} N\left[\frac{u - 2a - \mu T}{\sigma\sqrt{T}}\right]$$

$$P\left(Z_T > u,\ m_T^Z < a\right) = e^{\frac{2\mu a}{\sigma^2}} N\left[\frac{2a - u + \mu T}{\sigma\sqrt{T}}\right]$$

where $a = \ln \frac{H}{S}$ $\mu = \left(r - D - \frac{1}{2}\sigma^2\right)$ and $u = \ln K/S$.

Recalling our restricted densities in equations (2.29) and (2.30) and taking the derivative of equation (2.33)

$$\frac{\partial}{\partial w} P(W_T > w, m_T^X > a)$$

$$= \frac{\partial}{\partial w} N\left[\frac{-w + \mu T}{\sigma\sqrt{T}}\right] - \frac{\partial}{\partial w} e^{\frac{2\mu a}{\sigma^2}} N\left[\frac{2a - w + \mu T}{\sigma\sqrt{T}}\right]$$

we have

$$f_{do}(w, a, T) = P(W(T) \in dw,\ m_0^T > a) = \frac{1}{\sigma\sqrt{T}} n\left(\frac{w - \mu T}{\sigma\sqrt{T}}\right)$$
$$- e^{\frac{2\mu a}{\sigma^2}} n\left(\frac{w - 2a - \mu T}{\sigma\sqrt{T}}\right)$$

where $a \leq \min(w, 0)$ is the down barrier. Similarly,

$$f_{up}(w, a, T) = P(W(T) \in dw,\ M_0^T < a)$$

where $a \geq \max(w, 0)$ is the up barrier, we can also derive the relevant density functions.

Taking the derivative of equation (2.17) with respect to w

$$\frac{\partial}{\partial w}\tilde{P}\{\hat{M}(T) \leq a, \hat{X}(T) \leq w\}$$
$$= \frac{\partial}{\partial w} N\left(\frac{w - \mu T}{\sigma\sqrt{T}}\right) - \frac{\partial}{\partial w} e^{\frac{2\mu a}{\sigma^2}} N\left(\frac{w - 2a - \mu T}{\sigma\sqrt{T}}\right)$$

we can write

$$f_{up}(w, a, T) = P(W(T) \in dw,\ M_0^T < a)$$
$$= \frac{1}{\sigma\sqrt{T}} n\left(\frac{w - \mu T}{\sigma\sqrt{T}}\right) - e^{\frac{2\mu a}{\sigma^2}} n\left(\frac{w - 2a - \mu T}{\sigma\sqrt{T}}\right)$$

With Rubinstein and Reiner's (1991) notation, the density function is

$$g(u) = \frac{e^{\frac{2\mu a}{\sigma^2}}}{\sigma\sqrt{t}} n\left(\frac{u - \eta 2a - \eta\mu t}{\sigma\sqrt{t}}\right)$$

and $\eta = 1$ for down density and $\eta = -1$ for up density.

Finally, we need the density of the first passage time for the rebate. The difficulty is that the rebate is payable at a random time if the barrier is hit and the option is void. Therefore, we need the density of the first passage time for the underlying asset returns. As we explained in Section 3.2, the first passage time density can be obtained by differentiating (u) with respect to the time variable (elapsed time).

This density is

$$h(\tau) = \frac{-\eta a}{\sigma\tau\sqrt{2\pi\tau}} e^{-\frac{1}{2}v^2} \quad v = \frac{-\eta a + \eta\mu\tau}{\sigma\sqrt{\tau}} \tag{3.3}$$

If the barrier is approached from above (for down density) $\eta = 1$, and if the barrier is approached from below (for up density) $\eta = -1$. When the barrier is approached from above, $a < 0$ because $a = \ln H/S$ and $S > H$. This makes the density positive again. The reverse is also true for $\eta = -1$ case.

The value of the rebate can be calculated as a product of the cumulative probability of hitting time and the rebate R and simply discounting it with a risk-free rate.

3.2. Call Options (In)

3.2.1. *Down and in call C_{di}*

The holder is entitled to receive a standard call payoff if the barrier is breached from above. This implies the underlying (stock) price is above the barrier initially, where S denotes the initial asset price at time $\tau = 0$. If the asset price remains above the barrier at all times, a rebate is paid at expiration, and the option expires worthless. The buyer of the option thinks that the market will fall and the option will be triggered and be valuable in this case. Actually, it behaves more like a put, though it has the name "call." If the underlying asset price rises later, the option becomes more valuable; otherwise (if it keeps falling), the payoff could be zero. In a sense, it is preferable to calendar spread because there is no need to determine or guess the timing of fall and rise; the only necessary thing is fall and rise during the option's lifetime.

$$C_{di}(S > H)$$

Payoff Condition:

$$\max(0, S(t) - K) \quad \text{for } \tau \leq t,\ S(\tau) \leq H$$

$$\text{Rebate } \tau > t \quad \text{or } S(\tau) > H \text{ for all } \tau$$

However, we may have two cases by construction, irrespective of the barrier hit at $\tau \leq t$; $K > H$ and $K < H$, which may have different

Table 3.1. Conditional payoff structure for down-and-in call.

$K > H$	Conditional on	Payoff	Probability
$S(t) > K$	$S(\tau) \leq H$ for some $\tau \leq t$	$S(t) - K$	$P(S(t) > K, S(\tau) \leq H)$
$S(t) \leq K$	$S(\tau) \leq H$ for some $\tau \leq t$	0	
$S(\tau) > H$	For all $\tau \leq t$	Rebate	$+P(S(t) > H) -$ $P(S(t) > H, S(\tau) \leq H)$
$K < H$			
$S(t) > H$	$S(\tau) \leq H$ for some $\tau \leq t$	$S(t) - K$	$P(S(t) > H, S(\tau) \leq H)$
$S(t) \leq H$	$S(t) > K$	$S(t) - K$	$+P(H \geq S(t) > K)$
$S(\tau) \leq K$		0	
$S(\tau) > H$	For all $\tau \leq t$	Rebate	$+P(S(t) > H) -$ $P(S(t) > H, S(\tau) \leq H)$

payoff implications after hitting the barrier. Table 3.1 summarizes the possible cases and payoffs.

Pricing: There are two different situations to be calculated; $K > H$ and $K < H$.

3.2.1.1. *Down and in call* $C_{di} K > H$ *case*

Depending on $S(\tau) \leq H$ for some $\tau \leq t$, we receive the payoff $S_t - K$ for $S_t > K$. But, for $S(\tau) > H$ for all $\tau \leq t$ we receive the rebate.

Therefore, we need the probability of

$$P(S(t) > K, S(\tau) \leq H)$$

and

$$P(S(t) > H) - P(S(t) > H, S(\tau) \leq H)$$

Since it is $K > H$ to be entitled to receive the payoff, it is adequate to cross the barrier and remain above the strike. The relevant densities are $g(u)$ and $f(u) - g(u)$, where the integral variable starts from $\ln K/S$ for $g(u)$ and $\ln H/S$ for $f(u) - g(u)$ and we use the down density for $g(u)$ as $\eta = 1$.

For the first probability, we evaluate the following integral with $S_t = Se^u$

$$[3] = \exp(-rt) \int_{\ln\frac{K}{S}}^{\infty} (\varphi Se^u - \varphi K) g(u) du \quad \varphi = 1$$

because the barrier must be hit, and the asset price must be above the strike at maturity. It is the integral [3] with Rubinstein and Reiner (1991) notation.

Since

$$v = \frac{u - 2a - \mu t}{\sigma\sqrt{t}}$$

$$v\sigma\sqrt{t} + 2a + \mu t = u$$

we write the equation as

$$\exp(-rt)\frac{1}{\sqrt{2\pi}} \int_{(\ln\frac{K}{S}-2a-\mu t)/\sigma\sqrt{t}}^{\infty} (Se^{v\sigma\sqrt{t}+2a+\mu t} - K)$$

$$\times \exp\left\{\frac{2\mu a}{\sigma^2}\right\} \exp\left(-\frac{v^2}{2}\right) dv$$

where

$$v = \frac{u - \eta 2a - \eta\mu t}{\sigma\sqrt{t}} \quad a = \ln\frac{H}{S} \quad \mu = \left(r - D - \frac{1}{2}\sigma^2\right) \quad \eta = 1$$

and $dv\sigma\sqrt{t} = du$.

Let's evaluate the first term.

Canceling r and drawing D from $\mu = (r - D - \frac{1}{2}\sigma^2)$

$$\frac{Se^{-Dt}}{\sqrt{2\pi}} \int_{(\ln\frac{K}{S}-2a-\mu t)/\sigma\sqrt{t}}^{\infty} \left(e^{v\sigma\sqrt{t}-\frac{1}{2}\sigma^2 t}\right)$$

$$\times \exp\left\{\frac{2\mu a}{\sigma^2} + 2a\right\} \exp\left(-\frac{v^2}{2}\right) dv$$

$$\frac{Se^{-Dt}}{\sqrt{2\pi}} \int_{(\ln\frac{K}{S}-2a-\mu t)/\sigma\sqrt{t}}^{\infty} \exp\left\{2a\left(\frac{\mu}{\sigma^2} + 1\right)\right\} \exp\left(-\frac{(v - \sigma\sqrt{t})^2}{2}\right) dv$$

Since the lower limit of the integral is $\ln K/S$, the lower limit for v is

$$v = \frac{\ln \frac{K}{S} - 2a - \left(r - D - \frac{1}{2}\sigma^2\right)t}{\sigma\sqrt{t}}$$

$$= \frac{\ln \frac{K}{S} - \ln(H/S)^2 - \left(r - D - \frac{1}{2}\sigma^2\right)t}{\sigma\sqrt{t}}$$

$$v = \frac{-\ln \frac{S}{K} - 2\ln H/S - \left(r - D - \frac{1}{2}\sigma^2\right)t}{\sigma\sqrt{t}}$$

$$= -\frac{\ln \frac{H^2}{SK} + \left(r - D - \frac{1}{2}\sigma^2\right)t}{\sigma\sqrt{t}}$$

and adding the term $-\sigma\sqrt{t}$

$$= -\frac{\ln \frac{H^2}{SK} + \left(r - D - \frac{1}{2}\sigma^2\right)t}{\sigma\sqrt{t}} - \sigma\sqrt{t}$$

we obtain the lower limit as

$$v = -\frac{\ln \frac{H^2}{SK} + \left(r - D + \frac{1}{2}\sigma^2\right)t}{\sigma\sqrt{t}}$$

So the first part is

$$\frac{Se^{-Dt}}{\sqrt{2\pi}} \int_{-\infty}^{\frac{\ln \frac{H^2}{SK} + \left(r - D + \frac{1}{2}\sigma^2\right)t}{\sigma\sqrt{t}}} \exp\left\{2a\left(\frac{\mu}{\sigma^2} + 1\right)\right\} \exp\left(-\frac{v^2}{2}\right) dv$$

As we apply the transformation in Rubinstein, Reiner (1991)

$$\lambda = \frac{\mu}{\sigma^2} + 1 \tag{3.4}$$

the expression of $\exp\left(2a\left(\frac{\mu}{\sigma^2} + 1\right)\right)$ using $a = \ln,\ H/S$ is

$$e^{(\ln\ H/S))^{2\lambda}} = \left(\frac{H}{S}\right)^{2\lambda}$$

Also, if we draw μ from $\lambda = \frac{\mu}{\sigma^2} + 1$ we obtain

$$\mu = \lambda\sigma^2 - \sigma^2$$

$$\mu = (\lambda - 1)\sigma^2 = \left(r - D - \frac{1}{2}\sigma^2\right)$$

$$\lambda = \frac{r - D}{\sigma^2} + \frac{1}{2} \rightarrow 2\lambda = 2\left(\frac{r - D}{\sigma^2}\right) + 1$$

and putting back in the formula, we obtain the integral limit as

$$\frac{\ln \frac{H^2}{SK} + \left(r - D - \frac{1}{2}\sigma^2\right)t}{\sigma\sqrt{t}} + \sigma\sqrt{t}$$

$$= \frac{\ln \frac{H^2}{SK} + \left(\lambda\sigma^2 - \sigma^2\right)t}{\sigma\sqrt{t}} + \sigma\sqrt{t}$$

$$= y = \frac{\ln \frac{H^2}{SK} + \lambda\sigma^2 t}{\sigma\sqrt{t}} = \frac{\ln \frac{H^2}{SK}}{\sigma\sqrt{t}} + \lambda\sigma\sqrt{t}$$

Therefore, the first part is

$$Se^{-Dt}(H/S)^{2\lambda}\frac{1}{\sqrt{2\pi}}\int_{-\infty}^{y} e^{-\frac{1}{2}v^2}dv = Se^{-Dt}\left(\frac{H}{S}\right)^{2\lambda}N(y)$$

We do a similar algebra for the second integral.

$$Ke^{-rt}\frac{1}{\sqrt{2\pi}}\int_{\ln\ K/S}^{\infty} \exp\left\{2a\frac{\mu}{\sigma^2}\right\}e^{-\frac{1}{2}v^2}dv$$

Since

$$\mu = \lambda\sigma^2 - \sigma^2 \exp\left\{\frac{2a\mu}{\sigma^2}\right\} = \exp\ [a(2\lambda - 2)]$$

$$K(H/S)^{2\lambda-2}e^{-rt}\frac{1}{\sqrt{2\pi}}\int_{(\ln\ \frac{K}{S} - 2a - \mu t)/\sigma\sqrt{t}}^{\infty} e^{-\frac{1}{2}v^2}dv$$

$$K(H/S)^{2\lambda-2}e^{-rt}\frac{1}{\sqrt{2\pi}}\int_{-[y-\sigma\sqrt{t}]}^{\infty} e^{-\frac{1}{2}v^2}dv$$

$$v = \frac{\ln\frac{K}{S} - 2a - \mu t}{\sigma\sqrt{t}} = -\frac{\ln\frac{S}{K} + \ln(H/S)^2 + \left(\lambda\sigma^2 - \sigma^2\right)t}{\sigma\sqrt{t}}$$

$$v = -\frac{\ln\frac{H^2}{SK} + \left(\lambda\sigma^2 - \sigma^2\right)t}{\sigma\sqrt{t}} = -[y - \sigma\sqrt{t}]$$

we have

$$y - \sigma\sqrt{t} = \frac{\ln\frac{H^2}{SK}}{\sigma\sqrt{t}} + \lambda\sigma\sqrt{t} - \sigma\sqrt{t}$$

and we can write

$$K(H/S)^{2\lambda-2}e^{-rt}\frac{1}{\sqrt{2\pi}}\int_{-\infty}^{[y-\sigma\sqrt{t}]} e^{-\frac{1}{2}v^2}dv$$

$$= e^{-rt}K\left(\frac{H}{S}\right)^{2\lambda-2} N(y - \sigma\sqrt{t})$$

The first integral using the Rubinstein and Reiner (1991) notation with $\eta = 1$ $\varphi = 1$

$$[3] = \phi Se^{-Dt}\left(\frac{H}{S}\right)^{2\lambda} N(\eta y) - \phi K\left(\frac{H}{S}\right)^{2\lambda-2} e^{-rt}N(\eta y - \eta\sigma\sqrt{t})$$

where

$$y = \frac{\ln\frac{H^2}{SK}}{\sigma\sqrt{t}} + \lambda\sigma\sqrt{t}$$

This is the probability that

$$P(S_t > K,\ S(\tau) \leq H) = \left(\frac{H}{S}\right)^{\frac{2\mu}{\sigma^2}} N\left(\frac{2a - x + \mu t}{\sigma\sqrt{t}}\right)$$

That is,

$$e^{-rt}E\left[\max(S_t - K, 0)1_{(S_t>K,\ S(\tau)\leq H)}\right]$$

We can easily and practically calculate the integral [3] as

$$\left(\frac{H}{S}\right)^{\frac{2\mu}{\sigma^2}} N\left(\frac{\ln\frac{H^2}{SK} + \mu t}{\sigma\sqrt{t}}\right)$$

and the result is

$$[3] = e^{-Dt}S_0\left(\frac{H}{S}\right)^{\frac{2(r-D)}{\sigma^2}+1} N\left(\frac{\ln\frac{H^2}{SK}+\mu t}{\sigma\sqrt{t}}\right)$$

$$-e^{-rt}K\left(\frac{H}{S}\right)^{\frac{2(r-D)}{\sigma^2}-1} N\left(\frac{\ln\frac{H^2}{SK}+\mu t}{\sigma\sqrt{t}}\right)$$

where $\mu = r - D + \frac{1}{2}\sigma^2$ and $\mu = r - D - \frac{1}{2}\sigma^2$ for the first and last terms, respectively.

This is the same with

$$\phi S e^{-Dt}\left(\frac{H}{S}\right)^{\frac{2(r-D)}{\sigma^2}+1} N(y) - \phi K\left(\frac{H}{S}\right)^{\frac{2(r-D)}{\sigma^2}-1} e^{-rt}N(y-\sigma\sqrt{t})$$

Now, we calculate the value of the rebate. This is the probability of not hitting the barrier. We can define this simply as $P\,(S(t) > H)$. However, there may be paths at which the asset price breaches the barrier, but again, it gets above the barrier at expiration. This is

$$P\,(S(t) > H\,|S(\tau) \le H\,)$$

Therefore, we must subtract the probability of the cases where the barrier is hit. The relevant probability is

$$P\,(S(t) > H) - P\,(S\,(t) > H, \quad S(\tau) \le H)$$

The expected present value of the rebate is then given with the integral [5] with Rubinstein and Reiner (1991) notation

$$[5] = e^{-rt}R\int_{\ln\, H/S}^{\infty}\{f(u) - g(u)\}\,du$$

$$= e^{-rt}R\left\{N(\eta x_1 - \eta\sigma\sqrt{t}) - \left(\frac{H}{S}\right)^{2\lambda-2} N(\eta y_1 - \eta\sigma\sqrt{t})\right\}$$

We know that

$$f(u) = \frac{1}{\sigma\sqrt{2\pi t}}\exp\left(-\frac{v^2}{2}\right)$$

$$v = \frac{u-\mu t}{\sigma\sqrt{t}} \quad \mu = \left(r - D - \frac{1}{2}\sigma^2\right)$$

Writing

$$\frac{1}{\sqrt{2\pi}}\int_{\frac{-\ln\frac{S}{H}-\left(r-D-\frac{1}{2}\sigma^2\right)t}{\sigma\sqrt{t}}}^{\infty} e^{-\frac{v^2}{2}}dv$$

we obtain

$$\frac{1}{\sqrt{2\pi}}\int_{-\infty}^{\frac{\ln\frac{S}{H}+\left(r-D-\frac{1}{2}\sigma^2\right)t}{\sigma\sqrt{t}}} e^{-\frac{v^2}{2}}dv$$

After a simple algebra

$$\frac{\ln\frac{S}{H}+\left(r-D-\frac{1}{2}\sigma^2\right)t}{\sigma\sqrt{t}}=\frac{\ln\frac{S}{H}+(\lambda\sigma^2-\sigma^2)t}{\sigma\sqrt{t}}=\frac{\ln\frac{S}{H}+\lambda\sigma^2 t}{\sigma\sqrt{t}}-\sigma\sqrt{t}$$

$$x_1=\frac{\ln\frac{S}{H}+\lambda\sigma^2 t}{\sigma\sqrt{t}}=\frac{\ln\frac{S}{H}}{\sigma\sqrt{t}}+\lambda\sigma\sqrt{t}$$

the upper limit of the integral can be expressed

$$x_1-\sigma\sqrt{t}$$

where

$$x_1=\frac{\ln\frac{S}{H}}{\sigma\sqrt{t}}+\lambda\sigma\sqrt{t}$$

$$e^{-rt}RN(\eta x_1-\eta\sigma\sqrt{t})$$

with $\eta=1$.

For $g(u)$, we write

$$-\frac{e^{2\mu a/\sigma^2}}{\sqrt{2\pi}}\int_{\ln H/S}^{\infty} e^{-\frac{v^2}{2}}dv$$

and

$$v=\frac{u-2a-\mu t}{\sigma\sqrt{t}}$$

Then

$$-v=\frac{-\ln\frac{S}{H}-\ln\left(\frac{H}{S}\right)^2-(\lambda\sigma^2-\sigma^2)t}{\sigma\sqrt{t}}$$

With some algebra

$$\frac{-\ln\frac{S}{H}-\ln\left(\frac{H}{S}\right)^2-(\lambda\sigma^2-\sigma^2)t}{\sigma\sqrt{t}}=\frac{-\ln\frac{H}{S}-(\lambda\sigma^2-\sigma^2)t}{\sigma\sqrt{t}}$$
$$=-\frac{\ln\frac{H}{S}+(\lambda\sigma^2-\sigma^2)t}{\sigma\sqrt{t}}$$

and changing the integral limits and defining

$$y_1=\frac{\ln\frac{H}{S}}{\sigma\sqrt{t}}+\lambda\sigma\sqrt{t}$$

we obtain the upper integral limit as

$$\frac{\ln\frac{H}{S}+(\lambda\sigma^2-\sigma^2)t}{\sigma\sqrt{t}}=\frac{\ln\frac{H}{S}}{\sigma\sqrt{t}}+\lambda\sigma\sqrt{t}-\sigma\sqrt{t}=y_1-\sigma\sqrt{t}$$

Then, the rebate value is

$$[5]=e^{-rt}R\left\{N\left(\eta x_1-\eta\acute{o}\sqrt{t}\right)-\left(\frac{H}{S}\right)^{2\lambda-2}N(\eta y_1-\eta\sigma\sqrt{t})\right\}$$

where

$$e^{2\mu a/\sigma^2}=\left(\frac{H}{S}\right)^{2\lambda-2}$$

and $\lambda=\frac{\mu}{\sigma^2}+1$.

Once again, by applying the cumulative probability distributions with the proper integral limits, we can simply write the expected value of the rebate as

$$P(S(t)>H)-P(S(t)>H,S(\tau)\leq H)$$
$$e^{-rT}*R*\left[N\left(\frac{\ln\frac{S}{H}+(r-D-\frac{1}{2}\sigma^2)t}{\sigma\sqrt{t}}\right)\right.$$
$$\left.-\left(\frac{H}{S}\right)^{\frac{2(r-D)}{\sigma^2}-1}N\left(\frac{2\ln\frac{H}{S}-\ln H/S+(r-D-\frac{1}{2}\sigma^2)t}{\sigma\sqrt{t}}\right)\right]$$

In summary, the value of C_{di} for $K > H$ and $\eta = 1$

$$C_{di}^{K>H} = [3] + [5]$$

$$C_{di}^{K>H} = Se^{-Dt}\left(\frac{H}{S}\right)^{2\lambda} N(\eta y) - K\left(\frac{H}{S}\right)^{2\lambda-2} e^{-rt} N\left(\eta y - \eta\sigma\sqrt{t}\right)$$
$$+ e^{-rt} R \left\{ N\left(\eta x_1 - \eta\sigma\sqrt{t}\right) - \left(\frac{H}{S}\right)^{2\lambda-2} N(\eta y_1 - \eta\sigma\sqrt{t}) \right\}$$

where

$$y = \frac{\ln \frac{H^2}{SK} + \lambda\sigma^2 t}{\sigma\sqrt{t}} = \frac{\ln \frac{H^2}{SK}}{\sigma\sqrt{t}} + \lambda\sigma\sqrt{t}$$

$$x_1 = \frac{\ln \frac{S}{H} + \lambda\sigma^2 t}{\sigma\sqrt{t}} = \frac{\ln \frac{S}{H}}{\sigma\sqrt{t}} + \lambda\sigma\sqrt{t}$$

$$y_1 = \frac{\ln \frac{H}{S}}{\sigma\sqrt{t}} + \lambda\sigma\sqrt{t}$$

$$\lambda = 1 + \frac{\mu}{\sigma^2}$$

3.2.1.2. *Down and in call C_{di} $K < H$ case*

To be entitled to receive the payoff, we need $S(\tau) \leq H$ for some $\tau \leq t$. Therefore, the asset price must breach the barrier and be greater than K at maturity. As before, never hitting the barrier requires rebate payment. The relevant probabilities to be considered for $K < H$ case is:

$$P(S(\tau) \leq H, S(t) > H)$$
$$P(H \geq S(t) > K)$$

and

$$P(S(t) > H) - P(S(t) > H, S(\tau) \leq H)$$

for the rebate. The last probability is the same with the $K > H$ case. Therefore, the rebate is equal to [5] as before.

The relevant density for the first probability is again $g(u)$ ($\eta = 1$) down density. But the integration lower limit is $\ln H/S$. This covers all the cases where the integral variable is above $\ln H/S (S > H)$.

The second probability covers the region between $H - K$. Since the probability of $P(H \geq S(t) > K)$ is

$$P(H \geq S(t) > K) = P(S(t) > K) - P(S(t) > H)$$

we may consider the integrals of $g(u)$ with $\ln H/S$ and $f(u)$ with $\ln K/S$ and $\ln H/S$, and we can calculate the cumulative probability of this region as

$$P(S(t) > K) - P(S(t) > H)$$

The density to be used is $f(u)$ for both probabilities but with different integral limits $\ln K/S$ and $\ln H/S$, respectively.

$$\begin{aligned}
[1] &= e^{-rt} \int_{\ln K/S}^{\infty} \phi(Se^u - K) f(u) du \\
&= \phi S e^{-Dt} N(\phi x) - \phi e^{-rt} K N(\phi x - \phi\sigma\sqrt{t}) \\
x &= \frac{\ln S/K}{\sigma\sqrt{t}} + \lambda\sigma\sqrt{t}\, \phi = \eta = 1
\end{aligned}$$

or

$$\begin{aligned}
x &= \frac{\ln \frac{S}{K} + \left(r - D + \frac{1}{2}\sigma^2\right) t}{\sigma\sqrt{t}} \\
[2] &= e^{-rt} \int_{\ln H/S}^{\infty} \phi(Se^u - K) f(u) du = \phi S e^{-Dt} N(\phi x_1) \\
&\quad - \phi e^{-rt} K N(\phi x_1 - \phi\sigma\sqrt{t}) \\
x_1 &= \frac{\ln \frac{S}{H} + \lambda\sigma^2 t}{\sigma\sqrt{t}} = \frac{\ln \frac{S}{H}}{\sigma\sqrt{t}} + \lambda\sigma\sqrt{t}
\end{aligned}$$

On top of those, we have to add the situations requiring the first probability:

$$P(S(\tau) \leq H, S(t) > H)$$

That is, in addition to the region $H - K$, which is given by [1–2], we have to add the possibility of breaching the barrier and staying over the barrier at maturity. This is the integral

$$[4] = e^{-rt}\int_{\ln H/S}^{\infty}(Se^{u}-K)g(u)du = \phi Se^{-Dt}(H/S)^{2\lambda}N(\eta y_1)$$
$$-\phi e^{-rt}K(H/S)^{2\lambda-2}N(\eta y_1-\eta\sigma\sqrt{t})$$
$$y_1 = \frac{\ln\frac{H}{S}}{\sigma\sqrt{t}}+\lambda\sigma\sqrt{t}$$

with $g(u)$ the down density but for integral limit $\ln H/S$ this time.

Finally, the value of $C_{di}^{K<H}$ is

$$C_{di}^{K<H} = 1-2+4+5\,\eta = \phi = 1$$

If we simply use the cumulative distribution probabilities. [1] is simply BS price with $\ln K/S$ and [2] is also BS price with $\ln H/S$. The last one is our restricted probability with $\ln H/S$.

$$\mu = r-D+\frac{1}{2}\sigma^2 \quad \text{and} \quad \mu = r-D-\frac{1}{2}\sigma^2$$

$$\begin{aligned}
C_{di}^{K<H} &= Se^{-Dt}N\left[\frac{\ln\frac{S}{K}+(r-D+\frac{1}{2}\sigma^2)t}{\sigma\sqrt{t}}\right]\\
&\quad - e^{-rt}KN\left[\frac{\ln\frac{S}{K}+\left(r-D-\frac{1}{2}\sigma^2\right)t}{\sigma\sqrt{t}}\right]\\
&\quad - Se^{-Dt}N\left[\frac{\ln\frac{S}{H}+\left(r-D+\frac{1}{2}\sigma^2\right)t}{\sigma\sqrt{t}}\right]\\
&\quad + e^{-rt}KN\left[\frac{\ln\frac{S}{H}+\left(r-D-\frac{1}{2}\sigma^2\right)t}{\sigma\sqrt{t}}\right]\\
&\quad + e^{-Dt}S_0\left(\frac{H}{S}\right)^{\frac{2(r-D)}{\sigma^2}+1}N\left(\frac{\ln\frac{H}{S}+\left(r-D+\frac{1}{2}\sigma^2\right)t}{\sigma\sqrt{t}}\right)
\end{aligned}$$

$$- e^{-rt} K \left(\frac{H}{S}\right)^{\frac{2(r-D)}{\sigma^2}-1} N\left(\frac{\ln \frac{H}{S} + \left(r - D - \frac{1}{2}\sigma^2\right)t}{\sigma\sqrt{t}}\right)$$

$$+ e^{-rT} * R$$

$$* \left[N\left(\frac{\ln \frac{S}{H} + (r - D - \frac{1}{2}\sigma^2)t}{\sigma\sqrt{t}}\right)\right.$$

$$\left. - \left(\frac{H}{S}\right)^{\frac{2(r-D)}{\sigma^2}-1} N\left(\frac{\ln \frac{H}{S} + (r - D - \frac{1}{2}\sigma^2)t}{\sigma\sqrt{t}}\right)\right]$$

3.2.2. *Up-and-in call* C_{ui}

The initial asset price is below the barrier for up and in call. If the price breaches the barrier from below, the holder of the option is entitled to receive the call payoff; otherwise receives a rebate at expiration.

Similarly, we may have two different cases by construction: $K > H$ and $K < H$. Table 3.2 gives the whole structure for up-and-in calls.

$$C_{ui}\ (S < H)$$

Table 3.2. Conditional payoff structure for up-and-in call.

$K > H$	Conditional on	Payoff	Probability
$S(t) > K$		$S(t) - K$	$P\left(S(t) > K\right)$
$S(t) \leq K$	$S(\tau) \geq H$ for some $\tau \leq t$	0	
$S(\tau) < H$	For all $\tau \leq t$	Rebate	$+P(S(t) < H) - P(S(t) < H, S(\tau) \geq H)$
$K < H$			
$S(t) \geq H$		$S(t) - K$	$P\left(S(t) \geq H\right)$
$S(t) > K$	$S(\tau) \geq H$ for	$S(t) - K$	$+P(H > S(t) > K, S(\tau) \geq H)$
$S(t) < H$	some $\tau \leq t$		
$S(\tau) \leq K$		0	
$S(\tau) < H$	For all $\tau \leq t$	Rebate	$+P(S(t) < H) - P(S(t) < H, S(\tau) \geq H)$

Payoff Condition:

$\max(0, S(t) - K)$ for $\tau \le t,\ S(\tau) \ge H$
Rebate for $\tau \le t,\ S(\tau) < H$

3.2.2.1. *Up and in call* C_{ui} $K > H$ *case*

Since $K > H$, the relevant probability is $P(S(t) > K)$. The option has a value if and only if $S(t) > K$. If this condition is satisfied, it already means that the option has been knocked in. For this probability, the relevant density function is $f(u)$, and the lower integral limit is $\ln K/S$. Therefore, the first component is integral [1]

$$[1] = e^{-rt} \int_{\ln\ K/S}^{\infty} \phi\,(Se^u - K)\, f(u)du = \phi S e^{-Dt} N(\phi x)$$
$$- \phi e^{-rt} K N(\phi x - \phi\sigma\sqrt{t})$$

Similarly, for the rebate, we need the probability of $P(S(t) < H)$. But we have to deduct the cases that $P(S(\tau) \ge H)$ for some $\tau \le t$ but $P(S(t) < H$ which is

$$P(S(t) < H) - P(S(\tau) \ge H \quad S(t) < H)$$

This means the relevant density is $f(u) - g(u)$ with $\eta = -1$ and

$$v = \frac{u + 2a + \mu t}{\sigma\sqrt{t}}$$

$$[5] = e^{-rt} R \left\{ N\left(\eta x_1 - \eta\sigma\sqrt{t}\right) - \left(\frac{H}{S}\right)^{2\lambda - 2} N(\eta y_1 - \eta\sigma\sqrt{t}) \right\} \eta = -1$$

recalling

$$x_1 = \frac{\ln \frac{S}{H} + \lambda\sigma^2 t}{\sigma\sqrt{t}}$$

$$y_1 = \frac{\ln \frac{H}{S}}{\sigma\sqrt{t}} + \lambda\sigma\sqrt{t}$$

For $P(S(t) < H)$, the upper integral limit is ln H/S, and the probability is

$$N\left(\frac{-\ln\frac{S}{H}-\mu t}{\sigma\sqrt{t}}\right)=N\left(\frac{-\ln\frac{S}{H}-(\lambda\sigma^2-\sigma^2)t}{\sigma\sqrt{t}}\right)$$
$$=-\frac{\ln\frac{S}{H}+\lambda\sigma^2 t}{\sigma\sqrt{t}}+\sigma\sqrt{t}=-x_1+\sigma\sqrt{t}$$

or

$$N\left(\frac{-\ln\frac{S}{H}-\left((r-D-\frac{1}{2}\sigma^2)\right)t}{\sigma\sqrt{t}}\right)$$

For

$$P(S(\tau)\geq H \qquad S(t)<H)$$

the probability is

$$\left(\frac{H}{S}\right)^{\frac{2\mu}{\sigma^2}}N\left(\frac{u-2a-\mu t}{\sigma\sqrt{t}}\right)$$
$$\left(\frac{H}{S}\right)^{\frac{2\mu}{\sigma^2}}N\left(\frac{-\ln H/S-\mu T}{\sigma\sqrt{t}}\right)=\left(\frac{H}{S}\right)^{\frac{2\mu}{\sigma^2}}N\left(-\frac{\ln\frac{H}{S}+\lambda\sigma^2 t}{\sigma\sqrt{t}}+\sigma\sqrt{t}\right)$$
$$=-y_1+\sigma\sqrt{t}$$

Therefore, the price of $C_{ui}^{K>H}(S<H)$ is

$$C_{ui}^{K>H}(S<H)=[1]+[5]\,\eta=-1\,\phi=1$$
$$C_{ui}^{K>H}=Se^{-Dt}N(x)-e^{-rt}KN\left(x-\sigma\sqrt{t}\right)$$
$$+e^{-rt}R\left\{N(-x_1+\sigma\sqrt{t})-\left(\frac{H}{S}\right)^{2\lambda-2}N(-y_1+\sigma\sqrt{t})\right\}$$

where the first part is exactly the Black–Scholes price.

3.2.2.2. *Up and in call* C_{ui} $K < H$ *case*

We need the probability for the values greater than H; $P(S(t) \geq H)$

This integral contains all the values over H, and the payoff condition is satisfied.

$$[2] = e^{-rt} \int_{\ln\ H/S = \phi S e^{-Dt} N(\phi x_1) - \phi e^{-rt} K N(\phi x_1 - \phi\sigma\sqrt{t})}^{\infty} \phi(Se^u - K) f(u) du$$

where $\phi = 1$.

For the region $H - K$, we need the probability

$$\begin{aligned} &P(H > S(t) > K;\ S(\tau) \geq H) \\ &\quad = P(S(t) < H, S(\tau) \geq H) - P(S(t) < K, S(\tau) \geq H) \end{aligned}$$

That means the asset price must breach the barrier first, then fall and remain over K. Then, the difference $H - K$ has a value where the barrier is breached, and the asset price remains less than H but greater than K.

Therefore, the density is $g(u)$ for both cases. The positive value is integral [4] with a lower limit ln K/S, and the negative value is integral [3] with a lower limit ln K/S.

So, the price of $C_{ui}^{K<H}$

$$C_{ui}^{K<H}(S < H) = [2] - [3] + [4] + [5]\, \eta = -1 \qquad \phi = 1$$

Note that the integral limits of [3] are actually $-\infty, \ln\frac{K}{S}$, and similarly, they are $-\infty, \ln\frac{H}{S}$ for integral [4]. We obtain the same by simply attaching $\eta = -1$ to previous integrals.

The barrier must be hit, and the asset price must be above it since the barrier is higher than the strike by construction. It is the integral [4] with Rubinstein and Reiner's (1991) notation.

We write the equation as

$$\begin{aligned} &\exp(-rt)\frac{1}{\sqrt{2\pi}} \int_{-\infty}^{\ln H/S} (Se^u - K)\exp\left\{\frac{2\mu a}{\sigma^2}\right\} \\ &\exp -\frac{1}{2}\left(\frac{u - 2a - \mu t}{\sigma\sqrt{t}}\right)^2 du \end{aligned}$$

because we want the asset values less than H.

$$\exp(-rt)\frac{1}{\sqrt{2\pi}}\int_{-\infty}^{(-\ln\frac{H}{S}-\mu t)/\sigma\sqrt{t}}\left(Se^{v\sigma\sqrt{t}+2a+\mu t}-K\right)\exp\left\{\frac{2\mu a}{\sigma^2}\right\}$$
$$\times\exp\left(-\frac{v^2}{2}\right)dv$$

where

$$v=\frac{u-2a-\mu t}{\sigma\sqrt{t}}\quad a=\ln\frac{H}{S}\quad\mu=\left(r-D-\frac{1}{2}\sigma^2\right)$$

and $dv\sigma\sqrt{t}=du$. Let's evaluate the first term.

Canceling r and drawing D from $\mu=(r-D-\frac{1}{2}\sigma^2)$

$$\frac{Se^{-Dt}}{\sqrt{2\pi}}\int_{-\infty}^{(-\ln\frac{H}{S}-\mu t)/\sigma\sqrt{t}}\left(e^{v\sigma\sqrt{t}-\frac{1}{2}\sigma^2 t}\right)\exp\left\{\frac{2\mu a}{\sigma^2}+2a\right\}\exp\left(-\frac{v^2}{2}\right)dv$$

$$\frac{Se^{-Dt}}{\sqrt{2\pi}}\int_{-\infty}^{(-\ln\frac{H}{S}-\mu t)/\sigma\sqrt{t}}\exp\left\{2a\left(\frac{\mu}{\sigma^2}+1\right)\right\}\exp\left(-\frac{\left(v-\sigma\sqrt{t}\right)^2}{2}\right)dv$$

$$=\frac{-\ln\frac{H}{S}-\left(r-D-\frac{1}{2}\sigma^2\right)t}{\sigma\sqrt{t}}-\sigma\sqrt{t}$$

we obtain the upper limit as

$$v=\frac{-\ln\frac{H}{S}-\left(r-D+\frac{1}{2}\sigma^2\right)t}{\sigma\sqrt{t}}$$

So the first part is

$$\frac{Se^{-Dt}}{\sqrt{2\pi}}\int_{-\infty}^{\frac{-\ln\ \frac{H}{S}-\left(r-D+\frac{1}{2}\sigma^2\right)t}{\sigma\sqrt{t}}}\exp\left\{2a\left(\frac{\mu}{\sigma^2}+1\right)\right\}\exp\left(-\frac{v^2}{2}\right)dv$$

As we apply the transformation in Rubinstein and Reiner (1991) $\lambda=\frac{\mu}{\sigma^2}+1$ the expression of

$\exp\left(2a(\frac{\mu}{\sigma^2}+1)\right)$ using $a = \ln H/S$ is

$$e^{(\ln\ H/S))^{2\lambda}} = \left(\frac{H}{S}\right)^{2\lambda}$$

Also, if we draw μ from $\lambda = \frac{\mu}{\sigma^2}+1$ we obtain

$$\left(r - D - \frac{1}{2}\sigma^2\right) = \mu = \lambda\sigma^2 - \sigma^2$$

and putting back in the formula we obtain the integral limit as

$$\frac{-\ln\frac{H}{S} - \left(r - D - \frac{1}{2}\sigma^2\right)t}{\sigma\sqrt{t}} - \sigma\sqrt{t} = -\frac{\ln\frac{H}{S} + \left(r - D + \frac{1}{2}\sigma^2\right)t}{\sigma\sqrt{t}} =$$

Therefore, the first part is

$$Se^{-Dt}(H/S)^{2\lambda}\frac{1}{\sqrt{2\pi}}\int_{-\infty}^{-\frac{\ln\ \frac{H}{S}+\left(r-D+\frac{1}{2}\sigma^2\right)t}{\sigma\sqrt{t}}} e^{-\frac{1}{2}v^2}dv$$

$$= Se^{-Dt}\left(\frac{H}{S}\right)^{2\lambda}N(-y_1)$$

$$-y_1 = -\frac{\ln\frac{H}{S}}{\sigma\sqrt{t}} - \lambda\sigma\sqrt{t} = -\frac{\ln\frac{H}{S} + \left(r - D + \frac{1}{2}\sigma^2\right)t}{\sigma\sqrt{t}}$$

We do a similar algebra for the second integral.

$$Ke^{-rt}\frac{1}{\sqrt{2\pi}}\int_{\ln K/S}^{-\frac{\ln\frac{H}{S}+\left(r-D-\frac{1}{2}\sigma^2\right)t}{\sigma\sqrt{t}}} \exp\left\{2a\frac{\mu}{\sigma^2}\right\}e^{-\frac{1}{2}v^2}dv$$

Since

$$\mu = \lambda\sigma^2 - \sigma^2 \exp\left\{\frac{2a\mu}{\sigma^2}\right\} = \exp\left[2a(\lambda - 1)\right]$$

$$K(H/S)^{2\lambda-2}e^{-rt}\frac{1}{\sqrt{2\pi}}\int_{-\infty}^{(-\ln\frac{H}{S}-\mu t)/\sigma\sqrt{t}} e^{-\frac{1}{2}v^2}dv$$

$$\frac{-\ln\frac{H}{S} - \left(r - D - \frac{1}{2}\sigma^2\right)t}{\sigma\sqrt{t}} - \sigma\sqrt{t} = -\frac{\ln\frac{H}{S} + \left(r - D + \frac{1}{2}\sigma^2\right)t}{\sigma\sqrt{t}}$$

$$-\frac{\ln\frac{H}{S} + \left(r - D - \frac{1}{2}\sigma^2\right)t}{\sigma\sqrt{t}} = -\frac{\ln\ \frac{H}{S} + \left(r - D + \frac{1}{2}\sigma^2\right)t}{\sigma\sqrt{t}}$$

$$+\sigma\sqrt{t} = -[y_1 - \sigma\sqrt{t}] - \frac{\ln\frac{H}{S} + \left(\lambda\sigma^2 - \sigma^2\right)t}{\sigma\sqrt{t}}$$

$$-y_1 + \sigma\sqrt{t} = -\frac{\ln\frac{H}{S}}{\sigma\sqrt{t}} - \lambda\sigma\sqrt{t} + \sigma\sqrt{t}$$

we can write:

$$K(H/S)^{2\lambda-2}e^{-rt}\frac{1}{\sqrt{2\pi}}\int_{-\infty}^{[-y_1+\sigma\sqrt{t}]} e^{-\frac{1}{2}v^2}dv$$

$$= e^{-rt}K\left(\frac{H}{S}\right)^{2\lambda-2}N(-y_1+\sigma\sqrt{t})$$

$$Se^{-Dt}e^{\frac{2\mu a}{\sigma^2}+2a}\frac{1}{\sqrt{2\pi}}\int_{-\infty}^{-y_1}\exp\left(-\frac{1}{2}v^2\right)dv$$

$$= \phi Se^{-Dt}\left(\frac{H}{S}\right)^{2\lambda}N(\eta y_1) \quad \eta = -1$$

$[4] = \phi Se^{-Dt}\left(\frac{H}{S}\right)^{2\lambda}N(\eta y_1) - e^{-rt}K\left(\frac{H}{S}\right)^{2\lambda-2}N(-y_1+\sigma\sqrt{t})\eta = -1$ for up-and-in option.

Applying the same for [3] and density $g(u)$

$$\exp(-rt)\frac{1}{\sqrt{2\pi}}\int_{-\infty}^{\ln K/S}(Se^u - K)\exp\left\{\frac{2\mu a}{\sigma^2}\right\}\exp$$

$$-\frac{1}{2}\left(\frac{u-2a-\mu t}{\sigma\sqrt{t}}\right)^2 du$$

we write the price as

$$C_{ui}^{K<H}(S<H) = [2] - [3] + [4] + [5] \quad \eta = -1, \quad \phi = 1$$

3.3. Put Options (In)

3.3.1. *Down and in put $P_{di}(S > H)$*

Like down and in calls, the option is effective if the asset price breaches the barrier and is void otherwise. The only difference is the payoff, which is put and has value if the asset price ends up below

Table 3.3. Conditional payoff structure for down-and-in put.

$K > H$	Conditional on	Payoff	Probability
$S(\tau) > H$	For all $\tau \leq t$	Rebate	$P(S(t) > H) - P(S(t) > H, S(\tau) \leq H)$
$S(t) \leq H$		$K - S(t)$	$P(S(t) \leq H)$
$S(\tau) \leq H$ $K > S > H$	For some $\tau \leq t$	$K - S(t)$	$P(S(\tau) \leq H,\ S(t) > H) - P(S(t) > K,$ $S(\tau) \leq H)$
$S(t) > K$		0	
$K < H$			
$S(t) > H$		Rebate	$P(S(t) > H) - P(S(t) > H, S(\tau) \leq H)$
$S(t) > K$		0	
$S(\tau) \leq K$	For all $\tau \leq t$	$K - S(t)$	$P(S(t) < K)$

the exercise price at expiration. Table 3.3 gives the whole structure for down-and-in puts.

$$P_{di}\ (S > H)$$

Payoff Condition:

$\max(0, K - S(t))$ for some $\tau \leq t,\ S(\tau) \leq H$
Rebate for all $\tau \leq t,\ S(\tau) > H$

3.3.1.1. *Down-and-in put $K > H$ case*

The first row is the probability of a rebate. This is the integral [5]. Since the density is down and the payoff function is for put, we will be using $\eta = 1$ and $\phi = -1$.

$$N\left(\frac{-\ln\frac{H}{S} + \mu t}{\sigma\sqrt{t}}\right) - \left(\frac{H}{S}\right)^{\frac{2\mu}{\sigma^2}} N\left(\frac{-\ln H/S + 2\ln\frac{H}{S} + \mu t}{\sigma\sqrt{t}}\right)$$

$$= N(x_1) - \left(\frac{H}{S}\right)^{\frac{2\mu}{\sigma^2}} N(y_1 - \sigma\sqrt{t})$$

So, the rebate is:

$$[5] = e^{-rt}R\left\{N(x_1) - \left(\frac{H}{S}\right)^{2\lambda-2} N(y_1 - \sigma\sqrt{t})\right\}$$

The value of the payoff in the second row is calculated by integral [2]. Because the density is $f(u)$ and the upper integral limit is $\ln H/S$ for the payoff.

$$[2] = e^{-rt} \int_{-\infty}^{\ln H/S} (K - Se^u) f(u) du \ \phi = -1$$

First term

$$e^{-rt} \frac{K}{\sigma\sqrt{2\pi t}} \int_{-\infty}^{\frac{\ln H/S - \mu t}{\sigma\sqrt{t}}} e^{-\frac{1}{2}v^2} dv$$

$$\frac{\ln H/S - \mu t}{\sigma\sqrt{t}} = -\left[\frac{\ln\frac{S}{H}}{\sigma\sqrt{t}} + \lambda\sigma\sqrt{t}\right] + \sigma\sqrt{t} = -x_1 + \sigma\sqrt{t}$$

$$Ke^{-rt} N\left(-x_1 + \sigma\sqrt{t}\right) = Ke^{-rt} N\left(\phi x_1 - \phi\sigma\sqrt{t}\right) \quad \phi = -1$$

The second term, with

$$e^{u - \frac{1}{2}v^2}$$

and

$$-\left[\frac{\ln\frac{S}{H}}{\sigma\sqrt{t}} + \lambda\sigma\sqrt{t}\right] + \sigma\sqrt{t} - \sigma\sqrt{t} = -x_1$$

will be obtained as

$$Se^{-Dt} N(\phi x_1) \, \phi = -1$$

$$[2] = Ke^{-rt} N(-x_1 + \sigma\sqrt{t}) - Se^{-Dt} N\left(-x_1\right)$$

Finally, the density for the third row is $g(u)$. Depending on the hitting condition, we take the asset prices more than H but less than K where the integration limits are $\ln H/S$ and $\ln K/S$. This is the region $K - H$ and computed by the integrals [4] and [3]

$$[4] = e^{-rt} \int_{\ln H/S}^{\infty} (K - Se^u) g(u) du = \phi Se^{-Dt} (H/S)^{2\lambda} N(\eta y_1)$$
$$-\phi e^{-rt} K (H/S)^{2\lambda - 2} N(\eta y_1 - \eta\sigma\sqrt{t})$$

$$[3] = \exp(-rt)\int_{\ln K/S}^{\infty}(K - Se^{u})g(u)du = \phi S e^{-Dt}\left(\frac{H}{S}\right)^{2\lambda} N(\eta y)$$
$$-\phi K\left(\frac{H}{S}\right)^{2\lambda-2} e^{-rt}N(\eta y - \eta\sigma\sqrt{t})$$

where $\phi = -1$ $\eta = 1$.

Therefore, the value of $P_{di}^{K>H}$ is

$$P_{di}^{K>H} = [2] - [3] + [4] + [5]$$

3.3.1.2. *Down-and-in put P_{di} $K < H$ case*

For $P_{di}^{K<H}$, there is only one payoff condition because if the put option is in the money, this probability also contains the hitting probability. The option cannot be in the money if it does not breach the barrier. So, we can calculate $P(S(t) < K)$ with $f(u)$, $\phi = -1$ and integral upper limit with $\ln K/S$. This is integral [1] with $\eta = 1$ and $\phi = -1$.

$$[1] = e^{-rt}\int_{\ln K/S}^{\infty}\phi(Se^{u} - K)f(u)du = \phi S e^{-Dt}N(\phi x)$$
$$- \phi e^{-rt}KN(\phi x - \phi\sigma\sqrt{t})$$

Writing

$$e^{-rt}\int_{-\infty}^{\ln K/S}(K - Se^{u})f(u)du = e^{-rt}KN(-x + \sigma\sqrt{t}) - Se^{-Dt}N(-x)$$

where

$$x = \frac{\ln\frac{S}{K} + \left(r - D + \frac{1}{2}\sigma^{2}\right)t}{\sigma\sqrt{t}} = \frac{\ln\frac{S}{K}}{\sigma\sqrt{t}} + \lambda\sigma\sqrt{t}$$

$P_{di}^{K<H}$ price is

$$P_{di}^{K<H} = [1] + [5]$$

Table 3.4. Conditional payoff structure for up-and-in put.

$K > H$	Conditional on	Payoff	Probability
$S(\tau) < H$	For all $\tau \leq t$	Rebate	$P(S(t) < H) - P(S(t) < H, S(\tau) \geq H)$
$S(t) \leq H$		$K - S(t)$	$P(S(\tau) \geq H,\ S(t) < H)$
$K > S \geq H$	For some $\tau \leq t$	$K - S(t)$	$P(S(t) < K) - P(S(t) < H)$
$S(t) > K$		0	
$K < H$			
$S(t) < H$		Rebate	$P(S(t) < H) - P(S(t) < H, S(\tau) \geq H)$
$S(\tau) \geq H$	For some $\tau \leq t$	$K - S(t)$	$P(S(t) < K,\ S(\tau) \geq H)$

3.3.2. *Up-and-in put* P_{ui} $(S < H)$

The option is in if the barrier is crossed from below at any time until expiration. Table 3.4 summarizes the probabilities and payoffs.

Payoff Condition:

$\max(0, K - S(t))$ for some $\tau \leq t,\ S(\tau) \geq H$
Rebate for all $\tau \leq t,\ S(\tau) < H$

3.3.2.1. *Up-and-in put* P_{ui} $K < H$ *case*

To be entitled to receive the payoff, the asset price must breach the barrier first; then, it must fall below K. This is the only probability to be considered. The relevant density is $g(u)$ with $\eta = -1$, and the integral upper limit is $\ln K/S$. $(\phi = -1)$. Therefore, the price is

$$P_{ui}^{K<H} = [3] + [5] \quad \eta = -1 \quad \phi = -1$$

The probability is

$$P(S(t) < K,\ S(\tau) \geq H)$$

$$\left(\frac{H}{S}\right)^{\frac{2\mu}{\sigma^2}} N\left(\frac{u - 2a - \mu t}{\sigma\sqrt{t}}\right)$$

$$[3] = \exp(-rt)\left(\frac{H}{S}\right)^{\frac{2\mu}{\sigma^2}} \int_{-\infty}^{\ln K/S} (K - Se^{u}) \frac{1}{\sigma\sqrt{2\pi t}} e^{-\frac{1}{2}\left(\frac{u-2a-\mu t}{\sigma\sqrt{t}}\right)^2} du$$

$$= \exp(-rt)\left(\frac{H}{S}\right)^{\frac{2\mu}{\sigma^2}} \int_{-\infty}^{\left(-\frac{\ln H^2/SK+\mu t}{\sigma\sqrt{t}}\right)} (K - Se^{v\sigma\sqrt{t}+2a+\mu t})$$

$$\times \frac{1}{\sqrt{2\pi}} e^{-\frac{1}{2}(v)^2} dv$$

$$= \exp(-rt)K\frac{1}{\sqrt{2\pi}}\left(\frac{H}{S}\right)^{\frac{2\mu}{\sigma^2}} \int_{-\infty}^{\left(-\frac{\ln H^2/SK+\mu t}{\sigma\sqrt{t}}\right)} e^{-\frac{1}{2}(v)^2} dv$$

$$-\left(\frac{H}{S}\right)^{2(\frac{\mu}{\sigma^2}+1)} \frac{Se^{-Dt}}{\sqrt{2\pi}} \int_{-\infty}^{\left(-\frac{\ln H^2/SK+\mu t}{\sigma\sqrt{t}}\right)} e^{-\frac{1}{2}(v-\sigma\sqrt{t})^2} dv$$

$$= e^{-rt}K\left(\frac{H}{S}\right)^{2\lambda-2} N\left(-y+\sigma\sqrt{t}\right) - Se^{-Dt}\left(\frac{H}{S}\right)^{2\lambda} N(-y)$$

We do similar calculations for rebates but with different integral limits, with the sign $\eta = -1$.

3.3.2.2. *Up-and-in put P_{ui} $K > H$ case*

The first probability is that the asset price may hit the barrier but remain below it. This is

$$P(S(\tau) \geq H,\ S(t) < H)$$

and requires density $g(u)$ with upper limit $\ln H/S$. This is integral [4]. For the second probability, the asset price must be in the region $K > S > H$. So, we need the values between $K - H$. Then, the relevant density is (u) with upper limits $\ln K/S$ and $\ln H/S$, respectively. This is the difference between integrals [1] and [2]. Together with the rebate, the $P_{ui}^{K>H}$ price is

$$P_{ui}^{K>H} = [1] - [2] + [4] + [5] \quad \{\eta = -1 \quad \phi = -1\}$$

3.4. Call Options (Out)

3.4.1. *Down-and-out call* $C_{do}(S > H)$

Assume we are holding a covered call (short call, long stock) and would like to liquidate the position because the stock price falls sharply (see Rubinstein and Reiner, 1991). We could do the same thing with a down-and-out call, which automatically liquidates the position.

If the asset price breaches the barrier from above, the option holder is not entitled to receive the payoff, and she may be paid a rebate at hitting time. If the price remains above the barrier until maturity, she is entitled to receive the standard call payoff at expiration. Consider a manufacturer who needs a certain amount of raw material in 6 months. If she believes that the asset prices will rise, a down-and-out barrier call is the most suitable candidate to buy because it provides upside protection at a lower price than a vanilla call. However, if the prices fall, this would be a perfect opportunity to buy with the option expiring worthless. The only risk is the immediate increase in the raw material prices after the fall because of the vanished protection after the knock-out.

$$C_{do}\ (S > H)$$

Payoff Condition:

$\max(0, S(t) - K)$ for all $\tau \leq t,\ S(\tau) > H$
Rebate for some $\tau \leq t,\ S(\tau) \leq H$ at knock-out time (hit time)

One crucial difference relative to "in" options is the density function of the first passage time used to calculate the expected value of rebate payment. Since the parties are not in a position to wait until expiration and the option may be out at any time, we need the density of the first passage time given in Section 3.2.

The full terms are presented in Table 3.5.

3.4.1.1. *Down-and-out call* $K > H$ *case*

The asset price must be above K at expiration. Then, we must subtract the probabilities that the asset price breaches the barrier at

Table 3.5. Conditional payoff structure for down-and-out call.

$K > H$	Conditional on	Payoff	Probability
$S(\tau) > H$	For all $\tau \leq t$	$S(t) - K$	$P(S(t) > K) - P(S(t) > K, S(\tau) \leq H)$
$H < S(\tau) \leq K$	For all $\tau \leq t$	0	
$S(\tau) \leq H$	For some $\tau \leq t$	Rebate	$P(\tau_m \leq t)$
$K < H$			
$S(\tau) > H$	For all $\tau \leq t$	$S(t) - K$	$P(S(t) > H) - P(S(t) > H, S(\tau) \leq H)$
$S(\tau) \leq H$	For some $\tau \leq t$	Rebate	$P(\tau_m \leq t)$

some time $\tau \leq t$ but $S(t) > K$ at expiration. But these are the integrals [1] and [3] with densities $f(u)$ and $g(u)$. If we add the rebate, the price for $C_{do}^{K>H}$ is

$$C_{do}^{K>H} = [1] - [3] + [6] \; \eta = 1 \; \phi = 1$$

where

$$[6] = R \int_0^t e^{-r\tau} h(\tau) d\tau$$
$$= R \left\{ \left(\frac{H}{S}\right)^{a+b} N(\eta z) + \left(\frac{H}{S}\right)^{a-b} N(\eta z - 2\eta b \sigma \sqrt{t}) \right\}$$

and

$$z = \frac{\ln H/S}{\sigma\sqrt{t}} + b\sigma\sqrt{t} \quad a = \frac{\mu}{\sigma^2} \quad b = \frac{\sqrt{\mu^2 + 2(\ln r)\sigma^2}}{\sigma^2}$$

$$P(S(t) > K) - P(S(t) > K, S(\tau) \leq H) =$$

$$N\left(\frac{-\ln\frac{K}{S} + \mu t}{\sigma\sqrt{t}}\right) - \left(\frac{H}{S}\right)^{\frac{2\mu}{\sigma^2}} N\left(\frac{\ln\frac{S}{K} + 2\ln H/S + \mu t}{\sigma\sqrt{t}}\right)$$

This is very similar to the case $K > H$. But we discard the price levels of $K < S < H$; otherwise, the option gets void. Therefore, the lower limit of integrals is $\ln H/S$. The densities are the same, but integrals are [2] and [4]. So, the $C_{do}^{K<H}$price is

$$C_{do}^{K<H} = [2] - [4] + [6] \ \eta = 1 \ \phi = 1$$

$$P(S(t) > H) - P(S(t) > H, S(\tau) \leq H)$$

$$N\left(\frac{-\ln\frac{H}{S}+\mu t}{\sigma\sqrt{t}}\right) - \left(\frac{H}{S}\right)^{\frac{2\mu}{\sigma^2}} N\left(\frac{\ln\frac{S}{H}+2\ln H/S + \mu t}{\sigma\sqrt{t}}\right)$$

3.4.2. *Up-and-out call C_{uo}*

$$C_{uo}(S < H)$$

Payoff Condition:

$\max(0, S(t) - K)$ for all $\tau \leq t,\ S(\tau) < H$
Rebate for some $\tau \leq t,\ S(\tau) \geq H$ at knock-out time (hit time)

3.4.2.1. *Up-and-out call $\boldsymbol{K > H}$ case*

This is the simplest case because there is only one probability. When the asset price hits the barrier from below, the option pays only a rebate. So, the price is the expected present value of the rebate

$$C_{uo}^{K>H} = [6] \ \eta = -1 \ \phi = 1$$

3.4.2.2. *Up-and-out call $\boldsymbol{K < H}$ case*

The payoff is positive only in the region $K < S < H$.

We need the price levels and probabilities for the region $H - K$.

One probability is $P(S(t) > K)$, but we have to deduct the cases that $P(S(t) > H)$. The relevant density is $f(u)$ and the integrals are [1] and [2]:

$$P(S(t) > K) - P(S(t) > H)$$

These integrals cover up the cases at expiration. We have to deduct the cases where the barrier is not breached through the time at some time τ.

This is related to the probabilities

$$P(S(t) > K,\ S(\tau) \leq H) \quad \text{and} \quad P(S(t) > H,\ S(\tau) \leq H)$$

which correspond to integrals [3] and [4].

If we add the integral [3], we must subtract [4]; otherwise, we would have calculated the probability twice. In other words, we would have subtracted the probability of being greater than H at maturity but less than H until maturity from the probability of being greater than K at maturity but less than H in between. Then, we would have covered up all the probabilities between $H - K$. Adding the rebate, the price of $C_{uo}^{K<H}$ is

$$C_{uo}^{K<H} = [1] - [2] + [3] - [4] + [6] \quad \eta = -1\ \phi = 1$$

Note that the probability of $S(\tau) \leq H$ is not the same in $P(S(t) > K,$ $S(\tau) \leq H)$ and $P(S(t) > H,\ S(\tau) \leq H)$ for they are joint probabilities and the subtraction contributes a value to the price and avoids double counting.

$$P(S(t) > K,\ S(\tau) \leq H) = \left(\frac{H}{S}\right)^{\frac{2\mu}{\sigma^2}} N\left(\frac{\ln\frac{K}{S} - 2\ln H/S - \mu t}{\sigma\sqrt{t}}\right)$$

$$P(S(t) > H,\ S(\tau) \leq H) = \left(\frac{H}{S}\right)^{\frac{2\mu}{\sigma^2}} N\left(\frac{\ln\frac{H}{S} - 2\ln H/S - \mu t}{\sigma\sqrt{t}}\right)$$

3.5. Put Options (Out)

3.5.1. *Down-and-out put P_{do}*

$$P_{do}\ (S > H)$$

Payoff Condition:

$\max(0, K - S(t))$ for all $\tau \leq t,\ S(\tau) > H$

Rebate for some $\tau \leq t,\ S(\tau) \leq H$ at knock-out time. Tables 3.6 and 3.7 produce the conditional payoff structure for down-and-out and up-and-out puts.

3.5.1.1. *Down-and-out put $K < H$ case*

To have a positive payoff, the asset price must first cross the barrier, but this ends the process, and the option becomes void. Therefore, the price of $P_{do}^{K<H}$ consists only of the rebate.

$$P_{do}^{K<H} = [6] \quad \eta = 1 \quad \phi = -1$$

Table 3.6. Conditional payoff structure for down-and-out put.

$K > H$	Conditional on	Payoff	Probability
$S(\tau) > H$	For all $\tau \leq t$	$K - S(t)$	$P(S(t) < K) - P(S(t) < H)$
$H < S(\tau) \leq K$	For all $\tau \leq t$	0	$P(S(\tau) > H,\ S(t) < K)-$ $P(S(\tau) > H,\ S(t) < H)$
$S(\tau) \leq H$	For some $\tau \leq t$	Rebate	$P(\tau_m \leq t)$
$K < H$			
$S(\tau) > H$	For all $\tau \leq t$	0	
$S(\tau) \leq H$	For some $\tau \leq t$	Rebate	$P(\tau_m \leq t)$

3.5.1.2. *Down-and-out put* $\mathbf{K > H}$ *case*

The first part is related to the difference $K - H$ at maturity. This is the difference between

$$P(S < K) - P(S < H)$$

with different sign $\phi = -1$. Therefore, the relevant densities are $f(u)$ with upper integral limits $\ln K/S$ $\ln H/S$ (or with $\phi = -1$ for put payoff) and the integrals are [1] and [2].

Since the relevant probabilities for the first part are

$$P(S < K) - P(S < H) = N\left(\frac{\ln\frac{K}{S} - \mu t}{\sigma\sqrt{t}}\right) - \left(\frac{\ln\frac{H}{S} - \mu t}{\sigma\sqrt{t}}\right)$$

the integrals are

$$[1] = Ke^{-rt}N(-x + \sigma\sqrt{t}) - Se^{-Dt}N(-x)$$

$$[2] = Ke^{-rt}N(-x_1 + \sigma\sqrt{t}) - Se^{-Dt}N(-x_1)$$

The other part requires adding the probability the barrier will not be hit until maturity. That is the minimum of the underlying remains above H, $S(\tau) > H$ but less than K. These are the probabilities

$$P(S(\tau) > H,\ S(t) < K)$$

and

$$P(S(\tau) > H,\ S(t) < H)$$

and equal to integrals [3] and [4] with density $g(u)$. This compensates for the range of $K - H$.

$$P\left(S(t) < K,\ S(\tau) > H\right) = \left(\frac{H}{S}\right)^{\frac{2\mu}{\sigma^2}} N\left(\frac{-\ln\frac{K}{S} + 2\ln H/S + \mu t}{\sigma\sqrt{t}}\right)$$

$$P\left(S(t) < H,\ S(\tau) > H\right) = \left(\frac{H}{S}\right)^{\frac{2\mu}{\sigma^2}} N\left(\frac{-\ln\frac{H}{S} + 2\ln H/S + \mu t}{\sigma\sqrt{t}}\right)$$

$$[3] = \left(\frac{H}{S}\right)^{2\lambda-2} Ke^{-rt}N\left(y - \sigma\sqrt{t}\right) - \left(\frac{H}{S}\right)^{2\lambda} Se^{-Dt}N\left(y\right)$$

$$[4] = \left(\frac{H}{S}\right)^{2\lambda-2} Ke^{-rt}N\left(y_1 - \sigma\sqrt{t}\right) - Se^{-Dt}N\left(y_1\right)$$

Therefore, the price of $P_{do}^{K>H}$ is

$$P_{do}^{K>H} = [1] - [2] + [3] - [4] + [6] \quad \eta = 1 \quad \phi = -1$$

3.5.2. *Up-and-out put* P_{uo}

$$P_{uo}\left(S < H\right)$$

Payoff Condition:

$\max(0, K - S(t))$ for all $\tau \leq t,\ S(\tau) < H$
Rebate for some $\tau \leq t,\ S(\tau) \geq H$ at knock-out time

Table 3.7. Conditional payoff structure for up-and-out put.

$K > H$	Conditional on	Payoff	Probability
$S(\tau) < H$	For all $\tau \leq t$	$K - S(t)$	$P(S(t) < H) - P(S(t) > H,$ $S(\tau) \geq H)$
$S(\tau) \geq H$	For some $\tau \leq t$	Rebate	$P(\tau_m \leq t)$
$K < H$			
$K > S(\tau) < H$	For all $\tau \leq t$	$K - S(t)$	$P(S(t) < K) - P(S(t) < K,$ $S(\tau) \geq H)$
$S(\tau) \geq H$	For some $\tau \leq t$	Rebate	$P(\tau_m \leq t)$

3.5.2.1. *Up-and-out put* $\boldsymbol{K > H}$ *case*

The asset price must be less than H at all times. The integrals are

$$[2] - [4] = P(S(t) < H) - P(S(t) < H, S(\tau) \geq H)$$

with upper limit $\ln H/S$ and densities $f(u)$ and $g(u)$, respectively.

Therefore, the price of $P_{uo}^{K>H}$ with rebate is

$$P_{uo}^{K>H} = [2] - [4] + [6] \; \eta = -1 \; \phi = -1$$

The cumulative probabilities are

$$P(S(t) < H) = N\left(\frac{\ln\frac{H}{S} - \mu t}{\sigma\sqrt{t}}\right)$$

$$P(S(t) < H, S(\tau) \geq H) = \left(\frac{H}{S}\right)^{\frac{2\mu}{\sigma^2}} N\left(\frac{\ln\frac{H}{S} - 2\ln\frac{H}{S} - \mu t}{\sigma\sqrt{t}}\right)$$

3.5.2.2. *Up-and-out put* $\boldsymbol{K < H}$ *case*

Now, the integrals are

$$[1] - [3] = P(S(t) < K) - P(S(t) < K, S(\tau) \geq H)$$

with minus sign $\eta = -1$ $\phi = -1$ and upper limit $\ln K/S$. So, the price of $P_{uo}^{K<H}$ with rebate is

$$P_{uo}^{K<H} = [1] - [3] + [6] \; \eta = -1 \; \phi = -1$$

3.6. The Summary and the Proof of Rebate Formula for Knock-Out Options

The summary of all barrier options is presented in Table 3.8 as follows:

$$\begin{aligned}[1] &= e^{-rt}\int_{\ln K/S}^{\infty}(Se^{u} - K)f(u)du \\ &= \phi Se^{-Dt}N(\phi x) - \phi e^{-rt}KN(\phi x - \phi\sigma\sqrt{t})\end{aligned}$$

Table 3.8. Summary.

Option	Value	η	ϕ
C_{di} $K > H$	[3] + [5]	1	1
C_{di} $K < H$	[1] − [2] + [4] + [5]	1	1
C_{ui} $K > H$	[1] + [5]	−1	1
C_{ui} $K < H$	[2] − [3] + [4] + [5]	−1	1
P_{di} $K > H$	[2] − [3] + [4] + [5]	1	−1
P_{di} $K < H$	[1] + [5	1	−1
P_{ui} $K > H$	[1] − [2] + [4] + [5]	−1	−1
P_{ui} $K < H$	[3] + [5]	−1	−1
C_{do} $K > H$	[1] − [3] + [6]	1	1
C_{do} $K < H$	[2] − [4] + [6]	1	1
C_{uo} $K > H$	[6]	−1	1
C_{uo} $K < H$	[1] − [2] + [3] − [4] + [6]	−1	1
P_{do} $K > H$	[1] − [2] + [3] − [4] + [6]	1	−1
P_{do} $K < H$	[6]	1	−1
P_{uo} $K > H$	[2] − [4] + [6]	−1	−1
P_{uo} $K < H$	[1] − [3] + [6]	−1	−1

$$
\begin{aligned}
[2] &= e^{-rt} \int_{\ln H/S}^{\infty} (Se^u - K)\, f(u) du \\
&= \phi S e^{-Dt} N(\phi x_1) - \phi e^{-rt} K N(\phi x_1 - \phi\sigma\sqrt{t}) \\
[3] &= \exp(-rt) \int_{\ln K/S}^{\infty} (Se^u - K) g(u) du \\
&= \phi S e^{-Dt} \left(\frac{H}{S}\right)^{2\lambda} N(\eta y) - \phi K \left(\frac{H}{S}\right)^{2\lambda-2} e^{-rt} N(\eta y - \eta\sigma\sqrt{t}) \\
[4] &= e^{-rt} \int_{\ln H/S}^{\infty} (Se^u -) g(u) du \\
&= \phi S e^{-Dt} (H/S)^{2\lambda} N(\eta y_1) - \phi e^{-rt} K (H/S)^{2\lambda-2} N(\eta y_1 - \eta\sigma\sqrt{t}) \\
[5] &= e^{-rt} R \int_{\ln H/S}^{\infty} \{f(u) - g(u)\}\, du \\
&= e^{-rt} R \left\{ N\left(\eta x_1 - \eta\sigma\sqrt{t}\right) - \left(\frac{H}{S}\right)^{2\lambda-2} N(\eta y_1 - \eta\sigma\sqrt{t}) \right\}
\end{aligned}
$$

$$x = \frac{\ln S/K}{\sigma\sqrt{t}} + \lambda\sigma\sqrt{t} \quad \phi = \eta = 1$$

$$y = \frac{\ln \frac{H^2}{SK} + \lambda\sigma^2 t}{\sigma\sqrt{t}} = \frac{\ln \frac{H^2}{SK}}{\sigma\sqrt{t}} + \lambda\sigma\sqrt{t}$$

$$x_1 = \frac{\ln \frac{S}{H} + \lambda\sigma^2 t}{\sigma\sqrt{t}} = \frac{\ln \frac{S}{H}}{\sigma\sqrt{t}} + \lambda\sigma\sqrt{t}$$

$$y_1 = \frac{\ln \frac{H}{S}}{\sigma\sqrt{t}} + \lambda\sigma\sqrt{t}$$

$$[6] = R\int_0^t e^{-r\tau} h(\tau) d\tau$$

$$= R\left\{\left(\frac{H}{S}\right)^{a+b} N(\eta z) + \left(\frac{H}{S}\right)^{a-b} N(\eta z - 2\eta b\sigma\sqrt{t})\right\}$$

$$z = \frac{\ln H/S}{\sigma\sqrt{t}} + b\sigma\sqrt{t} \quad a = \frac{\mu}{\sigma^2} \; b = \frac{\sqrt{\mu^2 + 2r\sigma^2}}{\sigma^2}$$

Proof of [6]. Assume $\eta = 1$. Ignoring the multiplication by R for a while, let's write

$$[6] = e^{-r\tau} \int_0^t \frac{-a}{\sigma\tau\sqrt{2\pi\tau}} e^{-\frac{1}{2}v^2} d\tau \;\; v = \frac{-a + \mu\tau}{\sigma\sqrt{\tau}}$$

Substitute $z = 1/\tau$. Then

$$dz = -z^2 d\tau$$

$$\tau \to 0 \;\; z \to \infty$$

$$\tau \to t \;\; z \to 1/t$$

and we obtain

$$\frac{a}{\sigma z^2\sqrt{2\pi\frac{1}{z^3}}} \int_\infty^{1/t} e^{-r\tau} e^{-\frac{1}{2}\left(\frac{-a+\mu\tau}{\sigma\sqrt{\tau}}\right)^2} dz$$

$$= \frac{a}{\sigma\sqrt{2\pi z}} \int_\infty^{1/t} e^{-r\tau} e^{-\frac{1}{2}\left(\frac{-a+\mu/z}{\sigma/\sqrt{z}}\right)^2} dz$$

$$\frac{a}{\sigma\sqrt{2\pi z}}\int_{\infty}^{1/t} e^{-\frac{r}{z}} e^{-\frac{1}{2}\left(\frac{-az+\mu}{\sigma\sqrt{z}}\right)^2} dz$$

$$\exp\left(-\frac{2r\sigma^2}{2\sigma^2 z} - \frac{(-az+\mu)^2}{2\sigma^2 z}\right) = \exp\left(-\frac{1}{2}\frac{\left(2r\sigma^2 + (-az+\mu)^2\right)}{\sigma^2 z}\right)$$

$$-\frac{1}{2}\frac{\left(2r\sigma^2 + (-az+\mu)^2\right)}{\sigma^2 z} = -\frac{1}{2}\frac{(2r\sigma^2 + a^2z^2 + \mu^2 - 2\mu az)}{\sigma^2 z}$$

Since $= \ln H/S$, the last term can be written as

$$\exp\left(-\frac{-2\mu az}{2\sigma^2 z}\right) = (H/S)^{\frac{\mu}{\sigma^2}} = (H/S)^c$$

where $c = \mu/\sigma^2$. Now, let's substitute

$$y = \sqrt{z}\ dy = \frac{1}{2\sqrt{z}}\ dzy \to \frac{1}{\sqrt{t}}$$

and let

$$v^2 = 2r\sigma^2 + \mu^2$$

$$\frac{2a(H/S)^c}{\sigma\sqrt{2\pi}}\int_{\infty}^{1/\sqrt{t}} e^{-\frac{1}{2}\frac{\left(a^2y^2+v^2/y^2\right)}{\sigma^2}} dy$$

Changing sign

$$-\frac{2a(H/S)^c}{\sigma\sqrt{2\pi}}\int_{-\infty}^{-1/\sqrt{t}} e^{-\frac{1}{2}\frac{\left(a^2y^2+v^2/y^2\right)}{\sigma^2}} dy$$

We can write

$$-\frac{1}{2}\frac{\left(a^2y^2 + \frac{v^2}{y^2}\right)}{\sigma^2} = -\frac{1}{2}\frac{\left(-ay - \frac{v}{y}\right)^2}{\sigma^2} + \frac{2av}{2\sigma^2}$$

to adjust the integral limits. Then, we have to add av/σ^2 to complete the square. Defining

$$b = \frac{v}{\sigma^2} = \frac{\sqrt{2r\sigma^2 + \mu^2}}{\sigma^2}$$

we write

$$-\frac{2a(H/S)^{c+b}}{\sigma\sqrt{2\pi}}\int_{-\infty}^{-1/\sqrt{t}} e^{-\frac{1}{2}\frac{\left(-ay-\frac{v}{y}\right)^2}{\sigma^2}}dy$$

$$x = -ay - \frac{v}{y}$$

$$ay^2 + xy + v = 0$$

Then,

$$y = \frac{-x \pm \sqrt{x^2 - 4av}}{2a}$$

and the differential is

$$dy = \frac{1}{2a}\left[-1 - \frac{x}{\sqrt{x^2 - 4av}}\right]dx$$

This makes the sign positive again for two integrals.

Finally, replacing $-1/\sqrt{t}$ for

$$x = -ay - \frac{v}{y}$$

we obtain

$$x = \frac{a}{\sqrt{t}} + \frac{vt}{\sqrt{t}}$$

$$\frac{2a(H/S)^{c+b}}{2a\sigma\sqrt{2\pi}}\int_{-\infty}^{\frac{a}{\sqrt{t}}+\frac{vt}{\sqrt{t}}} e^{-\frac{1}{2}\frac{x^2}{\sigma^2}}dx + \frac{2a(H/S)^{c+b}}{2a\sigma\sqrt{2\pi}}$$

$$\times \int_{-\infty}^{\frac{a}{\sqrt{t}}+\frac{vt}{\sqrt{t}}} \frac{x}{\sqrt{x^2-4av}} e^{-\frac{1}{2}\frac{x^2}{\sigma^2}}dx$$

Making the change of variable last time

$$z = \frac{x}{\sigma} = \frac{a}{\sigma\sqrt{t}} + \frac{vt}{\sigma\sqrt{t}}$$

$$dz\sigma = dx$$

$$\frac{2a\sigma\left(\frac{H}{S}\right)^{c+b}}{2a\sigma\sqrt{2\pi}}\int_{\infty}^{\frac{a}{\sigma\sqrt{t}}+\frac{vt}{\sigma\sqrt{t}}} e^{-\frac{1}{2}z^2}dz = \frac{\left(\frac{H}{S}\right)^{c+b}}{\sqrt{2\pi}}\int_{-\infty}^{\frac{a}{\sigma\sqrt{t}}+\frac{vt}{\sigma\sqrt{t}}} e^{-\frac{1}{2}z^2}dz$$

we obtain the result as

$$(H/S)^{c+b}N(z)$$

where

$$z = \frac{a}{\sigma\sqrt{t}} + \frac{vt}{\sigma\sqrt{t}} = \frac{\ln H/S}{\sigma\sqrt{t}} + \frac{vt}{\sigma\sqrt{t}} = \frac{\ln\frac{H}{S} + t\sqrt{2r\sigma^2+\mu^2}}{\sigma\sqrt{t}}$$

$$= \frac{\ln H/S}{\sigma\sqrt{t}} + b\sigma\sqrt{t}$$

$$c = \frac{\mu}{\sigma^2}\ b = \frac{\sqrt{2r\sigma^2+\mu^2}}{\sigma^2} \quad v = \sqrt{2r\sigma^2+\mu^2}$$

with Rubinstein and Reiner's (1991) notation (except r, instead of $\log r$).

For the second term, we can write

$$\frac{(H/S)^{c+b}}{\sigma\sqrt{2\pi}}\int_{-\infty}^{\frac{a}{\sqrt{t}}+v\sqrt{t}} \frac{x}{\sqrt{x^2-4av}}e^{-\frac{1}{2}\frac{x^2}{\sigma^2}}dx$$

$$s^2 = x^2 - 4av \quad 2sds = 2xdx$$

Since

$$s^2 = x^2 - 4av$$

$$s^2 = \frac{a^2}{t} + v^2t + 2av - 4av = \left(\frac{a}{\sqrt{t}} - v\sqrt{t}\right)^2$$

$$s \to \frac{a}{\sqrt{t}} - v\sqrt{t}$$

$$\frac{(H/S)^{c+b}}{\sigma\sqrt{2\pi}}\int_{-\infty}^{\frac{a}{\sqrt{t}}-v\sqrt{t}} e^{-\frac{1}{2}\left(\frac{s^2+4av}{\sigma^2}\right)}ds$$

$$= \frac{(H/S)^{c+b}}{\sigma\sqrt{2\pi}}\int_{-\infty}^{\left(\frac{a}{\sqrt{t}}-v\sqrt{t}\right)} e^{-\frac{1}{2}\left(\frac{s^2}{\sigma^2}\right)}e^{-\frac{1}{2}\left(\frac{4av}{\sigma^2}\right)}ds$$

But

$$e^{-\frac{1}{2}\left(\frac{4av}{\sigma^2}\right)} = \left(\frac{H}{S}\right)^{-2v/\sigma^2} = \left(\frac{H}{S}\right)^{-2b}$$

and makes the coefficient term

$$\frac{(H/S)^{c-b}}{\sigma\sqrt{2\pi}}$$

Finally changing variable

$$n = \frac{s}{\sigma} \quad dn\sigma = ds$$

$$\frac{(H/S)^{c-b}}{\sqrt{2\pi}} \int_{-\infty}^{\frac{a}{\sigma\sqrt{t}} - \frac{vt}{\sigma\sqrt{t}}} e^{-\frac{1}{2}n^2} dn$$

$$\left(\frac{H}{S}\right)^{c-b} N(z - 2b\sigma\sqrt{t})$$

where

$$z - 2b\sigma\sqrt{t} = \frac{a}{\sigma\sqrt{t}} - \frac{vt}{\sigma\sqrt{t}} = \frac{\ln H/S}{\sigma\sqrt{t}} - \frac{vt}{\sigma\sqrt{t}}$$

and

$$z - 2b\sigma\sqrt{t} = \frac{\ln\frac{H}{S}}{\sigma\sqrt{t}} + b\sigma\sqrt{t} - 2b\sigma\sqrt{t} = \frac{\ln\frac{H}{S}}{\sigma\sqrt{t}} - b\sigma\sqrt{t} = \frac{\ln H/S}{\sigma\sqrt{t}} - \frac{vt}{\sigma\sqrt{t}}$$

Finally, the last integral [6] is

$$[6] = R\left\{\left(\frac{H}{S}\right)^{c+b} N(\eta z) + \left(\frac{H}{S}\right)^{c-b} N(\eta z - \eta 2b\sigma\sqrt{t})\right\}$$

and

$$z = \frac{\ln\frac{H}{S}}{\sigma\sqrt{t}} + b\sigma\sqrt{t}$$

The rebate function may sometimes be time-dependent and take the form

$$R(\tau) = R(\xi e^{\kappa\tau} - 1)$$

where $\xi \geq 1$ and κ is a growth parameter. This requires the integration of

$$R\int_0^t e^{-r\tau}(\xi e^{\kappa\tau} - 1)h(\tau)d\tau$$

which yields a similar solution to [6] with slightly different parameters.

The lack of barrier continuity (discontinuity) creates hedging problems in barrier options (circuit breaker effect). Hsu (1997), Carr *et al.* (1998), Carr and Chou (1996, 2002), and Derman *et al.* (2000) are the primary references for barrier hedging.

In the absence of the fixed payout, R, one interesting consequence is that the sum of the down-and-out and down-and-in options will give the standard option payout. So, we can write the following identity for the standard option payout.

$$C = C_{do} + C_{di}$$

$$P = P_{do} + P_{di}$$

For example, when the stock price rises, the down-and-in option will be useless, but the down-and-out option will be alive. Therefore, if the option is in the money, it will pay like a standard option. In this way, we would have obtained cheaper option positions by decreasing the number of paths that the stock will move.

3.7. PDE Solutions of Barrier Options

In this section, we have benefited from Professor Sam Howison's working paper on "Barrier Options."

Barrier option pricing requires the solution of the same Black–Scholes partial differential equation but with slightly different boundary conditions. The boundary condition for the option payoff is the same; however, another boundary condition involves the barrier, and the option payoff is zero when the underlying hits the barrier from above (down-and-out) or below (up-and-out). First, we will consider the case for a down-and-out call.

3.7.1. *Down-and-out call PDE solution*

The DO Barrier option has an explicit formula. We consider the case where the lower barrier is set below the exercise price.

$$K > B_{-}$$

Suppose that we are above the barrier at time t and $S > B_{-}$ and we hold the down-and-out call.

Then $C_{do}(S,t)$ satisfies the Black–Scholes equation

$$\frac{\partial C_{do}(S,t)}{\partial t}+\frac{1}{2}\sigma^2 S^2\frac{\partial^2 C_{do}(S,t)}{\partial S^2}+(r-D)S\frac{\partial C_{do}(S,t)}{\partial S}$$
$$-rC_{do}(S,t)=0 \tag{3.5}$$

for $\infty > S > B_-$ and the option does not exist for $S < B_-$.

The terminal condition is $C_{do}(S,T) = \max(S_T - K,0)$. For $S \to \infty$

$$C_{do}(S,T) \cong Se^{-D(T-t)} - e^{-r(T-t)}K$$

Here, the valuation problem differs from that of a vanilla call. The boundary condition is $S = B_-$ rather than $S = 0$. If $S = B_-$.

$$C_{do}(B_-,t) = 0$$

This completes the formulation.

Reduction to the heat equation

$$S = B_-e^x \quad t = T - \frac{2\tau}{\sigma^2} \quad C_{do} = B_-e^{\alpha x+\beta\tau}u(x,\tau)$$

with

$$\alpha = e^{\frac{1}{2}(k'+1)} \quad \beta = -\frac{1}{4}\left(k'-1\right)^2 - k \quad k = \frac{2r}{\sigma^2} \quad k' = \frac{2(r-D)}{\sigma^2}$$

$$\frac{\partial u}{\partial \tau} = \frac{\partial^2 u}{\partial x^2} \quad 0 < x < \infty \quad \tau > 0 \tag{3.6}$$

and

$$u(x,0) = U(x) = \max\left(e^{\frac{1}{2}(k'+1)x} - \frac{K}{B_-}e^{\frac{1}{2}(k'-1)x}, 0\right)$$

$$x \geq 0 \tag{3.7}$$

$$u(0,t) = 0 \tag{3.8}$$

The equation (3.2) is invariant under reflection, replacing x by $-x$. Thus, if $u(x,\tau)$ is a solution of equation (3.6), so is $u(-x,\tau)$.

In the method of images, we solve a semi-infinite heat equation problem by first solving an infinite problem made up of two semi-infinite problems with equal and opposite initial temperature distributions; one half is hot, the other cold.

We can apply this method to the barrier option problem. We reflect the initial data about the point $x = 0$ (the "join" of the two bars, corresponding to the barrier) at the same time changing its sign, satisfying equation (3.8). Thus, instead of solving equations (3.6)–(3.8) on the interval $0 < x < \infty$, we solve equation (3.6) for all x but subject to

$$u(x,0) = \begin{cases} U(x) & x > 0 \\ -U(-x) & x < 0 \end{cases} \tag{3.9}$$

that is

$$u(x,0) = \begin{cases} \max(e^{\frac{1}{2}(k'+1)x} - \frac{K}{B_-}e^{\frac{1}{2}(k'-1)x}, 0) & x > 0 \\ -\max(e^{-\frac{1}{2}(k'+1)x} - \frac{K}{B_-}e^{-\frac{1}{2}(k'-1)x}, 0) & x < 0 \end{cases} \tag{3.10}$$

and in this way, we guarantee that $u\,(0,\tau) = 0$. This is the solution of the heat equation.

Now, consider a vanilla call with the same exercise price and maturity with no barrier; $C_v(S,t;K)$ and $U_v(x,\tau)$ for the corresponding solution of the heat equation. The payoff $C_v(S,t;K)$ is zero for all S below the strike; this translates into $U_v(x,0) = 0$ for $x < \ln\,(K/B_-)$.

When we set the barrier below the strike, we ensure that $\ln\,(K/B_-) > 0$. So if we extend our down and out call payoff $U(x)$ into $x < 0$ by setting it equal to zero there ($x < \ln\,(K/B_-)$), we have exactly the transformed payoff of the vanilla call $U_v(x)$. Then we can write equation (3.10) as

$$u\,(x,0) = U_v(x) - U_v(-x)$$

holding for all x. The solution to the barrier problem is

$$u(x,\tau) = U_v(x,\tau) - U_v(-x,\tau)$$

This always vanishes at $x = 0$. (Why?)

Now, return to the variables S and t.

$$C_v(S,t;K) = C_v(B_-e^x, t(\tau);K) = B_-e^{\alpha x+\beta\tau}U_v(x,\tau)$$
$$U_v(x,\tau) = e^{-\alpha x-\beta\tau}C_v(B_-e^x, t(\tau);K)/B_-$$
$$U_v(-x,\tau) = e^{\alpha x-\beta\tau}C_v(B_-e^{-x}, t(\tau);K)/B_-$$

Since

$$C_{do} = B_- e^{\alpha x + \beta\tau} u(x,\tau)$$

$$C_{do} = B_- e^{\alpha x + \beta\tau} [U_v(x,\tau) - U_v(-x,\tau)]$$

$$C_{do} = B_- e^{\alpha x + \beta\tau} \left[\frac{e^{-\alpha x - \beta\tau} C_v\left(B_- e^{x}, t; K\right)}{B_-} - \frac{e^{\alpha x - \beta\tau} C_v\left(B_- e^{-x}, t; K\right)}{B_-} \right]$$

$$e^{x} = \frac{S}{B_-} \quad e^{-x} = \frac{B_-}{S}$$

$$C_{do} = C_v(S,t;K) - e^{2\alpha x} C_v(B_- e^{-x}, t; K)$$

$$C_{do} = C_v(S,t;K) - \left(\frac{S}{B_-}\right)^{2\alpha} C_v\left(\frac{B_-^2}{S}, t; K\right)$$

Thus, when the strike is above the barrier, the barrier option value is revealed as the vanilla call less an image contribution or reflection, which enables us to satisfy the barrier condition. Now, suppose that the barrier is above the strike. In this case, we would have discarded the instances where the asset price is above the strike (and the option has value) but below the barrier. Thus, the reflected solution does not vanish above the barrier at maturity because the vanilla call still has a value below the barrier. We may cure this situation by truncating the payoff of the vanilla call at the barrier level.

When we truncate the payoff at B, we have to add the value for interval $B - K$. This value is equal to $B - K$ times the digital barrier call with an exercise price B and the same maturity. Therefore, we modify the down-and-out call price where the barrier is above strike as

$$C_{do} = C_v\left(S,t;B_-\right) - \left(\frac{B_-}{S}\right)^{\frac{2\mu}{\sigma^2}} C_v\left(\frac{B_-^2}{S}, t; B_-\right)$$
$$+ \left(B_- - K\right) \left[C_{dig}\left(S,t;B_-\right) - \left(\frac{B_-}{S}\right)^{\frac{2\mu}{\sigma^2}} C_{dig}\left(\frac{B_-^2}{S}, t; B_-\right) \right]$$

The digital down and out formula when the strike is above the barrier

$$C_{do}^{dig}\left(S,t;B_-\right) = C_{dig}\left(S,t;K\right) - \left(\frac{B_-}{S}\right)^{\frac{2\mu}{\sigma^2}} C_{dig}\left(\frac{B_-^2}{S}, t; K\right) \quad (3.11)$$

and when the strike is below the barrier

$$C_{do}^{dig}\left(S,t;B_-\right)=C_{dig}\left(S,t;B_-\right)-\left(\frac{B_-}{S}\right)^{\frac{2\mu}{\sigma^2}}C_{dig}\left(\frac{B_-^2}{S},t;B_-\right)\tag{3.12}$$

3.7.2. *The down-and-in call PDE solution*

If the barrier is triggered, the option is in, and it automatically becomes a vanilla call. Investors who think that the market will fall and rise again during the option's lifetime could prefer this type of option. It could be a better strategy than a calendar spread because there is no need to estimate when the fall and rise will occur, and by using the barrier parity, we can easily price the down and in option.

$$\begin{aligned}C_v&=C_{do}+C_{di}\\C_{di}&=C_v-C_{do}\\C_{di}&=C_v(S,t;K)-C_v\left(S,t;\ K\right)+\left(\frac{S}{B_-}\right)^{2\alpha}C_v\left(\frac{B_-^2}{S},t;\ K\right)\\&=\left(\frac{S}{B_-}\right)^{2\alpha}C_v\left(\frac{B_-^2}{S},t;K\right)\end{aligned}\tag{3.13}$$

The parity logic is clear: if the barrier is hit, the down and in option becomes a vanilla call. Similarly, the down-and-out option becomes vanilla if the barrier is never hit.

3.7.3. *Down-and-out puts*

The holder receives the payoff of a vanilla put if the asset never hits the lower barrier and the option is in the money. Suppose the barrier is above the strike, and the option never pays off. So, the strike must be well above the barrier to make sense.

The idea is simple: long a put barrier with strike K and short a barrier with strike B_-. This covers up the payoff between $K - B_-$

region. Therefore, the formula is

$$P_{do} = P_v(S,t;K) - \left(\frac{S}{B_-}\right)^{2\alpha} P_v\left(\frac{B_-^2}{S},t;K\right) - P_v(S,t;B_-) + \left(\frac{S}{B_-}\right)^{2\alpha} P_v\left(\frac{B_-^2}{S},t;B_-\right) \quad (3.14)$$

3.7.4. *Green function in PDE solution* (Kwok, 2008, pp. 184–187)

Let's take the Black–Scholes partial differential equation as

$$-\frac{\partial C_{do}(x,\tau)}{\partial \tau} + \frac{1}{2}\sigma^2\frac{\partial^2 C_{do}(x,\tau)}{\partial x^2} + \left(r - D - \frac{\sigma^2}{2}\right)\frac{\partial C_{do}(x,\tau)}{\partial x} - rC_{do}(x,\tau) = 0$$

defined in the semi-infinite domain with $x = \ln S\ (S_T)$.

Boundary conditions are

$$C(\ln B_-,\tau) = 0 \quad C(x,0) = \max(e^x - K, 0)$$

The Green function in the infinite domain $-\infty < x < \infty$ is given by

$$G_0(x,\tau;\varepsilon) = \frac{e^{-r\tau}}{\sigma\sqrt{2\pi\tau}}\exp\left(-\frac{(x+\mu\tau-\varepsilon)^2}{2\sigma^2\tau}\right)$$

where $\mu = r - \frac{\sigma^2}{2}$ and satisfies the initial condition

$$\lim_{\tau\to 0^+} G_0(y,\tau;\varepsilon) = \delta(y-\varepsilon)$$

However, we would like to solve the restricted Green function in the semi-infinite domain $\ln B_- < x < \infty$ with boundary condition $C(\ln B_-,\tau) = 0$.

Now, assume the solution has the following form

$$G(x,\tau;\varepsilon) = G_0(x,\tau;\varepsilon) - \psi(\varepsilon)G_0(x,\tau;\eta) \tag{3.15}$$

We need to find $\psi(\varepsilon)$ and η in terms of ε such that the boundary condition is satisfied as

$$G(\ln B_-,\tau;\varepsilon) = 0$$

Since $G_0(x,\tau;\varepsilon)$ and $\psi(\varepsilon)G_0(x,\tau;\eta)$ both satisfy the Black–Scholes PDE, so $G(x,\tau;\varepsilon)$ does. Also, for

$$\eta \notin (\ln B_-,\infty)$$

that is, barrier has been hit, we write $\lim_{\tau\to 0^+} G_0(x,\tau;\eta) = 0$ for all $x > \ln B_-$ and this satisfies the initial condition. Imposing the boundary condition along the barrier

$$G\left(\ln B_-,\tau;\varepsilon\right) = G_0\left(\ln B_-,\tau;\varepsilon\right) - \psi(\varepsilon)G_0(\ln B_-,\tau;\eta) = 0$$

$$\psi(\varepsilon) = \frac{G_0(\ln B_-,\tau;\varepsilon)}{G_0(\ln B_-,\tau;\eta)} \tag{3.16}$$

$$\psi(\varepsilon) = \frac{\exp\left(-\frac{(x+\mu\tau-\varepsilon)^2}{2\sigma^2\tau}\right)}{\exp\left(-\frac{(x+\mu\tau-\eta)^2}{2\sigma^2\tau}\right)}$$

$$= \exp\left(\frac{-x^2-\varepsilon^2-\mu^2\tau^2-2x\mu\tau+2x\varepsilon+2\varepsilon\mu\tau+x^2+\eta^2}{2\sigma^2\tau}\right.$$

$$\left.\frac{+\mu^2\tau^2+2x\mu\tau-2x\eta-2\eta\mu\tau}{2\sigma^2\tau}\right)$$

$$\psi(\varepsilon) = \exp\left(\frac{-\varepsilon^2+2\ln B_-\varepsilon-2\ln B_-\eta+2\varepsilon\mu\tau-2\eta\mu\tau+\eta^2}{2\sigma^2\tau}\right)$$

$$= \frac{(\eta-\varepsilon)(\eta+\varepsilon)+2\ln B_-(\varepsilon-\eta)+2\mu\tau(\varepsilon-\eta)}{2\sigma^2\tau}$$

$$\psi(\varepsilon) = \frac{(\varepsilon-\eta)[2\ln B_-+2\mu\tau]-(\varepsilon-\eta)(\eta+\varepsilon)}{2\sigma^2\tau}$$

But the right-hand side must be the function of only ε. Therefore, by choosing $\eta = 2\ln B_{-}\varepsilon$. We obtain

$$\psi(\varepsilon) = \exp\left(\frac{(2\varepsilon - 2\ln B_{-})[2(\ln B_{-} + \mu\tau) - (2\varepsilon - 2\ln B_{-})2\ln B_{-}]}{2\sigma^2\tau}\right)$$

$$= \exp\frac{2(\varepsilon - \ln B_{-})[2\mu\tau]}{2\sigma^2\tau}$$

$$\psi(\varepsilon) = \exp\frac{2\mu}{\sigma^2}(\varepsilon - \ln B_{-}) \tag{3.17}$$

The parameter η can be interpreted as the mirror image of ε with respect to its barrier $x = \ln B_{-}$.

Replacing the relevant equations in the second term

$$\psi(\varepsilon)\, G_0(x, \tau; \eta) = \exp\frac{2\mu}{\sigma^2}(\varepsilon - \ln B_{-})\frac{e^{-r\tau}}{\sigma\sqrt{2\pi\tau}}$$
$$\times \exp\left(-\frac{(x + \mu\tau - (2\ln B_{-} - \varepsilon))^2}{2\sigma^2\tau}\right)$$

After writing

$$\exp\left(-\frac{[(x + \mu\tau - (2\ln B - \varepsilon)]^2}{2\sigma^2\tau} + \frac{4\mu\tau}{2\sigma^2\tau}(\varepsilon - \ln B)\right)$$

and adding

$$+ 4x^2 - 4x^2 - 4\mu\tau(\ln B - x) + 4\mu\tau(\ln B - x)$$

$$\exp\left(\frac{4\mu\tau\,(\ln B - \ln S)}{2\sigma^2\tau}\right) = \exp\left(\frac{2\mu\ln(B/S)}{\sigma^2}\right) = \left(\frac{B}{S}\right)^{2\mu/\sigma^2}$$

we obtain

$$G_0(x, \tau; \eta) = \left(\frac{B}{S}\right)^{2\mu/\sigma^2}\frac{e^{-r\tau}}{\sigma\sqrt{2\pi\tau}}\exp\left(-\frac{((x - \varepsilon) + \mu\tau - 2(x - \ln B))^2}{2\sigma^2\tau}\right)$$

Finally, in the semi-infinite domain, the Green function is

$$G_0(x,\tau;\eta)$$

$$= \left(\frac{B}{S}\right)^{2\mu/\sigma^2} \frac{e^{-r\tau}}{\sigma\sqrt{2\pi\tau}}\exp\left(-\frac{(-(x-\varepsilon)-\mu\tau+2(x-\ln B))^2}{2\sigma^2\tau}\right)$$

$$u=\varepsilon-x \quad \beta=\ln B-x=\ln,(B/S)$$

$$G_0(x,\tau;\eta)=\frac{e^{-r\tau}}{\sigma\sqrt{2\pi\tau}}\left(\frac{B}{S}\right)^{2\mu/\sigma^2}\exp\left(-\frac{(u-\mu\tau-2\beta))^2}{2\sigma^2\tau}\right)$$

$$G(x,\tau;\varepsilon)=\frac{e^{-r\tau}}{\sigma\sqrt{2\pi\tau}}\left[\exp\left(-\frac{(u-\mu\tau)^2}{2\sigma^2\tau}\right)-\left(\frac{B}{S}\right)^{\frac{2\mu}{\sigma^2}}\right.$$

$$\left.\exp\left(-\frac{(u-2\beta-\mu\tau)^2}{2\sigma^2\tau}\right)\right] \tag{3.18}$$

Assuming the barrier is below the strike $K=\max(B,K)$

$$C_{do}(x,\tau;\varepsilon)=\int_{\ln K}^{\infty}G(x,\tau;\varepsilon)\,(e^{\varepsilon}-K,0)\,d\varepsilon$$

Since $u=\varepsilon-x \quad du=d\varepsilon \quad e^{\varepsilon}=e^{x}e^{u}=Se^{u}$

$$C_{do}(x,\tau;u)=\frac{e^{-r\tau}}{\sigma\sqrt{2\pi\tau}}\int_{\ln K/S}^{\infty}\left[\exp\left(-\frac{(u-\mu\tau)^2}{2\sigma^2\tau}\right)-\left(\frac{B}{S}\right)^{2\mu/\sigma^2}\right.$$

$$\left.\times\exp\left(-\frac{(u-2\beta-\mu\tau)^2}{2\sigma^2\tau}\right)\right](Se^{u}-K,0)\,du$$

Calculating the integral yields

$$C_{do}(x,\tau)=Se^{-D\tau}\left[N(d_1)-\left(\frac{B}{S}\right)^{\delta+1}N(d_3)\right]$$

$$-e^{-r\tau}K\left[N(d_2)-\left(\frac{B}{S}\right)^{\delta-1}N(d_4)\right] \tag{3.19}$$

where

$$d_1 = \frac{\ln\frac{S}{K} + \left(r - D + \frac{1}{2}\sigma^2\right)\tau}{\sigma\sqrt{\tau}} \qquad d_2 = d_1 - \sigma\sqrt{\tau}$$

$$d_3 = d_1 + \frac{2}{\sigma\sqrt{\tau}}\ln\left(\frac{B}{S}\right) \qquad d_4 = d_2 + \frac{2}{\sigma\sqrt{\tau}}\ln\left(\frac{B}{S}\right) \qquad \delta = 2r/\sigma^2$$

precisely the same one we have calculated in a probabilistic context.

3.8. Conclusion

We have provided the formulae of vanilla barrier options expressed first by Merton (1973) and then in a paper by Rubinstein and Reiner (1991). Also, a wide range of literature deriving the barrier formulae in different contexts and notations exists. Shreve (2004), Zhang (1998), Konstandatos (2008), and Jeanblanc *et al.* (2009) bring more rigor to the presentation of formulae. For the derivations using the PDE solutions, we refer to Zvan *et al.* (2000), Kwok (2008), and Howison (1998). Boyle and Lau (1994), Ritchken (1995), Broadie and Glasserman (1997), Ahn *et al.* (1999), Kou (2003), Duan *et al.* (2003), Fusai *et al.* (2006), Howison and Steinberg (2007), and Feng and Linetsky (2008) examine discrete barriers using various numerical methods such as adaptive mesh model, Markov chains, Hilbert transforms and Binomial model. Leisen (1999) examines the barrier option pricing in a setup containing jump risk; Roberts and Shortland (1997) and Lo *et al.* (2003) approach the pricing of barriers with time-dependent parameters. A hybrid approach to pricing is presented by Wang *et al.* (2009).

Chapter 4

Why Barriers?

4.1. Introduction

Barrier options are one of the path-dependent options whose payoff is conditional, such as standard call and put options. When the underlying asset value hits a specific barrier value, it has the features of being "in" or "out." Theoretical foundations and formulations of barrier options are given by Snyder (1969), Merton (1973), Rubinstein and Reiner (1991), Daniel and Benson (1991), and Hudson (1991). Rich (1994) also examines the subject in detail.

Barrier options are among the oldest exotic options and have been traded OTC in the US market since 1967. Interest has increased considerably since 1992, and the overall option transaction volume in the first half of 2023 is over 65 trillion dollars. Therefore, the transaction volume of barrier options is estimated to be approximately 3 trillion dollars (BIS, https://stats.bis.org/statx/srs/table/d5.1).

Barrier options have attracted intense interest as instruments to satisfy the complex needs of various investor groups, especially in stock markets. In particular, these options are cheaper than vanilla calls and puts, and are a more attractive instrument for investors. Since knock-in or knock-out features disable some price ranges and the realization possibilities of these prices, they provide cheaper option prices. In other words, barrier options provide value beyond investors' standard "bullish" or "bearish" expectations. Due to these features, we classify barrier options into "path-dependent" and "trigger options."

A vanilla barrier can be classified into two groups: knock-in and knock-out. However, since each group is classified into two different ways, "up" or "down," there are four different types. Considering that each has a call or put feature, we get eight different types of vanilla barrier options. In this section, we see how barrier options can be used by investors and the motivation behind them. The work by Zhang (1997, pp. 203–340) is recommended for a detailed review.

4.2. The Uses of Barriers

4.2.1. *Down-and-out call*

Suppose the S&P Index is at 1,000. The investor predicts that the index will develop above 1,000 in the medium and long term, but may go even lower if it falls to 850. If the index goes even lower, the investor will not need option protection and will buy cheaply. Therefore, the option does not need to be active at 850 price levels. The investor can choose an index level such as 1,250 and invest in a "down-and-out-call" option with a barrier level of 850. If the index goes up, protection is provided by making purchases at the 1,250 level. All the monitorings in the examples are daily and the notional amount is $1 million.

MATLAB commands produce the down-and-out barrier call and vanilla call prices as $13.69 and $13.78, respectively.

Underlying Asset	S&P Index
Currency	USD
Initial spot value	1,000 points
Exercise price	1,250 points
Contract date	29.02.2024
Maturity	30.11.2024
Barrier	850 points
Volatility	0.20
Risk-free rate	5%

MATLAB commands are as follows:

```
Rates = 0.05;
Settle = datetime(2024,2,29);
Maturity = datetime(2024,11,31);
```

```
Compounding = -1;
Basis = 0;
>> RateSpec = intenvset('ValuationDate', Settle,
'StartDates', Settle, 'EndDates', Maturity, ...
'Rates', Rates, 'Compounding', Compounding, 'Basis',
Basis)
RateSpec =
 struct with fields:
      FinObj: 'RateSpec'
    Compounding: -1
       Disc: 0.9633
       Rates: 0.0500
      EndTimes: 0.7473
    StartTimes: 0
      EndDates: 739576
    StartDates: 739302
   ValuationDate: 739302
       Basis: 0
   EndMonthRule: 1
>> AssetPrice = 1000;
Volatility = 0.30;
StockSpec = stockspec(Volatility, AssetPrice)
StockSpec =
 struct with fields:
       FinObj: 'StockSpec'
       Sigma: 0.3000
     AssetPrice: 1000
    DividendType:
   DividendAmounts: 0
   ExDividendDates:
>> Strike = 1250;
OptSpec = 'call';
Barrier = 850;
BarrierSpec = 'DO';
Price = barrierbybls(RateSpec, StockSpec, OptSpec,
Strike, Settle,...
Maturity, BarrierSpec, Barrier)
Price =
  13.6933
```

```
>> blsprice(1000,1250,0.05,274/365,0.2)
ans =
  13.7756
```

Generally, for knock-out type barrier options,

- a longer time to maturity,
- a higher volatility, and
- a barrier value closer to the spot value

will mean a lower option premium.

If the investor's prediction in our example comes true and the share prices rise above 1,250, he will have an "in-the-money" option. Below 1,250, the option will be "out-of-the-money," and if it drops to 850, it will be out. However, the investor will fund his long position at low prices.

4.2.2. *Up-and-out call*

Let's assume the spot market is at 1,000. The portfolio manager expects a good return from the upward trend of his portfolio. However, at the same time, it wants to protect against the upward rise due to the purchases it plans to make. An up-and-out barrier call may be a good investment choice in this case. For example, an up-and-out call with a value of 1,060 strike and a 1,200 barrier will allow the investor to buy at $1,060 unless the barrier value is hit. If the barrier value is reached, the option will be worthless, but the investor's portfolio value will increase, and there will be no need for protection. Price information can be recovered with the following MATLAB commands.

Underlying Asset	S&P Index
Initial spot value	1,000 points
Exercise price	1,060 points
Contract date	20.02.2024
Maturity	31.03.2024
Barrier	1,200 points
Volatility	0.30
Risk-free rate	10%

```
BarrierOpt = fininstrument(‘‘Barrier, ‘Strike’,1060,
‘ExerciseDate’,datetime(2024,3,31), ‘OptionType,’
‘‘call",‘ExerciseStyle’,"european",‘BarrierType’,"UO",
‘BarrierValue’,1200,‘Name’,
"barrier_option")
>> BlackScholesModel = finmodel("BlackScholes",
‘Volatility’,0.30)
>> Settle = datetime(2024,2,20);
Maturity = datetime(2024,3,31);
Rate = 0.10;
myRC = ratecurve(‘zero’, Settle, Maturity, Rate,
‘Basis’,1)
>> outPricer = finpricer("FiniteDifference",‘Model’,
BlackScholesModel,‘DiscountCurve’,myRC,‘SpotPrice’,1000)
>> [Price, outPR] = price(outPricer, BarrierOpt,["all"])
Price = 10.2652
The Black-Scholes price is $20.8523.
```

4.2.3. *Up-and-in call*

Our investor predicts that the index value will rise in the next 6 months. However, it tolerates a 5% increase in the index, and if the increase is above this level, it needs protection for its portfolio investment. Vanilla or up-and-in-barrier calls are suitable instruments for this.

Underlying Asset	S&P Index
Initial spot value	1,000 points
Exercise price	1,000 points
Contract date	29.02.2024
Maturity	31.08.2024
Barrier	1,050 points
Volatility	0.30
Risk-free rate	10%

The call price will be $108.88, and the up-and-in barrier call price will be $65.2078. The option will not be active during the index value's rise up to 1,050, and the investor will have covered his purchases with a limited loss. As can be seen, the knock-in option provides a significant price advantage to the investor. The investor will make a substantial profit if the index hits the barrier. Still, it may also happen that the index returns to its previous price levels until the end of maturity and becomes out-of-the-money.

4.2.4. *Down-and-in call*

Our investor predicts that the index value will decrease significantly, but he is not concerned with a limited decline. For example, if the index value is 1,000, he plans to buy at levels up to 900. However, when the index reaches 900, creating a portfolio at a lower level of 800 is possible with a down-and-in barrier call option.

The down-and-in barrier call price is 29.22, and the Black–Scholes price is 208.99. As can be seen, the barrier option has a serious price advantage over the vanilla option. If the barrier level is reached and the price rebounds, the advantage continues, but if the price decline continues, there is a risk that the option will turn into an out-of-the-money option.

Underlying Asset	S&P Index
Initial spot value	1,000 points
Exercise price	800 points
Contract date	20.02.2024
Maturity	31.03.2024
Barrier	900 points
Volatility	0.30
Risk-free rate	10%

4.2.5. *Down-and-in put*

This time, our investor is anxious about his portfolio investment, which may lose value if the index drops too much. However, she may tolerate a 5% depreciation. Then, she requires protection against the index losing value beyond this. For this, down-and-in put would be a suitable choice.

Underlying Asset	S&P Index
Initial spot value	950 points
Exercise price	880 points
Contract date	20.02.2024
Maturity	31.08.2024
Barrier	900 points
Volatility	0.30
Risk-free rate	10%

The barrier put price is 6.8194, and the vanilla put price is 9.3821. The option will not be activated for index values higher than 900, and values lower than 950 will incur a loss. However, if the index hits 900 and falls below 880, the investor can compensate for his loss. Though the option premium is relatively low, the investor may stop her loss only at the 880 level.

Generally, for knock-in type barrier options,

- a longer time to maturity,
- a higher volatility, and
- a barrier value closer to the spot value

will mean a higher option premium.

4.2.6. *Down-and-out put*

In this scheme, the option will be void when the S&P Index value hits the barrier value of 980, and the investor will receive nothing. However, if the index remains above 980, the investor will receive the difference between 1,400 and the spot value. The premium for the down-and-out put is much cheaper than the vanilla put value.

Underlying Asset	S&P Index
Initial spot value	1,400 points
Exercise price	1,400 points
Contract date	29.02.2024
Maturity	31.08.2024
Barrier	980 points
Volatility	0.30
Risk-free rate	10%

```
Price = barrierbybls(RateSpec, StockSpec, OptSpec, Strike,
Settle,...
Maturity, BarrierSpec, Barrier)
Price = 55.8443
[a,b]=blsprice(1400,1400,0.1,0.5,0.3)
call = 152.6910 put = 84.4122
```

For example, if the index is 1,100, the return from the option, if not knocked out, is

$$(1400 - 1100)/1400 = 21.43\%$$

and the premium is

$$P_{DO} = 55.8443/1400 = 3.98\% \quad P = 84.41/1400 = 6.03\%$$

So, the investor's profit is equal to

$$1{,}000{,}000 * (21.43 - 3.98)\% = \$174{,}500$$

4.3. Hedging Barriers

Barrier options are much more challenging to hedge than vanilla options. Barrier options, in particular, have high gamma, implying that there is a possibility of a high loss of value for the writer when the underlying asset price is in the vicinity of barrier value. In that region, dynamic hedging is both expensive and inaccurate, and static hedging is an attractive alternative (Derman and Kani, 1993 and Derman *et al.*, 2000).

As is well known, dynamic hedging has two main difficulties. The first one is the impossibility of continuous hedging. Therefore, traders adjust their portfolios at discrete time intervals, which may cause minor errors that may compound over the option's life. The second disadvantage of the method is the transaction costs, which may grow with the adjustment frequency and erode the profit margin significantly.

Derman *et al.* (2000) show that static option replication is free of these difficulties and may be very useful in these three areas:

Trading: It is particularly suited to hedging exotic high-gamma options which require frequent and costly dynamic hedging.

Structuring: A static replicating portfolio with the same payoff can be created at a lower cost as an exotic option. An exotic option that is not offered in the market may also be created.

Valuation: In the presence of transaction costs, volatility smiles, liquidity, and other market conditions that violate the assumptions of Black–Scholes, the market value of the replicating portfolio may provide a practical and fair value of the option (see the introduction part of Derman *et al.* (2000)).

4.3.1. *Static hedging of barriers*

Derman *et al.*'s (2000) basic idea is that if two portfolios are worth something on a specific boundary, they must also be the same inside the boundary. By following this principle, they replicate the target option on and inside the boundary with the standard options, practically for a limited number of time steps. The (hedging) cost of replicating is the price (value) of the target option. The process gives us the fixed portfolio weights for each standard option and each maturity.

4.3.1.1. *Up-and-out barrier call*

We can start with an example of the European "up-and-out call" from Hull and White (2009). Let's consider a 9 month up-and-out European call on a non-dividend paying stock where the stock price (S_0) is 50, the strike price (K) is 50, the barrier is 60($K < H$), the risk-free rate is 10% and the volatility is 30%.

The value of this "up-and-out" barrier call is 0.3136. Assume that the financial institution selling the option will hedge it with standard options using static option replication.

Let's first find the values of "vanilla" options to be used in the hedging process:

	Call Prices
Option A: blsprice (50, 50, 0.10, 0.75, 0.30):	6.9924
Option B: blsprice (50, 60, 0.10, 0.75, 0.30):	3.0846
Option C: blsprice (50, 60, 0.10, 0.5, 0.30):	1.8330
Option D: blsprice (50, 60, 0.10, 0.25, 0.30):	0.6144

The method proceeds as follows (see Derman *et al.* (1994) and Hull and White (2009) for the technique and the example):

1. First, we divide the life of the option into N steps of length Δt.
2. Second, we choose one unit of 9-month maturity standard call option with a strike 50 to match the first boundary (long position).
3. Third, we choose a standard call option with a strike 60 and a maturity at time $N\Delta t$ to match the boundary at $\{H, (N-1)\Delta t\}$ (short position).
4. Then, we choose a standard call option with a strike 60 and a maturity at the time $(N-1)\Delta t$ to match the boundary at H, $(N-2)\Delta t$, and so on.

The values of the up-and-out option on the boundary with $K < H$ condition is

$$f(S, N\Delta t) = \max(S - K, 0) \text{ when } S < H \text{ for all } t,\ 0 \le t \le T$$
$$f(S, N\Delta t) = 0 \text{ when } S \ge H \text{ for all } t,\ 0 \le t \le T$$

Let's assume three time steps ($N = 3$) and $\Delta t = 0.25, 0.5, 0.75$. If the underlying price is $S_0 = 60$, then the price of Option A and Option B with blsprice (S, K, r, t, σ) formula are blsprice (60, 50, 0.10, 0.25, 0.30) $C_0 = 11.5433$ and blsprice (60, 60, 0.10, 0.25, 0.30) $C_0 = 4.3325$, respectively. Therefore, at a point of $(N-1)\Delta t = 0.5$, i.e., with a maturity of 0.25, the financial institution should sell 11.5433/ 4.3325 = 2.66435 units of Option B to make the portfolio value zero.

In this case, when the underlying price is $K < S < H$, the barrier payoff will be met by the vanilla call, and if $S \ge H$ barrier payoff and portfolio payoff will all be zero, making the hedge work perfectly.

Now, let's take option C. We are at $(N-2)\Delta t = 0.25$ time point. When the underlying price is $S_0 = 60$, option C's current value (by that time) is blsprice (60, 60, 0.10, 0.25, 0.30) $C_0 = 4.3325$ because the maturity of option C is 0.5 (i.e., the remaining maturity is 0.25).

However, we have option A (long) and option B (short) in our portfolio and values are

Option B: blsprice (60, 60, 0.10, 0.5, 0.30) = 6.5439
Option A: price (60, 50, 0.10, 0.5, 0.30) = 13.2207, respectively, at point 0.25

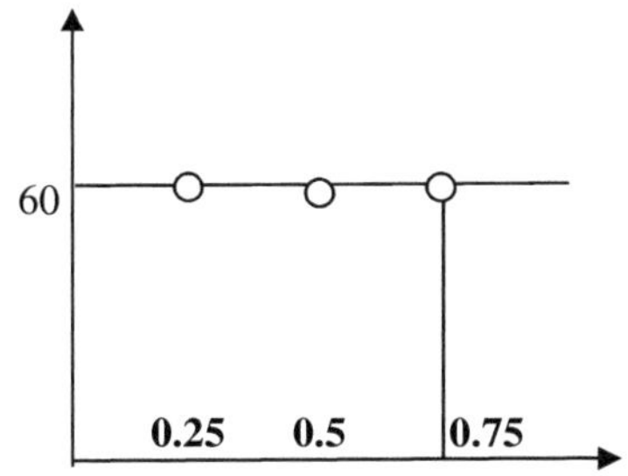

Figure 4.1. Boundary of the barrier option.

So, the overall portfolio value is $-2.66435 * 6.5439 + 13.2207 = -4.21454$. Therefore, the institution should buy $4.21454/4.3325 = 0.97277$ units of option C. Only in this case would the portfolio value be zero if the barrier is hit when the price is 60.

Finally, let's check the portfolio value at $\Delta t = 0$ point. If the underlying price is $S_0 = 60$, the prices will be as follows (Figure 4.1):

Option A: blsprice (60, 50, 0.10, 0.75, 0.30) = 14.7696
Option B: blsprice (60, 60, 0.10, 0.75, 0.30) = 8.3909
Option C: blsprice (60, 60, 0.10, 0.5, 0.30) = 6.5439

Then, the overall portfolio value is $+14.7696 - 8.3909 * 2.66435 + 6.5439 * 0.97277 = -1.221$.

Once again, the price of option D at this price level is blsprice (60, 60, 0.10, 0.25, 0.30), $C_0 = 4.3325$.

Therefore, the institution should buy $1.221/4.3325 = 0.28182$ units of option D. In this case, the value of the portfolio replicating the up-and-out barrier call is calculated as (using the initial option prices)

$$6.9924 - 2.66435 * 3.0846 + 0.97277 * 1.833$$
$$+ 0.28182 * 0.6144 = 0.73178$$

So, the cost of hedging is 0.73178. The actual barrier value is 0.3136, and the difference is due to the small number of time steps on the boundary. When the number of time steps is increased to 100, the cost of the hedge approaches 0.32, which is almost the benchmark value of the original target option.

The portfolio is unwound when any part of the boundary is reached. The hedging process does not require frequent rebalancing and provides significant savings on transaction costs.

4.3.1.2. *Down-and-out barrier call*

There is a difference between hedging up-and-out and down-and-out barrier calls. Assuming the strike and the initial price are the same or in a close neighborhood of each other, it gets "in-the-money" when the price goes up toward the barrier simultaneously. However, when the initial price decreases, it moves in the "out-of-the-money" direction. In this case, a vanilla call may hedge approximately the short "down-and-out" barrier position. For example, the price of "DOC" (down-and-out call) is 7.7274 for

$$S_0 = 60 \quad K = 60 \quad H = 50 \quad r = 0.1 \quad T = 0.75 \quad \sigma = 0.30$$

and the vanilla call price at $K = 60$ is 8.3909. The reason for the small difference is the possibility of turning out the prices after hitting the barrier at some time and exceeding the strike at maturity.

It can be shown that "down-and-out" calls can be hedged using a standard call option at the barrier's strike and a standard put option, always making the portfolio value zero at each time step with various strike levels. We have found the approximate hedge value as 7.7279 with the following price structure:

Option A: blsprice (60, 60, 0.10, 0.75, 0.30): 8.3909 (long)
Option B: blsprice (60, 44.326, 0.10, 0.75, 0.30): 0.4171 (short)
Option C: blsprice (60, 44.641, 0.10, 0.5, 0.30): 0.2310 (short)
Option D: blsprice (60, 42.273, 0.10, 0.25, 0.30): 0.0149 (short)

The method works as follows: When the price is at the barrier level (50) at the time step $\Delta t = 0.5$, the call value is

$$\text{blsprice}(50,\ 60,\ 0.10,\ 0.25,\ 0.30) = 0.6144$$

The strike level making the portfolio level zero is 44.326 for the put option with maturity $T = 0.75$:

$$\text{blsprice}(50,\ 44.326,\ 0.10,\ 0.25,\ 0.30) = 0.6144$$

Now, we are at $\Delta t = 0.25$, and option values are

$$\text{blsprice}(50, 60, 0.10, 0.50, 0.30) = 1.8330$$

$$\text{blsprice}(50, 44.326, 0.10, 0.50, 0.30) = 1.1597$$

So, we need another put option for 1.8330–1.1597 = 0.6733 value and make this zero again.

The strike of this put option is 44.641, and the maturity is $T = 0.5$:

$$\text{blsprice}(50,\ 44.641,\ 0.10,\ 0.25,\ 0.30) = 0.6733$$

Finally, we are at $\Delta t = 0$, and when the price is 50, option values are

$$\text{blsprice}(50, 60, 0.10, 0.75, 0.30) = 3.0846$$
$$\text{blsprice}(50, 44.326, 0.10, 0.75, 0.30) = 1.5317$$
$$\text{blsprice}(50, 44.641, 0.10, 0.50, 0.30) = 1.2340$$

So, we need another put option for $3.0846 - 1.5317 - 1.2340 = 0.3189$ value and make this zero again. The strike of this put option is 42.273, and the maturity is $T = 0.25$:

$$\text{blsprice}(50, 42.273, 0.10, 0.25, 0.30) = 0.3189$$

By completing the hedge with long $\text{C}(K)$ and three short $\text{P}(K_1)$, $\text{P}(K_2)$, $\text{P}(K_3)$, we catch the "DOC" price almost perfectly.

4.3.1.3. *Down-and-out barrier put (DOP)*

This section constructs a hedge for a "down-and-out" barrier put using standard put options. The principle is the same: hedge on and inside the boundary. For example, let's assume $S_0 = K = 60$, $H = 50$, $r = 10\%$ $\sigma = 30\%$ $T = 0.75$, similar to the previous examples. The option price of DOP is 0.30602. Now, the selling institution will use the Static Options Replication proposed by Derman *et al.* (2000) as follows.

The prices of vanilla put options to be used for hedging on the boundary are as follows:

Put Prices

Option A: blsprice (60, 60, 0.10, 0.75, 0.30): 4.0555
Option B: blsprice (60, 50, 0.10, 0.75, 0.30): 1.1567
Option C: blsprice (60, 50, 0.10, 0.5, 0.30): 0.7822
Option D: blsprice (60, 50, 0.10, 0.25, 0.30): 0.3088

It is inadequate to replicate the barrier option by only one put option with maturity $T = 0.75$ and a strike $K = 60$. We will use three time steps $\Delta t = 0.25, 0.5, 0.75$ and three put options, which make the portfolio value "0" with the strike level equal to the barrier: $K = H$, i.e., on the boundary.

If $S0 = 50$, the value of option A, (blsprice (50, 60, 0.10, 0.25, 0.30) $= P_0$) is 9.1330 and option B is (blsprice (50, 50, 0.10, 0.25, 0.30) $= P_0$) 2.3759, respectively. The number of option B to be shorted is

$$-\frac{9.133}{2.3759} = -3.844$$

to make the portfolio value zero at that point.

When the underlying price is less than 60 and above 50, the payoff is represented by the vanilla put, and option A provides what we need. When the price is 50, the barrier option is out, yet the vanilla option A still has some value, which is netted off by the short position of option B.

Now, we are at $\Delta t = 0.25$ dir. If the underlying price is $S_0 = 50$, the value of the third option, i.e., option C, is blsprice(50, 50, 0.10, 0.25, 0.30) $= P_0 = 2.3759$.

However, our portfolio has options A (long) and B (short). The value of these options is

B: blsprice (50, 50, 0.10, 0.5, 0.30) = 3.0147
A: blsprice (50, 60, 0.10, 0.5, 0.30) = 8.9067

So, the portfolio's value is $-3.844 * 3.0147 + 8.9067 = -2.6818$. The institution has to buy $2.6818/2.3759 = 1.12875$ units of option C. Accordingly, when the price is 50, the portfolio's value will be zero.

Finally, let's evaluate the positions at $\Delta t = 0$ point. When the price is $S_0 = 50$, the values of the options are

Option A: blsprice (50,60,0.10,0.75,0.30) = 8.7492
Option B: blsprice (50,50,0.10,0.75,0.30) = 3.3796 and $-3.3796 * 3.844 = -12.9912$ as a total value
Option C: blsprice (50,50,0.10,0.5,0.30) = 3.0147

That is, $3.0147 * 1.12875 = 3.4028$ as a total value. The overall portfolio value is

$$+8.7492 - 3.3796 * 3.844 + 3.0147 * 1.12875 = -0.8392$$

At that point ($S_0 = 50$), the value of option D is 2.3759 dir. Therefore, the institution should buy $0.8392/2.3759 = 0.3532$ units of option D to make the portfolio value zero.

So, with the weights and the initial option prices with ($S_0 = 60$), the value of the portfolio replicating the DOP barrier option is

$$4.0555 - 3.8439 * 1.1567 + 1.12875 * 0.7822$$
$$+ 0.3532 * 0.3088 = 0.601198$$

The original DOP value is 0.30602, and the difference between the values is due to the frequency of the hedging points on the boundary. The hedging cost is 0.3509 and 0.31 for the hedging frequencies 20 and 100 time points, respectively.

As always, the options will be automatically closed when they are matured.

4.3.1.4. *Up-and-out barrier put*

The same reasoning is valid for the UOPs and the DOPs, as mentioned in the previous section for the calls. Assuming the strike and the initial price are the same or in a close neighborhood of each other, it gets "out-of-the-money" and "out" when the price goes up toward the barrier simultaneously. However, when the initial price decreases, it moves "in-the-money" direction and remains "in." Therefore, one standard put option and various call options with different strikes at each time step may provide a very close hedge. Here is another example of a UOP Barrier with

$$S_0 = 55 \quad K = 55 \quad H = 60 \quad r = 10\% \quad \sigma = 30\% \quad T = 1$$

We will use four time points this time.

Table 4.1 shows the values of portfolios at each time step when the underlying price is $S_0 = H = 60$. If the price hits the barrier, the

Table 4.1. Hedging on the boundary.

Option	Type	Strike/ maturity	Value of the portfolio				
			$\Delta t = 0$	$\Delta t = 0.25$	$\Delta t = 0.5$	$\Delta t = 0.75$	$\Delta t = 1$
A	+P	55/1	2.6452	2.3224	1.8535	1.1207	0
B	−C	69.505/1	−5.9703	−4.4360	−2.8142	−1.1206	0
C	+C	70.44/0.75	4.1476	+2.5689	0.9607	0	
D	−C	74.71/0.5	−1.6656	−0.4554	0		
E	+C	71.216/0.25	0.8431	0			
			0	0	0	0	0

option is out, and the portfolio generates no liability. If the barrier is not hit, the standard put option matches the barrier payoff inside the barrier. Hence, computing the prices of each option,

Option A: blsprice (55, 55, 0.10, 1, 0.30): 3.9697
Option B: blsprice (55, 69.505, 0.10, 1, 0.30): 3.7669 (−)
Option C: blsprice (55, 70.44, 0.10, 0.75, 0.30): 2.3546
Option D: blsprice (55, 74.71, 0.10, 0.5, 0.30): 0.7290 (−)
Option E: blsprice (55, 71.216, 0.10, 0.25, 0.30): 0.2384

will yield a replicating cost of 2.067 as the hedging value where the price of the "up-and-out" barrier put is 2.1167.

4.3.2. *Put–call symmetry*

Car *et al.* (1998) present the hedging principles of single barriers with vanilla options using the put–call symmetry. This symmetry is assumed to hold when the underlying reaches the barrier. They first concentrate on down-and-out calls since the corresponding results can be recovered using the parity condition

$$\mathrm{OC}(K, H) = \mathrm{C}(K) - \mathrm{IC}(K, H) \tag{4.1}$$

where $\mathrm{OC}(K, H)$, and $\mathrm{IC}(K, H)$ are out-call and in-call, respectively, with strike K and barrier H.

4.3.2.1. *Down-and-out calls*

A DOC with a strike K and barrier $H < K$ becomes worthless if the barrier is hit at any time during its life. To hedge a down-and-out call, we must match the terminal payoff and the payoff along the barrier. We may simply purchase a standard call $C(K)$ to hedge the terminal payoff.

When $F = H$, the DOC is worthless, but our current hedge has a positive value. Thus, we need to sell off an instrument with the same value when the forward price equals the barrier value. From put–call symmetry (see Appendix C), we know that

$$C(K) = KH^{-1}\mathrm{P}(H^2K^{-1})\ K_P = H^2K^{-1} \tag{4.2}$$

Thus, we need to write KH^{-1} puts with a strike at H^2K^{-1} to complete the hedge:

$$\text{DOC}(K, H) = C(K) - KH^{-1}P(H^2K^{-1}) \quad H < K$$

If the barrier is hit before maturity, the replicating portfolio should be liquidated by selling the call and buying back KH^{-1} puts. If the barrier is not hit, a long call gives the same terminal payoff with the DOC, and the puts expire worthless as $H^2K^{-1} < H$.

The hedging formula is long call and short put via the PCS formula

$$\text{DOC} = C(K) - KH^{-1}P(H^2K^{-1})$$
$$\text{DOC} = C(100) - 1.0526P(90.25)$$

with $K = 100$ $H = 95$ $S_0 = 100$ $r = r_f(d)$ $\sigma = 0.3$ $T = 1$
C(100) = blsprice (100, 100, 0.0, 1, 0.3) = 11.9235
P(90.25) = blsprice (100, 90.25, 0.0, 1, 0.3) = 7.1184
1.0526 ∗ P(90.25) = 7.4928

The difference is the value of the "down-and-out" European barrier call option, which is 4.4307 (4.4295 with MATLAB).

4.3.2.2. *Up-and-out calls*

An up-and-out call UOC has a knockout barrier above the current forward price. When the barrier is at or below the strike ($H \leq K$), the UOC is always worthless. Therefore, we consider barriers set above the strike ($H > K$), which implies the option has intrinsic value before it is knocked out.

Our replicating portfolio contains a standard call at strike K and a short position in KH^{-1} puts with strike H^2K^{-1}. However, this causes problems at expiration if the barrier has not been hit, and the put option may be in-the-money. Considering

$$C(K) = [F - K]B + P(K)$$
$$\text{OC}(K, H) = C(K) - \text{IC}(K, H)$$

we can write the replicating portfolio with up-and-in securities as

$$\begin{aligned}\mathrm{UOC}(K,H) &= C(K) - \mathrm{UIC}(K,H)\\ \mathrm{UIC}(K,H) + \mathrm{UIB}(H) &= \mathrm{UIP}(K,H) + \mathrm{UIS}(K)\\ \mathrm{UOC}(K,H) &= C(K) - [H-K]\mathrm{UIB}(H) - \mathrm{UIP}(K,H) \qquad (4.3)\end{aligned}$$

where the up-and-in bond $\mathrm{UIB}(H)$ pays \$1 at expiration if the barrier has been hit before maturity.

To see if the portfolio matches with the payoff $\mathrm{UOC}(K,H)$, first, we assume the barrier is never touched. Then, the standard long call position $\mathrm{C}(K)$ provides the required payoff, and the remaining up-and-in instruments expire worthless. Conversely, if the UOC knocks out, the other put and bond instruments knock in. Therefore, the right side of the equation could be written in terms of put–call parity. Since $F = H$, the parity dictates

$$\mathrm{C}(K) - [F-K] - \mathrm{P}(K) = 0$$

So, the portfolio exactly matches the payoff of $\mathrm{UOC}(K,H)$. The advantage of hedging $\mathrm{UOC}(K,H)$ with up-and-in puts and bonds is that the equation holds for any continuous process for the underlying price. However, the disadvantage is that there might not be enough up-and-in instruments trading in the market. However, an $\mathrm{UIP}(K,H)$ can be replicated with KH^{-1} calls struck at H^2K^{-1} and an $\mathrm{UIB}(H)$ can be replicated by buying two binary calls struck at H and H^{-1} European calls struck at H:

$$\mathrm{UIB}(H) = 2\mathrm{BC}(H) + H^{-1}\mathrm{C}(H) \quad H > F$$

The intuition is that since the probability of finishing in the money is 50%, two binaries are enough to replicate. However, the positive skew of terminal price distribution implies that the probabilities are slightly less than 0.5, and we require a small correction with $H^{-1}\mathrm{C}(H)$. Then, we can write

$$\begin{aligned}\mathrm{UOC}(K,H) = \mathrm{C}(K) &- [H-K][2\mathrm{BC}(H) + H^{-1}\mathrm{C}(H)]\\ &- KH^{-1}\mathrm{C}(H^2K^{-1})\\ &H > K, F \qquad (4.4)\end{aligned}$$

It is also well known that binary calls can be synthesized using an infinite number of vertical spreads of standard calls:

$$\mathrm{BC}(H) = \lim_{n\to\infty} n\left[\mathrm{C}(H) - \mathrm{C}\left(H + \frac{1}{n}\right)\right] \tag{4.5}$$

As a result, the up-and-out call can be replicated using standard calls alone. However, the replication strategy of binary calls in (3.5) is not so practical. To remedy this, Carr *et al.* (1998) use Richardson extrapolation. Suppose $F = S = 100$ $K = 105(H)$ $r = r_f = 4\%$ $\sigma = 20\%$ $T = 0.25$ years. The exact binary call value is \$0.292384. Defining VS(n) as the value of n vertical call spreads with strikes 105 and $105 + \frac{1}{n}$ $n = 1, 2, 3$, we can calculate the vertical spread value as

$$\mathrm{VS}(1) = 0.276446 \quad \mathrm{VS}(2) = 0.284331 \quad \mathrm{VS}(3) = 0.286997$$

Applying Richardson extrapolation, Marchuk and Shaidurov (1983, p. 24) can be seen for the derivation of Richardson weights:

$$\mathrm{BC}(105) = 6\mathrm{C}(105) - 0.5\mathrm{C}(106) + 8\mathrm{C}(105.5) - 13.5\mathrm{C}(105.33)$$

Now, we can replicate an UOC(K, H) with $K = 100$ $H = 105$:

$$\begin{aligned}\mathrm{UOC}(K, H) = {} & \mathrm{C}(K) - [H - K][2\mathrm{BC}(H) + H^{-1}\mathrm{C}(H)] \\ & - KH^{-1}\mathrm{C}(H^2K^{-1}) \quad H > K, F\end{aligned}$$

by purchasing C(100), selling 5 $[2\mathrm{BC}(105) + 105^{-1}\mathrm{C}(105)]$ and selling 0.9524 calls struck at $H^2K^{-1} = 110.25$. This portfolio must provide a zero value along the barrier and the call payoff at maturity. For down-and-in bonds, we can use binary puts and a binary put can be recovered with

$$\mathrm{BP}(H) = \lim_{n\to\infty} n\left[\mathrm{P}\left(H + \frac{1}{n}\right) - \mathrm{P}(H)\right]$$

through the Richardson extrapolation with similar weights.

4.3.3. *Summary of strategies by using put–call symmetry*

Table 4.2 presents a list of strategies. Remember that all the barrier positions exclude the rebate payments.

Table 4.2. Summary of hedging strategies for single barriers.

Barrier	Hedging strategy	
Down-and-out call	Buy a call with strike K and sell KH^{-1} puts with strike $\frac{H^2}{K}$. If the barrier is hit, close the positions.	$K \geq H$
	Buy Call with strike K, sell $H - K$ units DIB, and sell put struck at K.	$K < H$
Up-and-out call	Buy a call with strike K, sell KH^{-1} calls with strike H^2/K sell $H - K$ units extrapolated calls, and H^{-1} calls with strike (H). If the barrier is hit, close all the positions.	$H > K$
	Not applicable.	$K < H$
Up-and-in call	Do nothing until the barrier is hit. When it is, purchase a standard call with the same strike as the up-and-in call initially sold.	$K \geq H$
	Buy KH^{-1} calls with strike H^2/K, buy $H - K$ units UIB.	$K < H$
Down-and-in call	Buy KH^{-1} puts with strike H^2/K. If the barrier is hit, sell the puts and buy a call at the same strike as the down-and-in call initially sold. If the barrier is never touched, all options will expire worthless. (Remember the parity condition C = DIC + DOC.)	$K \geq H$
	Buy a put with strike K, buy $H - K$ units, down-and-in bond.	$K < H$
Down-and-in put	Do nothing until the barrier is hit. When it is, purchase a standard put with the same strike as the down-and-in put initially sold.	$H > K$
	Buy KH^{-1} puts with strike H^2/K and buy $K - H$ DIB(H).	$K \geq H$
Down-and-out put	Not applicable.	$K < H$
	Buy $P(K)$, sell KH^{-1} puts with strike H^2/K and sell $K - H$ DIB(H).	$K \geq H$
Up-and-in put	Buy KH^{-1} calls with strike H^2/K. If the barrier is touched, sell the calls and buy a put at the same strike as the up-and-in put initially sold. If the barrier is never touched, all options will expire worthless.	$K \leq H$
	Buy call struck at K and buy $(K - H)$ UIB(H). If not touched, close the positions.	$K > H$
Up-and-out put	Sell KH^{-1} calls with strike H^2/K and buy a put with strike K. If the barrier is touched, close the positions (remember the parity condition $P =$ UIP + UOP).	$K \leq H$
	Buy $P(K)$, sell $(K - H)$ UIB(H) and sell $C(K)$.	$K > H$

4.4. Conclusion

The barrier options have high gamma positions when the underlying price is around the barrier. Therefore, they may become risky for the writers and must be hedged properly. In this section, we have explained essential tools for hedging barrier options and discussed the various uses of barriers. Derman *et al.* (2000) propose static hedging, which is based on hedging on the boundary of the option where the boundary is the barrier value. Bowie and Carr (1994) and Carr and Chou (1996, 1998, 2002) approach hedging via put–call symmetry and simply show how to hedge single barriers with vanilla options. Andersen *et al.* (2002), Bermin (2022), Poulsen (2006), Nalholm and Poulsen (2006), and Ilhan and Sircar (2006) are among the leading resources examining the hedging of barrier options. Also, many resources on exotic option pricing contain chapters on barrier option pricing. Among those, we refer to Bouzouba and Osseiran (2010), Buchen (2012), Briys *et al.* (1998), Cheuk and Vorst (1996), Clewlow and Strickland (1997, 1998), Das (1996), and Nelken (1996).

Chapter 5

Partial and Rainbow Barriers

5.1. Introduction

This chapter is based on Heynen and Kat's "Partial Barrier Options" (1994c) and Carr's "Two Extensions to Barrier Option Valuation" (1995) papers. Using the basic principles and densities in their papers, we have derived all the formulas not entirely given in the documents.

Sometimes, investors may need the monitoring period limited to only part of the relevant option's lifetime. For example, an investor buying an up-and-in call might want the monitoring period to start sometime after the option's starting date to make the option cheaper. Other restrictions on the monitoring period can make the option expensive. On the other hand, for up-and-in calls, it also allows the barrier to be chosen closer to the spot price, increasing the option premium.

Partial barrier options also provide the building blocks to package various other partial exotic options, such as partial ladder options. A ladder option is an ordinary put or call option with the additional feature that it is locked in if the underlying price hits one of several barrier levels.

Suppose we want to construct a ladder call with $K < H_1 < H_2$. Such an option can be packaged by

(1) buying an ordinary call with strike K
(2) writing an up-and-in put with strike K and barrier H_1
(3) buying an up-and-in put with strike H_1 and barrier H_1

(4) writing an up-and-in put with strike H_1 and barrier H_2
(5) buying an up-and-in put with strike H_2 and barrier H_2.

$K = 100$	$H_1 = 105$ hits $S_t = 103$	$H_1 = 105$ hits $S_t = 108$	$H_2 = 110$ hits $S_t = 108$	$H_2 = 110$ hits $S_t = 112$
Ladder pays	$105 - 100 = 5$	$108 - 100 = 8$	$110 - 100 = 10$	$110 - 100 = 12$
1 receives	$103 - 100 = 3$	$108 - 100 = 8$	$108 - 100 = 8$	$112 - 100 = 12$
2	$\max(100 - 103, 0) = 0$	$\max(100 - 108, 0) = 0$	$\max(100 - 108, 0) = 0$	0
3 receives	$\max(105 - 103, 0) = 2$	$\max(105 - 108, 0) = 0$	$\max(105 - 108, 0) = 0$	0
4	0	0	$\max(105 - 108, 0) = 0$	0
5	0	0 $\max(110 - 108, 0) = 2$	0	

Together with the third option, we are locked in a profit of $H_1 - K$ with a potential upside profit opportunity. The fourth and fifth options do the same for the second barrier level. This lock-in feature may cause ladder options to become expensive, and as suggested by Heynen and Kat (1994c), a remedy is to restrict the lifetime of the options. Since ladder options are usually used to solve market exit timing problems, choosing the monitoring period as the last part of the option's lifetime is sufficient.

5.2. Valuation

The following known SDE gives the risk-neutral price process for the underlying asset:

$$d \ln\left(\frac{S_t}{S_0}\right) = \left(r - \delta - \frac{1}{2}\sigma^2\right) dt + \sigma dW_t$$

First, we take the options with a monitoring period starting at time 0 and ending at an arbitrary date t_1 before expiration. That means the monitoring period is the initial period, and Heynen and Kat refer to this type of partial barrier options as Type A options.

The maximum price of the underlying asset over the monitoring period is $M_0^{t_1}$.

The price of an up-and-out call (UOC) can be written as

$$\mathrm{UOC}(A) = e^{-rT} E\left[(S_T - K)1_{S_T>K, M_0^{t_1}<H}\right] \quad S_0 < H$$

This can be written under two different probability measures as

$$\mathrm{UOC}(A) = S_0 \tilde{E}\left[1_{S_T>K, M_0^{t_1}<H}\right] - e^{-rT} K E[1_{S_T>K, M_0^{t_1}<H}]$$

where we use $\widetilde{E}$ as expectation under the probability measure where the stock is taken as numeraire and change the drift from $\left(r - \delta - \frac{1}{2}\sigma^2\right)$ to $\left(r - \delta + \frac{1}{2}\sigma^2\right)$.

$$\begin{aligned}
d\widetilde{W} &= dW^S + \sigma dt \\
dS &= (r - q)Sdt + \sigma S d\widetilde{W} \\
dS &= (r - q + \sigma^2)Sdt + \sigma S dW^S
\end{aligned}$$

Using Ito's lemma and finding $d(\ln S)$ yields

$$\ln\,(S_T/S_0) = \left(r - q + \frac{1}{2}\sigma^2\right) dt + \sigma dW^S$$

Similarly, a down-and-out call (DOC)(A) can be written as

$$\mathrm{DOC}(A) = e^{-rT} E\left[(S_T - K)1_{S_T>K, m_0^{t_1}>H}\right] \quad S_0 > H$$

$$\mathrm{DOC}(A) = S_0 \widetilde{E}\left[1_{S_T>K, m_0^{t_1}>H}\right] - e^{-rT} K E\left[1_{S_T>K, m_0^{t_1}>H}\right]$$

where $m_0^{t_1}$ is the minimum price over the initial monitoring period.

The price is

$$\begin{aligned}
&OC(A) \\
&= S_0\left[N\left(d_1, \theta e_1; \theta\sqrt{t_1/T}\right) - \left(\frac{H}{S_0}\right)^{\frac{2r}{\sigma^2}+1} N\left(f_1, \theta e_1'; \theta\sqrt{t_1/T}\right)\right]
\end{aligned}$$

$$-e^{-rT}K\left[N\left(d_2,\theta e_2;\theta\sqrt{t_1/T}\right)\right.$$

$$\left.-\left(\frac{H}{S_0}\right)^{\frac{2r}{\sigma^2}-1}N(f_2,\theta e_2';\theta\sqrt{t_1/T})\right]$$

where $\theta=-1$ for UOC, $\theta=1$ for DOC.

$$d_1=\frac{-\ln\frac{K}{S_0}+\left(r+\frac{1}{2}\sigma^2\right)T}{\sigma\sqrt{T}}=\frac{\ln\frac{S_0}{K}+\left(r+\frac{1}{2}\sigma^2\right)T}{\sigma\sqrt{T}}$$

$$d_2=d_1-\sigma\sqrt{T}$$

$$e_1=\frac{-\ln\frac{H}{S_0}+\left(r+\frac{1}{2}\sigma^2\right)t_1}{\sigma\sqrt{t_1}}$$

$$e_2=e_1-\sigma\sqrt{t_1}$$

$$e_1'=e_1+\frac{2\ln\frac{H}{S_0}}{\sigma\sqrt{t_1}}\quad e_2'=e_1'-\sigma\sqrt{t_1}$$

$$f_1=\frac{-\ln\frac{K}{S_0}+2\ln\frac{H}{S_0}+\left(r+\frac{1}{2}\sigma^2\right)T}{\sigma\sqrt{T}}$$

$$f_2=f_1-\sigma\sqrt{T}$$

We need to evaluate the following probability distributions

$$E\left[1_{S_T>K,M_0^{t_1}<H}\right]$$
$$E\left[1_{S_T>K,m_0^{t_1}>H}\right]$$

5.3. Calculation of Probabilities and Densities

In this section, we have benefited from Carr's (1995) paper, "Two extensions to barrier option valuation." After finding the basic probabilities, we can price early-starting (Type A) and forward-starting (Type B) partial barrier options.

By the reflection principle, on a probability space $(\Omega, \mathcal{F}, P_0)$ and under the measure P_0

$$\begin{aligned} P_0(M_{01} > b, X_1 < k) &= P_0(M_{01} > b, X_1 > 2b - k) \\ &= P_0(X_1 > 2b - k) \end{aligned}$$

and because of the symmetry, we can write the cumulative distribution function and the density function (derivative of cumulative distribution with respect to k) as

$$P_0(-X_1 < k - 2b) = N\left(\frac{k-2b}{t_1^{1/2}}\right)$$

$$P_0(M_{01} > b, X_1 \in dk) = \frac{1}{t_1^{1/2}} N'\left(\frac{k-2b}{t_1^{1/2}}\right) = \frac{1}{t_1^{1/2}} n\left(\frac{k-2b}{t_1^{1/2}}\right)$$

respectively.

To add drift μ to the process X, we define a new probability measure P equivalent to P_0 by its Radon–Nicodym derivative

$$\frac{dP}{dP_0} = \mu X_1 - \frac{1}{2}\mu_1^2 t_1$$

Then, by Girsanov's theorem', X has drift μ under P.

$$E\left[1_{(M_{01}>b, X_1<k)}\right] = E_0\left[\frac{dP}{dP_0} 1_{(M_{01}>b, X_1<k)}\right]$$

$$E_0\left[\mu X_1 - \frac{1}{2}\mu_1^2 t_1 1_{(M_{01}>b, X_1<k)}\right]$$

$$= E_0\left[\left(\mu X_1 - \frac{1}{2}\mu_1^2 t_1\right) P_0\left(M_{01} > b, X_1 < k\right)\right]$$

$$= e^{-\frac{1}{2}\mu_1^2 t_1}\int_{-\infty}^{k} e^{\mu z} P_0\left(M_{01} > b, X_1 \in dz\right)$$

$$e^{-\frac{1}{2}\mu_1^2 t_1}\int_{-\infty}^{k} \frac{e^{\mu z}}{t_1^{1/2}} N'\left(\frac{z-2b}{t_1^{1/2}}\right) dz = e^{-\frac{1}{2}\mu_1^2 t_1}\int_{-\infty}^{k} e^{\mu z} n_z\left(2b, t_1\right) dz$$

$$n_z\left(\mu, \sigma^2\right) = \frac{1}{\sigma\sqrt{2\pi}} e^{-\frac{1}{2}\left(\frac{z-\mu}{\sigma}\right)^2}$$

$$\int_{-\infty}^{k} e^{-\frac{1}{2}\mu_1^2 t_1} e^{\mu z} n_z\left(2b, t_1\right) = \int_{-\infty}^{k} e^{-\frac{1}{2}\mu_1^2 t_1} e^{\mu z} e^{-\frac{1}{2}\left(\frac{z-2b}{t_1^{1/2}}\right)^2} dz$$

$$-\frac{1}{2}\mu_1^2 t_1 + \mu z - \frac{1}{2t_1}(z^2 + 4b^2 - 4bz)$$

$$= -\frac{1}{2t_1}\mu_1^2 t_1^2 + \frac{2\mu z t_1}{2t_1} - \frac{1}{2t_1}\left(z^2 + 4b^2 - 4bz\right)$$

If we add and subtract $\frac{4\mu b t_1}{2t_1}$

$$-\frac{1}{2t_1}\mu_1^2 t_1^2 + \frac{2\mu z t_1}{2t_1} - \frac{1}{2t_1}(z^2 + 4b^2 - 4bz) - \frac{4\mu b t_1}{2t_1} + \frac{4\mu b t_1}{2t_1}$$

$$-\frac{1}{2t_1}(z - 2b - \mu t_1)^2 + 2\mu b$$

That is,

$$\int_{-\infty}^{k} e^{-\frac{1}{2}\mu_1^2 t_1} e^{\mu z} e^{-\frac{1}{2}\left(\frac{z-2b}{t_1^{1/2}}\right)^2} dz = e^{2\mu b}\int_{-\infty}^{k} e^{-\frac{1}{2}\left(\frac{z-2b-\mu t_1}{t_1^{1/2}}\right)^2} dz$$

$$= E\left[1_{(M_{01} > b, X_1 < k)}\right] = P\left(\left(M_{01} > b, X_1 < k\right)\right)$$

$$= e^{2\mu b} N\left(\frac{k - 2b - \mu t_1}{t_1^{1/2}}\right)$$

For arbitrary σ and $dX_1 = \mu dt_1 + \sigma dW_{t_1}$

$$E\left[1_{(M_{01}>b,X_1<k)}\right] = P\left((M_{01} > b, X_1 < k)\right)$$
$$= e^{2\mu b/\sigma^2} N\left(\frac{k - 2b - \mu t_1}{\sigma\sqrt{t_1}}\right)$$

Letting $k \uparrow b$ yields

$$E\left[1_{(M_{01}>b,X_1<b)}\right] = P\left((M_{01} > b, X_1 < b)\right) = e^{2\mu b/\sigma^2} N\left(\frac{-b - \mu t_1}{\sigma\sqrt{t_1}}\right)$$

Let $M_{12} = \max_{t_1 \le t \le t_2} X_t$ $m_{12} = \min_{t_1 \le t \le t_2} X_t$ denote the maximum and minimum of the process X_t in $[t_1, t_2]$.

$$P(M_{01} > b, X_1 < k_1, M_{12} < b, X_2 < k_2)$$
$$= P\left(M_{01} > b, X_1 < k_1, X_2 < k_2\right)$$
$$- P\left(M_{01} > b, X_1 < k_1, M_{12} > b, X_2 < k_2\right)$$

The probability that $M_{12} < b$, $X_2 < k_2$ provided that $M_{01} > b$, $X_1 < k_1$, is equal to the probability $P(M_{01} > b, X_1 < k_1, X_2 < k_2)$ minus the probability that $X_2 < k_2$ but the stock value hits the barrier in the period $M_{12} > b$ (maximum exceeds the barrier). Remember that the asset may have hit the barrier b in $[0,\ t_1]$ and can also be $X_1 < k_1$ at t_1.

By the reflection principle, the 1st probability on the right-hand side is

$$P_0\left(M_{01} > b, X_1 < k_1, X_2 < k_2\right) = P\left(X_1 > 2b - k_1, X_2 > 2b - k_2\right)$$

Again, by symmetry,

$$P_0\left(-X_1 < k_1 - 2b,\ -X_2 < k_2 - 2b\right) = N_2\left(\frac{k_1 - 2b}{t_1^{1/2}}, \frac{k_2 - 2b}{t_2^{1/2}}; \sqrt{\frac{t_1}{t_2}}\right) \tag{5.1}$$

$$N_2\left(x_1, x_2; \rho\right) = \frac{1}{2\pi\sqrt{1-\rho^2}} \int_{-\infty}^{x_1} \int_{-\infty}^{x_2}$$
$$\times \exp\left\{-\frac{1}{2(1-\rho^2)}\left[z_1^2 - 2\rho z_1 z_2 + z_2^2\right]\right\} dz_2 dz_1$$

The second probability

$$P_0\left(M_{01} > b, X_1 < k_1, M_{12} > b,\ X_2 < k_2\right)$$

$$= P\left(M_{01} > b, X_1 < k_1, m_{12} < b,\ X_2 < k_2\right)$$

$$P\left(X_1 > 2b - k_1,\ X_2 < k_2\right) = P\left(-X_1 < k_1 - 2b,\ X_2 < k_2\right)$$

$$N_2\left(\frac{k_1 - 2b}{t_1^{1/2}}, \frac{k_2}{t_2^{1/2}}; -\sqrt{\frac{t_1}{t_2}}\right) \tag{5.2}$$

This is the bivariate normal distribution with a minus correlation coefficient because of $-X_1$ and X_2. Also $X_2 < k_2$ supersedes the $m_{12} < b$. Substituting

$$P_0\left(M_{01} > b, X_1 < k_1, M_{12} < b, X_2 < k_2\right)$$

$$= N_2\left(\frac{k_1 - 2b}{t_1^{1/2}}, \frac{k_2 - 2b}{t_2^{1/2}}; \sqrt{\frac{t_1}{t_2}}\right) - N_2\left(\frac{k_1 - 2b}{t_1^{1/2}}, \frac{k_2}{t_2^{1/2}}; -\sqrt{\frac{t_1}{t_2}}\right) \tag{5.3}$$

Differentiating with respect to k_1 and k_2 yields

$$P_0\left(M_{01} > b, X_1 \in dk_1, M_{12} < b, X_2 \in dk_2\right)$$

$$= n_{z_1 z_2}\left(\begin{pmatrix} 2b \\ 2b \end{pmatrix}, \begin{pmatrix} t_1 & t_1 \\ t_1 & t_2 \end{pmatrix}\right) - n_{z_1 z_2}\left(\begin{pmatrix} 2b \\ 0 \end{pmatrix}, \begin{pmatrix} t_1 & -t_1 \\ -t_1 & t_2 \end{pmatrix}\right) dk_1 dk_2$$

Let's define a new probability measure to add drift.

$$\frac{dP}{dP_0} = \exp\left\{\mu X_2 - \frac{1}{2}\mu^2 t_2\right\}$$

Now, X has drift μ under P. Under the new measure P

$$P\left(M_{01} > b, X_1 < k_1, M_{12} < b, X_2 < k_2\right)$$

$$= E\left[1\left(M_{01} > b, X_1 < k_1, M_{12} < b, X_2 < k_2\right)\right] =$$

$$E_0\left[\frac{dP}{dP_0} 1\left(M_{01} > b, X_1 < k_1, M_{12} < b, X_2 < k_2\right)\right]$$

$$E_0\left[\exp\left\{\mu X_2 - \frac{1}{2}\mu^2 t_2\right\} 1\left(M_{01} > b, X_1 < k_1, M_{12} < b, X_2 < k_2\right)\right]$$

By writing

$$\int_{-\infty}^{k_1}\int_{-\infty}^{k_2}\exp\left\{\mu z_2-\frac{1}{2}\mu^2 t_2\right\}$$
$$\times\left[P_0\left(M_{01}>b,X_1\in dk_1,M_{12}<b,X_2\in dk_2\right)\right]$$

and using the relationship from a multivariate normal distribution, we obtain

$$\int_{-\infty}^{k_1}\int_{-\infty}^{k_2}\exp\left\{\mu z_2-\frac{1}{2}\mu^2 t_2\right\}\left[n_{z_1z_2}\left(\begin{pmatrix}2b\\2b\end{pmatrix},\begin{pmatrix}t_1 & t_1\\ t_1 & t_2\end{pmatrix}\right)\right.$$
$$\left.-n_{z_1z_2}\left(\begin{pmatrix}2b\\0\end{pmatrix},\begin{pmatrix}t_1 & -t_1\\ -t_1 & t_2\end{pmatrix}\right)\right]dz_1dz_2$$
$$=\int_{-\infty}^{k_1}\int_{-\infty}^{k_2}\left[e^{2\mu b}n_{z_1z_2}\left(\begin{pmatrix}2b+\mu t_1\\2b+\mu t_2\end{pmatrix},\begin{pmatrix}t_1 & t_1\\ t_1 & t_2\end{pmatrix}\right)\right.$$
$$\left.-n_{z_1z_2}\left(\begin{pmatrix}2b-\mu t_1\\ \mu t_2\end{pmatrix},\begin{pmatrix}t_1 & -t_1\\ -t_1 & t_2\end{pmatrix}\right)\right]dz_1dz_2$$

By writing

$$\int_{-\infty}^{k_1}\int_{-\infty}^{k_2}\exp\left(\mu X_2-\frac{1}{2}\mu^2 t_2\right)P_0$$
$$\times\left(M_{01}>b,X_1\in dz_1,M_{12}\leq b,X_2\in dz_2\right)$$
$$\int_{-\infty}^{k_1}\int_{-\infty}^{k_2}\exp\left(\mu X_2-\frac{1}{2}\mu^2 t_2\right)$$
$$\left[n_{z_1z_2}\left(\begin{pmatrix}2b\\2b\end{pmatrix},\begin{pmatrix}t_1 & t_1\\ t_1 & t_2\end{pmatrix}\right)-n_{z_1z_2}\left(\begin{pmatrix}2b\\0\end{pmatrix},\begin{pmatrix}t_1 & -t_1\\ -t_1 & t_2\end{pmatrix}\right)\right]dz_2dz_1$$

(For proof, see Carr (1995), App. A.4, p. 34)

$$\exp\left(w'x\right)n_x\left(\mu,\Omega\right)=\exp\left(w'\mu+\frac{1}{2}w'\Omega w\right)n_x\left(\mu+\Omega w,\Omega\right)$$

$$\exp\left(w'\mu+\frac{1}{2}w'\Omega w\right)=\exp\left(\begin{pmatrix}0 & \mu\end{pmatrix}\begin{pmatrix}2b\\2b\end{pmatrix}\right.$$
$$\left.+\frac{1}{2}\begin{pmatrix}0 & \mu\end{pmatrix}\begin{pmatrix}t_1 & t_1\\t_1 & t_2\end{pmatrix}\begin{pmatrix}0\\\mu\end{pmatrix}\right)$$

$$n_x\left(\mu+\Omega w,\Omega\right)=\begin{pmatrix}2b\\2b\end{pmatrix}+\begin{pmatrix}t_1 & t_1\\t_1 & t_2\end{pmatrix}\begin{pmatrix}0\\\mu\end{pmatrix}=\begin{pmatrix}2b+\mu t_1\\2b+\mu t_2\end{pmatrix}$$

Then we have,

$$\int_{-\infty}^{k_1}\int_{-\infty}^{k_2}\left[\exp\ (2\mu b)\,n_{z_1z_2}\left(\begin{pmatrix}2b+\mu t_1\\2b+\mu t_2\end{pmatrix},\begin{pmatrix}t_1 & t_1\\t_1 & t_2\end{pmatrix}\right)\right.$$
$$\left.-n_{z_1z_2}\left(\begin{pmatrix}2b-\mu t_1\\\mu t_2\end{pmatrix},\begin{pmatrix}t_1 & -t_1\\-t_1 & t_2\end{pmatrix}\right)\right]dz_2dz_1$$

The exp $(2\mu b)$ term is the coefficient of only the first bivariate density. Because the minus term

$$-\frac{1}{2}\mu^2t_2$$

is canceled out with the $\frac{1}{2}\mu^2t_2$ coming out of the multiplication $\frac{1}{2}\begin{pmatrix}0 & \mu\end{pmatrix}\begin{pmatrix}t_1 & t_1\\t_1 & t_2\end{pmatrix}\begin{pmatrix}0\\\mu\end{pmatrix}$.

For the second bivariate density, we can write

$$\exp\left(w'\mu+\frac{1}{2}w'\Omega w\right)=\exp\left(\begin{pmatrix}0 & \mu\end{pmatrix}\begin{pmatrix}2b\\0\end{pmatrix}\right.$$
$$\left.+\begin{pmatrix}0 & \mu\end{pmatrix}\begin{pmatrix}t_1 & -t_1\\-t_1 & t_2\end{pmatrix}\begin{pmatrix}0\\\mu\end{pmatrix}\right)$$

This time, there is no exp $(2\mu b)$ term, and

$$-\frac{1}{2}\mu^2t_2$$

is also canceled out. But the $n_x\left(\mu+\Omega w,\Omega\right)$ is

$$\begin{pmatrix}2b\\0\end{pmatrix}+\begin{pmatrix}t_1 & -t_1\\-t_1 & t_2\end{pmatrix}\begin{pmatrix}0\\\mu\end{pmatrix}=\begin{pmatrix}2b-\mu t_1\\\mu t_2\end{pmatrix}$$

Integration would give the cumulative bivariate normal distribution function:

$$e^{2\mu b}N_2\left(\frac{k_1-2b-\mu t_1}{\sqrt{t_1}},\frac{k_2-2b-\mu t_2}{\sqrt{t_2}};\sqrt{\frac{t_1}{t_2}}\right)$$

$$-N_2\left(\frac{k_1-2b+\mu t_1}{\sqrt{t_1}},\frac{k_2-\mu t_2}{\sqrt{t_2}};-\sqrt{\frac{t_1}{t_2}}\right)$$

which corresponds to

$$e^{\frac{2\mu b}{\sigma^2}}N_2\left(\frac{k_1-2b-\mu t_1}{\sigma\sqrt{t_1}},\frac{k_2-2b-\mu t_2}{\sigma\sqrt{t_2}};\sqrt{\frac{t_1}{t_2}}\right)$$

$$-N_2\left(\frac{k_1-2b+\mu t_1}{\sigma\sqrt{t_1}},\frac{k_2-\mu t_2}{\sigma\sqrt{t_2}};-\sqrt{\frac{t_1}{t_2}}\right)$$

for the process with variance σ^2 under the measure P.

Though the barrier is hit in the protection period and the stock price is less than k_1 at t_1, it is not hit in the unprotected period, and the stock price is less than k_2 at maturity.

For arbitrary σ the probability $P(M_{01} > b, X_1 < k_1, M_{12} < b, X_2 < k_2)$ is

$$e^{\frac{2\mu b}{\sigma^2}}N_2\left(\frac{k_1-2b-\mu t_1}{\sigma\sqrt{t_1}},\frac{k_2-2b-\mu t_2}{\sigma\sqrt{t_2}};\sqrt{\frac{t_1}{t_2}}\right)$$

$$-N_2\left(\frac{k_1-2b+\mu t_1}{\sigma\sqrt{t_1}},\frac{k_2-\mu t_2}{\sigma\sqrt{t_2}};-\sqrt{\frac{t_1}{t_2}}\right)$$

Letting $k_1 \uparrow b$ and $k_2 \uparrow b$ yields

$$e^{\frac{2\mu b}{\sigma^2}}N_2\left(\frac{-b-\mu t_1}{\sigma\sqrt{t_1}},\frac{-b-\mu t_2}{\sigma\sqrt{t_2}};\sqrt{\frac{t_1}{t_2}}\right)$$

$$-N_2\left(\frac{-b+\mu t_1}{\sigma\sqrt{t_1}},\frac{b-\mu t_2}{\sigma\sqrt{t_2}};-\sqrt{\frac{t_1}{t_2}}\right) \tag{5.4}$$

Also, for

$$E[1_{(M_{01}>b,X_1<k)}]$$

$$= P\left((M_{01} > b, X_1 < k)\right) = e^{2\mu b/\sigma^2}N\left(\frac{k-2b-\mu t_1}{\sigma\sqrt{t_1}}\right)$$

when $k \uparrow b$ we can write

$$E\left[1_{(M_{01}>b, X_1<b)}\right] = P\left((M_{01} > b, X_1 < b)\right) = e^{2\mu b/\sigma^2} N\left(\frac{-b-\mu t_1}{\sigma\sqrt{t_1}}\right)$$

Let's calculate the probability of hitting the barrier in an unprotected period. This is

$$P\left(M_{01} > b, X_1 < b, \tau < t_2\right) = P\left(M_{01} > b, X_1 < b, M_{12} > b\right)$$

$$= P\left(M_{01} > b, X_1 < b\right) - \left(M_{01} > b, X_1 < b, M_{12} < b\right)$$

$$e^{2\mu b/\sigma^2} N\left(\frac{-b-\mu t_1}{\sigma\sqrt{t_1}}\right) - e^{\frac{2\mu b}{\sigma^2}} N_2\left(\frac{-b-\mu t_1}{\sigma\sqrt{t_1}}, \frac{-b-\mu t_2}{\sigma\sqrt{t_2}}; \sqrt{\frac{t_1}{t_2}}\right)$$

$$+ N_2\left(\frac{-b+\mu t_1}{\sigma\sqrt{t_1}}, \frac{b-\mu t_2}{\sigma\sqrt{t_2}}; -\sqrt{\frac{t_1}{t_2}}\right)$$

Using the bivariate identity, the first two terms can be expressed as

$$e^{2\mu b/\sigma^2} N\left(\frac{-b-\mu t_1}{\sigma\sqrt{t_1}}\right) - e^{\frac{2\mu b}{\sigma^2}} N_2\left(\frac{-b-\mu t_1}{\sigma\sqrt{t_1}}, \frac{-b-\mu t_2}{\sigma\sqrt{t_2}}; \sqrt{\frac{t_1}{t_2}}\right)$$

$$= e^{\frac{2\mu b}{\sigma^2}} N_2\left(\frac{-b-\mu t_1}{\sigma\sqrt{t_1}}, \frac{b+\mu t_2}{\sigma\sqrt{t_2}}; -\sqrt{\frac{t_1}{t_2}}\right)$$

Though the barrier is hit in the protection period, the stock price is less than the barrier at time t_1, if the barrier is hit in the unprotected period, the option is knocked out.

$$\begin{aligned} P(M_{01} > b, X_1 < b, M_{12} > b) &= e^{\frac{2\mu b}{\sigma^2}} N_2\left(\frac{-b-\mu t_1}{\sigma\sqrt{t_1}}, \frac{b+\mu t_2}{\sigma\sqrt{t_2}}; -\sqrt{\frac{t_1}{t_2}}\right) \\ &+ N_2\left(\frac{-b+\mu t_1}{\sigma t_1^{1/2}}, \frac{b-\mu t_2}{\sigma t_2^{1/2}}; -\sqrt{\frac{t_1}{t_2}}\right) \end{aligned} \tag{5.5}$$

Now, we calculate the probability

$$P\left(X_2 < k_2, X_1 < b,\ \tau > t_2\right)$$

That is, the barrier is not hit during the unprotected period.

$$P\left(X_2 < k_2, X_1 < b,\ \tau > t_2\right)$$

$$= P\left(M_{01} < b, X_1 < b,\ X_2 < k_2,\ \tau > t_2\right)$$

$$+P(M_{01} > b, X_1 < b,\ X_2 < k_2,\ \tau > t_2)$$

$$= P(M_{02} < b,\ X_2 < k_2) + P(M_{01} > b, X_1 < b,\ X_2 < k_2,\ \tau > t_2)$$

By the reflection principle, we know the probability of $P(M_{02} < b,\ X_2 < k_2)$ with drift and variance is

$$P(M_{02} < b,\ X_2 < k_2) = P(X_2 < k_2) - P((M_{02} > b, X_2 < k_2))$$

$$= N\left(\frac{k_2 - \mu t_2}{\sigma\sqrt{t_2}}\right) - e^{2\mu b/\sigma^2} N\left(\frac{k_2 - 2b - \mu t_2}{\sigma\sqrt{t_2}}\right) \tag{5.6}$$

The probability of $P(M_{01} > b, X_1 < b,\ X_2 < k_2,\ \tau > t_2)$ from (3.4) is

$$e^{\frac{2\mu b}{\sigma^2}} N_2\left(\frac{k_1 - 2b - \mu t_1}{\sigma\sqrt{t_1}}, \frac{k_2 - 2b - \mu t_2}{\sigma\sqrt{t_2}}; \sqrt{\frac{t_1}{t_2}}\right)$$

$$-N_2\left(\frac{k_1 - 2b + \mu t_1}{\sigma\sqrt{t_1}}, \frac{k_2 - \mu t_2}{\sigma\sqrt{t_2}}; -\sqrt{\frac{t_1}{t_2}}\right)$$

but since $b = k_1$

$$e^{\frac{2\mu b}{\sigma^2}} N_2\left(\frac{-b - \mu t_1}{\sigma\sqrt{t_1}}, \frac{k_2 - 2b - \mu t_2}{\sigma\sqrt{t_2}}; \sqrt{\frac{t_1}{t_2}}\right)$$

$$-N_2\left(\frac{-b + \mu t_1}{\sigma\sqrt{t_1}}, \frac{k_2 - \mu t_2}{\sigma\sqrt{t_2}}; -\sqrt{\frac{t_1}{t_2}}\right)$$

So, in total,

$$N\left(\frac{k_2 - \mu t_2}{\sigma\sqrt{t_2}}\right) - e^{\frac{2\mu b}{\sigma^2}} N\left(\frac{k_2 - 2b - \mu t_2}{\sigma\sqrt{t_2}}\right)$$

$$+ e^{\frac{2\mu b}{\sigma^2}} N_2\left(\frac{-b - \mu t_1}{\sigma\sqrt{t_1}}, \frac{k_2 - 2b - \mu t_2}{\sigma\sqrt{t_2}}; \sqrt{\frac{t_1}{t_2}}\right)$$

$$- N_2\left(\frac{-b + \mu t_1}{\sigma\sqrt{t_1}}, \frac{k_2 - \mu t_2}{\sigma\sqrt{t_2}}; -\sqrt{\frac{t_1}{t_2}}\right)$$

Since

$$N\left(\frac{k_2-\mu t_2}{\sigma\sqrt{t_2}}\right)-N_2\left(\frac{-b+\mu t_1}{\sigma\sqrt{t_1}},\frac{k_2-\mu t_2}{\sigma\sqrt{t_2}};-\sqrt{\frac{t_1}{t_2}}\right)$$

$$=N_2\left(\frac{b-\mu t_1}{\sigma\sqrt{t_1}},\frac{k_2-\mu t_2}{\sigma\sqrt{t_2}};\sqrt{\frac{t_1}{t_2}}\right)$$

$$e^{\frac{2\mu b}{\sigma^2}}N_2\left(\frac{-b-\mu t_1}{\sigma t_1^{1/2}},\frac{k_2-2b-\mu t_2}{\sigma t_2^{1/2}};\sqrt{\frac{t_1}{t_2}}\right)$$

$$-e^{\frac{2\mu b}{\sigma^2}}N\left(\frac{k_2-2b-\mu t_2}{\sigma\sqrt{t_2}}\right)$$

$$=-e^{\frac{2\mu b}{\sigma^2}}N_2\left(\frac{b+\mu t_1}{\sigma t_1^{1/2}},\frac{k_2-2b-\mu t_2}{\sigma t_2^{1/2}};-\sqrt{\frac{t_1}{t_2}}\right)$$

$$P\left(X_2<k_2,X_1<b,\tau>t_2\right)$$

$$=N_2\left(\frac{b-\mu t_1}{\sigma\sqrt{t_1}},\frac{k_2-\mu t_2}{\sigma\sqrt{t_2}};\sqrt{\frac{t_1}{t_2}}\right)$$

$$-e^{\frac{2\mu b}{\sigma^2}}N_2\left(\frac{b+\mu t_1}{\sigma\sqrt{t_1}},\frac{k_2-2b-\mu t_2}{\sigma\sqrt{t_2}};-\sqrt{\frac{t_1}{t_2}}\right) \tag{5.7}$$

Letting $k_2\uparrow b$

$$P\left(X_1<b,\tau>t_2\right)=N_2\left(\frac{b-\mu t_1}{\sigma\sqrt{t_1}},\frac{b-\mu t_2}{\sigma\sqrt{t_2}};\sqrt{\frac{t_1}{t_2}}\right)$$

$$-e^{\frac{2\mu b}{\sigma^2}}N_2\left(\frac{b+\mu t_1}{\sigma\sqrt{t_1}},\frac{-b-\mu t_2}{\sigma\sqrt{t_2}};-\sqrt{\frac{t_1}{t_2}}\right) \tag{5.8}$$

Then, we obtain the probability

$$P(X_2>k_2,X_1<b,\ \tau>t_2)$$
$$=P(X_1<b,\ \tau>t_2)-P(X_2<k_2,X_1<b,\ \tau>t_2)$$

as

$$
\begin{aligned}
&= N_2\left(\frac{b-\mu t_1}{\sigma\sqrt{t_1}}, \frac{b-\mu t_2}{\sigma\sqrt{t_2}}; \sqrt{\frac{t_1}{t_2}}\right) \\
&\quad - e^{\frac{2\mu b}{\sigma^2}} N_2\left(\frac{b+\mu t_1}{\sigma\sqrt{t_1}}, \frac{-b-\mu t_2}{\sigma\sqrt{t_2}}; -\sqrt{\frac{t_1}{t_2}}\right) \\
&\quad - N_2\left(\frac{b-\mu t_1}{\sigma\sqrt{t_1}}, \frac{k_2-\mu t_2}{\sigma\sqrt{t_2}}; \sqrt{\frac{t_1}{t_2}}\right) \\
&\quad + e^{\frac{2\mu b}{\sigma^2}} N_2\left(\frac{b+\mu t_1}{\sigma\sqrt{t_1}}, \frac{k_2-2b-\mu t_2}{\sigma\sqrt{t_2}}; -\sqrt{\frac{t_1}{t_2}}\right) \qquad (5.9)
\end{aligned}
$$

5.3.1. *Calculation of* $E[\mathbf{1}_{m_0^{t_1}>H}]$, $E[\mathbf{1}_{M_0^{t_1}<H}]$, $E[\mathbf{1}_{m_{t_1}^T>H}]$, $E[\mathbf{1}_{M_{t_1}^T<H}]$

The first two expectations take the protection period between the current time and an arbitrary time before expiration, and the last two are taken for a forward starting protection period. $\boldsymbol{m_0^{t_1}}, \boldsymbol{m_{t_1}^T}$, $\boldsymbol{M_0^{t_1}}, \boldsymbol{M_{t_1}^T}$, and $\boldsymbol{m = \ln \frac{H}{S_0}}$ refer to a minimum, maximum, and the barrier levels respectively. All values are relative to the initial stock price.

(1) $$E[\mathbf{1}_{m_0^{t_1}>H}]$$

Consider the probability of

$$
\begin{aligned}
&\boldsymbol{P}\left(\boldsymbol{m_0^{t_1}} > \boldsymbol{m}, \boldsymbol{X} > \boldsymbol{k}\right) \\
&\boldsymbol{P}\left(\boldsymbol{m_0^{t_1}} > \boldsymbol{m}, \boldsymbol{X} > \boldsymbol{k}\right) = \boldsymbol{P}(\boldsymbol{X} > \boldsymbol{k}) - \boldsymbol{P}\left(\boldsymbol{m_0^{t_1}} < \boldsymbol{m}, \boldsymbol{X} > \boldsymbol{k}\right) \\
&\boldsymbol{N}\left(\frac{-\ln\ K/S + \mu t_1}{\sigma\sqrt{t_1}}\right) \\
&\quad - e^{2\mu m/\sigma^2} \boldsymbol{N}\left(\frac{-\ln\ \frac{K}{S} + 2\ln\ H/S + \mu t_1}{\sigma}\sqrt{t_1}\right)
\end{aligned}
$$

So, when $\boldsymbol{k \uparrow m}$

$$P\left(m_0^{t_1} > m\right) = P\left(m_0^{t_1} > \ln\frac{H}{S_0}\right) = N\left(\frac{-m+\mu t_1}{\sigma\sqrt{t_1}}\right) - e^{2\mu m/\sigma^2} N\left(\frac{m+\mu t_1}{\sigma\sqrt{t_1}}\right)$$

$$\boldsymbol{E}\left[\mathbf{1}_{m_0^{t_1}>H}\right] = \boldsymbol{N}\left(\frac{\ln\frac{S_0}{H} + (r-\frac{1}{2}\sigma^2)t_1}{\sigma\sqrt{t_1}}\right) - \left(\frac{H}{S_0}\right)^{\frac{2r}{\sigma^2}-1} \boldsymbol{N}\left(\frac{\ln\frac{H}{S_0} + (r-\frac{1}{2}\sigma^2)t_1}{\sigma\sqrt{t_1}}\right)$$

$$\boldsymbol{E}\left[\mathbf{1}_{m_0^{t_1}>H}\right] = \boldsymbol{N}(e_2) - \left(\frac{H}{S_0}\right)^{\frac{2r}{\sigma^2}-1} \boldsymbol{N}(e_2')$$

$$\widetilde{\boldsymbol{E}}\left[\mathbf{1}_{m_0^{t_1}>H}\right] = \boldsymbol{N}(e_1) - \left(\frac{H}{S_0}\right)^{\frac{2r}{\sigma^2}+1} \boldsymbol{N}(e_1') \tag{5.10}$$

(2) $$\boldsymbol{E}[\mathbf{1}_{M_0^{t_1}<H}]$$

By substituting

$$\boldsymbol{m} = -\boldsymbol{M} \quad \boldsymbol{\mu} = -\boldsymbol{\mu}$$

we obtain

$$\boldsymbol{N}\left(\frac{M-\mu t_1}{\sigma\sqrt{t_1}}\right) - e^{2\mu M/\sigma^2} \boldsymbol{N}\left(\frac{-M-\mu t_1}{\sigma\sqrt{t_1}}\right)$$

$$\boldsymbol{N}\left(\frac{\ln\frac{H}{S_0} - \mu t_1}{\sigma\sqrt{t_1}}\right) - e^{\frac{2\mu M}{\sigma^2}} \boldsymbol{N}\left(\frac{-\ln\frac{H}{S_0} - \mu t_1}{\sigma\sqrt{t_1}}\right)$$

$$= \boldsymbol{N}\left(-\frac{\ln\frac{S_0}{H} + \mu t_1}{\sigma\sqrt{t_1}}\right) - e^{\frac{2\mu M}{\sigma^2}} \boldsymbol{N}\left(-\frac{\ln\frac{H}{S_0} + \mu t_1}{\sigma\sqrt{t_1}}\right)$$

$$\boldsymbol{E}\left[\mathbf{1}_{\boldsymbol{M_0^{t_1}<H}}\right] = \boldsymbol{N}(-\boldsymbol{e_2}) - \left(\frac{\boldsymbol{H}}{\boldsymbol{S_0}}\right)^{\frac{\mathbf{2}r}{\sigma^{\mathbf{2}}}-\mathbf{1}} \boldsymbol{N}(-\boldsymbol{e_2'})$$

$$\widetilde{E}\left[1_{M_0^{t_1}<H}\right] = N(-e_1) - \left(\frac{H}{S_0}\right)^{\frac{2r}{\sigma^2}+1} N(-e_1') \tag{5.11}$$

(3) $$E\left[1_{m_{t_1}^T>H}\right]$$

This probability can be written as

$$\begin{aligned}\widetilde{E}\left[1_{S_T>H,m_{t_1}^T>H}\right] &= \widetilde{E}\left[1_{m_{t_1}^T>H}\right] \\ &= P\left(m_{01}<b, X_1>k_1, m_{12}>b, X_2>k_2\right) \\ &\quad + P\left(m_{01}>b, X_1>k_1, m_{12}>b, X_2>k_2\right)\end{aligned}$$

Following Carr, for arbitrary σ, we write the probability of $P(M_{01} > b, X_1 < k_1, M_{12} < b, X_2 < k_2)$ as

$$\begin{aligned}&e^{\frac{2\mu b}{\sigma^2}} N_2\left(\frac{k_1-2b-\mu t_1}{\sigma t_1^{1/2}}, \frac{k_2-2b-\mu t_2}{\sigma t_2^{1/2}}; \sqrt{\frac{t_1}{t_2}}\right) \\ &\quad - N_2\left(\frac{k_1-2b+\mu t_1}{\sigma t_1^{1/2}}, \frac{k_2-\mu t_2}{\sigma t_2^{1/2}}; -\sqrt{\frac{t_1}{t_2}}\right)\end{aligned}$$

But since now our probability is

$$P\left(m_{01}<b, X_1>k_1, m_{12}>b,\ X_2>k_2\right)$$

we can write

$$\begin{aligned}&e^{\frac{2\mu b}{\sigma^2}} N_2\left(\frac{-k_1+2b+\mu t_1}{\sigma\sqrt{t_1}}, \frac{-k_2+2b+\mu t_2}{\sigma\sqrt{t_2}}; \sqrt{\frac{t_1}{t_2}}\right) \\ &\quad - N_2\left(\frac{-k_1+2b-\mu t_1}{\sigma\sqrt{t_1}}, \frac{-k_2+\mu t_2}{\sigma\sqrt{t_2}}; -\sqrt{\frac{t_1}{t_2}}\right)\end{aligned}$$

Letting $k_1 \uparrow b$ $P(m_{01} < b, X_1 > b, m_{12} > b,\ X_2 > k_2)$ is

$$e^{\frac{2\mu b}{\sigma^2}} N_2\left(\frac{b+\mu t_1}{\sigma\sqrt{t_1}}, \frac{-k_2+2b+\mu t_2}{\sigma\sqrt{t_2}}; \sqrt{\frac{t_1}{t_2}}\right)$$
$$- N_2\left(\frac{b-\mu t_1}{\sigma\sqrt{t_1}}, \frac{-k_2+\mu t_2}{\sigma\sqrt{t_2}}; -\sqrt{\frac{t_1}{t_2}}\right)$$

Now for

$$P(m_{01} > b, X_1 > k_1, m_{12} > b,\ X_2 > k_2) = P(m_{02} > b,\ X_2 > k_2)$$

$$P(m_{02} > b, X_2 > k_2) = P(X_2 > k_2) - P(m_{02} < b, X_2 > k_2)$$
$$= N\left(\frac{-k_2+\mu t_2}{\sigma\sqrt{t_2}}\right) - e^{\frac{2\mu b}{\sigma^2}} N\left(\frac{-k_2+2b+\mu t_2}{\sigma\sqrt{t_2}}\right)$$

Collecting the terms

$$\widetilde{E}\left[1_{S_T > H, m^T_{t_1} > H}\right]$$
$$= \widetilde{E}\left[1_{m^T_{t_1} > H}\right] = P(m_{01} < b, X_1 > k_1, m_{12} > b, X_2 > k_2)$$
$$+ P(m_{01} > b, X_1 > k_1, m_{12} > b, X_2 > k_2)$$
$$= e^{\frac{2\mu b}{\sigma^2}} N_2\left(\frac{b+\mu t_1}{\sigma\sqrt{t_1}}, \frac{-k_2+2b+\mu t_2}{\sigma\sqrt{t_2}}; \sqrt{\frac{t_1}{t_2}}\right)$$
$$- N_2\left(\frac{b-\mu t_1}{\sigma\sqrt{t_1}}, \frac{-k_2+\mu t_2}{\sigma\sqrt{t_2}}; -\sqrt{\frac{t_1}{t_2}}\right) + N\left(\frac{-k_2+\mu t_2}{\sigma\sqrt{t_2}}\right)$$
$$- e^{\frac{2\mu b}{\sigma^2}} N\left(\frac{-k_2+2b+\mu t_2}{\sigma\sqrt{t_2}}\right)$$

Using the bivariate identity, we can write:

$$-e^{\frac{2\mu b}{\sigma^2}} \left[N\left(\frac{-k_2+2b+\mu t_2}{\sigma\sqrt{t_2}}\right)\right.$$
$$\left. - N_2\left(\frac{b+\mu t_1}{\sigma\sqrt{t_1}}, \frac{-k_2+2b+\mu t_2}{\sigma\sqrt{t_2}}; \sqrt{\frac{t_1}{t_2}}\right)\right]$$

$$= -e^{\frac{2\mu b}{\sigma^2}} N_2\left(\frac{-b-\mu t_1}{\sigma\sqrt{t_1}}, \frac{-k_2+2b+\mu t_2}{\sigma\sqrt{t_2}}; -\sqrt{\frac{t_1}{t_2}}\right)$$

$$N\left(\frac{-k_2+\mu t_2}{\sigma\sqrt{t_2}}\right) - N_2\left(\frac{b-\mu t_1}{\sigma\sqrt{t_1}}, \frac{-k_2+\mu t_2}{\sigma\sqrt{t_2}}; -\sqrt{\frac{t_1}{t_2}}\right)$$

$$= N_2\left(\frac{-b+\mu t_1}{\sigma\sqrt{t_1}}, \frac{-k_2+\mu t_2}{\sigma\sqrt{t_2}}; \sqrt{\frac{t_1}{t_2}}\right)$$

$$\widetilde{E}\left[1_{m_{t_1}^T > H}\right] = N_2\left(\frac{-b+\mu t_1}{\sigma\sqrt{t_1}}, \frac{-k_2+\mu t_2}{\sigma\sqrt{t_2}}; \sqrt{\frac{t_1}{t_2}}\right) - e^{\frac{2\mu b}{\sigma^2}} N_2\left(\frac{-b-\mu t_1}{\sigma\sqrt{t_1}}, \frac{-k_2+2b+\mu t_2}{\sigma\sqrt{t_2}}; -\sqrt{\frac{t_1}{t_2}}\right)$$

Letting $k_2 \uparrow b$ we obtain

$$\boldsymbol{\widetilde{E}[1_{m_{t_1}^T > H}] = N_2\left(\frac{-b+\mu t_1}{\sigma\sqrt{t_1}}, \frac{-b+\mu t_2}{\sigma\sqrt{t_2}}; \sqrt{\frac{t_1}{t_2}}\right) - e^{\frac{2\mu b}{\sigma^2}} N_2\left(\frac{-b-\mu t_1}{\sigma\sqrt{t_1}}, \frac{b+\mu t_2}{\sigma\sqrt{t_2}}; -\sqrt{\frac{t_1}{t_2}}\right)}$$

$$\boldsymbol{e_1 = \frac{\ln S_0/H + \left(r+\frac{1}{2}\sigma^2\right) t_1}{\sigma\sqrt{t_1}}}$$

$$\boldsymbol{g_1 = \frac{\ln S_0/H + \left(r+\frac{1}{2}\sigma^2\right) T}{\sigma\sqrt{T}}}$$

$$\boldsymbol{e_1' = \frac{\ln H/S_0 + \left(r+\frac{1}{2}\sigma^2\right) t_1}{\sigma\sqrt{t_1}}}$$

$$\boldsymbol{-e_1' = \frac{\ln S_0/H - \left(r+\frac{1}{2}\sigma^2\right) t_1}{\sigma\sqrt{t_1}}}$$

$$\boldsymbol{g_1' = \frac{-\ln H/S_0 + \left(r+\frac{1}{2}\sigma^2\right) T}{\sigma\sqrt{T}} + \frac{2\ln H/S_0}{\sigma\sqrt{T}} = \frac{\ln H/S_0 + \left(r+\frac{1}{2}\sigma^2\right) T}{\sigma\sqrt{T}}}$$

$$\boldsymbol{\widetilde{E}[1_{m_{t_1}^T>H}] = N\left(g_1, e_1; \sqrt{\frac{t_1}{T}}\right) - \left(\frac{H}{S_0}\right)^{\frac{2r}{\sigma^2}+1}}$$

$$\boldsymbol{\times N\left(g_1', -e_1'; -\sqrt{\frac{t_1}{T}}\right)}$$

$$\boldsymbol{E[1_{m_{t_1}^T>H}] = N\left(g_2, e_2; \sqrt{\frac{t_1}{T}}\right) - \left(\frac{H}{S_0}\right)^{\frac{2r}{\sigma^2}-1}}$$

$$\boldsymbol{\times N\left(g_2', -e_2'; -\sqrt{\frac{t_1}{T}}\right)} \tag{5.12}$$

(4) $$\boldsymbol{E\left[1_{M_{t_1}^T<H}\right]}$$

This probability can be written

$$P\left(S_{t_1}^{-\mu} < x,\ M_{t_1}^T < H\right) = P(X_1 < b,\ X_2 < b,\ \tau > T)$$

But from Carr (1995), we know that

$$\boldsymbol{P\left(X_1 < b, X_2 < k_2, \tau > t_2\right)}$$

$$\begin{aligned}
&P(X_2 < k_2, X_1 < b,\ \tau > t_2)\\
&\quad = P(M_{01} < b, X_1 < b,\ X_2 < k_2,\ \tau > t_2)\\
&\qquad + P(M_{01} > b, X_1 < b,\ X_2 < k_2,\ \tau > t_2)\\
&\quad = P(M_{02} < b, X_2 < k_2) + P(M_{01} > b, X_1 < b, X_2 < k_2, \tau > t_2)\\
&N\left(\frac{k_2 - \mu t_2}{\sigma\sqrt{t_2}}\right) - e^{\frac{2\mu b}{\sigma^2}} N\left(\frac{k_2 - 2b - \mu t_2}{\sigma\sqrt{t_2}}\right)\\
&\qquad + e^{\frac{2\mu b}{\sigma^2}} N_2\left(\frac{-b - \mu t_1}{\sigma\sqrt{t_1}}, \frac{k_2 - 2b - \mu t_2}{\sigma\sqrt{t_2}}; \sqrt{\frac{t_1}{t_2}}\right)\\
&\qquad - N_2\left(\frac{-b + \mu t_1}{\sigma\sqrt{t_1}}, \frac{k_2 - \mu t_2}{\sigma\sqrt{t_2}}; -\sqrt{\frac{t_1}{t_2}}\right)
\end{aligned}$$

Letting $k_2 \uparrow b$ yields

$$N\left(\frac{b-\mu t_2}{\sigma\sqrt{t_2}}\right) - e^{\frac{2\mu b}{\sigma^2}} N\left(\frac{-b-\mu t_2}{\sigma\sqrt{t_2}}\right)$$
$$+ e^{\frac{2\mu b}{\sigma^2}} N_2\left(\frac{-b-\mu t_1}{\sigma\sqrt{t_1}}, \frac{-b-\mu t_2}{\sigma\sqrt{t_2}}; \sqrt{\frac{t_1}{t_2}}\right)$$
$$- N_2\left(\frac{-b+\mu t_1}{\sigma\sqrt{t_1}}, \frac{b-\mu t_2}{\sigma\sqrt{t_2}}; -\sqrt{\frac{t_1}{t_2}}\right)$$

Using the bivariate identity, we find the probability as

$$\boldsymbol{E}[\mathbf{1}_{M_{t_1}^T<H}] = \boldsymbol{N_2}\left(\frac{b-\mu t_1}{\sigma\sqrt{t_1}}, \frac{b-\mu t_2}{\sigma\sqrt{t_2}}; \sqrt{\frac{t_1}{t_2}}\right)$$
$$- \left(\frac{H}{S_0}\right)^{\frac{2\mu}{\sigma^2}} \boldsymbol{N_2}\left(\frac{b+\mu t_1}{\sigma\sqrt{t_1}}, \frac{-b-\mu t_2}{\sigma\sqrt{t_2}}; -\sqrt{\frac{t_1}{t_2}}\right)$$

$$\widetilde{\boldsymbol{E}}[\mathbf{1}_{M_{t_1}^T<H}] = \boldsymbol{N_2}\left(-e_1, -g_1; \sqrt{\frac{t_1}{t_2}}\right) - \left(\frac{H}{S_0}\right)^{\frac{2r}{\sigma^2}+1}$$
$$\times \boldsymbol{N_2}\left(e_1', -g_1'; -\sqrt{\frac{t_1}{t_2}}\right)$$

$$\boldsymbol{E}[\mathbf{1}_{M_{t_1}^T<H}] = \boldsymbol{N_2}\left(-e_2, -g_2; \sqrt{\frac{t_1}{t_2}}\right) - \left(\frac{H}{S_0}\right)^{\frac{2r}{\sigma^2}-1}$$
$$\times \boldsymbol{N_2}\left(e_2', -g_2'; -\sqrt{\frac{t_1}{t_2}}\right) \tag{5.13}$$

$$-e_2 = -\frac{\ln S_0/H + \left(r - \frac{1}{2}\sigma^2\right) t_1}{\sigma\sqrt{t_1}}$$

$$-g_2 = -\frac{\ln S_0/H + \left(r - \frac{1}{2}\sigma^2\right) T}{\sigma\sqrt{T}}$$

$$e_2' = \frac{\ln H/S_0 + \left(r - \frac{1}{2}\sigma^2\right) t_1}{\sigma\sqrt{t_1}}$$

$$-g_2' = -\frac{\ln H/S_0 + \left(r - \frac{1}{2}\sigma^2\right) T}{\sigma\sqrt{T}}$$

5.4. Type A Options

5.4.1. *Type A down and out partial barrier call*

The monitoring period starts at $t = 0$ and ends at an arbitrary time t_1 for $[0, t_1]$ period. It can be out only in this period. After this period, the option turns out to be a vanilla-type option with its unique payoff function.

The probabilities for $[0, t_1]$ period:

$$P(S_{t_1} > x, m_0^{t_1} < b) = P(S_{t_1} < 2b - x)$$

$$= N\left(\frac{2b - x}{\sigma\sqrt{t_1}}\right)$$

with drift term and barrier H where $b = \ln H/S_0$.

$$P\left(S_{t_1}^{\mu} > x, m_0^{t_1} < b\right) = e^{2\mu b/\sigma^2} N\left(\frac{2b - x + \mu t_1}{\sigma\sqrt{t_1}}\right)$$

$$P\left(S_{t_1}^{\mu} > x, m_0^{t_1} > b\right)$$

$$= P\left(S_{t_1}^{\mu} > x\right) - P\left(S_{t_1}^{\mu} > x, m_0^{t_1} < b\right)$$

$$= N\left(\frac{-x + \mu t_1}{\sigma\sqrt{t_1}}\right) - e^{2\mu b/\sigma^2} N\left(\frac{2b - x + \mu t_1}{\sigma\sqrt{t_1}}\right)$$

For a special case $b = x$, since $m_0^{t_1} > b$, we can write $S_{t_1}^{\mu} > b$. In this case, the cumulative probability is

$$P\left(m_0^{t_1} > b\right) = N\left(\frac{-b + \mu t_1}{\sigma\sqrt{t_1}}\right) - e^{2\mu b/\sigma^2} N\left(\frac{b + \mu t_1}{\sigma\sqrt{t_1}}\right)$$

Now, let's write the partial barrier's payoff as

$$\text{DOC}(A) = e^{-rT} E\left[(S_T - K)1_{S_T > K, m_0^{t1} > H}\right] \quad S_0 > H$$

$$\times E[1_{S_T > K, m_0^{t1} > H}]$$

The probabilities for $[0, t_1]$

$$P(S_{t_1}^{\mu} > x) - P(S_{t_1}^{\mu} > x, m_0^{t_1} < b)$$

$$= N\left(\frac{-x + \mu t_1}{\sigma\sqrt{t_1}}\right) - e^{2\mu b/\sigma^2} N\left(\frac{2b - x + \mu t_1}{\sigma\sqrt{t_1}}\right)$$

Since it is the first period $[0, t_1]$ monitored, the relevant value for asset price is H and must always be above this level. Therefore, we can change the probability accordingly as

$$P\left(S_{t_1}^{\mu} > H\right) - P\left(S_{t_1}^{\mu} > H, m_0^{t_1} < H\right)$$

$$= P\left(\ln \frac{S_{t_1}^{\mu}}{S_0} > \ln \frac{H}{S_0}\right) - P\left(\ln \frac{S_{t_1}^{\mu}}{S_0} > \ln \frac{H}{S_0}, \ln \frac{m_0^{t_1}}{S_0} < \ln \frac{H}{S_0}\right)$$

$$N\left(\frac{-x + \mu t_1}{\sigma\sqrt{t_1}}\right) - e^{2\mu b/\sigma^2} N\left(\frac{2b - x + \mu t_1}{\sigma\sqrt{t_1}}\right)$$

where x also starts from $\ln \frac{H}{S_0}$.

$$N\left(\frac{\ln \frac{S_0}{H} + \mu t_1}{\sigma\sqrt{t_1}}\right) - \left(\frac{H}{S_0}\right)^{2\mu/\sigma^2} N\left(\frac{2\ln \frac{H}{S_0} - \ln \frac{H}{S_0} + \mu t_1}{\sigma\sqrt{t_1}}\right)$$

Our final integral is

$$\frac{1}{\sigma\sqrt{2\pi(T - t_1)}} \int_{\ln \frac{K}{S_{t_1}}}^{\infty} e^{-\frac{1}{2}\left(\frac{(z-\mu(T-t_1))}{\sigma\sqrt{T-t_1}}\right)^2} \left[N\left(\frac{\ln \frac{S_0}{H} + \mu t_1}{\sigma\sqrt{t_1}}\right)\right.$$

$$\left. - \left(\frac{H}{S_0}\right)^{2\mu/\sigma^2} N\left(\frac{2\ln \frac{H}{S_0} - \ln \frac{H}{S_0} + \mu t_1}{\sigma\sqrt{t_1}}\right)\right] dz$$

$$\begin{aligned} x &= \ln\left(S_{t_1}/S_0\right) \\ z &= \ln\left(S_T/S_{t_1}\right) \end{aligned} \tag{5.14}$$

and since S_{t_1} has to start from $S_{t_1} = H$, the lower limit of the integral is $\ln \frac{K}{H}$.

$$\frac{1}{\sigma\sqrt{2\pi(T - t_1)}} \int_{\ln \frac{K}{H}}^{\infty} e^{-\frac{1}{2}\left(\frac{(z-\mu(T-t_1))}{\sigma\sqrt{T-t_1}}\right)^2} \left[N\left(\frac{\ln \frac{S_0}{H} + \mu t_1}{\sigma\sqrt{t_1}}\right)\right.$$

$$\left. - \left(\frac{H}{S_0}\right)^{2\mu/\sigma^2} N\left(\frac{2\ln \frac{H}{S_0} - \ln \frac{H}{S_0} + \mu t_1}{\sigma\sqrt{t_1}}\right)\right] dz$$

$$\int_{-\infty}^{\frac{\ln\frac{S_0}{H}+\mu t_1}{\sigma\sqrt{t_1}}} f(x)N\left(\frac{(\ln H/K+\mu(T-t_1))}{\sigma\sqrt{T-t_1}}\right)dx$$

$$-\left(\frac{H}{S_0}\right)^{2\mu/\sigma^2}\int_{-\infty}^{\frac{2\ln\frac{H}{S_0}-\ln\frac{H}{S_0}+\mu t_1}{\sigma\sqrt{t_1}}} f(x)N\left(\frac{(\ln H/K+\mu(T-t_1))}{\sigma\sqrt{T-t_1}}\right)dx$$

Using the bivariate identity,

$$\int_{-\infty}^{h} f(x)N\left(\frac{(k-\rho x)}{\sqrt{1-\rho^2}}\right)dx = N(h,k;\rho)$$

$$e_1 = \frac{\ln\frac{S_0}{H}+\mu t_1}{\sigma\sqrt{t_1}} \quad \mu = r+\frac{1}{2}\sigma^2$$

$$k = d_1 = \frac{(\ln H/K+\mu(T-t_1))}{\sigma\sqrt{T-t_1}} * \sqrt{\frac{T-t_1}{T}} + \sqrt{\frac{t_1}{T}}\frac{\ln\frac{S_0}{H}+\mu t_1}{\sigma\sqrt{t_1}}$$

$$= \frac{\ln\frac{S_0}{K}+\mu T}{\sigma\sqrt{T}}$$

$$\rho = \sqrt{\frac{t_1}{T}} - \left(\frac{H}{S_0}\right)^{2\mu/\sigma^2}\int_{-\infty}^{\frac{2\ln\frac{H}{S_0}-\ln\frac{H}{S_0}+\mu t_1}{\sigma\sqrt{t_1}}} f(x)$$

$$\times N\left(\frac{(\ln H/K+\mu(T-t_1))}{\sigma\sqrt{T-t_1}}\right)dx$$

$$e_1' = \frac{\ln\frac{H}{S_0}+\mu t_1}{\sigma\sqrt{t_1}} = e_1 + \frac{2\ln\frac{H}{S_0}}{\sigma\sqrt{t_1}} \quad \mu = r+\frac{1}{2}\sigma^2$$

$$k = f_1 = \frac{(\ln H/K+\mu(T-t_1))}{\sigma\sqrt{T-t_1}} * \sqrt{\frac{T-t_1}{T}} + \sqrt{\frac{t_1}{T}}\frac{\ln\frac{H}{S_0}+\mu t_1}{\sigma\sqrt{t_1}}$$

$$= \frac{\ln\frac{H^2}{KS_0}+\mu T}{\sigma\sqrt{T}}$$

$$\text{DOC }(A) = S_0\left[N(e_1, d_1; \rho) - \left(\frac{H}{S_0}\right)^{2\mu/\sigma^2} N\left(e_1', f_1; \rho\right)\right]$$
$$-e^{-rT}K\left[N(e_2, d_2; \rho) - \left(\frac{H}{S_0}\right)^{2\mu/\sigma^2} N\left(e_2', f_2; \rho\right)\right] \qquad (5.15)$$

$\mu = r + \frac{1}{2}\sigma^2$ for the first two terms and $\mu = r - \frac{1}{2}\sigma^2$ for the last two terms.

5.4.2. *Type A up and out partial barrier call*

Here, we should consider that the maximum value of the barrier variable must remain below the barrier throughout the monitoring period.

Let Z_t be a Brownian motion. We can write

$$M_0^{t_1} = \max_{0\leq t\leq T}(\sigma Z_{t1} + \mu t_1) = -\min_{0\leq t\leq T}(\sigma(-Z_{t1}) + (-\mu)t_1)$$

Since Z_t and $-Z_t$ have the same distribution, the maximum of $S_{t_1}^{\mu}$ is distributed the same as the minimum of $S_{t_1}^{-\mu}$. Substituting μ with $-\mu$, b with $-b = B$ and x with $-x$

$$P\left(S_{t_1} > x, m_0^{t_1} < b\right) \rightarrow P\left(-S_{t_1} < -x, -m_0^{t_1} > B\right)$$
$$\rightarrow P\left(S_{t_1} < x, M_0^{t_1} > B\right)$$

The probabilities for the period $[0, t_1]$

$$P(S_{t_1} < x, M_0^{t_1} > B) = P(S_{t_1} < x - 2B)$$
$$= N\left(\frac{x - 2B}{\sigma\sqrt{t_1}}\right)$$

and with a drift term

$$P(S_{t_1}^{-\mu} < x, M_0^{t_1} > B) = e^{2\mu B/\sigma^2} \quad N\left(\frac{x - 2B - \mu t_1}{\sigma\sqrt{t_1}}\right)$$

Since $S_{t_1}^{\mu}$ and $S_{t_1}^{-\mu}$ are identically distributed

$$P(S_{t_1}^{-\mu} < x, \quad M_0^{t_1} < B)$$

$$= P(S_{t_1}^{\mu} < x) - P(S_{t_1}^{\mu} < x, \quad M_0^{t_1} > B)$$

$$= N\left(\frac{x - \mu t_1}{\sigma\sqrt{t_1}}\right) - e^{2\mu B/\sigma^2} N\left(\frac{x - 2B - \mu t_1}{\sigma\sqrt{t_1}}\right)$$

For a special case, $B = x$, and for $M_0^{t_1} < B$ we may write $S_{t_1}^{\mu} < B$. In this case, the cumulative probability is

$$N\left(\frac{B - \mu t_1}{\sigma\sqrt{t_1}}\right) - e^{2\mu B/\sigma^2} N\left(\frac{-B - \mu t_1}{\sigma\sqrt{t_1}}\right)$$

Now, we can write the payoff function of the up-and-out partial barrier call.

$$\text{UOC}(A) = e^{-rT} E\left[(S_T - K)1_{S_T > K, M_0^{t_1} < H}\right] \quad S_0 < H$$

$$E\left[1_{S_T > K, M_0^{t1} < H}\right]$$

The probabilities for $[0, t_1]$ period are

$$P\left(S_{t_1}^{\mu} < x\right) - P\left(S_{t_1}^{\mu} < x, M_0^{t_1} > B\right)$$

$$= N\left(\frac{x - \mu t_1}{\sigma\sqrt{t_1}}\right) - e^{2\mu B/\sigma^2} N\left(\frac{x - 2B - \mu t_1}{\sigma\sqrt{t_1}}\right)$$

where x also starts from $\ln \frac{H}{S_0}$.

$$P\left(S_{t_1}^{\mu} < H\right) - P\left(S_{t_1}^{\mu} < H, M_0^{t_1} > H\right)$$

$$= P\left(\ln \frac{S_{t_1}^{\mu}}{S_0} < \ln \frac{H}{S_0}\right) - P\left(\ln \frac{S_{t_1}^{\mu}}{S_0} < \ln \frac{H}{S_0}, \ln \frac{M_0^{t_1}}{S_0} > \ln \frac{H}{S_0}\right)$$

$$N\left(\frac{\ln \frac{H}{S_0} - \mu t_1}{\sigma\sqrt{t_1}}\right) - \left(\frac{H}{S_0}\right)^{2\mu/\sigma^2} N\left(\frac{\ln \frac{H}{S_0} - 2\ln \frac{H}{S_0} - \mu t_1}{\sigma\sqrt{t_1}}\right)$$

$$x = \ln\left(S_{t_1}/S_0\right)$$

and S_{t_1} will start from $S_{t_1} = H$

$$z = \ln\left(S_T/S_{t_1}\right)$$

the lower limit of the integral is $\ln \frac{K}{H}$.

Because when the first barrier observation period ends, the S_{t_1} value should not be above the barrier value H.

$$\frac{1}{\sigma\sqrt{2\pi(T-t_1)}}\int_{\ln\frac{K}{H}}^{\infty} e^{-\frac{1}{2}\left(\frac{(z-\mu(T-t_1))}{\sigma\sqrt{T-t_1}}\right)^2}\left[N\left(-\frac{\ln\frac{S_0}{H}+\mu t_1}{\sigma\sqrt{t_1}}\right)\right.$$
$$\left.-\left(\frac{H}{S_0}\right)^{2\mu/\sigma^2}N\left(\frac{\ln\frac{S_0}{H}-\mu t_1}{\sigma\sqrt{t_1}}\right)\right]dz$$

$$\int_{-\infty}^{-\frac{\ln\frac{S_0}{H}+\mu t_1}{\sigma\sqrt{t_1}}} f(x)N\left(\frac{(\ln H/K+\mu(T-t_1))}{\sigma\sqrt{T-t_1}}\right)dx$$
$$-\left(\frac{H}{S_0}\right)^{2\mu/\sigma^2}\int_{-\infty}^{\frac{-\ln\frac{H}{S_0}-\mu t_1}{\sigma\sqrt{t_1}}} f(x)N\left(\frac{(\ln H/K+\mu(T-t_1))}{\sigma\sqrt{T-t_1}}\right)dx$$

$$-e_1=-\frac{\ln\frac{S_0}{H}+\mu t_1}{\sigma\sqrt{t_1}}\quad \mu=r+\frac{1}{2}\sigma^2$$

$$d_1=\frac{(\ln H/K+\mu(T-t_1))}{\sigma\sqrt{T-t_1}}*\sqrt{\frac{T-t_1}{T}}+\sqrt{\frac{t_1}{T}}\frac{\ln\frac{S_0}{H}+\mu t_1}{\sigma\sqrt{t_1}}$$
$$=\frac{\ln\frac{S_0}{K}+\mu T}{\sigma\sqrt{T}}$$

$$N(-e_1,d_1;-\rho)$$

$$\rho=\sqrt{\frac{t_1}{T}}$$

Second integral is

$$-\left(\frac{H}{S_0}\right)^{2\mu/\sigma^2}\int_{-\infty}^{\frac{-\ln\frac{H}{S_0}-\mu t_1}{\sigma\sqrt{t_1}}} f(x)N\left(\frac{(\ln H/K+\mu(T-t_1))}{\sigma\sqrt{T-t_1}}\right)dx$$

$$-e_1'=-\frac{\ln\frac{H}{S_0}+\mu t_1}{\sigma\sqrt{t_1}}=\mu=r+\frac{1}{2}\sigma^2$$

$$f_1 = \frac{(\ln H/K + \mu(T - t_1))}{\sigma\sqrt{T - t_1}} * \sqrt{\frac{T - t_1}{T}} + \sqrt{\frac{t_1}{T}} \frac{\ln \frac{H}{S_0} + \mu t_1}{\sigma\sqrt{t_1}}$$

$$= \frac{\ln \frac{H^2}{KS_0} + \mu T}{\sigma\sqrt{T}}$$

$$\text{UOC } (A) = S_0 \left[N(-e_1, d_1; -\rho) - \left(\frac{H}{S_0}\right)^{2\mu/\sigma^2} N(-e_1', f_1; -\rho) \right]$$

$$- e^{-rT} K \left[N(-e_2, d_2; -\rho) - \left(\frac{H}{S_0}\right)^{2\mu/\sigma^2} N(-e_2', f_2; -\rho) \right]$$

$$\rho = \sqrt{\frac{t_1}{T}} \tag{5.16}$$

$\mu = r + \frac{1}{2}\sigma^2$ for the first two terms and $\mu = r - \frac{1}{2}\sigma^2$ for the last two terms.

5.5. Type B Options

When the barrier observation period starts before the expiration date, such as t_1, and ends at the expiration date T, the barrier situation can be interpreted in two different ways. One interpretation is that the option is "in" or "out" only if the barrier is hit or crossed. For example, let the share value and the barrier start moving at the same level or values close to each other. If the share value is below the barrier at point t_1, nothing happens. Because the option is designed to be "in" or "out" if the stock value hits or crosses the barrier during the barrier observation period. The other interpretation states that it is not crucial whether the stock value hits the barrier and that the actual function of the barrier should be to separate the "in" and "out" zones of the option. According to this interpretation, the option is knocked out immediately if the share value is below the barrier during the observation period (Heynen and Kat, 1994c).

The first case will be designated as a B1-type option. The important thing here is hitting the barrier, so there will be no difference between "up" and "down" options.

For B2 type options, we are interested in out or in regions. We are not interested in an actual barrier hit or crossing but in the location of the asset relative to the barrier. We will be concerned with the up-and-out option when the out region is above the barrier. We will consider the down-and-out option when the out region is below the barrier.

5.5.1. *Type B1 partial barrier call options*

Now, we look at options with an arbitrary date t_1, which starts before expiration and ends at maturity T or t_2 and where the option knocks in or out when the underlying hits or crosses the barrier. Here, the relevant thing is whether the barrier is hit or not. Heynen and Kat refer to these options as B1-type barrier options. Since the relevant thing is only hitting or crossing the barrier, it does not matter whether the crossing is from up or down; therefore, there is no difference between up and down options.

When $K > H$ $B1$ knock-out call $OC(B1+)$ price can be formulated as follows;

$$\begin{aligned} OC(B1+) &= e^{-rT}E\left[(S_T - K)\,1_{S_T>K,m_{t_1}^T>H}\right] \\ &= S_0\widetilde{E}\left[1_{S_T>K,m_{t_1}^T>H}\right] - e^{-rT}KE\left[1_{S_T>K,m_{t_1}^T>H}\right] \end{aligned} \tag{5.17}$$

When $K < H$ $B1$ knock-out call $OC(B1-)$ price can be formulated as follows:

$$\begin{aligned} \boldsymbol{OC\,(B1-)} &= \boldsymbol{e^{-rT}E\left[(S_T - K)\,1_{S_T>K,M_{t_1}^T<H}\right]} \\ &\quad \boldsymbol{+\,e^{-rT}E\left[(S_T - K)\,1_{m_{t_1}^T>H}\right]} \\ &= \boldsymbol{S_0\widetilde{E}\left[1_{S_T>K,M_{t_1}^T<H}\right] - e^{-rT}KE\left[1_{S_T>K,M_{t_1}^T<H}\right]} \\ &\quad \boldsymbol{+\,S_0\widetilde{E}\left[1_{m_{t_1}^T>H}\right] - e^{-rT}KE\left[1_{m_{t_1}^T>H}\right]} \end{aligned} \tag{5.18}$$

$$OC(B1+) = S_0\left[N(e_1, d_1; \rho) - \left(\frac{H}{S_0}\right)^{2\mu/\sigma^2} N(-e_1', f_1; -\rho)\right]$$
$$- e^{-rT}K\left[N(e_2, d_2; \rho) - \left(\frac{H}{S_0}\right)^{2\mu/\sigma^2} N\big(-e_2', f_2; -\rho\big)\right]$$

$$\boldsymbol{OC(B1-) = S_0\left[N(-e_1, -g_1; \rho) - \left(\frac{H}{S_0}\right)^{2\mu/\sigma^2} N(e_1', -g_1'; -\rho)\right]}$$
$$\boldsymbol{- e^{-rT}K\left[N(-e_2, -g_2; \rho) - \left(\frac{H}{S_0}\right)^{\frac{2\mu}{\sigma^2}} N(e_2', -g_2'; -\rho)\right]}$$
$$\boldsymbol{- S_0\left[N(-e_1, -d_1; \rho) - \left(\frac{H}{S_0}\right)^{\frac{2\mu}{\sigma^2}} N(e_1', -f_1; -\rho)\right]}$$
$$\boldsymbol{+ e^{-rT}K\left[N(-e_2, -d_2; \rho) - \left(\frac{H}{S_0}\right)^{\frac{2\mu}{\sigma^2}} N(e_2', -f_2; -\rho)\right]}$$
$$\boldsymbol{+ S_0\left[N(e_1, g_1; \rho) - \left(\frac{H}{S_0}\right)^{2\mu/\sigma^2} N(-e_1', g_1'; -\rho)\right]}$$
$$\boldsymbol{- e^{-rT}K\left[N(e_2, g_2; \rho) - \left(\frac{H}{S_0}\right)^{\frac{2\mu}{\sigma^2}} N(-e_2', g_2'; -\rho)\right]}$$

When $K > H$, the price of a type B1 knock-out call $OC(B1+)$ can be written as

$$e^{-rT}E[(S_T - K)1_{S_T>K, m_{t_1}^T>H}]$$
$$= S_0 E[\xi 1_{S_T>K, m_{t_1}^T>H}] - e^{-rT}KE[1_{S_T>K, m_{t_1}^T>H}]$$

We cannot add the probability of $M_{t_1}^T < H$ since it violates the payoff condition.

Let's calculate the probability by decomposing as follows

$$\widetilde{E}[1_{S_T>K, m_{t_1}^T>H}] = P\left(m_{01} < b, X_1 > k_1, m_{12} > b, X_2 > k_2\right)$$
$$+ P\left(m_{01} > b, X_1 > k_1, m_{12} > b, X_2 > k_2\right)$$

Following Carr, we write for arbitrary σ the probability $P\left(M_{01} > b, X_1 < k_1, M_{12} < b,\ X_2 < k_2\right)$ as

$$e^{\frac{2\mu b}{\sigma^2}} N_2\left(\frac{k_1 - 2b - \mu t_1}{\sigma\sqrt{t_1}}, \frac{k_2 - 2b - \mu t_2}{\sigma\sqrt{t_2}}; \sqrt{\frac{t_1}{t_2}}\right)$$
$$- N_2\left(\frac{k_1 - 2b + \mu t_1}{\sigma\sqrt{t_1}}, \frac{k_2 - \mu t_2}{\sigma\sqrt{t_2}}; -\sqrt{\frac{t_1}{t_2}}\right)$$

But since now our probability is

$$P\left(m_{01} < b, X_1 > k_1, m_{12} > b, X_2 > k_2\right)$$
$$e^{\frac{2\mu b}{\sigma^2}} N_2\left(\frac{-k_1 + 2b + \mu t_1}{\sigma\sqrt{t_1}}, \frac{-k_2 + 2b + \mu t_2}{\sigma\sqrt{t_2}}; \sqrt{\frac{t_1}{t_2}}\right)$$
$$- N_2\left(\frac{-k_1 + 2b - \mu t_1}{\sigma\sqrt{t_1}}, \frac{-k_2 + \mu t_2}{\sigma\sqrt{t_2}}; -\sqrt{\frac{t_1}{t_2}}\right)$$

Letting $k_1 \uparrow b$

$$P(m_{01} < b, X_1 > b, m_{12} > b,\ X_2 > k_2)$$
$$e^{\frac{2\mu b}{\sigma^2}} N_2\left(\frac{b + \mu t_1}{\sigma\sqrt{t_1}}, \frac{-k_2 + 2b + \mu t_2}{\sigma\sqrt{t_2}}; \sqrt{\frac{t_1}{t_2}}\right)$$
$$- N_2\left(\frac{b - \mu t_1}{\sigma\sqrt{t_1}}, \frac{-k_2 + \mu t_2}{\sigma\sqrt{t_2}}; -\sqrt{\frac{t_1}{t_2}}\right)$$

Now, the probability for $P(m_{02} > b,\ X_2 > k_2)$ is

$$P\left(m_{01} > b, X_1 > k_1, m_{12} > b,\ X_2 > k_2\right) = P\left(m_{02} > b, X_2 > k_2\right)$$

$$P(m_{02} > b, X_2 > k_2) = P(X_2 > k_2) - P(m_{02} < b, X_2 > k_2)$$

$$= N\left(\frac{-k_2 + \mu t_2}{\sigma\sqrt{t_2}}\right) - e^{\frac{2\mu b}{\sigma^2}} N_2\left(\frac{-k_2 + 2b + \mu t_2}{\sigma\sqrt{t_2}}; \sqrt{\frac{t_1}{t_2}}\right)$$

Collecting the terms

$$e^{\frac{2\mu b}{\sigma^2}} N_2\left(\frac{b+\mu t_1}{\sigma\sqrt{t_1}}, \frac{-k_2+2b+\mu t_2}{\sigma\sqrt{t_2}}; \sqrt{\frac{t_1}{t_2}}\right)$$

$$- N_2\left(\frac{b-\mu t_1}{\sigma\sqrt{t_1}}, \frac{-k_2+\mu t_2}{\sigma\sqrt{t_2}}; -\sqrt{\frac{t_1}{t_2}}\right)$$

$$+ N\left(\frac{-k_2+\mu t_2}{\sigma\sqrt{t_2}}\right) - e^{\frac{2\mu b}{\sigma^2}} N_2\left(\frac{-k_2+2b+\mu t_2}{\sigma\sqrt{t_2}}; \sqrt{\frac{t_1}{t_2}}\right)$$

$$-e^{\frac{2\mu b}{\sigma^2}}\left[N_2\left(\frac{-k_2+2b+\mu t_2}{\sigma\sqrt{t_2}}; \sqrt{\frac{t_1}{t_2}}\right)\right.$$

$$\left. - N_2\left(\frac{b+\mu t_1}{\sigma\sqrt{t_1}}, \frac{-k_2+2b+\mu t_2}{\sigma\sqrt{t_2}}; \sqrt{\frac{t_1}{t_2}}\right)\right]$$

$$= -e^{\frac{2\mu b}{\sigma^2}} N_2\left(\frac{-b-\mu t_1}{\sigma\sqrt{t_1}}, \frac{-k_2+2b+\mu t_2}{\sigma\sqrt{t_2}}; -\sqrt{\frac{t_1}{t_2}}\right)$$

$$N\left(\frac{-k_2+\mu t_2}{\sigma\sqrt{t_2}}\right) - N_2\left(\frac{b-\mu t_1}{\sigma\sqrt{t_1}}, \frac{-k_2+\mu t_2}{\sigma\sqrt{t_2}}; -\sqrt{\frac{t_1}{t_2}}\right)$$

$$= N_2\left(\frac{-b+\mu t_1}{\sigma\sqrt{t_1}}, \frac{-k_2+\mu t_2}{\sigma\sqrt{t_2}}; \sqrt{\frac{t_1}{t_2}}\right)$$

$$\widetilde{E}\left[1_{S_T>K, m_{t_1}^T>H}\right] = N_2\left(\frac{-b+\mu t_1}{\sigma\sqrt{t_1}}, \frac{-k_2+\mu t_2}{\sigma\sqrt{t_2}}; \sqrt{\frac{t_1}{t_2}}\right)$$

$$- e^{\frac{2\mu b}{\sigma^2}} N_2\left(\frac{-b-\mu t_1}{\sigma\sqrt{t_1}}, \frac{-k_2+2b+\mu t_2}{\sigma\sqrt{t_2}}; -\sqrt{\frac{t_1}{t_2}}\right)$$

Therefore, the price is

$$OC(B1+)$$

$$= S_0 e^{-qT}\left[N_2\left(\frac{\ln S_0/H+\widetilde{\mu}t_1}{\sigma\sqrt{t_1}}, \frac{\ln S_0/K+\widetilde{\mu}t_2}{\sigma\sqrt{t_2}}; \sqrt{\frac{t_1}{t_2}}\right)\right.$$

$$\left. - (H/S_0)^{\frac{2r}{\sigma^2}+1} N_2\left(\frac{-\ln H/S_0-\widetilde{\mu}t_1}{\sigma\sqrt{t_1}}, \frac{\ln H^2/KS_0+\widetilde{\mu}t_2}{\sigma\sqrt{t_2}}; -\sqrt{\frac{t_1}{t_2}}\right)\right]$$

$$- Ke^{-rT}\left[N_2\left(\frac{\ln S_0/H+\mu t_1}{\sigma\sqrt{t_1}},\frac{\ln S_0/K+\mu t_2}{\sigma\sqrt{t_2}};\sqrt{\frac{t_1}{t_2}}\right)\right.$$

$$\left.-(H/S_0)^{\frac{2r}{\sigma^2}-1}N_2\left(\frac{-\ln H/S_0-\mu t_1}{\sigma\sqrt{t_1}},\frac{\ln H^2/KS_0+\mu t_2}{\sigma\sqrt{t_2}};-\sqrt{\frac{t_1}{t_2}}\right)\right] \tag{5.19}$$

where $\widetilde{\mu}=r-q+\frac{1}{2}\sigma^2$ $\mu=r-q-\frac{1}{2}\sigma^2$.

$$OC(B1+)=S_0\left[N(e_1,d_1;\rho)-\left(\frac{H}{S_0}\right)^{2\mu/\sigma^2}N(-e_1',f_1;-\rho)\right]$$

$$-e^{-rT}K\left[N(e_2,d_2;\rho)-\left(\frac{H}{S_0}\right)^{2\mu/\sigma^2}N\big(-e_2',f_2;-\rho\big)\right]$$

Now, let's calculate the price when $K<H$. Let's call it $OC\,(B1-)$

This time, the price of a type B1 knock-out call can be written as

$$e^{-rT}E\left[(S_T-K)\,1_{S_T>K,M_{t_1}^T<H}\right]+e^{-rT}E\left[1_{m_{t_1}^T>H}\right]$$

for $K<H$ case. The second probability is due to the condition that the share price may be located at both regions and $K<H$.

Let's calculate the probability by decomposing as follows. From Carr, using equation (5.9)

$$P\,(X_2>k_2,X_1<b,\tau>t_2)$$

$$=P\,(X_1<b,\tau>t_2)-P\,(X_2<k_2,X_1<b,\tau>t_2)$$

$$N_2\left(\frac{b-\mu t_1}{\sigma\sqrt{t_1}},\frac{b-\mu t_2}{\sigma\sqrt{t_2}};\sqrt{\frac{t_1}{t_2}}\right)-e^{\frac{2\mu b}{\sigma^2}}N_2\left(\frac{b+\mu t_1}{\sigma\sqrt{t_1}},\frac{-b-\mu t_2}{\sigma\sqrt{t_2}};-\sqrt{\frac{t_1}{t_2}}\right)$$

$$-N_2\left(\frac{b-\mu t_1}{\sigma\sqrt{t_1}},\frac{k_2-\mu t_2}{\sigma\sqrt{t_2}};\sqrt{\frac{t_1}{t_2}}\right)$$

$$+e^{\frac{2\mu b}{\sigma^2}}N_2\left(\frac{b+\mu t_1}{\sigma\sqrt{t_1}},\frac{k_2-2b-\mu t_2}{\sigma\sqrt{t_2}};-\sqrt{\frac{t_1}{t_2}}\right)$$

For the second probability, we know that

$$\widetilde{E}[1_{m_{t_1}^T>H}]=N\left(g_1,e_1;\sqrt{\frac{t_1}{T}}\right)-\left(\frac{H}{S_0}\right)^{\frac{2r}{\sigma^2}+1}N\left(g_1',-e_1';-\sqrt{\frac{t_1}{T}}\right)$$

Therefore, the price of OC (B1-) for $K < H$ is

$$
\begin{aligned}
&OC(B1-)\\
&= S_0e^{-qT}\left[N_2\left(-\frac{\ln\frac{S_0}{H}+\widetilde{\mu}t_1}{\sigma\sqrt{t_1}}, -\frac{\ln S_0/H+\widetilde{\mu}t_2}{\sigma\sqrt{t_2}}; \sqrt{\frac{t_1}{t_2}}\right)\right.\\
&\quad -\left(\frac{H}{S_0}\right)^{\frac{2r}{\sigma^2}+1} N_2\left(\frac{\ln\frac{H}{S_0}+\widetilde{\mu}t_1}{\sigma\sqrt{t_1}}, \frac{-\ln\frac{H}{S_0}-\widetilde{\mu}t_2}{\sigma\sqrt{t_2}}; -\sqrt{\frac{t_1}{t_2}}\right)\\
&\quad - N_2\left(-\frac{\ln\frac{S_0}{H}+\widetilde{\mu}t_1}{\sigma\sqrt{t_1}}, -\frac{\ln\frac{S_0}{K}+\widetilde{\mu}t_2}{\sigma\sqrt{t_2}}; \sqrt{\frac{t_1}{t_2}}\right)\\
&\quad +\left(\frac{H}{S_0}\right)^{\frac{2r}{\sigma^2}+1} N_2\left(\frac{\ln\frac{H}{S_0}+\widetilde{\mu}t_1}{\sigma\sqrt{t_1}}, -\frac{\ln H^2/KS_0+\widetilde{\mu}t_2}{\sigma\sqrt{t_2}}; -\sqrt{\frac{t_1}{t_2}}\right)\\
&\quad + N_2\left(\frac{\ln\frac{S_0}{H}+\widetilde{\mu}t_1}{\sigma\sqrt{t_1}}, \frac{\ln S_0/H+\widetilde{\mu}t_2}{\sigma\sqrt{t_2}}; \sqrt{\frac{t_1}{t_2}}\right)\\
&\quad \left.-\left(\frac{H}{S_0}\right)^{\frac{2r}{\sigma^2}+1} N_2\left(-\frac{\ln\frac{H}{S_0}+\widetilde{\mu}t_1}{\sigma\sqrt{t_1}}, \frac{\ln\frac{H}{S_0}+\widetilde{\mu}t_2}{\sigma\sqrt{t_2}}; -\sqrt{\frac{t_1}{t_2}}\right)\right]\\
&\quad -Ke^{-rT}\left[N_2\left(-\frac{\ln\frac{S_0}{H}+\mu t_1}{\sigma\sqrt{t_1}}, -\frac{\ln S_0/H+\mu t_2}{\sigma\sqrt{t_2}}; \sqrt{\frac{t_1}{t_2}}\right)\right.\\
&\quad -\left(\frac{H}{S_0}\right)^{\frac{2r}{\sigma^2}-1} N_2\left(\frac{\ln\frac{H}{S_0}+\mu t_1}{\sigma\sqrt{t_1}}, \frac{-\ln\frac{H}{S_0}-\mu t_2}{\sigma\sqrt{t_2}}; -\sqrt{\frac{t_1}{t_2}}\right)\\
&\quad - N_2\left(-\frac{\ln\frac{S_0}{H}+\mu t_1}{\sigma\sqrt{t_1}}, \frac{\ln\frac{S_0}{K}+\mu t_1}{\sigma\sqrt{t_2}}; \sqrt{\frac{t_1}{t_2}}\right)\\
&\quad +\left(\frac{H}{S_0}\right)^{\frac{2r}{\sigma^2}-1} N_2\left(\frac{\ln\frac{H}{S_0}+\mu t_1}{\sigma\sqrt{t_1}}, -\frac{\ln H^2/KS_0+\mu t_2}{\sigma\sqrt{t_2}}; -\sqrt{\frac{t_1}{t_2}}\right)\\
&\quad + N_2\left(\frac{\ln\frac{S_0}{H}+\widetilde{\mu}t_1}{\sigma\sqrt{t_1}}, \frac{\ln S_0/H+\widetilde{\mu}t_2}{\sigma\sqrt{t_2}}; \sqrt{\frac{t_1}{t_2}}\right)\\
&\quad \left.-\left(\frac{H}{S_0}\right)^{\frac{2r}{\sigma^2}-1} N_2\left(-\frac{\ln\frac{H}{S_0}+\widetilde{\mu}t_1}{\sigma\sqrt{t_1}}, \frac{\ln\frac{H}{S_0}+\widetilde{\mu}t_2}{\sigma\sqrt{t_2}}; -\sqrt{\frac{t_1}{t_2}}\right)\right]
\end{aligned}
$$

$$
\begin{aligned}
&OC(B1-)\\
&= S_0 e^{-qT}\left[N_2\left(-e_1,-g_1;\sqrt{\frac{t_1}{t_2}}\right)-\left(\frac{H}{S_0}\right)^{\frac{2r}{\sigma^2}+1}\right.\\
&\quad \times N_2\left(e_1',-g_1';-\sqrt{\frac{t_1}{t_2}}\right)-N_2\left(-d_1,-e_1;\sqrt{\frac{t_1}{t_2}}\right)\\
&\quad +\left(\frac{H}{S_0}\right)^{\frac{2r}{\sigma^2}+1}N_2\left(e_1',-f_1;-\sqrt{\frac{t_1}{t_2}}\right)\\
&\quad \left.+N_2\left(e_1,g_1;\sqrt{\frac{t_1}{t_2}}\right)-\left(\frac{H}{S_0}\right)^{\frac{2r}{\sigma^2}+1}N_2\left(-e_1',g_1';-\sqrt{\frac{t_1}{t_2}}\right)\right]\\
&\quad -Ke^{-rT}\left[N_2\left(-e_2,-g_2;\sqrt{\frac{t_1}{t_2}}\right)-\left(\frac{H}{S_0}\right)^{\frac{2r}{\sigma^2}+1}\right.\\
&\quad \times N_2\left(e_2',-g_2';-\sqrt{\frac{t_1}{t_2}}\right)-N_2\left(-d_2,-e_2;\sqrt{\frac{t_1}{t_2}}\right)\\
&\quad +\left(\frac{H}{S_0}\right)^{\frac{2r}{\sigma^2}+1}N_2\left(e_2',-f_2;-\sqrt{\frac{t_1}{t_2}}\right)+N_2\left(e_2,g_2;\sqrt{\frac{t_1}{t_2}}\right)\\
&\quad \left.-\left(\frac{H}{S_0}\right)^{\frac{2r}{\sigma^2}+1}N_2\left(-e_2',g_2';-\sqrt{\frac{t_1}{t_2}}\right)\right] \qquad (5.20)
\end{aligned}
$$

5.5.2. *Type B2 partial barrier call options*

For the $B2$ type UOC option, we take $K < H$; otherwise, the option would be worthless. Therefore, the price of UOC($B2$)

$$
\begin{aligned}
\mathrm{UOC}(B2) &= e^{-rT}E\left[(S_T-K)1_{S_T>K,M_{t_1}^T<H}\right]\\
&= S_0E\left[\xi 1_{S_T>K,M_{t_1}^T<H}\right]-e^{-rT}KE\left[1_{S_T>K,M_{t_1}^T<H}\right]\\
&= S_0\widetilde{E}\left[1_{S_T>K,M_{t_1}^T<H}\right]-e^{-rT}KE\left[1_{S_T>K,M_{t_1}^T<H}\right]
\end{aligned}
$$

The probability

$$P(X_2 > k_2, X_1 < b, \tau > t_2)$$
$$= P(X_1 < b, \tau > t_2) - P(X_2 < k_2, X_1 < b, \tau > t_2)$$

is exactly the one that we want to calculate. (Why?) This is equal to

$$N_2\left(\frac{b-\mu t_1}{\sigma\sqrt{t_1}}, \frac{b-\mu t_2}{\sigma\sqrt{t_2}}; \sqrt{\frac{t_1}{t_2}}\right) - e^{\frac{2\mu b}{\sigma^2}} N_2\left(\frac{b+\mu t_1}{\sigma\sqrt{t_1}}, \frac{-b-\mu t_2}{\sigma\sqrt{t_2}}; -\sqrt{\frac{t_1}{t_2}}\right)$$
$$- N_2\left(\frac{b-\mu t_1}{\sigma\sqrt{t_1}}, \frac{k_2-\mu t_2}{\sigma\sqrt{t_2}}; \sqrt{\frac{t_1}{t_2}}\right)$$
$$+ e^{\frac{2\mu b}{\sigma^2}} N_2\left(\frac{b+\mu t_1}{\sigma\sqrt{t_1}}, \frac{k_2-2b-\mu t_2}{\sigma\sqrt{t_2}}; -\sqrt{\frac{t_1}{t_2}}\right)$$

UOC($B2$)

$$= S_0 e^{-qT}\left[N_2\left(\frac{b-\widetilde{\mu} t_1}{\sigma\sqrt{t_1}}, \frac{b-\widetilde{\mu} t_2}{\sigma\sqrt{t_2}}; \sqrt{\frac{t_1}{t_2}}\right)\right.$$
$$- e^{\frac{2\mu b}{\sigma^2}} N_2\left(\frac{b+\widetilde{\mu} t_1}{\sigma\sqrt{t_1}}, \frac{-b-\widetilde{\mu} t_2}{\sigma\sqrt{t_2}}; -\sqrt{\frac{t_1}{t_2}}\right)$$
$$- N_2\left(\frac{b-\widetilde{\mu} t_1}{\sigma\sqrt{t_1}}, \frac{k_2-\widetilde{\mu} t_2}{\sigma\sqrt{t_2}}; \sqrt{\frac{t_1}{t_2}}\right)$$
$$\left.+ e^{\frac{2\mu b}{\sigma^2}} N_2\left(\frac{b+\widetilde{\mu} t_1}{\sigma\sqrt{t_1}}, \frac{k_2-2b-\widetilde{\mu} t_2}{\sigma\sqrt{t_2}}; -\sqrt{\frac{t_1}{t_2}}\right)\right]$$
$$- e^{-rT} K\left[N_2\left(\frac{b-\mu t_1}{\sigma\sqrt{t_1}}, \frac{b-\mu t_2}{\sigma\sqrt{t_2}}; \sqrt{\frac{t_1}{t_2}}\right)\right.$$
$$- e^{\frac{2\mu b}{\sigma^2}} N_2\left(\frac{b+\mu t_1}{\sigma\sqrt{t_1}}, \frac{-b-\mu t_2}{\sigma\sqrt{t_2}}; -\sqrt{\frac{t_1}{t_2}}\right)$$
$$- N_2\left(\frac{b-\mu t_1}{\sigma\sqrt{t_1}}, \frac{k_2-\mu t_2}{\sigma\sqrt{t_2}}; \sqrt{\frac{t_1}{t_2}}\right)$$
$$\left.+ e^{\frac{2\mu b}{\sigma^2}} N_2\left(\frac{b+\mu t_1}{\sigma\sqrt{t_1}}, \frac{k_2-2b-\mu t_2}{\sigma\sqrt{t_2}}; -\sqrt{\frac{t_1}{t_2}}\right)\right]$$

UOC($B2$)

$$
\begin{aligned}
&= S_0 e^{-qT}\left[N_2\left(-e_1, -g_1; \sqrt{\frac{t_1}{T}}\right) - \left(\frac{H}{S}\right)^{\frac{2r}{\sigma^2}+1}\right.\\
&\times N_2\left(e_1', -g_1'; -\sqrt{\frac{t_1}{T}}\right)\\
&\left. - N_2\left(-e_1, -d_1; \sqrt{\frac{t_1}{T}}\right) + \left(\frac{H}{S}\right)^{\frac{2r}{\sigma^2}+1} N_2\left(e_1', -f_1; -\sqrt{\frac{t_1}{T}}\right)\right]\\
&- e^{-rT}K\left[N_2\left(-e_2, -g_2; \sqrt{\frac{t_1}{T}}\right) - \left(\frac{H}{S}\right)^{\frac{2r}{\sigma^2}-1}\right.\\
&\times N_2\left(e_2', -g_2'; -\sqrt{\frac{t_1}{T}}\right) - N_2\left(-e_2, -d_2; \sqrt{\frac{t_1}{T}}\right)\\
&\left. + \left(\frac{H}{S}\right)^{\frac{2r}{\sigma^2}-1} N_2\left(e_2', -f_2; -\sqrt{\frac{t_1}{T}}\right)\right] \qquad (5.21)
\end{aligned}
$$

where

$$
\widetilde{\mu} = r - q + \frac{1}{2}\sigma^2 \quad \mu = r - q - \frac{1}{2}\sigma^2 \quad K < H
$$

Now, the price of a type $B2$ DOC with $K < H$ can be calculated as follows

$$
\begin{aligned}
&\mathrm{DOC}\,(B2) = e^{-rT} E\left[(S_T - K) 1_{S_T > K, m_{t_1}^T > H}\right]\\
&= S_0 E\left[\xi 1_{S_T > K, m_{t_1}^T > H}\right] - e^{-rT} K E\left[1_{S_T > K, m_{t_1}^T > H}\right]\\
&S_0 \widetilde{E}\left[1_{S_T > K, m_{t_1}^T > H}\right] - e^{-rT} K E\left[1_{S_T > K, m_{t_1}^T > H}\right]\\
&\widetilde{E}\left[1_{S_T > K, m_{t_1}^T > H}\right] = P\left(S_{t_1} > H, S_T > K, m_{t_1}^T > H\right)\\
&= P\left(S_{t_1} > H, S_T > K\right) - P\left(S_{t_1} > H, S_T > K, m_{t_1}^T < H\right)
\end{aligned}
$$

But since for $m_{t_1}^T < H$, $S_{t_1} > H$ and $S_T > K$ is not adequate for our desired result, that must be written as

$$P\left(S_{t_1} > H, S_T > H\right) - P\left(S_{t_1} > H, S_T > H, m_{t_1}^T < H\right)$$

because of the condition that $K < H$.

That is

$$\int_b^\infty \int_b^\infty n_{z1z2}\left[\begin{pmatrix} -\mu t_1 \\ -\mu t_2 \end{pmatrix} \begin{pmatrix} \sigma^2 t_1 & \sigma^2 t_1 \\ \sigma^2 t_1 & \sigma^2 t_2 \end{pmatrix}\right] dz_1 dz_2$$
$$- e^{\frac{2\mu b}{\sigma^2}} \int_{-\infty}^b \int_b^\infty n_{z1z2}\left[\begin{pmatrix} \mu t_1 \\ -(2b+\mu t_2) \end{pmatrix} \begin{pmatrix} \sigma^2 t_1 & -\sigma^2 t_1 \\ -\sigma^2 t_1 & \sigma^2 t_2 \end{pmatrix}\right] dz_1 dz_2$$

Because

$$P\left(S_T > H, m_{t_1}^T < H\right) = e^{2\mu b/\sigma^2} N\left(\frac{-k + 2b + \mu t_2}{\sigma\sqrt{t_2}}\right)$$

Integrating yields

$$N\left(\frac{-b+\mu t_1}{\sigma\sqrt{t_1}}, \frac{-b+\mu t_2}{\sigma\sqrt{t_2}}; \sqrt{\frac{t_1}{t_2}}\right)$$
$$- \left(\frac{H}{S}\right)^{\frac{2r}{\sigma^2}+1} N\left(\frac{b-\mu t_1}{\sigma\sqrt{t_1}}, \frac{b+\mu t_2}{\sigma\sqrt{t_2}}; -\sqrt{\frac{t_1}{t_2}}\right)$$

DOC($B2$)

$$= S_0 e^{-qT}\left[N\left(e_1, g_1; \sqrt{\frac{t_1}{t_2}}\right) - \left(\frac{H}{S}\right)^{\frac{2r}{\sigma^2}+1} N\left(-e_1, g_1'; -\sqrt{\frac{t_1}{t_2}}\right)\right]$$
$$- e^{-rT} K\left[N\left(e_2, g_2; \sqrt{\frac{t_1}{t_2}}\right) - \left(\frac{H}{S}\right)^{\frac{2r}{\sigma^2}-1} N\left(-e_2, g_2'; -\sqrt{\frac{t_1}{t_2}}\right)\right]$$

If $K > H$ there is no difference between the DOC($B2$) and DOC ($B1+$) and we can use

$$\mathrm{DOC}(B1) = e^{-rT} E\left[(S_T - K)\, 1_{S_T > K, m_{t_1}^T > H}\right] \quad K > H$$

$$\mathrm{DOC}(B1+) = S_0\left[N(e_1, d_1; \rho) - \left(\frac{H}{S_0}\right)^{2\mu/\sigma^2} N\left(-e_1', f_1; -\rho\right)\right]$$
$$- e^{-rT} K\left[N(e_2, d_2; \rho) - \left(\frac{H}{S_0}\right)^{2\mu/\sigma^2} N\left(-e_2', f_2; -\rho\right)\right]$$

as given by equation (5.19).

We can summarize the cumulative normal distribution integral limits as follows:

$$\boldsymbol{e_1} = \frac{\ln \boldsymbol{S_0/H} + \left(\boldsymbol{r - q + \frac{1}{2}\sigma^2}\right) \boldsymbol{t_1}}{\boldsymbol{\sigma\sqrt{t_1}}}$$

$$\boldsymbol{e_1'} = \frac{\ln \boldsymbol{H/S_0} + \left(\boldsymbol{r - q + \frac{1}{2}\sigma^2}\right) \boldsymbol{t_1}}{\boldsymbol{\sigma\sqrt{t_1}}}$$

$$\boldsymbol{e_2} = \frac{\ln \boldsymbol{S_0/H} + \left(\boldsymbol{r - q - \frac{1}{2}\sigma^2}\right) \boldsymbol{t_1}}{\boldsymbol{\sigma\sqrt{t_1}}}$$

$$\boldsymbol{e_2'} = \frac{\ln \boldsymbol{H/S_0} + \left(\boldsymbol{r - q - \frac{1}{2}\sigma^2}\right) \boldsymbol{t_1}}{\boldsymbol{\sigma\sqrt{t_1}}}$$

$$\boldsymbol{g_1} = \frac{\ln \boldsymbol{S_0/H} + \left(\boldsymbol{r - q + \frac{1}{2}\sigma^2}\right) \boldsymbol{T}}{\boldsymbol{\sigma\sqrt{T}}}$$

$$\boldsymbol{g_1'} = \frac{\ln \boldsymbol{H/S_0} + \left(\boldsymbol{r - q + \frac{1}{2}\sigma^2}\right) \boldsymbol{T}}{\boldsymbol{\sigma\sqrt{T}}}$$

$$\boldsymbol{g_2} = \frac{\ln \boldsymbol{S_0/H} + \left(\boldsymbol{r - q - \frac{1}{2}\sigma^2}\right) \boldsymbol{T}}{\boldsymbol{\sigma\sqrt{T}}}$$

$$\boldsymbol{g_2'} = \frac{\ln \boldsymbol{H/S_0} + \left(\boldsymbol{r - q - \frac{1}{2}\sigma^2}\right) \boldsymbol{T}}{\boldsymbol{\sigma\sqrt{T}}}$$

$$f_1 = \frac{\ln \frac{H^2}{KS_0} + \left(r - q + \frac{1}{2}\sigma^2\right) T}{\sigma\sqrt{T}}$$

$$f_2 = \frac{\ln \frac{H^2}{KS_0} + \left(r - q - \frac{1}{2}\sigma^2\right) T}{\sigma\sqrt{T}}$$

$$\boldsymbol{d_1} = \frac{\ln \boldsymbol{S_0/K} + \left(\boldsymbol{r - q + \frac{1}{2}\sigma^2}\right) \boldsymbol{T}}{\boldsymbol{\sigma\sqrt{T}}}$$

$$\boldsymbol{d_2} = \frac{\ln \boldsymbol{S_0/K} + \left(\boldsymbol{r - q - \frac{1}{2}\sigma^2}\right) \boldsymbol{T}}{\boldsymbol{\sigma\sqrt{T}}}$$

Until now, we have focused on "out" options. A knock-in option can be priced via an ordinary option since a knock-in option plus a knock-out option with the same strike, maturity, barrier, and monitoring period yields the price of an otherwise identical ordinary option. Therefore, partial knock-in call (put) prices can be simply calculated as the difference between the ordinary calls (puts) and the knock-out partial barrier prices.

5.6. Rainbow Barriers

This section is based on the paper by Carr (1995), namely "Two Extensions to Barrier Option Valuation and Heynen and Kat (1994a). We explain the situation where there are two assets: the barrier is in terms of the first asset, and the payoff is based on the second asset. The final payoff of one type of asset depends on another asset, whether it hits the barrier or not, until the option's maturity T.

Let $B > S_{10}$ initially, i.e., the barrier is selected for the first asset. The (call) payoff is

$$\max(S_{2T} - K, 0)$$

if $S_{1t} < B$ for all $t \in [0, T]$.

Carr (1995) gives an example of a gold mine operated by a US investor in Canada that was exposed to foreign exchange risk. (Rise in Canadian dollar increases the running costs of the mine.) However, if gold prices rise, the gold producer may be able to afford the rising production costs of the mine. Therefore, she can buy an UOC rainbow barrier where S_1 is the gold price, and S_2 is the Canadian dollars. If S_1 does not increase, the option compensates the investor against the unfavorable rise of the Canadian dollar. If S_1 increases, the option is knocked out.

We know that the value of a standard call on foreign exchange is

$$c_0 = e^{-r_2 T} S_{20} N\left(\frac{\ln\left(\frac{S_{20}}{K}\right) + \left(r - r_2 + \frac{1}{2}\sigma_2^2\right)T}{\sigma_2\sqrt{T}}\right)$$

$$- e^{-rT} K N\left(\frac{\ln\left(\frac{S_{20}}{K}\right) + \left(r - r_2 - \frac{1}{2}\sigma_2^2\right)T}{\sigma_2\sqrt{T}}\right)$$

and the value of UOC can be decomposed as

$$U_0^{oc} = c_0 - U_0^{ic}$$

Carr proves that the price of up and in rainbow barrier call can be expressed as

$$U_0^{ic} = e^{-r_2 T} S_{20}\left[\left(\frac{B}{S_{10}}\right)^{2\frac{r - r_1 + \sigma_{12}}{\sigma_1^2} - 1}\right.$$

$$N_2\left(\frac{\ln\left(\frac{S_{10}}{B}\right) - \left(r - r_1 - \frac{1}{2}\sigma_1^2 + \sigma_{12}\right)T}{\sigma_1\sqrt{T}},\right.$$

$$\left.\times \frac{\ln\left(\frac{S_{20}}{K}\right) + \rho\frac{\sigma_2}{\sigma_1} 2\ln\left(\frac{B}{S_{10}}\right) + \left(r - r_2 + \frac{1}{2}\sigma_2^2\right)T}{\sigma_2\sqrt{T}}; -\rho\right)$$

$$+ N_2\left(\frac{\ln\left(\frac{S_{10}}{B}\right) + \left(r - r_1 - \frac{1}{2}\sigma_1^2 + \sigma_{12}\right)T}{\sigma_1\sqrt{T}},\right.$$

$$\left.\left.\times \frac{\ln\left(\frac{S_{20}}{K}\right) + \left(r - r_2 + \frac{1}{2}\sigma_2^2\right)T}{\sigma_2\sqrt{T}}; \rho\right)\right]$$

$$- e^{-rT} K\left[\left(\frac{B}{S_{10}}\right)^{2\frac{r - r_1}{\sigma_1^2} - 1} N_2\left(\frac{\ln\left(\frac{S_{10}}{B}\right) - \left(r - r_1 - \frac{1}{2}\sigma_1^2\right)T}{\sigma_1\sqrt{T}},\right.\right.$$

$$\times \frac{\ln\left(\frac{S_{20}}{K}\right) + \rho\frac{\sigma_2}{\sigma_1}2\ln\left(\frac{B}{S_{10}}\right) + \left(r - r_2 - \frac{1}{2}\sigma_2^2\right)T}{\sigma_2\sqrt{T}}; -\rho\Bigg)$$

$$+ N_2\left(\frac{\ln\left(\frac{S_{10}}{B}\right) + \left(r - r_1 - \frac{1}{2}\sigma_1^2\right)T}{\sigma_1\sqrt{T}},\right.$$

$$\left.\times \frac{\ln\left(\frac{S_{20}}{K}\right) + \left(r - r_2 - \frac{1}{2}\sigma_2^2\right)T}{\sigma_2\sqrt{T}}; \rho\right)\Bigg] \tag{5.22}$$

The first term is the price of the "rainbow gap call," paying the second asset price at expiration if

$$S_{2T} > K$$

and the first asset price breached the barrier (note that this is part of the up-and-in call). The second term is the value of a short position in a "rainbow digital call, "which pays the holder the amount K under the same conditions.

Proof (Carr, 1995):

We write the following processes under the risk-neutral probability measure P^0:

$$\frac{dS_{1t}}{S_{1t}} = (r - r_1)\,dt + \sigma_1 dW_{1t}^0$$

$$\frac{dS_{2t}}{S_{2t}} = (r - r_2)\,dt + \sigma_2\left(\rho dW_{1t}^0 + \sqrt{1-\rho^2}dW_{2t}^0\right)$$

$$cov\left(\frac{dS_{1t}}{S_{1t}}, \frac{dS_{2t}}{S_{2t}}\right) = \sigma_{12}dt,\ t \in [0, T]$$

$$E\left[dW_{1t}^0 dW_{2t}^0\right] = 0$$

where dW_{1t}^0 and dW_{2t}^0 are independent Brownian motions and the solutions of SDEs as

$$S_{1t} = S_{10}e^{\left(r - r_1 - \frac{1}{2}\sigma_1^2\right)t + \sigma_1 W_{1t}^0}$$

$$S_{2t} = S_{20}e^{\left(r - r_2 - \frac{1}{2}\sigma_2^2\right)t + \sigma_2\left(\rho W_{1t}^0 + \sqrt{1-\rho^2}W_{2t}^0\right)}\quad t \in [0, T]$$

The value of a European up-and-in call is $(S_{1t} < B)$

$$U_0^{ic} = e^{-rT} E^0 \left\{ \max(0, S_{2T} - K) 1_{\max_{0 \le t \le T} S_{1t} > B} \right\}$$

$$= e^{-rT} E^0 \left\{ \left[S_{2T} 1_{S_{2T} > K} - K 1_{S_{2T} > K} \right] 1_{\max_{0 \le t \le T} S_{1t} > B} \right\}$$

$$= e^{-rT} E^0 \Big\{ \Big[S_{20} e^{\left(r - r_2 - \frac{1}{2}\sigma_2^2\right)T + \sigma_2 \left(\rho W_{1T}^0 + \sqrt{1-\rho^2} W_{2T}^0\right)}$$

$$\times 1_{S_{2T} > K, \max_{0 \le t \le T} S_{1t} > B_,} \Big] \Big\}$$

$$\times \; - e^{-rT} E^0 \Big\{ \Big[K 1_{S_{2T} > K, \max_{0 \le t \le T} S_{1t} > B_,} \Big] \Big\}$$

$$= e^{-r_2 T} S_{20} E^0 \Big\{ \Big[\xi 1_{S_{2T} > K, \max_{0 \le t \le T} S_{1t} > B_,} \Big] \Big\}$$

$$- e^{-rT} K E^0 \Big\{ \Big[1_{S_{2T} > K, \max_{0 \le t \le T} S_{1t} > B_,} \Big] \Big\}$$

The Radon–Nikodym derivative is

$$\xi = e^{-\frac{1}{2}\sigma_2^2 T + \sigma_2 \left(\rho W_{1T}^0 + \sqrt{1-\rho^2} W_{2T}^0\right)}$$

$$= e^{-\frac{1}{2}\rho^2 \sigma_2^2 T + \sigma_2 \rho W_{1T}^0 - \left(1-\rho^2\right)\frac{1}{2}\sigma_2^2 T + \sigma_2 \sqrt{1-\rho^2} W_{2T}^0} \tag{5.23}$$

$$e^{\sigma_2 \rho W_{1T}^0 - \frac{1}{2}\rho^2 \sigma_2^2 T + \sqrt{1-\rho^2} W_{2T}^0 \; - \frac{1}{2}\left(1-\rho^2\right)\sigma_2^2 T}$$

where we have added $\pm \frac{1}{2}\rho^2 \sigma_2^2 T$.

Let's define an equivalent probability measure P^1 by

$$\xi = \frac{dP^1}{dP^0}$$

From Girsanov theorem, we can write

$$W_{1t}^1 = W_{1t}^0 - \rho \sigma_2 t$$

$$W_{2t}^1 = W_{2t}^0 - \sqrt{1-\rho^2}\sigma_2 t$$

So, under the probability measure, P^1, stochastic differential equations, and their solutions are

$$\frac{dS_{1t}}{S_{1t}} = (r - r_1)\, dt + \sigma_1 d\left(W_{1t}^1 + \rho \sigma_2 t\right)$$

$$= (r - r_1 + \rho \sigma_1 \sigma_2)\, dt + \sigma_1 dW_{1t}^1 = (r - r_1 + \sigma_{12})\, dt + \sigma_1 dW_{1t}^1$$

$$\frac{dS_{2t}}{S_{2t}} = (r - r_2)\, dt$$
$$+ \sigma_2 \left(\rho d(W_{1t}^1 + \rho\sigma_2 t) + \sqrt{1-\rho^2} d(W_{2t}^1 + \sqrt{1-\rho^2}\sigma_2 t) \right)$$

$$\frac{dS_{2t}}{S_{2t}} = (r - r_2)\, dt + \sigma_2 \rho dW_{1t}^1$$
$$+ \left(\rho^2 \sigma_2^2 dt + \sigma_2 \sqrt{1-\rho^2} dW_{2t}^1 + (1 - \rho^2)\sigma_2^2 dt) \right)$$
$$= \left(r - r_2 + \sigma_2^2\right) dt + \sigma_2 \rho dW_{1t}^1 + \sigma_2 \sqrt{1-\rho^2} dW_{2t}^1$$
$$= \left(r - r_2 + \sigma_2^2\right) dt + \sigma_2 \left(\rho dW_{1t}^1 + \sqrt{1-\rho^2} dW_{2t}^1 \right)$$

and

$$S_{1t} = S_{10} e^{\left(r - r_1 - \frac{1}{2}\sigma_1^2 + \sigma_{12}\right)t + \sigma_1 W_{1t}^1}$$
$$S_{2t} = S_{20} e^{\left(r - r_2 + \frac{1}{2}\sigma_2^2\right)t + \sigma_2\left(\rho W_{1t}^1 + \sqrt{1-\rho^2} W_{2t}^1\right)}$$

respectively. Therefore, up-and-in call price can be stated as

$$U_0^{ic} = e^{-r_2 T} S_{20} E^1\{[1_{S_{2T} > K, \max_{0\le t\le T} S_{1t} > B},]\}$$
$$- e^{-rT} K E^0\{[1_{S_{2T} > K, \max_{0\le t\le T} S_{1t} > B},]\}$$

$$U_0^{ic} = e^{-r_2 T} S_{20} P^1 \left(S_{2T} > K, \max_{0\le t\le T} S_{1t} > B \right)$$
$$- e^{-rT} K P^0 \left(S_{2T} > K, \max_{0\le t\le T} S_{1t} > B \right)$$

Considering

$$X_{1t} = \ln\left(\frac{S_{1t}}{S_{10}}\right) X_{10} = 0$$

and using Ito's Lemma

$$dX_{1t} = \frac{1}{S_{1t}} dS_{1t} - \frac{1}{2}\frac{1}{S_{1t}^2} dS_{1t}^2$$

we can write the drift terms under the different probability measures as

$$dX_{1t} = \left(r - r_1 - \frac{1}{2}\sigma_1^2\right) dt + \sigma_1 dW_{1t}^0$$

$$\mu_1^0 = \left(r - r_1 - \frac{1}{2}\sigma_1^2\right)$$

$$dX_{1t} = \left(r - r_1 - \frac{1}{2}\sigma_1^2 + \sigma_{12}\right) dt + \sigma_1 dW_{1t}^1$$

$$\mu_1^1 = \left(r - r_1 - \frac{1}{2}\sigma_1^2 + \sigma_{12}\right)$$

$$dX_{2t} = \left(r - r_2 - \frac{1}{2}\sigma_2^2\right) dt + \sigma_2 \left(\rho dW_{1t}^0 + \sqrt{1-\rho^2} dW_{2t}^0\right)$$

$$\mu_2^0 = \left(r - r_2 - \frac{1}{2}\sigma_2^2\right)$$

$$dX_{2t} = \left(r - r_2 + \frac{1}{2}\sigma_2^2\right) dt + \sigma_2 \left(\rho dW_{1t}^1 + \sqrt{1-\rho^2} dW_{2t}^1\right)$$

$$\mu_2^1 = \left(r - r_2 + \frac{1}{2}\sigma_2^2\right)$$

and

$$dX_{1t} = \mu_1^0 dt + \sigma_1 dW_{1t}^0$$

$$dX_{1t} = \mu_1^1 dt + \sigma_1 dW_{1t}^1$$

$$dX_{2t} = \mu_2^0 dt + \sigma_2 \left(\rho dW_{1t}^0 + \sqrt{1-\rho^2} dW_{2t}^0\right)$$

$$dX_{2t} = \mu_2^1 dt + \sigma_2 \left(\rho dW_{1t}^1 + \sqrt{1 - \rho^2} dW_{2t}^1\right)$$

That is, different drifts are under different probability measures.

Let's define a new probability measure $\overline{P}^0$ equivalent to P^0 and write the Radon–Nikodym derivative as

$$\xi = \frac{d\overline{P}^0}{dP^0} = \exp\left\{-\frac{\mu_1^0}{\sigma_1}W_{1T}^0 - \frac{1}{2}\left(\frac{\mu_1^0}{\sigma_1}\right)^2 T\right\}$$

and

$$\zeta = \frac{dP^0}{d\overline{P}^0} = \exp\left\{\frac{\mu_1^0}{\sigma_1}W_{1T}^0 + \frac{1}{2}\left(\frac{\mu_1^0}{\sigma_1}\right)^2 T\right\}$$

Using Girsanov's Theorem we can write

$$\overline{W}_{1T}^0 = W_{1T}^0 + \frac{\mu_1^0}{\sigma_1}T$$

$$W_{1T}^0 = \overline{W}_{1T}^0 - \frac{\mu_1^0}{\sigma_1}T \quad W_{2T}^0 = \overline{W}_{2T}^0$$

$$dX_{1t} = \mu_1^0 dt + \sigma_1 d\left(\overline{W}_{1t}^0 - \frac{\mu_1^0}{\sigma_1}t\right) = \sigma_1 d\overline{W}_{1t}^0$$

$$dX_{2t} = \mu_2^0 dt + \sigma_2\left(\rho d\left(\overline{W}_{1t}^0 - \frac{\mu_1^0}{\sigma_1}t\right) + \sqrt{1-\rho^2}\overline{W}_{2t}^0\right)$$

$$dX_{2t} = \left(\mu_2^0 - \frac{\sigma_2}{\sigma_1}\rho\mu_1^0\right)dt + \sigma_2\left(\rho d\overline{W}_{1t}^0 + \sqrt{1-\rho^2}\overline{W}_{2t}^0\right)$$

and finally

$$dX_{2t} = \overline{\mu}_2^0 dt + \sigma_2\left(\rho d\overline{W}_{1t}^0 + \sqrt{1-\rho^2}\overline{W}_{2t}^0\right)$$

where

$$\overline{\mu}_2^0 = \left(\mu_2^0 - \frac{\sigma_2}{\sigma_1}\rho\mu_1^0\right) \overline{\mu}_1^0 = 0$$

Similarly, let's define another probability measure equivalent to measure P^1 by

$$\xi = \frac{d\overline{P}^1}{dP^1} = \exp\left\{-\frac{\mu_1^1}{\sigma_1}W_{1T}^0 - \frac{1}{2}\left(\frac{\mu_1^1}{\sigma_1}\right)^2 T\right\}$$

Using Girsanov's Theorem, we can write

$$W_{1t}^1 = \overline{W}_{1t}^1 - \frac{\mu_1^1}{\sigma_1}t \quad W_{2t}^1 = \overline{W}_{2t}^1$$

So, we write similarly

$$dX_{1t} = \mu_1^1 dt + \sigma_1 d\left(\overline{W}_{1t}^1 - \frac{\mu_1^1}{\sigma_1}t\right) = \sigma_1 d\overline{W}_{1t}^1$$

$$dX_{2t} = \mu_2^1 dt + \sigma_2\left(\rho d\left(\overline{W}_{1t}^1 - \frac{\mu_1^0}{\sigma_1}t\right) + \sqrt{1-\rho^2}d\overline{W}_{2t}^1\right)$$

$$dX_{2t} = \left(\mu_2^1 - \frac{\sigma_2}{\sigma_1}\rho\mu_1^1\right)dt + \sigma_2\left(\rho d\overline{W}_{1t}^1 + \sqrt{1-\rho^2}\overline{W}_{2t}^1\right)$$

$$dX_{2t} = \overline{\mu}_2^1 dt + \sigma_2\left(\rho d\overline{W}_{1t}^1 + \sqrt{1-\rho^2}\overline{W}_{2t}^1\right)$$

where

$$\overline{\mu}_2^1 = \left(\mu_2^1 - \frac{\sigma_2}{\sigma_1}\rho\mu_1^1\right) \; \overline{\mu}_1^1 = 0 \tag{5.24}$$

Also, note that

$$\begin{aligned}\frac{dP^0}{d\overline{P}^0} &= \exp\left\{\frac{\mu_1^0}{\sigma_1}W_{1T}^0 + \frac{1}{2}\left(\frac{\mu_1^0}{\sigma_1}\right)^2 T\right\} \\ &= \exp\left\{\frac{\mu_1^0}{\sigma_1}\left(\overline{W}_{1T}^0 - \frac{\mu_1^0}{\sigma_1}T\right) + \frac{1}{2}\left(\frac{\mu_1^0}{\sigma_1}\right)^2 T\right\} \\ &= \exp\left\{\frac{\mu_1^0}{\sigma_1}\overline{W}_{1T}^0 - \frac{1}{2}\left(\frac{\mu_1^0}{\sigma_1}\right)^2 T\right\}\end{aligned}$$

Now, we can calculate the probabilities and the expectations as shown by Carr (1995) on pp. 16–19. Let

$$I^0 = P^0\left(\max_{0\le t\le T} S_{1t} > B, S_{2T} > K\right)$$

Dividing by S_{10} and S_{20} yields

$$I^0 = P^0\left(\max_{0\le t\le T} X_{1t} > b, X_{2T} > k\right)$$

where

$$X_{it} = \ln\left(\frac{S_{it}}{S_{i0}}\right) \quad b = \ln\left(\frac{B}{S_{10}}\right) \quad k = \ln\left(\frac{K}{S_{20}}\right)$$

Let

$$M_T^x = \max_{0\le t\le T} X_{1t}$$

$$I^0 = P^0\left(X_{2T} > k, M_T^x > b\right) = E^0\left[1_{(X_{2T}>k, M_T^x>b)}\right]$$

By changing the probability measure, we can write

$$E^0\left[1_{(X_{2T}>k, M_T^x>b)}\right] = \overline{E}^0\left[\frac{dP^0}{d\overline{P}^0}1_{(X_{2T}>k, M_T^x>b)}\right]$$

$$= \overline{E}^0\left[\exp\left\{\frac{\mu_1^0}{\sigma_1}\overline{W}_{1T}^0 - \frac{1}{2}\left(\frac{\mu_1^0}{\sigma_1}\right)^2 T\right\}1_{(X_{2T}>k, M_T^x>b)}\right]$$

Since $\overline{W}_{1T}^0$ (X_{1T}^0) is driftless and

$$dX_{1t} = \mu_1^0 dt + \sigma_1 d\left(\overline{W}_{1t}^0 - \frac{\mu_1^0}{\sigma_1}t\right) = \sigma_1 d\overline{W}_{1t}^0$$

$$X_{1t} = \sigma_1 \overline{W}_{1t}^0$$

$$\overline{E}^0\left[\exp\left\{\frac{\mu_1^0}{\sigma_1}\overline{W}_{1T}^0 - \frac{1}{2}\left(\frac{\mu_1^0}{\sigma_1}\right)^2 T\right\}1_{(X_{2T}>k, M_T^x>b)}\right]$$

$$= \exp\left\{-\frac{1}{2}\left(\frac{\mu_1^0}{\sigma_1}\right)^2 T\right\}\overline{E}^0\left[\exp\left\{-\frac{\mu_1^0}{\sigma_1^2}X_{1T}\right\}1_{(X_{2T}>k, M_T^x>b)}\right] \tag{5.25}$$

But this is an expectation containing both X_{1T}, X_{2T}, and M_T^x and can be expressed as

$$\exp\left\{-\frac{1}{2}\left(\frac{\mu_1^0}{\sigma_1}\right)^2 T\right\}\int_{-\infty}^{\infty}\exp\left\{\frac{\mu_1^0}{\sigma_1^2}x_1\right\}\overline{P}^0$$

$$\times\left(X_{2T} > k, \sigma_1\overline{W}_{1T}^0 \in dx_1, M_T^x > b\right)$$

Since

$$dX_{2t} = \overline{\mu}_2^0 dt + \sigma_2(\rho d\overline{W}_{1t}^0 + \sqrt{1-\rho^2}\overline{W}_{2t}^0)$$

the inside of the probability can be stated as

$$\exp\left\{-\frac{1}{2}\left(\frac{\mu_1^0}{\sigma_1}\right)^2 T\right\}\int_{-\infty}^{\infty} e^{\frac{\mu_1^0}{\sigma_1^2}x_1}$$
$$\times\,\overline{P}^0(\overline{\mu}_2^0 T + \sigma_2\rho\overline{W}_{1T}^0 + \sigma_2\sqrt{1-\rho^2}\overline{W}_{2T}^0$$
$$> k, \sigma_1\overline{W}_{1T}^0 \in dx_1, M_T^x > b)$$
$$\exp\left\{-\frac{1}{2}\left(\frac{\mu_1^0}{\sigma_1}\right)^2 T\right\}$$
$$\int_{-\infty}^{\infty} e^{\frac{\mu_1^0}{\sigma_1^2}x_1}\overline{P}^0\left(\overline{\mu}_2^0 T + \frac{\sigma_2}{\sigma_1}\rho x_1 + \sigma_2\sqrt{1-\rho^2}\overline{W}_{2T}^0 > k\right),$$
$$\sigma_1\overline{W}_{1T}^0 \in dx_1, M_T^x > b \tag{5.26}$$

It is possible to separate $\overline{W}_{2T}^0$ and $\overline{W}_{1T}^0$ since they are uncorrelated Brownian motions by construction. Therefore, we can write

$$\exp\left\{-\frac{1}{2}\left(\frac{\mu_1^0}{\sigma_1}\right)^2 T\right\}\int_{-\infty}^{\infty} e^{\frac{\mu_1^0}{\sigma_1^2}x_1}\overline{P}^0\left(\sigma_2\overline{W}_{2T}^0 > \frac{k-\overline{\mu}_2^0 T - \frac{\sigma_2}{\sigma_1}\rho x_1}{\sqrt{1-\rho^2}}\right)$$
$$\times\,\overline{P}^0(\sigma_1\overline{W}_{1T}^0 \in dx_1, M_T^x > b)$$

and with different integral limits for two integration regions:

$$\exp\left\{-\frac{1}{2}\left(\frac{\mu_1^0}{\sigma_1}\right)^2 T\right\}\int_{-\infty}^{b} e^{\frac{\mu_1^0}{\sigma_1^2}x_1}\overline{P}^0\left(\sigma_2\overline{W}_{2T}^0 > \frac{k-\overline{\mu}_2^0 T - \frac{\sigma_2}{\sigma_1}\rho x_1}{\sqrt{1-\rho^2}}\right)$$
$$\times\,\overline{P}^0\left(\sigma_1\overline{W}_{1T}^0 \in dx_1, M_T^x > b\right)$$
$$+\exp\left\{-\frac{1}{2}\left(\frac{\mu_1^0}{\sigma_1}\right)^2 T\right\}\int_{b}^{\infty} e^{\frac{\mu_1^0}{\sigma_1^2}x_1}\overline{P}^0$$
$$\times\left(\sigma_2\overline{W}_{2T}^0 > \frac{k-\overline{\mu}_2^0 T - \frac{\sigma_2}{\sigma_1}\rho x_1}{\sqrt{1-\rho^2}}\right)\overline{P}^0(\sigma_1\overline{W}_{1T}^0 \in dx_1, M_T^x > b)$$

Remember that the probability of $P\left(W < x,\ M_T^W > b\right)$ is

$$P\left(W < x, M_T^W > b\right) = e^{\frac{2\mu b}{\sigma^2}} N\left(\frac{x - 2b - \mu T}{\sigma\sqrt{T}}\right)$$

But since for $\overline{\mu}^0 = 0$ from equation (5.24)

$$\overline{P}^0\left(W < x, M_T^W > b\right) = \overline{P}^0(W > 2b - x) = N\left(\frac{x - 2b}{\sigma\sqrt{T}}\right)$$

$$\overline{P}^0(-W < x - 2b) = N\left(\frac{x - 2b}{\sigma\sqrt{T}}\right)$$

For the negative, integral region, the derivation is

$$\overline{P}^0\left(\sigma_1 \overline{W}^0_{1T} \in dx_1, M_T^W > b\right) = \frac{1}{\sigma_1\sqrt{T}} N'\left(\frac{2b - x_1}{\sigma_1\sqrt{T}}\right)$$

and

$$\overline{P}^0\left(\sigma_2 \overline{W}^0_{2T} > \frac{k - \overline{\mu}_2^0 T - \frac{\sigma_2}{\sigma_1}\rho x_1}{\sqrt{1-\rho^2}}\right) = \frac{1}{\sigma_2\sqrt{T}} N'\left(\frac{x_2}{\sigma_2\sqrt{T}}\right)$$

where

$$x_2 = \frac{k - \overline{\mu}_2^0 T - \frac{\sigma_2}{\sigma_1}\rho x_1}{\sqrt{1-\rho^2}}$$

So, the first part of the integral is

$$\exp\left\{-\frac{1}{2}\left(\frac{\mu_1^0}{\sigma_1}\right)^2 T\right\} \int_{-\infty}^{b} e^{\frac{\mu_1^0}{\sigma_1^2} x_1} \int_{\frac{k - \overline{\mu}_2^0 T - \frac{\sigma_2}{\sigma_1}\rho x_1}{\sqrt{1-\rho^2}}}^{\infty} \frac{1}{\sigma_2\sqrt{T}} N'\left(\frac{x_2}{\sigma_2\sqrt{T}}\right) dx_2$$

$$\frac{1}{\sigma_1\sqrt{T}} N'\left(\frac{2b - x_1}{\sigma_1\sqrt{T}}\right) dx_1 \tag{5.27}$$

and x_1 is up to b.

The second part is

$$\exp\left\{-\frac{1}{2}\left(\frac{\mu_1^0}{\sigma_1}\right)^2 T\right\}\int_b^\infty e^{\frac{\mu_1^0}{\sigma_1^2}x_1}\int_{\frac{k-\overline{\mu}_2^0 T-\frac{\sigma_2}{\sigma_1}\rho x_1}{\sqrt{1-\rho^2}}}^\infty \frac{1}{\sigma_2\sqrt{T}}N'\left(\frac{x_2}{\sigma_2\sqrt{T}}\right)dx_2$$

$$\frac{1}{\sigma_1\sqrt{T}}N^{'}\left(\frac{x_1}{\sigma_1\sqrt{T}}\right)dx_1 \tag{5.28}$$

using the reflection principle, x_1 is from b to infinity. Now, writing

$$\left[-\frac{1}{2}\left(\frac{\mu_1^0}{\sigma_1}\right)^2 T+\frac{\mu_1^0}{\sigma_1^2}x_1-\frac{1}{2}\left(\frac{2b-x_1}{\sigma_1\sqrt{T}}\right)^2\right]$$

$$=\left[-\frac{1}{2}\left(\frac{\mu_1^0}{\sigma_1}\right)^2 T+\frac{\mu_1^0}{\sigma_1^2}x_1-\frac{1}{2}\frac{4b^2-4bx_1+x_1^2}{\sigma_1^2}\right]$$

$$=\left[-\frac{1}{2}\left(\frac{\mu_1^0}{\sigma_1}\right)^2 \frac{T^2}{T}+\frac{2T\mu_1^0}{2T\sigma_1^2}x_1-\frac{4b^2-4bx_1+x_1^2}{2\sigma_1^2 T}\right]$$

$$=\left[-\frac{4b^2-4bx_1+x_1^2+\left(\mu_1^0 T\right)^2-2T\mu_1^0 x_1}{2\sigma_1^2 T}\right]$$

and by adding

$$\mp\frac{4b\mu_1^0 T}{2\sigma_1^2 T}$$

we obtain

$$\frac{1}{\sigma_1\sqrt{T}\sqrt{2\pi}}\exp\left(\frac{2b\mu_1^0}{\sigma_1^2}\right)\exp\left\{-\frac{1}{2}\left(\frac{x_1-(2b+\mu_1^0 T)}{\sigma_1\sqrt{T}}\right)^2\right\}$$

Similarly, for the second integral

$$\exp\left\{-\frac{1}{2}\left(\frac{\mu_1^0}{\sigma_1}\right)^2 T+\frac{\mu_1^0}{\sigma_1^2}x_1-\frac{1}{2}x_1^2\right\}=\left[-\frac{x_1^2+\left(\mu_1^0 T\right)^2-2T\mu_1^0 x_1}{2\sigma_1^2 T}\right]$$

$$=\frac{1}{\sigma_1\sqrt{T}\sqrt{2\pi}}\exp\left\{-\frac{1}{2}\left(\frac{x_1-\mu_1^0 T}{\sigma_1\sqrt{T}}\right)^2\right\}$$

Substituting in I^0 yields

$$I^0 = \exp\left(\frac{2b\mu_1^0}{\sigma_1^2}\right)\int_{-\infty}^{b}\int_{\frac{k-\overline{\mu}_2^0 T-\frac{\sigma_2}{\sigma_1}\rho x_1}{\sqrt{1-\rho^2}}}^{\infty}\frac{1}{\sigma_2\sqrt{T}}N'\left(\frac{x_2}{\sigma_2\sqrt{T}}\right)dx_2 +$$

$$\int_{b}^{\infty}\int_{\frac{k-\overline{\mu}_2^0 T-\frac{\sigma_2}{\sigma_1}\rho x_1}{\sqrt{1-\rho^2}}}^{\infty}\frac{1}{\sigma_2\sqrt{T}}N'\left(\frac{x_2}{\sigma_2\sqrt{T}}\right)dx_2\frac{1}{\sigma_1\sqrt{T}}N'\left(\frac{x_1-\mu_1^0 T}{\sigma_1\sqrt{T}}\right)dx_1$$

$$\frac{1}{\sigma_1\sqrt{T}}N'\left(\frac{x_1-(2b+\mu_1^0 T)}{\sigma_1\sqrt{T}}\right)dx_1 \tag{5.29}$$

Changing the integral variables, we can write

$$y_1 = \frac{x_1-(2b+\mu_1^0 T)}{\sigma_1\sqrt{T}} \quad x_1 \to b \; y_1 \to \frac{-b-\mu_1^0 T}{\sigma_1\sqrt{T}}$$

From bivariate identity, we know that

$$y = w\sqrt{1-\rho^2}+\rho x$$

or

$$w = \frac{y-\rho x}{\sqrt{1-\rho^2}}$$

and

$$y = y_2 \quad w = -\frac{x_2}{\sigma_2\sqrt{T}} \quad x = \frac{x_1-(2b+\mu_1^0 T)}{\sigma_1\sqrt{T}}$$

and considering the sign of y_2 will be negative because we change the order of integral limits and the correlation is negative:

$$y_2 = -\left[\frac{x_2}{\sigma_2\sqrt{T}}\sqrt{1-\rho^2}+\rho\left(\frac{x_1-(2b+\mu_1^0 T)}{\sigma_1\sqrt{T}}\right)\right]$$

$$= -\frac{1}{\sigma_2\sqrt{T}}\left[x_2\sqrt{1-\rho^2}+\frac{\sigma_2}{\sigma_1}\rho\left(x_1-(2b+\mu_1^0 T)\right)\right]$$

Replacing x_2

$$= -\frac{1}{\sigma_2\sqrt{T}}\left[\frac{k-\overline{\mu}_2^0 T-\frac{\sigma_2}{\sigma_1}\rho x_1}{\sqrt{1-\rho^2}}\sqrt{1-\rho^2}+\frac{\sigma_2}{\sigma_1}\rho\left(x_1-\left(2b+\mu_1^0 T\right)\right)\right]$$

$$y_2 = \frac{1}{\sigma_2\sqrt{T}}\left[-k+\overline{\mu}_2^0 T+2b\frac{\sigma_2}{\sigma_1}\rho+\frac{\sigma_2}{\sigma_1}\rho\mu_1^0 T\right]$$

we obtain the first integral as

$$\exp\left(\frac{2b\mu_1^0}{\sigma_1^2}\right)\int_{-\infty}^{\frac{-b-\mu_1^0 T}{\sigma_1\sqrt{T}}}\int_{-\infty}^{\frac{-k+\overline{\mu}_2^0 T+2b\frac{\sigma_2}{\sigma_1}\rho+\frac{\sigma_2}{\sigma_1}\rho\mu_1^0 T}{\sigma_2\sqrt{T}}} n_y\left(\mu_y,\Omega_y\right)dy_2 dy_1$$

$$= \exp\left(\frac{2b\mu_1^0}{\sigma_1^2}\right)N_2(y_1,y_2;-\rho)$$

where μ_y is the zero-mean vector, and Ω_y is the variance-covariance matrix

$$\Omega_y = \begin{bmatrix} 1 & -\rho \\ -\rho & 1 \end{bmatrix}$$

For the second integral, we write

$$\int_b^{\infty}\int_{\frac{k-\overline{\mu}_2^0 T-\frac{\sigma_2}{\sigma_1}\rho x_1}{\sqrt{1-\rho^2}}}^{\infty}\frac{1}{\sigma_2\sqrt{T}}N'\left(\frac{x_2}{\sigma_2\sqrt{T}}\right)dx_2\frac{1}{\sigma_1\sqrt{T}}N'\left(\frac{x_1-\mu_1^0 T}{\sigma_1\sqrt{T}}\right)dx_1$$

$$\Omega_y = \begin{bmatrix} 1 & \rho \\ \rho & 1 \end{bmatrix}$$

$$y = w\sqrt{1-\rho^2}+\rho x$$

and

$$y = y_2 \; w = -\frac{x_2}{\sigma_2\sqrt{T}} \quad x = -\frac{x_1-\mu_1^0 T}{\sigma_1\sqrt{T}}$$

Here, both variables have a negative sign but a positive correlation.

The first integral limit is

$$\frac{-b+\mu_1^0 T}{\sigma_1\sqrt{T}}$$

$$y_2 = -\frac{x_2}{\sigma_2\sqrt{T}}\sqrt{1-\rho^2} + \rho\left(\frac{-x_1+\mu_1^0 T}{\sigma_1\sqrt{T}}\right)$$

$$= \frac{1}{\sigma_2\sqrt{T}}\left[-x_2\sqrt{1-\rho^2} + \sigma_2\rho\left(\frac{-x_1+\mu_1^0 T}{\sigma_1\sqrt{T}}\right)\right]$$

$$\frac{1}{\sigma_2\sqrt{T}}\left[-\frac{k-\overline{\mu}_2^0 T - \frac{\sigma_2}{\sigma_1}\rho x_1}{\sqrt{1-\rho^2}}\sqrt{1-\rho^2} - \frac{\sigma_2}{\sigma_1}\rho\left(x_1-\mu_1^0 T\right)\right]$$

$$= \frac{1}{\sigma_2\sqrt{T}}\left[-k+\overline{\mu}_2^0 T + \frac{\sigma_2}{\sigma_1}\rho\mu_1^0 T\right]$$

$$y_2 = \frac{-k+\overline{\mu}_2^0 T + \frac{\sigma_2}{\sigma_1}\rho\mu_1^0 T}{\sigma_2\sqrt{T}}$$

$$\int_{-\infty}^{\frac{-b+\mu_1^0 T}{\sigma_1\sqrt{T}}}\int_{-\infty}^{\frac{-k+\overline{\mu}_2^0 T+\frac{\sigma_2}{\sigma_1}\rho\mu_1^0 T}{\sigma_2\sqrt{T}}} n_y\left(\mu_y,\Omega_y\right)dy_2dy_1 = N_2\left(y_1,y_2;\rho\right)$$

Finally, it is

$$\exp\left(\frac{2b\mu_1^0}{\sigma_1^2}\right)\int_{-\infty}^{\frac{-b-\mu_1^0 T}{\sigma_1\sqrt{T}}}\int_{-}^{\frac{-k+\overline{\mu}_2^0 T+2b\frac{\sigma_2}{\sigma_1}\rho+\frac{\sigma_2}{\sigma_1}\rho\mu_1^0 T}{\sigma_2\sqrt{T}}} \infty n_y(\mu_y,\Omega_y)dy_2dy_1$$

$$+\int_{-\infty}^{\frac{-b+\mu_1^0 T}{\sigma_1\sqrt{T}}}\int_{-\infty}^{\frac{-k+\overline{\mu}_2^0 T+\frac{\sigma_2}{\sigma_1}\rho\mu_1^0 T}{\sigma_2\sqrt{T}}} n_y\left(\mu_y,\Omega_y\right)dy_2dy_1$$

$$= \exp\left(\frac{2b\mu_1^0}{\sigma_1^2}\right)N_2\left(y_1^-,y_2;-\rho\right) + N_2\left(y_1^+,y_3;\rho\right)$$

$$\left(\frac{B}{S_{10}}\right)^{2\frac{r-r_1-\frac{1}{2}\sigma_1^2}{\sigma_1^2}} N_2\left(\frac{\ln\left(\frac{S_{10}}{B}\right)-\left(r-r_1-\frac{1}{2}\sigma_1^2\right)T}{\sigma_1\sqrt{T}},\right.$$

$$\left.\times\frac{\ln\left(\frac{S_{20}}{K}\right)+\left(r-r_2-\frac{1}{2}\sigma_2^2\right)T+2\ln\left(\frac{B}{S_{10}}\right)\frac{\sigma_2}{\sigma_1}\rho}{\sigma_2\sqrt{T}};-\rho\right)$$

$$+N_2\left(\frac{\ln\left(\frac{S_{10}}{B}\right)+\left(r-r_1-\frac{1}{2}\sigma_1^2\right)T}{\sigma_1\sqrt{T}},\right.$$

$$\left.\frac{\ln\left(\frac{S_{20}}{K}\right)+\left(r-r_2-\frac{1}{2}\sigma_2^2\right)T}{\sigma_2\sqrt{T}};\rho\right)$$

Since

$$\overline{\mu}_2^0=\mu_2^0-\frac{\sigma_2}{\sigma_1}\rho\mu_1^0$$

and

$$\mu_2^0=\left(r-r_2-\frac{1}{2}\sigma_2^2\right)$$

we simplify as

$$\begin{aligned}
&-k+\overline{\mu}_2^0T+2b\frac{\sigma_2}{\sigma_1}\rho+\frac{\sigma_2}{\sigma_1}\rho\mu_1^0T\\
&\quad=-k+\left(\mu_2^0-\frac{\sigma_2}{\sigma_1}\rho\mu_1^0\right)T+2b\frac{\sigma_2}{\sigma_1}\rho+\frac{\sigma_2}{\sigma_1}\rho\mu_1^0T\\
&\quad=-k+\mu_2^0T+2b\frac{\sigma_2}{\sigma_1}\rho
\end{aligned}$$

$$\begin{aligned}
-k+\overline{\mu}_2^0T+\frac{\sigma_2}{\sigma_1}\rho\mu_1^0T&=-k+\left(\mu_2^0-\frac{\sigma_2}{\sigma_1}\rho\mu_1^0\right)T+\frac{\sigma_2}{\sigma_1}\rho\mu_1^0T\\
&=-k+\mu_2^0T
\end{aligned}$$

Similarly, for

$$
\begin{aligned}
I^1 &= P^1\left(\max_{0\le t\le T} S_{1t} > B,\ S_{2T} > K\right)\\
&= \exp\left(\frac{2b\mu_1^1}{\sigma_1^2}\right)\int_{-\infty}^{\frac{-b-\mu_1^1 T}{\sigma_1\sqrt{T}}}\int_{-\infty}^{\frac{-k+\overline{\mu}_2^1 T+2b\frac{\sigma_2}{\sigma_1}\rho+\frac{\sigma_2}{\sigma_1}\rho\mu_1^1 T}{\sigma_2\sqrt{T}}} n_y\left(\mu_y,\Omega_y\right)dy_2\ dy_1\\
&\quad+\int_{-\infty}^{\frac{-b+\mu_1^1 T}{\sigma_1\sqrt{T}}}\int_{-\infty}^{\frac{-k+\overline{\mu}_2^1 T+\frac{\sigma_2}{\sigma_1}\rho\mu_1^1 T}{\sigma_2\sqrt{T}}} n_y\left(\mu_y,\Omega_y\right)dy_2 dy_1 =
\end{aligned}
$$

$$
\begin{aligned}
&\exp\left(\frac{2b\mu_1^1}{\sigma_1^2}\right)N_2\left(y_1^-,y_2;-\rho\right)+N_2\left(y_1^+,y_3;\rho\right)\\
&= \left(\frac{B}{S_{10}}\right)^{2\frac{r-r_1-\frac{1}{2}\sigma_1^2+\sigma_{12}}{\sigma_1^2}} N_2\left(\frac{\ln\left(\frac{S_{10}}{B}\right)-\left(r-r_1-\frac{1}{2}\sigma_1^2+\sigma_{12}\right)T}{\sigma_1\sqrt{T}},\right.\\
&\qquad\left.\frac{\ln\left(\frac{S_{20}}{K}\right)+\left(r-r_2+\frac{1}{2}\sigma_2^2\right)T+2\ln\left(\frac{B}{S_{10}}\right)\frac{\sigma_2}{\sigma_1}\rho}{\sigma_2\sqrt{T}};-\rho\right)\\
&\qquad+N_2\left(\frac{\ln\left(\frac{S_{10}}{B}\right)+\left(r-r_1-\frac{1}{2}\sigma_1^2+\sigma_{12}\right)T}{\sigma_1\sqrt{T}},\right.\\
&\qquad\qquad\left.\frac{\ln\left(\frac{S_{20}}{K}\right)+\left(r-r_2+\frac{1}{2}\sigma_2^2\right)T}{\sigma_2\sqrt{T}};\rho\right)
\end{aligned}
$$

Finally, the up-and-in rainbow barrier call price is

$$
\begin{aligned}
U_0^{ic} &= S_{20}e^{-r_2 T}P^1\left(\max_{0\le t\le T} S_{1t} > B, S_{2T} > K\right)\\
&\qquad -Ke^{-rT}P^0\left(\max_{0\le t\le T} S_{1t} > B, S_{2T} > K\right)
\end{aligned}
$$

$$
\begin{aligned}
&= S_{20}e^{-r_2T}\left[\left(\frac{B}{S_{10}}\right)^{2\frac{r-r_1-\frac{1}{2}\sigma_1^2+\sigma_{12}}{\sigma_1^2}}\right.\\
&N_2\left(\frac{\ln\left(\frac{S_{10}}{B}\right)-\left(r-r_1-\frac{1}{2}\sigma_1^2+\sigma_{12}\right)T}{\sigma_1\sqrt{T}}\right.\\
&\qquad\left.\times\frac{\ln\left(\frac{S_{20}}{K}\right)+\left(r-r_2+\frac{1}{2}\sigma_2^2\right)T+2\ln\left(\frac{B}{S_{10}}\right)\frac{\sigma_2}{\sigma_1}\rho}{\sigma_2\sqrt{T}};-\rho\right)\\
&\qquad+N_2\left(\frac{\ln\left(\frac{S_{10}}{B}\right)+\left(r-r_1-\frac{1}{2}\sigma_1^2+\sigma_{12}\right)T}{\sigma_1\sqrt{T}},\right.\\
&\qquad\qquad\left.\left.\times\frac{\ln\left(\frac{S_{20}}{K}\right)+\left(r-r_2+\frac{1}{2}\sigma_2^2\right)T}{\sigma_2\sqrt{T}};\rho\right)\right]-Ke^{-rT}\\
&\left[\left(\frac{B}{S_{10}}\right)^{2\frac{r-r_1-\frac{1}{2}\sigma_1^2}{\sigma_1^2}}N_2\left(\frac{\ln\left(\frac{S_{10}}{B}\right)-\left(r-r_1-\frac{1}{2}\sigma_1^2\right)T}{\sigma_1\sqrt{T}},\right.\right.\\
&\qquad\left.\times\frac{\ln\left(\frac{S_{20}}{K}\right)+\left(r-r_2-\frac{1}{2}\sigma_2^2\right)T+2\ln\left(\frac{B}{S_{10}}\right)\frac{\sigma_2}{\sigma_1}\rho}{\sigma_2\sqrt{T}};-\rho\right)\\
&\qquad+N_2\left(\frac{\ln\left(\frac{S_{10}}{B}\right)+\left(r-r_1-\frac{1}{2}\sigma_1^2\right)T}{\sigma_1\sqrt{T}},\right.\\
&\qquad\qquad\left.\left.\times\frac{\ln\left(\frac{S_{20}}{K}\right)+\left(r-r_2-\frac{1}{2}\sigma_2^2\right)T}{\sigma_2\sqrt{T}};\rho\right)\right]
\end{aligned}
\tag{5.30}
$$

The reader may find another derivation in Wystup (2007) with bivariate joint density and univariate density functions.

5.7. Conclusion

In this chapter, we have examined the derivation of partial barrier and rainbow barrier option price formulae given by Heynen and Kat

(1994a, 1994b, and 1994c) and Carr (1995). We reviewed the formulae of partial barriers in two groups: early starting monitoring period (Type A) and forward starting monitoring period (Type B). On top of that, we have seen the formula differ when the strike is above or below the barrier value. We have not mentioned much about partial barrier put options, which may be thought of as exercises left to the reader. Unfortunately, there are few resources on the detailed derivation of partial barrier formulae. Carr (1995) and Wystup (2007) were the best; I benefited the most from them. For partial barrier absorption probabilities, we refer to Park and Schuurman (1983), Veestraeten (2004), Guillaume (2004), and Lee et al. (2022). Zhang (1995) can also be recommended for outside barrier options.

Chapter 6

Double Barrier Options

6.1. Introduction

Besides the vanilla-type barrier options studied in Chapter 3, there are many other types of barrier options containing some exotic features. These include but are not limited to, double barrier or corridor options, time-dependent barrier options, forward-start barriers, protected barriers, Asian barrier options, and so on.

These options mainly increase the functionality and flexibility of vanilla-type barrier options. Moreover, the premiums of exotic barrier options are generally lower than those of vanilla ones, which makes them very attractive products for hedgers and speculators. In this chapter, we will derive the price formulas of some of the double barrier options.

Let $A(A > 0)$ and $B(B \geq A)$ be two barriers and $A < S_0 < B$. Set $X_t = \ln S_t$ $a = \ln A$ and $b = \ln B$. For any real number y, let τ_y be the first hitting time to the barrier, i.e.,

$$\tau_y = \min \{t : X_t = y\}$$

Then, we can classify the types of double-barrier options into eight groups (See Luo, 2001, pp. 125–138).

6.2. The Classification of Double Barrier Options

(1) *Upper-barrier knock-in*: The option holder is eligible to receive a vanilla payoff if the upper barrier is breached before the lower

barrier is breached, and the option becomes worthless otherwise. To be eligible for the payoff, whether call or put, the necessary condition is:

$\tau_b < \tau_a$ and $\tau_b \leq T$. If $\tau_a < \tau_b$ or $\tau_b > T$, the option is worthless.

(2) *Lower-barrier knock-in*: The situation is just the opposite of upper-barrier knock-in. The option holder is eligible to receive a vanilla payoff if the lower barrier is breached before the upper barrier is breached, and the option becomes worthless otherwise. To be eligible for the payoff, whether call or put, the necessary condition is:

$\tau_a < \tau_b$ and $\tau_a \leq T$. If $\tau_b < \tau_a$ or $\tau_a > T$, the option is worthless.

(3) *Upper- barrier knock-out*: The holder of the upper-barrier knock-out option is eligible to receive a vanilla payoff if the upper barrier is not breached before the lower barrier is breached, and the option becomes worthless otherwise. Then, the condition can be stated as $\tau_b > \tau_a$ or $\tau_b > T$ to receive the vanilla payoff; otherwise, the option is worthless.
(4) *Lower-barrier knock-out*: The holder of the lower-barrier knock-out option is eligible to receive a vanilla payoff if the lower barrier is not breached before the upper barrier is breached, and the option becomes worthless otherwise. Then, the condition can be stated as $\tau_a > \tau_b$ or $\tau_a > T$ to receive the vanilla payoff; otherwise, the option is worthless.
(5) *One-touch knock-in* (*OTI*): This is one of the easiest types of double barriers. The holder of the OTI option is eligible to receive a vanilla payoff if at least one of the barriers is breached until maturity, i.e., $\tau_b \leq T$ or $\tau_a \leq T$.
(6) *Double-touch knock-in* (*DTI*) (*double knock-in*): The holder of the option is eligible to receive the vanilla option's payoff if and only if **both** of the barriers are breached until maturity T, i.e., if $\tau_a \leq T$ and $\tau_b \leq T$.
(7) *One-touch knock-out* (*double knock-out*): The holder of the option is eligible to receive the vanilla option's payoff if and only if none of the barriers is breached until maturity T, i.e., if $\tau_a > T$ and $\tau_b > T$. In other words, if one of the barriers is breached (one touch), the option is knocked out and becomes worthless.

(8) *Double-touch knock-out*: The holder of the option is eligible to receive the vanilla option's payoff if and only if at least one of the barriers is not breached until maturity T, i.e., if $\tau_a > T$ or $\tau_b > T$. In other words, the option becomes worthless if both barriers are breached until maturity.

First, we study double barrier options with changing boundaries, based on Kunitomo-Ikeda's "Options with Curved Boundaries." In the second sub-section, we provide some derivations for the corridor options by referring to Antoon Pelsser's paper "Pricing Double Barrier Options: An Analytical Approach." The last sub-section concisely wraps up the double-barrier formulae with reference to Luo (2001).

6.3. Double Barriers with Curved Boundaries: Kunitomo Ikeda Approach

A comprehensive paper on double barrier options is "Pricing Options with Curved Boundaries" by Kunitomo and Ikeda (1992). This paper evaluates option contracts restricted by two knockout boundaries and provides an analytical valuation formula. To derive an analytical formula, they first extend the formula originally derived by Levy (1948). Then, they use some classical results on the Brownian motion by Anderson (1960) in sequential analysis and translate them to the geometric Brownian motion case.

6.3.1. *Generalized Levy formula*

Let the underlying asset price $S(t)$ at time t follow the geometric Brownian motion

$$dS = \mu S dt + \sigma S dW(t)$$

and let the upper and lower absorbing boundaries in the interval $[0, t]$ be

$$\begin{aligned} y &= Be^{\delta_1 u} \\ y &= Ae^{\delta_2 u} \end{aligned} \tag{6.1}$$

where $B \geq A > 0$. The condition $Be^{\delta_1 t} \geq Ae^{\delta_2 t}$ implies that the two boundaries do not intersect in the interval $[0, t]$. If the asset price

$S(t)$ starts at S_0 and hits the lower or upper barrier before time t, the option contract is nullified (knocked out). However, if the asset price does not breach the two boundaries, the option holder is eligible to receive the payoff of the standard option contract at time t. So, to derive the fair price of the option contract, we need the transition density function of the stochastic process $\{S(t)\}$ with two curved boundaries. Let

$$L(t) = \min_{0 \le u \le t} S(u) \quad M(t) = \max_{0 \le u \le t} S(u)$$

be the minimum and maximum asset price in the interval $[0, t]$ respectively. Then, we have the following probability for $(L(t), M(t), S(t))$.

Theorem 6.1 (Kunitomo and Ikeda, 1992, p. 278). *Suppose $S(t)$ follows a geometric Brownian motion with $S(0) = S_0$ and let*

$$I \subset [Ae^{\delta_2 t}, Be^{\delta_1 t}]$$

Then the probability that $Ae^{\delta_2 t} < L(t) \le M(t) < Be^{\delta_1 t}$ for all $t \in [0, T]$ and $S(T) \in I$ is

$$P_1 = \int_I \left(\sum_{n=-\infty}^{\infty} k_n(y) \right) \frac{dy}{y}$$

where

$$k_n(y)$$
$$= \left(\frac{B^n}{A^n}\right)^{c_{1n}} \left(\frac{A}{S_0}\right)^{c_{2n}} \varphi\left(\frac{\ln y - \ln\left(S_0 B^{2n}/A^{2n}\right) - \left(\mu - \frac{1}{2}\sigma^2\right)T}{\sigma\sqrt{T}}\right)$$
$$- \left(\frac{A^{n+1}}{S_0 B^n}\right)^{c_{3n}} \varphi\left(\frac{\ln y - \ln\left(A^{2n+2}/B^{2n} S_0\right) - \left(\mu - \frac{1}{2}\sigma^2\right)T}{\sigma\sqrt{T}}\right)$$

$$c_{1n} = 2\frac{\mu - \delta_2 - n(\delta_1 - \delta_2)}{\sigma^2} - 1$$

$$c_{2n} = 2n\frac{(\delta_1 - \delta_2)}{\sigma^2}$$

$$c_{3n} = 2\frac{\mu - \delta_2 + n(\delta_1 - \delta_2)}{\sigma^2} - 1 \tag{6.2}$$

and $\varphi(.)$ is the density function of standard normal distribution.

This is a generalization of Levy (1948). We can make the transformations as follows:

$$X(t) = \ln S(t) \; dX(t) = dS(t)/S(t)$$

$$\mu' = \mu - \frac{1}{2}\sigma^2$$

and the minimum and the maximum of $X(u)$ in the interval $[0, t]$

$$L(t) = \min_{0 \le u \le t} S(u) \to l(u) = \min_{0 \le u \le t} X(u)$$

$$M(t) = \max_{0 \le u \le t} S(u) \to m(u) = \max_{0 \le u \le t} X(u)$$

Theorem 6.2 (Kunitomo and Ikeda, 1992, p. 279). *Suppose $X(t)$ follows a geometric Brownian motion with $X(0) = x_0$ and let*

$$I \subset [\gamma_2 + \delta_2 T, \;\; \gamma_1 + \delta_1 T]$$

Then, the probability that

$$\gamma_2 + \delta_2 t < l(t) \le m(t) < \gamma_1 + \delta_1 t$$

for all $t \in [0, T]$ and $X(T) \in I$ is

$$P_2 = \int_I \left(\sum_{n=-\infty}^{\infty} k_n'(x) \right) dx$$

where

$$\begin{aligned}
k_n'(x) = {} & \frac{1}{\sqrt{2\pi T}} \exp\left(-\frac{1}{2T\sigma^2} \{[x - x_0 - \mu' T - 2n(\gamma_1 - \gamma_2)]^2 \right. \\
& + 4nT[n(\gamma_1 - \gamma_2)(\delta_1 - \delta_2) + \gamma_1\delta_2 - \gamma_2\delta_1 - \mu'(\gamma_1 - \gamma_2) \\
& \left. + x_0(\delta_1 - \delta_2)]\} \right) \\
& - \frac{1}{\sqrt{2\pi T}} \exp\left(-\frac{1}{2T\sigma^2} \{[x + x_0 - \mu' T - 2\gamma_2 - 2n(\gamma_2 - \gamma_1)]^2 \right. \\
& \left. + 4T[n(\gamma_1 - \gamma_2) - \gamma_2 + x_0]\,[n(\delta_1 - \delta_2) - \delta_2 + \mu']\} \right)
\end{aligned}$$

If we set

$$x_0 = \delta_1 = \delta_2 = \mu' = 0 \ \sigma = 1$$

the kernel density becomes

$$k'_n(x) = \varphi\left(\frac{x - 2n(\gamma_1 - \gamma_2)}{\sqrt{T}}\right) - \varphi\left(\frac{x - 2\gamma_2 + 2n(\gamma_1 - \gamma_2)}{\sqrt{T}}\right) \quad (6.3)$$

This is known as the Levy formula in probability theory. However, Kunitomo and Ikeda use geometric Brownian motion and curved boundaries ($\delta_1, \delta_2 \neq 0$), which can be regarded as a non-trivial extension of the Levy formula.

Proof. Kunitomo and Ikeda first prove the Theorem 6.1 for $\mu' = 0$ and $\sigma = 1$.

Let $Y(t)$ be the standard Brownian motion with $N(0,t)$, $E[Y(t)]^2 = t$ and $Y(0) = 0$. $T, \gamma_1, \gamma_2, \delta_1, \delta_2$ are real numbers and let $\gamma_1 > \gamma_2 \quad \gamma_1 + \delta_1 T \geq \gamma_2 + \delta_2 T$ and $T > 0$.

Let also τ_1 and τ_2 be the first hitting times of the upper boundary line

$$x = \gamma_1 + \delta_1 t \quad (0 \leq t \leq T)$$

and the lower boundary line

$$x = \gamma_2 + \delta_2 t \quad (0 \leq t \leq T)$$

respectively. Then, we define the probability

$$P_1(T, y) = P\{\tau_1 < \tau_2 < T | Y(T) = y\} \quad (6.4)$$

which is the conditional probability that $Y(t) \geq \gamma_1 + \delta_1 t$ for a smaller t than any t for which $Y(t) \leq \gamma_2 + \delta_2 t$ given $Y(T) = y(\leq \gamma_1 + \delta_1 t)$. That is, the probability of hitting the upper barrier is earlier than hitting the lower barrier.

This conditional probability is given by

$$P_1(T,y) = \sum_{n=1}^{\infty} \exp\left[-\frac{2}{T}\{n^2\gamma_1(\gamma_1+\delta_1 T - y) + [n-1]^2 \times \gamma_2(\gamma_2+\delta_2 T - y) - n(n-1)[\gamma_1(\gamma_2+\delta_2 T - y) + \gamma_2(\gamma_1+\delta_1 T - y)]\}\right]$$

$$- \sum_{n=1}^{\infty} \exp\left[-\frac{2}{T}\{n^2\gamma_1\,(\gamma_1+\delta_1 T - y) + \gamma_2(\gamma_2+\delta_2 T - y) - n(n-1)\gamma_1(\gamma_2+\delta_2 T - y) - n(n+1) \times\ \gamma_2(\gamma_1+\delta_1 T - y)\}\right] \quad (6.5)$$

in Anderson (1960).

We want to calculate the probability of a path breaching the upper line before the lower line for $0 \le t \le T$ and $Y(T)$ is in an interval. The unconditional density of $Y(t)$ at $t = T$ is $\varphi\left(\frac{y}{\sqrt{T},}\right)$ and the interval is

$$I \subset [\gamma_2 + \delta_2 T,\ \gamma_1 + \delta_1 T]$$

at time T.

Then, we can write

$$P(\tau_1 < \tau_2 < T,\ Y(T) \in I) = P\{\tau_1 < \tau_2 < T | Y(T) = y\} \times P\{Y(T) = y\}$$

$$\begin{aligned} P(\tau_1 < \tau_2 < T,\ Y(T) \in I) &= \int_I \varphi\left(\frac{y}{\sqrt{T}}\right) P_1(T,y)dy \\ &= \frac{1}{\sqrt{2\pi T}} \int_I e^{-\frac{1}{2}y^2/T} P_1(T,y)dy \end{aligned} \quad (6.6)$$

Let's calculate the integrals. We need the integration of the following terms with respect to y. (Let's ignore the coefficient $\frac{1}{\sqrt{2\pi T}}$ for the time being.)

$$P(\tau_1 < \tau_2 < T,\ Y(T) \in I)$$

$$= \sum_{n=1}^{\infty} \exp\left[-\frac{y^2}{2T} - \frac{2}{T}\{n^2\gamma_1(\gamma_1 + \delta_1 T - y)\right.$$

$$+ [n-1]^2\gamma_2(\gamma_2 + \delta_2 T - y) - n(n-1)[\gamma_1(\gamma_2 + \delta_2 T - y)$$

$$\left.\left. + \gamma_2(\gamma_1 + \delta_1 T - y)\right]\right\}\Big]$$

$$- \sum_{n=1}^{\infty} \exp\left[-\frac{y^2}{2T} - \frac{2}{T}\{n^2[\gamma_1(\gamma_1 + \delta_1 T - y) + \gamma_2(\gamma_2 + \delta_2 T - y)]\right.$$

$$\left. - n(n-1)\gamma_1(\gamma_2 + \delta_2 T - y) - n(n+1)\gamma_2(\gamma_1 + \delta_1 T - y)\right\}\Big]$$

For the first term, ignoring $2T$ in the denominator, we write the numerator as follows:

$$-\{y^2 + 4n^2\gamma_1(\gamma_1 + \delta_1 T - y) + 4[n-1]^2\gamma_2(\gamma_2 + \delta_2 T - y)$$
$$- 4n(n-1)[\gamma_1(\gamma_2 + \delta_2 T - y) + \gamma_2(\gamma_1 + \delta_1 T - y)]\}$$

Let's open the terms in parenthesis; the ones including y are:

$$-(y^2 - 4n^2\gamma_1 y - 4(n^2 - 2n + 1)y\gamma_2 + 4(n^2 - n)\gamma_1 y$$
$$+ 4(n^2 - n)\gamma_2 y) = -(y^2 + 4n\gamma_2 y - 4\gamma_2 y - 4n\gamma_1 y)$$

To write this statement $(y - 2\gamma_2 - 2n(\gamma_1 - \gamma_2))^2$, we have to add and subtract

$$-4\gamma_2^2 - 4n^2(\gamma_1 - \gamma_2)^2 - 8n\gamma_2(\gamma_1 - \gamma_2)$$

The second group terms are:

$$4n^2\gamma_1(\gamma_1 + \delta_1 T) + 4[n-1]^2\gamma_2(\gamma_2 + \delta_2 T)$$
$$- 4n(n-1)[\gamma_1(\gamma_2 + \delta_2 T) + \gamma_2(\gamma_1 + \delta_1 T)] - 4\gamma_2^2$$
$$- 4n^2(\gamma_1 - \gamma_2)^2 - 8n\gamma_2(\gamma_1 - \gamma_2)$$

The remaining terms are:

$$\begin{aligned}
&4n^2\gamma_1^2 + 4n^2\gamma_1\delta_1 T + 4\left(n^2 - 2n + 1\right)\gamma_2\left(\gamma_2 + \delta_2 T\right)\\
&\quad - 4n(n-1)(\gamma_1\gamma_2 + \gamma_1\delta_2 T) - 4n(n-1)\gamma_2\left(\gamma_1 + \delta_1 T\right)\\
&\quad - 4\gamma_2^2 - 4n^2(\gamma_1 - \gamma_2)^2 - 8n\gamma_2(\gamma_1 - \gamma_2)\\
&= 4n^2\gamma_1\delta_1 T + 4n^2\gamma_2\delta_2 T - 4n^2\gamma_1\delta_2 T - 4n^2\gamma_2\delta_1 T\\
&\quad - 8n\gamma_2\delta_2 T + 4\gamma_2\delta_2 T + 4n\gamma_1\delta_2 T + 4n\gamma_2\delta_1 T
\end{aligned}$$

adding and subtracting $4n\gamma_2\delta_2 T$ and grouping the terms

$$\begin{aligned}
&4n^2\delta_1(\gamma_1 - \gamma_2)T - 4n^2\delta_2(\gamma_1 - \gamma_2)T - 8n\gamma_2\delta_2 T + 4\gamma_2\delta_2 T + 4n\gamma_1\delta_2 T\\
&\quad + 4n\gamma_2\delta_1 T + 4n\gamma_2\delta_2 T - 4n\gamma_2\delta_2 T\\
&= 4n^2\delta_1\left(\gamma_1 - \gamma_2\right)T - 4n^2\delta_2\left(\gamma_1 - \gamma_2\right)T + 4n(\gamma_1 - \gamma_2)\delta_2 T\\
&\quad + 4\gamma_2\delta_2 T + 4n\gamma_2(\delta_1 - \delta_2)T\\
&= 4n^2\left(\gamma_1 - \gamma_2\right)\left(\delta_1 - \delta_2\right)T + 4n\left(\gamma_1 - \gamma_2\right)\delta_2 T + 4n\gamma_2\left(\delta_1 - \delta_2\right)T\\
&\quad + 4\gamma_2\delta_2 T
\end{aligned}$$

Taking in a parenthesis, these terms can be restated as

$$4T\left[\left(\gamma_1 - \gamma_2\right)n + \gamma_2\right]\left[\left(\delta_1 - \delta_2\right)n + \delta_2\right]$$

Remembering that the integral is in the form of

$$P\left(\tau_1 < \tau_2 < T,\ Y(T) \in I\right) = \frac{1}{\sqrt{2\pi T}}\int_I e^{-\frac{1}{2}y^2} P_1\left(T, y\right) dy$$

the first integral can be stated in the form of

$$\begin{aligned}
&\frac{1}{\sqrt{2\pi T}}\int_I \sum_{i=1}^{\infty} \exp\left\{-\frac{1}{2T}((y - 2\gamma_2 - 2n(\gamma_1 - \gamma_2)^2\right.\\
&\qquad\left. + 4T[(\gamma_1 - \gamma_2)n + \gamma_2][(\delta_1 - \delta_2)n + \delta_2])\right\} dy \qquad (6.7)
\end{aligned}$$

Let's calculate the second integral now.

$$\frac{1}{\sqrt{2\pi T}}\int_I\sum_{i=1}^{\infty}\exp\left[-\frac{y^2}{2T}-\frac{2}{T}\{n^2[\gamma_1(\gamma_1+\delta_1T-y)\right.$$
$$+\gamma_2(\gamma_2+\delta_2T-y)]-n(n-1)\gamma_1(\gamma_2+\delta_2T-y)$$
$$\left.-n(n+1)\gamma_2(\gamma_1+\delta_1T-y)\}\right]dy$$

With similar algebra, we can write

$$-\frac{1}{2T}(y^2+4n^2[\gamma_1(\gamma_1+\delta_1T-y)+\gamma_2(\gamma_2+\delta_2T-y)]$$
$$-4n(n-1)\gamma_1(\gamma_2+\delta_2T-y)-4n(n+1)\gamma_2(\gamma_1+\delta_1T-y))$$

The terms with y are

$$y^2-4n^2\gamma_1y-4n^2\gamma_2y+4n(n-1)\gamma_1y+4n(n+1)\gamma_2y$$
$$=y^2-4n(\gamma_1-\gamma_2)y$$

To write this term as

$$(y-2n(\gamma_1-\gamma_2))^2$$

we have to add and subtract $4n^2(\gamma_1-\gamma_2)^2$. Therefore, the first term for the second integral is

$$-\frac{1}{2T}(y-2n(\gamma_1-\gamma_2))^2$$

The other terms with $-4n^2(\gamma_1-\gamma_2)^2$ are

$$-4n^2(\gamma_1-\gamma_2)^2+4n^2[\gamma_1(\gamma_1+\delta_1T)+\gamma_2(\gamma_2+\delta_2T)]$$
$$-4n(n-1)\gamma_1(\gamma_2+\delta_2T)-4n(n+1)\gamma_2(\gamma_1+\delta_1T)$$
$$-4n^2\gamma_1^2-4n^2\gamma_2^2+8n^2\gamma_1\gamma_2+4n^2\gamma_1^2+4n^2\gamma_1\delta_1T+4n^2\gamma_2^2$$
$$+4n^2\gamma_2\delta_2T-4n^2\gamma_1\gamma_2-4n^2\gamma_1\delta_2T+4n\gamma_1\gamma_2+4n\gamma_1\delta_2T$$
$$-4n^2\gamma_2\delta_1T-4n\gamma_1\gamma_2-4n\gamma_2\delta_1T$$

and the remaining terms are

$$4n^2\gamma_1\delta_1 T + 4n^2\gamma_2\delta_2 T - 4n^2\gamma_1\delta_2 T + 4n\gamma_1\delta_2 T \\ - 4n^2\gamma_2\delta_1 T - 4n\gamma_2\delta_1 T$$

This can be grouped as

$$\begin{aligned} &4n^2\gamma_1(\delta_1 - \delta_2)T - 4n^2\gamma_2(\delta_1 - \delta_2) + 4n\gamma_1\delta_2 T - 4n\gamma_2\delta_1 T \\ &4n^2(\delta_1 - \delta_2)(\gamma_1 - \gamma_2)T + 4n\gamma_1\delta_2 T - 4n\gamma_2\delta_1 T \\ &\quad = 4nT[n(\delta_1 - \delta_2)(\gamma_1 - \gamma_2) + (\gamma_1\delta_2 - \gamma_2\delta_1)] \end{aligned}$$

The exponential term of the density becomes

$$-\frac{1}{2T}[(y - 2n(\gamma_1 - \gamma_2))^2 + 4nT[n(\delta_1 - \delta_2)(\gamma_1 - \gamma_2) \\ + (\gamma_1\delta_2 - \gamma_2\delta_1)]] \tag{6.8}$$

Finally, the complete integral is

$$\begin{aligned} &P(\tau_1 < \tau_2 < T,\ Y(T) \in I) = \frac{1}{\sqrt{2\pi T}} \int_I e^{-\frac{1}{2}y^2} P_1(T, y)dy \\ &= \frac{1}{\sqrt{2\pi T}} \int_I \sum_{i=1}^{\infty} \exp\left\{ -\frac{1}{2T}\left((y - 2\gamma_2 - 2n(\gamma_1 - \gamma_2)^2\right.\right. \\ &\quad \left.\left. + 4T[(\gamma_1 - \gamma_2)n + \gamma_2][(\delta_1 - \delta_2)n + \delta_2]\right)\right\} dy \\ &\quad - \frac{1}{\sqrt{2\pi T}} \int_I \sum_{i=1}^{\infty} \exp\left\{ -\frac{1}{2T}\left[(y - 2n(\gamma_1 - \gamma_2))^2\right.\right. \\ &\quad \left.\left. + 4nT[n(\delta_1 - \delta_2)(\gamma_1 - \gamma_2) + (\gamma_1\delta_2 - \gamma_2\delta_1)]\right]\right\} dy \end{aligned} \tag{6.9}$$

Another probability is the conditional probability that $Y(t) \leq \gamma_2 + \delta_2 t$ for a smaller t $(t \leq T)$ than any t for which $Y(t) \geq \gamma_1 + \delta_1 t$ given $Y(T) = y(\geq \gamma_2 + \delta_2 t)$ which means that the hitting time to the lower barrier is earlier than the hitting time to the upper barrier when the value of y is above the lower barrier. This conditional probability can be shown by

$$P_2(T,y) = P\{\tau_2 < \tau_1 < T \,|\, Y(T) = y\} \tag{6.10}$$

This is obtained by replacing (γ_1, δ_1) by $(-\gamma_2, -\delta_2)$ in (6.7).

Therefore, the unconditional joint probability that $Y(t) \leq \gamma_2 + \delta_2 t$ for a smaller t $(t \leq T)$ than any t for which $Y(t) \geq \gamma_1 + \delta_1 t$ and $Y(T) \in I$ is

$$P\left(\tau_2 < \tau_1 < T,\ Y(T) \in I\right)$$

$$= P\{\tau_2 < \tau_1 < T \,|Y(T) = y\}.P\{Y(T) = y\}$$

$$P\left(\tau_2 < \tau_1 < T,\ Y(T) \in I\right) = \int_I \varphi\left(\frac{y}{\sqrt{T}}\right) P_2\left(T, y\right) dy$$

$$= \frac{1}{\sqrt{2\pi T}} \int_I e^{-\frac{1}{2T}y^2} P_2\left(T, y\right) dy \tag{6.11}$$

where

$$P_2(T,y) = \sum_{n=1}^{\infty} \exp\left(-\frac{2}{T}\left\{[n^2\gamma_2(\gamma_2 + \delta_2 T - y)]\right.\right.$$

$$+ (n-1)^2\gamma_1(\gamma_1 + \delta_1 T - y) - n(n-1)\left[\gamma_2\left(\gamma_1 + \delta_1 T - y\right)\right.$$

$$\left.\left.\left. + \ \gamma_1(\gamma_2 + \delta_2 T - y)\right]\right\}\right)$$

$$-\sum_{n=1}^{\infty} \exp\left(-\frac{2}{T}\{n^2[\gamma_2(\gamma_2 + \delta_2 T - y\right) + \gamma_1(\gamma_1 + \delta_1 T - y)]$$

$$-n(n-1)\gamma_2(\gamma_1 + \delta_1 T - y) - n(n+1)\gamma_1(\gamma_2 + \delta_2 T - y)\}) \tag{6.12}$$

To compute the unconditional joint probability, we do a similar algebra as we did above and compute the inside of the integral as follows:

$$P(\tau_2 < \tau_1 < T,\ Y(T) \in I) = \frac{1}{\sqrt{2\pi T}} \int_I e^{-\frac{1}{2}y^2} P_2(T,y)dy$$

$$= \sum_{n=1}^{\infty} \exp\left(-\frac{1}{2T}y^2 - \frac{2}{T}\{[n^2\gamma_2(\gamma_2 + \delta_2 T - y)] + (n-1)^2\gamma_1\right.$$

$$\times (\gamma_1 + \delta_1 T - y) - n(n-1)[\gamma_2(\gamma_1 + \delta_1 T - y)$$

$$+ \gamma_1(\gamma_2 + \delta_2 T - y)]\}\Big)$$

$$- \sum_{n=1}^{\infty} \exp\left(-\frac{1}{2T}y^2 - \frac{2}{T}\{n^2[\gamma_2(\gamma_2 + \delta_2 T - y) + \gamma_1\right.$$

$$\times (\gamma_1 + \delta_1 T - y)] - n(n-1)\gamma_2(\gamma_1 + \delta_1 T - y)$$

$$\left. - n(n+1)\gamma_1(\gamma_2 + \delta_2 T - y)\}\right)$$

For the first integral, let's write the terms including y first:

$$\begin{aligned} &-(y^2 - 4n^2 y\gamma_2 - 4n^2 y\gamma_1 + 8ny\gamma_1 - 4y\gamma_1 + 4n^2 y\gamma_2 \\ &\quad - 4ny\gamma_2 + 4n^2 y\gamma_1 - 4ny\gamma_1) \\ &= -\left(y^2 + 4ny\gamma_1 - 4y\gamma_1 - 4ny\gamma_2\right) \end{aligned}$$

To write this in

$$-\left(y - 2\gamma_1 + 2n(\gamma_1 - \gamma_2)\right)^2$$

we add and subtract

$$4\gamma_1^2 + 4n^2(\gamma_1 - \gamma_2)^2 - 8n\gamma_1(\gamma_1 - \gamma_2)$$

Then, adding and subtracting $2\gamma_2$

$$-(y - 2\gamma_1 + 2n(\gamma_1 - \gamma_2) + 2\gamma_2 - 2\gamma_2)^2$$

we obtain

$$\begin{aligned} &-(y - 2\gamma_2 + 2n(\gamma_1 - \gamma_2) - 2(\gamma_1 - \gamma_2))^2 \\ &= -(y - 2\gamma_2 + 2(n-1)(\gamma_1 - \gamma_2))^2 \end{aligned}$$

Now, let's write the other terms:

$$\begin{aligned} &-4\gamma_1^2 - 4n^2(\gamma_1 - \gamma_2)^2 + 8n\gamma_1(\gamma_1 - \gamma_2) + 4n^2\gamma_2^2 + 4n^2\gamma_2\delta_2 T \\ &\quad + 4n^2\gamma_1^2 - 8n\gamma_1^2 + 4\gamma_1^2 + 4n^2\gamma_1\delta_1 T - 8n\gamma_1\delta_1 T + 4\gamma_1\delta_1 T \\ &\quad - 4n^2\gamma_1\gamma_2 - 4n^2\gamma_2\delta_1 T + 4n\gamma_1\gamma_2 + 4n\delta_1\gamma_2 T - 4n^2\gamma_1\gamma_2 \\ &\quad - 4n^2\gamma_1\delta_2 T + 4n\gamma_1\gamma_2 + 4n\gamma_1\delta_2 T \end{aligned}$$

After canceling the same terms and writing $8n\gamma_1\delta_1 T = 4n\gamma_1\delta_1 T + 4n\gamma_1\delta_1 T$

$$= 4n^2\gamma_2\delta_2 T + 4n^2\gamma_1\delta_1 T - 4n^2\gamma_2\delta_1 T - 4n^2\gamma_1\delta_2 T - 4n\gamma_1\delta_1 T$$
$$- 4n\gamma_1\delta_1 T + 4n\gamma_1\delta_2 T + 4n\delta_1\gamma_2 T + 4\gamma_1\delta_2 T + 4n\gamma_2\delta_1 T$$
$$4n^2\gamma_1(\delta_1 - \delta_2)T - 4n^2\gamma_2(\delta_1 - \delta_2)T - 4n\delta_1(\gamma_1 - \gamma_2)T$$
$$- 4n\gamma_1(\delta_1 - \delta_2)T + 4\gamma_1\delta_2 T$$
$$= 4n^2(\gamma_1 - \gamma_2)(\delta_1 - \delta_2)T - 4n\delta_1(\gamma_1 - \gamma_2)T$$
$$- 4n\gamma_1(\delta_1 - \delta_2)T + 4\gamma_1\delta_2 T$$

But this is

$$4T[(\gamma_1 - \gamma_2)n - \gamma_1][(\delta_1 - \delta_2)n - \delta_1]$$

So, we have obtained the exponential term of the first integral as

$$\frac{1}{\sqrt{2\pi T}}\int_I \left[\exp\left(-\frac{1}{2T}\{(y - 2\gamma_2 + 2(n-1)(\gamma_1 - \gamma_2)\right)^2\right.$$
$$\left. + 4T[(\gamma_1 - \gamma_2)n - \gamma_1][(\delta_1 - \delta_2)n - \delta_1]\})\right] dy$$

By applying a similar algebra, the complete integral and the density can be obtained as

$$P(\tau_2 < \tau_1 < T,\ Y(T) \in I)$$
$$= \frac{1}{\sqrt{2\pi T}}\int_I \left[\exp\left(-\frac{1}{2T}\{(y - 2\gamma_2 + 2(n-1)(\gamma_1 - \gamma_2))^2\right.\right.$$
$$\left.\left. + 4T[(\gamma_1 - \gamma_2)n - \gamma_1][(\delta_1 - \delta_2)n - \delta_1]\}\right)\right] dy$$
$$- \frac{1}{\sqrt{2\pi T}}\int_I \left[\exp\left(-\frac{1}{2T}\{(y + 2n(\gamma_1 - \gamma_2))^2\right.\right.$$
$$\left.\left. + 4Tn[n(\gamma_1 - \gamma_2)(\delta_1 - \delta_2) + (\gamma_2\delta_1 - \gamma_1\delta_2)]\}\right)\right] dy \quad (6.13)$$

Having defined the hitting probabilities, now we can consider that the joint probability that $Y(T) \in I$ and (or $Y(T) \in [\gamma_2 + \delta_2 T, \gamma_1 + \delta_1 T]$)

$$\gamma_2 + \delta_2 T < l(t) \le m(t) < \gamma_1 + \delta_1 T$$

for any $t \le T$ is given by

$$P(T) = P(\tau_1 > T,\ \tau_2 > T,\ Y(T) \in I)$$

But this is equal to

$$\begin{aligned} P(Y(T) \in I) &- P(\tau_1 < \tau_2 < T,\ Y(T) \in I) \\ &\quad - P(\tau_2 < \tau_1 < T,\ Y(T) \in I) \\ P(Y(T) \in I) &- \frac{1}{\sqrt{2\pi T}} \int_I e^{-\frac{1}{2}y^2} P_1(T,y)dy \\ &\quad - \frac{1}{\sqrt{2\pi T}} \int_I e^{-\frac{1}{2}y^2} P_2(T,y)dy \end{aligned} \tag{6.14}$$

Rearranging the terms in the equation yields the probability as

$$\begin{aligned} P(T) = \frac{1}{\sqrt{2\pi T}} \int_I & \sum_{n=-\infty}^{+\infty} \exp\left(-\frac{1}{2T}\{[y - 2n(\gamma_1 - \gamma_2)]^2\right. \\ & + 4Tn[n(\gamma_1 - \gamma_2)(\delta_1 - \delta_2) + (\gamma_1\delta_2 - \gamma_2\delta_1)]\} \\ & - \sum_{n=-\infty}^{+\infty} \exp\left(-\frac{1}{2T}\{[y - 2\gamma_2 + 2n(\gamma_1 - \gamma_2)]^2\right. \\ & \left.\left. + 4Tn[(n(\gamma_1 - \gamma_2) - \gamma_2)(n(\delta_1 - \delta_2) - \delta_2)]\}\right)\right) dy \end{aligned} \tag{6.15}$$

It is time to define a Brownian motion with drift. Let $X(t)$ be the Brownian motion starting at x_0 with drift parameter μ^* and instantaneous variance σ^2. Therefore, we need the joint probability that $X(T) \in I$ and (or $X(T) \in [\gamma_2 + \delta_2 T, \gamma_1 + \delta_1 T]$)

$$\gamma_2 + \delta_2 T < l(t) \le m(t) < \gamma_1 + \delta_1 T$$

for any $t \le T$. Using the Girsanov theorem, we change the measure as follows: first, making a change of variable, we write

$$y = \frac{x - x_0}{\sigma} \quad dy = \frac{dx}{\sigma}$$

and multiply the inside of the integral by the Radon–Nikodym derivative

$$\xi = \exp\left(\frac{\mu^*}{\sigma^2}(x - x_0) - \frac{\mu^{*2}T}{2\sigma^2}\right)$$

and we obtain

$$P^*(T) = \int_I \frac{1}{\sigma}\exp\left(\frac{\mu^*}{\sigma^2}(x - x_0) - \frac{\mu^{*2}T}{2\sigma^2}\right) * k\left(\frac{\gamma_1 - x_0 + \delta_1 T}{\sigma}, \frac{\gamma_2 - x_0 + \delta_2 T}{\sigma}, \frac{x - x_0}{\sigma}\right) dx$$

where

$$\begin{aligned} &k[\gamma_1 + \delta_1 T, \gamma_2 + \delta_2 T, x] \\ &= \frac{1}{\sqrt{2\pi T}}\left[\sum_{-\infty}^{\infty} \exp\left(-\frac{1}{2T}\{[x - 2n(\gamma_1 - \gamma_2)]^2\right.\right. \\ &\quad \left. + 4Tn[n(\gamma_1 - \gamma_2)(\delta_1 - \delta_2) + (\gamma_1\delta_2 - \gamma_2\delta_1)]\}\right) \\ &\quad - \sum_{-\infty}^{\infty} \exp\left(-\frac{1}{2T}\{[x - 2\gamma_2 + 2n(\gamma_1 - \gamma_2)]^2\right. \\ &\quad \left.\left. + 4T[(n(\gamma_1 - \gamma_2) - \gamma_2)(n(\delta_1 - \delta_2) - \delta_2)]\}\right)\right] \end{aligned} \tag{6.16}$$

Then, we rearrange the inside of the integral as follows.

Multiplying

$$\exp\left(-\frac{1}{2T}\{[y - 2n(\gamma_1 - \gamma_2)]^2 + 4Tn[n(\gamma_1 - \gamma_2)(\delta_1 - \delta_2) + (\gamma_1\delta_2 - \gamma_2\delta_1)]\}\right)$$

by

$$\exp\left(\frac{\mu^*}{\sigma^2}(x - x_0) - \frac{\mu^{*2}T}{2\sigma^2}\right)$$

and substituting

$$y = \frac{x - x_0}{\sigma} \quad \frac{\gamma_1 - x_0 + \delta_1 T}{\sigma} \quad \frac{\gamma_2 - x_0 + \delta_2 T}{\sigma}$$

we obtain

$$\exp\left(\frac{\mu^*}{\sigma^2}(x - x_0) - \frac{\mu^{*2}T}{2\sigma^2}\right)$$

$$\exp\left\{-\frac{1}{2T}\left(\left(\frac{x - x_0}{\sigma} - 2n\left(\frac{\gamma_1 - x_0}{\sigma} - \frac{\gamma_2 - x_0}{\sigma}\right)\right)\right)^2\right.$$

$$+ 4Tn\left[n\left(\frac{\gamma_1 - x_0}{\sigma} - \frac{\gamma_2 - x_0}{\sigma}\right)\frac{1}{\sigma}(\delta_1 - \delta_2)\right.$$

$$\left.\left. + \left(\frac{\gamma_1 - x_0}{\sigma}\delta_2/\sigma - \frac{\gamma_2 - x_0}{\sigma}\delta_1/\sigma\right)\right]\right\}$$

The first part would yield

$$\frac{-[x - x_0 - 2n(\gamma_1 - \gamma_2) - \mu^* T]^2}{2\sigma^2 T}$$

by adding and subtracting

$$\frac{4n(\gamma_1 - \gamma_2)\mu^* T}{2\sigma^2 T}$$

The other term in the exponent is

$$\frac{4n(\gamma_1 - \gamma_2)\mu^* T}{2\sigma^2 T} + 4Tn\left[n\left(\frac{\gamma_1 - x_0}{\sigma} - \frac{\gamma_2 - x_0}{\sigma}\right)\frac{1}{\sigma}(\delta_1 - \delta_2)\right.$$

$$\left. + \left(\frac{\gamma_1 - x_0}{\sigma}\delta_2/\sigma - \frac{\gamma_2 - x_0}{\sigma}\delta_1/\sigma\right)\right]$$

We find the terms one by one as

(1)

$$\frac{-4Tn}{2T\sigma^2}\left[(\gamma_1\delta_2 - \gamma_2\delta_1) + x_0(\delta_1 - \delta_2)\right]$$

$$= \frac{2n}{\sigma^2}\left[-(\gamma_1 - x_0)\delta_2 + (\gamma_2 - x_0)\delta_1\right]$$

(2)

$$\frac{-4Tn^2}{2T\sigma^2}\left[(\gamma_1-\gamma_2)\right](\delta_1-\delta_2)=\frac{2n}{\sigma^2}\left[-n(\gamma_1-\gamma_2)(\delta_1-\delta_2)\right]$$

(3)

$$\frac{4n(\gamma_1-\gamma_2)\mu^*T}{2\sigma^2T}=\frac{2n(\gamma_1-\gamma_2)\mu^*}{\sigma^2}$$

the other half of the first equation is

$$\frac{2n}{\sigma^2}\left[(\gamma_1-\gamma_2)\mu^*-n(\gamma_1-\gamma_2)(\delta_1-\delta_2)-(\gamma_1-x_0)\delta_2-(\gamma_2-x_0)\delta_1\right]$$

because $\gamma_1\to\gamma_1-x_0$ and $\gamma_2\to\gamma_2-x_0$.

By applying a similar algebra, we may write the probability under measure P^* as

$$\begin{aligned}
&P^*(T)\\
&=\int_I\left(\sum_{-\infty}^{\infty}\varphi\left[\frac{x-x_0-2n(\gamma_1-\gamma_2)-\mu^*T}{\sigma\sqrt{T}}\right]\exp\left\{\frac{2n}{\sigma^2}[(\gamma_1-\gamma_2)\mu^*\right.\right.\\
&\quad\left.\times-n(\gamma_1-\gamma_2)(\delta_1-\delta_2)-(\gamma_1-x_0)\delta_2+(\gamma_2-x_0)\delta_1]\right\}\\
&\quad-\sum_{-\infty}^{\infty}\varphi\left[\frac{x+x_0-2\gamma_2+2n(\gamma_1-\gamma_2)-\mu^*T}{\sigma\sqrt{T}}\right]\\
&\quad\times\exp\left\{\frac{2\mu^*}{\sigma^2}[(\gamma_2-x_0)-n(\gamma_1-\gamma_2)]\right\}\\
&\quad\left.\times\exp\left\{\frac{2}{\sigma^2}[-n(\gamma_1-\gamma_2)+(\gamma_2-x_0)][n(\delta_1-\delta_2)-\delta_2]\right\}\right)dx \quad \square
\end{aligned} \tag{6.17}$$

Turning back to $S(t)$ by transforming $S(t)=\exp(X(t))$, we can write the drift parameter as

$$\mu=\mu^*+\frac{1}{2}\sigma^2$$

Letting $A = \exp\ (\gamma_2)\ B = \exp(\gamma_1)$ the joint probability that $S(T) \in I$ and

$$Ae^{\delta_2 t} < L(t) \leq M(t) < Be^{\delta_1 t}$$

for any $t \leq T$ is given by

$$\begin{aligned}
P^{**}(T) = \int_I \Bigg(&\sum_{-\infty}^{\infty} \varphi \left[\frac{\ln y - \ln\left(\frac{S_0 B^{2n}}{A^{2n}}\right) - \left(\mu - \frac{1}{2}\sigma^2\right) T}{\sigma\sqrt{T}} \right] \\
&\times \left(\frac{B^n}{A^n}\right)^{\frac{2\mu}{\sigma^2}-1} \left[\left(\frac{A^n}{B^n}\right)^{\delta_1-\delta_2} \left(\frac{S_0}{B}\right)^{\delta_2} \left(\frac{A}{S_0}\right)^{\delta_1} \right]^{\frac{2n}{\sigma^2}} \\
&- \sum_{-\infty}^{\infty} \varphi \left[\frac{\ln y - \ln\left(\frac{A^{2n+2}}{S_0 B^{2n}}\right) - (\mu - \frac{1}{2}\sigma^2)T}{\sigma\sqrt{T}} \right] \left(\frac{A^{n+1}}{B^n S_0}\right)^{\frac{2\mu}{\sigma^2}-1} \\
&\times \left(\frac{A^{n+1}}{B^n S_0}\right)^{\frac{2}{\sigma^2}[n(\delta_1-\delta_2)-\delta_2]} \Bigg) \frac{dy}{y} \qquad (6.18)
\end{aligned}$$

For example, the term

$$\exp\left\{ \frac{2\mu^*}{\sigma^2} \left[(\gamma_2 - x_0) - n(\gamma_1 - \gamma_2) \right] \right\}$$

can be opened as

$$\begin{aligned}
&\exp\left\{ \frac{2(\mu - \frac{1}{2}\sigma^2)}{\sigma^2} \left[(\ln A - \ln S_0) - n(\ln B - \ln A) \right] \right\} \\
&= \exp\left\{ \frac{2(\mu - \frac{1}{2}\sigma^2)}{\sigma^2} \left[(\ln(A/S_0)) - (\ln(B^n/A^n) \right] \right\} \\
&= \exp\left(\ln\left(\frac{A/S_0}{B^n/A^n}\right)^{\frac{2\mu}{\sigma^2}-1} \right) = \left(\frac{AA^n}{B^n S_0}\right)^{\frac{2\mu}{\sigma^2}-1} = \left(\frac{A^{n+1}}{B^n S_0}\right)^{\frac{2\mu}{\sigma^2}-1}
\end{aligned}$$

This formula can be further reduced to the form

$$k_n(y)$$
$$= \left(\frac{B^n}{A^n}\right)^{c_{1n}} \left(\frac{A}{S_0}\right)^{c_{2n}} \varphi\left(\frac{\ln y \; - \ln\left(S_0 B^{2n}/A^{2n}\right) - \left(\mu - \frac{1}{2}\sigma^2\right) T}{\sigma\sqrt{T}}\right)$$
$$- \left(\frac{A^{n+1}}{S_0 B^n}\right)^{c_{3n}} \varphi\left(\frac{\ln y - \ln\left(\frac{A^{2n+2}}{B^{2n} S_0}\right) - \left(\mu - \frac{1}{2}\sigma^2\right) T}{\sigma\sqrt{T}}\right) \tag{6.19}$$

For example, multiplying with $A^{-\delta_2} A^{\delta_2}$ yields

$$\left(\frac{B^n}{A^n}\right)^{\frac{2\mu}{\sigma^2}-1} \left[\left(\frac{A^n}{B^n}\right)^{\delta_1-\delta_2} \left(\frac{S_0}{B}\right)^{\delta_2} \left(\frac{A}{S_0}\right)^{\delta_1} A^{-\delta_2} A^{\delta_2}\right]^{\frac{2n}{\sigma^2}}$$
$$= \left(\frac{B^n}{A^n}\right)^{\frac{2\mu}{\sigma^2}-1} \left(\frac{B^n}{A^n}\right)^{-\frac{2n}{\sigma^2}(\delta_1-\delta_2)} \left(\frac{A}{S_0}\right)^{\frac{2n}{\sigma^2}(\delta_1-\delta_2)} \left(\frac{B^n}{A^n}\right)^{-\frac{2}{\sigma^2}\delta_2}$$

Collecting the terms yields

$$c_{1n} = 2\left[\frac{\mu - n\left(\delta_1 - \delta_2\right) - \delta_2}{\sigma^2}\right] - 1$$
$$c_{2n} = \frac{2n}{\sigma^2}(\delta_1 - \delta_2)$$

In equation (6.19), we write

$$\left(\frac{A^{n+1}}{B^n S_0}\right)^{\frac{2\mu}{\sigma^2}-1} \left(\frac{A^{n+1}}{B^n S_0}\right)^{\frac{2}{\sigma^2}[n(\delta_1-\delta_2)-\delta_2]} = \left(\frac{A^{n+1}}{B^n S_0}\right)^{\frac{2}{\sigma^2}[\mu+n(\delta_1-\delta_2)-\delta_2]-1}$$
$$c_{3n} = \frac{2}{\sigma^2}\left[\mu + n\left(\delta_1 - \delta_2\right) - \delta_2\right] - 1$$

and the exponent is c_{3n} in equation (6.19).

Kunitomo and Ikeda provide one corollary with two results.
(i) Assume $S(0) = S_0$ for $I \subset [Ae^{\delta_2 t}, \infty]$ with $A > 0$. Then the probability that $Ae^{\delta_2 t} < L(t)$ for all $t \in [0, T]$ and $S(T) \in I$ is

$$P_3 = \int_{Ae^{\delta_2 t}}^{\infty} \left(\varphi \left[\frac{\ln y - \ln S_0 \ - (\mu - \frac{1}{2}\sigma^2)T}{\sigma\sqrt{T}} \right] \right.$$
$$\left. - \varphi \left[\frac{\ln y - \ln\left(\frac{A^2}{S_0}\right) - (\mu - \frac{1}{2}\sigma^2)T}{\sigma\sqrt{T}} \right] \left(\frac{A}{S_0}\right)^{\frac{2}{\sigma^2}[(\mu - \delta_2 - \frac{1}{2}\sigma^2)]} \right) \frac{dy}{y} \tag{6.20}$$

(ii) Assume $S(0) = S_0$ for $I \subset \left[-\infty, Be^{\delta_1 t}\right]$ with $B > 0$. Then, the probability that
$M(t) < Be^{\delta_1 t}$ for all $t \in [0, T]$ and $S(T) \in I$ is

$$P_4 = \int_{-\infty}^{Be^{\delta_1 t}} \left(\varphi \left[\frac{\ln y - \ln S_0 \ - (\mu - \frac{1}{2}\sigma^2)T}{\sigma\sqrt{T}} \right] \right.$$
$$\left. - \varphi \left[\frac{\ln y - \ln\left(\frac{B^2}{S_0}\right) - (\mu - \frac{1}{2}\sigma^2)T}{\sigma\sqrt{T}} \right] \left(\frac{B}{S_0}\right)^{\frac{2}{\sigma^2}[(\mu - \delta_1 - \frac{1}{2}\sigma^2)]} \right) \frac{dy}{y} \tag{6.21}$$

These results can be obtained by letting B go to infinity, or A go to zero in Theorem 2.1 in Kunitomo and Ikeda (1992).

Practically, that means to assume $n = 0$, and we obtain equations (6.20) and (6.21).

6.3.2. *Option formulae*

Now, the double knock-out call (DKOC) option price is given in Kunitomo and Ikeda (Theorem 3.1, 1992). The call price is $(T - t = \tau)$

$$c(t) = e^{-r\tau} E\left\{\max(S(T) - K, 0) \mid S(t) = S\right\}$$
$$c(t) = e^{-r\tau} \int_K^F s(T) f(s(T) ds(T) - e^{-r\tau} K \int_K^F f(s(T) ds(T)$$

where $F = Be^{\delta_1 T}$, $\mu = r + \sigma^2$ for the first integral(why?) and $\mu = r$ is the second integral.

Theorem 6.3 (Kunitomo and Ikeda, 1992). *The value of the call option at t which is nullified before its maturity date whenever the underlying asset price reaches the upper boundary $Be^{\delta_1 u}$ or the lower boundary $Ae^{\delta_2 u}$ for any $u \in [t, T]$ is given by*

$$
\begin{aligned}
c(t) = S \sum_{n=-\infty}^{\infty} & \left\{ \left(\frac{B^n}{A^n}\right)^{c_{1n}^*} \left(\frac{A}{S_0}\right)^{c_{2n}} [N(d_{1n}) - N(d_{2n})] \right. \\
& \left. -\left(\frac{A^{n+1}}{S_0 B^n}\right)^{c_{3n}^*} [N(d_{3n}) - N(d_{4n})] \right\} \\
& - e^{-r\tau} K \sum_{n=-\infty}^{\infty} \left\{ \left(\frac{B^n}{A^n}\right)^{c_{1n}^*-2} \left(\frac{A}{S_0}\right)^{c_{2n}} \right. \\
& \times [N(d_{1n} - \sigma\sqrt{\tau}) - N(d_{2n} - \sigma\sqrt{\tau})] \\
& \left. - \left(\frac{A^{n+1}}{S_0 B^n}\right)^{c_{3n}^*-2} [N(d_{3n} - \sigma\sqrt{\tau}) - N(d_{4n} - \sigma\sqrt{\tau})] \right\}
\end{aligned}
$$

where

$$
\begin{aligned}
c_{1n}^* &= 2\left[\frac{(r+\sigma^2) - n(\delta_1 - \delta_2) - \delta_2}{\sigma^2}\right] - 1 \\
&= 2\left[\frac{(r - n(\delta_1 - \delta_2) - \delta_2}{\sigma^2}\right] + 1 \\
c_{3n}^* &= \frac{2}{\sigma^2}\left[(r+\sigma^2) + n(\delta_1 - \delta_2) - \delta_2\right] - 1 \\
&= \frac{2}{\sigma^2}\left[r + n(\delta_1 - \delta_2) - \delta_2\right] + 1
\end{aligned}
$$

$$d_{1n} = \frac{\ln\left(S_0 B^{2n}/K A^{2n}\right) + \left(r + \frac{1}{2}\sigma^2\right)\tau}{\sigma\sqrt{\tau}}$$

$$d_{2n} = \frac{\ln\left(S_0 B^{2n}/F A^{2n}\right) + \left(r + \frac{1}{2}\sigma^2\right)\tau}{\sigma\sqrt{\tau}}$$

$$d_{3n} = \frac{\ln\left(A^{2n+2}/B^{2n} S_0 K\right) + \left(r + \frac{1}{2}\sigma^2\right)\tau}{\sigma\sqrt{\tau}}$$

$$d_{4n} = \frac{\ln\left(A^{2n+2}/B^{2n} S_0 F\right) + \left(r + \frac{1}{2}\sigma^2\right)\tau}{\sigma\sqrt{\tau}} \tag{6.22}$$

To write the cumulative normal distribution in that form, first, we write

$$S_0 \int_K^F \xi\ f(s(T)ds(T)$$

where ξ is the Radon–Nikodym derivative we use to change the probability measure.

$$S_0 \int_K^F \xi\ f(s(T)ds(T)$$

$$= S_0 \left[\int_{-\infty}^F \xi\ f(s(T)ds(T) - \int_{-\infty}^K \xi\ f(s(T)ds(T)\right]$$

$$\int_{-\infty}^F \xi\ f(s(T)ds(T) - \int_{-\infty}^K \xi\ f(s(T)ds(T) + 1 - 1$$

$$= 1 - \int_{-\infty}^K \xi\ f(s(T)ds(T) - \left(1 - \int_{-\infty}^F \xi\ f(s(T)ds\,(T)\right)$$

$$1 - N\left[\frac{\ln K - \ln\left(\frac{S_0 B^{2n}}{A^{2n}}\right) - \left(\mu - \frac{1}{2}\sigma^2\right)\tau}{\sigma\sqrt{\tau}}\right]$$

$$= N\left[\frac{-\ln K + \ln\left(\frac{S_0 B^{2n}}{A^{2n}}\right) + \left(r + \sigma^2 - \frac{1}{2}\sigma^2\right)\tau}{\sigma\sqrt{\tau}}\right]$$

$$N\left[\frac{\ln\left(\frac{S_0B^{2n}}{KA^{2n}}\right)+\left(r+\frac{1}{2}\sigma^2\right)\tau}{\sigma\sqrt{\tau}}\right]$$

$$=N\left(d_{1n}\right)-\left(1-\int_{-\infty}^{F}\xi\ f(s(T)ds(T)\right)$$

$$=-\left(1-N\left[\frac{\ln F-\ln\left(\frac{S_0B^{2n}}{A^{2n}}\right)-\left(r+\sigma^2-\frac{1}{2}\sigma^2\right)\tau}{\sigma\sqrt{\tau}}\right]\right)$$

$$=-N\left(d_{2n}\right)$$

$$S_0\left[1-\int_{-\infty}^{K}f(s(T)ds(T)-\left(1-\int_{-\infty}^{F}f(s(T)ds(T)\right)\right]$$

$$1-N\left[\frac{\ln K-\ln\left(\frac{A^{2n+2}}{S_0B^{2n}}\right)-\left(\mu-\frac{1}{2}\sigma^2\right)\tau}{\sigma\sqrt{\tau}}\right]=N\left(d_{3n}\right)$$

$$-\left(1-N\left[\frac{\ln F-\ln\left(\frac{A^{2n+2}}{S_0B^{2n}}\right)-\left(\mu-\frac{1}{2}\sigma^2\right)\tau}{\sigma\sqrt{\tau}}\right]\right)=-N\left(d_{4n}\right) \tag{6.23}$$

where $\mu=r+\sigma^2$.

For the second group of integrals, we apply the density

$$k_n(y)$$

$$=\left(\frac{B^n}{A^n}\right)^{c_{1n}}\left(\frac{A}{S_0}\right)^{c_{2n}}\varphi\left(\frac{\ln y-\ln\ \left(S_0B^{2n}/A^{2n}\right)-\left(\mu-\frac{1}{2}\sigma^2\right)T}{\sigma\sqrt{T}}\right)$$

$$-\left(\frac{A^{n+1}}{S_0B^n}\right)^{c_{3n}}\varphi\left(\frac{\ln y\ -\ln\left(\frac{A^{2n+2}}{B^{2n}S_0}\right)-\left(\mu-\frac{1}{2}\sigma^2\right)T}{\sigma\sqrt{T}}\right)$$

to

$$-Ke^{-rT}\left[\int_{-\infty}^{F} f(s(T)ds(T) - \int_{-\infty}^{K} f(s(T)ds(T)\right] =$$

$$-Ke^{-rT}\left[1-\int_{-\infty}^{K} f(s(T)ds(T) - \left(1 - \int_{-\infty}^{F} f(s(T)ds(T)\right)\right]$$

By applying the same algebra to the second term in the option formula, using equation (6.20) *for* $\mu = r$, *we obtain the complete pricing formula.*

Similarly, the price of a double barrier knockout European put option at t can be given as

$$p(t) = e^{-r\tau}E\left\{\max(K - S(T), 0) \mid S(t) = S\right\}$$

$$p(t) = e^{-r\tau}K\int_{F'}^{K} f(s(T)ds(T) - e^{-r\tau}\int_{F'}^{K} s(T)f(s(T)ds(T)$$

where $F' = Ae^{\delta_2 T}$.

Theorem 6.4 (Kunitomo and Ikeda, 1992). *The value of the put option at* t, *which is nullified before its maturity date whenever the underlying asset price reaches the upper boundary* $Be^{\delta_1 u}$ *or the lower boundary* $Ae^{\delta_2 u}$ *for any* $u \in [t, T]$ *is given by*

$$p(t) = -S\sum_{n=-\infty}^{\infty}\left\{\left(\frac{B^n}{A^n}\right)^{c_{1n}^*}\left(\frac{A}{S_0}\right)^{c_{2n}}\left[N\left(d'_{1n}\right) - N\left(d'_{2n}\right)\right]\right.$$
$$\left. - \left(\frac{A^{n+1}}{S_0 B^n}\right)^{c_{3n}^*}\left[N\left(d'_{3n}\right) - N\left(d'_{4n}\right)\right]\right\}$$
$$+ e^{-r\tau}K\sum_{n=-\infty}^{\infty}\left\{\left(\frac{B^n}{A^n}\right)^{c_{1n}^*-2}\left(\frac{A}{S_0}\right)^{c_{2n}}\right.$$
$$\times\left[N\left(d'_{1n} - \sigma\sqrt{\tau}\right) - N\left(d'_{2n} - \sigma\sqrt{\tau}\right)\right] - \left(\frac{A^{n+1}}{S_0 B^n}\right)^{c_{3n}^*-2}$$
$$\left.\times\left[N\left(d'_{3n} - \sigma\sqrt{\tau}\right) - N\left(d'_{4n} - \sigma\sqrt{\tau}\right)\right]\right\}$$

where

$$d'_{1n} = \frac{\ln\left(S_0 B^{2n}/F' A^{2n}\right) + \left(r + \frac{1}{2}\sigma^2\right)\tau}{\sigma\sqrt{\tau}}$$

$$d'_{2n} = \frac{\ln\left(S_0 B^{2n}/K A^{2n}\right) + \left(r + \frac{1}{2}\sigma^2\right)\tau}{\sigma\sqrt{\tau}}$$

$$d'_{3n} = \frac{\ln\left(A^{2n+2}/B^{2n} S_0 F'\right) + \left(r + \frac{1}{2}\sigma^2\right)\tau}{\sigma\sqrt{\tau}}$$

$$d'_{4n} = \frac{\ln\left(A^{2n+2}/B^{2n} S_0 K\right) + \left(r + \frac{1}{2}\sigma^2\right)\tau}{\sigma\sqrt{\tau}} \tag{6.24}$$

As an example, with the following parameters and for $n = -1,\ 0,\ 1$

$$S_0 = 1000 \quad K = 1000 \quad r = 0.05 \quad \tau = \frac{1}{12} \quad \sigma = 0.2$$
$$A = 400 \quad B = 1600 \quad \delta_1 = 0.1 \quad \delta_2 = -0.1$$

a Matlab code (provided in the Appendix) yields $c = 25.1207$. *For* $\tau = \frac{1}{4}$, $c = 46.1496$. *Kunitomo and İkeda (1992, pp. 284–287) provide a wide range of double barrier call option prices with different parameters.*

6.4. Pelsser's Analytical Approach

6.4.1. *Transition densities*

Pelsser (2000) derives analytical formulae for pricing various double-barrier options. He uses contour integration to solve the inverse of the Laplace transforms analytically. Then, the need for a numerical inversion routine of Laplace transforms is eliminated. Consider a stochastic process

$$z = \mu dt + \sigma dW$$

and a transition density function $p(t, x; s, y)$. This is the probability density that the process starts at time t at $z(t) = x$, survives until time s, and takes the value $z(s) = y$ at time s. Assume we have a lower barrier at "0" and an upper barrier l where $0 \leq x, y \leq l$ and $t \leq s$.

This transition density function satisfies forward and backward Kolmogorov equations. Let's write the backward equation as

$$p_t + \mu p_x + \frac{1}{2}\sigma^2 p_{xx} = 0$$

subject to the boundary conditions

$$p(t, 0; \dots) = p(t, l; \dots) = 0 \quad p(s, x; s, y) = \delta(y - x)$$

where $\delta(y - x)$ is the Dirac delta function. In this case, the density function collapses into a delta function at time $t = s$, implying no uncertainty in the process. If the process hits one of the two barriers, it gets killed, and the probability of returning to y at time s is zero. So, the probability density function characterizes the survival of the process until time s. The forward equation is

$$-p_s - \mu p_y + \frac{1}{2}\sigma^2 p_{yy} = 0$$

subject to the boundary conditions

$$p(..; s, 0) = p(..; s, l) = 0 \quad p(t, x; t, y) = \delta(x - y)$$

The solution to the backward and forward equations can be found in Cox and Miller (1965, pp. 213–225). A Fourier series solution suggested by the method of separation of variables is

$$p(x, t) = e^{\kappa x - \lambda t} \sin\left\{\frac{n\pi(x + b)}{a + b}\right\} \tag{6.25}$$

They choose the sine function in this form because the boundary conditions are satisfied when $x = a$ or $x = -b$ (not zero). The forward equation is satisfied by choosing

$$\kappa = \frac{\mu}{\sigma^2} \quad \lambda = \lambda_n = \frac{1}{2}\left(\frac{\mu^2}{\sigma^2} + \frac{n^2\pi^2\sigma^2}{(a + b)^2}\right) \tag{6.26}$$

A linear superposition of the terms is given by

$$p(x, t) = e^{\frac{\mu}{\sigma^2}x} \sum_{n=1}^{\infty} a_n e^{-\lambda_n t} \sin\left\{\frac{n\pi(x + b)}{a + b}\right\} \tag{6.27}$$

where the coefficients a_n have to be determined from the initial condition $p(x, 0) = \delta(x)$ (see Cox and Miller, 1965, pp. 213–225) and

$$a_n = \frac{2}{a+b} \sin\left(\frac{n\pi b}{a+b}\right)$$

For an arbitrary initial value x_0, we replace a, b and x by $a - x_0$, $b + x_0$ and $x - x_0$, respectively. We can use the solution as

$$p(t, x_0; s, x)) = e^{\frac{\mu}{\sigma^2}(x-x_0)} \frac{2}{l} \sum_{n=1}^{\infty} e^{-\lambda_n(s-t)} \sin\left(\frac{n\pi(b+x_0)}{a+b}\right)$$

$$\sin\left\{\frac{n\pi(x - x_0 + (b + x_0)))}{a+b}\right\}$$

$$p\,(t, x_0; s, x) = e^{\frac{\mu}{\sigma^2}(x-x_0)} \frac{2}{l} \sum_{n=1}^{\infty} e^{-\lambda_n(s-t)} \sin\left(\frac{n\pi(x_0)}{l}\right) \sin\left\{\frac{n\pi x}{l}\right\}$$

$$p(t, x; s, y) = e^{\frac{\mu}{\sigma^2}(y-x)} \frac{2}{l} \sum_{n=1}^{\infty} e^{-\lambda_n(s-t)} \sin\left(\frac{n\pi y}{l}\right) \sin\left\{\frac{n\pi x)}{l}\right\}$$

$$a = l \quad b = 0$$

$$\lambda_n = \frac{1}{2}\left(\frac{\mu^2}{\sigma^2} + \frac{n^2\pi^2\sigma^2}{l^2}\right) \tag{6.28}$$

as given in Pelsser (2000).

Since the term λ_n grows quadratically in n, $e^{-\lambda_n(s-t)}$ approaches zero quickly, and very few terms are needed for an accurate solution.

6.4.2. *Barrier densities*

Let $g^+(t, x; s)$ denote the probability density function of first hitting the upper barrier at time s before the lower barrier is hit, given that the process started at (t, x). Let $g^-(t, x; s)$ denote the probability density function of first hitting the lower barrier before the upper barrier is hit.

We can write the identity as

$$\int_t^T g^+(t, x; s)ds + \int_t^T g^-(t, x; s)ds + \int_0^l p(t, x; T, y)dy = 1 \tag{6.29}$$

for all $T > t$. Taking the derivative with respect to T yields

$$g^+(t,x;T) + g^-(t,x;Ts) = -\frac{\partial}{\partial T}\int_0^l p(t,x;T,y)dy$$

$$g^+(t,x;s) + g^-(t,x;s)$$

$$= e^{\frac{\mu}{\sigma^2}(l-x)}\frac{\sigma^2}{l^2}\sum_{n=1}^{\infty} e^{-\lambda_n(s-t)} n\pi \sin\left\{n\pi\frac{l-x)}{l}\right\}$$

$$+ e^{-x\frac{\mu}{\sigma^2}}\frac{\sigma^2}{l^2}\sum_{n=1}^{\infty} e^{-\lambda_n(s-t)} n\pi \sin\left\{n\pi\frac{x)}{l}\right\}$$

$$\int_0^l p(t,x;T,y)dy = \int_0^l e^{\frac{\mu}{\sigma^2}(y-x)}\frac{2}{l}\sum_{n=1}^{\infty} e^{-\lambda_n(s-t)} \sin\left(\frac{n\pi y}{l}\right)$$

$$\times \sin\left\{\frac{n\pi x)}{l}\right\} dy$$

$$e^{\frac{\mu}{\sigma^2}(y-x)}dy = dv \sum_{n=1}^{\infty} e^{-\lambda_n(s-t)} \sin\left(\frac{n\pi y}{l}\right) \sin\left\{\frac{n\pi x)}{l}\right\} = u$$

$$uv - \int v du \tag{6.30}$$

Since uv part goes to zero because of the sinus terms, we have

$$-\frac{2}{l}\int_0^l \frac{\sigma^2}{\mu} e^{\frac{\mu}{\sigma^2}(y-x)} \sum_{n=1}^{\infty} e^{-\lambda_n(s-t)}\frac{n\pi}{l}\cos\left(\frac{n\pi y}{l}\right)\sin\left\{\frac{n\pi x)}{l}\right\} dy$$

Once again, applying partial integration

$$-\frac{2}{l^2}\frac{\sigma^4}{\mu^2} e^{\frac{\mu}{\sigma^2}(y-x)} \sum_{n=1}^{\infty} e^{-\lambda_n(s-t)} n\pi\cos\left(\frac{n\pi y}{l}\right)\sin\left\{\frac{n\pi x)}{l}\right\}\Bigg|_0^l$$

$$-\int_0^l \frac{2}{l^2}\frac{\sigma^4}{\mu^2} e^{\frac{\mu}{\sigma^2}(y-x)} \sum_{n=1}^{\infty} e^{-\lambda_n(s-t)}\frac{n^2\pi^2}{l}\sin\left(\frac{n\pi y}{l}\right)\sin\left\{\frac{n\pi x)}{l}\right\} dy$$

Since

$$\cos\left(\frac{n\pi l}{l}\right)\sin\left\{\frac{n\pi x)}{l}\right\} = -\sin\left\{\frac{n\pi(l-x))}{l}\right\}$$

we write

$$\frac{2}{l^2}\frac{\sigma^4}{\mu^2}e^{\frac{\mu}{\sigma^2}(l-x)}\sum_{n=1}^{\infty}e^{-\lambda_n(s-t)}n\pi\,\sin\left\{\frac{n\pi(l-x))}{l}\right\}$$

$$+\frac{2}{l^2}\frac{\sigma^4}{\mu^2}e^{\frac{\mu}{\sigma^2}(-x)}\sum_{n=1}^{\infty}e^{-\lambda_n(s-t)}n\pi\,\sin\left\{\frac{n\pi x))}{l}\right\}$$

$$-\frac{n^2\pi^2}{l^2}\frac{\sigma^4}{\mu^2}\int_0^l p(t,x;T,y)dy$$

That is

$$\left(1+\frac{n^2\pi^2}{l^2}\frac{\sigma^4}{\mu^2}\right)\int_0^l p(t,x;T,y)dy$$

$$=\frac{2}{l^2}\frac{\sigma^4}{\mu^2}e^{\frac{\mu}{\sigma^2}(l-x)}\sum_{n=1}^{\infty}e^{-\lambda_n(s-t)}n\pi\sin\left\{\frac{n\pi(l-x))}{l}\right\}$$

$$+\frac{2}{l^2}\frac{\sigma^4}{\mu^2}e^{-\frac{\mu}{\sigma^2}x}\sum_{n=1}^{\infty}e^{-\lambda_n(s-t)}n\pi\,\sin\left\{\frac{n\pi x))}{l}\right\}$$

Taking the (minus) derivative with respect to s would yield

$$\frac{\frac{2}{l^2}\frac{\sigma^4}{\mu^2}\left(\frac{1}{2}\left(\frac{\mu^2}{\sigma^2}+\frac{n^2\pi^2\sigma^2}{l^2}\right)\right)}{\left(1+\frac{n^2\pi^2}{l^2}\frac{\sigma^4}{\mu^2}\right)}=\frac{\sigma^2}{l^2}$$

and we have equation (6.30).

6.4.2.1. *Derivation of* $\boldsymbol{g^+(t,x;s)}$

$g^+(t,x;s)$ satisfies the backward equation

$$g_t^+ + \mu g_x^+ + \frac{1}{2}\sigma^2 g_{xx}^+ = 0$$

By setting $\tau = s - t$, we can write

$$g^+(t,x;s) = g^+(\tau,x)$$

$$-g_\tau^+ + \mu g_x^+ + \frac{1}{2}\sigma^2 g_{xx}^+ = 0 \qquad (6.31)$$

subject to the boundary conditions

$$g^+(\tau, l) = \delta(\tau) \quad g^+(0, x) = \delta(l - x)\ g^+(\tau, 0) = 0$$

To obtain a solution for equation (6.31), let's consider the Laplace transform:

$$\gamma^+(x, v) = \int_0^\infty e^{-v\tau} g^+(\tau, x) d\tau \quad v \geq 0$$

Substituting in (6.31)

$$-\int e^{-v\tau} g_\tau^+ d\tau + \int e^{-v\tau} \mu g_x^+ d\tau + \int e^{-v\tau} \frac{1}{2}\sigma^2 g_{xx}^+ d\tau = 0$$

and applying partial integration to the first integral we obtain

$$-v\gamma^+ + \mu\gamma_x^+ + \frac{1}{2}\sigma^2\gamma_{xx}^+ = 0$$

subject to

$$g^+(0, l) = \gamma^+(l) = 1$$

because

$$g^+(0, l) = \gamma^+(l) = \int_0^\infty e^{-v.0} g^+(0, l) d\tau = \int_0^\infty \delta(l - x) d\tau = 1$$

and

$$g^+(\tau, 0) = \gamma^+(0) = 0$$

because

$$\gamma^+(0) = \int_0^\infty e^{-v\tau} g^+(\tau, 0) d\tau = \int_0^\infty e^{-v\tau} \cdot 0 d\tau = 0$$

Now the PDE is of second-order ordinary differential equation, and the solution can be expressed as

$$\gamma^+(x) = e^{-\frac{\mu}{\sigma^2}x}(A\sinh(\theta x) + B\cosh(\theta x))$$

where

$$\theta(v) = \frac{1}{\sigma^2}\sqrt{\mu^2 + \sigma^2 v} \tag{6.32}$$

From boundary conditions $\gamma^+(0) = 0$ and $\gamma^+(l) = 1$, we can determine A and B as

$$B = 0 \quad A = \frac{e^{\frac{\mu}{\sigma^2} l}}{\sinh(\theta l)}$$

Then, the complete solution is

$$\gamma^+(x, v) = e^{\frac{\mu}{\sigma^2}(l-x)} \frac{\sinh(\theta(v)x)}{\sinh(\theta(v)l)} \tag{6.33}$$

To obtain the density for the upper barrier, we need the inversion of this Laplace transform $\gamma^+(x, v)$. This can be done by using Bromwich's integral (Duffy, 1994, Ch. 1.4, pp. 11–50)

$$g^+(\tau, x) = \frac{1}{2\pi i} \int_{c-i\infty}^{c+i\infty} e^{\tau z} \gamma^+(x; z) dz$$

Now, z is a complex variable, and x is treated as a parameter. Pelsser (1997) handles the integral as contour integral and transforms the line integral into contour integral by adding a circular arc in the second and third quadrants where integral limit c lies to the right of any of the singularities of the function $\gamma^+(x, z)$.

Pelsser (2000) uses Cauchy's Residue Theorem' to solve the integral.

Cauchy's Residue Theorem'. If $f(z)$ is analytic inside a closed contour C except at points z_k where f has singularities, then

$$\oint_C f(z)dz = 2\pi i. \sum_k \quad \text{residue of } f(z) \text{ at } z_k$$

at z_k. The residue of a singularity z_k equals the coefficient a_{-1} of the Laurent series

$$f(z) = \sum_{n=-\infty}^{\infty} a_n (z - z_k)^n$$

around a singularity z_k. The largest negative power (-1) in the Laurent expansion gives the order of singularity. Then, the residue can be computed as

$$\text{Res}(z_k) = \lim_{z \to z_k} (z - z_k) f(z)$$

and the line integral must be equal, by the residue theorem, to the sum of residues of the singularities enclosed in the contour.

We need to find the singularities of the function $e^{\tau z}\gamma^+(x;z)$. They are the terms making the denominator of $\gamma^+(x;z)$ zero. Using the identity $\sinh(z) = -i\sin(iz)$, we find that $\sinh(\theta(z)l)$ is zero if $i\theta(z)l = k\pi$ for k integer. Solving for z yields

$$z_k = -\frac{1}{2}\left(\frac{\mu^2}{\sigma^2} + \frac{k^2\pi^2\sigma^2}{l^2}\right) \tag{6.34}$$

Using

$$\theta(z) = \frac{1}{\sigma^2}\sqrt{\mu^2 + 2\sigma^2 z}$$

we write

$$\theta^2 = \frac{1}{\sigma^4}(\mu^2 + 2\sigma^2 z_k)$$

Taking $i\theta(z)l = k\pi$ and

$$-\theta^2 l^2 = k^2\pi^2$$

yields equation (6.34). The residue for each singularity can be obtained as follows:

$$\mathrm{Res}(z_k) = \lim_{z\to z_k} e^{\tau z} e^{\frac{\mu}{\sigma^2}(l-x)} \sinh(\theta x)\frac{(z - z_k)}{\sinh(\theta l)}$$

Taking the limit by using l'Hospital's rule yields

$$= \lim_{z\to z_k} e^{\tau z} e^{\frac{\mu}{\sigma^2}(l-x)} \sinh(\theta x)\frac{1}{\cosh(\theta l)\frac{\partial\theta}{\partial z}l}$$

$$\frac{\partial\theta}{\partial z} = \frac{2\sigma^2}{2\sigma^2}\left(\mu^2 + 2\sigma^2 z\right)^{-1/2} = \frac{1}{\sqrt{\mu^2 + 2\sigma^2 z}}$$

$$= \lim_{z\to z_k} e^{\tau z} e^{\frac{\mu}{\sigma^2}(l-x)} \sinh(\theta x)\frac{\sigma^2}{\cosh(\frac{k\pi i l}{l})\frac{\sigma^2}{\sqrt{\mu^2+2\sigma^2 z}}l}$$

$$= \lim_{z\to z_k} e^{\tau z} e^{\frac{\mu}{\sigma^2}(l-x)} \sinh(\theta x)\frac{\sigma^2\theta}{\cosh\left(\frac{k\pi i l}{l}\right)l}$$

$$= \lim_{z\to z_k} e^{\tau z} e^{\frac{\mu}{\sigma^2}(l-x)} \sinh(\theta x)\frac{\sigma^2(k\pi i)/l}{\cosh(\frac{k\pi i l}{l})l}$$

Since $\theta = \frac{k\pi i}{l}$

$$\frac{\theta\sigma^2}{l} = \frac{k\pi i\sigma^2}{l^2}$$

$$\cosh\left(\frac{k\pi i l}{l}\right) = (-1)^k$$

$$= e^{\tau z_k} e^{\frac{\mu}{\sigma^2}(l-x)} \sinh\left(k\pi i \frac{x}{l}\right)(-1)^k \frac{\sigma^2}{l^2} k\pi i$$

$$\sinh\left(k\pi i \frac{x}{l}\right) = -i\sin\left(i^2 k\pi \frac{x}{l}\right)$$

$$= -i^2 e^{\tau z_k} e^{\frac{\mu}{\sigma^2}(l-x)} \cdot \sin\left(-k\pi \frac{x}{l}\right)(-1)^k \frac{\sigma^2}{l^2} k\pi$$

Using

$$\sin\left(-k\pi \frac{x}{l}\right)(-1)^k = \sin\left(k\pi \frac{l-x}{l}\right)$$

we obtain

$$\text{Res}(z_k) = e^{\tau z_k} e^{\frac{\mu}{\sigma^2}(l-x)} \frac{\sigma^2}{l^2} \sin\left(k\pi \frac{l-x}{l}\right) k\pi$$

Summing up all the residues gives the following density function of hitting the upper barrier before hitting the lower one:

$$g^+(t, x; s) = e^{\frac{\mu}{\sigma^2}(l-x)} \frac{\sigma^2}{l^2} \sum_{k=1}^{\infty} e^{z_k(s-t)} k\pi \sin\left(k\pi \frac{l-x}{l}\right) \tag{6.35}$$

6.4.2.2. *Derivation of* $\boldsymbol{g^-}$

Laplace transform γ^- satisfies the same PDE with boundary conditions $\gamma^-(0) = 1$, $\gamma^-(l) = 0$. Solution is

$$\gamma^-(x; z) = e^{-\frac{\mu}{\sigma^2}x} \frac{\sinh(\theta(z)(l-x))}{\sinh(\theta(z)l)} \tag{6.36}$$

It can be observed that

$$\gamma^{-}(x) = e^{-2\frac{\mu}{\sigma^2}x}\gamma^{+}(l-x)$$

since

$$\gamma^{+}(x,z) = e^{\frac{\mu}{\sigma^2}(l-x)}\frac{\sinh(\theta(z)x)}{\sinh(\theta(z)l)}$$

Substituting in equation (6.36) yields

$$e^{-2\frac{\mu}{\sigma^2}x}e^{\frac{\mu}{\sigma^2}(l-(l-x))}\frac{\sigma^2}{l^2}\sum_{k=1}^{\infty}e^{z_k(s-t)}k\pi\sin\left(k\pi\frac{l-(l-x)}{l}\right)$$

$$g^{-}(t,x;s) = e^{-\frac{\mu}{\sigma^2}x}\frac{\sigma^2}{l^2}\sum_{k=1}^{\infty}e^{z_k(s-t)}k\pi\sin\left(k\pi\frac{x}{l}\right) \tag{6.37}$$

6.4.3. *Valuation formulae*

For the option maturity T, let's take $\mu = r - d - \frac{1}{2}\sigma^2$ and $L < S(t) < U$. Then dividing by L and taking logarithms yields $x = z(t) = \ln S(t)/L$ and $l = \ln U/L$. In Pelsser (2000), it is assumed that we receive an amount K_U if the upper barrier is hit first, an amount K_L if the lower barrier is hit first, and an amount K if neither barrier is hit until maturity. This is the most straightforward double barrier (European) option, which pays a constant amount at maturity. Then, the value of this option (as a constant payoff) is given by

$$\begin{aligned} C_{CPM}(t) = e^{-r(T-t)}(&K_U P^{+}(T) + K_L P^{-}(T) \\ &+ K(1 - P^{+}(T) - P^{-}(T)) \end{aligned}$$

where $P^{\pm}(T)$ is the cumulative hitting probability and can be given by the integral

$$\begin{aligned} P^{\pm}(T) &= \int_t^T g^{\pm}(t,x;s)ds = \int_t^{\infty} g^{\pm}(t,x;s)ds - \int_T^{\infty} g^{\pm}(t,x;s)ds \\ &= \gamma^{\pm}(x;0) - \int_T^{\infty} g^{\pm}(t,x;s)\,ds \end{aligned}$$

Integrating term-by-term yields

$$P^+(T)$$
$$= e^{\frac{\mu}{\sigma^2}(l-x)}\left\{\frac{\sinh\left(\frac{\mu}{\sigma^2}x\right)}{\sinh\left(\frac{\mu}{\sigma^2}l\right)} - \frac{\sigma^2}{l^2}\sum_{k=1}^{\infty}\frac{e^{-\lambda_k(T-t)}}{\lambda_k}k\pi\sin\left(k\pi\frac{l-x}{l}\right)\right\}$$

$$P^-(T)$$
$$= e^{-\frac{\mu}{\sigma^2}x}\left\{\frac{\sinh\left(\frac{\mu}{\sigma^2}(l-x)\right)}{\sinh\left(\frac{\mu}{\sigma^2}l\right)} - \frac{\sigma^2}{l^2}\sum_{k=1}^{\infty}\frac{e^{-\lambda_k(T-t)}}{\lambda_k}k\pi\sin\left(k\pi\frac{x}{l}\right)\right\}$$

Here, we used equations (6.33) and (6.36)

$$\gamma^{\pm}(x;0) \to \gamma^+(x,z) = e^{\frac{\mu}{\sigma^2}(l-x)}\frac{\sinh(\theta(z)x)}{\sinh(\theta(z)l)}$$

$$\gamma^-(x;z) = e^{-\frac{\mu}{\sigma^2}x}\frac{\sinh(\theta(z)(l-x))}{\sinh(\theta(z)l)}$$

$$\gamma^+(x,0) = e^{\frac{\mu}{\sigma^2}(l-x)}\frac{\sinh\left(\frac{\mu}{\sigma^2}x\right)}{\sinh\left(\frac{\mu}{\sigma^2}l\right)}$$

$$\gamma^-(x,0) = e^{-\frac{\mu}{\sigma^2}x}\frac{\sinh\left(\frac{\mu}{\sigma^2}(l-x)\right)}{\sinh\left(\frac{\mu}{\sigma^2}l\right)}$$

The value of the rebate is simply the payment multiplied by one minus the probability of hitting the barriers.

6.4.4. *Rebate at hit*

The value of rebate for hitting the upper barrier is

$$V_{RAHU}(t) = K_U\int_t^T e^{-r(s-t)}g^+(t,x;s)ds \tag{6.38}$$

Since $e^{-r(s-t)}$ is the inside term, we can write

$$r + \lambda_k = \frac{1}{2}\left(\frac{2\sigma^2 r + \mu^2}{\sigma^2} + \frac{k^2\sigma^2\pi^2}{l^2}\right) = \frac{1}{2}\left(\frac{\mu'^2}{\sigma^2} + \frac{k^2\sigma^2\pi^2}{l^2}\right) = \lambda'_k$$

where

$$\mu' = \sqrt{2\sigma^2 r + \mu^2}$$

and

$$\theta(z) = \frac{1}{\sigma^2}\sqrt{\mu'^2 + 2\sigma^2 z}$$

If $g^{'+}$ is the barrier density with drift μ', we obtain:

$$K_U\left[\int_t^{\infty} g^{+'}(t,x;s)\,ds - \int_T^{\infty} g^{+'}(t,x;s)\,ds\right]$$

$$V_{RAHU}(t)$$

$$= K_U e^{\frac{\mu}{\sigma^2}(l-x)}\left\{\frac{\sinh\left(\frac{\mu'}{\sigma^2}x\right)}{\sinh\left(\frac{\mu'}{\sigma^2}l\right)} - \frac{\sigma^2}{l^2}\sum_{k=1}^{\infty}\frac{e^{-\lambda'_k(T-t)}}{\lambda'_k}k\pi\sin\left(k\pi\frac{l-x}{l}\right)\right\} \tag{6.39}$$

Similarly, the value of the rebate is found to be

$$V_{RAHL}(t) = K_L e^{-\frac{\mu}{\sigma^2}x}\left\{\frac{\sinh\left(\frac{\mu'}{\sigma^2}(l-x)\right)}{\sinh\left(\frac{\mu'}{\sigma^2}l\right)}\right.$$

$$\left. - \frac{\sigma^2}{l^2}\sum_{k=1}^{\infty}\frac{e^{-\lambda'_k(T-t)}}{\lambda'_k}k\pi\sin\left(k\pi\frac{x}{l}\right)\right\} \tag{6.40}$$

if the lower barrier is hit first.

6.4.5. *Double knock-out option*

The payoff of the DKOC option is max $(S_T - K, 0)$ if neither barrier is hit during the option's lifetime, zero otherwise. Then, the value of the option is given by

$$V_{\mathrm{DKOC}}(t) = e^{-r(T-t)}\int_0^l \max(Le^y - K, 0)p(t,x;T,y)dy \tag{6.41}$$

(Remember that $L < S(t) < U$ corresponds to $1 < \frac{S(t)}{L} < U/L$ therefore $0 < y < l$)

The option is in the money if

$$Le^y > K \quad y > \ln K/L \ = d$$

$$V_{\text{DKOC}}(t) = e^{-r(T-t)} \int_d^l (Le^y - K) p(t, x; T, y) dy$$

$$= e^{-r(T-t)} \left(L \int_d^l e^y p(t, x; T, y) dy - K \int_d^l p(t, x; T, y) dy \right)$$

where $p(t, x; s, y)$ is given by equation (6.28) as

$$p\left(t, x; s, y\right) = e^{\frac{\mu}{\sigma^2}(y-x)} \frac{2}{l} \sum_{n=1}^{\infty} e^{-\lambda_n (s-t)} \sin\left(\frac{n\pi y}{l}\right) \sin\left\{\frac{n\pi x)}{l}\right\}$$

We need to find primitives for the terms of the form $e^{ay}\sin(by)$. This is given by

$$\int e^{ay} \sin(by) dy = e^{ay} \frac{a \sin(by) \ - b\cos(by)}{a^2 + b^2}$$

Because,

$$\int e^{ay} \sin(by) dy = -\frac{1}{b} \cos(by) e^{ay} + \frac{a}{b} \int \cos(by) \ e^{ay} dy$$

$$= -\frac{1}{b} \cos(by) \ e^{ay} + \frac{a}{b} e^{ay} \frac{1}{b} \sin(by)$$

$$- \frac{a^2}{b^2} \int e^{ay} \sin(by) dy$$

If we set

$$Q(\alpha, y) = \int e^{\alpha y} p(t, x; T, y) dy$$

we obtain for $Q(\alpha, y)$

$$Q(\alpha, y) = \frac{2}{l} e^{\frac{\mu}{\sigma^2}(y-x)} e^{\alpha y} \sum_{k=1}^{\infty} e^{-\lambda_k (T-t)} \sin\left(k\pi \frac{x}{l}\right)$$

$$\left(\frac{\left(\frac{\mu}{\sigma^2} + \alpha\right) \sin\left(k\pi \frac{y}{l}\right) - \frac{k\pi}{l} \cos\left(k\pi \frac{y}{l}\right)}{\left(\frac{\mu}{\sigma^2} + \alpha\right)^2 + \frac{k^2\pi^2}{l^2}} \right) \tag{6.42}$$

where $x = \frac{S(0)}{L}$, $a = \frac{\mu}{\sigma^2} + \alpha$, and $b = \frac{k\pi}{l}$.

Then, the value of the DKOC can be expressed as

$$V_{\mathrm{DKOC}}(t) = e^{-r(T-t)}(L(Q(1,l) - Q(1,d)) - K(Q(0,l) - Q(0,d))) \tag{6.43}$$

and the value of the double knock-out put (DKOP) can be expressed as

$$\begin{aligned} V_{\mathrm{DKOP}}(t) &= e^{-r(T-t)} \int_0^d (K - Le^y)\, p\,(t,x;T,y)\,dy \\ &= e^{-r(T-t)} \left(K \int_0^d p\,(t,x;T,y)\,dy - L \int_0^d e^y p\,(t,x;T,y)\,dy \right) \\ V_{\mathrm{DKOP}}(t) &= e^{-r(T-t)}(K(Q(0,d) - Q(0,0)) - L(Q(1,d) \\ &\quad - Q(1,0))) \end{aligned} \tag{6.44}$$

A Matlab code is given in the appendix for the double barrier knock-out call option. Since the formula includes infinite sums, the truncation must be set for the correct number of k. As the terms of $e^{-\lambda_k(s-t)}$ decline very fast, Pelsser (2000) gives the number as

$$k > \sqrt{\frac{-2\frac{\ln \varepsilon}{s-t} - \frac{\mu^2}{\sigma^2}}{\frac{\pi^2\sigma^2}{l^2}}}$$

where ε is the order of error for the calculation. We have truncated at $k = 25$ in the code (see the Appendix).

6.5. Wrapping Up: Valuation Formulas from Luo (2001)

6.5.1. *Standard double barrier options*

We will give a summary of Luo (2001) in this subsection for the double barrier options defined in the introduction. First, we present some notations given by Luo (2001) on pp. 127–128. Luo's work is based on the formulae of hitting probabilities of Brownian motion given by Sidenius (1998).

Let the normal density be

$$\varphi(x;\lambda,v) = \frac{1}{\sqrt{2\pi v^2}}\exp\left(-\frac{(x-\lambda)^2}{2v^2}\right)$$

$$dS_t = (r-q)\,S_t dt + \sigma S_t dW_t$$

$$dX_t = \left(r-q-\frac{1}{2}\sigma^2\right)dt + \sigma dW_t$$

$$X_t = X_0 + \left(r-q-\frac{1}{2}\sigma^2\right)t + \sigma W_t$$

where $X_t = \log S_t$ and $N(x)$ is the cumulative standard normal distribution function. We also set two barriers $A(A > 0) B > A\ A \leq S_0 \leq B$ and $a = \log A\ b = \log B$.

For any real number y, τ_y is the time that X_t hits y for the first time, i.e., $\tau_y = \min\{t, X_t = y\}$. In other terms, this is the time the process S_t hits the e^y for the first time.

Setting $X_0 = x_0\ n \geq 1$ and $\mu = \left(r-q-\frac{1}{2}\sigma^2\right)$

$$\alpha_n^+ = 2nb - 2(n-1)a - x_0$$

$$\alpha_n^- = 2na - 2(n-1)b - x_0$$

$$\beta_n^+ = 2n(b-a) + x_0$$

$$\beta_n^- = 2n(a-b) + x_0$$

Denoting by $x \bigvee y$ and $x \bigwedge y$ the maximum and the minimum of two numbers x and y, respectively, the double barrier formulas are as follows; all the definitions are given in the introduction of this chapter.

(1) *Upper-barrier knock-in*: The necessary condition is

$\tau_b < \tau_a$ and $\tau_b \leq T$. If $\tau_a < \tau_b$ or $\tau_b > T$, the option is worthless.

(a) *Call option*:

$$\begin{aligned} V_{ui} = C_{ui} = {} & L(x_0; b \vee \log K, +\infty) \\ & + \sum_{n=1}^{\infty}[L(\alpha_n^+; b \wedge \log K, b) - L(\beta_n^+; b \wedge \log K, b) \\ & - L(\alpha_n^-; b \vee \log K, +\infty) + L(\beta_n^-; b \vee \log K, +\infty)] \end{aligned}$$

(b) *Put option*:

$$\begin{aligned}
V_{ui} = P_{ui} &= L(x_0; b, b \vee \log K) \\
&+ \sum_{n=1}^{\infty} [L(\alpha_n^+; -\infty, b \wedge \log K) \\
&- L(\beta_n^+; -\infty, b \wedge \log K) \\
&- L(\alpha_n^-; b, b \vee \log K) + L(\beta_n^-; b, b \vee \log K)]
\end{aligned}$$

where

$$\begin{aligned}
L(c; G, H) &= \exp(-rT) \int_G^H (e^x - K) \exp\left[-\alpha(x - x_0) - \beta T\right] \\
&\times \varphi(x; c, \sigma^2 T)dx = \exp\left(\frac{\mu}{\sigma^2}(c - x_0) - rT\right) \\
&* \left\{\left[\exp\left[\left(\mu + \frac{1}{2}\sigma^2\right)T + c\right] N\left(\frac{c + (\mu + \sigma^2)T - G}{\sigma\sqrt{T}}\right)\right.\right. \\
&\left. - KN\left(\frac{c + \mu T - G}{\sigma\sqrt{T}}\right)\right] - \left[\exp\left[\left(\mu + \frac{1}{2}\sigma^2\right)T + c\right]\right. \\
&\left.\left. \times\ N\left(\frac{c + (\mu + \sigma^2)T - H}{\sigma\sqrt{T}}\right) - KN\left(\frac{c + \mu T - H}{\sigma\sqrt{T}}\right)\right]\right\}
\end{aligned}$$

and

$$\mu = r - q - \frac{1}{2}\sigma^2 \tag{6.45}$$

Let's start with the last integral

$$\begin{aligned}
&L(c; G, H) \\
&= -\exp(-rT)K \left[\int_{-\infty}^H \exp\left[-\alpha(x - x_0) - \beta T\right] \varphi\left(x; c, \sigma^2 T\right) dx\right. \\
&\left. - \int_{-\infty}^G \exp\left[-\alpha(x - x_0) - \beta T\right] \varphi\left(x; c, \sigma^2 T\right) dx\right]
\end{aligned}$$

$$\exp\left[-\alpha\left(x-x_0\right)-\beta T\right]\varphi\left(x;c,\sigma^2T\right)$$
$$=\frac{\mu}{\sigma^2}\left(x-x_0\right)-\frac{\mu^2T}{2\sigma^2}-\frac{1}{2\sigma^2T}(x-c)^2$$

But this can be written as

$$-\frac{1}{2\sigma^2T}(x-c-\mu T)^2-\frac{\mu}{\sigma^2}x_0+\frac{c\mu}{\sigma^2}$$

So, the first coefficient is

$$\exp\Big(\left(c-x_0\right)\frac{\mu}{\sigma^2}-rT\Big)$$

and the integral is

$$-K\left[\int_{-\infty}^{H}\varphi\left(x;c,\sigma^2T\right)dx)-\int_{-\infty}^{G}\varphi\left(x;c,\sigma^2T\right)dx)\right]$$
$$=-KN\left(\frac{H-c-\mu T}{\sigma\sqrt{T}}\right)+KN\left(\frac{G-c-\mu T}{\sigma\sqrt{T}}\right)$$
$$-K\left[-(1-N\left(\frac{H-c-\mu T}{\sigma\sqrt{T}}\right)+(1-N\left(\frac{G-c-\mu T}{\sigma\sqrt{T}}\right)\right]$$
$$=-\exp\Big(\left(c-x_0\right)\frac{\mu}{\sigma^2}-rT\Big)K\left[N\left(\frac{c+\mu T-G}{\sigma\sqrt{T}}\right)\right.$$
$$\left.-N\left(\frac{c+\mu T-H}{\sigma\sqrt{T}}\right)\right]$$

The first term contains e^x term.

$$=\exp\left(-rT\right)\left[\int_{-\infty}^{H}\exp(x)\exp[-\alpha\left(x-x_0\right)-\beta T]\varphi\left(x;c,\sigma^2T\right)dx\right.$$
$$\left.-\int_{-\infty}^{G}\exp(x)\exp[-\alpha\left(x-x_0\right)-\beta T]\varphi(x;c,\sigma^2T)dx\right]$$

$$-\frac{1}{2\sigma^2T}(x-c)^2-\frac{\mu}{\sigma^2}x_0+\frac{\mu}{\sigma^2}x+x-\frac{\mu^2}{2\sigma^2}T=-\frac{1}{2\sigma^2T}(x-c)^2$$
$$-\frac{\mu^2}{2\sigma^2}T^2-\frac{\mu}{\sigma^2}x_0+\frac{2(\sigma^2+\mu)T}{2\sigma^2T}x-rT$$

To write the square term as

$$-\frac{1}{2\sigma^2 T}\left(x - c - (\mu + \sigma^2)\right)^2$$

we have to add and subtract

$$\frac{2c\left(\mu+\sigma^2\right)T}{2\sigma^2 T} + \frac{2\mu\sigma^2 T^2 + \sigma^4 T^2}{2\sigma^2 T}$$

$$\frac{2\mu\sigma^2 T^2 + \sigma^4 T^2}{2\sigma^2 T} \to \exp\left(\mu + \frac{1}{2}\sigma^2\right)T$$

$$\frac{2c\left(\mu+\sigma^2\right)T}{2\sigma^2 T} - \frac{\mu}{\sigma^2}x_0 - rT = c\frac{\mu}{\sigma^2} + c - \frac{\mu}{\sigma^2}x_0 - rT$$

Rearranging all the terms we obtain

$$\exp\left[\left(\mu + \frac{1}{2}\sigma^2\right)T + c\right]\exp\left(\frac{\mu}{\sigma^2}(c - x_0)\right)$$

$$\exp\left(-rT\right)\left[\int_{-\infty}^{H}\exp(x)\exp\left[-\alpha\left(x - x_0\right) - \beta T\right]\varphi\left(x; c, \sigma^2 T\right)dx\right.$$

$$\left. - \int_{-\infty}^{G}\exp(x)\exp\left[-\alpha\left(x - x_0\right) - \beta T\right]\varphi\left(x; c, \sigma^2 T\right)dx\right]$$

$$= \exp\left[\left(\mu + \frac{1}{2}\sigma^2\right)T + c\right]\exp\left(\frac{\mu}{\sigma^2}(c - x_0)\right)$$

$$\times\left[\int_{-\infty}^{H}\varphi\left(x; c, \sigma^2 T\right)dx - \int_{-\infty}^{G}\varphi\left(x; c, \sigma^2 T\right)dx\right]$$

$$\exp\left[\left(\mu + \frac{1}{2}\sigma^2\right)T + c\right]\exp\left(\frac{\mu}{\sigma^2}(c - x_0)\right)$$

$$\times\left[N\left(\frac{H - (c + (\mu + \sigma^2)T)}{\sigma\sqrt{T}}\right) - N\left(\frac{G - (c + (\mu + \sigma^2)T)}{\sigma\sqrt{T}}\right)\right]$$

which is

$$\exp\left[\left(\mu+\frac{1}{2}\sigma^2\right)T+c\right]\exp\left(\frac{\mu}{\sigma^2}(c-x_0)\right)$$
$$\times\left[N\left(\frac{(c+\left(\mu+\sigma^2\right)T-G}{\sigma\sqrt{T}}\right)-N\left(\frac{(c+\left(\mu+\sigma^2\right)T-H}{\sigma\sqrt{T}}\right)\right]$$

and together with the first integral, yields equation (6.45).

Also, we can write

$$L\left(c;G,+\infty\right)=\lim_{H\to\infty}L(c;G,H)$$

and

$$L\ \ (c;-\infty,H)=\lim_{G\to-\infty}L(c;G,H)$$
$$=\exp\left(\frac{\mu}{\sigma^2}\left(c-x_0\right)-rT\right)\left[\exp\left[\left(\mu+\frac{1}{2}\sigma^2\right)T+c\right]\right.$$
$$\left.\times N\left(\frac{H-c-\left(\mu+\sigma^2\right)T}{\sigma\sqrt{T}}\right)-KN\left(\frac{H-c-\mu T}{\sigma\sqrt{T}}\right)\right]$$

Since

$$P\left(\tau_b<\tau_a,\tau_b<T,\ X_T\in dx\right)=q\left(x,T\right)dx$$
$$q(x,T)=$$

$e^{-\alpha(x-x_0)-\beta T}*\left\{\sum_{n=1}^{\infty}\left(\varphi(x;\alpha_n^+,\sigma^2T\right)-\varphi(x;\beta_n^+,\sigma^2T)\right\}$ for $x<b$

$e^{-\alpha(x-x_0)-\beta T}*\{\varphi(x;x_0,\sigma^2T)-\sum_{n=1}^{\infty}(\varphi(x;\alpha_n^-,\sigma^2T)-\varphi(x;\beta_n^-,\sigma^2T))\}$ for $x>b$

The call price is

$$C_{ui}=\exp(-rT)E\left[1_{\tau_b<\tau_a,\tau_b<T}\max(S_T-K)\right]$$
$$=\exp\left(-rT\right)\int_{-\infty}^{\infty}(e^x-K)q(x,t)dx$$

For $\ln K \le b$ case

$$\exp(-rT)\int_{\ln K}^{b}(e^{x}-K)q(x,t)dx+\exp(-rT)\int_{b}^{\infty}(e^{x}-K)q(x,t)dx$$

(2) *Lower barrier knock-in*:

(a) *Call option*:

$$\begin{aligned}V_{li}=C_{li}&=L\left(x_0;a\wedge \log K,a\right)+\sum_{n=1}^{\infty}[L\left(\alpha_n^-;a\vee \log K,+\infty\right)\\&-L\left(\beta_n^-;a\vee \log K,+\infty\right)-L\left(\alpha_n^+;a\wedge \log K,a\right)\\&+L\left(\beta_n^+;a\wedge \log K,a\right)]\end{aligned}$$

(b) *Put option*:

$$\begin{aligned}V_{li}=P_{li}&=L\left(x_0;-\infty,a\wedge \log K\right)+\sum_{n=1}^{\infty}[L(\alpha_n^-;a,a\vee \log K)\\&-L(\beta_n^-;a,a\vee \log K)-L(\alpha_n^+;-\infty,a\wedge \log K)\\&+L(\beta_n^+;-\infty,a\wedge \log K)]\end{aligned}$$

(3) *Upper-barrier knock-out for calls and puts*:

$$V_{uo}=V_0-V_{ui}$$

where V_0 is the standard BSM formula for calls and puts.

(4) *Lower-barrier knock-out for calls and puts*:

$$V_{lo}=V_0-V_{li}$$

(5) *One-touch knock-in (OTI)*:

$$V_{\text{oti}}=V_{ui}+V_{li}$$

(6) *Double-touch knock-in (DTI)*:

$$V_{\text{dti}}=(V_{\text{dki}})=V_{sui}+V_{sli}-V_{\text{oti}}$$

The letter s in front of the subscripts on the right-hand side of the equation denotes that the barrier is a "single" type. Therefore, the price is the summation of the up-and-in barrier and the down-and-in barrier minus the price of the OTI double barrier. This avoids double counting.

(7) *One-touch knock-out (double knock out)*:

$$V_{\text{oto}}\,(\equiv V_{\text{dko}}) = V_0 - V_{\text{oti}}$$

(8) *Double-touch knock-out*:

$$V_{\text{dto}} = V_0 - V_{\text{dti}}$$

Proof of Upper barrier knock-in formula:
Let $\alpha = -\mu/\sigma^2$ and $\beta = \mu^2/2\sigma^2$
We write

$$P\left(\tau_b < \tau_a, \tau_b < T,\ X_T \in dx\right) = q\left(x;T\right)dx$$

with reference to Sidenius (1998) where

$$\begin{aligned} q\left(x;T\right) &= \exp(-\alpha\left(x - x_0\right) - \beta T) \\ &\quad \times \left\{\sum_{n=1}^{\infty}\left[\varphi\left(x;\alpha_n^+,\sigma^2 T\right) - \varphi\left(x;\beta_n^+,\sigma^2 T\right)\right]\right\} \end{aligned}$$

for $x < b$

and

$$\begin{aligned} q(x;T) &= \exp(-\alpha\left(x - x_0\right) - \beta T) \\ &\quad \times \left\{\varphi\left(x;x_0,\sigma^2 T\right) - \sum_{n=1}^{\infty}\left[\varphi\left(x;\alpha_n^-,\sigma^2 T\right) - \varphi\left(x;\beta_n^-,\sigma^2 T\right)\right]\right\} \end{aligned}$$

for $x > b$

By writing $S_T = \exp(X_T)$ or $x = \ln S_T$

$$\begin{aligned} V_{ui} &= \exp(-rT)\ E\left[1_{\tau_b < \tau_a, \tau_b < T} \max(S_T - K, 0)\right] \\ &= \exp(-rT) \int_{-\infty}^{+\infty} \max(\exp(x)\ - K, 0)\, q(x;T) dx \end{aligned}$$

Case 1: $\log K \le b$. Then we write

$$V_{ui} = \exp(-rT)\int_{\log K}^{b}(\exp(x)-K)q(x;T)dx + \int_{b}^{+\infty}(\exp(x)-K)q(x;T)dx$$

For $x < b$, we can write the first probability density of $q(x;T)$

$$\int_{\log\ K}^{b}(\exp(x)-K)q(x;T)dx = \sum_{n=1}^{\infty}[L(\alpha_n^+; b\wedge \log K, b) - L(\beta_n^+; b\wedge \log K, b)]$$

For the second probability

$$\begin{aligned}\int_{b}^{\infty}&(\exp(x)-K)q\,(x;T)\,dx \\ &= \int_{b}^{\infty}(\exp(x)-K)\exp(-\alpha(x-x_0)-\beta T) \\ &\quad \times \left\{\varphi(x;x_0,\sigma^2 T) - \sum_{n=1}^{\infty}\left[\varphi\left(x;\alpha_n^-,\sigma^2 T\right) - \varphi\left(x;\beta_n^-,\sigma^2 T\right)\right]\right\}\end{aligned}$$

which is equal to

$$L(x_0; b\vee \log K, +\infty) - \sum_{n=1}^{\infty}[L(\alpha_n^-; b\vee \log K, +\infty) + L(\beta_n^-; b\vee \log K, +\infty)]$$

Then, it gives the formula in (6.17).

Case 2: $\log K > b$. We write

$$V_{\text{dui}} = \exp(-rT)\int_{\log K\vee b}^{+\infty}(\exp(x)-K)q\,(x;T)\,dx$$

Noting that $(c; b\vee \log K, b) = 0$, the above gives the formula in (1).

Using the density in Sidenius (1998) for lower barrier knock-in options

$$
\begin{aligned}
P\left(\tau_a<\tau_b, \tau_a<T,\ X_T \in dx\right) &= p\left(x; T\right) dx \\
p(x; T) &= \exp\left(-\alpha\left(x-x_0\right)-\beta T\right) \\
&\quad \times\left\{\sum_{n=1}^{\infty}\left[\varphi\left(x; \alpha_n^{-}, \sigma^2 T\right)-\varphi\left(x; \beta_n^{-}, \sigma^2 T\right)\right]\right\}
\end{aligned}
$$

for $x > a$

and

$$
\begin{aligned}
p\left(x; T\right) &= \exp\left(-\alpha\left(x-x_0\right)-\beta T\right) \\
&\quad \times\left\{\varphi\left(x; x_0, \sigma^2 T\right)-\sum_{n=1}^{\infty}\left[\varphi\left(x; \alpha_n^{+}, \sigma^2 T\right)-\varphi\left(x; \beta_n^{+}, \sigma^2 T\right)\right]\right\}
\end{aligned}
$$

for $x < a$

we can obtain the formula in (2).

For the remaining six types of double barrier options, we only need the relationship between the double barrier options, single barrier options, and the standard type of calls and puts, as stated in Luo (2001).

For example, for a OTI double barrier option, we can write the probability that one of the two barriers is breached before T is equal to the sum of breaching the upper or lower barriers separately, i.e.,

$$
P\left(\tau_a \wedge \tau_b \leq T\right)=P\left(\tau_a<\tau_b, \tau_a \leq T\right)+P(\tau_b<\tau_a, \tau_b \leq T)
$$

So, the price is

$$
V_{oti}=V_{ui}+V_{li}
$$

Also, the one-touch knock-out option is where none of the two barriers are breached until maturity. That means

$$
\begin{aligned}
P\left(\tau_a \wedge \tau_b>T\right) &= 1-P\left(\tau_a \wedge \tau_b \leq T\right) \\
V_{\text{oto}} &= V_0-V_{\text{oti}}
\end{aligned}
$$

where V_0 is the vanilla type (BS) option price.

In Sidenius (1998, p. 74), the double knock-out barrier call price is 1.7678 with parameters

$$S_0 = 100 \quad K = 100 \quad r = 0.1 \quad T = 0.25 \quad \sigma = 0.2 \quad d = 0.05$$
$$L = 90 \quad U = 115$$

We have used only two terms ($n = 2$) to calculate the double barrier call option prices. The prices are (see the Matlab codes in Appendix)

$$V_{ui} = 2.7228 \quad V_{li} = 0.0671$$

Then, the double knock-in price is $V_{oti} = 2.7898$, and the DKOC is the BS price (4.5576) minus 2.7898, which is 1.7678. The upper and lower knock-out barriers can be found easily by subtracting the values of double knock-in barriers from the BS price.

6.5.2. *Double barrier binary options*

Similar to standard double barrier options, the same type of double barrier binary options can be defined as an asset or nothing and cash or nothing options. For example, an asset or nothing upper barrier knock-in double barrier binary option (too long a name) pays its holder the amount of the asset if the upper barrier is hit before the lower barrier during the lifetime of the option and the underlying price exceeds the exercise price at maturity and pays nothing otherwise.

Regarding Luo (2001, p. 133, Proposition 2), a cash-or-nothing double-barrier binary option price can be given as

$$\begin{aligned} &Q(c; M, G, H) \\ &= \exp(-rT)\int_G^H M \exp[-\alpha(x - x_0) - \beta T]\varphi(x; c, \sigma^2 T)dx \\ &= M\exp\left(\frac{\mu}{\sigma^2}(c - x_0) - rT\right)\left[N\left(\frac{c + \mu T - G}{\sigma\sqrt{T}}\right)\right. \\ &\quad \left. - N\left(\frac{c + \mu T - H}{\sigma\sqrt{T}}\right)\right] \end{aligned}$$

where M is the cash payoff of the option if $S_T > K$ at expiry and the prespecified barrier-hitting conditions are satisfied. The asset or nothing double-barrier binary option is also given as;

$$
\begin{aligned}
J(c; G, H) &\\
&= \exp(-rT) \int_G^H \exp(x) \exp\left[-\alpha (x - x_0) - \beta T\right] \varphi\left(x; c, \sigma^2 T\right) dx \\
&= \exp\left(\frac{\mu}{\sigma^2}(c - x_0) + c + \left(\mu - r + \frac{1}{2}\sigma^2\right) T\right. \\
&\quad \times \left[N\left(\frac{c + (\mu + \sigma^2)T - G}{\sigma\sqrt{T}}\right) - N\left(\frac{c + (\mu + \sigma^2)T - H}{\sigma\sqrt{T}}\right)\right]
\end{aligned}
$$

We have just replaced the function $L(c; G, H)$ with $Q(c; M, G, H)$ and $J(c; G, H)$.

6.5.3. *Rebates*

There are two types of rebate payments: at maturity or hitting time to barriers. If it is paid at the time of maturity, the current value of the rebate is the product of the relevant hitting probability times the rebate amount discounted by the risk-free rate. If the payment is made when the underlying price hits the barrier, the hitting time is random, making the discounting a random process. The present value of the rebate becomes an expectation of the randomly discounted rebate value. The reader is referred to Sidenius (1998) for closed-form formulae of rebates.

6.6. Conclusion

In this chapter, we have examined double barrier options, particularly the double knock-out barrier options. We have seen that there are eight types of double barriers, and if we can find the price of the knock-in or knock-out option, the other one's price can be found simply by subtracting from the price of the vanilla option. Kunitomo and Ikeda (1992), Geman and Yor (1996), Sidenius (1998), Pelsser (2000), and Luo (2001) are the fundamental papers that we can use in obtaining the prices of various types of double barrier options. Bhagavatula and Carr (1995) and Lo and Hui (2007) are the primary sources for valuing double barrier options with time-dependent parameters using Fourier series expansion—Buchen and Konstandatos (2009) value double barriers with arbitrary payoffs and curved boundaries.

Chapter 7

Exotic Barriers

7.1. Step-Barriers

Step barrier options are options where the barriers increase or decrease monotonically as a function of time. These are generally called standard barrier options. Step barriers where the barrier observation period is not continuous are called partial step barriers. Our primary source for pricing step barriers is Guillaume's article "Analytical Valuation of Options on Joint Minima and Maxima" (2004). When the size increases, i.e., the number of barriers, a crucial difficulty occurs in pricing step-barriers. In this case, obtaining the cumulative normal distribution functions of the joint distribution becomes difficult, and Monte Carlo methods may be required.

This sub-section is based on Tristan Guillaume's excellent paper, "Analytical valuation of options on joint minima and maxima," revised version 2004. First, we will present the analytical framework given by Guillaume (2004) and present a detailed derivation of some parts of the formulae of step barriers in the same paper.

7.1.1. *Analytical framework*

Depending on the number of barriers, we may write the price of a path-dependent European call as

$$\begin{aligned} &C\left(S, T, K, r, \sigma, \delta, A_1, A_2 \ldots A_m\right) \\ &\quad = e^{-rT} E^Q\left((S_T - K) 1_{A_1, A_2 \ldots A_m, S_T > K} \mid S_0\right) \end{aligned}$$

where δ is the dividend yield, E^Q is the expectation under an equivalent martingale measure Q, and $A_1, A_2 \ldots A_m$ are path-dependent conditions (barriers). Then, splitting the expectation and applying the Girsanov theorem, we have

$$\begin{aligned}
&C(S,T,K,r,\sigma,\delta,A_1,A_2\ldots A_m)\\
&\quad = e^{-rT}E^Q\left(S_T 1_{A_1,A_2\ldots A_m,S_T>K} \mid S_0\right)\\
&\qquad - e^{-rT}E^Q\left(K 1_{A_1,A_2\ldots A_m,S_T>K} \mid S_0\right)\\
&e^{-rT}E^Q\left(S_0 e^{(r-\delta-\sigma^2/2)T+\sigma W_T} 1_{\{A_1,A_2\ldots A_m,S_T>K\}}\right)\\
&\qquad - e^{-rT}KE^Q\left(1_{\{A_1,A_2\ldots A_m,S_T>K\}}\right)\\
&\frac{d\tilde{Q}}{dQ} = e^{-\frac{\sigma^2}{2}T+\sigma W_T}\\
&C(S,T,K,r,\sigma,\delta,A_1,A_2\ldots A_m)\\
&\quad = S_0 e^{-\delta T}\tilde{Q}(A_1,A_2\ldots A_m,S_T>K)\\
&\qquad - e^{-rT}KQ(A_1,A_2\ldots A_m,S_T>K) \qquad (7.1)
\end{aligned}$$

where $\tilde{Q}$ is the new probability measure with numeraire S.

Defining $x_T = \ln\frac{S_T}{S_0}$ $k = \ln \mathrm{K}$, the call and put prices are expressed as

$$\begin{aligned}
&C(S,T,K,r,\sigma,\delta,A_1,A_2\ldots A_m)\\
&\quad = S_0 e^{-\delta T}\tilde{Q}(A_1,A_2\ldots A_m,x_T>k)\\
&\qquad - e^{-rT}KQ(A_1,A_2\ldots A_m,x_T>k)\\
&P(S,T,K,r,\sigma,\delta,A_1,A_2\ldots A_m)\\
&\quad = -S_0 e^{-\delta T}\tilde{Q}(A_1,A_2\ldots A_m,x_T<k)\\
&\qquad + e^{-rT}KQ(A_1,A_2\ldots A_m,x_T<k)
\end{aligned}$$

Under the $Q-$measure, the drift is $\mu = r-\delta-\sigma^2/2$ and under the $\tilde{Q}-$measure, the drift is $\tilde{\mu} = r-\delta+\sigma^2/2$.

Since the step barriers require more than two variables, we need higher-dimension Gaussian distributions, and univariate $N(a)$ and bivariate $N_2(a,b;\rho)$ will not be sufficient for pricing.

If $X = (X_1, X_2, \dots X_n)$ is a vector of n joint standardized Gaussian random variables with a symmetric positive-definite variance-covariance matrix Σ, the density of X is given by

$$f(x_1 \dots x_n) = \frac{e^{-\frac{X^T \Sigma^{-1} X}{2}}}{(2\pi)^{n/2}\sqrt{|\Sigma|}}$$

For example, the density for three standardized Gaussian random variables can be written as

$$f(a, b, c; \rho_{12}, \rho_{23}, \rho_{13}) = \frac{\exp\{-(\lambda_1 a^2 + \lambda_2 b^2 + \lambda_3 c^2 + 2\lambda_4 ab + 2\lambda_5 bc + 2\lambda_6 ac)\}}{(2\pi)^{3/2}\sqrt{|\Sigma|}}$$

where $|\Sigma| = 1 - \rho_{12}^2 - \rho_{23}^2 - \rho_{13}^2 + 2\rho_{12}\rho_{23}\rho_{13}$ and

$$\lambda_1 = \frac{1-\rho_{23}^2}{|\Sigma|} \quad \lambda_2 = \frac{1-\rho_{13}^2}{|\Sigma|} \quad \lambda_3 = \frac{1-\rho_{12}^2}{|\Sigma|} \quad \lambda_4 = \frac{\rho_{23}\rho_{13}-\rho_{12}}{|\Sigma|}$$

$$\lambda_5 = \frac{\rho_{12}\rho_{13}-\rho_{23}}{|\Sigma|} \quad \lambda_6 = \frac{\rho_{12}\rho_{23}-\rho_{13}}{|\Sigma|}$$

Assuming two disjoint periods and two maximums the probability of $Q\left(M_0^1 < h_1, M_1^2 < h_2, X_{T_2} < k\right)$ can be stated as

$$E^Q\{1_{\{M_0^1<h_1,\ X_{T_1}<h_1\}} E^Q(1_{\{M_1^2<h_2,\ X_{T_2}<k\}} \mid X_{T_1})\} = \int_{-\infty}^{h_1} \Psi(u)\Phi(u)du$$

where

$$E^Q 1_{\{M_0^1<h_1,\ X_{T_1}<h_1\}} = \Psi(u) = \frac{e^{-\frac{1}{2}\left(\frac{u-\mu T_1}{\sigma\sqrt{T_1}}\right)^2}}{\sigma\sqrt{2\pi T_1}} - e^{\frac{2\mu h_1}{\sigma^2}} \frac{e^{-\frac{1}{2}\left(\frac{u-2h_1-\mu T_1}{\sigma\sqrt{T_1}}\right)^2}}{\sigma\sqrt{2\pi T_1}} \tag{7.2}$$

$$\Phi(u) = E^Q\left(1_{\{M_1^2<h_2,\ X_{T_2}<k\}} \mid X_{T_1}\right) = N\left(\frac{k-u-\mu(T_2-T_1)}{\sigma\sqrt{T_2-T_1}}\right) - e^{2\mu(h_2-u)/\sigma^2} N\left(\frac{k-2h_2+u-\mu(T_2-T_1)}{\sigma\sqrt{T_2-T_1}}\right) \tag{7.3}$$

The density $\Psi(u)$ can be calculated easily. For the cumulative distribution, we need some algebra:

$$E^Q\left(1_{\{M_1^2<h_2,\ X_{T_2}<k\}}\,|\,X_{T_1}\right) = P\left(X_{T_2}<k\right)$$
$$-P\left(X_{T_2}<k, M_1^2>h_2\right)$$

$$\ln\left(\frac{S_T}{S_{T_1}}\frac{S_{T_1}}{S_0}\right) < \ln K/S_0 = k$$
$$S_T = S_{T_2}$$
$$v+u < \ln K/S_0$$
$$v < k-u$$

So, $P(X_{T_2}<k) = P\left(v<k-u\right)$ since $X_{T_2} = X_T$. Then, the first term can be written as

$$N\left(\frac{k-u-\mu(T_2-T_1)}{\sigma\sqrt{T_2-T_1}}\right)$$

Similarly,

$$P\left(X_{T_2}<k, M_1^2>h_2\right) = P\left(v<k-u, M_1^2>h_2\right)$$
$$\ln\left(\frac{M_1^2}{S_{T_1}}\frac{S_{T_1}}{S_0}\right) > \ln H_2/S_0$$
$$x > h_2-u$$

So, the exponent is

$$e^{2\mu(h_2-u)/\sigma^2}$$

and cumulative normal distribution is

$$N\left(\frac{k-u-2(h_2-u)-\mu(T_2-T_1)}{\sigma\sqrt{T_2-T_1}}\right)$$
$$= N\left(\frac{k+u-2h_2-\mu(T_2-T_1)}{\sigma\sqrt{T_2-T_1}}\right)$$

and we are done.

Now, let $T_0 < T_1 < T_2 < T_3$ be different dates during the option life $[T_0, T_3]$.

Then, we can write

$$Q\left(X_{T_1} < a, X_{T_2} < b, X_{T_3} < c\right)$$

$$= \int_{-\infty}^{a}\int_{-\infty}^{b} \frac{\exp\left\{-\left[\frac{\left(\frac{x-\mu T_1}{\sigma\sqrt{T_1}}\right)^2 - 2\rho_{12}\left(\frac{x-\mu T_1}{\sigma\sqrt{T_1}}\right)\left(\frac{y-\mu T_2}{\sigma\sqrt{T_2}}\right) + \left(\frac{y-\mu T_2}{\sigma\sqrt{T_2}}\right)^2}{2\left(1-\rho_{12}^2\right)}\right]\right\}}{2\pi\sigma^2\sqrt{T_1 T_2(1-\rho_{12}^2)}}$$

$$\times N\left(\frac{c - y - \mu\left(T_3 - T_2\right)}{\sigma\sqrt{(T_3 - T_2)}}\right) dydx \tag{7.4}$$

where $\rho_{12} = \sqrt{T_1/T_2}$. With some algebra, it can be stated as

$$Q\left(X_{T_1} < a, X_{T_2} < b, X_{T_3} < c\right) = \int_{-\infty}^{\frac{a-\mu T_1}{\sigma\sqrt{T_1}}}\int_{-\infty}^{\frac{b-\mu T_2}{\sigma\sqrt{T_2}}}\int_{-\infty}^{\frac{c-\mu T_3}{\sigma\sqrt{T_3}}}$$

$$\frac{\exp\left\{\left[\frac{-x^2}{2} - \frac{1}{2}\left(\frac{y-\rho_{12}x}{\sqrt{(1-\rho_{12}^2)}}\right)^2 - \frac{1}{2}\left(\frac{z-\rho_{23}y}{\sqrt{(1-\rho_{23}^2)}}\right)^2\right]\right\}}{(2\pi)^{3/2}\sqrt{(1-\rho_{12}^2)(1-\rho_{23}^2)}} dzdydx \tag{7.5}$$

where

$$\rho_{23} = \sqrt{T_2/T_3}$$

This can be stated succinctly as

$$N_3\left(\frac{a-\mu T_1}{\sigma\sqrt{T_1}}, \frac{b-\mu T_2}{\sigma\sqrt{T_2}}, \frac{c-\mu T_3}{\sigma\sqrt{T_3}};\ \rho_{12}, \rho_{23}\right)$$

Now, let us write

$$\frac{x-\mu T_1}{\sigma\sqrt{T_1}} = u\left(\frac{y-\mu T_2}{\sigma\sqrt{T_2}}\right) = v\ \frac{c-\mu T_3}{\sigma\sqrt{T_3}} = z$$

and

$$\frac{c-y-\mu\left(T_3-T_2\right)}{\sigma\sqrt{(T_3-T_2)}}=\frac{c-\mu\left(T_3\right)-\left(y-\mu T_2\right)}{\sigma\sqrt{(T_3-T_2)}}$$

$$\frac{c-\mu T_3}{\sigma\sqrt{T_3}\sqrt{(1-T_2/T_3)}}-\frac{y-\mu T_2}{\sigma\sqrt{T_3}\sqrt{(1-T_2/T_3)}}$$

$$\frac{z}{\sqrt{(1-\rho_{23}^2)}}-\frac{\left(y-\mu T_2\right)\sqrt{T_2}}{\sigma\sqrt{T_2}\sqrt{T_3}\sqrt{(1-T_2/T_3)}}=\frac{z-\rho_{23}v}{\sqrt{(1-\rho_{23}^2)}}$$

Squared terms can be written as follows

$$\frac{-\frac{u^2}{2}+2uv\rho_{12}-\frac{v^2}{2}}{2\left(1-\rho_{12}^2\right)}$$

By adding

$$\frac{u^2\rho_{12}^2}{2(1-\rho_{12}^2)}-\frac{u^2\rho_{12}^2}{2(1-\rho_{12}^2)}$$

we can obtain

$$-\frac{u^2}{2}-\frac{\left(v-\rho_{12}u\right)^2}{2\left(1-\rho_{12}^2\right)}$$

since

$$\frac{-u^2}{2\left(1-\rho_{12}^2\right)}+\frac{u^2\rho_{12}^2}{2(1-\rho_{12}^2)}=-\frac{u^2(1-\rho_{12}^2)}{2\left(1-\rho_{12}^2\right)}=-\frac{u^2}{2}$$

Finally, it becomes

$$Q\left(X_{T_1}<a,X_{T_2}<b,X_{T_3}<c\right)=\int_{-\infty}^{\frac{a-\mu T_1}{\sigma\sqrt{T_1}}}\int_{-\infty}^{\frac{b-\mu T_2}{\sigma\sqrt{T_2}}}\int_{-\infty}^{\frac{c-\mu T_3}{\sigma\sqrt{T_3}}}$$

$$\times\frac{\exp\left\{\left[\frac{-u^2}{2}-\left(\frac{v-\rho_{12}u}{2\left(1-\rho_{12}^2\right)}\right)^2-\left(\frac{z-\rho_{23}v}{2\left(1-\rho_{23}^2\right)}\right)^2\right]\right\}}{(2\pi)^{3/2}\sqrt{(1-\rho_{12}^2)(1-\rho_{23}^2)}}dzdydx$$

$$=N_3\left(\frac{a-\mu T_1}{\sigma\sqrt{T_1}},\frac{b-\mu T_2}{\sigma\sqrt{T_2}},\frac{c-\mu T_3}{\sigma\sqrt{T_3}};\rho_{12},\rho_{23}\right)$$

For another time point $T_3 < T_4$

$$N_4\left(\frac{a-\mu T_1}{\sigma\sqrt{T_1}}, \frac{b-\mu T_2}{\sigma\sqrt{T_2}}, \frac{c-\mu T_3}{\sigma\sqrt{T_3}}, \frac{d-\mu T_4}{\sigma\sqrt{T_4}}; \rho_{12}, \rho_{23}, \rho_{34}\right)$$
$$= Q\left(X_{T_1} < a, X_{T_2} < b, X_{T_3} < c, X_{T_4} < d\right)$$
$$= \int_{-\infty}^{\frac{a-\mu T_1}{\sigma\sqrt{T_1}}} \int_{-\infty}^{\frac{b-\mu T_2}{\sigma\sqrt{T_2}}} \int_{-\infty}^{\frac{c-\mu T_3}{\sigma\sqrt{T_3}}} \int_{-\infty}^{\frac{d-\mu T_4}{\sigma\sqrt{T_4}}} dzdydxdw$$
$$\frac{\exp\left\{\left[\frac{-w^2}{2} - \left(\frac{x-\rho_{12}w}{2\left(1-\rho_{12}^2\right)}\right)^2 - \left(\frac{y-\rho_{23}x}{2\left(1-\rho_{23}^2\right)}\right)^2 - \left(\frac{z-\rho_{34}y}{2\left(1-\rho_{34}^2\right)}\right)^2\right]\right\}}{(2\pi)^{4/2}\sqrt{(1-\rho_{12}^2)(1-\rho_{23}^2)(1-\rho_{34}^2)}}$$
$$\rho_{34} = \sqrt{T_3/T_4} \tag{7.6}$$

and in the more general case, we can write

$$Q\left(X_{T_1} < x_1, X_{T_2} < x_2, X_{T_3} < x_3, \ldots X_{T_d} < x_d\right)$$
$$= N_d\left(\frac{x_1-\mu T_1}{\sigma\sqrt{T_1}}, \frac{x_2-\mu T_2}{\sigma\sqrt{T_2}}, \frac{x_3-\mu T_3}{\sigma\sqrt{T_3}}, \ldots \frac{x_d-\mu T_d}{\sigma\sqrt{T_4}};\right.$$
$$\left. \times\ \rho_{12}, \rho_{23}, \ldots \rho_{d-1,d}\right)$$
$$= \int_{-\infty}^{\frac{x_1-\mu T_1}{\sigma\sqrt{T_1}}} \int_{-\infty}^{\frac{x_2-\mu T_2}{\sigma\sqrt{T_2}}} \int_{-\infty}^{\frac{x_3-\mu T_3}{\sigma\sqrt{T_3}}} \cdots \int_{-\infty}^{\frac{x_d-\mu T_d}{\sigma\sqrt{T_4}}} dy_d dy_{d-1} \ldots dy_1$$
$$\times \frac{\exp\left\{\left[\frac{-y_1^2}{2} - \sum_{k=1}^{d-1}\left(\frac{y_{k+1}-\rho_{k,k+1}y_k}{2\left(1-\rho_{k,k+1}^2\right)}\right)^2\right]\right\}}{(2\pi)^{d/2}\sqrt{\left(1-\rho_{12}^2\right)\left(1-\rho_{23}^2\right)\ldots\left(1-\rho_{d-1,d}^2\right)}} \tag{7.7}$$

7.1.2. *Standard step-up-and-out put option*

The analytical valuation of d-dimensional step barriers requires a d-dimensional joint distribution of the maximum and terminal values of a geometric Brownian motion for step-up barriers and the minimum and terminal values of a geometric Brownian motion for step-down barriers, respectively (Guillaume, 2004).

Let us define four barriers for a standard step-up barrier option

$$H_1 < H_2 < H_3 < H_4$$

and 4 disjoint time intervals $[T_0, T_1][T_1, T_2][T_2, T_3][T_3, T_4]$. Assuming the option is put, we need the joint probability that the asset price will not hit the barrier H_1 in $[T_0, T_1]$, H_2 in $[T_1, T_2]\dots$ H_4 in $[T_3, T_{4,}]$ and the asset price is below the strike at maturity. This is the probability of

$$Q(M_0^1 < h_1, M_1^2 < h_2, M_2^3 < h_3, M_3^4 < h_4, X_4 < k)$$

$$X_T = \ln S_T/S_0 \quad k = \ln K/S_0 \quad h_i = \ln H_i/S_0 \quad M_i^j = \max_{t\in[T_i,T_j]} X_t$$

Let us consider first the 2-step case. We can write the probability as

$$\begin{aligned}
&Q\left(M_0^1 < h_1, M_1^2 < h_2, X_{T_2} < k\right) \\
&= E^Q\left\{1_{\{M_0^1<h_1,\ X_{T_1}<h_1\}} E^Q\left(1_{\{M_1^2<h_2,\ X_{T_2}<k\}} \mid X_{T_1}\right)\right\} \\
&= \int_{-\infty}^{h_1} \Psi(u)\Phi(u)du
\end{aligned}$$

where

$$\begin{aligned}
E^Q 1_{\{M_0^1<h_1,\ X_{T_1}<h_1\}} &= \Psi(u) \\
&= \frac{e^{-\frac{1}{2}\left(\frac{u-\mu T_1}{\sigma\sqrt{T_1}}\right)^2}}{\sigma\sqrt{2\pi T_1}} - e^{2\mu h_1/\sigma^2}\frac{e^{-\frac{1}{2}\left(\frac{u-2h_1-\mu T_1}{\sigma\sqrt{T_1}}\right)^2}}{\sigma\sqrt{2\pi T_1}}
\end{aligned}$$

$$\begin{aligned}
\Phi(u) &= E^Q\left(1_{\{M_1^2<h_2,\ X_{T_2}<k\}} \mid X_{T_1}\right) \\
&= N\left(\frac{k-u-\mu(T_2-T_1)}{\sigma\sqrt{T_2-T_1}}\right) \\
&\quad - e^{2\mu(h_2-u)/\sigma^2} N\left(\frac{k-2h_2+u-\mu(T_2-T_1)}{\sigma\sqrt{T_2-T_1}}\right)
\end{aligned}$$

Since

$$-\frac{1}{2}\left(\frac{u-\mu T_1}{\sigma\sqrt{T_1}}\right)^2 - \frac{2\mu u}{\sigma^2} = -\frac{1}{2}\left(\frac{u+\mu T_1}{\sigma\sqrt{T_1}}\right)^2$$

$$-\frac{1}{2}\left(\frac{u \pm 2h_\alpha - \mu T_1}{\sigma\sqrt{T_1}}\right)^2 + \frac{2\mu}{\sigma^2}\left(h_\lambda \mp h_\alpha - u\right)$$

$$= -\frac{1}{2}\left(\frac{u \pm 2h_\alpha + \mu T_1}{\sigma\sqrt{T_1}}\right)^2 + \frac{2\mu}{\sigma^2}\left(h_\lambda \pm h_\alpha\right)$$

and

$$\int_{-\infty}^{a}\int_{-\infty}^{b} \frac{e^{-\frac{1}{2}\left\{\left(\frac{u}{\sigma\sqrt{T_1}}\right)^2 + \left(\frac{v \mp u}{\sigma\sqrt{T_2 - T_1}}\right)^2\right\}}}{\sigma^2 2\pi\sqrt{T_1(T_2 - T_1)}} dv du$$

$$= N_2\left(\frac{a}{\sigma\sqrt{T_1}}, \frac{b}{\sigma\sqrt{T_2}}; \pm\rho_{12}\right)$$

the integral yields

$$N_2\left(\frac{h_1 - \mu T_1}{\sigma\sqrt{T_1}}, \frac{k - \mu T_2}{\sigma\sqrt{T_2}}; \rho_{12}\right)$$

$$- e^{\frac{2\mu h_2}{\sigma^2}} N_2\left(\frac{h_1 + \mu T_1}{\sigma\sqrt{T_1}}, \frac{k - 2h_2 - \mu T_2}{\sigma\sqrt{T_2}}; -\rho_{12}\right)$$

$$- e^{\frac{2\mu h_1}{\sigma^2}} N_2\left(\frac{-h_1 - \mu T_1}{\sigma\sqrt{T_1}}, \frac{k - 2h_1 - \mu T_2}{\sigma\sqrt{T_2}}; \rho_{12}\right)$$

$$+ e^{\frac{2\mu(h_2 - h_1)}{\sigma^2}} N_2\left(\frac{-h_1 + \mu T_1}{\sigma\sqrt{T_1}}, \frac{k - 2h_2 + 2h_1 - \mu T_2}{\sigma\sqrt{T_2}}; -\rho_{12}\right)$$

where $\rho_{12} = \sqrt{T_1/T_2}$. We can start by writing

$$\int_{-\infty}^{h_1} \left(\frac{e^{-\frac{1}{2}\left(\frac{u-\mu T_1}{\sigma\sqrt{T_1}}\right)^2}}{\sigma\sqrt{2\pi T_1}} - e^{2\mu h_1/\sigma^2} \frac{e^{-\frac{1}{2}\left(\frac{u-2h_1-\mu T_1}{\sigma\sqrt{T_1}}\right)^2}}{\sigma\sqrt{2\pi T_1}} \right)$$

$$\times \left[N\left(\frac{k-u-\mu(T_2-T_1)}{\sigma\sqrt{T_2-T_1}} \right) - e^{2\mu(h_2-u)/\sigma^2} \right.$$

$$\left. \times N\left(\frac{k-2h_2+u-\mu(T_2-T_1)}{\sigma\sqrt{T_2-T_1}} \right) \right] du$$

which will produce four different integrals and four bivariate cumulative distribution functions. The first integral is

$$\int_{-\infty}^{h_1} \left(\frac{e^{-\frac{1}{2}\left(\frac{u-\mu T_1}{\sigma\sqrt{T_1}}\right)^2}}{\sigma\sqrt{2\pi T_1}} \right) \left[N\left(\frac{k-u-\mu(T_2-T_1)}{\sigma\sqrt{T_2-T_1}} \right) \right] du$$

$$N\left(\frac{y-\rho x}{\sqrt{1-\rho^2}} \right) = N\left(\frac{k-u-\mu(T_2-T_1)}{\sigma\sqrt{T_2-T_1}} \right)$$

$$y = \frac{k-u-\mu(T_2-T_1)}{\sigma\sqrt{T_2-T_1}} \sqrt{1-\rho^2} + \rho x$$

Since

$$x = \frac{h_1-\mu T_1}{\sigma\sqrt{T_1}} \to y = \frac{k-\mu T_2}{\sigma\sqrt{T_2}}$$

we obtain the integral as

$$N_2\left(\frac{h_1-\mu T_1}{\sigma\sqrt{T_1}}, \frac{k-\mu T_2}{\sigma\sqrt{T_2}}; \rho_{12} \right)$$

The second integral is

$$-\int_{-\infty}^{h_1} \left(\frac{e^{-\frac{1}{2}\left(\frac{u-\mu T_1}{\sigma\sqrt{T_1}}\right)^2}}{\sigma\sqrt{2\pi T_1}} \right) \times \left[e^{2\mu(h_2-u)/\sigma^2} N\left(\frac{k-2h_2+u-\mu(T_2-T_1)}{\sigma\sqrt{T_2-T_1}} \right) \right] du$$

The minus term in the exponent $e^{2\mu(h_2-u)/\sigma^2}$ makes

$$\left(\frac{u+\mu T_1}{\sigma\sqrt{T_1}} \right)^2$$

So, $x = \frac{h_1+\mu T_1}{\sigma\sqrt{T_1}}$ and

$$y = \frac{k-2h_2+u-\mu(T_2-T_1)}{\sigma\sqrt{T_2-T_1}} \sqrt{1-\rho^2} + \rho x$$

and

$$y = \frac{k-2h_2-\mu T_2}{\sigma\sqrt{T_2}}$$

$$-e^{\frac{2\mu h_2}{\sigma^2}} N_2\left(\frac{h_1+\mu T_1}{\sigma\sqrt{T_1}}, \frac{k-2h_2-\mu T_2}{\sigma\sqrt{T_2}}; -\rho_{12} \right)$$

with $\rho = -\rho_{12}$. The last two integrations are implemented with the density and cumulative density functions:

$$-e^{2\mu h_1/\sigma^2} \frac{e^{-\frac{1}{2}\left(\frac{u-2h_1-\mu T_1}{\sigma\sqrt{T_1}}\right)^2}}{\sigma\sqrt{2\pi T_1}} N\left(\frac{k-u-\mu(T_2-T_1)}{\sigma\sqrt{T_2-T_1}} \right)$$

and

$$e^{2\mu h_1/\sigma^2} \frac{e^{-\frac{1}{2}\left(\frac{u-2h_1-\mu T_1}{\sigma\sqrt{T_1}}\right)^2}}{\sigma\sqrt{2\pi T_1}} N\left(\frac{k-2h_2+u-\mu(T_2-T_1)}{\sigma\sqrt{T_2-T_1}} \right)$$

in similar ways. We leave the last two equations (integrals) as exercises for the reader.

The next calculation is for the 3-step case. We consider the joint probability in the 3rd time step as:

$$Q\left(M_0^1 < h_1,\ M_1^2 < h_2,\ M_2^3 < h_3,\ X_{T_3} < k\right)$$

This is the conditional expectation of

$$E^Q\left\{1_{\{M_0^1<h_1, M_1^2<h_2, X_{T_2}<h_2\}} E^Q\left(1_{\{M_2^3<h_3, X_{T_3}<k\}} \mid X_{T_2}\right)\right\}$$

This can be written in integral form as

$$\begin{aligned} &\int_{-\infty}^{h_1}\int_{-\infty}^{h_2} \Psi^1(u,v)\,\Phi(v)\,dvdu - e^{\frac{2\mu}{\sigma^2}h_2}\int_{-\infty}^{h_1}\int_{-\infty}^{h_2} \Psi^2(u,v)\,\Phi(v)\,dvdu \\ &\quad - e^{\frac{2\mu}{\sigma^2}h_1}\int_{-\infty}^{-h_1}\int_{-\infty}^{h_2} \Psi^3(u,v)\,\Phi(v)\,dvdu \\ &\quad + e^{\frac{2\mu}{\sigma^2}(h_2-h_1)}\int_{-\infty}^{-h_1}\int_{-\infty}^{h_2} \Psi^4(u,v)\,\Phi(v)\,dvdu \end{aligned} \tag{7.8}$$

Since

$$\begin{aligned} 1_{\{M_2^3<h_3,\ X_{T_3}<k\}} &= P\left\{M_2^3 < h_3,\ X_{T_3} < k\right\} \\ &= P\left\{X_{T_3} < k\right\} - \left\{M_2^3 > h_3,\ X_{T_3} < k\right\} \end{aligned}$$

$$P\left\{X_{T_3} < k\right\} \to \ln\left(\frac{S_T}{S_{T_2}}\frac{S_{T_2}}{S_{T_1}}\frac{S_{T_1}}{S_0}\right) < \ln K/S_0$$

$$\ln\left(\frac{S_T}{S_{T_2}}\right) < \ln K/S_0 - v - u = \ln\frac{K}{S_0} - (v-u) - u$$

$$y < \ln K/S_0 - v$$

$$y < k - v$$

we obtain the cumulative distribution as

$$N\left(\frac{k - v - \mu(T_3 - T_2)}{\sigma\sqrt{T_3 - T_2}}\right)$$

Similarly, we can write

$$\ln\left(\frac{M_2^3}{S_{T_2}}\frac{S_{T_2}}{S_{T_1}}\frac{S_{T_1}}{S_0}\right) < \ln H_3/S_0$$

$$\ln\left(\frac{M_2^3}{S_{T_2}}\right) < \ln H_3/S_0 - (v-u) - u$$

$$x < h_3 - v$$

$$N\left(\frac{k - v - 2(h_3 - v) - \mu(T_3 - T_2)}{\sigma\sqrt{T_3 - T_2}}\right)$$

$$= N\left(\frac{k - 2h_3 + v - \mu(T_3 - T_2)}{\sigma\sqrt{T_3 - T_2}}\right)$$

Hence, $\Phi(v)$ is

$$\Phi(v) = N\left(\frac{k - v - \mu(T_3 - T_2)}{\sigma\sqrt{T_3 - T_2}}\right)$$

$$-e^{\frac{2\mu}{\sigma^2}(h_3 - v)} N\left(\frac{k - 2h_3 + v - \mu(T_3 - T_2)}{\sigma\sqrt{T_3 - T_2}}\right)$$

Now, for density functions, we can write

$$1_{\left\{M_0^1 < h_1,\ M_1^2 < h_2,\ X_{T_2} < h_2\right\}} = P\left(M_0^1 < h_1, M_1^2 < h_2,\ X_{T_2} < h_2\right)$$

$$P\left(M_0^1 < h_1, X_{T_1} < h_1\right)$$

$$= \frac{1}{\sigma\sqrt{2\pi T_1}} e^{-\frac{1}{2}\left(\frac{u - \mu T_1}{\sigma\sqrt{T_1}}\right)^2} - e^{\frac{2\mu h_1}{\sigma^2}} \frac{1}{\sigma\sqrt{2\pi T_1}} e^{-\frac{1}{2}\left(\frac{u - 2h_1 - \mu T_1}{\sigma\sqrt{T_1}}\right)^2}$$

$$P\left(M_1^2 < h_2,\ X_{T_2} < h_2 \,|X_{T_1} \in dx_1\right)$$

$$= P\left(X_{T_2} < h_2 \,|X_{T_1} \in dx_1\right) - P\left(M_1^2 > h_2,\ X_{T_2} < h_2 \,|X_{T_1} \in dx_1\right)$$

$$= \frac{1}{\sigma\sqrt{2\pi(T_2 - T_1)}} e^{-\frac{1}{2}\left(\frac{v - u - \mu(T_2 - T_1)}{\sigma\sqrt{(T_2 - T_1)}}\right)^2}$$

$$- e^{\frac{2\mu(h_2 - u)}{\sigma^2}} \frac{1}{\sigma\sqrt{2\pi(T_2 - T_1)}} e^{-\frac{1}{2}\left(\frac{v + u - 2h_2 - \mu(T_2 - T_1)}{\sigma\sqrt{(T_2 - T_1)}}\right)^2}$$

where $X_{T_2} = \ln S_{T_2}/S_0 = v$.

Here, we have used a similar argument:

$$P\left(v < h_2 - u, M_1^2 < h_2 - u\right)$$

$$\ln\left(\frac{M_1^2}{S_{T_1}}\frac{S_{T_1}}{S_0}\right) < \ln H_2/S_0$$

$$x < h_2 - u$$

$$\left(\frac{1}{\sigma\sqrt{2\pi T_1}}e^{-\frac{1}{2}\left(\frac{u-\mu T_1}{\sigma\sqrt{T_1}}\right)^2} - e^{\frac{2\mu h_1}{\sigma^2}}\frac{1}{\sigma\sqrt{2\pi T_1}}e^{-\frac{1}{2}\left(\frac{u-2h_1-\mu T_1}{\sigma\sqrt{T_1}}\right)^2}\right)$$

$$\left(\frac{1}{\sigma\sqrt{2\pi(T_2-T_1)}}e^{-\frac{1}{2}\left(\frac{v-u-\mu(T_2-T_1)}{\sigma\sqrt{(T_2-T_1)}}\right)^2}\right.$$

$$\left. - e^{\frac{2\mu(h_2-u)}{\sigma^2}}\frac{1}{\sigma\sqrt{2\pi(T_2-T_1)}}e^{-\frac{1}{2}\left(\frac{v+u-2h_2-\mu(T_2-T_1)}{\sigma\sqrt{(T_2-T_1)}}\right)^2}\right)$$

The integral upper limits are h_1 an d h_2. After finding the relevant densities, we can multiply each one with another and calculate the bivariate densities. The multiplications are presented in the following four density functions without the exponential coefficients. The first one is

$$\frac{1}{\sigma\sqrt{2\pi T_1}}e^{-\frac{1}{2}\left(\frac{u-\mu T_1}{\sigma\sqrt{T_1}}\right)^2}\frac{1}{\sigma\sqrt{2\pi(T_2-T_1)}}e^{-\frac{1}{2}\left(\frac{v-u-\mu(T_2-T_1)}{\sigma\sqrt{(T_2-T_1)}}\right)^2}$$

$$\Psi^1(u,v) = \frac{e^{-\frac{1}{2}\left\{\left(\frac{u-\mu T_1}{\sigma\sqrt{T_1}}\right)^2+\left(\frac{v-u-\mu(T_2-T_1)}{\sigma\sqrt{T_2-T_1}}\right)^2\right\}}}{\sigma^2 2\pi\sqrt{T_1(T_2-T_1)}}$$

The second one is

$$-\frac{1}{\sigma\sqrt{2\pi T_1}}e^{-\frac{1}{2}\left(\frac{u-\mu T_1}{\sigma\sqrt{T_1}}\right)^2}e^{\frac{2\mu(h_2-u)}{\sigma^2}}\frac{1}{\sigma\sqrt{2\pi(T_2-T_1)}}$$

$$\times e^{-\frac{1}{2}\left(\frac{v+u-2h_2-\mu(T_2-T_1)}{\sigma\sqrt{(T_2-T_1)}}\right)^2}$$

With $e^{\frac{-2\mu u}{\sigma^2}}$ the first term becomes

$$-\frac{1}{2}\left(\frac{u+\mu T_1}{\sigma\sqrt{T_1}}\right)^2$$

with coefficient $e^{\frac{2\mu(h_2)}{\sigma^2}}$

$$\Psi^2(u,v) = \frac{e^{-\frac{1}{2}\left\{\left(\frac{u+\mu T_1}{\sigma\sqrt{T_1}}\right)^2+\left(\frac{v+u-2h_2-\mu(T_2-T_1)}{\sigma\sqrt{T_2-T_1}}\right)^2\right\}}}{\sigma^2 2\pi\sqrt{T_1(T_2-T_1)}}$$

The third term is

$$-e^{\frac{2\mu h_1}{\sigma^2}}\frac{1}{\sigma\sqrt{2\pi T_1}}e^{-\frac{1}{2}\left(\frac{u-2h_1-\mu T_1}{\sigma\sqrt{T_1}}\right)^2}\frac{1}{\sigma\sqrt{2\pi(T_2-T_1)}}e^{-\frac{1}{2}\left(\frac{v-u-\mu(T_2-T_1)}{\sigma\sqrt{(T_2-T_1)}}\right)^2}$$

Since the upper integral limit is h_1, this becomes

$$e^{-\frac{1}{2}\left(\frac{-h_1-\mu T_1}{\sigma\sqrt{T_1}}\right)^2}$$

So, it can start from $-h_1$. The second term must be $v-u \to v-h_1$, but since u is $-h_1$, we must add $-2h_1$. Therefore, the density is

$$\Psi^3(u,v) = \frac{e^{-\frac{1}{2}\left\{\left(\frac{u-\mu T_1}{\sigma\sqrt{T_1}}\right)^2+\left(\frac{v-u-2h_1-\mu(T_2-T_1)}{\sigma\sqrt{T_2-T_1}}\right)^2\right\}}}{\sigma^2 2\pi\sqrt{T_1(T_2-T_1)}}$$

with coefficient $e^{\frac{2\mu h_1}{\sigma^2}}$.

The last one is

$$e^{\frac{2\mu h_1}{\sigma^2}}\frac{1}{\sigma\sqrt{2\pi T_1}}e^{-\frac{1}{2}\left(\frac{u-2h_1-\mu T_1}{\sigma\sqrt{T_1}}\right)^2}e^{\frac{2\mu(h_2-u)}{\sigma^2}}\frac{1}{\sigma\sqrt{2\pi(T_2-T_1)}}$$

$$e^{-\frac{1}{2}\left(\frac{v+u-2h_2-\mu(T_2-T_1)}{\sigma\sqrt{(T_2-T_1)}}\right)^2}$$

Since

$$-\frac{1}{2}\left(\frac{u \pm 2h_\alpha - \mu T_1}{\sigma\sqrt{T_1}}\right)^2 + \frac{2\mu}{\sigma^2}(h_\lambda \mp h_\alpha - u)$$

$$= -\frac{1}{2}\left(\frac{u \pm 2h_\alpha + \mu T_1}{\sigma\sqrt{T_1}}\right)^2 + \frac{2\mu}{\sigma^2}(h_\lambda \pm h_\alpha)$$

$$-\frac{1}{2}\left(\frac{u - 2h_1 - \mu T_1}{\sigma\sqrt{T_1}}\right)^2 + \frac{2\mu}{\sigma^2}(h_2 + h_1 - u)$$

$$= -\frac{1}{2}\left(\frac{u - 2h_1 + \mu T_1}{\sigma\sqrt{T_1}}\right)^2 + \frac{2\mu}{\sigma^2}(h_2 - h_1)$$

By adding and subtracting h_1, we obtain

$$\left(\frac{2\mu}{\sigma^2}(h_2 - h_1 + 2h_1 - u)\right) = \frac{2\mu}{\sigma^2}(h_2 - h_1) + \frac{2\mu}{\sigma^2}(2h_1 - u)$$

This makes

$$= -\frac{1}{2}\left(\frac{u - 2h_1 + \mu T_1}{\sigma\sqrt{T_1}}\right)^2 + \frac{2\mu}{\sigma^2}(h_2 - h_1)$$

and

$$e^{\frac{2\mu h_1}{\sigma^2}} \frac{1}{\sigma\sqrt{2\pi T_1}} e^{-\frac{1}{2}\left(\frac{u-2h_1+\mu T_1}{\sigma\sqrt{T_1}}\right)^2} e^{\frac{2\mu(h_2-u)}{\sigma^2}} \frac{1}{\sigma\sqrt{2\pi(T_2-T_1)}}$$

$$e^{-\frac{1}{2}\left(\frac{v+u-2h_2+2h_1-2h_1-\mu(T_2-T_1)}{\sigma\sqrt{(T_2-T_1)}}\right)^2}$$

$$e^{\frac{2\mu h_1}{\sigma^2}} \frac{1}{\sigma\sqrt{2\pi T_1}} e^{-\frac{1}{2}\left(\frac{u-2h_1+\mu T_1}{\sigma\sqrt{T_1}}\right)^2} e^{\frac{2\mu(h_2-u)}{\sigma^2}} \frac{1}{\sigma\sqrt{2\pi(T_2-T_1)}}$$

$$e^{-\frac{1}{2}\left(\frac{v-2h_2+2h_1-\mu T_2+u-2h_1+\mu T_1)}{\sigma\sqrt{(T_2-T_1)}}\right)^2}$$

Then, once again, the first integral upper limit is $-h_1$, and the density is

$$\frac{1}{2}\left\{\left(\frac{u + \mu T_1}{\sigma\sqrt{T_1}}\right)^2\right\}$$

Since the second term is

$$\frac{1}{2}\left(\frac{v+u-2h_2-\mu(T_2-T_1)}{\sigma\sqrt{(T_2-T_1)}}\right)^2$$

$$e^{-\frac{1}{2}\left(\frac{v-2h_2+2h_1-\mu T_2+u-2h_1+\mu T_1)}{\sigma\sqrt{(T_2-T_1)}}\right)^2}$$

the densities are

$$\frac{u+\mu T_1}{\sigma\sqrt{T_1}}=\frac{-h_1+\mu T_1}{\sigma\sqrt{T_1}}$$
$$\frac{v-2h_2+2h_1-\mu T_2}{\sigma\sqrt{T_2}}=\frac{-h_2+2h_1-\mu T_2}{\sigma\sqrt{T_2}}$$

and u is $-h_1$, we have to add $2h_1$ to make it positive. Therefore, the last density can be stated as

$$\Psi^4(u,v)=\frac{e^{-\frac{1}{2}\left\{\left(\frac{u+\mu T_1}{\sigma\sqrt{T_1}}\right)^2+\left(\frac{v+u-2h_2+2h_1-\mu(T_2-T_1)}{\sigma\sqrt{T_2-T_1}}\right)^2\right\}}}{\sigma^2 2\pi\sqrt{T_1(T_2-T_1)}}$$

where the coefficient is $e^{\frac{2\mu}{\sigma^2}(h_2-h_1)}$

Using identities

$$-\frac{1}{2}\left\{\left(\frac{u\pm\mu T_1}{\sigma\sqrt{T_1}}\right)^2+\left(\frac{v\pm u\pm 2h_\beta\pm 2h_\alpha-\mu(T_2-T_1)}{\sigma\sqrt{T_2-T_1}}\right)^2\right\}$$

$$+\frac{2\mu}{\sigma^2}(h_\lambda\mp h_\beta\mp h_\alpha-v)$$

$$=-\frac{1}{2}\left\{\left(\frac{u\mp\mu T_1}{\sigma\sqrt{T_1}}\right)^2+\left(\frac{v\pm u\pm 2h_\beta\pm 2h_\alpha+\mu(T_2-T_1)}{\sigma\sqrt{T_2-T_1}}\right)^2\right\}$$

$$+\frac{2\mu}{\sigma^2}(h_\lambda\pm h_\beta\pm h_\alpha)$$

and

$$\int_{-\infty}^{a}\int_{-\infty}^{b}\int_{-\infty}^{c}\frac{e^{-\frac{1}{2}\left\{\left(\frac{u}{\sigma\sqrt{T_1}}\right)^2+\left(\frac{v\pm u}{\sigma\sqrt{T_2-T_1}}\right)^2+\left(\frac{w\pm v}{\sigma\sqrt{T_3-T_2}}\right)^2\right\}}}{\sigma^3(2\pi)^{3/2}\sqrt{T_1(T_2-T_1)(T_3-T_2)}}dwdvdu$$

$$= N_3\left(\frac{a}{\sigma\sqrt{T_1}},\frac{b}{\sigma\sqrt{T_2}},\frac{c}{\sigma\sqrt{T_3}};\mp\rho_{12},\mp\rho_{23}\right) \tag{7.9}$$

we can write the probability of

$$Q\left(M_0^1<h_1,\ M_1^2<h_2,\ M_2^3<h_3,\ X_{T_3}<k\right)$$

as four different integrals in an expression composed of 8 terms involving trivariate Gaussian cumulative distribution. The formula is

$$N_3\left(\frac{h_1-\mu T_1}{\sigma\sqrt{T_1}},\frac{h_2-\mu T_2}{\sigma\sqrt{T_2}},\frac{k-\mu T_3}{\sigma\sqrt{T_3}};\rho_{12},\rho_{23}\right)$$
$$-e^{\frac{2\mu h_2}{\sigma^2}}N_3\left(\frac{h_1+\mu T_1}{\sigma\sqrt{T_1}},\frac{-h_2-\mu T_2}{\sigma\sqrt{T_2}},\frac{k-2h_2-\mu T_3}{\sigma\sqrt{T_3}};-\rho_{12},\rho_{23}\right)$$
$$-e^{\frac{2\mu h_1}{\sigma^2}}N_3\left(\frac{-h_1-\mu T_1}{\sigma\sqrt{T_1}},\frac{h_2-2h_1-\mu T_2}{\sigma\sqrt{T_2}},\frac{k-2h_1-\mu T_3}{\sigma\sqrt{T_3}};\rho_{12},\rho_{23}\right)$$
$$+e^{\frac{2\mu(h_2-h_1)}{\sigma^2}}N_3\left(\frac{-h_1+\mu T_1}{\sigma\sqrt{T_1}},\frac{-h_2+2h_1-\mu T_2}{\sigma\sqrt{T_2}}\frac{k-2h_2+2h_1-\mu T_3}{\sigma\sqrt{T_3}};-\rho_{12},\rho_{23}\right)$$
$$-e^{\frac{2\mu h_3}{\sigma^2}}N_3\left(\frac{h_1+\mu T_1}{\sigma\sqrt{T_1}},\frac{h_2+\mu T_2}{\sigma\sqrt{T_2}},\frac{k-2h_3-\mu T_3}{\sigma\sqrt{T_3}};\rho_{12},-\rho_{23}\right)$$
$$+e^{\frac{2\mu(h_3-h_2)}{\sigma^2}}N_3\left(\frac{h_1-\mu T_1}{\sigma\sqrt{T_1}},\frac{-h_2+\mu T_2}{\sigma\sqrt{T_2}},\frac{k+2h_2-2h_3-\mu T_3}{\sigma\sqrt{T_3}};\ -\rho_{12},-\rho_{23}\right)$$
$$+e^{\frac{2\mu(h_3-h_1)}{\sigma^2}}$$
$$N_3\left(\frac{-h_1+\mu T_1}{\sigma\sqrt{T_1}},\frac{h_2-2h_1+\mu T_2}{\sigma\sqrt{T_2}},\frac{k+2h_1-2h_3-\mu T_3}{\sigma\sqrt{T_3}};\rho_{12},-\rho_{23}\right)$$
$$-e^{\frac{2\mu(h_3-h_2+h_1)}{\sigma^2}}$$
$$N_3\left(\frac{-h_1-\mu T_1}{\sigma\sqrt{T_1}},\frac{-h_2+2h_1+\mu T_2}{\sigma\sqrt{T_2}},\frac{k-2h_3+2h_2-2h_1-\mu T_3}{\sigma\sqrt{T_3}};\ -\rho_{12},\ -\rho_{23}\right) \tag{7.10}$$

where

$$\int_{-\infty}^{a}\int_{-\infty}^{b}\int_{-\infty}^{c}\frac{e^{-\frac{x^2}{2}-\frac{(y-\rho_{12}x)^2}{2(1-\rho_{12}^2)}-\frac{(z-\rho_{23}y)^2}{2(1-\rho_{23}^2)}}}{(2\pi)^{3/2}\sqrt{(1-\rho_{12}^2)(1-\rho_{23}^2)}}dzdydx$$

$$= N_3\left(a,b,c;\rho_{12},\rho_{23}\right)$$

We can quickly evaluate the step-up and out put option with this formula, including three different barrier levels $H_1 < H_2 < H_3$.

Let's do the first integral:

$$\int_{-\infty}^{h_1}\int_{-\infty}^{h_2}\Psi^1\left(u,v\right)\Phi\left(v\right)dvdu$$

$$= \int_{-\infty}^{h_1}\int_{-\infty}^{h_2}\frac{e^{-\frac{1}{2}\left\{\left(\frac{u-\mu T_1}{\sigma\sqrt{T_1}}\right)^2+\left(\frac{v-u-\mu(T_2-T_1)}{\sigma\sqrt{T_2-T_1}}\right)^2\right\}}}{\sigma^2 2\pi\sqrt{T_1(T_2-T_1)}}$$

$$\times N\left(\frac{k-v-\mu(T_3-T_2)}{\sigma\sqrt{T_3-T_2}}\right)dvdu$$

Taking the squares yields

$$-\frac{1}{2}\left\{\left(\frac{u-\mu T_1}{\sigma\sqrt{T_1}}\right)^2+\left(\frac{v-u-\mu\left(T_2-T_1\right)}{\sigma\sqrt{T_2-T_1}}\right)^2\right\}$$

$$= -\frac{1}{2}\left\{x^2+\left(\frac{v-\mu T_2-(u-\mu T_1)}{\sigma\sqrt{T_2-T_1}}\right)^2\right\}$$

$$-\frac{1}{2}\left(\frac{v-\mu T_2-(u-\mu T_1)}{\sigma\sqrt{T_2-T_1}}\right)^2$$

$$= -\frac{1}{2}\left\{\left(\frac{u-\mu T_1}{\sigma\sqrt{T_2-T_1}}\right)^2+\left(\frac{v-\mu T_2}{\sigma\sqrt{T_2-T_1}}\right)^2-2\frac{(u-\mu T_1)(v-\mu T_2)}{\sigma^2 T_2\left(1-\rho_{12}^2\right)}\right\}$$

$$= -\frac{1}{2}\left\{\frac{\left(u-\mu T_1\right)^2}{\sigma^2 T_2\left(1-\rho_{12}^2\right)}+\frac{\left(v-\mu T_2\right)^2}{\sigma^2 T_2\left(1-\rho_{12}^2\right)}-2\frac{\left(u-\mu T_1\right)\left(v-\mu T_2\right)}{\sigma^2 T_2\left(1-\rho_{12}^2\right)}\right\}$$

$$= -\frac{1}{2}\left\{\frac{\left(u-\mu T_1\right)^2 T_1}{\sigma^2 T_1 T_2(1-\rho_{12}^2)}+\frac{\left(v-\mu T_2\right)^2}{\sigma^2 T_2(1-\rho_{12}^2)}-2\frac{\left(u-\mu T_1\right)\left(v-\mu T_2\right)T_1}{\sigma^2 T_1 T_2(1-\rho_{12}^2)}\right\}$$

Manipulating further yields

$$-\frac{1}{2}\left\{\frac{\left(\frac{u-\mu T_1}{\sigma\sqrt{T_1}}\right)^2\rho_{12}^2}{(1-\rho_{12}^2)}+\frac{\left(\frac{v-\mu T_2}{\sigma\sqrt{T_2}}\right)^2}{(1-\rho_{12}^2)}-2\frac{(u-\mu T_1)(v-\mu T_2)T_1}{\sigma\sqrt{T_1}\sigma\sqrt{T_2}\sqrt{T_1}\sqrt{T_2}(1-\rho_{12}^2)}\right\}$$

$$=-\frac{1}{2}\left\{\frac{\left(\frac{u-\mu T_1}{\sigma\sqrt{T_1}}\right)^2\rho_{12}^2}{(1-\rho_{12}^2)}+\frac{\left(\frac{v-\mu T_2}{\sigma\sqrt{T_2}}\right)^2}{(1-\rho_{12}^2)}-2\frac{(u-\mu T_1)(v-\mu T_2)\sqrt{T_1}}{\sigma\sqrt{T_1}\sigma\sqrt{T_2}(1-\rho_{12}^2)\sqrt{T_2}}\right\}$$

$$=-\frac{1}{2}\left\{\frac{(x)^2\rho_{12}^2}{(1-\rho_{12}^2)}+\frac{(y)^2}{(1-\rho_{12}^2)}-2\frac{xy\rho_{12}}{(1-\rho_{12}^2)}\right\}$$

$$-\frac{1}{2}\left\{\frac{(y-\rho_{12}x)^2}{(1-\rho_{12}^2)}\right\}$$

The denominator will be as

$$\sigma^2 2\pi\sqrt{T_1(T_2-T_1)}\sigma\sqrt{T_3-T_2}\sigma\sqrt{2\pi}$$
$$=\sigma^3(2\pi)^{3/2}\sqrt{T_1}\sqrt{T_2}\sqrt{T_3}\sqrt{(1-\rho_{12}^2)(1-\rho_{23}^2)}$$

Then, it is induced into the form of

$$\int_{-\infty}^{h_1}\int_{-\infty}^{h_2}\Psi^1(u,v)\,\Phi(v)\,dvdu$$

$$=\int_{-\infty}^{h_1}\int_{-\infty}^{h_2}\frac{e^{-\frac{1}{2}\left\{\left(\frac{u-\mu T_1}{\sigma\sqrt{T_1}}\right)^2+\frac{\left(\frac{u-\mu T_1}{\sigma\sqrt{T_1}}\right)^2+\left(\frac{v-\mu T_2}{\sigma\sqrt{T_2}}\right)^2-2\rho_{12}\left(\frac{u-\mu T_1}{\sigma\sqrt{T_1}}\right)\left(\frac{v-\mu T_2}{\sigma\sqrt{T_2}}\right)}{(1-\rho_{12}^2)}\right\}}}{\sigma^2 2\pi\sqrt{T_1T_2(1-\rho_{12}^2)}}$$
$$\times N\left(\frac{k-v-\mu(T_3-T_2)}{\sigma\sqrt{T_3-T_2}}\right)dvdu$$

This integral can be further manipulated and reduced to the form

$$Q\left(X_{T_1}<h_1,X_{T_2}<h_2,X_{T_3}<k\right)$$
$$=\int_{-\infty}^{\frac{h_1-\mu T_1}{\sigma\sqrt{T_1}}}\int_{-\infty}^{\frac{h_2-\mu T_2}{\sigma\sqrt{T_2}}}\int_{-\infty}^{\frac{k-\mu T_3}{\sigma\sqrt{T_3}}}\frac{e^{\left\{-\frac{1}{2}x^2-\frac{(y-\rho_{12}x)^2}{2(1-\rho_{12}^2)}-\frac{(z-\rho_{23}y)^2}{2(1-\rho_{23}^2)}\right\}}}{(2\pi)^{3/2}\sqrt{(1-\rho_{12}^2)(1-\rho_{23}^2)}}dzdydx$$

where

$$x = \frac{u - \mu T_1}{\sigma\sqrt{T_1}} \quad du = dx\sigma\sqrt{T_1}$$

$$y = \frac{v - \mu T_2}{\sigma\sqrt{T_2}} \quad dv = dy\sigma\sqrt{T_2}$$

$$z = \frac{w - \mu T_3}{\sigma\sqrt{T_3}} \quad dz = dw\sigma\sqrt{T_3}$$

which is equal to

$$N_3(a, b, c; \rho_{12}, \rho_{23})$$

By squaring

$$-\frac{1}{2}\left(\frac{k - v - \mu\,(T_3 - T_2)}{\sigma\sqrt{T_3 - T_2}}\right)^2 = -\frac{1}{2}\left(\frac{w - \mu T_3 - (v - \mu T_2)}{\sigma\sqrt{T_3 - T_2}}\right)^2$$

$$= -\frac{1}{2}\left\{\frac{(w - \mu T_3)^2}{\sigma^2 T_3\left(1 - \frac{T_2}{T_3}\right)} + \frac{(v - \mu T_2)^2}{\sigma^2 T_3\left(1 - \frac{T_2}{T_3}\right)} - 2\frac{(w - \mu T_3)(v - \mu T_2)}{\sigma^2 T_3\left(1 - \frac{T_2}{T_3}\right)}\right\}$$

$$-\frac{1}{2}\left\{\frac{\left(\frac{(w-\mu T_3)}{\sigma\sqrt{T_3}}\right)^2}{\left(1 - \rho_{23}^2\right)} + \frac{(v - \mu T_2)^2 T_2}{\sigma^2 T_2 T_3\left(1 - \rho_{23}^2\right)}\right.$$

$$\left.-2\frac{(w - \mu T_3)(v - \mu T_2)\sqrt{T_2}}{\sigma^2\sqrt{T_3}\sqrt{T_3}\sqrt{T_2}\left(1 - \rho_{23}^2\right)}\right\}$$

$$-\frac{1}{2}\left\{\frac{\left(\frac{(w-\mu T_3)}{\sigma\sqrt{T_3}}\right)^2}{\left(1 - \rho_{23}^2\right)} + \frac{\left(\frac{(v-\mu T_2)}{\sigma\sqrt{T_2}}\right)^2\rho_{23}^2}{\left(1 - \rho_{23}^2\right)} - 2\frac{\frac{(w-\mu T_3)}{\sigma\sqrt{T_3}})\frac{(v-\mu T_2)}{\sigma\sqrt{T_2}}\rho_{23}}{\left(1 - \rho_{23}^2\right)}\right\}$$

$$= -\frac{1}{2}\left\{\frac{(z - y\rho_{23})^2}{\left(1 - \rho_{23}^2\right)}\right\}$$

Therefore, the first integral is

$$N_3\left(\frac{h_1 - \mu T_1}{\sigma\sqrt{T_1}}, \frac{h_2 - \mu T_2}{\sigma\sqrt{T_2}}, \frac{k - \mu T_3}{\sigma\sqrt{T_3}}; \rho_{12}, \rho_{23}\right)$$

As for the second integral

$$\frac{e^{-\frac{1}{2}\left\{\left(\frac{u+\mu T_1}{\sigma\sqrt{T_1}}\right)^2+\left(\frac{v+u-2h_2-\mu(T_2-T_1)}{\sigma\sqrt{T_2-T_1}}\right)^2\right\}}}{\sigma^2 2\pi\sqrt{T_1(T_2-T_1)}} N\left(\frac{k-v-\mu(T_3-T_2)}{\sigma\sqrt{T_3-T_2}}\right)$$

$$= e^{-\frac{1}{2}\left\{\left(\frac{u+\mu T_1}{\sigma\sqrt{T_1}}\right)^2+\left(\frac{v+u-2h_2-\mu(T_2-T_1)}{\sigma\sqrt{T_2-T_1}}\right)^2+\left(\frac{w-v-\mu(T_3-T_2)}{\sigma\sqrt{T_3-T_2}}\right)^2\right\}}$$

$$-\frac{1}{2}\left\{\left(\frac{u+\mu T_1}{\sigma\sqrt{T_1}}\right)^2+\left(\frac{v+u-2h_2-\mu(T_2-T_1)}{\sigma\sqrt{T_2-T_1}}\right)^2\right.$$

$$\left.+\left(\frac{w-v-\mu(T_3-T_2)}{\sigma\sqrt{T_3-T_2}}\right)^2\right\}$$

$$= -\frac{1}{2}\left\{x^2+\left(\frac{(v-2h_2-\mu T_2)+(u+\mu T_1))}{\sigma\sqrt{T_2}\sqrt{1-\rho_{12}^2}}\right)^2\right.$$

$$\left.+\left(\frac{w-\mu T_3-2h_2+2h_2-(v-\mu T_2)}{\sigma\sqrt{T_3}\sqrt{1-\rho_{23}^2}}\right)^2\right\}$$

where

$$x=\frac{u+\mu T_1}{\sigma\sqrt{T_1}} \quad y=\frac{(v-2h_2-\mu T_2)}{\sigma\sqrt{T_2}} \quad z=\frac{w-2h_2-\mu T_3}{\sigma\sqrt{T_3}}$$

Taking the squares and with some algebra, we obtain the integral as

$$-\frac{1}{2}\left(\frac{(v-2h_2-\mu T_2)+(u+\mu T_1))}{\sigma\sqrt{T_2}\sqrt{1-\rho_{12}^2}}\right)^2 = -\frac{1}{2}\frac{y^2+x^2\rho_{12}^2+2xy\rho_{12}}{1-\rho_{12}^2}$$

$$= -\frac{(y+\rho_{12}x)^2}{2(1-\rho_{12}^2)}-\frac{1}{2}\left(\frac{w-\mu T_3-(v-\mu T_2)}{\sigma\sqrt{T_3}\sqrt{1-\rho_{23}^2}}\right)^2$$

$$= -\frac{\left(\frac{w-\mu T_3)}{\sigma\sqrt{T_3}}\right)^2 + \left(\frac{y\sigma\sqrt{T_2}+2h_2)}{\sigma\sqrt{T_3}}\right)^2 - 2\left(\frac{w-\mu T_3)}{\sigma\sqrt{T_3}}\right)\left(\frac{y\sigma\sqrt{T_2}+2h_2)}{\sigma\sqrt{T_3}}\right)}{2\left(1-\rho_{23}^2\right)}$$

$$= -\frac{z^2 + y^2\rho_{23}^2 + \frac{4h_2^2}{\sigma^2 T_3} + \frac{4y\sigma\sqrt{T_2}h_2}{\sigma\sqrt{T_3}} - 2zy\rho_{23} - \frac{4zh_2}{\sigma T_3}}{2\left(1-\rho_{23}^2\right)}$$

$$= -\frac{1}{2\left(1-\rho_{23}^2\right)}\left(z - y\rho_{23} - \frac{2h_2}{\sigma\sqrt{T_3}}\right)^2$$

So, the last variable's upper integral limit is

$$\frac{k-2h_2-\mu T_3}{\sigma\sqrt{T_3}}$$

$$\int_{-\infty}^{\frac{h_1+\mu T_1}{\sigma\sqrt{T_1}}}\int_{-\infty}^{\frac{-h_2-\mu T_2}{\sigma\sqrt{T_2}}}\int_{-\infty}^{\frac{k-2h_2-\mu T_3}{\sigma\sqrt{T_3}}} \frac{e^{\left\{-\frac{1}{2}x^2 - \frac{(y+\rho_{12}x)^2}{2(1-\rho_{12}^2)} - \frac{(z-\rho_{22}y)^2}{2(1-\rho_{23}^2)}\right\}}}{(2\pi)^{3/2}\sqrt{(1-\rho_{12}^2)(1-\rho_{23}^2)}} dzdydx$$

$$\sigma^2 2\pi\sqrt{2\pi}\sigma\sqrt{T_3-T_2}\sqrt{T_1(T_2-T_1)} \rightarrow (2\pi)^{3/2}\sqrt{(1-\rho_{12}^2)(1-\rho_{23}^2)}$$

and the correlation coefficient ρ_{12} is $-\sqrt{\frac{T_1}{T_2}}$.

Therefore, the second integral is

$$-e^{\frac{2\mu h_2}{\sigma^2}} N_3\left(\frac{h_1+\mu T_1}{\sigma\sqrt{T_1}}, \frac{-h_2-\mu T_2}{\sigma\sqrt{T_2}}, \frac{k-2h_2-\mu T_3}{\sigma\sqrt{T_3}}; -\rho_{12}, \rho_{23}\right)$$

We may apply similar steps for the remaining six integrals, and we leave them as exercises to the reader.

The probability $Q\left(X_{T_1} < h_1, X_{T_2} < h_2, X_{T_3} < k\right)$ is given by Guillaume (2004) as

$$N_3\left(\frac{h_1-\mu T_1}{\sigma\sqrt{T_1}}, \frac{h_2-\mu T_2}{\sigma\sqrt{T_2}}, \frac{k-\mu T_3}{\sigma\sqrt{T_3}}; \rho_{12}, \rho_{23}\right)$$
$$- e^{\frac{2\mu h_2}{\sigma^2}} N_3\left(\frac{h_1+\mu T_1}{\sigma\sqrt{T_1}}, \frac{-h_2-\mu T_2}{\sigma\sqrt{T_2}}, \frac{k-2h_2-\mu T_3}{\sigma\sqrt{T_3}}; -\rho_{12}, \rho_{23}\right)$$

$$
\begin{aligned}
&- e^{\frac{2\mu h_1}{\sigma^2}} N_3\left(\frac{-h_1-\mu T_1}{\sigma\sqrt{T_1}}, \frac{h_2-2h_1-\mu T_2}{\sigma\sqrt{T_2}},\right.\\
&\qquad\left.\times\frac{k-2h_1-\mu T_3}{\sigma\sqrt{T_3}}; \rho_{12}, \rho_{23}\right)\\
&+ e^{\frac{2\mu(h_2-h_1)}{\sigma^2}} N_3\left(\frac{-h_1+\mu T_1}{\sigma\sqrt{T_1}}, \frac{2h_1-h_2-\mu T_2}{\sigma\sqrt{T_2}},\right.\\
&\qquad\left.\times\frac{k-2h_2+2h_1-\mu T_3}{\sigma\sqrt{T_3}}; -\rho_{12}, \rho_{23}\right)\\
&- e^{\frac{2\mu h_3}{\sigma^2}} N_3\left(\frac{h_1+\mu T_1}{\sigma\sqrt{T_1}}, \frac{h_2+\mu T_2}{\sigma\sqrt{T_2}}, \frac{k-2h_3-\mu T_3}{\sigma\sqrt{T_3}}; \rho_{12}, -\rho_{23}\right)\\
&+ e^{\frac{2\mu(h_3-h_2)}{\sigma^2}} N_3\left(\frac{h_1-\mu T_1}{\sigma\sqrt{T_1}}, \frac{-h_2+\mu T_2}{\sigma\sqrt{T_2}},\right.\\
&\qquad\left.\times\frac{k-2h_3+2h_2-\mu T_3}{\sigma\sqrt{T_3}}; -\rho_{12}, -\rho_{23}\right)\\
&+ e^{\frac{2\mu(h_3-h_1)}{\sigma^2}} N_3\left(\frac{-h_1+\mu T_1}{\sigma\sqrt{T_1}}, \frac{h_2-2h_1+\mu T_2}{\sigma\sqrt{T_2}},\right.\\
&\qquad\left.\times\frac{k-2h_3+2h_1-\mu T_3}{\sigma\sqrt{T_3}}; \rho_{12}, -\rho_{23}\right)\\
&- e^{\frac{2\mu(h_3+h_1-h_2)}{\sigma^2}} N_3\left(\frac{-h_1-\mu T_1}{\sigma\sqrt{T_1}}, \frac{-h_2+2h_1+\mu T_2}{\sigma\sqrt{T_2}}\right.\\
&\qquad\left.\times\frac{k-2h_3+2h_2-2h_1-\mu T_3}{\sigma\sqrt{T_3}}; -\rho_{12}, -\rho_{23}\right)
\end{aligned}
$$

Then, the European step up-and-out put price is

$$
\begin{aligned}
p_0 &= e^{-rT} KQ\left(X_{T_1} < h_1, X_{T_2} < h_2, X_{T_3} < k\right)\\
&\quad - S_0\tilde{Q}\left(X_{T_1} < h_1, X_{T_2} < h_2, X_{T_3} < k\right)
\end{aligned}
$$

for three distinct monitoring periods.

The formula for the four-dimensional standard step up-and-out put option is given by Guillaume (2004, pp. 10–14) and requires 16 different integrations.

We only give the densities and the cumulative distribution function required for the integration.

The densities are:

$$f_1 = \frac{e^{-\frac{1}{2}\left\{\left(\frac{u-\mu T_1}{\sigma\sqrt{T_1}}\right)^2\right\}}}{(2\pi)^{1/2}\sigma\sqrt{T_1}} - e^{\frac{2\mu h_1}{\sigma^2}} \frac{e^{-\frac{1}{2}\left\{\left(\frac{u-2h_1-\mu T_1}{\sigma\sqrt{T_1}}\right)^2\right\}}}{(2\pi)^{1/2}\sigma\sqrt{T_1}}$$

$$f_2 = \frac{e^{-\frac{1}{2}\left\{\left(\frac{v-u-\mu(T_2-T_1)}{\sigma\sqrt{T_2-T_1}}\right)^2\right\}}}{(2\pi)^{1/2}\sigma\sqrt{(T_2-T_1)}} - e^{\frac{2\mu}{\sigma^2}(h_2-u)} \frac{e^{-\frac{1}{2}\left\{\left(\frac{v+u-2h_2-\mu(T_2-T_1)}{\sigma\sqrt{T_2-T_1}}\right)^2\right\}}}{(2\pi)^{1/2}\sigma\sqrt{(T_2-T_1)}}$$

$$f_3 = \frac{e^{-\frac{1}{2}\left\{\left(\frac{w-v-\mu(T_3-T_2)}{\sigma\sqrt{T_3-T_2}}\right)^2\right\}}}{(2\pi)^{1/2}\sigma\sqrt{(T_3-T_2)}} - e^{\frac{2\mu}{\sigma^2}(h_3-v)} \frac{e^{-\frac{1}{2}\left\{\left(\frac{w+v-2h_3-\mu(T_3-T_2)}{\sigma\sqrt{T_3-T_2}}\right)^2\right\}}}{(2\pi)^{1/2}\sigma\sqrt{(T_3-T_2)}}$$

The cumulative distribution function is

$$\Phi(v) = N\left(\frac{k-w-\mu(T_4-T_3)}{\sigma\sqrt{T_4-T_3}}\right) - e^{\frac{2\mu}{\sigma^2}(h_4-w)} N\left(\frac{k-2h_4+w-\mu(T_4-T_3)}{\sigma\sqrt{T_4-T_3}}\right) \qquad (7.11)$$

and the integrals are

$$\int_{-\infty}^{h_1}\int_{-\infty}^{h_2}\int_{-\infty}^{h_3} \Psi^1(u,v,w)\,\Phi(w)\,dwdvdu$$

$$- e^{\frac{2\mu}{\sigma^2}h_2} \int_{-\infty}^{h_1}\int_{-\infty}^{-h_2}\int_{-\infty}^{h_3} \Psi^2(u,v,w)\,\Phi(w)\,dwdvdu - e^{\frac{2\mu}{\sigma^2}h_1}$$

$$\int_{-\infty}^{-h_1}\int_{-\infty}^{h_2-2h_1}\int_{-\infty}^{h_3} \Psi^3(u,v,w)\,\Phi(w)\,dwdvdu$$

$$+ e^{\frac{2\mu}{\sigma^2}(h_2-h_1)} \int_{-\infty}^{-h_1}\int_{-\infty}^{-h_2+2h_1}\int_{-\infty}^{h_3} \Psi^4(u,v,w)\,\Phi(w)\,dwdvdu$$

$$- e^{\frac{2\mu}{\sigma^2}h_3} \int_{-\infty}^{h_1}\int_{-\infty}^{h_2}\int_{-\infty}^{h_3} \Psi^5(u,v,w)\,\Phi(w)\,dwdvdu$$

$$+\, e^{\frac{2\mu}{\sigma^2}(h_3-h_2)} \int_{-\infty}^{h_1} \int_{-\infty}^{-h_2} \int_{-\infty}^{h_3} \Psi^6\,(u,v,w)\,\Phi\,(w)\,dwdvdu$$

$$+\, e^{\frac{2\mu}{\sigma^2}(h_3-h_1)} \int_{-\infty}^{-h_1} \int_{-\infty}^{h_2-2h_1} \int_{-\infty}^{h_3} \Psi^7\,(u,v,w)\,\Phi\,(w)\,dwdvdu$$

$$-\, e^{\frac{2\mu}{\sigma^2}(h_3+h_1-h_2)} \int_{-\infty}^{-h_1} \int_{-\infty}^{-h_2+2h_1} \int_{-\infty}^{h_3} \Psi^8\,(u,v,w)\,\Phi\,(w)\,dwdvdu$$

where

$$\Psi^1\,(u,v,w) = \frac{e^{-\frac{1}{2}\left\{\left(\frac{u-\mu T_1}{\sigma\sqrt{T_1}}\right)^2+\left(\frac{v-u-\mu(T_2-T_1)}{\sigma\sqrt{T_2-T_1}}\right)^2+\left(\frac{w-v-\mu(T_3-T_2)}{\sigma\sqrt{T_3-T_2}}\right)^2\right\}}}{\sigma^3(2\pi)^{3/2}\sqrt{T_1(T_2-T_1)(T_3-T_2)}}$$

$$\Psi^2\,(u,v,w) = \frac{e^{-\frac{1}{2}\left\{\left(\frac{u+\mu T_1}{\sigma\sqrt{T_1}}\right)^2+\left(\frac{v+u-\mu(T_2-T_1)}{\sigma\sqrt{T_2-T_1}}\right)^2+\left(\frac{w-v-2h_2-\mu(T_3-T_2)}{\sigma\sqrt{T_3-T_2}}\right)^2\right\}}}{\sigma^3(2\pi)^{3/2}\sqrt{T_1(T_2-T_1)(T_3-T_2)}}$$

$$\Psi^3\,(u,v,w) = \frac{e^{-\frac{1}{2}\left\{\left(\frac{u-\mu T_1}{\sigma\sqrt{T_1}}\right)^2+\left(\frac{v-u-\mu(T_2-T_1)}{\sigma\sqrt{T_2-T_1}}\right)^2+\left(\frac{w-v-2h_1-\mu(T_3-T_2)}{\sigma\sqrt{T_3-T_2}}\right)^2\right\}}}{\sigma^3(2\pi)^{3/2}\sqrt{T_1(T_2-T_1)(T_3-T_2)}}$$

$$\Psi^4\,(u,v,w) = \frac{e^{-\frac{1}{2}\left\{\left(\frac{u+\mu T_1}{\sigma\sqrt{T_1}}\right)^2+\left(\frac{v+u-\mu(T_2-T_1)}{\sigma\sqrt{T_2-T_1}}\right)^2+\left(\frac{w-v+2h_1-2h_2-\mu(T_3-T_2)}{\sigma\sqrt{T_3-T_2}}\right)^2\right\}}}{\sigma^3(2\pi)^{3/2}\sqrt{T_1(T_2-T_1)(T_3-T_2)}}$$

$$\Psi^5\,(u,v,w) = \frac{e^{-\frac{1}{2}\left\{\left(\frac{u+\mu T_1}{\sigma\sqrt{T_1}}\right)^2+\left(\frac{v-u+\mu(T_2-T_1)}{\sigma\sqrt{T_2-T_1}}\right)^2+\left(\frac{w+v-2h_3-\mu(T_3-T_2)}{\sigma\sqrt{T_3-T_2}}\right)^2\right\}}}{\sigma^3(2\pi)^{3/2}\sqrt{T_1(T_2-T_1)(T_3-T_2)}}$$

$$\Psi^6\,(u,v,w) = \frac{e^{-\frac{1}{2}\left\{\left(\frac{u-\mu T_1}{\sigma\sqrt{T_1}}\right)^2+\left(\frac{v+u+\mu(T_2-T_1)}{\sigma\sqrt{T_2-T_1}}\right)^2+\left(\frac{w+v-2h_3+2h_2-\mu(T_3-T_2)}{\sigma\sqrt{T_3-T_2}}\right)^2\right\}}}{\sigma^3(2\pi)^{3/2}\sqrt{T_1(T_2-T_1)(T_3-T_2)}}$$

$$\Psi^7\,(u,v,w) = \frac{e^{-\frac{1}{2}\left\{\left(\frac{u+\mu T_1}{\sigma\sqrt{T_1}}\right)^2+\left(\frac{v-u+\mu(T_2-T_1)}{\sigma\sqrt{T_2-T_1}}\right)^2+\left(\frac{w+v-2h_3+2h_1-\mu(T_3-T_2)}{\sigma\sqrt{T_3-T_2}}\right)^2\right\}}}{\sigma^3(2\pi)^{3/2}\sqrt{T_1(T_2-T_1)(T_3-T_2)}}$$

$$\Psi^8\,(u,v,w) = \frac{e^{-\frac{1}{2}\left\{\left(\frac{u-\mu T_1}{\sigma\sqrt{T_1}}\right)^2+\left(\frac{v+u+\mu(T_2-T_1)}{\sigma\sqrt{T_2-T_1}}\right)^2+\left(\frac{w+v-2h_3-2h_1+2h_2-\mu(T_3-T_2)}{\sigma\sqrt{T_3-T_2}}\right)^2\right\}}}{\sigma^3(2\pi)^{3/2}\sqrt{T_1(T_2-T_1)(T_3-T_2)}} \tag{7.12}$$

$$
\begin{aligned}
&Q\left(M_0^1 < h_1, M_1^2 < h_2, M_2^3 < h_3, M_3^4 < h_4,\ X_4 < k\right)\\
&\quad = N_4\left(\frac{h_1-\mu T_1}{\sigma\sqrt{T_1}}, \frac{h_2-\mu T_2}{\sigma\sqrt{T_2}}, \frac{h_3-\mu T_3}{\sigma\sqrt{T_3}},\right.\\
&\qquad\qquad \left.\times\frac{k-\mu T_4}{\sigma\sqrt{T_4}};\ \rho_{12},\rho_{23},\rho_{34}\right) - e^{\frac{2\mu h_2}{\sigma^2}}\\
&N_4\left(\frac{h_1+\mu T_1}{\sigma\sqrt{T_1}}, \frac{-h_2-\mu T_2}{\sigma\sqrt{T_2}}, \frac{h_3-2h_2-\mu T_3}{\sigma\sqrt{T_3}},\right.\\
&\qquad \left.\times\frac{k-2h_2-\mu T_4}{\sigma\sqrt{T_4}};-\rho_{12},\rho_{23},\rho_{34}\right) - e^{\frac{2\mu h_1}{\sigma^2}}\\
&N_4\left(\frac{-h_1-\mu T_1}{\sigma\sqrt{T_1}}, \frac{h_2-2h_1-\mu T_2}{\sigma\sqrt{T_2}}, \frac{-2h_1+h_3-\mu T_3}{\sigma\sqrt{T_3}},\right.\\
&\qquad \left.\times\frac{k-2h_1-\mu T_4}{\sigma\sqrt{T_4}};\rho_{12},\rho_{23},\rho_{34}\right) + e^{\frac{2\mu(h_2-h_1)}{\sigma^2}}\\
&N_4\left(\frac{-h_1+\mu T_1}{\sigma\sqrt{T_1}}, \frac{-h_2+2h_1-\mu T_2}{\sigma\sqrt{T_2}}, \frac{h_3-2h_2+2h_1-\mu T_3}{\sigma\sqrt{T_3}},\right.\\
&\qquad \left.\times\frac{k-2h_2+2h_1-\mu T_4}{\sigma\sqrt{T_4}};-\rho_{12},\rho_{23},\rho_{34}\right) - e^{\frac{2\mu h_3}{\sigma^2}}\\
&N_4\left(\frac{h_1+\mu T_1}{\sigma\sqrt{T_1}}, \frac{h_2+\mu T_2}{\sigma\sqrt{T_2}}, \frac{-h_3-\mu T_3}{\sigma\sqrt{T_3}},\right.\\
&\qquad \left.\times\frac{k-2h_3-\mu T_4}{\sigma\sqrt{T_4}};\rho_{12},-\rho_{23},\rho_{34}\right) + e^{\frac{2\mu(h_3-h_2)}{\sigma^2}}\\
&N_4\left(\frac{h_1-\mu T_1}{\sigma\sqrt{T_1}}, \frac{-h_2+\mu T_2}{\sigma\sqrt{T_2}}, \frac{2h_2-h_3-\mu T_3}{\sigma\sqrt{T_3}}\right.\\
&\qquad \left.\times\frac{k+2h_2-2h_3-\mu T_4}{\sigma\sqrt{T_4}};-\rho_{12},-\rho_{23},\rho_{34}\right) + e^{\frac{2\mu(h_3-h_1)}{\sigma^2}}\\
&N_4\left(\frac{-h_1+\mu T_1}{\sigma\sqrt{T_1}}, \frac{h_2-2h_1+\mu T_2}{\sigma\sqrt{T_2}}, \frac{2h_1-h_3-\mu T_3}{\sigma\sqrt{T_3}},\right.\\
&\qquad \left.\times\frac{k+2h_1-2h_3-\mu T_4}{\sigma\sqrt{T_3}};\rho_{12},-\rho_{23},\rho_{34}\right)
\end{aligned}
$$

$$
\begin{aligned}
&-e^{\frac{2\mu(h_3-h_2+h_1)}{\sigma^2}} N_4\left(\frac{-h_1-\mu T_1}{\sigma\sqrt{T_1}}, \frac{-h_2+2h_1+\mu T_2}{\sigma\sqrt{T_2}},\right.\\
&\qquad \times \frac{2h_2-2h_1-h_3-\mu T_3}{\sigma\sqrt{T_3}},\\
&\qquad \left.\times \frac{k-2h_3+2h_2-2h_1-\mu T_4}{\sigma\sqrt{T_4}}; -\rho_{12}, -\rho_{23}, \rho_{34}\right)\\
&-e^{\frac{2\mu h_4}{\sigma^2}} N_4\left(\frac{h_1+\mu T_1}{\sigma\sqrt{T_1}}, \frac{h_2+\mu T_2}{\sigma\sqrt{T_2}}, \frac{h_3+\mu T_3}{\sigma\sqrt{T_3}},\right.\\
&\qquad \left.\times \frac{k-2h_4-\mu T_4}{\sigma\sqrt{T_4}}; \rho_{12}, \rho_{23}, -\rho_{34}\right)\\
&+e^{\frac{2\mu(h_4-h_2)}{\sigma^2}} N_4\left(\frac{h_1-\mu T_1}{\sigma\sqrt{T_1}}, \frac{-h_2+\mu T_2}{\sigma\sqrt{T_2}}, \frac{-2h_2+h_3+\mu T_3}{\sigma\sqrt{T_3}},\right.\\
&\qquad \left.\times \frac{k-2h_4+2h_2-\mu T_4}{\sigma\sqrt{T_4}}; -\rho_{12}, \rho_{23}, -\rho_{34}\right)\\
&+e^{\frac{2\mu(h_4-h_1)}{\sigma^2}} N_4\left(\frac{-h_1+\mu T_1}{\sigma\sqrt{T_1}}, \frac{h_2-2h_1+\mu T_2}{\sigma\sqrt{T_2}}, \frac{-2h_1+h_3+\mu T_3}{\sigma\sqrt{T_3}},\right.\\
&\qquad \left.\times \frac{k+2h_1-2h_4-\mu T_4}{\sigma\sqrt{T_4}}; \rho_{12}, \rho_{23}, -\rho_{34}\right)\\
&-e^{\frac{2\mu(h_4-h_2+h_1)}{\sigma^2}} N_4\left(\frac{-h_1-\mu T_1}{\sigma\sqrt{T_1}}, \frac{-h_2+2h_1+\mu T_2}{\sigma\sqrt{T_2}},\right.\\
&\qquad \times \frac{h_3-2h_2+2h_1+\mu T_3}{\sigma\sqrt{T_3}}\\
&\qquad \left.\times \frac{k-2h_4+2h_2-2h_1-\mu T_4}{\sigma\sqrt{T_4}}; -\rho_{12}, \rho_{23}, -\rho_{34}\right)\\
&-e^{\frac{2\mu(h_4-h_3)}{\sigma^2}} N_4\left(\frac{h_1-\mu T_1}{\sigma\sqrt{T_1}}, \frac{h_2-\mu T_2}{\sigma\sqrt{T_2}}, \frac{-h_3+\mu T_3}{\sigma\sqrt{T_3}},\right.\\
&\qquad \left.\times \frac{k+2h_3-2h_4-\mu T_4}{\sigma\sqrt{T_4}}; \rho_{12}, -\rho_{23}, -\rho_{34}\right) + e^{\frac{2\mu(h_4-h_3+h_2)}{\sigma^2}}
\end{aligned}
$$

$$N_4\left(\frac{h_1+\mu T_1}{\sigma\sqrt{T_1}},\frac{-h_2-\mu T_2}{\sigma\sqrt{T_2}},\frac{2h_2-h_3+\mu T_3}{\sigma\sqrt{T_3}},\right.$$

$$\left.\times\frac{k-2h_2-2h_4+2h_3-\mu T_4}{\sigma\sqrt{T_4}};-\rho_{12},-\rho_{23},-\rho_{34}\right)+e^{\frac{2\mu(h_4-h_3+h_1)}{\sigma^2}}$$

$$N_4\left(\frac{-h_1-\mu T_1}{\sigma\sqrt{T_1}},\frac{h_2-2h_1-\mu T_2}{\sigma\sqrt{T_2}},\frac{2h_1-h_3+\mu T_3}{\sigma\sqrt{T_3}},\right.$$

$$\left.\times\frac{k-2h_1-2h_4+2h_3-\mu T_4}{\sigma\sqrt{T_4}};\rho_{12},-\rho_{23},-\rho_{34}\right)-e^{\frac{2\mu(h_4-h_3+h_2-h_1)}{\sigma^2}}$$

$$N_4\left(\frac{-h_1+\mu T_1}{\sigma\sqrt{T_1}},\frac{-h_2+2h_1-\mu T_2}{\sigma\sqrt{T_2}},\frac{2h_2-2h_1-h_3+\mu T_3}{\sigma\sqrt{T_3}},\right.$$

$$\left.\times\frac{k-2h_4+2h_3-2h_2+2h_1-\mu T_4}{\sigma\sqrt{T_4}};-\rho_{12},-\rho_{23},-\rho_{34}\right) \tag{7.13}$$

7.1.3. *Standard step-down-and-out call option*

Guillaume (2004) gives the formula for the price of a four-dimensional step-down and out-call option in the Appendix section. Let $H_1 > H_2 > H_3 > H_4$ be the barrier levels for the period $0 > T_1 > T_2 > T_3 > T_4 = T$. The payoff function of the 4-step down and out barrier call is

$$\max(S_{T_4}-K,0)$$

provided that the barriers are not crossed in the relevant periods. For example, H_1 is not crossed before T_1, H_2 is not crossed between T_1 and T_2, H_3 is not crossed between T_2 and T_3, and so on. By construction, it is

$$S_0 > H_1 > H_2 > H_3 > H_4$$

The relevant joint cumulative distribution function is

$$Q(m_0^1 > h_1, m_1^2 > h_2, m_2^3 > h_3, m_3^4 > h_4, X_{T_4} > k)$$

where

$$m_a^b = \min_{t\in[a,b]} \ln\frac{S_t}{S_0} \quad h_i = \ln\frac{H_i}{S_0} \quad k = \ln\frac{K}{S_0} \quad X_{T_4} = X_T = \ln\frac{S_T}{S_0}$$

Applying the same method and solving

$$\begin{aligned} &E^Q\left\{1_{\{m_0^1>h_1,\, X_{T_1}>h_1\}} E^Q\left(1_{\{m_1^2>h_2,\ X_{T_2}>k\}} \,\Big|\, X_{T_1}\right)\right\} \\ &E^Q\left\{1_{\{m_0^1>h_1,\, m_1^2>h_2,\ X_{T_2}>h_2\}} E^Q\left(1_{\{m_2^3>h_3,\ X_{T_3}>k\}} \,\Big|\, X_{T_2}\right)\right\} \\ &E^Q\left\{1_{\{m_0^1>h_1,\, m_1^2>h_2, m_2^3>h_3, X_{T_3}>h_3\}} E^Q\left(1_{\{m_3^4>h_4,\ X_{T_4}>k\}} \,|\, X_{T_3}\right)\right\} \end{aligned} \tag{7.14}$$

we can obtain

$$Q(m_0^1 > h_1, m_1^2 > h_2, m_2^3 > h_3, m_3^4 > h_4, X_{T_4} > k)$$

as

$$N_4\left(\frac{-h_1+\mu T_1}{\sigma\sqrt{T_1}}, \frac{-h_2+\mu T_2}{\sigma\sqrt{T_2}}, \frac{-h_3+\mu T_3}{\sigma\sqrt{T_3}}, \frac{-k+\mu T_4}{\sigma\sqrt{T_4}}; \rho_{12}, \rho_{23}, \rho_{34}\right)$$

$$-\, e^{\frac{2\mu h_4}{\sigma^2}} N_4\left(\frac{-h_1-\mu T_1}{\sigma\sqrt{T_1}}, \frac{-h_2-\mu T_2}{\sigma\sqrt{T_2}}, \frac{-h_3-\mu T_3}{\sigma\sqrt{T_3}},\right.$$

$$\left.\times \frac{-k+2h_4+\mu T_4}{\sigma\sqrt{T_4}};\ \rho_{12}, \rho_{23}, -\rho_{34}\right) - e^{\frac{2\mu h_3}{\sigma^2}}$$

$$N_4\left(\frac{-h_1-\mu T_1}{\sigma\sqrt{T_1}}, \frac{-h_2-\mu T_2}{\sigma\sqrt{T_2}}, \frac{h_3+\mu T_3}{\sigma\sqrt{T_3}},\right.$$

$$\left.\times \frac{-k+2h_3+\mu T_4}{\sigma\sqrt{T_4}}; \rho_{12}, -\rho_{23}, \rho_{34}\right) + e^{\frac{2\mu(h_4-h_3)}{\sigma^2}}$$

$$N_4\left(\frac{-h_1+\mu T_1}{\sigma\sqrt{T_1}}, \frac{-h_2+\mu T_2}{\sigma\sqrt{T_2}}, \frac{h_3-\mu T_3}{\sigma\sqrt{T_3}},\right.$$

$$\left.\times \frac{-k-2h_3+2h_4+\mu T_4}{\sigma\sqrt{T_4}}; \rho_{12}, -\rho_{23}, -\rho_{34}\right)$$

$$-e^{\frac{2\mu h_2}{\sigma^2}} N_4\left(\frac{-h_1-\mu T_1}{\sigma\sqrt{T_1}}, \frac{h_2+\mu T_2}{\sigma\sqrt{T_2}}, \frac{-h_3+2h_2+\mu T_3}{\sigma\sqrt{T_3}},\right.$$

$$\left.\times \frac{-k+2h_2+\mu T_4}{\sigma\sqrt{T_4}}; -\rho_{12}, \rho_{23}, \rho_{34}\right)$$

$$+e^{\frac{2\mu(h_4-h_2)}{\sigma^2}} N_4\left(\frac{-h_1+\mu T_1}{\sigma\sqrt{T_1}}, \frac{h_2-\mu T_2}{\sigma\sqrt{T_2}}, \frac{2h_2-h_3-\mu T_3}{\sigma\sqrt{T_3}},\right.$$

$$\left.\times \frac{-k+2h_4-2h_2+\mu T_4}{\sigma\sqrt{T_4}}; -\rho_{12}, \rho_{23}, -\rho_{34}\right) + e^{\frac{2\mu(h_3-h_2)}{\sigma^2}}$$

$$N_4\left(\frac{-h_1+\mu T_1}{\sigma\sqrt{T_1}}, \frac{h_2-\mu T_2}{\sigma\sqrt{T_2}}, \frac{h_3-2h_2+\mu T_3}{\sigma\sqrt{T_3}},\right.$$

$$\left.\times \frac{-k+2h_3-2h_2+\mu T_4}{\sigma\sqrt{T_3}}; -\rho_{12}, -\rho_{23}, \rho_{34}\right)$$

$$-e^{\frac{2\mu(h_4-h_3+h_2)}{\sigma^2}} N_4\left(\frac{-h_1-\mu T_1}{\sigma\sqrt{T_1}}, \frac{h_2+\mu T_2}{\sigma\sqrt{T_2}}, \frac{-2h_2+h_3-\mu T_3}{\sigma\sqrt{T_3}},\right.$$

$$\left.\times \frac{-k-2h_3+2h_2+2h_4+\mu T_4}{\sigma\sqrt{T_4}}; -\rho_{12}, -\rho_{23}, -\rho_{34}\right)$$

$$-e^{\frac{2\mu h_1}{\sigma^2}} N_4\left(\frac{h_1+\mu T_1}{\sigma\sqrt{T_1}}, \frac{-h_2+2h_1+\mu T_2}{\sigma\sqrt{T_2}}, \frac{-h_3+2h_1+\mu T_3}{\sigma\sqrt{T_3}},\right.$$

$$\left.\times \frac{-k+2h_1+\mu T_4}{\sigma\sqrt{T_4}}; \rho_{12}, \rho_{23}, \rho_{34}\right)$$

$$+e^{\frac{2\mu(h_4-h_1)}{\sigma^2}} N_4\left(\frac{h_1-\mu T_1}{\sigma\sqrt{T_1}}, \frac{-h_2+2h_1-\mu T_2}{\sigma\sqrt{T_2}}, \frac{2h_1-h_3-\mu T_3}{\sigma\sqrt{T_3}},\right.$$

$$\left.\times \frac{-k+2h_4-2h_1+\mu T_4}{\sigma\sqrt{T_4}}; \rho_{12}, \rho_{23}, -\rho_{34}\right)$$

$$+e^{\frac{2\mu(h_3-h_1)}{\sigma^2}} N_4\left(\frac{h_1-\mu T_1}{\sigma\sqrt{T_1}}, \frac{-h_2+2h_1-\mu T_2}{\sigma\sqrt{T_2}}, \frac{-2h_1+h_3+\mu T_3}{\sigma\sqrt{T_3}},\right.$$

$$\left.\times \frac{-k-2h_1+2h_3+\mu T_4}{\sigma\sqrt{T_4}}; \rho_{12}, -\rho_{23}, \rho_{34}\right)$$

$$-e^{\frac{2\mu(h_4-h_3+h_1)}{\sigma^2}} N_4\left(\frac{h_1+\mu T_1}{\sigma\sqrt{T_1}}, \frac{-h_2+2h_1+\mu T_2}{\sigma\sqrt{T_2}}, \frac{h_3-2h_1-\mu T_3}{\sigma\sqrt{T_3}}, \times\frac{-k+2h_4+2h_1-2h_3+\mu T_4}{\sigma\sqrt{T_4}}; \rho_{12}, -\rho_{23}, -\rho_{34}\right)$$

$$+e^{\frac{2\mu(h_2-h_1)}{\sigma^2}}$$

$$N_4\left(\frac{h_1-\mu T_1}{\sigma\sqrt{T_1}}, \frac{h_2-2h_1+\mu T_2}{\sigma\sqrt{T_2}}, \frac{-h_3+2h_2-2h_1+\mu T_3}{\sigma\sqrt{T_3}}, \times\frac{-k+2h_2-2h_1+\mu T_4}{\sigma\sqrt{T_4}}; -\rho_{12}, \rho_{23}, \rho_{34}\right)$$

$$+e^{\frac{2\mu(h_4-h_2+h_1)}{\sigma^2}}$$

$$N_4\left(\frac{h_1+\mu T_1}{\sigma\sqrt{T_1}}, \frac{h_2-2h_1-\mu T_2}{\sigma\sqrt{T_2}}, \frac{2h_2-h_3-2h_1-\mu T_3}{\sigma\sqrt{T_3}}, \times\frac{-k-2h_2+2h_4+2h_1+\mu T_4}{\sigma\sqrt{T_4}}; -\rho_{12}, \rho_{23}, -\rho_{34}\right)$$

$$+e^{\frac{2\mu(h_3-h_2+h_1)}{\sigma^2}}$$

$$N_4\left(\frac{h_1+\mu T_1}{\sigma\sqrt{T_1}}, \frac{h_2-2h_1-\mu T_2}{\sigma\sqrt{T_2}}, \frac{-2h_2+h_3+2h_1+\mu T_3}{\sigma\sqrt{T_3}}, \times\frac{-k+2h_1-2h_2+2h_3+\mu T_4}{\sigma\sqrt{T_4}}; -\rho_{12}, -\rho_{23}, \rho_{34}\right)$$

$$-e^{\frac{2\mu(h_4-h_3+h_2-h_1)}{\sigma^2}}$$

$$N_4\left(\frac{h_1-\mu T_1}{\sigma\sqrt{T_1}}, \frac{h_2-2h_1+\mu T_2}{\sigma\sqrt{T_2}}, \frac{-2h_2+2h_1+h_3-\mu T_3}{\sigma\sqrt{T_3}}, \times\frac{-k+2h_4-2h_3+2h_2-2h_1+\mu T_4}{\sigma\sqrt{T_4}}; -\rho_{12}, -\rho_{23}, -\rho_{34}\right)$$

The price for the step-down barrier call is then,

$$\begin{aligned} c_{sdo} &= S_0 e^{-qT}\tilde{Q}\left(m_0^1 > h_1, m_1^2 > h_2, m_2^3 > h_3, m_3^4 > h_4, X_{T_4} > k\right) \\ &\quad - e^{-rT} K Q(m_0^1 > h_1, m_1^2 > h_2, m_2^3 > h_3, m_3^4 > h_4, X_{T_4} > k) \end{aligned} \tag{7.15}$$

where the drift term is $\tilde{\mu} = r - q + \frac{1}{2}\sigma^2$ for the probability measure $\tilde{Q}$ and $\mu = r - q - \frac{1}{2}\sigma^2$ for the probability measure Q.

For example, we can do the first integral as follows:

$$\int_{h_1}^{\infty}\int_{h_2}^{\infty}\int_{h_3}^{\infty} \frac{e^{-\frac{1}{2}\left\{\left(\frac{u-\mu T_1}{\sigma\sqrt{T_1}}\right)^2+\left(\frac{v-u-\mu(T_2-T_1)}{\sigma\sqrt{T_2-T_1}}\right)^2+\left(\frac{w-v-\mu(T_3-T_2)}{\sigma\sqrt{T_3-T_2}}\right)^2\right\}}}{\sigma^3(2\pi)^{3/2}\sqrt{T_1(T_2-T_1)(T_3-T_2)}}$$

$$N\left(\frac{-k-w+\mu(T_4-T_3)}{\sigma\sqrt{T_4-T_3}}\right) dwdvdu$$

$$\int_{-\infty}^{-h_1}\int_{-\infty}^{-h_2}\int_{-\infty}^{-h_3} \frac{e^{-\frac{1}{2}\left\{\left(\frac{u+\mu T_1}{\sigma\sqrt{T_1}}\right)^2+\left(\frac{v-u+\mu(T_2-T_1)}{\sigma\sqrt{T_2-T_1}}\right)^2+\left(\frac{w-v+\mu(T_3-T_2)}{\sigma\sqrt{T_3-T_2}}\right)^2\right\}}}{\sigma^3(2\pi)^{3/2}\sqrt{T_1(T_2-T_1)(T_3-T_2)}}$$

$$N\left(\frac{-k-w+\mu(T_4-T_3)}{\sigma\sqrt{T_4-T_3}}\right) dwdvdu =$$

$$\int_{-\infty}^{\frac{-h_1+\mu T_1}{\sigma\sqrt{T_1}}}\int_{-\infty}^{\frac{-h_2+\mu T_2}{\sigma\sqrt{T_2}}}\int_{-\infty}^{\frac{-h_3+\mu T_3}{\sigma\sqrt{T_3-T_2}}} \frac{e^{-\frac{1}{2}\left\{(x)^2+\left(\frac{y-\rho_{12}x)}{\sqrt{1-\rho_{12}^2}}\right)^2+\left(\frac{z-\rho_{23}y}{\sqrt{1-\rho_{23}^2}}\right)^2\right\}}}{(2\pi)^{3/2}\sqrt{(1-\rho_{12}^2)(1-\rho_{23}^2)}}$$

$$N\left(\frac{-k-w+\mu(T_4-T_3)}{\sigma\sqrt{T_4-T_3}}\right) dzdydx$$

Then, we obtain the first one as:

$$\int_{-\infty}^{\frac{-h_1+\mu T_1}{\sigma\sqrt{T_1}}}\int_{-\infty}^{\frac{-h_2+\mu T_2}{\sigma\sqrt{T_2}}}\int_{-\infty}^{\frac{-h_3+\mu T_3}{\sigma\sqrt{T_3}}}\int_{-\infty}^{\frac{-k+\mu T_4}{\sigma\sqrt{T_4}}}$$

$$\frac{e^{\left\{-\frac{1}{2}x^2-\frac{(y-\rho_{12}x)^2}{2\left(1-\rho_{12}^2\right)}-\frac{(z-\rho_{23}y)^2}{2\left(1-\rho_{23}^2\right)}-\frac{(q-\rho_{34}z)^2}{2\left(1-\rho_{34}^2\right)}\right\}}}{(2\pi)^2\sqrt{(1-\rho_{12}^2)(1-\rho_{23}^2)(1-\rho_{34}^2)}} dqdzdydx$$

$$x = \frac{a + \mu T_1}{\sigma\sqrt{T_1}} \quad a \to -h_1 \qquad y = \frac{b + \mu T_2}{\sigma\sqrt{T_2}} \quad b \to -h_2$$

$$z = \frac{c + \mu T_3}{\sigma\sqrt{T_3}} \quad c \to -h_3 \qquad q = \frac{d + \mu T_3}{\sigma\sqrt{T_3}} \quad d \to -k$$

all together yields

$$N_4\left(\frac{-h_1 + \mu T_1}{\sigma\sqrt{T_1}}, \frac{-h_2 + \mu T_2}{\sigma\sqrt{T_2}}, \frac{-h_3 + \mu T_3}{\sigma\sqrt{T_3}}, \frac{-k + \mu T_4}{\sigma\sqrt{T_4}}; \rho_{12}, \rho_{23}, \rho_{34}\right)$$

7.1.4. *Partial step barriers*

Guillaume (2004) shows that the sequence of monitored barriers need not be monotonically increasing or decreasing. A monitoring process may start at a forward time or finish earlier than maturity. For example, considering $T_0 < T_1 < T_2 < T_4 < T_5$, $[T_0, T_1]$ may be a non-monitored period and monitoring may start at $[T_1, T_2]$ and continues up to the end of T_4 for $[T_2, T_3]$ $[T_3, T_4]$ periods, $[T_4, T_5]$ being a silent period. This may be called forward-start early ending partial barrier. The ordering of the barriers may be chosen as $H_1 > H_2, H_2 < H_3, H_3 < H_1$.

If the option is a down-and-out call, the probability we need to calculate is

$$Q\left(m_1^2 > h_1, m_2^3 > h_2, m_3^4 > h_3, X_{T_5} > k\right) h_1 > h_2, h_2 < h_3, \ h_3 < h_1$$

This probability is equal to:

$$Q\left(m_1^2 > h_1, m_2^3 > h_2, X_{T_3} > h_3, m_3^4 > h_3, X_{T_4} > h_3, \ X_{T_5} > k\right)$$

(Why?) To find this probability, we need to solve

$$E^Q\left\{1_{\{m_1^2 > h_1,\, m_2^3 > h_2,\, X_{T_3} > h_3,\, m_3^4 > h_3,\, X_{T_4} > h_3\}} E^Q\left(1_{\{X_{T_5} > k\}} \mid X_{T_4}\right)\right\}$$

$$
\begin{gathered}
P(X_{T_1} > h_1) \\
P(X_{T_2} > h_1, m_1^2 > h_1) \\
P(X_{T_3} > h_3, m_2^3 > h_2) \\
P(X_{T_4} > h_3, m_3^4 > h_3) \\
P(X_{T_5} > k)
\end{gathered} \tag{7.16}
$$

Therefore, the lower integral limits are h_1, h_1, h_3, h_3, k (show with a graph).

$$
f_1 = \frac{e^{-\frac{1}{2}\left\{\left(\frac{u-\mu T_1}{\sigma\sqrt{T_1}}\right)^2\right\}}}{(2\pi)^{1/2}\sigma\sqrt{T_1}}
$$

$$
f_2 = \frac{e^{-\frac{1}{2}\left\{\left(\frac{v-u-\mu(T_2-T_1)}{\sigma\sqrt{T_2-T_1}}\right)^2\right\}}}{(2\pi)^{1/2}\sigma\sqrt{(T_2-T_1)}} - e^{\frac{2\mu}{\sigma^2}(h_1-u)}\frac{e^{-\frac{1}{2}\left\{\left(\frac{v+u-2h_1-\mu(T_2-T_1)}{\sigma\sqrt{T_2-T_1}}\right)^2\right\}}}{(2\pi)^{1/2}\sigma\sqrt{(T_2-T_1)}}
$$

$$
f_3 = \frac{e^{-\frac{1}{2}\left\{\left(\frac{w-v-\mu(T_3-T_2)}{\sigma\sqrt{T_3-T_2}}\right)^2\right\}}}{(2\pi)^{1/2}\sigma\sqrt{(T_3-T_2)}} - e^{\frac{2\mu}{\sigma^2}(h_2-v)}\frac{e^{-\frac{1}{2}\left\{\left(\frac{w+v-2h_2-\mu(T_3-T_2)}{\sigma\sqrt{T_3-T_2}}\right)^2\right\}}}{(2\pi)^{1/2}\sigma\sqrt{(T_3-T_2)}}
$$

$$
f_4 = \frac{e^{-\frac{1}{2}\left\{\left(\frac{x-w-\mu(T_4-T_3)}{\sigma\sqrt{T_4-T_3}}\right)^2\right\}}}{(2\pi)^{1/2}\sigma\sqrt{(T_4-T_3)}} - e^{\frac{2\mu}{\sigma^2}(h_3-w)}\frac{e^{-\frac{1}{2}\left\{\left(\frac{x+w-2h_3-\mu(T_4-T_3)}{\sigma\sqrt{T_4-T_3}}\right)^2\right\}}}{(2\pi)^{1/2}\sigma\sqrt{(T_4-T_3)}}
$$

$$
f_5 = \frac{e^{-\frac{1}{2}\left\{\left(\frac{y-x-\mu(T_5-T_4)}{\sigma\sqrt{T_5-T_4}}\right)^2\right\}}}{(2\pi)^{1/2}\sigma\sqrt{T_5-T_4}} \tag{7.17}
$$

The lower integral limits are h_1, h_1, h_2, h_3, k.

The solution requires quintivariate standard Gaussian distribution with eight terms:

$$N_5\left(\frac{-h_1+\mu T_1}{\sigma\sqrt{T_1}}, \frac{-h_1+\mu T_2}{\sigma\sqrt{T_2}}, \frac{-h_3+\mu T_3}{\sigma\sqrt{T_3}}, \frac{-h_3+\mu T_4}{\sigma\sqrt{T_4}}, \frac{-k+\mu T_5}{\sigma\sqrt{T_5}};\right.$$

$$\left.\rho_{12}, \rho_{23}, \rho_{34}, \rho_{45}\right)$$

$$-e^{\frac{2\mu h_1}{\sigma^2}} N_5\left(\frac{-h_1-\mu T_1}{\sigma\sqrt{T_1}}, \frac{h_1+\mu T_2}{\sigma\sqrt{T_2}}, \frac{2h_1-h_3+\mu T_3}{\sigma\sqrt{T_3}}, \frac{2h_1-h_3+\mu T_4}{\sigma\sqrt{T_4}},\right.$$

$$\left.\times\frac{-k+2h_1+\mu T_5}{\sigma\sqrt{T_5}}; -\rho_{12}, \rho_{23}, \rho_{34}, \rho_{45}\right)$$

$$-e^{\frac{2\mu h_2}{\sigma^2}} N_5\left(\frac{-h_1-\mu T_1}{\sigma\sqrt{T_1}}, \frac{-h_1-\mu T_2}{\sigma\sqrt{T_2}}, \frac{2h_2-h_3+\mu T_3}{\sigma\sqrt{T_3}},\right.$$

$$\times\frac{2h_2-h_3+\mu T_4}{\sigma\sqrt{T_4}}, \frac{-k+2h_2+\mu T_5}{\sigma\sqrt{T_5}};$$

$$\left.\times\rho_{12}, -\rho_{23}, \rho_{34}, \rho_{45}\right) + e^{\frac{2\mu(h_2-h_1)}{\sigma^2}}$$

$$N_5\left(\frac{-h_1+\mu T_1}{\sigma\sqrt{T_1}}, \frac{h_1-\mu T_2}{\sigma\sqrt{T_2}}, \frac{-h_3+2h_2-2h_1+\mu T_3}{\sigma\sqrt{T_3}},\right.$$

$$\frac{-h_3+2h_2-2h_1+\mu T_4}{\sigma\sqrt{T_4}}, \frac{-k+2h_2-2h_1+\mu T_5}{\sigma\sqrt{T_5}};$$

$$\left.\times-\rho_{12}, -\rho_{23}, \rho_{34}, \rho_{45}\right)$$

$$-e^{\frac{2\mu h_3}{\sigma^2}} N_5\left(\frac{-h_1-\mu T_1}{\sigma\sqrt{T_1}}, \frac{-h_1-\mu T_2}{\sigma\sqrt{T_2}}, \frac{-h_3-\mu T_3}{\sigma\sqrt{T_3}}, \frac{h_3+\mu T_4}{\sigma\sqrt{T_4}},\right.$$

$$\left.\times\frac{-k+2h_3+\mu T_5}{\sigma\sqrt{T_5}}; \rho_{12}, \rho_{23}, -\rho_{34}, \rho_{45}\right)$$

$$+e^{\frac{2\mu(h_3-h_1)}{\sigma^2}} N_5\left(\frac{-h_1+\mu T_1}{\sigma\sqrt{T_1}}, \frac{h_1-\mu T_2}{\sigma\sqrt{T_2}}, \frac{2h_1-h_3-\mu T_3}{\sigma\sqrt{T_3}},\right.$$

$$\times \frac{-2h_1+h_3+\mu T_4}{\sigma\sqrt{T_4}}, \frac{-k-2h_1+2h_3+\mu T_5}{\sigma\sqrt{T_5}};$$

$$\left. -\rho_{12}, \rho_{23}, -\rho_{34}, \rho_{45}\right)$$

$$+e^{\frac{2\mu(h_3-h_2)}{\sigma^2}} N_5\left(\frac{-h_1+\mu T_1}{\sigma\sqrt{T_1}}, \frac{-h_1+\mu T_2}{\sigma\sqrt{T_2}}, \frac{2h_2-h_3-\mu T_3}{\sigma\sqrt{T_3}},\right.$$

$$\times \frac{-2h_2+h_3+\mu T_4}{\sigma\sqrt{T_4}}, \frac{-k-2h_2+2h_3+\mu T_5}{\sigma\sqrt{T_5}};$$

$$\left. \times \rho_{12}, -\rho_{23}, -\rho_{34}, \rho_{45}\right)$$

$$-e^{\frac{2\mu(h_3-h_2+h_1)}{\sigma^2}} N_5\left(\frac{-h_1-\mu T_1}{\sigma\sqrt{T_1}}, \frac{h_1+\mu T_2}{\sigma\sqrt{T_2}}, \frac{2h_2-h_3-2h_1-\mu T_3}{\sigma\sqrt{T_3}},\right.$$

$$\frac{-2h_2+h_3+2h_1+\mu T_4}{\sigma\sqrt{T_4}}, \frac{-k+2h_3-2h_2+2h_1+\mu T_5}{\sigma\sqrt{T_5}};$$

$$\left. -\rho_{12}, -\rho_{23}, -\rho_{34}, \rho_{45}\right) \tag{7.18}$$

where

$$\int_{-\infty}^{a}\int_{-\infty}^{b}\int_{-\infty}^{c}\int_{-\infty}^{d}\int_{-\infty}^{e} \frac{e^{-\frac{u^2}{2}-\frac{(v-\rho_{12}u)^2}{2(1-\rho_{12}^2)}-\frac{(w-\rho_{23}v)^2}{2(1-\rho_{23}^2)}-\frac{(x-\rho_{34}w)^2}{2(1-\rho_{34}^2)}-\frac{(y-\rho_{45}x)^2}{2(1-\rho_{45}^2)}}}{(2\pi)^{5/2}\sqrt{(1-\rho_{12}^2)(1-\rho_{23}^2)(1-\rho_{34}^2)(1-\rho_{45}^2)}}$$

$$dydxdwdvdu = N_5\left(a, b, c, d, e; \rho_{12}, \rho_{23}, \rho_{34}, \rho_{45}\right)$$

For example, the first one is

$$\frac{e^{-\frac{1}{2}\left\{\left(\frac{u-\mu T_1}{\sigma\sqrt{T_1}}\right)^2\right\}}}{(2\pi)^{1/2}\sigma\sqrt{T_1}} \frac{e^{-\frac{1}{2}\left\{\left(\frac{v-u-\mu(T_2-T_1)}{\sigma\sqrt{T_2-T_1}}\right)^2\right\}}}{(2\pi)^{1/2}\sigma\sqrt{(T_2-T_1)}} \frac{e^{-\frac{1}{2}\left\{\left(\frac{w-v-\mu(T_3-T_2)}{\sigma\sqrt{T_3-T_2}}\right)^2\right\}}}{(2\pi)^{1/2}\sigma\sqrt{(T_3-T_2)}}$$

$$\frac{e^{-\frac{1}{2}\left\{\left(\frac{x-w-\mu(T_4-T_3)}{\sigma\sqrt{T_4-T_3}}\right)^2\right\}}}{(2\pi)^{1/2}\sigma\sqrt{(T_4-T_3)}}\frac{e^{-\frac{1}{2}\left\{\left(\frac{y-x-\mu(T_5-T_4)}{\sigma\sqrt{T_5-T_4}}\right)^2\right\}}}{(2\pi)^{1/2}\sigma\sqrt{T_5-T_4}}$$

That is

$$a=\frac{-h_1+\mu T_1}{\sigma\sqrt{T_1}}\quad b=\frac{-h_1+\mu T_2}{\sigma\sqrt{T_2}}\quad c=\frac{-h_3+\mu T_3}{\sigma\sqrt{T_3}}\quad d=\frac{-h_3+\mu T_4}{\sigma\sqrt{T_4}}$$

$$e=\frac{-k+\mu T_5}{\sigma\sqrt{T_5}}$$

and all correlations are positive.

The second one is

$$-\frac{e^{-\frac{1}{2}\left\{\left(\frac{u-\mu T_1}{\sigma\sqrt{T_1}}\right)^2\right\}}}{(2\pi)^{\frac{1}{2}}\sigma\sqrt{T_1}}e^{\frac{2\mu}{\sigma^2}(h_1-u)}$$

$$\frac{e^{-\frac{1}{2}\left\{\left(\frac{v+u-2h_1-\mu(T_2-T_1)}{\sigma\sqrt{T_2-T_1}}\right)^2\right\}}}{(2\pi)^{\frac{1}{2}}\sigma\sqrt{(T_2-T_1)}}$$

$$\frac{e^{-\frac{1}{2}\left\{\left(\frac{w-\mu T_3-(v-\mu T_2)}{\sigma\sqrt{T_3-T_2}}\right)^2\right\}}}{(2\pi)^{\frac{1}{2}}\sigma\sqrt{(T_3-T_2)}}$$

$$\frac{e^{-\frac{1}{2}\left\{\left(\frac{x-\mu T_4-(w-\mu T_3)}{\sigma\sqrt{T_4-T_3}}\right)^2\right\}}}{(2\pi)^{\frac{1}{2}}\sigma\sqrt{(T_4-T_3)}}\frac{e^{-\frac{1}{2}\left\{\left(\frac{y-\mu T_5-(x-\mu T_4)}{\sigma\sqrt{T_5-T_4}}\right)^2\right\}}}{(2\pi)^{1/2}\sigma\sqrt{T_5-T_4}}$$

The third one is

$$-\frac{e^{-\frac{1}{2}\left\{\left(\frac{u-\mu T_1}{\sigma\sqrt{T_1}}\right)^2\right\}}}{(2\pi)^{\frac{1}{2}}\sigma\sqrt{T_1}}\frac{e^{-\frac{1}{2}\left\{\left(\frac{v-u-\mu(T_2-T_1)}{\sigma\sqrt{T_2-T_1}}\right)^2\right\}}}{(2\pi)^{\frac{1}{2}}\sigma\sqrt{(T_2-T_1)}}e^{\frac{2\mu}{\sigma^2}(h_2-v)}$$

$$\times \frac{e^{-\frac{1}{2}\left\{\left(\frac{w+v-2h_2-\mu(T_3-T_2)}{\sigma\sqrt{T_3-T_2}}\right)^2\right\}}}{(2\pi)^{\frac{1}{2}}\sigma\sqrt{(T_3-T_2)}}$$

$$\frac{e^{-\frac{1}{2}\left\{\left(\frac{x-w-\mu(T_4-T_3)}{\sigma\sqrt{T_4-T_3}}\right)^2\right\}}}{(2\pi)^{\frac{1}{2}}\sigma\sqrt{(T_4-T_3)}}\frac{e^{-\frac{1}{2}\left\{\left(\frac{y-x-\mu(T_5-T_4)}{\sigma\sqrt{T_5-T_4}}\right)^2\right\}}}{(2\pi)^{1/2}\sigma\sqrt{T_5-T_4}}$$

The fourth one is

$$-\frac{e^{-\frac{1}{2}\left\{\left(\frac{u-\mu T_1}{\sigma\sqrt{T_1}}\right)^2\right\}}}{(2\pi)^{\frac{1}{2}}\sigma\sqrt{T_1}}\frac{e^{-\frac{1}{2}\left\{\left(\frac{v-u-\mu(T_2-T_1)}{\sigma\sqrt{T_2-T_1}}\right)^2\right\}}}{(2\pi)^{\frac{1}{2}}\sigma\sqrt{(T_2-T_1)}}$$

$$\times \frac{e^{-\frac{1}{2}\left\{\left(\frac{w-v-\mu(T_3-T_2)}{\sigma\sqrt{T_3-T_2}}\right)^2\right\}}}{(2\pi)^{\frac{1}{2}}\sigma\sqrt{(T_3-T_2)}} e^{\frac{2\mu}{\sigma^2}(h_3-w)}$$

$$\frac{e^{-\frac{1}{2}\left\{\left(\frac{x+w-2h_3-\mu(T_4-T_3)}{\sigma\sqrt{T_4-T_3}}\right)^2\right\}}}{(2\pi)^{\frac{1}{2}}\sigma\sqrt{(T_4-T_3)}}\frac{e^{-\frac{1}{2}\left\{\left(\frac{y-x-\mu(T_5-T_4)}{\sigma\sqrt{T_5-T_4}}\right)^2\right\}}}{(2\pi)^{1/2}\sigma\sqrt{T_5-T_4}}$$

By transforming

$$e^{\frac{2\mu}{\sigma^2}(h_3-w)} = e^{\frac{2\mu}{\sigma^2}(h_3-w+v)}e^{-\frac{2\mu}{\sigma^2}(v-u)}e^{-\frac{2\mu}{\sigma^2}u}$$

will yield

$$-e^{\frac{2\mu}{\sigma^2}h_3}\frac{e^{-\frac{1}{2}\left\{\left(\frac{u+\mu T_1}{\sigma\sqrt{T_1}}\right)^2\right\}}}{(2\pi)^{\frac{1}{2}}\sigma\sqrt{T_1}}\frac{e^{-\frac{1}{2}\left\{\left(\frac{v-u+\mu(T_2-T_1)}{\sigma\sqrt{T_2-T_1}}\right)^2\right\}}}{(2\pi)^{\frac{1}{2}}\sigma\sqrt{(T_2-T_1)}}\frac{e^{-\frac{1}{2}\left\{\left(\frac{w-v+\mu(T_3-T_2)}{\sigma\sqrt{T_3-T_2}}\right)^2\right\}}}{(2\pi)^{\frac{1}{2}}\sigma\sqrt{(T_3-T_2)}}$$

$$\frac{e^{-\frac{1}{2}\left\{\left(\frac{x+w-2h_3-\mu(T_4-T_3)}{\sigma\sqrt{T_4-T_3}}\right)^2\right\}}}{(2\pi)^{\frac{1}{2}}\sigma\sqrt{(T_4-T_3)}}\frac{e^{-\frac{1}{2}\left\{\left(\frac{y-x-\mu(T_5-T_4)}{\sigma\sqrt{T_5-T_4}}\right)^2\right\}}}{(2\pi)^{1/2}\sigma\sqrt{T_5-T_4}}$$

The transformation of variables yields

$$\frac{u+\mu T_1}{\sigma\sqrt{T_1}}\ \frac{v+\mu T_2}{\sigma\sqrt{T_2}}\ \frac{w+\mu T_3}{\sigma\sqrt{T_3}}\ \frac{x-2h_3-\mu T_4}{\sigma\sqrt{T_3}}\ \frac{y-2h_3-\mu T_5}{\sigma\sqrt{T_5}}$$

The only negative correlation is ρ_{34}. By changing the integral limits

$$\frac{u+\mu T_1}{\sigma\sqrt{T_1}}\ \frac{v+\mu T_2}{\sigma\sqrt{T_2}}\ \frac{w+\mu T_3}{\sigma\sqrt{T_3}}\ \frac{x-2h_3-\mu T_4}{\sigma\sqrt{T_3}}\ \frac{y-2h_3-\mu T_5}{\sigma\sqrt{T_5}}$$

$$\frac{-h_1-\mu T_1}{\sigma\sqrt{T_1}},\frac{-h_1-\mu T_2}{\sigma\sqrt{T_2}},\frac{-h_3-\mu T_3}{\sigma\sqrt{T_3}},\frac{h_3+\mu T_4}{\sigma\sqrt{T_4}},\frac{-k+2h_3+\mu T_5}{\sigma\sqrt{T_5}};$$

$$\rho_{12},\rho_{23},-\rho_{34},\rho_{45}$$

we find

$$-e^{\frac{2\mu h_3}{\sigma^2}}N_5\left(\frac{-h_1-\mu T_1}{\sigma\sqrt{T_1}},\frac{-h_1-\mu T_2}{\sigma\sqrt{T_2}},\frac{-h_3-\mu T_3}{\sigma\sqrt{T_3}},\frac{h_3+\mu T_4}{\sigma\sqrt{T_4}},\right.$$
$$\left.\frac{-k+2h_3+\mu T_5}{\sigma\sqrt{T_5}};\rho_{12},\rho_{23},-\rho_{34},\rho_{45}\right)$$

We left the remaining four integrals to the reader as an exercise.

7.1.5. *Outside step barriers*

The outside step barriers are the options where the barriers are monitored with respect to another asset other than the underlying. Assume there are assets S and V with risk-neutral drifts and volatilities $\mu_S,\mu_V,\sigma_S,\sigma_V$ respectively, following geometric Brownian motion. The correlation between S and V is ρ_{SV}, and the barriers are ordered as $H_1 < H_2 < H_3$ in terms of the asset V. Assuming the option is an up-and-out put option, we need to calculate the probability of

$$Q\left(M_0^1 < h_1, M_1^2 < h_2, M_2^3 < h_3, X_{T_3} < k\right) h_1 < h_2 < h_3$$

where

$$M_a^b = \max_{t\in[T_a,T_b]}\left[\ln\frac{V_t}{V_0}\right] \quad h_i=\ln\frac{H_i}{V_0} \quad k=\ln\frac{K}{S_0} \quad X_{T_3}=\ln\frac{S_{T_3}}{S_0}$$

The conditional expectation is

$$E^Q\left[1_{M_0^1<h_1,\, M_1^2<h_2,\, M_2^3<h_3,\, Y_{T_3}<h_3} E^Q\left(1_{X_{T_3}<k} \,\middle|\, Y_{T_3}\right)\right] \quad Y_{T_3} = \ln\frac{V_{T_3}}{V_0}$$

We know how to calculate the $E^Q\left[1_{M_0^1<h_1,\, M_1^2<h_2,\, M_2^3<h_3,\, Y_{T_3}<h_3}\right]$.

$E^Q\left(1_{X_{T_3}<k} \,\middle|\, Y_{T_3}\right)$ is the conditional expectation of $X_{T_3}(S_{T_3})$ on $Y_{T_3}(V_{T_3})$. The risk-neutral joint density of X_{T_3} and Y_{T_3} is

$$f_{X_{T_3},Y_{T_3}}(a,b)$$

$$= \frac{\exp\left\{-\frac{\left(\frac{a-\mu_V T_3}{\sigma_V\sqrt{T_3}}\right)^2 - 2\rho_{SV}\left(\frac{a-\mu_V T_3}{\sigma_V\sqrt{T_3}}\right)\left(\frac{b-\mu_S T_3}{\sigma_S\sqrt{T_3}}\right) + \left(\frac{b-\mu_S T_3}{\sigma_S\sqrt{T_3}}\right)^2}{2(1-\rho_{SV}^2)}\right\}}{2\pi\sigma_S\sigma_V T_3\sqrt{(1-\rho_{SV}^2)}}$$

Therefore, the conditional expectation is

$$f_{(X_{T_3}\,|\,Y_{T_3})} = \frac{\dfrac{\exp\left\{-\frac{\left(\frac{a-\mu_V T_3}{\sigma_V\sqrt{T_3}}\right)^2 - 2\rho_{SV}\left(\frac{a-\mu_V T_3}{\sigma_V\sqrt{T_3}}\right)\left(\frac{b-\mu_S T_3}{\sigma_S\sqrt{T_3}}\right) + \left(\frac{b-\mu_S T_3}{\sigma_S\sqrt{T_3}}\right)^2}{2(1-\rho_{SV}^2)}\right\}}{2\pi\sigma_S\sigma_V T_3\sqrt{(1-\rho_{SV}^2)}}}{\dfrac{\exp\left\{-\frac{1}{2}\left[\left(\frac{a-\mu_V T_3}{\sigma_V\sqrt{T_3}}\right)^2\right]\right\}}{\sigma_V\sqrt{2\pi T_3}}}$$

Using some algebra:

$$\frac{\exp\left\{+\frac{1}{2}\left(\frac{a-\mu_V T_3}{\sigma_V\sqrt{T_3}}\right)^2\frac{(1-\rho_{SV}^2)}{(1-\rho_{SV}^2)}\right.}{\sigma_S\sqrt{2\pi T_3(1-\rho_{SV}^2)}}$$

$$\left.\frac{-\frac{1}{2(1-\rho_{SV}^2)}\left[\left(\frac{a-\mu_V T_3}{\sigma_V\sqrt{T_3}}\right)^2 - 2\rho_{SV}\left(\frac{a-\mu_V T_3}{\sigma_V\sqrt{T_3}}\right)\left(\frac{b-\mu_S T_3}{\sigma_S\sqrt{T_3}}\right) + \left(\frac{b-\mu_S T_3}{\sigma_S\sqrt{T_3}}\right)^2\right]}{\sigma_S\sqrt{2\pi T_3(1-\rho_{SV}^2)}}\right\}$$

$$= \frac{\exp\left\{-\frac{1}{2(1-\rho_{SV}^2)}\left[\left(\frac{b-\mu_S T_3}{\sigma_S\sqrt{T_3}}\right) - \left(\frac{a-\mu_V T_3}{\sigma_V\sqrt{T_3}}\right)\rho_{SV}\right]^2\right\}}{\sigma_S\sqrt{2\pi T_3(1-\rho_{SV}^2)}}$$

and finally, we obtain (how?)

$$f_{(X_{T_3}|Y_{T_3})}(a \mid b) = \frac{\exp\left\{-\frac{\left[\left(b-\mu_S T_3-\rho_{SV}\frac{\sigma_S}{\sigma_V}(a-\mu_V T_3)\right)^2\right]}{2(1-\rho_{SV}^2)\sigma_S^2 T_3}\right\}}{\sigma_S\sqrt{2\pi(1-\rho_{SV}^2)T_3}}$$

where

$$(X_{T_3}|Y_{T_3}) \sim N\left(\mu_S T_3 + \rho_{SV}\frac{\sigma_S}{\sigma_V}\left(Y_{T_3} - \mu_V T_3\right); (1-\rho_{SV}^2)\sigma_S^2 T_3\right) \tag{7.19}$$

Performing the calculations, integrations yield:

$$E^Q\left[1_{M_0^1<h_1,\, M_1^2<h_2,\, M_2^3<h_3,\, Y_{T_3}<h_3} E^Q\left(1_{X_{T_3}<k} \mid Y_{T_3}\right)\right]$$

$$= N_4\left(\frac{h_1-\mu_V T_1}{\sigma_V\sqrt{T_1}}, \frac{h_2-\mu_V T_2}{\sigma_V\sqrt{T_2}}, \frac{h_3-\mu_V T_3}{\sigma_V\sqrt{T_3}}, \frac{k-\mu_S T_3}{\sigma_S\sqrt{T_3}}; \rho_{12}, \rho_{23}, \rho_{SV}\right)$$

$$- e^{\frac{2\mu_V h_2}{\sigma_V^2}} N_4\left(\frac{h_1+\mu_V T_1}{\sigma_V\sqrt{T_1}}, \frac{-h_2-\mu_V T_2}{\sigma_V\sqrt{T_2}}, \frac{-2h_2+h_3-\mu_V T_3}{\sigma_V\sqrt{T_3}},\right.$$

$$\left.\times\frac{k-2h_2\rho_{SV}\frac{\sigma_S}{\sigma_V}-\mu_S T_3}{\sigma_S\sqrt{T_3}}; -\rho_{12}, \rho_{23}, \rho_{SV}\right)$$

$$-e^{\frac{2\mu_V h_1}{\sigma_V^2}} N_4\left(\frac{-h_1-\mu_V T_1}{\sigma_V\sqrt{T_1}}, \frac{h_2-2h_1-\mu_V T_2}{\sigma_V\sqrt{T_2}}, \frac{-2h_1+h_3-\mu_V T_3}{\sigma_V\sqrt{T_3}},\right.$$

$$\left.\times\frac{k-2h_1\rho_{SV}\frac{\sigma_S}{\sigma_V}-\mu_S T_3}{\sigma_S\sqrt{T_3}}; \rho_{12}, \rho_{23}, \rho_{SV}\right)$$

$$+e^{\frac{2\mu_V(h_2-h_1)}{\sigma_V^2}} N_4\left(\frac{-h_1+\mu_V T_1}{\sigma_V\sqrt{T_1}}, \frac{-h_2+2h_1-\mu_V T_2}{\sigma_V\sqrt{T_2}},\right.$$

$$\times\frac{h_3-2h_2+2h_1-\mu_V T_3}{\sigma_V\sqrt{T_3}},$$

$$\left.\frac{k+2(h_1-h_2)-\mu_S T_3}{\sigma_S\sqrt{T_3}}; -\rho_{12}, \rho_{23}, \rho_{SV}\right)$$

$$-e^{\frac{2\mu_V h_3}{\sigma_V^2}} N_4\left(\frac{h_1+\mu_V T_1}{\sigma_V\sqrt{T_1}}, \frac{h_2+\mu_V T_2}{\sigma_V\sqrt{T_2}}, \frac{-h_3-\mu_V T_3}{\sigma_V\sqrt{T_3}},\right.$$
$$\left.\times\ \frac{k-2h_3\rho_{SV}\frac{\sigma_S}{\sigma_V}-\mu_S T_3}{\sigma_S\sqrt{T_3}}; \rho_{12}, -\rho_{23}, \rho_{SV}\right)$$

$$+e^{\frac{2\mu_V(h_3-h_2)}{\sigma_V^2}} N_4\left(\frac{h_1-\mu_V T_1}{\sigma_V\sqrt{T_1}}, \frac{-h_2+\mu_V T_2}{\sigma_V\sqrt{T_2}}, \frac{-h_3+2h_2-\mu_V T_3}{\sigma_V\sqrt{T_3}},\right.$$
$$\left.\times\ \frac{k+2(h_2-h_3)\rho_{SV}\frac{\sigma_S}{\sigma_V}-\mu_S T_3}{\sigma_S\sqrt{T_3}}; -\rho_{12}, -\rho_{23}, \rho_{SV}\right)$$

$$+e^{\frac{2\mu_V(h_3-h_1)}{\sigma_V^2}} N_4\left(\frac{-h_1+\mu_V T_1}{\sigma_V\sqrt{T_1}}, \frac{h_2-2h_1+\mu_V T_2}{\sigma_V\sqrt{T_2}}, \frac{2h_1-h_3-\mu_V T_3}{\sigma_V\sqrt{T_3}},\right.$$
$$\left.\times\ \frac{k+2(h_1-h_3)\rho_{SV}\frac{\sigma_S}{\sigma_V}-\mu_S T_3}{\sigma_S\sqrt{T_3}}; \rho_{12}, -\rho_{23}, \rho_{SV}\right)$$

$$-e^{\frac{2\mu_V(h_3-h_2+h_1)}{\sigma_V^2}}$$
$$N_4\left(\frac{-h_1-\mu_V T_1}{\sigma_V\sqrt{T_1}}, \frac{-h_2+2h_1+\mu_V T_2}{\sigma_V\sqrt{T_2}}, \frac{2h_2-2h_1-h_3-\mu_V T_3}{\sigma_V\sqrt{T_3}},\right.$$
$$\left.\times\ \frac{k+2(h_2-h_1-h_3)\rho_{SV}\frac{\sigma_S}{\sigma_V}-\mu_S T_3}{\sigma_S\sqrt{T_3}}; -\rho_{12}, -\rho_{23}, \rho_{SV}\right)$$

These are the probabilities

$$P(M_0^1 < h_1,\ Y_1 < h_1)$$
$$P(M_1^2 < h_2,\ Y_2 < h_2)$$
$$P(M_2^3 < h_3,\ Y_3 < h_3)$$
$$P(X_3 < k)$$

$$f_1 = \frac{e^{-\frac{1}{2}\left\{\left(\frac{u-\mu_V T_1}{\sigma\sqrt{T_1}}\right)^2\right\}}}{(2\pi)^{1/2}\sigma\sqrt{T_1}} - e^{\frac{2\mu_V h_1}{\sigma^2}}\frac{e^{-\frac{1}{2}\left\{\left(\frac{u-2h_1-\mu_V T_1}{\sigma\sqrt{T_1}}\right)^2\right\}}}{(2\pi)^{1/2}\sigma\sqrt{T_1}}$$

$$f_2 = \frac{e^{-\frac{1}{2}\left\{\left(\frac{v-u-\mu_V(T_2-T_1)}{\sigma\sqrt{T_2-T_1}}\right)^2\right\}}}{(2\pi)^{1/2}\sigma\sqrt{(T_2-T_1)}} - e^{\frac{2\mu_V}{\sigma^2}(h_2-u)}\frac{e^{-\frac{1}{2}\left\{\left(\frac{v+u-2h_2-\mu_V(T_2-T_1)}{\sigma\sqrt{T_2-T_1}}\right)^2\right\}}}{(2\pi)^{1/2}\sigma\sqrt{(T_2-T_1)}}$$

$$f_3 = \frac{e^{-\frac{1}{2}\left\{\left(\frac{w-v-\mu_V(T_3-T_2)}{\sigma\sqrt{T_3-T_2}}\right)^2\right\}}}{(2\pi)^{1/2}\sigma\sqrt{(T_3-T_2)}} - e^{\frac{2\mu_V}{\sigma^2}(h_3-v)}\frac{e^{-\frac{1}{2}\left\{\left(\frac{w+v-2h_3-\mu_V(T_3-T_2)}{\sigma\sqrt{T_3-T_2}}\right)^2\right\}}}{(2\pi)^{1/2}\sigma\sqrt{(T_3-T_2)}}$$

$$f_4 = \frac{e^{-\frac{1}{2}\left\{\left(\frac{z-\mu_S T_3-\rho_{SV}\frac{\sigma_S}{\sigma_V}(Y_{T_3}-\mu_V T_3))}{\sigma_S\sqrt{T_3}\sqrt{1-\rho_{SV}^2}}\right)^2\right\}}}{(2\pi)^{1/2}\sigma\sqrt{T_3(1-\rho_{SV}^2)}} \tag{7.20}$$

Here, we have a different correlation coefficient ρ_{SV} between the different assets' returns.

$$N_4(a,b,c,d;\rho_{12},\rho_{23},\rho_{SV})$$
$$= \int_{-\infty}^{a}\int_{-\infty}^{b}\int_{-\infty}^{c}\int_{-\infty}^{d}$$
$$\times \frac{e^{-\frac{w^2}{2}-\frac{1}{2}\left(\frac{x-\rho_{12}w}{\sqrt{(1-\rho_{12}^2)}}\right)^2-\frac{1}{2}\left(\frac{y-\rho_{23}x}{\sqrt{(1-\rho_{23}^2)}}\right)^2-\frac{1}{2}\left(\frac{z-\rho_{SV}y}{\sqrt{(1-\rho_{SV}^2)}}\right)^2}}{(2\pi)^2\sqrt{(1-\rho_{12}^2)(1-\rho_{23}^2)(1-\rho_{SV}^2)}}dzdydxdw$$

The option value is

$$p_{ou} = e^{-rT_3}KQ\left(M_0^1 < h_1, M_1^2 < h_2, M_2^3 < h_3,\ X_{T_3} < k\right)$$
$$- S_0e^{-DT_3}\tilde{Q}\left(M_0^1 < h_1, M_1^2 < h_2, M_2^3 < h_3,\ X_{T_3} < k\right)$$

where drift for asset S is $\tilde{\mu}_S = \mu_S + \sigma_S^2$ and $\widetilde{\mu}_V = \mu_V + \rho_{SV}\sigma_S\sigma_V$ due to Girsanov theorem.

The first one is

$$f_1 = \frac{e^{-\frac{1}{2}\left\{\left(\frac{u-\mu_V T_1}{\sigma\sqrt{T_1}}\right)^2\right\}}}{(2\pi)^{1/2}\sigma\sqrt{T_1}}\frac{e^{-\frac{1}{2}\left\{\left(\frac{v-u-\mu_V(T_2-T_1)}{\sigma\sqrt{T_2-T_1}}\right)^2\right\}}}{(2\pi)^{1/2}\sigma\sqrt{(T_2-T_1)}}$$

$$\times \frac{e^{-\frac{1}{2}\left\{\left(\frac{w-v-\mu_V(T_3-T_2)}{\sigma\sqrt{T_3-T_2}}\right)^2\right\}}}{(2\pi)^{1/2}\sigma\sqrt{(T_3-T_2)}}$$

$$\times \frac{e^{-\frac{1}{2}\left\{\left(\frac{m-\mu_S T_3-\rho_{SV}\frac{\sigma_S}{\sigma_V}(Y_{T_3}-\mu_V T_3))}{\sigma_S\sqrt{T_3}\sqrt{1-\rho_{SV}^2}}\right)^2\right\}}}{(2\pi)^{1/2}\sigma\sqrt{T_3(1-\rho_{SV}^2)}}$$

and immediately follows that the integration with upper integral limits h_1, h_2, h_3, k yields

$$N_4\left(\frac{h_1-\mu_V T_1}{\sigma_V\sqrt{T_1}}, \frac{h_2-\mu_V T_2}{\sigma_V\sqrt{T_2}}, \frac{h_3-\mu_V T_3}{\sigma_V\sqrt{T_3}}, \frac{k-\mu_S T_3}{\sigma_S\sqrt{T_3}}; \rho_{12}, \rho_{23}, \rho_{SV}\right)$$

For example

$$N\left[\frac{z-\rho_{SV}y}{\sqrt{1-\rho_{SV}^2}}\right] = N\left[\frac{k-\mu_S T_3-\rho_{SV}\frac{\sigma_S}{\sigma_V}(Y_{T_3}-\mu_V T_3))}{\sigma_S\sqrt{T_3}\sqrt{1-\rho_{SV}^2}}\right]$$

That is

$$z = \frac{k-\mu_S T_3-\rho_{SV}\frac{\sigma_S}{\sigma_V}(Y_{T_3}-\mu_V T_3))}{\sigma_S\sqrt{T_3}\sqrt{1-\rho_{SV}^2}}\sqrt{1-\rho_{SV}^2}+\rho_{SV}y$$

$$z = \frac{k-\mu_S T_3-\rho_{SV}\frac{\sigma_S}{\sigma_V}(Y_{T_3}-\mu_V T_3))}{\sigma_S\sqrt{T_3}}+\rho_{SV}\frac{(Y_{T_3}-\mu_V T_3)}{\sigma_V\sqrt{T_3}}$$

$$= \frac{k-\mu_S T_3}{\sigma_S\sqrt{T_3}}$$

The second one is

$$f_2 = -e^{\frac{2\mu_V h_1}{\sigma^2}}\frac{e^{-\frac{1}{2}\left\{\left(\frac{u-2h_1-\mu_V T_1}{\sigma\sqrt{T_1}}\right)^2\right\}}}{(2\pi)^{1/2}\sigma\sqrt{T_1}}\frac{e^{-\frac{1}{2}\left\{\left(\frac{v-u-\mu_V(T_2-T_1)}{\sigma\sqrt{T_2-T_1}}\right)^2\right\}}}{(2\pi)^{1/2}\sigma\sqrt{(T_2-T_1)}}$$

$$\times \frac{e^{-\frac{1}{2}\left\{\left(\frac{w-v-\mu_V(T_3-T_2)}{\sigma\sqrt{T_3-T_2}}\right)^2\right\}}}{(2\pi)^{1/2}\sigma\sqrt{(T_3-T_2)}}\frac{e^{-\frac{1}{2}\left\{\left(\frac{z-\mu_S T_3-\rho_{SV}\frac{\sigma_S}{\sigma_V}(Y_{T_3}-\mu_V T_3))}{\sigma_S\sqrt{T_3}\sqrt{1-\rho_{SV}^2}}\right)^2\right\}}}{(2\pi)^{1/2}\sigma\sqrt{T_3(1-\rho_{SV}^2)}}$$

To get the same variables, we have to add and subtract $2h_1$

$$\left(\frac{v - 2h_1 - u + 2h_1 - \mu_V(T_2 - T_1)}{\sigma\sqrt{T_2 - T_1}}\right)$$

$$= \frac{v - 2h_1 - \mu_V T_2 - (u - 2h_1 - \mu_V T_1)}{\sigma\sqrt{T_2 - T_1}}$$

$$\times \frac{w - 2h_1 - \mu_V T_3 - (v - 2h_1 - \mu_V T_2)}{\sigma\sqrt{T_3 - T_2}}$$

So, the first three upper integral limits are

$$\frac{-h_1 - \mu_V T_1}{\sigma_V\sqrt{T_1}}, \frac{h_2 - 2h_1 - \mu_V T_2}{\sigma_V\sqrt{T_2}}, \frac{h_3 - 2h_1 - \mu_V T_3}{\sigma_V\sqrt{T_3}}$$

The last one is

$$\frac{z - \mu_S T_3 - \rho_{SV}\frac{\sigma_S}{\sigma_V}\left(Y_{T_3} - \mu_V T_3\right))}{\sigma_S\sqrt{T_3}\sqrt{1 - \rho_{SV}^2}}\sqrt{1 - \rho_{SV}^2} + \rho_{SV}\frac{w - 2h_1 - \mu_V T_3}{\sigma_V\sqrt{T_3}}$$

where $Y_{T_3} = w$. So, the last one is

$$\frac{z - \mu_S T_3 - 2h_1\rho_{SV}\frac{\sigma_S}{\sigma_V}}{\sigma_S\sqrt{T_3}}$$

With the coefficient, it is

$$-e^{\frac{2\mu_V h_1}{\sigma_V^2}} N_4\left(\frac{-h_1 - \mu_V T_1}{\sigma_V\sqrt{T_1}}, \frac{h_2 - 2h_1 - \mu_V T_2}{\sigma_V\sqrt{T_2}}, \frac{-2h_1 + h_3 - \mu_V T_3}{\sigma_V\sqrt{T_3}},\right.$$

$$\left.\times \frac{k - 2h_1\rho_{SV}\frac{\sigma_S}{\sigma_V} - \mu_S T_3}{\sigma_S\sqrt{T_3}};\ \rho_{12}, \rho_{23}, \rho_{SV}\right)$$

7.2. Step Double Barriers

This is an exotic double-barrier option, which is also called a multi-barrier double-touch/no-touch (expanding or shrinking) tunnel or hot-dog option. (Guillaume, 2010). Since the double barrier evolves as a piecewise function of time, it is a step function of the time variable.

They can be embedded in various structured products such as range (tunnel) notes or loans, tower notes and loans (wedding cake or onion options), or range forward contracts.

The tower note is designed using the same principle as the tunnel note. However, it develops this principle further by allowing the investor to build up higher and higher coupons, like in a tower, depending on which range the underlying asset remains within. In their standard forms, all these range-type contracts expose the investors to a knock-out event called a "sudden death" risk. This risk can be handled using step double barrier options instead of standard ones. By this approach, clients can be further protected by making the trigger mechanism gradual, i.e., by removing only a fraction of the option payoff once one of the exit points is crossed.

The step double barrier options offer transparency, simplicity, and flexibility compared to standard double barriers.

We will refer to Guillaume (2010) for the formulae provided therein. We only present some calculation details and derivations for some formulae herein.

7.2.1. *Regular step double barrier options*

Let $\{t_0 = 0, \ldots t_n = T\}$ be a subdivision of the option lifetime $[0, T]$. Each time interval $[t_i, t_{i+1}]$ is associated with a constant double barrier $[D_i, U_i]$ where D_i is the lower, and U_i is the upper part. Each pair $[t_i, t_{i+1}]$, $[D_i, U_i]$ is prespecified in the contract.

A standard $n-$step double knock-out call or put is a contract that pays the same payoff as a call or put at maturity if the underlying asset price stays in the ranges $[D_i, U_i]$ in every time interval $[t_i, t_{i+1}]$; otherwise expires worthless.

A standard $n-$step double knock-in call or put is a contract that pays the same payoff as call or put at maturity provided that at least one of the upper or lower barriers has been hit before the option maturity; otherwise, it expires worthless.

A gradual knock-out and knock-in pattern is also possible.

TSDKO and TSDKI refer to two-step double-barrier knock-out and knock-in options, and DKO and DKI refer to standard double-barrier options.

When $D_1 = D_2$ and $U_1 = U_2$, we obtain the value of standard double barriers. A double barrier $[D_2, U_2]$ is referred wider than another double barrier if $D_1 \geq D_2$ and $U_1 \leq U_2$. Similarly, narrower than $[D_1, U_1]$ if $D_1 \leq D_2$ and $U_1 \geq U_2$.

The results are also valid if both barriers increase or decrease; $D_1 \geq D_2$ and $U_1 \geq U_2$ or $D_1 \leq D_2$ and $U_1 \leq U_2$.

We know what $S_0, r, \sigma, \delta, K$ mean and $[D_i, U_i]$ is the i-step of the double barrier, lower and the upper barrier, respectively.

t_2 : option expiry of the no-arbitrage value of a two-step double knock-out put (TSDKOP), an outside two-step double knock-out put (OTSDKOP), and two asset two-steps double knock-out put (TATS-DKOP).

t_3 : option expiry of the no-arbitrage value of an early-ending two-step double knock-out put (EETSDKOP), a forward-start two-step double knock-out put (FSTSDKOP), an outside early-ending two-step double knock-out (OEETSDKOP).

t_4 : option expiry of the no-arbitrage value of a window two-step double knock-out put (WTSDKOP).

$S_0^{(1)} S_0^{(2)}$ are the spot values of underlying assets, $\sigma_1, \sigma_2, \delta_1, \delta_2, \ \rho$ are the volatilities, pay-out rates and the correlation between the assets respectively. All acronyms are due to Guillaume (2010).

7.2.1.1. *TSDKOP*

The no-arbitrage value of a TSDKOP is given by

$$\begin{aligned}
&\text{TSDKOP}\,(S_0, r, \sigma, \delta, t_1, t_2, K, U_1, U_2, D_1, D_2) \\
&\quad = \exp(-rt_2) K \Phi_{TS}(\mu) - \exp(-\delta t_2) S_0 \Phi_{TS}(\tilde{\mu}) \\
&(\tilde{\mu}) = r - \delta + \frac{\sigma^2}{2} \quad \mu = r - \delta - \sigma^2/2
\end{aligned}$$

where

$$\begin{aligned}
\Phi_{TS}(\mu) = {} & \sum_{n_1=-\infty}^{\infty} \sum_{n_2=-\infty}^{\infty} \left(\frac{U_1^{n_1} U_2^{n_2}}{D_1^{n_1} D_2^{n_2}} \right)^{2\mu/\sigma^2} \\
& \times \left\{ N_2 \left[I_1(U_1 \wedge U_2), I_2(K); \sqrt{\frac{t_1}{t_2}} \right] - N_2 \left[I_1(D_1 \vee D_2), I_2(K); \sqrt{\frac{t_1}{t_2}} \right] \right. \\
& \left. - N_2 \left[I_1(U_1 \wedge U_2), I_2(D_2); \sqrt{\frac{t_1}{t_2}} \right] + N_2 \left[I_1(D_1 \vee D_2), I_2(D_2); \sqrt{\frac{t_1}{t_2}} \right] \right\}
\end{aligned}$$

$$- \sum_{n_1=-\infty}^{\infty} \sum_{n_2=-\infty}^{\infty} \left(\frac{D_1^{n_1} D_2^{n_2+1}}{S_0 U_1^{n_1} U_2^{n_2}} \right)^{2\mu/\sigma^2} \left\{ N_2 \left[I_3\left(U_1 \wedge U_2\right), I_4(K); -\sqrt{\frac{t_1}{t_2}} \right] \right.$$

$$- N_2 \left[I_3\left(D_1 \vee D_2\right), I_4(K); -\sqrt{\frac{t_1}{t_2}} \right] - N_2 \left[I_3\left(U_1 \wedge U_2\right), I_4\left(D_2\right); -\sqrt{\frac{t_1}{t_2}} \right]$$

$$\left. + N_2 \left[I_3\left(D_1 \vee D_2\right), I_4\left(D_2\right); -\sqrt{\frac{t_1}{t_2}} \right] \right\}$$

$$- \sum_{n_1=-\infty}^{\infty} \sum_{n_2=-\infty}^{\infty} \left(\frac{D_1^{n_1+1} U_2^{n_2}}{S_0 U_1^{n_1} D_2^{n_2}} \right)^{2\mu/\sigma^2} \left\{ N_2 \left[I_5(U_1 \wedge U_2), I_6(K); \sqrt{\frac{t_1}{t_2}} \right] \right.$$

$$- N_2 \left[I_5(D_1 \vee D_2), I_6(K); \sqrt{\frac{t_1}{t_2}} \right] - N_2 \left[I_5(U_1 \wedge U_2), I_6(D_2); \sqrt{\frac{t_1}{t_2}} \right]$$

$$\left. + N_2 \left[I_5(D_1 \vee D_2), I_6(D_2); \sqrt{\frac{t_1}{t_2}} \right] \right\}$$

$$+ \sum_{n_1=-\infty}^{\infty} \sum_{n_2=-\infty}^{\infty} \left(\frac{D_2^{n_2+1} U_1^{n_1}}{D_1^{n_1+1} U_2^{n_2}} \right)^{2\mu/\sigma^2} \left\{ N_2 \left[I_7\left(U_1 \wedge U_2\right), I_8(K); -\sqrt{\frac{t_1}{t_2}} \right] \right.$$

$$- N_2 \left[I_7\left(D_1 \vee D_2\right), I_8(K); -\sqrt{\frac{t_1}{t_2}} \right] - N_2 \left[I_7\left(U_1 \wedge U_2\right), I_8\left(D_2\right); -\sqrt{\frac{t_1}{t_2}} \right]$$

$$\left. + N_2 \left[I_7\left(D_1 \vee D_2\right), I_8\left(D_2\right); -\sqrt{\frac{t_1}{t_2}} \right] \right\}$$

$$I_1(X) = \left(\ln\left(\frac{X D_1^{2n_1}}{S_0 U_1^{2n_1}} \right) - \mu t_1 \right) \Big/ \sigma\sqrt{t_1}$$

$$I_2(X) = \left(\ln\left(\frac{X D_1^{2n_1} D_2^{2n_2}}{S_0 U_1^{2n_1} U_2^{2n_2}} \right) - \mu t_2 \right) \Big/ \sigma\sqrt{t_2}$$

$$I_3(X) = \left(\ln\left(\frac{X D_1^{2n_1}}{S_0 U_1^{2n_1}} \right) + \mu t_1 \right) \Big/ \sigma\sqrt{t_1}$$

$$I_4\left(X\right) = \left(\ln\left(\frac{X S_0 U_1^{2n_1} U_2^{2n_2}}{D_1^{2n_1} D_2^{2(n_2+1)}} \right) - \mu t_2 \right) \Big/ \sigma\sqrt{t_2}$$

$$I_5\left(X\right) = \left(\ln\left(\frac{X S_0 U_1^{2n_1}}{D_1^{2(n_1+1)}} \right) - \mu t_1 \right) \Big/ \sigma\sqrt{t_1}$$

$$I_6(X) = \left(\ln\left(\frac{XS_0U_1^{2n_1}D_2^{2n_2}}{U_2^{2n_2}D_1^{2(n_1+1)}}\right) - \mu t_2\right) \Big/ \sigma\sqrt{t_2}$$

$$I_7(X) = \left(\ln\left(\frac{XS_0U_1^{2n_1}}{D_1^{2(n_1+1)}}\right) + \mu t_1\right) \Big/ \sigma\sqrt{t_1}$$

$$I_8(X) = \left(\ln\left(\frac{XD_1^{2(n_1+1)}U_2^{2n_2}}{S_0U_1^{2n_1}D_2^{2(n_2+1)}}\right) - \mu t_2\right) \Big/ \sigma\sqrt{t_2} \tag{7.21}$$

The integration requires 16 terms. There are two different integrals, each requiring two densities. Also, there are two steps, and to separate the integral limits, we multiply the number of terms by two. Therefore, we will have 16 distributions. Guillaume (2010) uses the densities proposed by Kunitomo and Ikeda (1992).

$$\int_{\ln D_1}^{\ln U_1}\int_{\ln D_2}^{\ln K} = \int_{-\infty}^{\ln U_1} - \int_{-\infty}^{\ln D_1}\left(\int_{-\infty}^{\ln K} - \int_{-\infty}^{\ln D_2}\right)$$

$$\int_{-\infty}^{\ln U_1}\int_{-\infty}^{\ln K} - \int_{-\infty}^{\ln U_1}\int_{-\infty}^{\ln D_2} - \int_{-\infty}^{\ln D_1}\int_{-\infty}^{\ln K} - \int_{-\infty}^{\ln D_1}\int_{-\infty}^{\ln D_2}$$

The density used by Kunitomo and Ikeda is as follows. This density gives us the moves of the underlying asset between the lower and the upper barriers.

$$P^*(T) = \int_{\gamma_2}^{\gamma_1}\left(\sum_{-\infty}^{\infty}\varphi\left[\frac{x - x_0 - 2n(\gamma_1-\gamma_2) - \mu^*T}{\sigma\sqrt{T}}\right]\right.$$

$$\exp\left\{\frac{2n}{\sigma^2}[(\gamma_1-\gamma_2)\mu^* - n(\gamma_1-\gamma_2)(\delta_1-\delta_2)\right.$$

$$\left. - (\gamma_1 - x_0)\delta_2 + (\gamma_2 - x_0)\delta_1]\right\}$$

$$-\sum_{-\infty}^{\infty}\varphi\left[\frac{x + x_0 - 2\gamma_2 + 2n\left(\gamma_1-\gamma_2\right) - \mu^*T}{\sigma\sqrt{T}}\right]$$

$$\exp\left\{\frac{2\mu^*}{\sigma^2}[(\gamma_2 - x_0) - n(\gamma_1 - \gamma_2)]\right\}$$

$$\left.\exp\left\{\frac{2}{\sigma^2}[-n(\gamma_1 - \gamma_2) + (\gamma_2 - x_0)][n(\delta_1 - \delta_2) - \delta_2]\right\}\right) dx$$

However, since the barriers are constructed exponentially, we take the values δ_1, δ_2 as zero

$$\delta_1 = \delta_2 = 0$$

and $\gamma_1 = \ln U_1$ $\gamma_2 = \ln D_1$.

By rearranging the density

$$P^*(T) = \int_{\gamma_2}^{\gamma_1}\left(\sum_{-\infty}^{\infty}\varphi\left[\frac{x - x_0 - 2n(\gamma_1 - \gamma_2) - \mu^* T}{\sigma\sqrt{T}}\right]\right.$$

$$\times \exp\left\{\frac{2n}{\sigma^2}\left[(\gamma_1 - \gamma_2)\mu^*\right]\right\}$$

$$-\sum_{-\infty}^{\infty}\varphi\left[\frac{x + x_0 - 2\gamma_2 + 2n(\gamma_1 - \gamma_2) - \mu^* T}{\sigma\sqrt{T}}\right]$$

$$\left.\times \exp\left\{\frac{2\mu^*}{\sigma^2}\left[(\gamma_2 - x_0) - n(\gamma_1 - \gamma_2)\right]\right\}\right) dx$$

we obtain

$$P^*(T)$$

$$= \int_{\ln D_1}^{\ln U_1}\left(\sum_{-\infty}^{\infty}\frac{\exp\left(-\frac{1}{2}\left(\frac{x - x_0 - \ln {U_1}^{2n_1} + \ln {D_1}^{2n_1} - \mu t_1}{\sigma\sqrt{t_1}}\right)^2\right)}{\sigma\sqrt{2\pi t_1}}\left(\frac{{U_1}^{n_1}}{{D_1}^{n_1}}\right)^{\frac{2\mu}{\sigma^2}}\right.$$

$$\left.-\sum_{-\infty}^{\infty}\frac{\exp\left(-\frac{1}{2}\left(\frac{x + x_0 - \ln {D_1}^{2(n_1+1)} + \ln {U_1}^{2n_1} - \mu t_1}{\sigma\sqrt{T}}\right)\right)}{\sigma\sqrt{2\pi t_1}}\left(\frac{{D_1}^{n_1+1}}{S_0 {U_1}^{n_1}}\right)^{\frac{2\mu}{\sigma^2}}\right) dx \tag{7.22}$$

Then, we need to consider the second step for the period $t_2 - t_1$.

Let us start with the first group. This is the integral

$$\frac{1}{\sigma\sqrt{2\pi t_1}}\frac{1}{\sigma\sqrt{2\pi(t_2-t_1)}}\left(\frac{U_1{}^{n_1}}{D_1{}^{n_1}}\right)^{\frac{2\mu}{\sigma^2}}\left(\frac{U_2{}^{n_2}}{D_2{}^{2n_2}}\right)^{\frac{2\mu}{\sigma^2}}$$

$$\int_{-\infty}^{\ln U_1}\int_{-\infty}^{\ln K}\exp\left(-\frac{1}{2}\left(\frac{x-x_0-\ln U_1{}^{2n_1}+\ln D_1{}^{2n_1}-\mu t_1}{\sigma\sqrt{t_1}}\right)^2\right)$$

$$\exp\left(-\frac{1}{2}\left(\frac{y-x-\ln U_2{}^{2n_2}+\ln D_2{}^{2n_2}-\mu(t_2-t_1)}{\sigma\sqrt{t_2-t_1}}\right)^2\right)$$

So, the first variable is

$$\left(\frac{U_1{}^{n_1}}{D_1{}^{n_1}}\right)^{\frac{2\mu}{\sigma^2}}\int_{-\infty}^{\frac{\ln\left(\frac{U_1D_1{}^{2n_1}}{S_0U_1{}^{2n_1}}\right)-\mu t_1}{\sigma\sqrt{t_1}}}\int_{-\infty}^{\ln K}\frac{1}{\sqrt{2\pi}}e^{-\frac{1}{2}z^2}\dots$$

$$z=\frac{\ln\left(\frac{U_1D_1{}^{2n_1}}{S_0U_1{}^{2n_1}}\right)-\mu t_1}{\sigma\sqrt{t_1}}$$

Now, let us take the second density with the coefficient

$$\left(\frac{U_1{}^{2n_1}U_2{}^{2n_2}}{D_1{}^{2n_1}D_2{}^{2n_2}}\right)^{\frac{\mu}{\sigma^2}}$$

To obtain the z variable, we have to insert

$$\left(\frac{2\mu}{\sigma^2}\ln U_1{}^{2n_1}-\frac{2\mu}{\sigma^2}\ln D_1{}^{2n_1}-\frac{2\mu}{\sigma^2}\ln U_1{}^{2n_1}+\frac{2\mu}{\sigma^2}\ln D_1{}^{2n_1}-x_0+x_0\right)$$

$$\frac{y-\ln U_1{}^{2n_1}-\ln U_2{}^{2n_2}+\ln D_1{}^{2n_1}+\ln D_2{}^{2n_2}-x_0-}{\sigma\sqrt{t_2}\sigma\sqrt{1-t_1/t_2}}$$

$$\frac{\mu t_2-(x-\ln U_1{}^{2n_1}+\ln D_1{}^{2n_1}-x_0-\mu t_1)}{\sigma\sqrt{t_2}\sigma\sqrt{1-t_1/t_2}}$$

Finally, we have

$$\frac{y - \ln U_1{}^{2n_1} - \ln U_2{}^{2n_2} + \ln D_1{}^{2n_1} + \ln D_2{}^{2n_2} - x_0 - \mu t_2)}{\sigma\sqrt{t_2}}$$

$$-\sqrt{\frac{t_1}{t_2}}\frac{x - \ln U_1{}^{2n_1} + \ln D_1{}^{2n_1} - x_0 - \mu t_1)}{\sigma\sqrt{t_1}}$$

divided by $\sqrt{1-\rho^2}$ where $\rho = \sqrt{\frac{t_1}{t_2}}$.

Since the upper integral limit is $\ln K$ the second variable is

$$w = \frac{\ln K - \ln U_1{}^{2n_1} - \ln U_2{}^{2n_2} + \ln D_1{}^{2n_1} + \ln D_2{}^{2n_2} - x_0 - \mu t_2)}{\sigma\sqrt{t_2}}$$

$$= \frac{\ln\left(\frac{KD_1{}^{2n_1}D_2{}^{2n_2}}{U_1{}^{2n_1}U_2{}^{2n_2}S_0}\right) - \mu t_2}{\sigma\sqrt{t_2}}$$

$$\sum_{n_1=-\infty}^{\infty}\sum_{n_2=-\infty}^{\infty}\left(\frac{U_1{}^{n_1}U_2{}^{n_2}}{D_1{}^{n_1}D_2{}^{n_2}}\right)^{2\mu/\sigma^2}$$

$$\int_{-\infty}^{\frac{\ln\left(\frac{U_1D_1{}^{2n_1}}{S_0U_1{}^{2n_1}}\right)-\mu t_1}{\sigma\sqrt{t_1}}}\int_{-\infty}^{\frac{\ln\left(\frac{KD_1{}^{2n_1}D_2{}^{2n_2}}{U_1{}^{2n_1}U_2{}^{2n_2}S_0}\right)-\mu t_2}{\sigma\sqrt{t_2}}}$$

$$\frac{1}{\sqrt{2\pi}}e^{-\frac{1}{2}z^2-\frac{1}{2}\left(\frac{w-\rho z}{\sqrt{1-\rho^2}}\right)^2}dzdw$$

$$= \sum_{n_1=-\infty}^{\infty}\sum_{n_2=-\infty}^{\infty}\left(\frac{U_1{}^{n_1}U_2{}^{n_2}}{D_1{}^{n_1}D_2{}^{n_2}}\right)^{2\mu/\sigma^2} N_2(I_1\,(U_1), I_2(K); \rho)$$

$$I_1\,(U_1) = \frac{\ln\left(\frac{U_1D_1{}^{2n_1}}{S_0U_1{}^{2n_1}}\right) - \mu t_1}{\sigma\sqrt{t_1}}, \quad I_2(K) = \frac{\ln\left(\frac{KD_1{}^{2n_1}D_2{}^{2n_2}}{U_1{}^{2n_1}U_2{}^{2n_2}S_0}\right) - \mu t_2}{\sigma\sqrt{t_2}}$$

Since this group of integrals are

$$\int_{-\infty}^{\ln U_1}\int_{-\infty}^{\ln K} - \int_{-\infty}^{\ln U_1}\int_{-\infty}^{\ln D_2} - \int_{-\infty}^{\ln D_1}\int_{-\infty}^{\ln K} - \int_{-\infty}^{\ln D_1}\int_{-\infty}^{\ln D_2}$$

the other distributions are

$$-\sum_{n_1=-\infty}^{\infty}\sum_{n_2=-\infty}^{\infty} N_2(I_1\left(U_1\right), I_2\left(D_2\right);\rho)$$

$$-\sum_{n_1=-\infty}^{\infty}\sum_{n_2=-\infty}^{\infty} N_2(I_1(D_1), I_2(K);\rho)$$

$$+\sum_{n_1=-\infty}^{\infty}\sum_{n_2=-\infty}^{\infty} N_2(I_1(D_1), I_2(D_2);\rho)$$

each multiplied by

$$\left(\frac{{U_1}^{n_1}{U_2}^{n_2}}{{D_1}^{n_1}{D_2}^{n_2}}\right)^{\frac{2\mu}{\sigma^2}}$$

Now, let us take the second group of integrals for

$$\left(\frac{{U_1}^{n_1}}{{D_1}^{n_1}}\right)^{\frac{2\mu}{\sigma^2}}\frac{1}{\sigma\sqrt{2\pi t_1}}$$

$$\exp\left(-\frac{1}{2}\left(\frac{x-x_0-\ln {U_1}^{2n_1}+\ln {D_1}^{2n_1}-\mu t_1}{\sigma\sqrt{t_1}}\right)^2\right)$$

$$\exp\left(-\frac{1}{2}\left(\frac{y+x-\ln {D_2}^{2(n_2+1)}+\ln {U_2}^{2n_2}-\mu(t_2-t_1)}{\sigma\sqrt{t_2-t_1}}\right)\right)$$

$$\exp\left\{\frac{2\mu^*}{\sigma^2}\left[\left(\gamma_2-x\right)-n\left(\gamma_1-\gamma_2\right)\right]\right\}$$

By adding $-x_0 + x_0$

$$\exp\left(-\frac{1}{2}\left(\frac{y+x-\ln {D_2}^{2(n_2+1)}+\ln {U_2}^{2n_2}-\mu(t_2-t_1)}{\sigma\sqrt{t_2-t_1}}\right)\right)$$

$$\exp\left\{\frac{2\mu^*}{\sigma^2}\left[(\gamma_2 - x - x_0 + x_0) - n\left(\gamma_1-\gamma_2\right)\right]\right\}$$

$$\exp\left(-\frac{1}{2}\left(\frac{y+x-\ln {D_2}^{2(n_2+1)}+\ln {U_2}^{2n_2}-\mu(t_2-t_1)}{\sigma\sqrt{t_2-t_1}}\right)\right)$$

$$\times\left(\frac{{D_2}^{n_2+1}}{S_0{U_2}^{n_2}}\right)^{\frac{2\mu}{\sigma^2}}$$

and

$$\left(\frac{{U_1}^{n_1}}{{D_1}^{n_1}}\right)^{\frac{2\mu}{\sigma^2}}\frac{1}{\sigma\sqrt{2\pi t_1}}\exp\left(-\frac{1}{2}\left(\frac{x-x_0-\ln {U_1}^{2n_1}+\ln {D_1}^{2n_1}-\mu t_1}{\sigma\sqrt{t_1}}\right)^2\right)$$

$$\times\ \exp\left\{\frac{2\mu^*}{\sigma^2}\left[(-x+x_0)\right]\right\}$$

This makes the drift term $+\mu t_1$, but we have to add and subtract

$$\exp\left(\frac{2\mu}{\sigma^2}\ln\frac{{U_1}^{2n_1}}{{D_1}^{2n_1}}-\frac{2\mu}{\sigma^2}\ln\frac{{U_1}^{2n_1}}{{D_1}^{2n_1}}\right)$$

The positive term makes

$$\exp\left(-\frac{1}{2}\left(\frac{x-x_0-\ln {U_1}^{2n_1}+\ln {D_1}^{2n_1}+\mu t_1}{\sigma\sqrt{t_1}}\right)^2\right)$$

and the negative term makes

$$\left(\frac{{D_1}^{n_1}}{{U_1}^{n_1}}\right)^{\frac{2\mu}{\sigma^2}}$$

So, the coefficient is

$$\left(\frac{{D_1}^{n_1}}{{U_1}^{n_1}}\frac{{D_2}^{n_2+1}}{S_0{U_2}^{n_2}}\right)^{\frac{2\mu}{\sigma^2}}$$

Then the first variable is

$$z = \frac{\ln\left(\frac{U_1 {D_1}^{2n_1}}{S_0 {U_1}^{2n_1}}\right) + \mu t_1}{\sigma\sqrt{t_1}}$$

The second variable is

$$\exp\left(-\frac{1}{2}\left(\frac{y + x - \ln {D_2}^{2(n_2+1)} + \ln {U_2}^{2n_2} - \mu(t_2 - t_1)}{\sigma\sqrt{t_2 - t_1}}\right)\right)$$

$$= \exp\left(-\frac{1}{2}\left(\frac{y - \ln {D_2}^{2(n_2+1)} + \ln {U_2}^{2n_2} - \mu t_2 + x + \mu t_1}{\sigma\sqrt{t_2 - t_1}}\right)\right)$$

Adding

$$-x_0 - \ln {U_1}^{2n_1} + \ln {D_1}^{2n_1}$$

we obtain the $\frac{w-\rho z}{\sqrt{1-\rho^2}}$ term but with a negative correlation.

$$\frac{y + x_0 + \ln {U_1}^{2n_1} - \ln {D_1}^{2n_1} - \ln {D_2}^{2(n_2+1)} + \ln {U_2}^{2n_2} - \mu t_2 +}{\sigma\sqrt{t_2 - t_1}}$$

$$\frac{x - x_0 - \ln {U_1}^{2n_1} + \ln {D_1}^{2n_1} + \mu t_1}{\sigma\sqrt{t_2 - t_1}}$$

$$w = \frac{\ln K + \ln U_1^{2n_1} + \ln {U_2}^{2n_2} - \ln D_1^{2n_1} - \ln D_2^{2(n_2+1)} + \ln(S_0 - \mu t_2)}{\sigma\sqrt{t_2}}$$

$$= \frac{\ln\left(\frac{K S_0 {U_1}^{2n_1} {U_2}^{2n_2}}{{D_1}^{2n_1} {D_2}^{2(n_2+1)}}\right) - \mu t_2}{\sigma\sqrt{t_2}}$$

$$\sum_{n_1=-\infty}^{\infty} \sum_{n_2=-\infty}^{\infty} \left(\frac{{D_1}^{n_1} {D_2}^{n_2+1}}{{U_1}^{n_1} {U_2}^{n_2} S_0}\right)^{2\mu/\sigma^2}$$

$$\int_{-\infty}^{\frac{\ln\left(\frac{U_1 {D_1}^{2n_1}}{S_0 {U_1}^{2n_1}}\right)+\mu t_1}{\sigma\sqrt{t_1}}} \int_{-\infty}^{\frac{\ln\left(\frac{K S_0 {U_1}^{2n_1} {U_2}^{2n_2}}{{D_1}^{2n_1} {D_2}^{2(n_2+1)}}\right)-\mu t_2}{\sigma\sqrt{t_2}}} \frac{1}{\sqrt{2\pi}} e^{-\frac{1}{2}z^2 - \frac{1}{2}\left(\frac{w+\rho z}{\sqrt{1-\rho^2}}\right)^2} dz dw$$

$$= \sum_{n_1=-\infty}^{\infty} \sum_{n_2=-\infty}^{\infty} \left(\frac{D_1{}^{n_1} D_2{}^{n_2+1}}{U_1{}^{n_1} U_2{}^{n_2} S_0} \right)^{\frac{2\mu}{\sigma^2}} N_2(I_3(U_1), I_4(K); -\rho)$$

$$I_3(U_1) = \frac{\ln\left(\frac{U_1 D_1{}^{2n_1}}{S_0 U_1{}^{2n_1}} \right) + \mu t_1}{\sigma\sqrt{t_1}}, \quad I_4(K) = \frac{\ln\left(\frac{K S_0 U_1{}^{2n_1} U_2{}^{2n_2}}{D_1{}^{2n_1} D_2{}^{2(n_2+1)}} \right) - \mu t_2}{\sigma\sqrt{t_2}}$$

Since this group of integrals are

$$\int_{-\infty}^{\ln U_1} \int_{-\infty}^{\ln K} - \int_{-\infty}^{\ln U_1} \int_{-\infty}^{\ln D_2} - \int_{-\infty}^{\ln D_1} \int_{-\infty}^{\ln K} - \int_{-\infty}^{\ln D_1} \int_{-\infty}^{\ln D_2}$$

the other distributions are

$$- \sum_{n_1=-\infty}^{\infty} \sum_{n_2=-\infty}^{\infty} N_2(I_3(U_1), I_4(D_2); -\rho)$$

$$- \sum_{n_1=-\infty}^{\infty} \sum_{n_2=-\infty}^{\infty} N_2(I_3(D_1), I_4(K); -\rho)$$

$$+ \sum_{n_1=-\infty}^{\infty} \sum_{n_2=-\infty}^{\infty} N_2(I_3(D_1), I_4(D_2); -\rho)$$

each multiplied by

$$\left(\frac{D_1{}^{n_1} D_2{}^{n_2+1}}{U_1{}^{n_1} U_2{}^{n_2} S_0} \right)^{2\mu/\sigma^2}$$

The remaining derivations follow similarly.

The value of a two-step double knock-out call TSDKOC is obtained as follows:

$$\begin{aligned} &\text{TSDKOC } (S_0, r, \sigma, \delta, t_1, t_2, K, U_1, U_2, D_1, D_2) \\ &= \text{TSDKOP } (S_0, r, \sigma, \delta, t_1, t_2, U_2, U_1, U_2, D_1, D_2) \\ &\quad - \text{TSDKOP } (S_0, r, \sigma, \delta, t_1, t_2, K, U_1, U_2, D_1, D_2) \end{aligned} \tag{7.22}$$

The reason is clear. By writing the payoff functions of both put options, it will yield

$$\max(U_2 - S(T), 0) - \max(K - S(T), 0)$$

which is the call payoff with strike K:

$$\max\left(U_2 - K, 0\right)$$

where $S\left(T\right) < U_2$ condition must be satisfied for the option not to be knocked out.

7.2.1.2. *EETSDKOP*

An EETSDKOP is given by (Guillaume, 2010).

$$\begin{aligned}
&\mathrm{EETSDKOP}\left(S_0, r, \sigma, \delta, t_1, t_2, t_3, K, U_1, U_2, D_1, D_2\right)\\
&\quad = \exp\left(-rt_3\right) K \Phi_{\mathrm{EETS}}\left(\mu\right) - \exp\left(-\delta t_3\right) S_0 \Phi_{\mathrm{EETS}}\left(\tilde{\mu}\right)\\
&\Phi_{\mathrm{EETS}}\left(\mu\right) = \sum_{n_1=-\infty}^{\infty} \sum_{n_2=-\infty}^{\infty} \left(\frac{U_1^{n_1} U_2^{n_2}}{D_1^{n_1} D_2^{n_2}}\right)^{2\mu/\sigma^2}\\
&\left\{N_3\left[I_1\left(U_1 \wedge U_2\right), I_2\left(U_2\right), I_3(K); H_1\right]\right.\\
&\quad - N_3\left[I_1\left(D_1 \vee D_2\right), I_2\left(U_2\right), I_3(K); H_1\right]\\
&\quad - N_3\left[I_1\left(U_1 \wedge U_2\right), I_2\left(D_2\right), I_3(K); H_1\right]\\
&\quad \left. + N_3\left[I_1\left(D_1 \vee D_2\right), I_2\left(D_2\right), I_3(K); H_1\right]\right\}\\
&- \sum_{n_1=-\infty}^{\infty} \sum_{n_2=-\infty}^{\infty} \left(\frac{D_1^{n_1} D_2^{n_2+1}}{S_0 U_1^{n_1} U_2^{n_2}}\right)^{2\mu/\sigma^2}\\
&\left\{N_3\left[I_4\left(U_1 \wedge U_2\right), I_5\left(U_2\right), I_6(K); H_2\right]\right.\\
&\quad - N_3\left[I_4\left(D_1 \vee D_2\right), I_5\left(U_2\right), I_6(K); H_2\right]\\
&\quad - N_3\left[I_4\left(U_1 \wedge U_2\right), I_5\left(D_2\right), I_6(K); H_2\right]\\
&\quad \left. + N_3\left[I_4\left(D_1 \vee D_2\right), I_5\left(D_2\right), I_6(K); H_2\right]\right\}\\
&\quad - \sum_{n_1=-\infty}^{\infty} \sum_{n_2=-\infty}^{\infty} \left(\frac{D_1^{n_1+1} U_2^{n_2}}{S_0 U_1^{n_1} D_2^{n_2}}\right)^{2\mu/\sigma^2}\\
&\quad \left\{N_3\left[I_7\left(U_1 \wedge U_2\right), I_8\left(U_2\right), I_9(K); H_1\right]\right.\\
&\quad - N_3\left[I_7\left(D_1 \vee D_2\right), I_8\left(U_2\right), I_9(K); H_1\right]\\
&\quad - N_3\left[I_7\left(U_1 \wedge U_2\right), I_8\left(D_2\right), I_9(K); H_1\right]
\end{aligned}$$

$$+ N_3\left[I_7\left(D_1 \vee D_2\right), I_8\left(D_2\right), I_9(K); H_1\right]\}$$

$$+ \sum_{n_1=-\infty}^{\infty} \sum_{n_2=-\infty}^{\infty} \left(\frac{D_2^{n_2+1} U_1^{n_1}}{D_1^{n_1+1} U_2^{n_2}}\right)^{2\mu/\sigma^2}$$

$$\{N_3[I_{10}\left(U_1 \wedge U_2\right), I_{11}\left(U_2\right), I_{12}(K); H_2]$$

$$- N_3[I_{10}\left(D_1 \vee D_2\right), I_{11}\left(U_2\right), I_{12}(K); H_2]$$

$$- N_3\left[I_7\left(U_1 \wedge U_2\right), I_{11}\left(D_2\right), I_{12}(K); H_2\right]$$

$$+ N_3\left[I_7\left(D_1 \vee D_2\right), I_{11}\left(D_2\right), I_{12}(K); H_2\right]\}$$

$$I_1(X) = \left(\ln\left(\frac{X D_1^{2n_1}}{S_0 U_1^{2n_1}}\right) - \mu t_1\right) \Big/ \sigma\sqrt{t_1}$$

$$I_2(X) = \left(\ln\left(\frac{X D_1^{2n_1} D_2^{2n_2}}{S_0 U_1^{2n_1} U_2^{2n_2}}\right) - \mu t_2\right) \Big/ \sigma\sqrt{t_2}$$

$$I_3(X) = \left(\ln\left(\frac{X D_1^{2n_1} D_2^{2n_2}}{S_0 U_1^{2n_1} U_2^{2n_2}}\right) - \mu t_3\right) \Big/ \sigma\sqrt{t_3}$$

$$I_4(X) = \left(\ln\left(\frac{X D_1^{2n_1}}{S_0 U_1^{2n_1}}\right) + \mu t_1\right) \Big/ \sigma\sqrt{t_1}$$

$$I_5(X) = \left(\ln\left(\frac{X S_0 U_1^{2n_1} U_2^{2n_2}}{D_2^{2(n_2+1)} D_1^{2(n_1)}}\right) - \mu t_2\right) \Big/ \sigma\sqrt{t_2}$$

$$I_6(X) = \left(\ln\left(\frac{X S_0 U_1^{2n_1} U_2^{2n_2}}{D_1^{2n_1} D_2^{2(n_2+1)}}\right) - \mu t_3\right) \Big/ \sigma\sqrt{t_3}$$

$$I_7(X) = \left(\ln\left(\frac{X S_0 U_1^{2n_1}}{D_1^{2(n_1+1)}}\right) - \mu t_1\right) \Big/ \sigma\sqrt{t_1}$$

$$I_8(X) = \left(\ln\left(\frac{X S_0 U_1^{2(n_1)} D_2^{2n_2}}{U_2^{2n_2} D_1^{2(n_1+1)}}\right) - \mu t_2\right) \Big/ \sigma\sqrt{t_2}$$

$$I_9(X) = \left(\ln\left(\frac{X S_0 U_1^{2(n_1)} D_2^{2n_2}}{U_2^{2n_2} D_1^{2(n_1+1)}}\right) - \mu t_3\right) \Big/ \sigma\sqrt{t_3}$$

$$I_{10}(X) = \left(\ln\left(\frac{XS_0U_1^{2(n_1)}}{D_1^{2(n_1+1)}}\right) + \mu t_1\right) \Big/ \sigma\sqrt{t_1}$$

$$I_{11}(X) = \left(\ln\left(\frac{XD_1^{2(n_1+1)}U_2^{2n_2}}{S_0D_2^{2(n_2+1)}U_1^{2(n_1)}}\right) - \mu t_2\right) \Big/ \sigma\sqrt{t_2}$$

$$I_{12}(X) = \left(\ln\left(\frac{XD_1^{2(n_1+1)}U_2^{2n_2}}{S_0U_1^{2n_1}D_2^{2(n_2+1)}}\right) - \mu t_3\right) \Big/ \sigma\sqrt{t_3}$$

$$H_1 = \left\{\sqrt{\frac{t_1}{t_2}}, \sqrt{\frac{t_1}{t_3}}, \sqrt{\frac{t_2}{t_3}}\right\} \quad H_2 = \left\{-\sqrt{\frac{t_1}{t_2}}, -\sqrt{\frac{t_1}{t_3}}, \sqrt{\frac{t_2}{t_3}}\right\} \tag{7.23}$$

Let us write the relevant densities as

$$f_1 = \frac{1}{\sigma\sqrt{2\pi t_1}}\left[\exp\left(-\frac{1}{2}\left(\frac{x - x_0 - \ln U_1{}^{2n_1} + \ln D_1{}^{2n_1} - \mu t_1}{\sigma\sqrt{t_1}}\right)^2\right)\right.$$

$$\times \left(\frac{D_1{}^{n_1}}{U_1{}^{n_1}}\right)^{\frac{2\mu}{\sigma^2}} - \exp\left(-\frac{1}{2}\left(\frac{x + x_0 - \ln D_1{}^{2(n_1+1)} + \ln U_1{}^{2n_1} - \mu t_1}{\sigma\sqrt{T}}\right)\right)$$

$$\left.\times \left(\frac{D_1{}^{n_1+1}}{S_0U_1{}^{n_1}}\right)^{\frac{2\mu}{\sigma^2}}\right]$$

$$f_2 = \frac{1}{\sigma\sqrt{2\pi(t_2 - t_1)}}\exp\left(-\frac{1}{2}\left(\frac{y - x - \ln U_2{}^{2n_2} + \ln D_2{}^{2n_2} - \mu(t_2 - t_1)}{\sigma\sqrt{t_2 - t_1}}\right)^2\right)$$

$$\times \left(\frac{D_2{}^{n_2}}{U_2{}^{n_2}}\right)^{\frac{2\mu}{\sigma^2}}$$

$$-\exp\left(-\frac{1}{2}\left(\frac{y + x - \ln D_2{}^{2(n_2+1)} + \ln U_2{}^{2n_2} - \mu(t_2 - t_1)}{\sigma\sqrt{t_2 - t_1}}\right)\left(\frac{D_2{}^{n_2+1}}{S_0U_2{}^{n_2}}\right)^{\frac{2\mu}{\sigma^2}}\right)$$

$$f_3 = \frac{1}{\sigma\sqrt{2\pi(t_3 - t_2)}}\exp\left(-\frac{1}{2}\left(\frac{z - y - \mu(t_3 - t_2)}{\sigma\sqrt{t_3 - t_2}}\right)^2\right)$$

where

$$\int_{\ln D_1}^{\ln U_1}\int_{\ln D_2}^{\ln U_2}\int_{-\infty}^{\ln K} f_1f_2f_3dxdydz$$

However, this is split into two parts, yielding four different integrals. Once again, together with the densities, we obtain 16 cumulative distributions.

The group of integrals are

$$\left[\int_{-\infty}^{\ln U_1} - \int_{-\infty}^{\ln D_1}\left(\int_{-\infty}^{\ln U_2} - \int_{-\infty}^{\ln D_2}\right)\right]$$

$$\int_{-\infty}^{\ln K}\int_{-\infty}^{\ln U_1}\int_{-\infty}^{\ln U_2}\int_{-\infty}^{\ln K} - \int_{-\infty}^{\ln U_1}\int_{-\infty}^{\ln D_2}\int_{-\infty}^{\ln K}$$
$$- \int_{-\infty}^{\ln D_1}\int_{-\infty}^{\ln U_2}\int_{-\infty}^{\ln K} + \int_{-\infty}^{\ln D_1}\int_{-\infty}^{\ln D_2}\int_{-\infty}^{\ln K}$$

Let's take the first one, excluding the coefficient terms.

$$\exp\left(-\frac{1}{2}\left(\frac{x - x_0 - \ln {U_1}^{2n_1} + \ln {D_1}^{2n_1} - \mu t_1}{\sigma\sqrt{t_1}}\right)^2\right)$$

$$\exp\left(-\frac{1}{2}\left(\frac{y - x - \ln {U_2}^{2n_2} + \ln {D_2}^{2n_2} - \mu(t_2 - t_1)}{\sigma\sqrt{t_2 - t_1}}\right)^2\right)$$

$$\exp\left(-\frac{1}{2}\left(\frac{z - y - \mu(t_3 - t_2)}{\sigma\sqrt{t_3 - t_2}}\right)^2\right)$$

It is easy to see that the first variable is

$$u = \frac{x - x_0 - \ln {U_1}^{2n_1} + \ln {D_1}^{2n_1} - \mu t_1}{\sigma\sqrt{t_1}}$$
$$= \left(\ln\left(\frac{XD_1^{2n_1}}{S_0U_1^{2n_1}}\right) - \mu t_1\right) \Big/ \sigma\sqrt{t_1}$$

where $X = U_1$

$$I_1(U_1) = \left(\ln\left(\frac{U_1D_1^{2n_1}}{S_0U_1^{2n_1}}\right) - \mu t_1\right) \Big/ \sigma\sqrt{t_1}$$

To find the second one, we need some algebra

$$\frac{y - x - \ln {U_2}^{2n_2} + \ln {D_2}^{2n_2} - \mu(t_2 - t_1)}{\sigma\sqrt{t_2 - t_1}}$$

By adding and subtracting

$$-x_0 - \ln {U_1}^{2n_1} + \ln {D_1}^{2n_1}$$

we find

$$\frac{y - x_0 - \ln {U_1}^{2n_1} + \ln {D_1}^{2n_1} - \ln {U_2}^{2n_2} + \ln {D_2}^{2n_2} -}{\sigma\sqrt{t_2 - t_1}}$$

$$\frac{\mu t_2 - (x - \mu t_1 - x_0 - \ln {U_1}^{2n_1} + \ln {D_1}^{2n_1})}{\sigma\sqrt{t_2 - t_1}}$$

$$\frac{v - \rho_{12} u}{\sqrt{1 - \rho_{12}^2}}$$

Therefore,

$$v = \left(\ln\left(\frac{X D_1^{2n_1} D_2^{2n_2}}{S_0 U_1^{2n_1} U_2^{2n_2}}\right) - \mu t_2\right) \Big/ \sigma\sqrt{t_2}$$

where $X = U_2$ with ρ_{12} positive.

$$I_2\left(U_2\right) = \left(\ln\left(\frac{U_2 D_1^{2n_1} D_2^{2n_2}}{S_0 U_1^{2n_1} U_2^{2n_2}}\right) - \mu t_2\right) \Big/ \sigma\sqrt{t_2}$$

Finally, we deal with the last density.

$$\exp\left(-\frac{1}{2}\left(\frac{z - y - \mu(t_3 - t_2)}{\sigma\sqrt{t_3 - t_2}}\right)^2\right)$$

$$\frac{z + \ln\left(\frac{D_1^{2n_1} D_2^{2n_2}}{S_0 U_1^{2n_1} U_2^{2n_2}}\right) - \mu t_3 - \left(y + \ln\left(\frac{D_1^{2n_1} D_2^{2n_2}}{S_0 U_1^{2n_1} U_2^{2n_2}}\right) - \mu t_2\right)}{\sigma\sqrt{t_3 - t_2}}$$

we obtain

$$\frac{w - \rho_{23} v}{\sqrt{1 - \rho_{23}^2}}$$

where

$$w = \left(\ln\left(\frac{KD_1^{2n_1}D_2^{2n_2}}{S_0U_1^{2n_1}U_2^{2n_2}}\right) - \mu t_3\right) \Big/ \sigma\sqrt{t_3}$$

with positive ρ_{23}.

$$I_3(K) = \left(\ln\left(\frac{KD_1^{2n_1}D_2^{2n_2}}{S_0U_1^{2n_1}U_2^{2n_2}}\right) - \mu t_3\right) \Big/ \sigma\sqrt{t_3}$$

So, for the first group of integrals

$$\sum_{n_1=-\infty}^{\infty}\sum_{n_2=-\infty}^{\infty}\left(\frac{U_1^{n_1}U_2^{n_2}}{D_1^{n_1}D_2^{n_2}}\right)^{2\mu/\sigma^2}\{N_3[I_1(U_1\wedge U_2), I_2(U_2), I_3(K); H_1]$$

$$- N_3[I_1(D_1\vee D_2), I_2(U_2), I_3(K); H_1]$$

$$- N_3[I_1(U_1\wedge U_2), I_2(D_2), I_3(K); H_1]$$

$$+ N_3[I_1(D_1\vee D_2), I_2(D_2), I_3(K); H_1]\}$$

we can calculate the same distributions with different upper integral limits.

The value of an early-ending two-step double knock-out call (EETSDKOC)

$$\begin{aligned} &\text{EETSDKOC}\,(S_0, r, \sigma, \delta, t_1, t_2, t_3, K, U_1, U_2, D_1, D_2) \\ &= \text{EETSDKOP}\,(S_0, r, \sigma, \delta, t_1, t_2, t_3, A, U_1, U_2, D_1, D_2) \\ &\quad -\text{EETSDKOP}\,(S_0, r, \sigma, \delta, t_1, t_2, t_3, K, U_1, U_2, D_1, D_2) \end{aligned} \tag{7.24}$$

where $A \to \infty$ practically much larger than S_0.

7.2.1.3. *Forward-start two-step double knock-out put (FSTSDKOP)*

The no-arbitrage value of a FSTSDKOP is given by Guillaume (2010) as

$$\text{FSTSDKOP}\ (S_0, r, \sigma, \delta, t_1, t_2, t_3, K, U_1, U_2, D_1, D_2) =$$

$$\exp(-rt_3)K\Phi_{\text{FSTS}}(\mu) - \exp(-\delta t_3)S_0\Phi_{\text{FSTS}}(\tilde{\mu})$$

$$(\tilde{\mu}) = r - \delta + \frac{\sigma^2}{2}\ \mu = r - \delta - \sigma^2/2$$

where

$$\sum_{n_1=-\infty}^{\infty}\sum_{n_2=-\infty}^{\infty}\left(\frac{U_1^{n_1}U_2^{n_2}}{D_1^{n_1}D_2^{n_2}}\right)^{2\mu/\sigma^2} \{N_3\left[I_1\left(U_1\right), I_2\left(U_1\wedge U_2\right), I_3(K); H_1\right]$$

$$-N_3\left[I_1\left(U_1\right), I_2\left(U_1\wedge U_2\right), I_3\left(D_2\right); H_1\right]$$

$$-N_3\left[I_1\left(U_1\right), I_2\left(D_1\vee D_2\right), I_3(K); H_1\right]$$

$$+N_3\left[I_1\left(U_1\right), I_2\left(D_1\vee D_2\right), I_3\left(D_2\right); H_1\right]$$

$$-N_3\left[I_1\left(D_1\right), I_2\left(U_1\wedge U_2\right), I_3(K); H_1\right]$$

$$+N_3[I_1(D_1), I_2(U_1\wedge U_2), I_3(D_2); H_1]$$

$$+N_3[I_1(D_1), I_2(D_1\vee D_2), I_3(K); H_1]$$

$$-N_3[I_1(D_1), I_2(D_1\vee D_2), I_3(D_2); H_1]\}$$

$$-\sum_{n_1=-\infty}^{\infty}\sum_{n_2=-\infty}^{\infty}\left(\frac{D_1^{n_1}D_2^{n_2+1}}{S_0U_1^{n_1}U_2^{n_2}}\right)^{2\mu/\sigma^2}$$

$$\{N_3\left[I_4\left(U_1\right), I_5\left(U_1\wedge U_2\right), I_6(K); H_2\right]$$

$$-N_3\left[\left[I_4\left(U_1\right), I_5\left(U_1\wedge U_2\right), I_6\left(D_2\right); H_2\right]\right]$$

$$-N_3\left[I_4\left(U_1\right), I_5\left(D_1\vee D_2\right), I_6(K); H_2\right]$$

$$+N_3\left[I_4\left(U_1\right), I_5\left(D_1\vee D_2\right), I_6\left(D_2\right); H_2\right]$$

$$-N_3\left[I_4\left(D_1\right), I_5\left(U_1\wedge U_2\right), I_6(K); H_2\right]$$

$$+N_3\left[I_4\left(D_1\right), I_5\left(U_1\wedge U_2\right), I_6\left(D_2\right); H_2\right]$$

$$+N_3\left[I_4\left(D_1\right), I_5\left(D_1\vee D_2\right), I_6(K); H_2\right]$$

$$-N_3\left[I_4\left(D_1\right), I_5\left(D_1\vee D_2\right), I_6\left(D_2\right); H_2\right]\}$$

$$-\sum_{n_1=-\infty}^{\infty}\sum_{n_2=-\infty}^{\infty}\left(\frac{D_1^{n_1+1}U_2^{n_2}}{S_0U_1^{n_1}D_2^{n_2}}\right)^{2\mu/\sigma^2}$$

$$\{N_3\left[I_4\left(U_1\right), I_7\left(U_1\wedge U_2\right), I_8(K); H_3\right]$$

$$-N_3\left[I_4\left(U_1\right), I_7\left(U_1\wedge U_2\right), I_8\left(D_2\right); H_3\right]$$

$$
\begin{aligned}
&- N_3\left[I_4(U_1), I_7(D_1 \vee D_2), I_8(K); H_3\right] \\
&+ N_3\left[I_4(U_1), I_7(D_1 \vee D_2), I_8(D_2); H_3\right] \\
&- N_3\left[I_4(D_1), I_7(U_1 \wedge U_2), I_8(K); H_3\right] \\
&+ N_3\left[I_4(D_1), I_7(U_1 \wedge U_2), I_8(D_2); H_3\right] \\
&+ N_3\left[I_4(D_1), I_7(D_1 \vee D_2), I_8(K); H_3\right] \\
&- N_3\left[I_4(D_1), I_7(D_1 \vee D_2), I_8(D_2); H_3\right]\} \\
+ &\sum_{n_1=-\infty}^{\infty} \sum_{n_2=-\infty}^{\infty} \left(\frac{D_2^{n_2+1} U_1^{n_1}}{D_1^{n_1+1} U_2^{n_2}}\right)^{2\mu/\sigma^2} \\
&\{N_3\left[I_4(U_1), I_9(U_1 \wedge U_2), I_{10}(K); H_4\right] \\
&- N_3\left[I_4(U_1), I_9(U_1 \wedge U_2), I_{10}(D_2); H_4\right] \\
&- N_3\left[I_4(U_1), I_9(D_1 \vee D_2), I_{10}(K); H_4\right] \\
&+ N_3\left[I_4(U_1), I_9(D_1 \vee D_2), I_{10}(D_2); H_4\right] \\
&- N_3\left[I_4(D_1), I_9(U_1 \wedge U_2), I_{10}(K); H_4\right] \\
&+ N_3\left[I_4(D_1), I_9(U_1 \wedge U_2), I_{10}(D_2); H_4\right] \\
&+ N_3\left[I_4(D_1), I_9(D_1 \vee D_2), I_{10}(K); H_4\right] \\
&- N_3\left[I_4(D_1), I_9(D_1 \vee D_2), I_{10}(D_2); H_4\right]\}
\end{aligned}
$$

$$I_1(X) = \left(\ln\left(\frac{X}{S_0}\right) - \mu t_1\right) \Big/ \sigma\sqrt{t_1}$$

$$I_2(X) = \left(\ln\left(\frac{X D_1^{2n_1}}{S_0 U_1^{2n_1}}\right) - \mu t_2\right) \Big/ \sigma\sqrt{t_2}$$

$$I_3(X) = \left(\ln\left(\frac{X D_1^{2n_1} D_2^{2n_2}}{S_0 U_1^{2n_1} U_2^{2n_2}}\right) - \mu t_3\right) \Big/ \sigma\sqrt{t_3}$$

$$I_4(X) = \left(\ln\left(\frac{X}{S_0}\right) + \mu t_1\right) \Big/ \sigma\sqrt{t_1}$$

$$I_5(X) = \left(\ln\left(\frac{XD_1^{2n_1}}{U_1^{2(n_1)}}\right) + \mu t_2\right) \Big/ \sigma\sqrt{t_2}$$

$$I_6(X) = \left(\ln\left(\frac{XS_0U_1^{2n_1}U_2^{2n_2}}{D_1^{2n_1}D_2^{2(n_2+1)}}\right) - \mu t_3\right) \Big/ \sigma\sqrt{t_3}$$

$$I_7(X) = \left(\ln\left(\frac{XS_0U_1^{2n_1}}{D_1^{2(n_1+1)}}\right) - \mu t_2\right) \Big/ \sigma\sqrt{t_2}$$

$$I_8(X) = \left(\ln\left(\frac{XS_0U_1^{2(n_1)}D_2^{2n_2}}{U_2^{2n_2}D_1^{2(n_1+1)}}\right) - \mu t_3\right) \Big/ \sigma\sqrt{t_3}$$

$$I_9(X) = \left(\ln\left(\frac{XS_0U_1^{2(n_1)}}{D_1^{2(n_1+1)}}\right) + \mu t_2\right) \Big/ \sigma\sqrt{t_2}$$

$$I_{10}(X) = \left(\ln\left(\frac{XU_2^{2(n_2)}D_1^{2(n_1+1)}}{S_0U_1^{2(n_1)}D_2^{2(n_2+1)}}\right) - \mu t_3\right) \Big/ \sigma\sqrt{t_3}$$

$$H_1 = \left\{\sqrt{\frac{t_1}{t_2}}, \sqrt{\frac{t_1}{t_3}}, \sqrt{\frac{t_2}{t_3}}\right\} \quad H_2 = \left\{\sqrt{\frac{t_1}{t_2}}, -\sqrt{\frac{t_1}{t_3}}, -\sqrt{\frac{t_2}{t_3}}\right\}$$

$$H_3 = \left\{-\sqrt{\frac{t_1}{t_2}}, -\sqrt{\frac{t_1}{t_3}}, \sqrt{\frac{t_2}{t_3}}\right\} \quad H_4 = \left\{-\sqrt{\frac{t_1}{t_2}}, \sqrt{\frac{t_1}{t_3}}, -\sqrt{\frac{t_2}{t_3}}\right\} \tag{7.25}$$

The group of integrals are

$$\left[\int_{-\infty}^{\ln U_1} - \int_{-\infty}^{\ln D_1} \left(\int_{-\infty}^{\ln U_1} - \int_{-\infty}^{\ln D_1}\right)\right]\left(\int_{-\infty}^{\ln K} - \int_{-\infty}^{\ln D_2}\right)$$

$$\int_{-\infty}^{\ln U_1}\int_{-\infty}^{\ln U_1}\int_{-\infty}^{\ln K} - \int_{-\infty}^{\ln U_1}\int_{-\infty}^{\ln D_1}\int_{-\infty}^{\ln K}$$

$$-\int_{-\infty}^{\ln U_1}\int_{-\infty}^{\ln U_1}\int_{-\infty}^{\ln D_2} - \int_{-\infty}^{\ln D_1}\int_{-\infty}^{\ln U_1}\int_{-\infty}^{\ln K}$$

$$+\int_{-\infty}^{\ln D_1}\int_{-\infty}^{\ln D_1}\int_{-\infty}^{\ln K}+\int_{-\infty}^{\ln D_1}\int_{-\infty}^{\ln U_1}\int_{-\infty}^{\ln D_2}$$

$$-\int_{-\infty}^{\ln D_1}\int_{-\infty}^{\ln D_1}\int_{-\infty}^{\ln D_2}+\int_{-\infty}^{\ln U_1}\int_{-\infty}^{\ln D_1}\int_{-\infty}^{\ln D_2}$$

That means we will have 32 trivariate cumulative normal distributions, different from the number of early-ending ones.

The densities to be used are

$$f_1=\frac{1}{\sigma\sqrt{2\pi t_1}}\exp\left(-\frac{1}{2}\left(\frac{x-x_0-\mu t_1}{\sigma\sqrt{t_1}}\right)^2\right)$$

$$\begin{aligned}
f_2=&\frac{1}{\sigma\sqrt{2\pi(t_2-t_1)}}\\
&\times\left[\exp\left(-\frac{1}{2}\left(\frac{y-x-\ln {U_1}^{2n_1}+\ln {D_1}^{2n_1}-\mu(t_2-t_1)}{\sigma\sqrt{(t_2-t_1)}}\right)^2\right)\right.\\
&\times\left(\frac{{D_1}^{n_1}}{{U_1}^{n_1}}\right)^{\frac{2\mu}{\sigma^2}}\\
&-\exp\left(-\frac{1}{2}\left(\frac{y+x-\ln {D_1}^{2(n_1+1)}+\ln {U_1}^{2n_1}-\mu\,(t_2-t_1)}{\sigma\sqrt{(t_2-t_1)}}\right)\right)\\
&\left.\times\ \exp\left\{\frac{2\mu^*}{\sigma^2}\left[(\gamma_2-x)-n\,(\gamma_1-\gamma_2)\right]\right\}\right]
\end{aligned}$$

$$\begin{aligned}
f_3=&\frac{1}{\sigma\sqrt{2\pi(t_3-t_2)}}\\
&\times\exp\left(-\frac{1}{2}\left(\frac{z-y-\ln {U_2}^{2n_2}+\ln {D_2}^{2n_2}-\mu(t_3-t_2)}{\sigma\sqrt{t_3-t_2}}\right)^2\right)\\
&\times\left(\frac{{D_2}^{n_2}}{{U_2}^{n_2}}\right)^{\frac{2\mu}{\sigma^2}}
\end{aligned}$$

$$- \exp\left(-\frac{1}{2}\left(\frac{z+y-\ln {D_2}^{2(n_2+1)}+\ln {U_2}^{2n_2}-\mu(t_3-t_2)}{\sigma\sqrt{t_3-t_2}}\right)\right.$$

$$\left.\times \exp\left\{\frac{2\mu^*}{\sigma^2}\left[(\gamma_2-y)-n\left(\gamma_1-\gamma_2\right)\right]\right\}\right)$$

Now, we consider a different group of integral as

$$\int_{-\infty}^{\ln U_1}\int_{-\infty}^{\ln U_1}\int_{-\infty}^{\ln K} f_1 f_{2b} f_{3b} dx dy dz$$

by choosing the following densities:

$$\exp\left(-\frac{1}{2}\left(\frac{x-x_0-\mu t_1}{\sigma\sqrt{t_1}}\right)^2\right)$$

$$\exp\left(-\frac{1}{2}\left(\frac{y+x-\ln {D_1}^{2(n_1+1)}+\ln {U_1}^{2n_1}-\mu\left(t_2-t_1\right)}{\sigma\sqrt{(t_2-t_1)}}\right)\right)$$

$$\exp\left\{\frac{2\mu^*}{\sigma^2}\left[(\gamma_2-x)-n\left(\gamma_1-\gamma_2\right)\right]\right\}$$

$$\exp\left(-\frac{1}{2}\left(\frac{z+y-\ln {D_2}^{2(n_2+1)}+\ln {U_2}^{2n_2}-\mu(t_3-t_2)}{\sigma\sqrt{t_3-t_2}}\right)\right.$$

$$\left.\exp\left\{\frac{2\mu^*}{\sigma^2}\left[(\gamma_2-y)-n\left(\gamma_1-\gamma_2\right)\right]\right\}\right)$$

$$\exp\left(-\frac{1}{2}\left(\frac{y+x-\ln {D_1}^{2(n_1+1)}+\ln {U_1}^{2n_1}-\mu(t_2-t_1)}{\sigma\sqrt{(t_2-t_1)}}\right)\right)$$

$$\exp\left(\frac{2\mu}{\sigma^2}(-x-y-\ln {D_1}^{2(n_1+1)}+\ln {U_1}^{2n_1}+\ln {D_1}^{2(n_1+1)}-\ln {U_1}^{2n_1})\right)$$

$$\exp\left(-\frac{1}{2}\left(\frac{y+x-\ln {D_1}^{2(n_1+1)}+\ln {U_1}^{2n_1}+\mu(t_2-t_1)}{\sigma\sqrt{(t_2-t_1)}}\right)\right)$$

$$\times\frac{{U_1}^{2n_1}}{{D_1}^{2(n_1+1)}}\frac{{D_1}^{n_1+1}}{{U_1}^{n_1}}$$

$$-\frac{1}{2}\left(\frac{y+x_0-\ln {D_1}^{2(n_1+1)}+\ln {U_1}^{2n_1}+\mu t_2+(x-x_0-\mu t_1)}{\sigma\sqrt{(t_2-t_1)}}\right)$$

$$\times\left(\frac{{U_1}^{n_1}}{{D_1}^{(n_1+1)}}\right)^{2\mu/\sigma^2}$$

Therefore, the first variable is

$$u=\frac{x-x_0-\mu t_1}{\sigma\sqrt{t_1}}=\frac{\ln U_1/S_0-\mu t_1}{\sigma\sqrt{t_1}}$$

and the second variable is

$$I_9\left(U_1\wedge U_2\right)=v=\frac{y+x_0-\ln {D_1}^{2(n_1+1)}+\ln {U_1}^{2n_1}+\mu t_2}{\sigma\sqrt{t_2}}$$

$$=\frac{\ln\frac{U_1S_0{U_1}^{2n_1}}{{D_1}^{2(n_1+1)}}+\mu t_2}{\sigma\sqrt{t_2}}$$

with $-\rho_{12}$ and coefficient $\left(\frac{{U_1}^{n_1}}{{D_1}^{(n_1+1)}}\right)^{2\mu/\sigma^2}$.

The last density is

$$\exp\left(-\frac{1}{2}\left(\frac{z+y-\ln {D_2}^{2(n_2+1)}+\ln {U_2}^{2n_2}-\mu(t_3-t_2)}{\sigma\sqrt{t_3-t_2}}\right)\right.$$

$$\left.\exp\left\{\frac{2\mu^*}{\sigma^2}\left[(\gamma_2)-n\left(\gamma_1-\gamma_2\right)\right]\right\}\right)$$

$$\exp\left\{\frac{2\mu^*}{\sigma^2}\left[(\gamma_2)-n\left(\gamma_1-\gamma_2\right)\right]\right\}=\left(\frac{{D_2}^{(n_2+1)}}{{U_2}^{n_2}}\right)^{2\mu/\sigma^2}$$

So, the overall coefficient is

$$\left(\frac{{U_1}^{n_1}}{{D_1}^{(n_1+1)}}\frac{{D_2}^{(n_2+1)}}{{U_2}^{n_2}}\right)^{2\mu/\sigma^2}$$

$$\frac{z-x_0-\ln {D_2}^{2(n_2+1)}+\ln {U_2}^{2n_2}+\ln {D_1}^{2(n_1+1)}-\ln {U_1}^{2n_1}}{\sigma\sqrt{t_3-t_2}}$$

$$-\frac{\mu t_3+y-\ln {D_1}^{2(n_1+1)}+\ln {U_1}^{2n_1}+x_0+\mu t_2}{\sigma\sqrt{t_3-t_2}}$$

Then

$$w = \frac{\begin{array}{l} z - x_0 - \ln {D_2}^{2(n_2+1)} + \ln {U_2}^{2n_2} + \ln {D_1}^{2(n_1+1)} \\ - \ln {U_1}^{2n_1} - \mu t_3 \end{array}}{\sigma\sqrt{t_3}}$$

$$I_{10}(K) = w = \frac{\ln \frac{K {U_2}^{2n_2} {D_1}^{2(n_1+1)}}{S_0 {U_1}^{2n_1} {D_2}^{2(n_2+1)}} - \mu t_3}{\sigma\sqrt{t_3}}$$

So, the last group of integrals is

$$\begin{aligned} &+ \sum_{n_1=-\infty}^{\infty} \sum_{n_2=-\infty}^{\infty} \left(\frac{D_2^{n_2+1} U_1^{n_1}}{D_1^{n_1+1} U_2^{n_2}} \right)^{2\mu/\sigma^2} \\ &\quad \times \{ N_3 \left[I_1 \left(U_1 \right), I_9 \left(U_1 \wedge U_2 \right), I_{10}(K); H_4 \right] \\ &\quad - N_3 \left[I_1 \left(U_1 \right), I_9 \left(U_1 \wedge U_2 \right), I_{10} \left(D_2 \right); H_4 \right] \\ &\quad - N_3 \left[I_1 \left(U_1 \right), I_9 \left(D_1 \vee D_2 \right), I_{10}(K); H_4 \right] \\ &\quad + N_3 \left[I_1 \left(U_1 \right), I_9 \left(D_1 \vee D_2 \right), I_{10} \left(D_2 \right); H_4 \right] \\ &\quad - N_3 \left[I_1 \left(D_1 \right), I_9 \left(U_1 \wedge U_2 \right), I_{10}(K); H_4 \right] \\ &\quad + N_3 \left[I_1 \left(D_1 \right), I_9 \left(U_1 \wedge U_2 \right), I_{10} \left(D_2 \right); H_4 \right] \\ &\quad + N_3 \left[I_1 \left(D_1 \right), I_9 \left(D_1 \vee D_2 \right), I_{10}(K); H_4 \right] \\ &\quad - N_3 \left[I_1 \left(D_1 \right), I_9 \left(D_1 \vee D_2 \right), I_{10} \left(D_2 \right); H_4 \right] \} \end{aligned}$$

with $-\rho_{12}$, $-\rho_{23}$, and ρ_{13}.

The value of a forward-start two-step double knock-out call (FSTSDKOC) is obtained as follows:

$$\begin{aligned} &\text{FSTSDKOC} \left(S_0, r, \sigma, \delta, t_1, t_2, t_3, K, U_1, U_2, D_1, D_2 \right) \\ &\quad = \text{FSTSDKOP} \ \left(S_0, r, \sigma, \delta, t_1, t_2, t_3, U_2, U_1, U_2, D_1, D_2 \right) \\ &\quad\quad - \text{FSTSDKOP} \ \left(S_0, r, \sigma, \delta, t_1, t_2, t_3, K, U_1, U_2, D_1, D_2 \right) \end{aligned} \tag{7.26}$$

7.2.1.4. *Window two-step double knock-out put (WTSDKOP)*

The no-arbitrage value of a WTSDKOP is given by (Guillaume, 2010):

$$\mathrm{WTSDKOP}\left(S_0, r, \sigma, \delta, t_1, t_2, t_3, t_4, K, U_1, U_2, D_1, D_2\right)$$

$$\exp\left(-rt_4\right)K\Phi_{\mathrm{WSTS}}\left(\mu\right) - \exp\left(-\delta t_4\right)S_0\Phi_{\mathrm{WTS}}\left(\widetilde{\mu}\right)$$

$$\Phi_{\mathrm{WSTS}}\left(\mu\right) =$$

$$\sum_{n_1=-\infty}^{\infty}\sum_{n_2=-\infty}^{\infty}\left(\frac{U_1^{n_1}U_2^{n_2}}{D_1^{n_1}D_2^{n_2}}\right)^{\frac{2\mu}{\sigma^2}}$$

$$\{N_4\left[I_1\left(U_1\right), I_2\left(U_1 \wedge U_2\right), I_3\left(U_2\right), I_4(K); H_1\right]$$

$$- N_4\left[I_1\left(U_1\right), I_2\left(U_1 \wedge U_2\right), I_3\left(D_2\right), I_4(K); H_1\right]$$

$$- N_4\left[I_1\left(U_1\right), I_2\left(D_1 \vee D_2\right), I_3\left(U_2\right), I_4(K); H_1\right]$$

$$+ N_4\left[I_1\left(U_1\right), I_2\left(D_1 \vee D_2\right), I_3\left(D_2\right), I_4\left(K\right); H_1\right]$$

$$- N_4\left[I_1\left(D_1\right), I_2\left(U_1 \wedge U_2\right), I_3\left(U_2\right), I_4(K); H_1\right]$$

$$+ N_4\left[I_1\left(D_1\right), I_2\left(U_1 \wedge U_2\right), I_3\left(D_2\right), I_4(K); H_1\right]$$

$$+ N_4\left[I_1\left(D_1\right), I_2\left(D_1 \vee D_2\right), I_3\left(U_2\right), I_4(K); H_1\right]$$

$$- N_4\left[I_1\left(D_1\right), I_2\left(D_1 \vee D_2\right), I_3\left(D_2\right), I_4\left(K\right); H_1\right]\}$$

$$- \sum_{n_1=-\infty}^{\infty}\sum_{n_2=-\infty}^{\infty}\left(\frac{D_1^{n_1}D_2^{n_2+1}}{S_0U_1^{n_1}U_2^{n_2}}\right)^{\frac{2\mu}{\sigma^2}}$$

$$\times\ \{N_4\left[I_5\left(U_1\right), I_6\left(U_1 \wedge U_2\right), I_7\left(U_2\right), I_8(K); H_2\right]$$

$$- N_4\left[I_5\left(U_1\right), I_6\left(U_1 \wedge U_2\right), I_7\left(D_2\right), I_8(K); H_2\right]$$

$$- N_4\left[I_5\left(U_1\right), I_6\left(D_1 \vee D_2\right), I_7\left(U_2\right), I_8(K); H_2\right]$$

$$+ N_4\left[I_5\left(U_1\right), I_6\left(D_1 \vee D_2\right), I_7\left(D_2\right), I_8\left(K\right); H_2\right]$$

$$- N_4\left[I_5\left(D_1\right), I_6\left(U_1 \wedge U_2\right), I_7\left(U_2\right), I_8(K); H_2\right]$$

$$+ N_4\left[I_5\left(D_1\right), I_6\left(U_1 \wedge U_2\right), I_7\left(D_2\right), I_8(K); H_2\right]$$

$$+ N_4 \left[I_5(D_1), I_6(D_1 \vee D_2), I_7(U_2), I_8(K); H_2 \right]$$
$$- N_4 \left[I_5(D_1), I_6(D_1 \vee D_2), I_7(D_2), I_8(K); H_2 \right] \}$$
$$- \sum_{n_1=-\infty}^{\infty} \sum_{n_2=-\infty}^{\infty} \left(\frac{D_1^{n_1+1} U_2^{n_2}}{S_0 U_1^{n_1} D_2^{n_2}} \right)^{2\mu/\sigma^2}$$
$$\{ N_4 \left[I_5(U_1), I_9(U_1 \wedge U_2), I_{10}(U_2), I_{11}(K); H_3 \right]$$
$$- N_4 \left[I_5(U_1), I_9(U_1 \wedge U_2), I_{10}(D_2), I_{11}(K); H_3 \right]$$
$$- N_4 \left[I_5(U_1), I_9(D_1 \vee D_2), I_{10}(U_2), I_{11}(K); H_3 \right]$$
$$+ N_4 \left[I_5(U_1), I_9(D_1 \vee D_2), I_{10}(D_2), I_{11}(K); H_3 \right]$$
$$- N_4 \left[I_5(D_1), I_9(U_1 \wedge U_2), I_{10}(U_2), I_{11}(K); H_3 \right]$$
$$+ N_4 \left[I_5(D_1), I_9(U_1 \wedge U_2), I_{10}(D_2), I_{11}(K); H_3 \right]$$
$$+ N_4 \left[I_5(D_1), I_9(D_1 \vee D_2), I_{10}(U_2), I_{11}(K); H_3 \right]$$
$$- N_4 \left[I_5(D_1), I_9(D_1 \vee D_2), I_{10}(D_2), I_{11}(K); H_3 \right] \}$$
$$+ \sum_{n_1=-\infty}^{\infty} \sum_{n_2=-\infty}^{\infty} \left(\frac{D_2^{n_2+1} U_1^{n_1}}{D_1^{n_1+1} U_2^{n_2}} \right)^{2\mu/\sigma^2}$$
$$\{ N_4 \left[I_5(U_1), I_{12}(U_1 \wedge U_2), I_{13}(U_2), I_{14}(K); H_4 \right]$$
$$- N_4 \left[I_5(U_1), I_{12}(U_1 \wedge U_2), I_{13}(D_2), I_{14}(K); H_4 \right]$$
$$- N_4 \left[I_5(U_1), I_{12}(D_1 \vee D_2), I_{13}(U_2), I_{14}(K); H_4 \right]$$
$$+ N_4 \left[I_5(U_1), I_{12}(D_1 \vee D_2), I_{13}(D_2), I_{14}(K); H_4 \right]$$
$$- N_4 \left[I_5(D_1), I_{12}(U_1 \wedge U_2), I_{13}(U_2), I_{14}(K); H_4 \right]$$
$$+ N_4 \left[I_5(D_1), I_{12}(U_1 \wedge U_2), I_{13}(D_2), I_{14}(K); H_4 \right]$$
$$+ N_4 \left[I_5(D_1), I_{12}(D_1 \vee D_2), I_{13}(U_2), I_{14}(K); H_4 \right]$$
$$- N_4 \left[I_5(D_1), I_{12}(D_1 \vee D_2), I_{13}(D_2), I_{14}(K); H_4 \right] \}$$

where

$$N_4\left[b_1, b_2, b_3, b_4; \theta_{12}, \theta_{23}, \theta_{34}\right]$$

$$= \int_{-\infty}^{b_2}\int_{-\infty}^{b_3} \frac{\exp\left\{-\frac{x^2}{2} - \frac{1}{2(1-\theta_{23}^2)}(x_3 - \theta_{23}x_2)^2\right\}}{2\pi\sqrt{1-\theta_{23}^2}} N\left[\frac{b_1 - \theta_{12}x_2}{\sqrt{1-\theta_{12}^2}}\right]$$

$$N\left[\frac{b_4 - \theta_{34}x_3}{\sqrt{1-\theta_{34}^2}}\right] dx_2 dx_3$$

$$I_1(X) = \left(\ln\left(\frac{X}{S_0}\right) - \mu t_1\right) \Big/ \sigma\sqrt{t_1}$$

$$I_2(X) = \left(\ln\left(\frac{XD_1^{2n_1}}{S_0 U_1^{2n_1}}\right) - \mu t_2\right) \Big/ \sigma\sqrt{t_2}$$

$$I_3(X) = \left(\ln\left(\frac{XD_1^{2n_1}D_2^{2n_2}}{S_0 U_1^{2n_1}U_2^{2n_2}}\right) - \mu t_3\right) \Big/ \sigma\sqrt{t_3}$$

$$I_4(X) = \left(\ln\left(\frac{XD_1^{2n_1}D_2^{2n_2}}{S_0 U_1^{2n_1}U_2^{2n_2}}\right) - \mu t_4\right) \Big/ \sigma\sqrt{t_4}$$

$$I_5(X) = \left(\ln\left(\frac{X}{S_0}\right) + \mu t_1\right) \Big/ \sigma\sqrt{t_1}$$

$$I_6(X) = \left(\ln\left(\frac{XD_1^{2n_1}}{S_0 U_1^{2n_1}}\right) + \mu t_2\right) \Big/ \sigma\sqrt{t_2}$$

$$I_7(X) = \left(\ln\left(\frac{XS_0 U_1^{2n_1}U_2^{2n_2}}{D_1^{2n_1}D_2^{2(n_2+1)}}\right) - \mu t_3\right) \Big/ \sigma\sqrt{t_3}$$

$$I_8(X) = \left(\ln\left(\frac{XS_0 U_1^{2(n_1)}U_2^{2n_2}}{D_2^{2(n_2+1)}D_1^{2(n_1)}}\right) - \mu t_4\right) \Big/ \sigma\sqrt{t_4}$$

$$I_9(X) = \left(\ln\left(\frac{XS_0 U_1^{2(n_1)}}{D_1^{2(n_1+1)}}\right) - \mu t_2\right) \Big/ \sigma\sqrt{t_2}$$

$$I_{10}(X) = \left(\ln\left(\frac{XS_0D_2^{2(n_2)}U_1^{2(n_1)}}{D_1^{2(n_1+1)}U_2^{2(n_2)}}\right) - \mu t_3\right) \Big/ \sigma\sqrt{t_3}$$

$$I_{11}(X) = \left(\ln\left(\frac{XS_0D_2^{2(n_2)}U_1^{2(n_1)}}{D_1^{2(n_1+1)}U_2^{2(n_2)}}\right) - \mu t_4\right) \Big/ \sigma\sqrt{t_4}$$

$$I_{12}(X) = \left(\ln\left(\frac{XS_0U_1^{2(n_1)}}{D_1^{2(n_1+1)}}\right) + \mu t_2\right) \Big/ \sigma\sqrt{t_2}$$

$$I_{13}(X) = \left(\ln\left(\frac{XD_1^{2(n_1+1)}U_2^{2(n_2)}}{S_0D_2^{2(n_2+1)}U_1^{2(n_1)}}\right) - \mu t_3\right) \Big/ \sigma\sqrt{t_3}$$

$$I_{14}(X) = \left(\ln\left(\frac{XD_1^{2(n_1+1)}U_2^{2(n_2)}}{S_0D_2^{2(n_2+1)}U_1^{2(n_1)}}\right) - \mu t_4\right) \Big/ \sigma\sqrt{t_4}$$

$$H_1 = \left\{\sqrt{\frac{t_1}{t_2}}, \sqrt{\frac{t_1}{t_3}}, \sqrt{\frac{t_2}{t_3}}\right\} \quad H_2 = \left\{\sqrt{\frac{t_1}{t_2}}, -\sqrt{\frac{t_1}{t_3}}, \sqrt{\frac{t_2}{t_3}}\right\}$$

$$H_3 = \left\{-\sqrt{\frac{t_1}{t_2}}, \sqrt{\frac{t_1}{t_3}}, \sqrt{\frac{t_2}{t_3}}\right\} \quad H_4 = \left\{-\sqrt{\frac{t_1}{t_2}}, -\sqrt{\frac{t_1}{t_3}}, \sqrt{\frac{t_2}{t_3}}\right\} \tag{7.27}$$

The densities are

$$f_1 = \frac{1}{\sigma\sqrt{2\pi t_1}} \exp\left(-\frac{1}{2}\left(\frac{x - x_0 - \mu t_1}{\sigma\sqrt{t_1}}\right)^2\right)$$

$$f_2 = \frac{1}{\sigma\sqrt{2\pi(t_2 - t_1)}}$$

$$\times \left[\exp\left(-\frac{1}{2}\left(\frac{y - x - \ln U_1{}^{2n_1} + \ln D_1{}^{2n_1} - \mu(t_2 - t_1)}{\sigma\sqrt{(t_2 - t_1)}}\right)^2\right)\right.$$

$$\times \left(\frac{U_1{}^{n_1}}{D_1{}^{n_1}}\right)^{\frac{2\mu}{\sigma^2}}$$

$$- \exp\left(-\frac{1}{2}\left(\frac{y + x - \ln {D_1}^{2(n_1+1)} + \ln {U_1}^{2n_1} - \mu\,(t_2 - t_1)}{\sigma\sqrt{(t_2 - t_1)}}\right)\right)$$

$$\times\ \exp\left\{\frac{2\mu^*}{\sigma^2}\left[(\gamma_2 - x) - n\,(\gamma_1 - \gamma_2)\right]\right\}\Bigg]$$

$$f_3 = \frac{1}{\sigma\sqrt{2\pi(t_3 - t_2)}}$$

$$\exp\left(-\frac{1}{2}\left(\frac{z - y - \ln {U_2}^{2n_2} + \ln {D_2}^{2n_2} - \mu(t_3 - t_2)}{\sigma\sqrt{t_3 - t_2}}\right)^2\right)\left(\frac{{U_2}^{n_2}}{{D_2}^{n_2}}\right)^{\frac{2\mu}{\sigma^2}}$$

$$- \exp\left(-\frac{1}{2}\left(\frac{z + y - \ln {D_2}^{2(n_2+1)} + \ln {U_2}^{2n_2} - \mu(t_3 - t_2)}{\sigma\sqrt{t_3 - t_2}}\right)\right)$$

$$\times\ \exp\left\{\frac{2\mu^*}{\sigma^2}\left[(\gamma_2 - y) - n\,(\gamma_1 - \gamma_2)\right]\right\}$$

$$f_4 = \frac{1}{\sigma\sqrt{2\pi(t_4 - t_3)}}\exp\left(-\frac{1}{2}\left(\frac{w - z - \mu(t_4 - t_3)}{\sigma\sqrt{t_4 - t_3}}\right)^2\right)$$

$$\left[\int_{-\infty}^{\ln U_1} - \int_{-\infty}^{\ln D_1}\left(\int_{-\infty}^{\ln U_1} - \int_{-\infty}^{\ln D_1}\right)\right]\left(\int_{-\infty}^{\ln K} - \int_{-\infty}^{\ln D_2}\right)$$

$$\int_{-\infty}^{\ln U_1}\int_{-\infty}^{\ln U_1}\int_{-\infty}^{\ln U_2}\int_{-\infty}^{\ln K} - \int_{-\infty}^{\ln U_1}\int_{-\infty}^{\ln U_1}\int_{-\infty}^{\ln D_2}\int_{-\infty}^{\ln K}$$

$$- \int_{-\infty}^{\ln U_1}\int_{-\infty}^{\ln D_1}\int_{-\infty}^{\ln U_2}\int_{-\infty}^{\ln K} + \int_{-\infty}^{\ln U_1}\int_{-\infty}^{\ln D_1}\int_{-\infty}^{\ln D_2}\int_{-\infty}^{\ln K}$$

$$- \int_{-\infty}^{\ln D_1}\int_{-\infty}^{\ln U_1}\int_{-\infty}^{\ln U_2}\int_{-\infty}^{\ln K} + \int_{-\infty}^{\ln D_1}\int_{-\infty}^{\ln U_1}\int_{-\infty}^{\ln D_2}\int_{-\infty}^{\ln K}$$

$$+ \int_{-\infty}^{\ln D_1}\int_{-\infty}^{\ln D_1}\int_{-\infty}^{\ln U_2}\int_{-\infty}^{\ln K} - \int_{-\infty}^{\ln D_1}\int_{-\infty}^{\ln D_1}\int_{-\infty}^{\ln D_2}\int_{-\infty}^{\ln K}$$

Let us try the first group of integrals.

$$\frac{1}{\sigma\sqrt{2\pi t_1}}\exp\left(-\frac{1}{2}\left(\frac{x-x_0-\mu t_1}{\sigma\sqrt{t_1}}\right)^2\right)\frac{1}{\sigma\sqrt{2\pi(t_2-t_1)}}$$

$$\exp\left(-\frac{1}{2}\left(\frac{y-x-\ln {U_1}^{2n_1}+\ln {D_1}^{2n_1}-\mu(t_2-t_1)}{\sigma\sqrt{(t_2-t_1)}}\right)^2\right)\left(\frac{{U_1}^{n_1}}{{D_1}^{n_1}}\right)^{\frac{2\mu}{\sigma^2}}$$

$$\frac{1}{\sigma\sqrt{2\pi(t_3-t_2)}}$$

$$\exp\left(-\frac{1}{2}\left(\frac{z-y-\ln {U_2}^{2n_2}+\ln {D_2}^{2n_2}-\mu(t_3-t_2)}{\sigma\sqrt{t_3-t_2}}\right)^2\right)\left(\frac{{U_2}^{n_2}}{{D_2}^{n_2}}\right)^{\frac{2\mu}{\sigma^2}}$$

$$\frac{1}{\sigma\sqrt{2\pi(t_4-t_3)}}\exp\left(-\frac{1}{2}\left(\frac{w-z-\mu(t_4-t_3)}{\sigma\sqrt{t_4-t_3}}\right)^2\right)$$

The coefficient is

$$\left(\frac{{U_1}^{n_1}}{{D_1}^{n_1}}\frac{{U_2}^{n_2}}{{D_2}^{n_2}}\right)^{\frac{2\mu}{\sigma^2}}$$

$$u=\frac{x-x_0-\mu t_1}{\sigma\sqrt{t_1}}=\left(\ln\left(\frac{X}{S_0}\right)-\mu t_1\right)\Big/\sigma\sqrt{t_1}$$

$$I_1\left(U_1\right)=\left(\ln\left(\frac{U_1}{S_0}\right)-\mu t_1\right)\Big/\sigma\sqrt{t_1}$$

$$-\frac{1}{2}\left(\frac{y-x_0-\ln {U_1}^{2n_1}+\ln {D_1}^{2n_1}-\mu t_2-(x-x_0-\mu t_1)}{\sigma\sqrt{(t_2-t_1)}}\right)^2$$

$$v=\frac{y-x_0-\ln {U_1}^{2n_1}+\ln {D_1}^{2n_1}-\mu t_2}{\sigma\sqrt{t_2}}$$

$$I_2\left(U_1\right)=\left(\ln\left(\frac{U_1{D_1}^{2n_1}}{S_0{U_1}^{2n_1}}\right)-\mu t_2\right)\Big/\sigma\sqrt{t_2}$$

$$\frac{z - x_0 - \ln {U_2}^{2n_2} - \ln {U_1}^{2n_1} + \ln {D_2}^{2n_2} + \ln {D_1}^{2n_1}}{\sigma\sqrt{t_3 - t_2}}$$

$$-\frac{\mu t_3 - (y - x_0 - \ln {U_1}^{2n_1} + \ln {D_1}^{2n_1} - \mu t_2)}{\sigma\sqrt{t_3 - t_2}}$$

$$I_3\left(U_2\right) = \left(\ln\left(\frac{U_2 {D_1}^{2n_1} {D_2}^{2n_2}}{S_0 {U_1}^{2n_1} {U_2}^{2n_2}}\right) - \mu t_3\right) \Big/ \sigma\sqrt{t_3}$$

and finally,

$$\frac{w + \ln\left(\frac{{D_1}^{2n_1} {D_2}^{2n_2}}{S_0 {U_1}^{2n_1} {U_2}^{2n_2}}\right) - \mu t_4 - (z + \ln\left(\frac{{D_1}^{2n_1} {D_2}^{2n_2}}{S_0 {U_1}^{2n_1} {U_2}^{2n_2}}\right) - \mu t_3)}{\sigma\sqrt{t_4 - t_3}}$$

$$I_4(K) = \left(\ln\left(\frac{K {D_1}^{2n_1} {D_2}^{2n_2}}{S_0 {U_1}^{2n_1} {U_2}^{2n_2}}\right) - \mu t_4\right) \Big/ \sigma\sqrt{t_4}$$

with

$$H_1 = \rho_{12}, \rho_{23}, \rho_{34} = \left\{\sqrt{\frac{t_1}{t_2}}, \sqrt{\frac{t_2}{t_3}}, \sqrt{\frac{t_3}{t_4}}\right\}$$

Let us consider the next group of integrals

$$\frac{1}{\sigma\sqrt{2\pi t_1}} \exp\left(-\frac{1}{2}\left(\frac{x - x_0 - \mu t_1}{\sigma\sqrt{t_1}}\right)^2\right) \frac{1}{\sigma\sqrt{2\pi(t_2 - t_1)}}$$

$$\exp\left(-\frac{1}{2}\left(\frac{y - x - \ln {U_1}^{2n_1} + \ln {D_1}^{2n_1} - \mu(t_2 - t_1)}{\sigma\sqrt{(t_2 - t_1)}}\right)^2\right) \left(\frac{{U_1}^{n_1}}{{D_1}^{n_1}}\right)^{\frac{2\mu}{\sigma^2}}$$

$$- \exp\left(-\frac{1}{2}\left(\frac{z + y - \ln {D_2}^{2(n_2+1)} + \ln {U_2}^{2n_2} - \mu(t_3 - t_2)}{\sigma\sqrt{t_3 - t_2}}\right)\right)$$

$$\times \exp\left\{\frac{2\mu^*}{\sigma^2}\left[(\gamma_2 - y) - n\left(\gamma_1 - \gamma_2\right)\right]\right\}$$

$$\frac{1}{\sigma\sqrt{2\pi(t_4-t_3)}}\exp\left(-\frac{1}{2}\left(\frac{w-z-\mu(t_4-t_3)}{\sigma\sqrt{t_4-t_3}}\right)^2\right)$$

$$\exp\left\{\frac{2\mu^*}{\sigma^2}\left[(\gamma_2)-n\left(\gamma_1-\gamma_2\right)\right]\right\}\exp\left(\frac{2\mu^*}{\sigma^2}(-y-x+x-x_0+x_0)\right)$$

$$\exp\left(x-y\right)\exp(-x_0)\exp(-x+x_0)$$

This makes

$$\left(\frac{{U_1}^{n_1}}{S_0{D_1}^{n_1}}\right)^{\frac{2\mu}{\sigma^2}}$$

$$\exp\left(-\frac{1}{2}\left(\frac{x-x_0-\mu t_1}{\sigma\sqrt{t_1}}\right)^2\right)\exp\left(\frac{2\mu^*}{\sigma^2}(-x+x_0)\right)$$

$$=\exp\left(-\frac{1}{2}\left(\frac{x-x_0+\mu t_1}{\sigma\sqrt{t_1}}\right)^2\right)$$

$$\exp\left(-\frac{1}{2}\left(\frac{y-x-\ln {U_1}^{2n_1}+\ln {D_1}^{2n_1}-\mu\left(t_2-t_1\right)}{\sigma\sqrt{(t_2-t_1)}}\right)^2\right)$$

$$\exp\left(\frac{2\mu^*}{\sigma^2}(x-y)\right)$$

$$\exp\left(-\frac{1}{2}\left(\frac{y-x-\ln {U_1}^{2n_1}+\ln {D_1}^{2n_1}+\mu(t_2-t_1)}{\sigma\sqrt{(t_2-t_1)}}\right)^2\right)$$

with addition of $-\frac{2\mu^*}{\sigma^2}\ln {U_1}^{2n_1}+\frac{2\mu^*}{\sigma^2}\ln {D_1}^{2n_1}+\frac{2\mu^*}{\sigma^2}\ln {U_1}^{2n_1}-\frac{2\mu^*}{\sigma^2}\ln {D_1}^{2n_1}$.

This makes

$$\left(\frac{{U_1}^{n_1}{D_1}^{2n_1}}{S_0{D_1}^{n_1}{U_1}^{2n_1}}\right)^{\frac{2\mu}{\sigma^2}}=\left(\frac{{D_1}^{n_1}}{S_0{U_1}^{n_1}}\right)^{\frac{2\mu}{\sigma^2}}$$

Also, we obtain

$$\exp\left\{\frac{2\mu^*}{\sigma^2}\left[(\gamma_2)-n\left(\gamma_1-\gamma_2\right)\right]\right\}=\left(\frac{{D_2}^{n_2+1}}{{U_2}^{n_2}}\right)^{\frac{2\mu^*}{\sigma^2}}$$

Therefore, the coefficient is

$$\left(\frac{{D_1}^{n_1}}{S_0{U_1}^{n_1}}\frac{{D_2}^{n_2+1}}{{U_2}^{n_2}}\right)^{\frac{2\mu}{\sigma^2}}$$

and

$$u=\frac{x-x_0+\mu t_1}{\sigma\sqrt{t_1}}=\left(\ln\left(\frac{X}{S_0}\right)+\mu t_1\right)\Big/\sigma\sqrt{t_1}$$

$$I_5\left(U_1\right)=\left(\ln\left(\frac{U_1}{S_0}\right)+\mu t_1\right)\Big/\sigma\sqrt{t_1}$$

$$\exp\left(-\frac{1}{2}\left(\frac{y-x_0-\ln{U_1}^{2n_1}+\ln{D_1}^{2n_1}+\mu t_2-(x-x_0+\mu t_1)}{\sigma\sqrt{(t_2-t_1)}}\right)^2\right)$$

$$v=\frac{y-x_0-\ln{U_1}^{2n_1}+\ln{D_1}^{2n_1}+\mu t_2}{\sigma\sqrt{t_2}}$$

$$I_6\left(U_1\right)=\left(\ln\left(\frac{U_1{D_1}^{2n_1}}{S_0{U_1}^{2n_1}}\right)+\mu t_2\right)\Big/\sigma\sqrt{t_2}$$

$$\left(\frac{z+y-\ln{D_2}^{2(n_2+1)}+\ln{U_2}^{2n_2}-\mu(t_3-t_2)}{\sigma\sqrt{t_3-t_2}}\right)$$

$$\frac{z+x_0+\ln{U_2}^{2n_2}-\ln{D_2}^{2(n_2+1)}-\ln{D_1}^{2n_1}+\ln{U_1}^{2n_1}}{\sigma\sqrt{t_3-t_2}}$$

$$-\frac{\mu t_3+(y-x_0-\ln{U_1}^{2n_1}+\ln{D_1}^{2n_1}+\mu t_2)}{\sigma\sqrt{t_3-t_2}}$$

$$I_7\left(U_2\right)=\left(\ln\left(\frac{U_2S_0{U_2}^{2n_2}{U_1}^{2n_1}}{{D_1}^{2n_1}{D_2}^{2(n_2+1)}}\right)-\mu t_3\right)\Big/\sigma\sqrt{t_3}$$

and finally,

$$\exp\left(-\frac{1}{2}\left(\frac{w-z-\mu(t_4-t_3)}{\sigma\sqrt{t_4-t_3}}\right)^2\right)$$

$$\frac{w+\ln\left(\frac{S_0{U_2}^{2n_2}{U_1}^{2n_1}}{{D_1}^{2n_1}{D_2}^{2(n_2+1)}}\right)-\mu t_4-\left(z+\ln\left(\frac{S_0{U_2}^{2n_2}{U_1}^{2n_1}}{{D_1}^{2n_1}{D_2}^{2(n_2+1)}}\right)-\mu t_3\right)}{\sigma\sqrt{t_4-t_3}}$$

$$I_8(K)=\left(\ln\frac{KS_0{U_2}^{2n_2}{U_1}^{2n_1}}{{D_1}^{2n_1}{D_2}^{2(n_2+1)}}-\mu t_4\right)\Big/\sigma\sqrt{t_4}$$

where the correlations are

$$H_2=\rho_{12},-\rho_{23},\rho_{34}=\left\{\sqrt{\frac{t_1}{t_2}},-\sqrt{\frac{t_2}{t_3}},\sqrt{\frac{t_3}{t_4}}\right\}$$

The value of the window two-step double knock-out call (WTSDKOC) is obtained as

$$\begin{aligned}&\text{WTSDKOC }(S_0,r,\sigma,\delta,t_1,t_2,t_3,t_4,K,U_1,U_2,D_1,D_2)\\&\quad=\text{WTSDKOP}\,(S_0,r,\sigma,\delta,t_1,t_2,t_3,t_4,A,U_1,U_2,D_1,D_2)\\&\quad\quad-\text{WTSDKOP }(S_0,r,\sigma,\delta,t_1,t_2,t_3,t_4,K,U_1,U_2,D_1,D_2)\end{aligned}\tag{7.28}$$

7.2.1.5. *Outside two-step double knock-out put (OTSDKOP)*

The no-arbitrage value of an OTSDKOP is given by (Guillaume, 2010)

$$\text{OTSDKOP}\left(S_0^{(1)},S_0^{(2)},r,\sigma_1,\sigma_2,\delta_1,\delta_2,t_1,t_2,K,U_1,U_2,D_1,D_2\right)$$

$$\exp(-rt_2)K\Phi_{\text{WSTS}}(\mu)-\exp(-\delta_2t_2)S_0^{(2)}\Phi_{\text{WTS}}(\tilde{\mu})$$

$$\Phi_{\text{WSTS}}(\mu)=\mu_1=r-\delta_1-\frac{\sigma_1^2}{2}\quad\mu_2=r-\delta_2-\frac{\sigma_2^2}{2}$$

$$\tilde{\mu}_1 = r - \delta_1 + \sigma_1\sigma_2\rho_{12} - \frac{\sigma_1^2}{2}$$

$$\tilde{\mu}_2 = r - \delta_2 + \frac{\sigma_2^2}{2}$$

$$\Phi_{\mathrm{WSTS}}(\mu)$$

$$= \sum_{n_1=-\infty}^{\infty}\sum_{n_2=-\infty}^{\infty}\left(\frac{U_1^{n_1}U_2^{n_2}}{D_1^{n_1}D_2^{n_2}}\right)^{2\mu_1/\sigma_1^2}$$

$$\{N_3\left[I_1(U_1 \wedge U_2), I_2(U_2), I_3(K); H_1\right]$$

$$- N_3\left[I_1(D_1 \vee D_2), I_2(U_2), I_3(K); H_1\right]$$

$$- N_3\left[I_1(U_1 \wedge U_2), I_2(D_2), I_3(K); H_1\right]$$

$$+ N_3\left[I_1(D_1 \vee D_2), I_2(D_2), I_3(K); H_1\right]\}$$

$$- \sum_{n_1=-\infty}^{\infty}\sum_{n_2=-\infty}^{\infty}\left(\frac{D_1^{n_1}D_2^{n_2+1}}{S_0^{(1)}U_1^{n_1}U_2^{n_2}}\right)^{2\mu_1/\sigma_1^2}$$

$$\{N_3[I_4(U_1 \wedge U_2), I_5(U_2), I_6(K); H_2]$$

$$- N_3\left[[I_4(D_1 \vee D_2), I_5(U_2), I_6(K); H_2]\right]$$

$$- N_3\left[I_4(U_1 \wedge U_2), I_5(D_2), I_6(K); H_2\right]$$

$$+ N_3\left[I_4(D_1 \vee D_2), I_5(D_2), I_6(K); H_2\right]\}$$

$$- \sum_{n_1=-\infty}^{\infty}\sum_{n_2=-\infty}^{\infty}\left(\frac{D_1^{n_1+1}U_2^{n_2}}{S_0^{(1)}U_1^{n_1}D_2^{n_2}}\right)^{2\mu_1/\sigma_1^2}$$

$$\times \{N_3\left[I_7(U_1 \wedge U_2), I_8(U_2), I_9(K); H_1\right]$$

$$- N_3\left[I_7(D_1 \vee D_2), I_8(U_2), I_9(K); H_1\right]$$

$$- N_3\left[I_7(U_1 \wedge U_2), I_8(D_2), I_9(K); H_1\right]$$

$$+ N_3\left[I_7(D_1 \vee D_2), I_8(D_2), I_9(K); H_1\right] -\}$$

$$
\begin{aligned}
&+\sum_{n_1=-\infty}^{\infty}\sum_{n_2=-\infty}^{\infty}\left(\frac{D_2^{n_2+1}U_1^{n_1}}{D_1^{n_1+1}U_2^{n_2}}\right)^{2\mu_1/\sigma_1^2}\\
&\times\{N_3\left[I_{10}\left(U_1\wedge U_2\right),I_{11}\left(U_2\right),I_{12}(K);H_2\right]\\
&-N_3\left[I_{10}\left(D_1\vee D_2\right),I_{11}\left(U_2\right),I_{12}(K);H_2\right]\\
&-N_3\left[I_{10}\left(U_1\wedge U_2\right),I_{11}\left(D_2\right),I_{12}(K);H_2\right]\\
&+N_3\left[I_{10}\left(D_1\vee D_2\right),I_{11}\left(D_2\right),I_{12}(K);H_2\right]\}
\end{aligned}
$$

$$
I_1(X)=\left(\ln\left(\frac{XD_1^{2n_1}}{S_0^{(1)}U_1^{2n_1}}\right)-\mu_1t_1\right)\Big/\sigma_1\sqrt{t_1}
$$

$$
I_2(X)=\left(\ln\left(\frac{XD_1^{2n_1}D_2^{2n_2}}{S_0^{(1)}U_1^{2n_1}U_2^{2n_2}}\right)-\mu_1t_2\right)\Big/\sigma_1\sqrt{t_2}
$$

$$
I_3(X)=\frac{\left(\ln\left(\frac{X}{S_0^{(2)}}\right)-\mu_2t_2\right)}{\sigma_2\sqrt{t_2}}+\ln\left(\frac{D_1^{2\rho n_1}D_2^{2\rho n_2}}{U_2^{2\rho n_2}U_1^{2\rho n_1}}\right)\Big/\sigma_1\sqrt{t_2}
$$

$$
I_4(X)=\left(\ln\left(\frac{XD_1^{2n_1}}{S_0^{(1)}U_1^{2n_1}}\right)+\mu_1t_1\right)\Big/\sigma_1\sqrt{t_1}
$$

$$
I_5(X)=\left(\ln\left(\frac{XS_0^{(1)}U_1^{2n_1}U_2^{2n_2}}{D_1^{2n_1}D_2^{2(n_2+1)}}\right)-\mu_1t_2\right)\Big/\sigma_1\sqrt{t_2}
$$

$$
I_6(X)=\frac{\left(\ln\left(\frac{X}{S_0^{(2)}}\right)-\mu_2t_2\right)}{\sigma_2\sqrt{t_2}}+\ln\left(\frac{\left(S_0^{(1)}\right)^{2\rho}U_2^{2\rho n_2}U_1^{2\rho n_1}}{D_1^{2\rho n_1}D_2^{2\rho(n_2+1)}}\right)\Big/\sigma_1\sqrt{t_2}
$$

$$
I_7(X)=\left(\ln\left(\frac{XS_0^{(1)}U_1^{2n_1}}{D_1^{2(n_1+1)}}\right)-\mu_1t_1\right)\Big/\sigma_1\sqrt{t_1}
$$

$$I_8(X) = \left(\ln\left(\frac{XS_0^{(1)}{U_1}^{2n_1}D_2^{2n_2}}{U_2^{2n_2}D_1^{2(n_1+1)}}\right) - \mu_1 t_2\right) \Big/ \sigma_1\sqrt{t_2}$$

$$I_9(X) = \frac{\left(\ln\left(\frac{X}{S_0^{(2)}}\right) - \mu_2 t_2\right)}{\sigma_2\sqrt{t_2}} + \ln\left(\frac{\left(S_0^{(1)}\right)^{2\rho} D_2^{2\rho n_2}U_1^{2\rho n_1}}{U_2^{2\rho n_2}D_1^{2\rho(n_1+1)}}\right) \Big/ \sigma_1\sqrt{t_2}$$

$$I_{10}(X) = \left(\ln\left(\frac{XS_0^{(1)}{U_1}^{2n_1}}{D_1^{2(n_1+1)}}\right) + \mu_1 t_1\right) \Big/ \sigma_1\sqrt{t_1}$$

$$I_{11}(X) = \left(\ln\left(\frac{XD_1^{2(n_1+1)}U_2^{2n_2}}{S_0^{(1)}{U_1}^{2n_1}D_2^{2(n_2+1)}}\right) - \mu_1 t_2\right) \Big/ \sigma_1\sqrt{t_2}$$

$$I_{12}(X) = \frac{\left(\ln\left(\frac{X}{S_0^{(2)}}\right) - \mu_2 t_2\right)}{\sigma_2\sqrt{t_2}} + \ln\left(\frac{D_1^{2\rho(n_1+1)}U_2^{2\rho n_2}}{U_1^{2\rho n_1}D_2^{2\rho(n_2+1)}}\right) \Big/ \sigma_1\sqrt{t_2}$$

$$H_1 = \left\{\sqrt{\frac{t_1}{t_2}}, \rho\sqrt{\frac{t_1}{t_2}}, \rho\right\} \quad H_2 = \left\{-\sqrt{\frac{t_1}{t_2}}, -\rho\sqrt{\frac{t_1}{t_2}}, \rho\right\} \tag{7.29}$$

The densities are;

$$\int_{\gamma_2}^{\gamma_1} \left(\sum_{-\infty}^{\infty} \varphi\left[\frac{x - x_0 - 2n(\gamma_1 - \gamma_2) - \mu^* T}{\sigma\sqrt{T}}\right] \exp\left\{\frac{2n}{\sigma^2}\left[(\gamma_1 - \gamma_2)\,\mu^*\right]\right\}\right.$$
$$-\sum_{-\infty}^{\infty} \varphi\left[\frac{x + x_0 - 2\gamma_2 + 2n\,(\gamma_1 - \gamma_2) - \mu^* T}{\sigma\sqrt{T}}\right]$$
$$\left.\times \exp\left\{\frac{2\mu^*}{\sigma^2}\left[(\gamma_2 - x_0) - n\,(\gamma_1 - \gamma_2)\right]\right\}\right) dx$$

$$f_1 = \frac{1}{\sigma\sqrt{2\pi t_1}}$$
$$\times \exp\left(-\frac{1}{2}\left(\frac{x - x_0 - \ln {U_1}^{2n_1} + \ln {D_1}^{2n_1} - \mu_1 t_1}{\sigma\sqrt{t_1}}\right)^2\right)\left(\frac{{U_1}^{n_1}}{{D_1}^{n_1}}\right)^{\frac{2\mu_1}{\sigma^2}}$$

$$- \exp\left(-\frac{1}{2} \left(\frac{x + x_0 - \ln {D_1}^{2(n_1+1)} + \ln {U_1}^{2n_1} - \mu_1 t_1}{\sigma\sqrt{t_3 - t_2}} \right) \right.$$

$$\left. \times \exp\left\{ \frac{2\mu_1}{\sigma^2} \left[(\ln D_1 - x_0) - n\left(\ln U_1 - \ln D_1\right) \right] \right\} \right)$$

$$f_2 = \frac{\exp\left(-\frac{1}{2}\left(\frac{y - x - \ln {U_2}^{2n_2} + \ln {D_2}^{2n_2} - \mu_1(t_2 - t_1)}{\sigma\sqrt{t_2 - t_1}} \right)^2 \right)}{\sigma\sqrt{2\pi(t_2 - t_1)}} \left(\frac{{U_2}^{n_2}}{{D_2}^{n_2}} \right)^{\frac{2\mu_1}{\sigma^2}}$$

$$- \exp\left(-\frac{1}{2} \left(\frac{y + x - \ln {D_2}^{2(n_2+1)} + \ln {U_2}^{2n_2} - \mu_1(t_2 - t_1)}{\sigma\sqrt{t_2 - t_1}} \right) \right)$$

$$\times \exp\left\{ \frac{2\mu_1}{\sigma^2} \left[(\ln D_2 - x_0) - n\left(\ln U_2 - \ln D_2\right) \right] \right\}$$

The risk-neutral joint density of X_{T_2} and Y_{T_2} is

$$f_{X_{T_3}, Y_{T_3}}(a, b) = \left\{ \frac{\exp\left\{ -\frac{1}{2(1-\rho_{SV}^2)} \left[\left(\frac{a - \ln S_0^{(1)} - \mu_V T_2}{\sigma_V\sqrt{T_2}} \right)^2 \right] \right\}}{2\pi\sigma_S\sigma_V T_2\sqrt{(1-\rho_{SV}^2)}} \right.$$

$$\left. \frac{\left[-2\rho_{SV} \left(\frac{a - \ln S_0^{(1)} - \mu_V T_2}{\sigma_V\sqrt{T_2}} \right) \left(\frac{b - \ln S_0^{(2)} - \mu_S T_2}{\sigma_S\sqrt{T_2}} \right) + \left(\frac{b - \ln S_0^{(2)} - \mu_S T_2}{\sigma_S\sqrt{T_2}} \right)^2 \right]}{2\pi\sigma_S\sigma_V T_2\sqrt{(1-\rho_{SV}^2)}} \right\}$$

Therefore, the conditional expectation is

$$f_{(X_{T_3}|Y_{T_3})} = \exp \frac{\frac{\left\{ -\frac{1}{2(1-\rho_{SV}^2)} \left[\left(\frac{a - \ln S_0^1 - \mu_V T_2}{\sigma_V\sqrt{T_2}} \right)^2 \right] \right\}}{2\pi\sigma_S\sigma_V T_2\sqrt{(1-\rho_{SV}^2)}}}{\frac{\exp\left\{ -\frac{1}{2} \left[\left(\frac{a - \ln S_0^1 - \mu_V T_2}{\sigma_V\sqrt{T_2}} \right)^2 \right] \right\}}{\sigma_V\sqrt{2\pi T_2}}}$$

$$\frac{\dfrac{\left\{\left[-2\rho_{SV}\left(\frac{a-\ln S_0^{(1)}-\mu_V T_2}{\sigma_V\sqrt{T_2}}\right)\left(\frac{b-\ln S_0^{(2)}-\mu_S T_2}{\sigma_S\sqrt{T_2}}\right)+\left(\frac{b-\ln S_0^{(2)}-\mu_S T_2}{\sigma_S\sqrt{T_2}}\right)^2\right]\right\}}{2\pi\sigma_S\sigma_V T_2\sqrt{(1-\rho_{SV}^2)}}}{\dfrac{\exp\left\{-\frac{1}{2}\left[\left(\frac{a-\ln S_0^1-\mu_V T_2}{\sigma_V\sqrt{T_2}}\right)^2\right]\right\}}{\sigma_V\sqrt{2\pi T_2}}}$$

$$\exp\left\{\frac{+\frac{1}{2}\left(\frac{a-\ln S_0^{(1)}-\mu_V T_2}{\sigma_V\sqrt{T_2}}\right)^2\frac{(1-\rho_{SV}^2)}{(1-\rho_{SV}^2)}-}{\sigma_S\sqrt{2\pi T_2(1-\rho_{SV}^2)}}\right.$$

$$\frac{-\frac{1}{2(1-\rho_{SV}^2)}\left[\left(\frac{a-\ln S_0^{(1)}-\mu_V T_2}{\sigma_V\sqrt{T_2}}\right)^2+\left(\frac{b-\ln S_0^{(2)}-\mu_S T_2}{\sigma_S\sqrt{T_2}}\right)^2\right]}{\sigma_S\sqrt{2\pi T_2(1-\rho_{SV}^2)}}$$

$$\left.-\frac{2\rho_{SV}\left(\frac{a-\ln S_0^1-\mu_V T_2}{\sigma_V\sqrt{T_2}}\right)\left(\frac{b-\ln S_0^{(2)}-\mu_S T_2}{\sigma_S\sqrt{T_2}}\right)}{\sigma_S\sqrt{2\pi T_2(1-\rho_{SV}^2)}}\right\}$$

$$=\exp\left\{\frac{-\frac{1}{2(1-\rho_{SV}^2)}\left[\rho_{SV}^2\left(\frac{a-\ln S_0^1-\mu_V T_2}{\sigma_V\sqrt{T_2}}\right)^2\right]}{\sigma_S\sqrt{2\pi T_2(1-\rho_{SV}^2)}}\right.$$

$$-2\rho_{SV}\left(\frac{a-\ln S_0^{(1)}-\mu_V T_2}{\sigma_V\sqrt{T_2}}\right)\left(\frac{b-\ln S_0^{(2)}-\mu_S T_2}{\sigma_S\sqrt{T_2}}\right)$$

$$\left.+\left(\frac{b-\ln S_0^{(2)}-\mu_S T_2}{\sigma_S\sqrt{T_2}}\right)^2\right\}$$

$$=\frac{\exp\left\{-\frac{1}{2(1-\rho_{SV}^2)}\left[\left(\frac{b-\ln S_0^{(2)}-\mu_S T_2}{\sigma_S\sqrt{T_2}}\right)-\left(\frac{a-\ln S_0^{(1)}-\mu_V T_2}{\sigma_V\sqrt{T_2}}\right)\rho_{SV}\right]^2\right\}}{\sigma_S\sqrt{2\pi T_2(1-\rho_{SV}^2)}}$$

$$\frac{\exp\left\{-\frac{\left[b-\ln S_0^{(2)}-\mu_S T_2-\rho_{SV}\frac{\sigma_S}{\sigma_V}(a-\ln S_0^{(1)}-\mu_V T_2\right]^2}{2(1-\rho_{SV}^2)T_2\sigma_S^2}\right\}}{\sigma_S\sqrt{2\pi T_2(1-\rho_{SV}^2)}}$$

Finally, we obtain

$$f_{(X_{T_2}|Y_{T_2})}(a \mid b)$$

$$= \frac{\exp\left\{-\frac{\left[\left(b-\ln S_0^{(2)}-\mu_S T_2-\rho_{SV}\frac{\sigma_S}{\sigma_V}(a-\ln S_0^{(1)}-\mu_V T_2)\right)^2\right]}{2(1-\rho_{SV}^2)\sigma_S^2 T_2}\right\}}{\sigma_S\sqrt{2\pi(1-\rho_{SV}^2)T_2}} \tag{7.30}$$

where $(X_{T_2} \mid Y_{T_2}) \sim N\left(\mu_S T_2 + \rho_{SV}\frac{\sigma_S}{\sigma_V}(Y_{T_2}-\mu_V T_2); (1-\rho_{SV}^2)\sigma_S^2 T_2\right)$ and where

$$\mu_S = \mu_2 \quad \mu_V = \mu_1 \quad \sigma_S = \sigma_2 \quad \sigma_V = \sigma_1$$

$$f_3 = \frac{\exp\left\{-\frac{\left[\left(b-\ln S_0^{(2)}-\mu_2 T_2-\rho_{sv}\frac{\sigma_2}{\sigma_1}(a-\ln S_0^{(1)}-\mu_1 T_2)\right)^2\right]}{2(1-\rho_{SV}^2)\sigma_2^2 T_2}\right\}}{\sigma_2\sqrt{2\pi(1-\rho_{SV}^2)T_2}}$$

Then, we will have four groups of integrals, including four trivariate distributions each, therefore 16 distributions in total.

$$\left[\int_{-\infty}^{\ln U_1} - \int_{-\infty}^{\ln D_1}\left(\int_{-\infty}^{\ln U_2} - \int_{-\infty}^{\ln D_2}\right)\right]\left(\int_{-\infty}^{\ln K}\right)$$

As an example, we consider the first one.

$$\exp\left(-\frac{1}{2}\left(\frac{x-x_0-\ln {U_1}^{2n_1}+\ln {D_1}^{2n_1}-\mu_1 t_1}{\sigma_1\sqrt{t_1}}\right)^2\right)\left(\frac{{U_1}^{n_1}}{{D_1}^{n_1}}\right)^{\frac{2\mu_1}{\sigma^2}}$$

$$\exp\left(-\frac{1}{2}\left(\frac{y-x-\ln {U_2}^{2n_2}+\ln {D_2}^{2n_2}-\mu_1(t_2-t_1)}{\sigma_1\sqrt{t_2-t_1}}\right)^2\right)\left(\frac{{U_2}^{n_2}}{{D_2}^{n_2}}\right)^{\frac{2\mu_1}{\sigma^2}}$$

$$\exp\left\{-\frac{\left[\left(b-\ln S_0^{(2)}-\mu_2T_2-\rho_{sv}\frac{\sigma_2}{\sigma_1}(a-\ln S_0^1-\mu_1T_2)\right)^2\right]}{2(1-\rho_{SV}^2)\sigma_2^2T_2}\right\}$$

The coefficient is

$$\left(\frac{U_1{}^{n_1}}{D_1{}^{n_1}}\frac{U_2{}^{n_2}}{D_2{}^{n_2}}\right)^{\frac{2\mu_1}{\sigma^2}}$$

As can be easily seen, the first integral limit is

$$u=I_1\left(U_1\right)=\frac{\ln\left(\frac{U_1D_1{}^{2n_1}}{S_0{}^{(1)}U_1{}^{2n_1}}\right)-\mu_1t_1}{\sigma_1\sqrt{t_1}}$$

By completing

$$\frac{y-\rho x}{\sqrt{1-\rho^2}}$$

we obtain the second one as

$$v=I_2\left(U_2\right)=\frac{\ln\left(\frac{U_2D_1{}^{2n_1}D_2{}^{2n_2}}{S_0{}^{(1)}U_1{}^{2n_1}U_2{}^{2n_2}}\right)-\mu_1t_2}{\sigma_1\sqrt{t_2}}$$

$$f_3=\frac{\exp\left\{-\frac{\left[\left(b-\ln S_0^{(2)}-\mu_2T_2-\rho_{sv}\frac{\sigma_2}{\sigma_1}(a-\ln S_0^{(1)}-\mu_1T_2)\right)^2\right]}{2(1-\rho_{SV}^2)\sigma_2^2T_2}\right\}}{\sigma_2\sqrt{2\pi(1-\rho_{SV}^2)T_2}}$$

$$\frac{\frac{b-\ln S_0^{(2)}-\mu_2T_2-\rho_{sv}\frac{\sigma_2}{\sigma_1}(a-\ln S_0^{(1)}-\mu_1T_2)}{\sigma_2\sqrt{T_2}}}{\sqrt{(1-\rho_{SV}^2)}}$$

$$=\frac{\frac{b-\ln S_0^{(2)}-\mu_2T_2}{\sigma_2\sqrt{T_2}}-\rho_{sv}\frac{(a-\ln S_0^{(1)}-\mu_1T_2)}{\sigma_1\sqrt{T_2}}}{\sqrt{(1-\rho_{SV}^2)}}$$

To complete the circle, we need to add and subtract

$$\frac{\ln\left(\frac{D_1{}^{2n_1}D_2{}^{2n_2}}{U_1{}^{2n_1}U_2{}^{2n_2}}\right)}{\sigma_1\sqrt{t_2}}$$

where ρ_{sv} is added as an exponent. This makes

$$\frac{b-\ln S_0^{(2)}-\mu_2T_2}{\sigma_2\sqrt{T_2}}+\frac{\ln\left(\frac{D_1{}^{2\rho n_1}D_2{}^{2\rho n_2}}{S_0{}^{(1)}U_1{}^{2\rho n_1}U_2{}^{2\rho n_2}}\right)}{\sigma_1\sqrt{t_2}}$$

$$I_3(K)=\frac{\ln K/S_0^{(2)}-\mu_2T_2}{\sigma_2\sqrt{T_2}}+\frac{\ln\left(\frac{D_1{}^{2\rho n_1}D_2{}^{2\rho n_2}}{S_0{}^{(1)}U_1{}^{2\rho n_1}U_2{}^{2\rho n_2}}\right)}{\sigma_1\sqrt{t_2}}$$

Similarly, the remaining integrals can be obtained, as Guillaume (2010) has shown. The value of an outside two-step double knock-out call (OTSDKOC) is obtained as

$$\begin{aligned}&\text{OTSDKOC}\left(S_0^{(1)},S_0^{(2)},r,\sigma_1,\sigma_2,\delta_1,\delta_2,t_1,t_2,K,U_1,U_2,D_1,D_2\right)\\&\quad=\text{OTSDKOP}\left(S_0^{(1)},S_0^{(2)},r,\sigma_1,\sigma_2,\delta_1,\delta_2,t_1,t_2,A,U_1,U_2,D_1,D_2\right)\\&\qquad-\text{OTSDKOP}\left(S_0^{(1)},S_0^{(2)},r,\sigma_1,\sigma_2,\delta_1,\delta_2,t_1,t_2,K,U_1,U_2,D_1,D_2\right)\end{aligned}\tag{7.31}$$

7.2.1.6. *Outside early-ending two-step double knock-out put (OEETSDKOP)*

The no-arbitrage value of an OEETSDKOP is given by (Guillaume, 2010)

$$\text{OEETSDKOP}\left(S_0^{(1)},S_0^{(2)},r,\sigma_1,\sigma_2,\delta_1,\delta_2,t_1,t_2,t_3,K,U_1,U_2,D_1,D_2\right)$$

$$\exp(-rt_3)K\Phi_{\text{OEETS}}(\mu)-\exp(-\delta_2t_3)S_0^{(2)}\Phi_{\text{OEETS}}(\tilde{\mu})$$

$$\mu_1=r-\delta_1-\frac{\sigma_1^2}{2}\ \mu_2=r-\delta_2-\frac{\sigma_2^2}{2}$$

$$\tilde{\mu}_1=r-\delta_1+\sigma_1\sigma_2\rho_{12}-\frac{\sigma_1^2}{2}$$

$$\tilde{\mu}_2=r-\delta_2+\frac{\sigma_2^2}{2}$$

$$\Phi_{\text{OEETS}}(\mu)$$

$$= \sum_{n_1=-\infty}^{\infty} \sum_{n_2=-\infty}^{\infty} \left(\frac{U_1^{n_1} U_2^{n_2}}{D_1^{n_1} D_2^{n_2}} \right)^{2\mu_1/\sigma_1^2}$$

$$\{N_3 [I_1 (U_1 \wedge U_2), I_2 (U_2), I_3(K); H_1]$$

$$-N_3 [I_1 (D_1 \vee D_2), I_2 (U_2), I_3(K); H_1]$$

$$- N_3 [I_1 (U_1 \wedge U_2), I_2 (D_2), I_3(K); H_1]$$

$$+ N_3 [I_1 (D_1 \vee D_2), I_2 (D_2), I_3(K); H_1]\}$$

$$- \sum_{n_1=-\infty}^{\infty} \sum_{n_2=-\infty}^{\infty} \left(\frac{D_1^{n_1} D_2^{n_2+1}}{S_0^{(1)} U_1^{n_1} U_2^{n_2}} \right)^{2\mu_1/\sigma_1^2}$$

$$\{N_3 [I_4 (U_1 \wedge U_2), I_5 (U_2), I_6(K); H_2]$$

$$- N_3 [[I_4 (D_1 \vee D_2), I_5 (U_2), I_6(K); H_2]]$$

$$- N_3 [I_4 (U_1 \wedge U_2), I_5 (D_2), I_6(K); H_2]$$

$$+ N_3 [I_4 (D_1 \vee D_2), I_5 (D_2), I_6(K); H_2]\}$$

$$- \sum_{n_1=-\infty}^{\infty} \sum_{n_2=-\infty}^{\infty} \left(\frac{D_1^{n_1+1} U_2^{n_2}}{S_0^{(1)} U_1^{n_1} D_2^{n_2}} \right)^{2\mu_1/\sigma_1^2}$$

$$\{N_3 [I_7 (U_1 \wedge U_2), I_8 (U_2), I_9(K); H_1]$$

$$-N_3 [I_7 (D_1 \vee D_2), I_8 (U_2), I_9(K); H_1]$$

$$-N_3 [I_7 (U_1 \wedge U_2), I_8 (D_2), I_9(K); H_1]$$

$$+ N_3 [I_7 (D_1 \vee D_2), I_8 (D_2), I_9(K); H_1]\}$$

$$+ \sum_{n_1=-\infty}^{\infty} \sum_{n_2=-\infty}^{\infty} \left(\frac{D_2^{n_2+1} U_1^{n_1}}{D_1^{n_1+1} U_2^{n_2}} \right)^{2\mu_1/\sigma_1^2}$$

$$\{N_3 [I_{10} (U_1 \wedge U_2), I_{11} (U_2), I_{12}(K); H_2]$$

$$-N_3\left[I_{10}\left(D_1 \vee D_2\right), I_{11}\left(U_2\right), I_{12}(K); H_2\right]$$
$$-N_3\left[I_{10}\left(U_1 \wedge U_2\right), I_{11}\left(D_2\right), I_{12}(K); H_2\right]$$
$$+N_3\left[I_{10}\left(D_1 \vee D_2\right), I_{11}\left(D_2\right), I_{12}(K); H_2\right]\}$$

$$I_1(X)=\left(\ln\left(\frac{X D_1^{2n_1}}{S_0^{(1)} U_1^{2n_1}}\right)-\mu_1 t_1\right) \Big/ \sigma_1\sqrt{t_1}$$

$$I_2(X)=\left(\ln\left(\frac{X D_1^{2n_1} D_2^{2n_2}}{S_0^{(1)} U_1^{2n_1} U_2^{2n_2}}\right)-\mu_1 t_2\right) \Big/ \sigma_1\sqrt{t_2}$$

$$I_3(X)=\frac{\left(\ln\left(\frac{X}{S_0^{(2)}}\right)-\mu_2 t_3\right)}{\sigma_2\sqrt{t_3}}+\ln\left(\frac{D_1^{2\rho n_1} D_2^{2\rho n_2}}{U_2^{2\rho n_2} U_1^{2\rho n_1}}\right) \Big/ \sigma_1\sqrt{t_3}$$

$$I_4(X)=\left(\ln\left(\frac{X D_1^{2n_1}}{S_0^{(1)} U_1^{2n_1}}\right)+\mu_1 t_1\right) \Big/ \sigma_1\sqrt{t_1}$$

$$I_5(X)=\left(\ln\left(\frac{X S_0^{(1)} U_1^{2n_1} U_2^{2n_2}}{D_1^{2n_1} D_2^{2(n_2+1)}}\right)-\mu_1 t_2\right) \Big/ \sigma_1\sqrt{t_2}$$

$$I_6(X)=\frac{\left(\ln\left(\frac{X}{S_0^{(2)}}\right)-\mu_2 t_3\right)}{\sigma_2\sqrt{t_3}}+\ln\left(\frac{\left(S_0^{(1)}\right)^{2\rho} U_2^{2\rho n_2} U_1^{2\rho n_1}}{D_1^{2\rho n_1} D^{2\rho(n_2+1}{}_{2}}\right) \Big/ \sigma_1\sqrt{t_3}$$

$$I_7(X)=\left(\ln\left(\frac{X S_0^{(1)} U_1^{2n_1}}{D_1^{2(n_1+1)}}\right)-\mu_1 t_1\right) \Big/ \sigma_1\sqrt{t_1}$$

$$I_8(X)=\left(\ln\left(\frac{X S_0^{(1)} U_1^{2n_1} D_2^{2n_2}}{U_2^{2n_2} D_1^{2(n_1+1)}}\right)-\mu_1 t_2\right) \Big/ \sigma_1\sqrt{t_2}$$

$$I_9(X)=\frac{\left(\ln\left(\frac{X}{S_0^{(2)}}\right)-\mu_2 t_3\right)}{\sigma_2\sqrt{t_3}}+\ln\left(\frac{\left(S_0^{(1)}\right)^{2\rho} D_2^{2\rho n_2} U_1^{2\rho n_1}}{U_2^{2\rho n_2} D_1^{2\rho(n_1+1)}}\right) \Big/ \sigma_1\sqrt{t_3}$$

$$I_{10}(X) = \left(\ln\left(\frac{XS_0^{(1)}{U_1}^{2n_1}}{D_1^{2(n_1+1)}}\right) + \mu_1 t_1\right) \Big/ \sigma_1\sqrt{t_1}$$

$$I_{11}(X) = \left(\ln\left(\frac{XD_1^{2(n_1+1)}U_2^{2n_2}}{S_0^{(1)}{U_1}^{2n_1}D_2^{2(n_2+1)}}\right) - \mu_1 t_2\right) \Big/ \sigma_1\sqrt{t_2}$$

$$I_{12}(X) = \frac{\left(\ln\left(\frac{X}{S_0^{(2)}}\right) - \mu_2 t_3\right)}{\sigma_2\sqrt{t_3}} + \ln\left(\frac{D_1^{2\rho(n_1+1)}U_2^{2\rho n_2}}{U_1^{2\rho n_1}D_2^{2\rho(n_2+1)}}\right) \Big/ \sigma_1\sqrt{t_3}$$

$$H_1 = \left\{\sqrt{\frac{t_1}{t_2}}, \rho\sqrt{\frac{t_1}{t_3}}, \rho\sqrt{\frac{t_2}{t_3}}\right\} \; H_2 = \left\{-\sqrt{\frac{t_1}{t_2}}, -\rho\sqrt{\frac{t_1}{t_3}}, \rho\sqrt{\frac{t_2}{t_3}}\right\} \tag{7.32}$$

We consider the first group once again.

$$\exp\left(-\frac{1}{2}\left(\frac{x - x_0 - \ln {U_1}^{2n_1} + \ln {D_1}^{2n_1} - \mu_1 t_1}{\sigma_1\sqrt{t_1}}\right)^2\right)\left(\frac{{U_1}^{n_1}}{{D_1}^{n_1}}\right)^{\frac{2\mu_1}{\sigma^2}}$$

$$\exp\left(-\frac{1}{2}\left(\frac{y - x - \ln {U_2}^{2n_2} + \ln {D_2}^{2n_2} - \mu_1(t_2 - t_1)}{\sigma_1\sqrt{t_2 - t_1}}\right)^2\right)\left(\frac{{U_2}^{n_2}}{{D_2}^{n_2}}\right)^{\frac{2\mu_1}{\sigma^2}}$$

$$\frac{\exp\left\{-\frac{1}{2(1-\theta^2)}\left[\left(\frac{b-\ln S_0^{(2)}-\mu_2 T_3}{\sigma_2\sqrt{T_3}}\right) - \left(\frac{a-\ln S_0^1-\mu_1 T_2}{\sigma_1\sqrt{T_2}}\right)\rho_{12}\sqrt{\frac{t_2}{t_3}}\right]^2\right\}}{\sigma_S\sqrt{2\pi T_3(1-\theta^2)}}$$

where $\theta = \rho_{12}\sqrt{\frac{t_2}{t_3}}$.

The coefficient is

$$\left(\frac{{U_1}^{n_1}}{{D_1}^{n_1}}\frac{{U_2}^{n_2}}{{D_2}^{n_2}}\right)^{\frac{2\mu_1}{\sigma^2}}$$

$$I_1(U_1) = u = \frac{x - x_0 - \ln {U_1}^{2n_1} + \ln {D_1}^{2n_1} - \mu_1 t_1}{\sigma_1\sqrt{t_1}}$$

$$= \frac{\ln\left(\frac{U_1 {D_1}^{2n_1}}{S_0^{(1)}{U_1}^{2n_1}}\right) - \mu_1 t_1}{\sigma_1\sqrt{t_1}}$$

The next one is calculated by adding and subtracting the necessary terms.

$$= \frac{y - x_0 - \mu_1 t_2 - \ln {U_2}^{2n_2} + \ln {D_2}^{2n_2} - \ln {U_1}^{2n_1} + \ln {D_1}^{2n_1}}{\sigma_1\sqrt{t_2 - t_1}}$$

$$- \frac{(x - x_0 - \ln {U_1}^{2n_1} + \ln {D_1}^{2n_1} - \mu_1 t_1)}{\sigma_1\sqrt{t_2 - t_1}}$$

$$I_2\left(U_2\right) = v = \frac{\ln\left(\frac{U_2 {D_1}^{2n_1} {D_2}^{2n_2}}{S_0^{(1)} {U_1}^{2n_1} {U_2}^{2n_2}}\right) - \mu_1 t_2}{\sigma_1\sqrt{t_2}} \qquad \rho_{12} = \sqrt{\frac{t_1}{t_2}}$$

Now, since the correlation between period two and period three can be expressed as

$$\begin{aligned}
&\mathrm{Cov}\ X\left(t_2\right), Y\left(t_3\right) \\
&= \mathrm{Cov}\left(\mu_1 t_2 + \sigma_1\sqrt{t_2} Z_1, \mu_2 t_3 + \sigma_2\sqrt{t_2}\ \left(\rho_{12} Z_1 + \sqrt{1 - \rho_{12}^2} Z_2\right)\right. \\
&\qquad \left. + \sigma_2\sqrt{t_3 - t_2} Z_3\right) \\
&\sigma_1\sqrt{t_2}\sigma_2\sqrt{t_2}\rho_{12} = \rho_{12} t_2 \sigma_1 \sigma_2 \\
&\theta = \frac{\rho_{12} t_2 \sigma_1 \sigma_2}{\sigma_1\sqrt{t_2}\sigma_2\sqrt{t_3}} = \rho_{12}\sqrt{\frac{t_2}{t_3}}
\end{aligned}$$

we may write

$$\frac{\exp\left\{-\frac{\left[\left(\frac{b - \ln S_0^{(2)} - \mu_2 T_3}{\sigma_2\sqrt{T_3}}\right) - \left(\frac{a - \ln S_0^1 - \mu_1 T_2}{\sigma_1\sqrt{T_2}}\right)\rho_{12}\sqrt{\frac{t_2}{t_3}}\right]^2}{2(1 - \rho_{SV}^2)}\right\}}{\sigma_S\sqrt{2\pi T_3(1 - \theta^2)}}$$

With the addition of

$$\rho_{12}\sqrt{\frac{t_2}{t_2}}\ln\frac{\left(\frac{D_1^{2n_1}D_2^{2n_2}}{U_2^{2n_2}U_1^{2n_1}}\right)}{\sigma_1\sqrt{t_3}} - \rho_{12}\sqrt{\frac{t_2}{t_2}}\ln\frac{\left(\frac{D_1^{2n_1}D_2^{2n_2}}{U_2^{2n_2}U_1^{2n_1}}\right)}{\sigma_1\sqrt{t_3}}$$

$$\frac{b-\ln S_0^{(2)}-\mu_2 T_3}{\sigma_2\sqrt{T_3}} + \ln\left(\frac{D_1^{2\rho n_1}D_2^{2\rho n_2}}{U_2^{2\rho n_2}U_1^{2\rho n_1}}\right)\Big/\sigma_1\sqrt{t_3}$$

$$-\frac{\rho_{12}\sqrt{\frac{t_2}{t_3}}\left(a+\frac{D_1^{2n_1}D_2^{2n_2}}{U_2^{2n_2}U_1^{2\rho_1}}-\ln S_0^1-\mu_1 T_2\right)}{\sigma_1\sqrt{T_2}}$$

This is precisely the form of $\frac{w-\theta v}{\sqrt{1-\theta^2}}$

$$\frac{b-\ln S_0^{(2)}-\mu_2 T_3}{\sigma_2\sqrt{T_3}} + \ln\left(\frac{D_1^{2\rho n_1}D_2^{2\rho n_2}}{U_2^{2\rho n_2}U_1^{2\rho n_1}}\right)\Big/\sigma_1\sqrt{t_3}$$

$$-\frac{\rho_{12}\sqrt{\frac{t_2}{t_3}}\left(a+\frac{D_1^{2n_1}D_2^{2n_2}}{U_2^{2n_2}U_1^{2\rho_1}}-\ln S_0^1-\mu_1 T_2\right)}{\sigma_1\sqrt{T_2}}$$

Therefore, the last variable is

$$I_3(K) = w = \frac{\ln\left(\frac{K}{S_0^{(2)}}\right)-\mu_2 t_3}{\sigma_2\sqrt{t_3}} + \ln\left(\frac{D_1^{2\rho n_1}D_2^{2\rho n_2}}{U_2^{2\rho n_2}U_1^{2\rho n_1}}\right)\Big/\sigma_1\sqrt{t_3}$$

The remaining distributions are calculated similarly by using the above densities.

7.2.1.7. *Two-asset two-step double knock-out put (TATSDKOP)*

The no-arbitrage value of a TATSDKOP is given by (Guillaume, 2010)

$$\text{TATSDKOP}\left(S_0^{(1)}, S_0^{(2)}, r, \sigma_1, \sigma_2, \delta_1, \delta_2, t_1, t_2, K, U_1, U_2, D_1, D_2\right)$$

$$= \exp(-rt_2)K\Phi_{\text{TATS}}(\mu) - \exp(-\delta_2 t_2)S_0^{(2)}\Phi_{\text{TATS}}(\tilde{\mu})$$

$$\mu_1 = r - \delta_1 - \frac{\sigma_1^2}{2} \quad \mu_2 = r - \delta_2 - \frac{\sigma_2^2}{2}$$

$$\tilde{\mu}_1 = r - \delta_1 + \sigma_1\sigma_2\rho_{12} - \frac{\sigma_1^2}{2}$$

$$\tilde{\mu}_2 = r - \delta_2 + \frac{\sigma_2^2}{2}$$

$$\Phi_{\text{TATS}}(\mu) = \sum_{n_1=-\infty}^{\infty}\sum_{n_2=-\infty}^{\infty}\left(\frac{U_1^{n_1}}{D_1^{n_1}}\right)^{2\mu_1/\sigma_1^2}\left(\frac{U_2^{n_2}}{D_2^{n_2}}\right)^{2\mu_2/\sigma_2^2}$$

$$\{N_3[I_1(U_1), I_2(U_2), I_3(K); H_1]$$

$$- N_3[I_1(D_1), I_2(U_2), I_3(K); H_1]$$

$$- N_3[I_1(U_1), I_2(D_2), I_3(K); H_1]$$

$$+ N_3[I_1(D_1), I_2(D_2), I_3(K); H_1]$$

$$- N_3[I_1(U_1), I_2(U_2), I_3(D_2); H_1]$$

$$+ N_3[I_1(D_1), I_2(U_2), I_3(D_2); H_1]$$

$$+ N_3[I_1(U_1), I_2(D_2), I_3(D_2); H_1]$$

$$- N_3[I_1(D_1), I_2(D_2), I_3(D_2); H_1]\}$$

$$- \sum_{n_1=-\infty}^{\infty}\sum_{n_2=-\infty}^{\infty}\left(\frac{U_1^{n_1}}{D_1^{n_1}}\right)^{\left[\frac{2\mu_1}{\sigma_1^2} - \frac{4\rho\mu_2}{\sigma_1\sigma_2}\right]}\left(\frac{D_2^{n_2+1}}{S_0^{(2)}U_2^{n_2}}\right)^{2\mu_2/\sigma_2^2}$$

$$\{N_3[I_4(U_1), I_5(U_2), I_6(K); H_2]$$

$$- N_3[[I_4(D_1), I_5(U_2), I_6(K); H_2]]$$

$$- N_3[I_4(U_1), I_5(D_2), I_6(K); H_2]$$

$$+ N_3\left[I_4\left(D_1\right), I_5\left(D_2\right), I_6(K); H_2\right]$$

$$- N_3\left[I_4\left(U_1\right), I_5\left(U_2\right), I_6\left(D_2\right); H_2\right]$$

$$+ N_3\left[I_4\left(D_1\right), I_5\left(U_2\right), I_6\left(D_2\right); H_2\right]$$

$$+ N_3\left[I_4\left(U_1\right), I_5\left(D_2\right), I_6\left(D_2\right); H_2\right]$$

$$- N_3\left[I_4\left(D_1\right), I_5\left(D_2\right), I_6\left(D_2\right); H_2\right]\}$$

$$- \sum_{n_1=-\infty}^{\infty} \sum_{n_2=-\infty}^{\infty} \left(\frac{D_1^{n_1+1}}{S_0^{(1)} U_1^{n_1}}\right)^{2\mu_1/\sigma_1^2} \left(\frac{U_2^{n_2}}{D_2^{n_2}}\right)^{2\mu_2/\sigma_2^2}$$

$$\{N_3\left[I_7\left(U_1\right), I_8\left(U_2\right), I_9(K); H_1\right]$$

$$- N_3\left[I_7\left(D_1\right), I_8\left(U_2\right), I_9(K); H_1\right]$$

$$- N_3\left[I_7\left(U_1\right), I_8\left(D_2\right), I_9(K); H_1\right]$$

$$+ N_3\left[I_7\left(D_1\right), I_8\left(D_2\right), I_9(K); H_1\right]$$

$$- N_3\left[I_7\left(U_1\right), I_8\left(U_2\right), I_9\left(D_2\right); H_1\right]$$

$$+ N_3\left[I_7\left(D_1\right), I_8\left(U_2\right), I_9\left(D_2\right); H_1\right]$$

$$+ N_3\left[I_7\left(U_1\right), I_8\left(D_2\right), I_9\left(D_2\right); H_1\right]$$

$$- N_3\left[I_7\left(D_1\right), I_8\left(D_2\right), I_9\left(D_2\right); H_1\right]\}$$

$$+ \sum_{n_1=-\infty}^{\infty} \sum_{n_2=-\infty}^{\infty} \left(\frac{D_1^{n_1+1}}{S_0^{(1)} U_1^{n_1}}\right)^{\left[\frac{2\mu_1}{\sigma_1^2} - \frac{4\rho\mu_2}{\sigma_1\sigma_2}\right]} \left(\frac{D_2^{n_2+1}}{S_0^{(2)} U_2^{n_2}}\right)^{2\mu_2/\sigma_2^2}$$

$$\{N_3\left[I_{10}\left(U_1\right), I_{11}\left(U_2\right), I_{12}(K); H_2\right]$$

$$- N_3\left[I_{10}\left(D_1\right), I_{11}\left(U_2\right), I_{12}(K); H_2\right]$$

$$- N_3\left[I_{10}\left(U_1\right), I_{11}\left(D_2\right), I_{12}(K); H_2\right]$$

$$+ N_3\left[I_{10}\left(D_1\right), I_{11}\left(D_2\right), I_{12}(K); H_2\right]$$

$$- N_3\left[I_{10}\left(U_1\right), I_{11}\left(U_2\right), I_{12}\left(D_2\right); H_2\right]$$

$$+ N_3 \left[I_{10}(D_1), I_{11}(U_2), I_{12}(D_2); H_2 \right]$$
$$+ N_3 \left[I_{10}(U_1), I_{11}(D_2), I_{12}(D_2); H_2 \right]$$
$$- N_3 \left[I_{10}(D_1), I_{11}(D_2), I_{12}(D_2); H_2 \right] \}$$

$$I_1(X) = \left(\ln\left(\frac{X D_1^{2n_1}}{S_0^{(1)} U_1^{2n_1}} \right) - \mu_1 t_1 \right) \Big/ \sigma_1 \sqrt{t_1}$$

$$I_2(X) = \frac{\left(\ln\left(\frac{X}{S_0^{(2)}} \right) - \mu_2 t_1 \right)}{\sigma_2 \sqrt{t_1}} + \ln\left(\frac{D_1^{2\rho n_1}}{U_1^{2\rho n_1}} \right) \Big/ \sigma_1 \sqrt{t_1}$$

$$I_3(X) = \frac{\left(\ln\left(\frac{X D_2^{2n_2}}{S_0^{(2)} U_2^{2n_2}} \right) - \mu_2 t_2 \right)}{\sigma_2 \sqrt{t_2}} + \ln\left(\frac{D_1^{2\rho n_1}}{U_1^{2\rho n_1}} \right) \Big/ \sigma_1 \sqrt{t_2}$$

$$I_4(X) = I_1(X) - \frac{2\rho \mu_2 t_1}{\sigma_2}$$

$$I_5(X) = \frac{\left(\ln\left(\frac{X}{S_0^{(2)}} \right) + \mu_2 t_1 \right)}{\sigma_2 \sqrt{t_1}} + \ln\left(\frac{D_1^{2\rho n_1}}{U_1^{2\rho n_1}} \right) \Big/ \sigma_1 \sqrt{t_1}$$

$$I_6(X) = \frac{\left(\ln\left(\frac{X S_0^{(2)} U_2^{2n_2}}{D_2^{2(n_2+1)}} \right) - \mu_2 t_2 \right)}{\sigma_2 \sqrt{t_2}} + \ln\left(\frac{U_1^{2\rho n_1}}{D_1^{2\rho n_1}} \right) \Big/ \sigma_1 \sqrt{t_2}$$

$$I_7(X) = \left(\ln\left(\frac{X S_0^{(1)} U_1^{2n_1}}{D_1^{2(n_1+1)}} \right) - \mu_1 t_1 \right) \Big/ \sigma_1 \sqrt{t_1}$$

$$I_8(X) = \frac{\left(\ln\left(\frac{X}{S_0^{(2)}} \right) - \mu_2 t_1 \right)}{\sigma_2 \sqrt{t_1}} + \ln\left(\frac{\left(S_0^{(1)} \right)^{2\rho} U_1^{2\rho n_1}}{D_1^{2\rho(n_1+1)}} \right) \Big/ \sigma_1 \sqrt{t_1}$$

$$I_9(X) = \frac{\left(\ln\left(\frac{XD_2^{2n_2}}{S_0^{(2)}U_2^{2n_2}}\right) - \mu_2 t_2\right)}{\sigma_2\sqrt{t_2}} + \ln\left(\frac{\left(S_0^{(1)}\right)^{2\rho} U_1^{2\rho n_1}}{D_1^{2\rho(n_1+1)}}\right) \Big/ \sigma_1\sqrt{t_2}$$

$$I_{10}(X) = I_7(X) - \frac{2\rho\mu_2 t_1}{\sigma_2}$$

$$I_{11}(X) = \frac{\left(\ln\left(\frac{X}{S_0^{(2)}}\right) + \mu_2 t_1\right)}{\sigma_2\sqrt{t_1}} + \ln\left(\frac{\left(S_0^{(1)}\right)^{2\rho} U_1^{2\rho n_1}}{D_1^{2\rho(n_1+1)}}\right) \Big/ \sigma_1\sqrt{t_1}$$

$$I_{12}(X) = \frac{\left(\ln\left(\frac{XS_0^{(2)}U_2^{2n_2}}{D_2^{2(n_2+1)}}\right) - \mu_2 t_2\right)}{\sigma_2\sqrt{t_2}} + \ln\left(\frac{D_1^{2\rho(n_1+1)}}{\left(S_0^{(1)}\right)^{2\rho} U_1^{2\rho n_1}}\right) \Big/ \sigma_1\sqrt{t_2}$$

$$H_1 = \left\{\rho, \rho\sqrt{\frac{t_1}{t_2}}, \sqrt{\frac{t_1}{t_2}}\right\} \quad H_2 = \left\{\rho, -\rho\sqrt{\frac{t_1}{t_2}}, -\sqrt{\frac{t_1}{t_2}}\right\} \tag{7.33}$$

The value of a two-asset, two-step double knock-out call (TATS-DKOC) is obtained as

$$\begin{aligned}
&\text{TATSDKOC}\left(S_0^{(1)}, S_0^{(2)}, r, \sigma_1, \sigma_2, \delta_1, \delta_2, t_1, t_2, K, U_1, U_2, D_1, D_2\right) \\
&\quad = \text{TATSDKOP}\left(S_0^{(1)}, S_0^{(2)}, r, \sigma_1, \sigma_2, \delta_1, \delta_2, t_1, t_2, U_2, U_1, U_2, D_1, D_2\right) \\
&\quad - \text{TATSDKOP}\left(S_0^{(1)}, S_0^{(2)}, r, \sigma_1, \sigma_2, \delta_1, \delta_2, t_1, t_2, K, U_1, U_2, D_1, D_2\right)
\end{aligned} \tag{7.34}$$

7.3. Other Types of Exotic Barriers

Our knowledge of the types of barrier options is not limited to these options. In addition to the barrier types we have tried to explain, there are also different versions or combinations of them, and formulae for these have been developed by distinguished quants in the mathematical finance world. The two of these options are

Window Barrier Options and Window Double Barrier Options. The first is examined by Armstrong (2001), and the last is examined by Hui (1997) and Guillaume (2003). The window barrier options are regarded as the generalization of partial barriers. Here, monitoring a single constant barrier starts at some point after the start date of the option and terminates at a point before maturity. Hence, the name comes as the window. It is almost the same principle for window double barriers, and double barriers replace the single barrier. GuillaumeGuillaume (2003) gives the formulae of standard window double barrier options and partial window double barrier options for calls and puts.

Multitouch options are another type of barrier option. As it is well known, when the barrier is triggered, an "all or nothing" situation occurs, except when the rebate is paid. To provide a solution to the "sudden death" situation, various alternative options have been proposed. One of them is the soft barrier condition, where the knock-out or knock-in provision is defined for a specific range, and the different percentages of the payoff are paid depending on the highest or lowest level reached by the asset (Hart and Rose, 1994). In another approach, the time spent above or below the barrier determines the option payoff. This is the approach by Chesney *et al.* (1997), which is known as Parisian options (Haber, Schönbucher, and Wilmott, 1997), and by Linetsky (1999), known as the "step option." Multitouch options Guillaume (2023) provides an alternative way, and the payoff is designed according to the number of times the asset crosses the predefined barrier in various time intervals before maturity. The formulae require the calculation of many integrals, and the number of terms in the formula grows enormously, as provided by Guillaume (2023).

Another type of barrier option is structured with stochastic boundaries. It is called barrier options with stochastic barriers. Park and Beekman (1983), Rich (1993), and Che and Dassios (2012) examine the general procedures of stochastic barriers, mainly considering the GBM process and the jump and compound Poisson processes. Guillaume (2021) provides an informative introduction and closed-form formulae for the option with GBM processes and one-sided stochastic boundaries. For example, assume S_1, S_2, S_3, and S_4 are four correlated GBM processes. S_1, and S_2 are defined as lower or upper boundaries with respect to S_3 on two successive time intervals

$[t_0, t_1]$ and $[t_1, t_2]$. Then, a closed-form formula can be obtained for the joint probability that S_3 will not cross S_1 between $[t_0, t_1]$, and that S_3 will not cross S_2 between $[t_1, t_2]$ and that S_4 will stay above or below a prespecified constant (K) at a time $t_3 \geq t_2$. Setting the sequence of events this way allows the analytical valuation of the barrier option formulae in a much more general context.

7.4. Conclusion

In this chapter, we have examined some exotic barrier types, including step barriers, partial step barriers, and various types of step double barriers. We thank T. Guillaume for the pricing formulae of these exotic barriers, which require the calculation of many integrals using the first passage time densities and many multivariate cumulative distribution functions. The reader may find all the related formulae in Guillaume (2003, 2004, 2010, 2012, 2021, 2023). The formulae presented in the chapter can be implemented much faster and with much better accuracy by using the quadrature rules for the trivariate, quadrivariate and pentavariate normal cumulative distribution functions. These functions are derived and are clearly presented in Guillaume (2023) on Multitouch Options. These quadrature rules work better than the Halton low discrepancy sequences used in Guillaume (2004) (originally 2001). We have only provided a detailed derivation of a few formulae and a few of the terms in various formulae. We have also presented some exotic types of barrier options, such as window barriers, window double barriers, multi-touch barrier options, and barrier options with stochastic barriers, without providing the very long and complex formulae of the options. We refer to Ait-Sahalia, Imhoff, and Lai (2003) and Jun and Ku (2013) for American-type barriers. Roger and Zane (1999) value barrier options with moving barriers.

Appendix A

Review of Probability

A.1. Probability, σ-Algebra, and Random Variables

Definition A.1. Let Ω be a non-empty set, and let $\mathcal{F}$ be the collections of subsets of Ω. Then $\mathcal{F}$ is called a sigma-algebra (sigma-field) if

(i) The empty set $\emptyset$ belongs to $\mathcal{F}$.
(ii) If the set A belongs to $\mathcal{F}$, then the complement $\Omega \backslash A$ belongs to $\mathcal{F}$.
(iii) If $A_1, A_2, \ldots, A_n$ is a sequence of sets in $\mathcal{F}$ then their union $A_1 \bigcup A_2 \bigcup \ldots$ also belongs to $\mathcal{F}$.

Due to (ii) and (iii), we can also write

$$\bigcap_{n=1}^{\infty} A_n = \left(\bigcup_{n=1}^{\infty} A_n^c \right)^c$$

Example: Coin tossing
Let an event w be Head (H) and Tail (T); $w = H, T$. Assume we will have 3 tosses. Then, our event set will be

$$\Omega = \{\phi, \{HHH, HHT, HTH, HTT, THH, THT, TTH, TTT\}\}$$

This is our first σ-algebra $\mathcal{F}_0$, including $2^{2^0} = 2$ sets. Then, if we are told the outcome of the first coin toss only, we can resolve the sets

$$A_H = \{HHH, HHT, HTH, HTT\}$$

$$A_T = \{THH, THT, TTH, TTT\}$$

Then our $t = 1$ information set, i.e., σ-algebra $\mathcal{F}_1$, can be shown as

$$\mathcal{F}_1 = \Omega = \{\phi, A_H, A_T, A_H \cup A_T\}$$

where $A_H \cup A_T = \Omega$ and the number of sets in $\mathcal{F}_1$ is $2^{2^1} = 4$. A finer resolution is obtained if we know the first two coin tosses. The sets are

$$A_{HH} = \{HHH, HHT\} \; A_{HT} = \{HTH, HTT\}$$
$$A_{TH} = \{THH, THT\} \; A_{TT} = \{TTH, TTT\}$$

Now, $\mathcal{F}_2$ will contain $2^{2^2} = 16$ sets

$$\begin{aligned}\mathcal{F}_2 = \Omega = \{&\phi, A_H, A_T, A_H \cup A_T, A_{HH}, A_{HT}, A_{TH}, A_{TT}, A_{HH} \\ &\cup A_{TH}, A_{HH} \cup A_{TT}, A_{HT} \cup A_{TT}, A_{HT} \cup A_{TH}, A_{HH} \\ &\cup A_{HT} \cup A_{TH}, A_{HH} \cup A_{HT} \cup A_{TT}, A_{HH} \cup A_{TH} \\ &\cup A_{TT}, A_{HT} \cup A_{TH} \cup A_{TT}\}\end{aligned}$$

Finally, with the last coin toss, we will have resolved all the sets in Ω. $\mathcal{F}_3$ will contain all the subsets of Ω. The number of subsets is $2^{2^3} = 256$.

So, all this is about is how the information disseminates through the information sets called σ-algebras, and $\mathcal{F}_0, \mathcal{F}_1, \mathcal{F}_2, \mathcal{F}_3, \ldots$ which is indexed by time is called a filtration.

Example: Assume an urn contains 3 balls: white (w), black (b), and yellow (y). One ball is drawn randomly from the urn and placed back in the urn at time 1. Then, another ball is drawn at random (second draw) from the urn at time 2.

Now, our first sigma algebra is

$$\mathcal{F}_0 = \{\phi, \{ww, bb, yy, wb, wy, by, bw, wy, yw\}\}$$

When the first ball is drawn, the color of the ball is now certain. Then, the set is resolved as

$$\begin{aligned}\mathcal{F}_1 = \{&\phi, \Omega, \{ww, wb, wy\}, \{bb, by, bw\}, \{yy, yb, yw\}, \{ww, wb, wy\} \\ &\cup \{bb, by, bw\}, \{ww, wb, wy\} \cup \{yy, yb, yw\}, \{bb, by, bw\} \\ &\cup \{yy, yb, yw\}\}\end{aligned}$$

Then, $\mathcal{F}_1$ contains $2^{3^1} = 8$ subsets. When the last drawing is made, we get a finer resolution, and the number of subsets is 2^{3^2}=512 (Try! **Hint:** Use combinations).

Definition A.2. Let Ω be a nonempty set. Let T be a fixed positive number and assume for each $t \in [0, T]$ there is a σ-algebra $\mathcal{F}(t)$ on Ω. Assume further that $u \leq t$. Then, every set in $\mathcal{F}(u)$ is also in $\mathcal{F}(t)$. We call the σ-algebras $\mathcal{F}(t)$, $0 \leq t \leq T$ a filtration.

Definition A.3. Let $\mathcal{F}$ be a σ-algebra on Ω. A probability measure P is a function

$$P: \mathcal{F} \to [0, 1]$$

such that

(i) $P(\Omega) = 1$.
(ii) Whenever $A_1 \cup A_2 \cup \ldots$ is a sequence of countably additive disjoint sets in $\mathcal{F}$, then

$$P\left(\bigcup_{n=1}^{\infty} A_n\right) = \sum_{n=1}^{\infty} P(A_n)$$

The triple $(\Omega, \mathcal{F}, P)$ is called a probability space. We can also write for finitely many disjoint sets as

$$P\left(\bigcup_{n=1}^{N} A_n\right) = \sum_{n=1}^{N} P(A_n)$$

Naturally, it is also

$$P(A^c) = 1 - P(A)$$

Definition A.4. Let $\mathcal{F}$ be a σ-algebra on Ω and let $(\Omega, \mathcal{F}, P)$ be a probability space. A random variable is a real-valued function X defined on Ω with the property that for every Borel subset B of $\mathbb{R}$, the set

$$\{X \in B\} = \{w \in \Omega,\ X(w) \in B\}$$

is in the σ-algebra $\mathcal{F}$; $\{X \in B\} \in \mathcal{F}$. Then

$$X : \Omega \to \mathbb{R}$$

is said to be $\mathcal{F}$-measurable. (Every open and closed set and their unions and complements in $\mathbb{R}$ are called Borel sets.)

Definition A.5. Let X be a random variable on a probability space $(\Omega, \mathcal{F}, P)$. Every random variable

$$X : \Omega \to \mathbb{R}$$

gives rise to a probability measure

$$P_X(B) = P(X \in B)$$

on $\mathbb{R}$ defined on the σ-algebra of Borel sets $B \in \mathcal{B}(\mathbb{R})$. Then, $P_X(B)$ is called the distribution of X. The function

$$F_X : \mathbb{R} \to [0, 1]$$

is defined by

$$F_X(x) = P(X \leq x)$$

and it is called the distribution function of X.

Definition A.6. Let $f_X : \mathbb{R} \to \mathbb{R}$ be a Borel function such that for any Borel set $B \subset \mathbb{R}$

$$P(X \in B) = \int_B f_X(x)dx$$

X is defined as a random variable with a continuous distribution, and f_X is called the density function of X.

If there is a sequence of (finite or infinite) distinct real numbers $x_1, x_2 \ldots$ and with $B \subset \mathbb{R}$, then we can write

$$P(X \in B) = \sum_{x_i \in B} P(X = x_i)$$

Furthermore, X is said to have a discrete distribution with mass $P(X = x_i)$ at x_i.

Definition A.7. Let the events be $A, B \in \mathcal{F}$ with $P(B) \neq 0$. The conditional probability of A given B is defined by

$$P(A|B) = \frac{P(A \cap B)}{P(B)}$$

The events $A, B \in \mathcal{F}$ are called independent if we can write them as

$$P(A \cap B) = P(A)P(B)$$

In general, we can express the independency with

$$P(A_1 \cap A_2 \cap A_3 \ldots \cap A_n) = P(A_1)P(A_2)\ldots P(A_n)$$

for $n = 1, 2\ldots$

Definition A.8. Let X and Y be two random variables and let $A, B \in \mathcal{B}(\mathbb{R})$ be two Borel sets. Then X and Y are independent if $X \in A$ and $Y \in B$ are independent. We also say that n random variables $X_1, X_2, \ldots X_n$ are independent if for any Borel sets $B_1, B_2, \ldots B_n \in \mathcal{B}(\mathbb{R})$ the events

$$\{X_1 \in B_1\}, \ldots, \{X_n \in B_n\}$$

are independent.

Definition A.9. The σ-algebras $\mathcal{H}, \varepsilon \subset \mathcal{F}$ are called independent if any two events

$$A \in \mathcal{H} \quad B \in \varepsilon$$

are independent.

Definition A.10. The random variable X is said to be independent of a σ-algebra $\mathcal{H}$ if the σ-algebra generated by $X, \sigma(X)$ and $\mathcal{H}$ are independent.

Definition A.11. Let X be a random variable defined on probability space $(\Omega, \mathcal{F}, P)$. The expectation of X is given by

$$E[X] = \sum_{w \in \Omega} X(w)P(w)$$

This is the average value of X, where the probabilities are considered in averaging. If Ω is uncountably infinite, the expectation is calculated via integration.

Theorem A.1 (Shreve, 2004, pp. 16–19). *We quote the theorem in (Shreve, 2004) without proof.*

Let X be a random variable defined on probability space $(\Omega, \mathcal{F}, P)$

(i) If X takes finitely many values $x_0, x_1, \ldots, x_n$

$$E[X] = \int_{\Omega} X(w)dP(w) = \sum_{k=0}^{n} x_k P(X = x_k)$$

(ii) (Integrability). The random variable is said to be integrable if and only if

$$\int_{\Omega} |X(w)|dP(w) < \infty$$

(iii) (Comparison). If $X \leq Y$ almost surely ($P(X \leq Y) = 1$) and if the integrals $\int_{\Omega} |X(w)|dP(w) < \infty$ and $\int_{\Omega} |Y(w)|dP(w) < \infty$ are defined then

$$\int_{\Omega} X(w)dP(w) \leq \int_{\Omega} Y(w)dP(w)$$

(iv) (Linearity). If α and β are real constants and X and Y are integrable or if all constants and variables are nonnegative, then

$$\begin{aligned}&\int_{\Omega} (\alpha X(w) + \beta Y(w))dP(w)\\ &\quad = \alpha \int_{\Omega} X(w)dP(w) + \beta \int_{\Omega} Y(w)dP(w)\end{aligned}$$

(v) (Jensen's Inequality). If φ is a convex, real-valued function defined on $\mathbb{R}$ and if $E|X| < \infty$ (integrable)

$$\varphi(EX) \leq E\varphi(X)$$

A.2. Information and Conditioning

Definition A.12 (Conditional Expectation). For any integrable random variable X and any event $A \in \mathcal{F}$ with $P(A) \neq 0$, the conditional expectation of X is given by

$$E(X|A) = \frac{1}{P(A)} \int_{A} XdP$$

Definition A.13. Let X be an integrable random variable on a probability space $(\Omega, \mathcal{F}, P)$, and $\mathcal{H}$ is a sub-σ-algebra of $\mathcal{F}$. The conditional expectation of X given $\mathcal{H}$ denoted $E(X|\mathcal{H})$ is any random variable that satisfies

(i) Measurability; $E(X|\mathcal{H})$ is $\mathcal{H}$-measurable.
(ii) Partial averaging

$$\int_A X(w)dP(w) = \int_A E(X|\mathcal{H})(w)dP(w) \quad A \in \mathcal{H}$$

Theorem A.2 (Shreve, 2004, pp. 69–73). *We quote the theorem in (Shreve, 2004) without proof.*

Let $(\Omega, \mathcal{F}, P)$ be a probability space, and let $\mathcal{H}$ be a sub-σ-algebra of $\mathcal{F}$.

(i) *Linearity of conditional expectations*: If X and Y are integrable random variables and a and b are constants

$$E(aX + bY|\mathcal{H}) = aE(X|\mathcal{H}) + bE(Y|\mathcal{H})$$

(ii) *Taking out what is known*: If X and Y are integrable random variables and XY is integrable, and X is $\mathcal{H}$-measurable, then

$$E(XY|\mathcal{H}) = XE(Y|\mathcal{H})$$

(iii) *Iterated conditioning*: If $\mathcal{H}$ is a sub-σ-algebra of $\mathcal{F}$ ($\mathcal{H}$ contains less information than $\mathcal{F}, \mathcal{H} \subset \mathcal{F}$)

$$E\{E(X|\mathcal{F})|\mathcal{F})|\mathcal{H}\} = E(X|\mathcal{H})$$

(iv) *Independence*: If X is integrable and independent of $\mathcal{H}$, then

$$E(X|\mathcal{H}) = EX$$

(v) *Conditional Jensen's inequality*: If $\varphi(x)$ is a convex function of a dummy variable x and X is integrable, then

$$E[\varphi(X)|\mathcal{H}] \geq \varphi(E(X|\mathcal{H}))$$

Definition A.14. Let $(\Omega, \mathcal{F}, P)$ be a probability space, let T be a fixed positive number, and let $\mathcal{F}(t)$, $0 \leq t \leq T$ be a filtration of sub-σ-algebras of $\mathcal{F}$. Consider an adapted process $M(t)$, $0 \leq t \leq T$ (the value is known by the time t)

(i) If

$$E(M(t)|\mathcal{F}(s)) = M(s)$$

the adapted process is said to be a martingale. It bears no tendency to rise or fall.

(ii) If

$$E(M(t)|\mathcal{F}(s)) \geq M(s)$$

this process is sub-martingale. There is no tendency to fall, but it may rise.

(iii) If

$$E(M(t)|\mathcal{F}(s)) \leq M(s)$$

this process is super-martingale. There is no tendency to rise, but it may fall.

We refer to Feller (1971), Karlin and Taylor (1975), Protter (1992), Jacod and Shiryaev (2000), Oksendal (2003), and Shreve (2004) on the general theory of probability and the stochastic processes.

Appendix B

Matlab Codes

B.1. Double Barrier Knock-Out Call Option Price (Kunitomo-Ikeda, 1992)

```
function cdbb= Kundb (S0, K, r, sig, tau, A, B, del1, del2, n)
F=B*exp (del1*tau);
nvec= [-n: 1: n];
for i=1: length (nvec)
d1(i)=(log(S0*B^(nvec(i)*2)/(K*A^(nvec(i)*2))) +(r+sig^2/2)
*tau)/(sig*sqrt(tau))
d2(i)=(log(S0*B^(nvec(i)*2)/(F*A^(nvec(i)*2))) +(r+sig^2/2)
*tau)/(sig*sqrt(tau))
d3(i)=(log(A^(nvec(i)*2+2)/(K*S0*B^(nvec(i)*2))) +(r+sig^2/2)
*tau)/(sig*sqrt(tau))
d4(i)=(log(A^(nvec(i)*2+2)/(F*S0*B^(nvec(i)*2))) +(r+sig^2/2)
*tau)/(sig*sqrt(tau))
C1 (i) =2*(r-del2-nvec (i)*(del1-del2))/sig^2+1
C2 (i) =2*nvec (i)*(del1-del2)/sig^2
C3 (i) = 2*(r-del2+nvec (i)*(del1-del2))/sig^2+1
end
top1=0
for i=1: length (nvec)
top1=top1+(((B^nvec(i)/A^nvec(i))) ^c1(i))*((A/S0)^c2(i))
*((normcdf(d1(i))-normcdf(d2(i))))-
(((A^(nvec(i)+1)/(S0*B^nvec(i)))) ^c3(i))*...
   (normcdf (d3 (i))-normcdf (d4 (i)))
end
```

```
top2=0
for i=1: length (nvec)
top2=top2+(((B^nvec(i)/A^nvec(i))) ^(c1(i)-2)) *((A/S0) ^c2(i))
*((normcdf(d1(i)-sig*sqrt(tau))-normcdf(d2(i)-sig*sqrt(tau)))) -
((A^(nvec(i)+1)/(S0*B^nvec(i)))) ^(c3(i)-2)*...
  ((normcdf (d3 (i)-sig*sqrt (tau))-normcdf(d4(i)-sig*sqrt (tau))))
end
Cddb =S0*top1-K*top2*exp (-r*tau)
```

B.2. Double Barrier Knock-Out Call Option Price (Pelsser, 1997)

```
function vdbko= Pelsdko (S0, K, r, sig, tau, L, U, k)
mu=r-0.5*sig^2;
l=log (U/L); d=log (K/L); x=log (S0/L);
kvec= [1: k];
alfa= [0 1];
top1L=0;
top1D=0;
top2L=0;
top2D=0;
for i=1: length (kvec)
  lamk =0.5*(mu^2/sig^2+kvec (i) ^2*pi^2*sig^2/l^2)
  top1L=top1L+exp(-lamk*tau) *sin(kvec(i)*pi*x/l)
*(((mu/sig^2+alfa (2)) *sin(kvec(i)*pi*l/l)-(kvec(i)*pi/l)
*cos(kvec(i)*pi*l/l))...
    /((mu/sig^2+alfa (2)) ^2+kvec (i) ^2*pi^2/l^2))
  top1D=top1D+exp(-lamk*tau) *sin(kvec(i)*pi*x/l)
*(((mu/sig^2+alfa(2)) *sin(kvec(i)*pi*d/l)-(kvec(i)*pi/l)
*cos(kvec(i)*pi*d/l))...
    /((mu/sig^2+alfa (2)) ^2+kvec (i) ^2*pi^2/l^2))
  top2L=top2L+exp(-lamk*tau) *sin(kvec(i)*pi*x/l)
*(((mu/sig^2+alfa(1)) *sin(kvec(i)*pi*l/l)-(kvec(i)*pi/l)
*cos(kvec(i)*pi*l/l))...
    / ((mu/sig^2+alfa (1)) ^2+kvec (i) ^2*pi^2/l^2))
  top2D=top2D+exp(-lamk*tau) *sin(kvec(i)*pi*x/l)
*(((mu/sig^2+alfa(1)) *sin(kvec(i)*pi*d/l)-(kvec(i)*pi/l)
```

```
*cos(kvec(i)*pi*d/l))...
    / ((mu/sig^2+alfa (1))^2+kvec(I)^2*pi^2/l^2))
end
Q1L= (2/l) *exp (alfa (2) *l) *exp ((mu/sig^2) *(l-x)) *top1L
Q1D= (2/l) *exp (alfa (2) *d) *exp ((mu/sig^2) *(d-x)) *top1D
Q0L= (2/l) *exp (alfa (1) *l) *exp ((mu/sig^2) *(l-x)) *top2L
Q0D= (2/l) *exp (alfa (1) *d) *exp ((mu/sig^2) *(d-x)) *top2D
vdbko =exp (-r*tau) *(L*(Q1L-Q1D)-K*(Q0L-Q0D))
```

B.3. Upper Barrier Knock-In Call Option (Luo, 2001)

```
function VUI=LuoVUI2(S0, K, r, T, sig, d, U, L, m)
% upper barrier knock-in tau (b) <tau (a) tau (b) <=T
mu =r-d-0.5*sig^2; x0=log (S0); b=log (U); a=log (L); k=log (K);
n= [1: m];
topalp =0; topbep =0; topalm =0; topbem =0;
Lfist=exp(-r*T) *S0*exp((mu+0.5*sig^2) *T)
*normcdf((x0+(mu+sig^2) *T-b)/(sig*sqrt(T)))-exp(-r*T)
*K*normcdf((x0+mu*T-b)/(sig*sqrt(T)));

for i=1: length (n)
alfap =2*i*b-2*(i-1) *a-x0;
betp =2*i*(b-a) + x0;
alfam =2*i*a-2*(i-1) *b-x0;
betm =2*i*(a-b) + x0;
topalp =topalp +exp ((mu/sig^2) *(alfap-x0)-r*T) *exp
((mu+0.5*sig^2) *T+ alfap) *normcdf ((alfap+(mu+sig^2) *T-min
(k, b))/(sig* sqrt (T)))-...
   exp ((mu/sig^2)*(alfap-x0)-r*T) *K*normcdf (((alfap + mu*T-
min(k, b))/ (sig*sqrt (T))))...
   -exp ((mu/sig^2) *(alfap-x0)-r*T) *exp ((mu+0.5*sig^2) *T+
alfap) *normcdf (((alfap+ (mu+sig^2) *T-b))/ (sig*sqrt (T)))...
   +exp ((mu/sig^2) *(alfap-x0)-r*T) *K*normcdf ((alfap + mu*T-
b)/(sig*sqrt (T)));

   topbep =topbep +exp ((mu/sig^2) *(betp-x0)-r*T) *exp
((mu+0.5*sig^2) *T+ betp) *normcdf ((betp+ (mu+sig^2)
*T-min (k,b))/ (sig* sqrt (T)))-...
```

```
exp ((mu/sig^2)*(betp-x0)-r*T)*K*normcdf(((betp + mu*T-min
(k, b))/ (sig*sqrt (T))))...
 -exp ((mu/sig^2) *(betp-x0)-r*T) *exp ((mu+0.5*sig^2) *T +
betp) *normcdf ((betp+ (mu+sig^2) *T-b)/ (sig*sqrt (T)))...
  +K*normcdf ((betp + mu*T-b)/(sig*sqrt (T))) *exp((mu/sig^2)
*(betp-x0)-r*T);

 topalm =topalm + exp ((mu/sig^2) *(alfam-x0)-r*T) *exp
((mu+0.5*sig^2) *T+ alfam) *normcdf (((alfam+ (mu+sig^2) *T-
max (k, b))/ (sig* sqrt (T))))-...
  exp ((mu/sig^2) *(alfam-x0)-r*T) *K*normcdf ((alfam + mu*T-
b)/(sig*sqrt (T)));

 topbem =topbem + exp ((mu/sig^2) *(betm-x0)-r*T) *exp
((mu+0.5*sig^2)*T+ betm) *normcdf ((betm+ (mu+sig^2) *T-b)/
(sig* sqrt (T)))-...
  exp ((mu/sig^2)*(betm-x0)-r*T)*K*normcdf((betm + mu*T-b)/
(sig* sqrt (T)));
end
VUI=Lfist + topalp-topbep-topalm+ topbem %upper barrier
knock-in
vuo =blsprice (S0, K, r, T, sig, d)-VUI % upper barrier knock-out
```

B.4. Lower Barrier Knock-In Call Option (Luo, 2001)

```
function VLI=LuoVLI2(S0, K, r, T, sig, d, U, L, m)
% lower barrier knock-in
mu =r-d-0.5*sig^2; x0 =log (S0); b=log (U); a=log (L); k=log (K);
n= [1: m];
Topalp=0; topbep=0; topalm=0; topbem=0;
Lfist=exp(-r*T) *S0*exp((mu+0.5*sig^2) *T) *normcdf((a-x0-
(mu+sig^2) *T)/(sig*sqrt(T)))-exp(-r*T) *K*normcdf ((a-x0-
mu*T)/(sig*sqrt(T)))-...
exp (-r*T) *S0*exp ((mu+0.5*sig^2) *T) *normcdf ((min (a, k)-x0-
(mu+sig^2)*T)/(sig*sqrt(T)))+exp(-r*T)*K*normcdf ((min (a, k)-
x0-mu*T)/(sig*sqrt(T)));
```

```
for i=1: length (n)
alfap =2*i*b-2*(i-1) *a-x0;
betp =2*i*(b-a) + x0;
alfam =2*i*a-2*(i-1) *b-x0;
betm =2*i*(a-b) + x0;

Topalp=Topalp +exp ((mu/sig^2) *(alfap-x0)-r*T) *exp
((mu+0.5*sig^2) *T+ alfap) *normcdf((a-alfap-(mu+sig^2)
*T)/(sig*sqrt(T)))-...
  exp ((mu/sig^2) *(alfap-x0)-r*T) *K*normcdf ((a-alfap-mu*T)/
(sig* sqrt (T)))...
  -exp ((mu/sig^2) *(alfap-x0)-r*T) *exp ((mu+0.5*sig^2) *T+
alfap)*normcdf ((min (a,k)-alfap-(mu+sig^2) *T)/(sig* sqrt (T)))...
  +exp ((mu/sig^2) *(alfap-x0)-r*T) *K*normcdf ((min (a, k)
-alfap-mu*T)/ (sig* sqrt (T)));

 topbep=topbep +exp ((mu/sig^2) *(betp-x0)-r*T) *exp
((mu+0.5*sig^2) *T+ betp) *normcdf((a-betp-(mu+sig^2) *T)/
(sig*sqrt (T)))-...
  exp ((mu/sig^2) *(betp-x0)-r*T) *K*normcdf ((a-betp-mu*T)/
(sig*sqrt (T)))...
  -exp ((mu/sig^2) *(betp-x0)-r*T) *exp ((mu+0.5*sig^2)
*T+ betp) *normcdf ((min (a, k)-betp-(mu+sig^2) *T)/
(sig*sqrt (T)))...
  +exp ((mu/sig^2) *(betp-x0)-r*T) *K*normcdf ((min (a, k)-
betp-mu*T)/(sig* sqrt (T)));

 topalm =topalm + exp ((mu/sig^2) *(alfam-x0)-r*T) *exp
((mu+0.5*sig^2) *T +alfam) *normcdf ((alfam+ (mu+sig^2)
*T-max (k, a))/ (sig* sqrt (T)))-...
  exp ((mu/sig^2) *(alfam-x0)-r*T) *K*normcdf ((alfam + mu*T-
max (k, a))/ (sig*sqrt (T)));

 topbem =topbem+ exp ((mu/sig^2) *(betm-x0)-r*T) *exp
((mu+0.5*sig^2) *T + betm) *normcdf ((betm+ (mu+sig^2)
*T-max (k, a))/ (sig* sqrt (T)))-...
  exp ((mu/sig^2) *(betm-x0)-r*T) *K*normcdf ((betm + mu*T-
max (k,a))/ (sig*sqrt (T)));
end
```

```
VLI=Lfist+topalm+topbep-topalp-topbem
voti=VLI+LuoVUI2(S0, K, r, T, sig, d, U, L, m) %one touch
knock-in vui+vli
voto=blsprice (S0, K, r, T, sig, d)-voti % one touch knock-out
means double knock out
VLO=blsprice (S0, K, r, T, sig, d)-VLI % lower barrier knock-out
```

Appendix C

European Put-Call Symmetry

Carr *et al.* (1998) assume that the volatility of the forward price is a known function $\sigma(F_t, t)$ of the forward price F_t and time t. They also assume the following symmetry condition:

$$\sigma(F_t, t) = \sigma\left(\frac{F^2}{F_t}, t\right) \tag{C.1}$$

for all $F_t \geq 0$, where F is the current forward price (F_0) and

$$X_t = \ln\left(\frac{F_t}{F}\right)$$

In this setting, the volatility at any future date is assumed to be the same for any two levels (call and put strikes) whose geometric mean is the current forward $((F.F)^{1/2} = F$ or $(K_C K_P.)^{1/2} = F)$.

Letting $v(X_t, t) = \sigma(F_t, t)$ the equivalent condition for the symmetry of volatility is

$$v(x, t) = v(-x, t) \tag{C.2}$$

for all $x \in \mathbb{R}$ and $t \in [0, T]$. The symmetry condition is satisfied in models with a symmetric smile in the log of K/F. However, the volatility against K/F will be asymmetric with higher put volatility than call volatility for strikes equidistant from the forward.

Given frictionless markets, no arbitrage, zero drift, and the symmetry conditions, Carr *et al.* (1998) show that the following relationship holds:

$$C(K)K^{-\frac{1}{2}} = P(H)H^{-\frac{1}{2}} \tag{C.3}$$

where the geometric mean of the call strike K and the put strike H is the forward price F:

$$F = (KH)^{1/2}$$

Proof. Let $\sigma(F_t, t) = \sigma(F(t), t)$ be the local volatility, and the forward price process is

$$\frac{dF(t)}{F(t)} = \sigma(F(t), t)dW(t) \tag{C.4}$$

under the martingale measure. Let $B(0)$ be the price at time 0 of a bond paying one dollar at maturity T and let $C(0, K, T)$ and $P(0, K, T)$ be the initial value of a European call and put struck at K with maturity T. Let

$$\begin{aligned} G_C(K,T) &= B(0)^{-1}C(0,K,T) \\ G_P(K,T) &= B(0)^{-1}P(0,K,T) \end{aligned} \tag{C.5}$$

be the respective forward values quoted at 0 of these options for delivery in T years. Carr *et al.* (1998) show that both forward values satisfy the following forward partial differential equation:

$$\frac{\sigma^2(K,T)K^2}{2}\frac{\partial^2 G}{\partial K^2}(K,T) = \frac{\partial G}{\partial T}(K,T) \quad K > 0 \quad T > 0 \tag{C.6}$$

Let's write the call option's expected value under the equivalent martingale measure

$$G_C(K,T) = \int_K^{\infty} (F(T) - K)p(F(T), T; F(0), 0)dF(T) \tag{C.7}$$

where $p(F(T), T; F(0), 0)$ is the transition density of $F(T)$. The Kolmogorov equation governing this density is

$$\frac{1}{2}\frac{\partial^2}{\partial K^2}[\sigma^2(K,T)K^2 p(K,T;F(0),0)] = \frac{\partial}{\partial T}p(K,T;F(0),0)$$

Differentiating C.6 two times yields:

$$\frac{\partial G_C(K,T)}{\partial K} = -(F(T)-K)p(K,T;F(0),0)$$

$$\frac{\partial^2 G}{\partial K^2}(K,T) = p(K,T;F(0),0)$$

and substituting this in the Kolmogorov equation gives

$$\frac{1}{2}\frac{\partial^2}{\partial K^2}\left[\sigma^2(K,T)K^2\frac{\partial^2 G}{\partial K^2}(K,T)\right] = \frac{\partial}{\partial T}\frac{\partial^2 G}{\partial K^2}(K,T)$$

Now, integrating with respect to K twice gives

$$\frac{\sigma^2(K,T)K^2}{2}\frac{\partial^2 G}{\partial K^2}(K,T) = \frac{\partial G}{\partial T}(K,T) \tag{C.8}$$

The forward call (put) value is the unique solution of C.8, subject to the following boundary conditions:

For call options:

$$G_C(K,0) = \max\left[F(T=0)-K\right], \quad K>0$$
$$\lim_{K\to\infty} G_C(K,T) = 0 \quad T>0$$
$$\lim_{K\to 0} G_C(K,T) = F(0) \quad T>0$$

For put options:

$$G_P(K,0) = \max\left[K-F(T=0)\right] \quad K>0$$
$$\lim_{K\to\infty} G_P(K,T) \cong K \quad T>0$$
$$\lim_{K\to 0} G_P(K,T) = 0 \quad T>0$$

Let

$$u_C(x,T) = G_C(K,T)(KF(0))^{-1/2}$$
$$u_P(x,T) = G_P(K,T)(KF(0))^{-1/2}$$

be normalized call and put forward values, written as functions of $x = \ln(K/F(0))$ and maturity T. Then, $u_C(x,T)$ and $u_P(x,T)$ are the solutions of

$$\frac{v^2(x,T)}{2}\frac{\partial^2 u}{\partial x^2}(x,T) - \frac{v^2(x,T)}{8}u(x,T) = \frac{\partial u}{\partial T}(x,T) \tag{C.9}$$

where $v(x,T) = \sigma(F(0)e^x, T$. The normalized forward call value $u_C(x,T)$ is the unique solution to C.9 subject to the following boundary conditions

$$u_C(x,0) = \max\left[e^{-\frac{x}{2}} - e^{\frac{x}{2}}, 0\right] \quad x \in (-\infty, +\infty)$$
$$\lim_{x\to\infty} u_C(x,T) = 0 \quad T > 0$$
$$\lim_{x\to-\infty} u_C(x,T) = e^{-\frac{x}{2}} \quad T > 0$$

Similarly, for puts

$$u_P(x,0) = \max\left[e^{\frac{x}{2}} - e^{-\frac{x}{2}}, 0\right] \quad x \in (-\infty, +\infty)$$
$$\lim_{x\to\infty} u_P(x,T) = e^{\frac{x}{2}} \quad T > 0$$
$$\lim_{x\to-\infty} u_P(x,T) = 0 \quad T > 0$$

The symmetry condition is

$$v^2(x,T) = v^2(-x,T) \quad \text{for all } x \in (-\infty, +\infty).$$

We can proceed in the following way: $(F_0 = F)$

$$x = \ln K/F_0 \quad \to F_0 e^x = K \to \frac{dx}{dK} = \frac{1}{K}$$

$$G_C(K,T) = u_C(x,T)(KF)^{1/2}$$
$$\frac{\partial G_C(K,T)}{\partial K} = \frac{1}{2}F^{1/2}K^{-1/2}u + (KF)^{1/2}\frac{\partial u}{\partial x}\frac{\partial x}{\partial K}$$
$$\frac{\partial G_C(K,T)}{\partial K} = \frac{1}{2}F^{1/2}K^{-1/2}u + F^{1/2}K^{-1/2}\frac{\partial u}{\partial x}$$

$$\frac{\partial^2 G_C}{\partial K^2}(K,T) = -\frac{1}{4}F^{\frac{1}{2}}K^{-\frac{3}{2}}u + \frac{\partial u}{\partial x}\frac{\partial x}{\partial K}\frac{1}{2}F^{\frac{1}{2}}K^{-\frac{1}{2}}$$
$$-\frac{1}{2}F^{\frac{1}{2}}K^{-\frac{3}{2}}\frac{\partial u}{\partial x} + F^{1/2}K^{-1/2}\frac{\partial^2 u}{\partial x^2}\frac{\partial x}{\partial K}$$
$$\frac{\partial^2 G_C}{\partial K^2}(K,T) = -\frac{1}{4}F^{\frac{1}{2}}K^{-\frac{3}{2}}u + F^{1/2}K^{-3/2}\frac{\partial^2 u}{\partial x^2}$$

Substituting this in (C.9)

$$\frac{\sigma^2(K,T)K^2}{2}\frac{\partial^2 G}{\partial K^2}(K,T) = \frac{\partial G}{\partial T}(K,T)$$
$$\frac{\sigma^2(K,T)K^2}{2}\left[-\frac{1}{4}F^{\frac{1}{2}}K^{-\frac{3}{2}}u + F^{1/2}K^{-3/2}\frac{\partial^2 u}{\partial x^2}\right] = \frac{\partial u}{\partial T}(KF)^{1/2}$$
$$\frac{\partial u}{\partial T} = \frac{\sigma^2(K,T)}{2}\frac{\partial^2 u}{\partial x^2} - \frac{\sigma^2(K,T)}{8}u$$

Since $\sigma^2(K,T) = v^2(x,T)$, $v(x,T) = \sigma(F_0 e^x, T)$ we obtain

$$\frac{\partial u(x,T)}{\partial T} = \frac{v^2(x,T)}{2}\frac{\partial^2 u(x,T)}{\partial x^2} - \frac{v^2(x,T)}{8}u(x,T)$$

For boundary condition, we can write

$$G_C(K,0)$$
$$= \max[F(T=0) - K, 0] \to u_C(x,0) = G_C(K,0)(KF(0))^{-1/2}$$
$$(F(0) - F(0)e^x, 0)(F(0)F(0)e^x)^{-\frac{1}{2}}$$
$$= (1 - e^x, 0)e^{-\frac{x}{2}} = \max(e^{-\frac{x}{2}} - e^{\frac{x}{2}}, 0)$$

The symmetry condition is $v^2(x,T) = v^2(-x,T)$ for $x \in \mathbb{R}\, T > 0$ therefore, we can write

$$u_C(x,T) = u_P(-x,T) \quad x \in \mathbb{R}\, T > 0$$

Turning back to forward prices

$$G_C(K,T)(KF)^{-1/2} = u_C(x,T)$$
$$u_P(x,T) = G_P(K,T)(KF)^{-1/2}$$
$$u_C(x,T) = u_P(-x,T)$$

we can write

$$G_C(K_C, T)(K_C F)^{-1/2} = G_P(K_P, T)(K_P F)^{-1/2}$$

where $(K_C K_P)^{1/2} = F$. Once again, turning back to current prices from forward prices, we multiply by $B(0)$ and $F^{1/2,}$ and the result is

$$C(0,\, K_C, T){K_C}^{-1/2} = P(0, K_P, T){K_P}^{-\frac{1}{2}} \tag{C.10}$$

□

Bibliography

Ahn, D. H., Figlewski, S., and Gao, B. (1999). Pricing discrete barrier options with an adaptive mesh model. Working Paper.

Ait-Sahalia, F., Imhoff, L., and Lai, T. L. (2003). Fast and accurate valuation of American barrier options. *Journal of Computational Finance*, *7*, 129–145.

Andersen, L., Andreasen, J., and Eliezer, D. (2000). Static replication of barrier options: Some general results. SSRN.

Anderson, T. W. (1960). A modification of the sequential probability ratio test to reduce the sample size. *Annals of Mathematical Statistics*, *31*(1), 165–197.

Armstrong, G. F. (2001). Valuation formulae for window barrier options. *Applied Mathematical Finance*, *8*(4), 197–208.

Beaglehole, D. (1992). Down and out, up and in options. University of Iowa Working Paper.

Benson, R. and Daniel, N. (1991). Up, over and out. *Risk*, *4*(6), 17–19.

Bermin, H. P. (2002). A general approach to hedging options: Applications to barrier and partial barrier options. *Mathematical Finance*, *12*(3), 199–218.

Bhagavatula, R., and Carr, P. (1995). Valuing double barrier options with time-dependent parameters. Cornell University Working Paper.

Björk, T. (2004). *Arbitrage Theory in Continuous Time*. Oxford Finance.

Black, F. and Scholes, M. (1973). The pricing of options and corporate liabilities. *Journal of Political Economy*, *81*, 637–654.

Bouzoubaa, M. and Osseiran, A. (2010). *Exotic Options and Hybrids*. Wiley.

Bowie, J. and Carr, P. (1994). Static simplicity. *Risk*, *7*(8), 44–49.

Boyle, P. P. (1988). A lattice framework for option pricing with two state variables. *The Journal of Financial and Quantitative Analysis*, *23*(1), 1–12.

Boyle, P. P., Evnine, J., and Gibbs, S. (1989). Numerical evaluation of multivariate contingent claims. *The Review of Financial Studies*, *2*(2), 241–250.

Boyle, P. and Lau, S. (1994). Bumping up against the barrier with the binomial method. *Journal of Derivatives*, *1*(4), 6–14.

Briys, E., Bellalah, M., Mai, H. M., and de Varenne, F. (1998). *Options, Futures and Exotic Derivatives: Theory, Application and Practice.* John Wiley and Sons.

Broadie, M. and Glasserman, P. (1997). A continuity correction for discrete barrier options. *Mathematical Finance*, *7*(4), 325–348.

Buchen, P. (2012). *An Introduction to Exotic Option Pricing.* CRC Press.

Buchen, P. and Konstandatos, O. (2009). A new approach to pricing double barrier options with arbitrary payoffs and curved boundaries. *Applied Mathematical Finance*, *16*(6), 497–515.

Carr, P. (1995). Two extensions to barrier option valuation. *Applied Mathematical Finance*, *2*, 173–209.

Carr, P. and Chou, A. (1996). *Breaking Barriers.* A preliminary version.

Carr, P. and Chou, A. (2002). Hedging complex barrier options. Working paper.

Carr, P. C., Ellis, K., and Gupta, V. (1998). *Static Hedging of Exotic Options.* Working Paper: Johnson Graduate School of Management, Cornell University.

Chance, D. M. (2005). Reflection principle in finance. Teaching Notes.

Che, X. and Dassios, A. (2012). Stochastic boundary crossing probabilities for the Brownian motion. *Journal of Applied Probability*, *50*, 419–429.

Chesney, M., Jeanblanc, M., and Yor, M. (1997). Brownian excursions and Parisian barrier options. *Annals of Applied Probability*, *29*, 165–184.

Cheuk, H. T. and Vorst, C. T. (1996). Complex barrier options. *Journal of Derivatives*, *4*(1), 8–22.

Clewlow, L. and Strickland, C. (1997). *Exotic Options: The State of the Art.* Thomson Business Press.

Clewlow, L. and Strickland, C. (1998). *Implementing Derivatives Models.* John Wiley and Sons.

Cox, J. C. and Miller, H. D. (1965). *The Theory of Stochastic Processes.* Chapman & Hall/CRC.

Cox, J. C., Ross, S. A., and Rubinstein, M. (1979). Option pricing: A simplified approach. *Journal of Financial Economics*, *7*, 229–263.

Cox, J. C. and Rubinstein, M. (1985). *Option Markets.* Prentice-Hall.

Das, S. (1996). *Exotic Options.* LBC Information Services.

Delbaen, F. and Schachermayer, W. (1994). A general version of the fundamental theorem of asset pricing. *Matematische Annalen*, *300*, 463–520.

Delbaen, F. and Schachermayer, W. (1998). The fundamental theorem for unbounded processes. *Matematische Annalen*, *312*, 215–250.

Derman, E. and Kani, I. (1993). The ins and outs of barrier options. Goldman Sachs Quantitative Strategies Research Notes.

Derman, E., Ergener, D., and Kani, I. (2000). Static options replication. *Journal of Derivatives*, *2*(4), 78–95.

Duan, J. C., Dudley, E., Gauthier, G., and Simonato, J. G. (2003). Pricing discretely monitored barrier options by a Markov chain. *The Journal of Derivatives*, *10*(4), 9–31.

Duffy, G. D. (1994). *Transform Methods for Solving Partial Differential Equations.* CRC Press.

Elliott, J. R. and Kopp, E. P. (2004). *Mathematics of Financial Markets.* Springer.

Etheridge, A. (2002). *A Course in Financial Calculus.* Cambridge University Press.

Feller, W. (1971). *An Introduction to Probability Theory and Its Applications: Volume 2.* John Wiley and Sons.

Feng, L. and Linetsky, V. (2008). Pricing discretely monitored barrier options and defaultable bonds in Levy process models: A fast Hilbert transform approach. *Mathematical Finance*, *18*(3), 337–384.

Fusai, G., Abrahams, I. D., and Sgarra, C. (2006). An exact analytical solution for discrete barrier options. *Finance and Stochastics*, *10*(1), 1–26.

Geman, H. and Yor, M. (1996). Pricing and hedging double-barrier options: A probabilistic approach. *Mathematical Finance*, *6*(4), 365–378.

Guillaume, T. (2003). Window double barrier options. *Review of Derivatives Research*, 6, 47–75.

Guillaume, T. (2004). Analytical valuation of options on joint minima and maxima in high dimensions. *Applied Mathematical Finance*, *8*(4), 209–233.

Guillaume, T. (2010). Step double barrier options. *The Journal of Derivatives*, *18*(1), 59–80.

Guillaume, T. (2012). A few insights into cliquet options. *International Journal of Business*, *17*(2), 163–180.

Guillaume, T. (2021). Closed-form valuation of barrier options with stochastic barriers. *Annals of Operations Research.* https://doi.org/10.1007/s10479-020-03860-w.

Guillaume, T. (2023). Multitouch options. *Journal of Risk and Financial Management*, *16*, 300.

Haber, R. J., Schönbucher, P. J., and Wilmott, P. (1997). Pricing Parisian options. MFG Working Paper, Oxford University.

Harrison, J. and Kreps, J. (1979). Martingales and arbitrage in multiperiod securities markets. *Journal of Economic Theory*, 11, 418–443.

Harrison, J. and Pliska, S. (1981). Martingales and stochastic integrals in the theory of continuous trading. *Stochastic Processes and their Applications*, *11*, 215–260.

Harrison, J. and Pliska, S. (1983). Stochastic calculus model of continuous trading: Complete markets. *Stochastic Processes and their Applications*, *15*, 313–316.

Harrison, M. J. (1985). *Brownian Motion and Stochastic Flow Systems.* Wiley.

Hart, I. and Rose, M. (1994). Striking continuity. *Risk Magazine*, *7*, 51–56.

Heynen, R. and Kat, H. (1994a). Outside barrier options. MeesPierson working paper.

Heynen, R. and Kat, H. (1994b). Crossing barriers. *Risk*, *7*(6), 46–51.

Heynen, R. and Kat, H. (1994c). Partial barrier options. *Journal of Financial Engineering*, *3*(3/4), 253–274.

Heynen, R. C. and Kat, H. M. (1996). Discrete partial barrier options with a moving barrier. *The Journal of Financial Engineering, 5*, 199–209.

Heynen, R. and Kat, H. (1997). Barrier options. In L. Clewlow and C. Strickland (Eds.), *Exotic Options.* Thomson Business Press.

Howison, S. (2006). *Barrier Options.* Working Paper.

Howison, S. and Steinberg, M. (2007). A matched asymptotic expansions approach to continuity corrections for discretely sampled options. Part 1: Barrier options. *Applied Mathematical Finance, 14*(1), 63–89.

Hsu, H. (1997). Surprised parties. *RISK*, April.

Hudson, M. (1991). The value in going out. *Risk*, March, 31.

Hui, C. (1997). Time-dependent barrier option values. *The Journal of Futures Markets, 17*(6), 667–688.

Hull, J. C. (2009). *Options, Futures, and Other Derivatives.* Prentice Hall.

Ilhan, A. and Sircar, R. (2006). Optimal static-dynamic hedges for barrier options. *Mathematical Finance, 16*(2), 359–385.

Jacod, J. and Shiryaev, A. N. (2000). *Limit Theorems for Stochastic Processes.* Springer.

Jeanblanc, M., Yor, M., and Chesney, M. (2009). *Mathematical Methods for Financial Markets.* Springer Finance. https://doi.org/10.1007/978-1-84628-737-4.

Jun, D. and Ku, H. (2013). Valuation of American partial barrier options. *Review of Derivatives Research, 16*, 167–191.

Kamrad, B. and Ritchken, P. (1991). Multinomial approximating models for options with k state variables. *Management Science, 37*(12), 1640–1652.

Karlin, S. and Taylor, H. M. (1975). *A First Course in Stochastic Processes.* Academic Press.

Kat, H. and Verdonk, L. (1994). *Barrier Options and Binomial Trees.* MeesPierson working paper.

Konstandatos, O. (2003). *A New Framework for Pricing Barrier and Lookback Options* [Doctoral dissertation]. The University of Sydney.

Konstandatos, O. (2008). *Pricing Path-Dependent Options: A Comprehensive Mathematical Framework. Applications of Mathematics* (1st ed.). VDM-Verlag Dr Mueller Aktiengesellschaft & Co. Kg.

Kou, S. G. (2003). On pricing of discrete barrier options. *Statistica Sinica, 13*, 955–964.

Kunitomo, N. and Ikeda, M. (1992). Pricing options with curved boundaries. *Mathematical Finance, 2*, 275–298.

Kwok, Y. K. (2008). *Mathematical Models of Financial Derivatives.* Springer.

Lawrence, S. J. L. (2001). Various types of double-barrier options. *Journal of Computational Finance, 4*(3), 125–138.

Lee, H., Lee, G., and Song, S. (2022). Multi-step reflection principle and barrier options. *Journal of Futures Markets, 42*, 692–721.

Leisen, D. P. J. (1999). Valuation of barrier options in a Black-Scholes setup with jump risk. Discussion Paper B-446.

Levy, P. (1948). *Stochastic Processes and Brownian Motion.* Paris.

Linetsky, V. (1999). Step options. *Mathematical Finance, 9*(1), 55–96.

Lo, C. F., Lee, H. C., and Hui, C. H. (2003). A simple approach for pricing barrier options with time-dependent parameters. *Quantitative Finance*, *3*, 98–107.

Lo, C. F. and Hui, C. H. (2007). Valuing double barrier options with time-dependent parameters by Fourier series expansion. *International Journal of Applied Mathematics*, *36*(1), 1–5.

Merton, R. C. (1973). Theory of rational option pricing. *Bell Journal of Economics and Management Science*, *4*, 141–183.

Nalholm, M. and Poulsen, R. (2006). Static hedging and model risk for barrier options. *Journal of Futures Markets*, *26*(5), 417–520.

Nelken, I. (Ed.). (1996). *The Handbook of Exotic Options.* Irwin Professional Publishing.

Oksendal, B. (2003). *Stochastic Differential Equations.* Springer.

Park, C. and Schuurman, F. C. (1983). Partial-barrier absorption probabilities for the Wiener process. *Journal of Applied Probability*, *20*(1), 103–110.

Park, C. and Beekman, J. A. (1983). Stochastic barriers for the Wiener process. *Journal of Applied Probability*, *20*, 338–348.

Pelsser, A. (2000). Pricing double barrier options using Laplace transforms. *Finance and Stochastics*, *4*(1), 95–104.

Pliska, R. S. (1997). *Introduction to Mathematical Finance.* Blackwell Publishing.

Poulsen, R. (2006). Barrier options and their static hedges. *Quantitative Finance*, *6*(4), 327–335.

Privault, N. (2014). *Stochastic Finance.* Chapman Hall.

Protter, P. (1992). *Stochastic Integration and Differential Equations.* Springer.

Rich, D. (1993). The valuation and application of options with stochastic barriers. Virginia Polytechnic Institute working paper.

Rich, D. (1994). The mathematical foundations of barrier option pricing theory. *Advances in Futures and Options Research*, *7*, 267–311.

Ritchken, P. (1995). On pricing barrier options. *The Journal of Derivatives*, *3*, 19–28.

Roberts, G. O. and Shortland, C. F. (1997). Pricing barrier options with time-dependent coefficients. *Mathematical Finance*, *7*(1), 83–93.

Rogers, L. C. G. and Zane, O. (1999). *Valuing Moving Barrier Options.* Working Paper, University of Bath.

Rubinstein, M. and Reiner, E. (1991). Breaking down the barriers. *Risk*, *4*(8), 28–35.

Shreve, S. (2004). *Stochastic Calculus for Finance.* Springer.

Sidenius, J. (1998). Double barrier options: Valuation by path counting. *Journal of Computational Finance*, *1*(3), 63–79.

Snyder, G. (1969). Alternative forms of options. *Financial Analysts Journal*, Sept/Oct., 93–99.

Veestraeten, D. (2004). The conditional probability density function for a reflected Brownian motion. *Computational Economics*, *24*, 185–207.

Wang, M. L. A., Liu, Y. H., and Hsiao, Y. L. (2009). Barrier option pricing: A hybrid method approach. *Quantitative Finance*, *9*(3), 341–352.

Wystup, U. (2007). *FX Options and Structured Products.* John Wiley and Sons Ltd.

Zhang, P. G. (1995). A unified formula for outside barrier options. *The Journal of Financial Engineering*, *4*(4), 319–335.

Zhang, P. (1998). *Exotic Options: A Guide to Second Generation Options.* World Scientific Press.

Zvan, R., Vetzal, K. R., and Forsyth, P. A. (2000). PDE methods for pricing barrier options. *Journal of Economic Dynamics & Control*, *24*, 1563–1590.

Index

M

N

O

P

Q

R

S